Rome

"All you've got to do is decide to go
and the hardest part is over.

So go!"

TONY WHEELER, COFOUNDER – LONELY PLANET

THIS EDITION WRITTEN AND RESEARCHED BY
Duncan Garwood,
Abigail Blasi

Contents

Plan Your Trip — 4

Explore Rome — 56

Understand Rome — 265

Survival Guide — 317

Rome Maps — 353

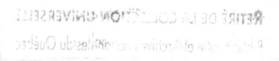

(left) Spanish Steps (p113)

(above) Pantheon (p82)

(right) Basilica di Santa Maria in Trastevere (p183)

Welcome to Rome

History, human genius and the hot midday sun have conspired to make Rome one of the world's most seductive and thrilling cities.

Artistic Grandeur

With an artistic heritage dating back to Etruscan times, Rome is one of the world's great art cities. Throughout history, it has played a starring role in the major upheavals of Western art and the results are here for all to see – amazing classical statues, stunning Renaissance frescoes and breathtaking baroque churches. Walk around the centre and even without trying you'll come across masterpieces by the greats of the artistic pantheon – sculptures by Michelangelo, paintings by Caravaggio, frescoes by Raphael and fountains by Bernini. In Rome, art is not locked away from view, it's quite literally all around you.

Historical Legacies

For much of its history Rome has been at the centre of world events. First, as *caput mundi* (capital of the world), the fearsome hub of the Roman Empire, then for centuries as the seat of papal power. It was a city that counted and this is writ large on its historic streets – martial ruins recall ancient glories, stately *palazzi* (mansions) evoke Renaissance intrigue and towering basilicas testify to artistic genius and papal ambition. Elsewhere, underground temples, buried houses and *maddonelle* (roadside shrines) tell of past lives and local beliefs.

Roman Feasting

A trip to Rome is as much about lapping up the lifestyle as it is about gorging on art and historic sights. And there's no better way of getting into the local spirit of things than by eating and drinking well. Food and wine are central to Roman social life and the hundreds of pizzerias, trattorias, restaurants and gelaterie that crowd the city centre do as much business catering to locals as to tourists and out-of-towners. Do as the Romans do, says the proverb, and there's nothing more Roman than enjoying a tasty wood-fired pizza in a packed pizzeria or dining alfresco on a glorious city-centre piazza.

Rome, the Capital

But there's more to Rome than history, fine art and great food. Rome is Italy's capital and largest city, and while history is all around, modern life is lived to the full. Rome is Italy's political and religious heartbeat and the influences of government and Church dominate the city. Many city-centre *palazzi* house government offices, while in the Vatican the dome of St Peter's Basilica reminds everyone of the pope's presence. Political intrigue is thick in the air and as tourists tuck into their pizza politicians hatch plots over spaghetti and wine.

Why I Love Rome

By Duncan Garwood, Author

Even after more than a decade of living in Rome, the city continues to amaze me. I still get a buzz every time I see the Colosseum and I still find it thrilling to visit places I read about as a school kid. But as much as the history, what I love is the way the city embraces the present, the way designer bars occupy 15th-century *palazzi* and neighbourhood markets take over beautiful historic piazzas. I also enjoy a good meal in a Roman trattoria, especially if accompanied by a bit of political banter and a bottle of local wine.

For more about our authors, see p384.

Top: View of St Peter's Basilica from the Capitoline Museums (p71)

Rome's
Top 13

Colosseum (p62)

1 Rome's most iconic monument, the Colosseum is a compelling sight. You'll know what it looks like but no photograph can prepare you for the thrill of seeing it for the first time. For 2000 years, this muscular arena has stood as the symbol of Roman power, as the striking embodiment of the terrible awe that Rome once inspired. As you climb its steeply stacked stands, try to imagine them full of frenzied spectators screaming for blood – a chilling thought.

◉ *Ancient Rome*

Palatino (p64)

2 Rome's seven hills offer some superb vantage points. One of the best is the Palatino (Palatine Hill), a gorgeous green expanse of evocative ruins, towering pine trees and sweeping views overlooking the Roman Forum. This is where it all began, where Romulus supposedly killed Remus and founded the city in 753 BC, and where the ancient Roman emperors lived in unimaginable luxury. Nowadays, it's a truly haunting spot, and as you walk the gravel paths you can almost sense the ghosts in the air.

◉ *Ancient Rome*

RICHARD I'ANSON / GETTY IMAGES ©

Museo e Galleria Borghese (p222)

3 Everybody's heard of Michelangelo and the Sistine Chapel, but Rome is as much about baroque art as it is about the Renaissance, and the lovely Museo e Galleria Borghese is the place to see it. You'll need to book ahead but it's a small price to pay to see Bernini's amazing baroque sculptures, as well as works by Canova, Caravaggio, Raphael and Titian. And when you've finished, the surrounding Villa Borghese park is the perfect place to digest what you've just seen.

☉ *Villa Borghese & Northern Rome*

Pantheon (p82)

4 The best preserved of Rome's ancient monuments, the Pantheon is a truly remarkable building. Its huge columned portico and thick-set walls impress, but it's only when you get inside that you get the full measure of the place. It's vast, and you'll feel very small as you look up at the record-breaking dome soaring above your head. Adding to the effect are the shafts of light that stream in through the central oculus (the circular opening at the dome's apex), illuminating the royal tombs set into the circular marble-clad walls.

☉ *Centro Storico*

Vatican Museums (p143)

5 Rome boasts many artistic highlights, but few are as overpowering as Michelangelo's frescoes in the Sistine Chapel. A kaleidoscopic barrage of colours and images, they come as the grand finale of the Vatican Museums, Rome's largest and most popular art museum. Inside the vast complex, kilometre upon kilometre of corridors are lined with classical sculptures, paintings and tapestries as they lead inexorably towards the Raphael Rooms, a suite of four rooms brilliantly frescoed by Raphael, and, beyond that, the Sistine Chapel. LEFT: SPIRAL STAIRCASE, VATICAN MUSEUMS

☉ *Vatican City, Borgo & Prati*

St Peter's Basilica *(p138)*

6 You don't have to be a believer to be bowled over by St Peter's Basilica, Rome's largest and most spectacular church. Everything about the place is astonishing, from the sweeping piazza that announces it to the grandiose facade and unbelievably opulent interior. Topping everything is Michelangelo's extraordinary dome, a mould-breaking masterpiece of Renaissance architecture and one of Rome's landmark sights. This is a building that was designed to awe, and even in this city full of churches it stands head and shoulders above everything else.

⊙ *Vatican City, Borgo & Prati*

An Evening in Trastevere
(p191)

7 One of the great joys of Rome is eating and drinking well, especially in summer when it's warm enough to dine alfresco, and the city's animated streets are packed until the early hours. And nowhere is better for a night out than the picture-perfect neighbourhood of Trastevere. Over the river from the historic centre, its medieval lanes, hidden piazzas and pastel-hued *palazzi* (mansions) harbour hundreds of bars, cafes, trattorias and restaurants catering to a nightly crowd of up-for-it Romans and spellbound visitors. RIGHT: PIAZZA SANTA MARIA IN TRASTEVERE AT NIGHT

✖ *Trastevere & Gianicolo*

RICHARD I'ANSON / GETTY IMAGES ©

Via Appia Antica

(p210)

8 The most famous of Rome's ancient roads, and one of the city's most sought-after addresses, the Appian Way is a gorgeous place to be on a clear, sunny morning. Running through lush green fields and littered with piles of greying ruins, it's the very picture of pastoral Italian beauty. But the bucolic scenery belies the road's bloodstained history. It was here that Spartacus and 6000 of his slave army were crucified, and it was here that the early Christians buried their dead in the catacombs.

⊙ *Southern Rome*

Capitoline Museums (p71)

9 In ancient times, the Campidoglio (Capitoline Hill) was home to Rome's two most important temples. Nowadays, the main reason to make the short, steep climb to the top is to admire the views and visit the Capitoline Museums on Piazza del Campidoglio. The world's oldest public museums, they harbour some fantastic classical statuary, including the celebrated Lupa Capitolina (Capitoline Wolf), an icon of early Etruscan art, and some really wonderful paintings. And make sure to bring your camera for the masonry littered around the entrance courtyard. BELOW: LUPA CAPITOLINA (CAPITOLINE WOLF) STATUE, CAPITOLINE MUSEUMS

◉ *Ancient Rome*

Roman Forum (p67)

10 To walk through the tumbledown ruins of the Roman Forum is to retrace the footsteps of the great figures of Roman history, people such as Julius Caesar and Pompey, who both led triumphal marches up Via Sacra, the Forum's central axis. The Forum is today one of Rome's most visited sights, but crowds are nothing new here. In ancient times this was the city's busy, chaotic centre, humming with activity as everyone from senators to slaves went about their daily business.

◉ *Ancient Rome*

Rome's Piazzas (p89)

11 Hanging out on Rome's showcase piazzas is part and parcel of Roman life. Having an ice cream at a pavement cafe on Piazza Navona, people-watching on Piazza del Popolo, queuing on St Peter's Square – these are all quintessential Roman experiences. For millennia, the city's piazzas have been at the centre of city life, hosting markets, ceremonies, games and even executions, and still today they attract cheerful crowds of locals, tourists, hipsters, diners and street artists. BELOW RIGHT: PIAZZA NAVONA

◉ *Showtime on Rome's Piazzas*

Trevi Fountain *(p115)*

12 A stop at Rome's largest and most famous fountain is a traditional rite of passage for visitors to Rome. Every day crowds gather to toss coins into the foutain's water and ensure that one day they'll return to the Eternal City. The fountain, designed by Nicola Salvi in the 18th century, is a gloriously over-the-top rococo affair depicting wild horses, mythical figures and cascading rock falls. Impressive at any time of the day, it's particularly spellbinding after dark when the lights come on and it's illuminated to stylish effect.

⊙ *Tridente, Trevi & the Quirinale*

People-Watching on the Spanish Steps *(p113)*

13 Rising up from Piazza di Spagna, the Spanish Steps are a favourite perch and a prime people-watching spot. Visitors have been hanging out here since the 18th century and still they come – local lotharios to flirt with the foreigners, red-faced tourists to catch their breath, street touts to sell their plastic tat. Below the Steps, well-heeled shoppers exercise their credit cards at the area's boutiques and flagship designer stores.

⊙ *Tridente, Trevi & the Quirinale*

What's New

All-Day Dining

The latest food-related fashion to sweep Rome is large multipurpose venues that open all day and function as bars, cafes, takeaways and *pasticcerie* (pastry shops), as well as restaurants. Standout examples include Romeo, a modish Prati eatery; Baccano near the Trevi Fountain, and Porto Fluviale, a bar-restaurant in trendy Ostiense. But the high temple of Rome's flourishing food scene is Eataly, a giant foodie complex that recently opened in a renovated train terminus.

Terme di Caracalla

You can now go underground at the Terme di Caracalla to visit a pagan temple and the tunnels where sweating slaves used to fuel a vast plumbing system. (p202)

Città dell'Acqua

Escape the crowds at the Trevi Fountain and search out the Città dell'Acqua, where you can poke around ancient waterworks and an excavated Roman street. (p123)

Pompi

If you like *dolci* (sweets), you'll love the new city-centre branch of Pompi, Rome's most celebrated tiramisu maker. (p128)

Le Artigiane

A shop with a difference, Le Artigiane is a showcase for local artisans, a browsers' dream full of handmade clothes, jewellery, and design objects. (p105)

Athea Inn

Bunk down in vibrant Testaccio at the Athea Inn, a great little B&B offering designer decor and value for money. (p264)

Metamorfosi

In the upmarket Parioli district, fine-dining Metamorfosi has proved a hit with Rome's gourmets. (p232)

Museo della Repubblica Romana e della Memoria Garibaldina

Opened on the Gianicolo to celebrate Italy's 150th anniversary, the small Museo della Repubblica Romana e della Memoria Garibaldina charts the crucial role Garibaldi played in the Italian unification movement. (p188)

Galleria d'Arte Moderna

Take a break from Rome's classic art for a taste of the modern at the Galleria d'Arte Moderna, beautifully housed in a light-filled convent. (p119)

Vice

A newcomer to Rome's ice-cream scene, Vice hits the road running with its smooth tastes and contemporary look. (p97)

For more recommendations and reviews, see **lonelyplanet. com/rome**

Need to Know

For more information, see Survival Guide (p317)

Currency

Euro (€)

Language

Italian

Visas

Not required by EU citizens. Not required by nationals of Australia, Canada, New Zealand and the USA for stays of up to 90 days.

Money

ATMs are widespread. Major credit cards are widely accepted but some smaller shops, trattorias and *pensioni* (small hotels or guesthouses) might not take them and the Vatican Museums ticket office doesn't accept them.

Mobile Phones

Local SIM cards can be used in European, Australian and unlocked US phones. Other phones must be set to roaming.

Time

Western European Time (GMT/UTC plus one hour).

Tourist Information

Information points (☺9.30am-7pm) around town for maps, brochures and the Roma Pass. Also a telephone line (☏06 06 08) for museum bookings, accommodation and transport help.

Daily Costs

Budget:
Under €70

➡ Dorm bed: €15–35

➡ Pizza plus beer: €15

➡ Save by drinking coffee standing at the bar

➡ Eat with an *aperitivo* to save money

Midrange:
€70-200

➡ Double room: €120–250

➡ Three-course restaurant meal: €30 or more

➡ OK to mix and match courses when eating out

➡ Roma Pass (a three-day card covering museum entry and public transport): €34

Top End:
Over €200

➡ Double room: €250 or more

➡ Tasting menu at a top restaurant: €100

➡ City-centre taxi ride: €10–15

➡ Auditorium concert tickets: €25–90

Advance Planning

Two months before Book high season accommodation.

Three to four weeks before Check for concerts at www.auditorium.it, www.operaroma.it, www.circoloartisti.it.

One to two weeks before Reserve tables at A-list restaurants. Sort out tickets to the pope's weekly audience at St Peter's.

Few days before Check www.estateromana.comune.roma.it for free summer events. Phone for tickets for the Museo e Galleria Borghese (compulsory) and book for the Vatican Museums (advisable to avoid queues).

Useful Websites

➡ **Lonely Planet** (www.lonelyplanet.com/rome) Destination lowdown, hotels and traveller forum.

➡ **060608** (www.060608.it) Rome's official tourist website.

➡ **Coopculture** (www.coopculture.it) Information and ticket booking for Rome's monuments.

➡ **Vatican Museums** (http://mv.vatican.va) Book tickets and avoid the queues.

➡ **Auditorium** (www.auditorium.com) Check concert listings.

WHEN TO GO

In spring and early autumn there's good weather and many festivals and outdoor events. It's also busy and peak rates apply.

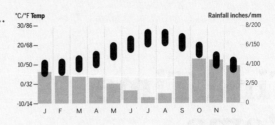

Arriving in Rome

Leonardo da Vinci (Fiumicino) Airport Direct trains to Stazione Termini 6.38am to 11.38pm, €14; slower trains to Trastevere, Ostiense and Tiburtina stations, 5.58am to 11.28pm, €8; buses to Stazione Termini 5.35am to 12.30am plus night services at 1.15am, 2.15am, 3.30am and 5am, €4–7; private transfers from €22 per person; taxis €48.

Ciampino Airport Buses to Stazione Termini 7.45am to 12.15am, €4; private transfers from €22 per person; taxis €30.

Stazione Termini Airport buses and trains, and international trains arrive at Stazione Termini. From here, continue by bus, metro or taxi.

For much more on **arrival**, see p318

Getting Around

Rome's public transport system includes buses, trams, metro and a suburban train network. The main hub is Stazione Termini, the only point at which the city's two main metro lines cross. The metro is quicker than surface transport but the network is limited and the bus is often a better bet. Children under 10 travel free.

➜ **Metro** Two main lines: A (orange) and B (blue). Runs 5.30am to 11.30pm (to 1.30am on Friday and Saturday).

➜ **Buses** Most routes pass through Stazione Termini. Buses run from 5.30am until midnight, with limited services throughout the night.

For much more on **getting around**, see p320

Sleeping

Rome is expensive and busy year-round, so you'll want to book as far ahead as you can to secure the best deal and the place you want.

Accommodation options range from palatial five-star hotels to hostels, B&Bs, convents and *pensioni.* Hostels are the cheapest, offering dorm beds and private rooms. Bed and breakfasts range from simple home-style set-ups to chic boutique outfits with prices to match, while religious institutions provide basic, value-for-money accommodation but may insist on a curfew. Hotels are plentiful and there are many budget, family-run *pensioni* in the Termini area.

Useful Websites

➜ **060608** (www.060608.it) Lists all official accommodation options (with prices).

➜ **Santa Susanna** (www.santasusanna.org/comingToRome/convents.html) Has information on religious accommodation.

➜ **Bed & Breakfast Association of Rome** (www.b-b.rm.it) Search for B&Bs and apartments.

For much more on **sleeping**, see p252

ORGANISED TOURS

Taking a tour is a good way of seeing a lot in a short time or investigating a sight in depth. There are many outfits running hop-on hop-off bus tours, typically costing about €20 per person. Both the Colosseum and Vatican Museums offer official guided tours, but for a more personalised service you'll be better off with a private guide. For more details, see p323.

First Time Rome

For more information, see Survival Guide (p317)

Checklist

➡ Check the validity of your passport

➡ Organise travel insurance

➡ Inform your credit/debit card company of your travel plans

➡ Check if you can use your mobile (cell) phone (p330)

➡ Book for popular sights such as the Vatican Museums and Museo e Galleria Borghese; also for A-list restaurants, concerts and accommodation

➡ If coming at Christmas or Easter check details of religious services at St Peter's Basilica and other big churches

What to Pack

➡ Passport

➡ Credit card

➡ Phrasebook

➡ Mobile-phone charger

➡ Camera

➡ Small day pack

➡ Trainers or comfy walking shoes

➡ Set of smart-casual evening clothes

➡ Universal adaptor

Top Tips for Your Trip

➡ Don't try to cover everything. Focus on a few sights/areas and leave the rest for next time.

➡ Rome's historic centre is made for leisurely strolling, so allow time for mapless wandering. Half the fun of Rome is discovering what's around the corner – and there's always something.

➡ When choosing where to eat, never judge a place by its appearance. Some of the best meals are had in modest-looking trattorias.

➡ When it's very hot – which it is in summer – adjust to the local rhythm: go out in the morning, rest after lunch and head out again late afternoon or early evening.

What to Wear

Appearances matter in Rome. That said, you'll need to dress comfortably because you'll be walking a lot. Suitable wear for men is generally trousers (pants) and shirts or polo shirts and, for women, skirts, trousers or dresses. Shorts, T-shirts and sandals are fine in summer but bear in mind that strict dress codes are enforced at St Peter's Basilica and the Vatican Museums. For evening wear, smart casual is the norm. A light sweater or waterproof jacket is useful in spring and autumn.

Be Forewarned

➡ Rome is a safe city but petty theft can be a problem and pickpockets are active in touristy areas and on crowded public transport. Use common sense and watch your valuables (see p330).

➡ There aren't any no-go areas, but keep your wits about you around Stazione Termini.

➡ August is Italy's main holiday period. Romans desert the city in droves and many shops and eateries close for a week or two around 15 August. Many museums close on Mondays.

➡ Expect queues at major sights such as the Colosseum, St Peter's Basilica and Vatican Museums. Booking tickets in advance costs extra but saves waiting time.

Money

Credit and debit cards are widely accepted but check before purchasing at smaller shops, trattorias, bars and *pensioni* (small hotels). Visa and MasterCard are the most widely recognised but Cirrus and Maestro are also well covered. American Express is only accepted by some major chains and big hotels, and few places take Diners Club.

ATMs (*bancomat*) are common, but be aware of transaction fees. If an ATM rejects your card, try another before assuming the problem is with your card.

For more information, see p328.

Taxes & Refunds

A 20% value-added tax known as IVA (*Imposta sul Valore Aggiunta*) is included in the price of most goods and services. Tax-free shopping is available at some shops – see p329 for more details.

All stays in the city are subject to an accommodation tax – the exact sum depends on the length of your sojourn and type of accommodation.

Tipping

Romans are not big tippers, but as a rough guide:

➡ **Taxis** Optional, but most people round up to the nearest euro.

➡ **Restaurants** Service (*servizio*) is generally included; if it's not, a euro or two is fine in pizzerias, 10% in restaurants.

➡ **Bars** Not necessary, although many people leave small change if drinking at the bar.

Language

You can get by with English, but you'll improve your experience by mastering a few basics. This is particularly true in restaurants where menus don't always have English translations. Most of the big museums and archaeological sites sell English-language guides but exhibits are rarely labelled well in English. See Language (p333) for more information.

Phrases to Learn Before You Go

 What's the local speciality?
Qual'è la specialità di questa regione?
kwa·*le* la spe·cha·lee·*ta* dee *kwes*·ta re·*jo*·ne

A bit like the rivalry between medieval Italian city-states, these days the country's regions compete in speciality foods and wines.

 Which combined tickets do you have?
Quali biglietti cumulativi avete?
kwa·lee bee·*lye*·tee koo·moo·la·*tee*·vee a·ve·te

Make the most of your euro by getting combined tickets to various sights; they are available in all major Italian cities.

 Where can I buy discount designer items?
C'è un outlet in zona? che oon *owt*·let in zo·na

Discount fashion outlets are big business in major cities – get bargain-priced seconds, samples and cast-offs for *la bella figura*.

 I'm here with my husband/boyfriend.
Sono qui con il mio marito/ragazzo.
so·no kwee kon eel *mee*·o ma·ree·to/ra·ga·tso

Solo women travellers may receive unwanted attention in some parts of Italy; if ignoring fails have a polite rejection ready.

Etiquette

Italy is quite a formal society and the niceties of social interaction are observed.

➡ **Greetings** Greet people in bars, shops, trattorias etc with a *buongiorno* (good morning) or *buonasera* (good evening).

➡ **Dress** Cover up when visiting churches and go smart when eating out.

➡ **Eating Out** Eat pasta with a fork, not a spoon; it's OK to eat pizza with your hands.

Roma Pass

The Roma Pass (€34; valid for three days) offers free and discounted entry to museums, galleries and archaeological sites, as well as free public transport. Available at tourist information points, it'll save you money if you use it for big sights such as the Colosseum and Capitoline Museums.

Top Itineraries

Day One

Ancient Rome (p60)

Start the day at the **Colosseum**, Rome's huge gladiatorial arena – try to get there early to avoid the queues. Then head down to the **Palatino** to poke around crumbling ruins and admire sweeping views. From the Palatino, follow on to the **Roman Forum**, an evocative area of tumble-down temples, sprouting columns and ruined basilicas.

 Lunch Sample regional specialities at the Enoteca Provincia Romana (p78).

Ancient Rome (p60)

After lunch climb the **Cordonata** to **Piazza del Campidoglio** and the **Capitoline Museums**. Here you'll find some stunning ancient sculpture and paintings by a selection of big-name artists. To clear your head afterwards, pop next door to **Il Vittoriano** and take the lift to the top for Rome's best 360-degree views.

 Dinner Dine on quality seafood at Vecchia Roma (p102).

Centro Storico (p80)

Spend the evening exploring the **Jewish Ghetto** where there are some wonderful eateries. Round the day off with a late drink at **Bartaruga**, near the Ghetto's much-loved turtle fountain.

Day Two

Vatican City, Borgo & Prati (p136)

On day two, hit the Vatican. First up, grab a *cornetto* (criossant) from **Dolce Maniera**, then plunge into the **Vatican Museums**. Once you've blown your mind on the Sistine Chapel and the other highlights, complete your tour at **St Peter's Basilica**. If the queues are bad, though, or you're suffering art overload, stop first for an early lunch.

 Lunch Grab a snack at Mondo Arancina (p156).

Centro Storico (p80)

Dedicate the afternoon to sniffing around the historic centre. Here you'll come across some of Rome's great sights, including **Piazza Navona** and the **Pantheon**. Art lovers can admire paintings by Caravaggio in the **Chiesa di San Luigi dei Francesi** and fashion-conscious shoppers can browse the boutiques on **Via del Governo Vecchio**.

 Dinner Romantic Casa Coppelle (p97) offers fine French-inspired food.

Centro Storico (p80)

After dinner stop in the centre for a taste of *dolce vita* bar life. Depending on what you're after, you could spend a relaxed evening at **Etablì** near Piazza Navona, join the student drinkers on **Campo de' Fiori**, or chat over coffee at **Caffè Sant'Eustachio**.

Relaxing in the gardens of the Villa Borghese (p225)

Day Three

Villa Borghese & Northern Rome (p220)

 Day three starts with a trip to the **Museo e Galleria Borghese** to marvel at amazing baroque sculpture. Afterwards, walk off what you've just seen in the shady avenues of **Villa Borghese** and check what's going on at Rome's buzzing cultural centre, the **Auditorium Parco della Musica**.

> **Lunch** Pop up to Piazzale Ponte Milvio in the Flaminio district (p231).

Tridente, Trevi & the Quirinale (p111)

In the afternoon investigate the area around **Piazza di Spagna**. Plan your moves while sitting on the **Spanish Steps** then dive down **Via dei Condotti** to window shop at the flagship designer stores. From Via del Corso, at the bottom, you can make your way up to the **Trevi Fountain**, where tradition dictates you throw in a coin to ensure your return to Rome.

> **Dinner** Trastevere (p189) heaves with restaurants, pizzerias and trattorias.

Trastevere & Gianicolo (p181)

Over the river, the charmingly photogenic **Trastevere** neighbourhood bursts with life in the evening as locals and tourists flock to its many eateries and bars. Get into the mood with an aperitif at **Freni e Frizioni** before pizza at **Pizzeria Dar Poeta** or a refined dinner at **Glass Hostaria**.

Day Four

Southern Rome (p208)

 On day four it's time to venture out to **Via Appia Antica**. The main attractions here are the catacombs and it's a wonderfully creepy sensation to duck down into these sinister pitch-black tunnels. Back above ground, you'll find the remains of an ancient racetrack at the nearby **Villa di Massenzio**.

> **Lunch** Book a table at highly regarded Trattoria Monti (p173).

Monti, Esquilino & San Lorenzo (p159)

Start the afternoon by visiting the **Museo Nazionale Romano: Palazzo Massimo alle Terme**, a superb museum full of classical sculpture and stunning mosaics. Then, drop by the monumental **Basilica di Santa Maggiore**, famous for its mosaics, and the **Basilica di San Pietro in Vincoli**, home to Michelangelo's muscular *Moses* sculpture. Finish up by exploring the pretty lanes of the **Monti** district.

> **Dinner** Head out to boho San Lorenzo (p176) and see what's cooking.

Monti, Esquilino & San Lorenzo (p159)

Step out with the students in **San Lorenzo**, where there's always something going on in the chic restaurants, cheap student haunts and bars. Further out, you'll find plenty of action in trendy **Pigneto**.

If You Like...

Museums & Galleries

Vatican Museums One of the world's great museums with a vast collection of classical art culminating in the Sistine Chapel. (p143)

Museo e Galleria Borghese Houses the best baroque sculpture in town and some seriously good Old Masters. (p222)

Museo Nazionale Romano: Palazzo Massimo alle Terme Fabulous Roman frescoes and wall mosaics are the highlight of this overlooked gem. (p161)

Capitoline Museums The world's oldest public museums are a must for anyone interested in ancient sculpture. (p71)

Museo Nazionale Etrusco di Villa Giulia A lovely museum housing a huge collection of Etruscan art and artefacts. (p228)

Palazzo e Galleria Doria Pamphilj Hidden behind a grimy exterior, this lavish private gallery is full of major works by big-name Italian artists. (p94)

Galleria Nazionale d'Arte Antica: Palazzo Barberini A sumptuous baroque palace laden with paintings by giants such as Caravaggio, Raphael and Hans Holbein. (p124)

Museo Nazionale Romano: Palazzo Altemps Classical sculpture is set against a backdrop of baroque frescoes at this excellent museum in the historic centre. (p90)

Museo dell'Ara Pacis A huge block of sculpted marble, the Ara Pacis is housed in a controversial modern pavilion. (p118)

LONELY PLANET / GETTY IMAGES ©

Ancient sculptures in the Capitoline Museums (p71)

MAXXI This gallery of contemporary art is worth seeing as much for its architecture as the art it displays. (p228)

Roman Relics

Colosseum One of the world's most famous buildings, this breathtaking arena encapsulates all the drama of ancient Rome. (p62)

Pantheon With its revolutionary design, this awe-inspiring Roman temple has served as an architectural blueprint for millennia. (p82)

Palatino Ancient emperors languished in luxury on the Palatino, the oldest and most exclusive part of imperial Rome. (p64)

Terme di Caracalla The hulking remains of this vast baths complex hint at the scale that ancient Rome was built to. (p202)

Ostia Antica An ancient port preserved over the millennia, Ostia Antica gives a good impression of a working Roman town. (p236)

Roman Forum This was ancient Rome's bustling centre, full of temples, basilicas, shops and streets. (p67)

Via Appia Antica March down Rome's oldest road, built in the 4th century BC, en route to the catacombs. (p210)

Imperial Forums The highlight of these sprawled ruins is the Mercati di Traiano, a multistorey shopping centre dating to the 2nd century. (p75)

Church Art

Sistine Chapel Michelangelo's frescoes are among the world's most famous works of art. (p143)

St Peter's Basilica Marvel at Michelangelo's *Pietà* and many other celebrated masterpieces. (p138)

Chiesa di Santa Maria della Vittoria Home to one of the greatest works of baroque art, Bernini's *Teresa traffita dall'amore di Dio*. (p122)

Chiesa di San Luigi dei Francesi An ornate baroque church boasting a trio of Caravaggio paintings. (p86)

Chiesa di Santa Prassede This small, off-the-radar church features brilliant Byzantine-inspired mosaics. (p164)

Basilica di San Pietro in Vincoli Face up to Michelangelo's muscular *Moses* sculpture. (p163)

Chiesa di Santa Maria del Popolo Works by Caravaggio, Raphael and Bernini adorn this magnificent Renaissance church. (p114)

Basilica di Santa Maria in Trastevere An ancient basilica celebrated for its golden apse mosaics. (p183)

Chiesa di Sant'Ignazio di Loyola Boasts a famous trompe l'œil ceiling fresco that plays with your sense of perception. (p97)

Eating with the Locals

Forno Roscioli A seriously good bakery serving glorious *pizza bianca* (pizza with salt and olive oil). (p100)

Da Felice A Testaccio favourite specialising in traditional Roman cuisine. (p206)

Pizzeria Da Remo Join the locals for a no-frills meal of textbook Roman pizza. (p205)

Glass Hostaria Dine on contemporary Italian food at this designer Trastevere restaurant. (p191)

For more top Rome spots, see the following:
➡ Eating (p34)
➡ Drinking & Nightlife (p43)
➡ Entertainment (p48)
➡ Shopping (p53)

Il Gelato Ice cream hits new heights at this ground-breaking gelateria. (p127)

Trattoria Monti A highly rated restaurant specialising in food from Le Marche region. (p173)

Cacio e Pepe Enjoy a no-nonsense lunch at this long-standing Prati favourite where hungry workers fill up on hearty Roman staples. (p156)

Going Underground

Basilica di San Clemente Descend into the bowels of this multilayered basilica to discover a pagan temple and 1st-century house. (p199)

Vatican Grottoes Extending beneath St Peter's Basilica, these underground chambers contain the tombs of several popes. (p138)

Catacombs Via Appia Antica is riddled with catacombs where the early Christians buried their dead. (p210)

Case Romane Poke around the houses where Saints John and Paul lived before they were executed. (p202)

Terme di Caracalla Explore an ancient temple and the underground tunnels where slaves once fed furnaces at this huge baths complex. (p202)

Palazzo Valentini A multimedia display brings excavated ruins to life beneath the seat of the Province of Rome. (p121)

PLAN YOUR TRIP IF YOU LIKE...

Parks & Gardens

Villa Borghese Rome's most central park, Villa Borghese is a refined oasis with a small lake, landscaped avenues and fine museums. (p225)

Villa Celimontana This tranquil pocket of greenery is a great escape from the hustle of the nearby Colosseum. (p203)

Villa Ada With its extensive woods and wild stretches, this sprawling park feels a million miles from Rome. (p229)

Villa Torlonia Locals love this small park with its swaying palm trees and neoclassical villas. (p230)

Orto Botanico Rome's 12-hectare botanical gardens rise up the Gianicolo Hill behind Trastevere. (p185)

Parco Savello Linger over romantic views among the orange trees at this perfumed garden in the hilltop Aventino neighbourhood. (p203)

Palazzi & Villas

Palazzo Farnese One of Rome's great Renaissance *palazzi* (mansions), now home to the French Embassy and stunning frescoes. (p90)

Villa Farnesina A refined Renaissance villa famous for its rich fresco decor. (p188)

Palazzo Barberini Home to the Galleria Nazionale d'Arte Antica, this sumptuous palace is a masterpiece of baroque architecture. (p124)

Palazzo del Quirinale The palatial residence of the Italian president was built by a phalanx of baroque architects. (p123)

Palazzo della Civiltà del Lavoro Known as the Square Colosseum, this icon of 1930s rationalism stars in the outlying EUR district. (p213)

Palazzo di Montecitorio Politicians flock to the ornate Bernini-designed palace, home of Italy's Chamber of Deputies. (p95)

Sweeping Views

Il Vittoriano Not recommended for vertigo sufferers, the summit of this marble monolith towers over the rest of Rome. (p76)

Gianicolo Rising above Trastevere, the Gianicolo Hill affords sweeping panoramas over Rome's rooftops. (p185)

Orti Farnesiani A viewing terrace in the Palatino's medieval gardens commands grandstand views over the Roman Forum. (p64)

St Peter's Basilica Climb the dome and you're rewarded with huge 360-degree views. (p138)

Priorato dei Cavalieri di Malta Look through the keyhole for a perfectly framed picture of St Peter's dome. (p204)

Castel Sant'Angelo Gaze over a sea of rooftops from this operatic castle, the setting for scenes in Puccini's *Tosca*. (p154)

Street Life

Trastevere Students, tourists, locals, diners, drinkers, junkies and street hawkers mingle on Trastevere's vivacious streets. (p181)

Spanish Steps Find a space and settle back to watch the ever-changing spectacle on the square below. (p113)

Piazza Navona This beautiful baroque arena provides the stage for a colourful cast of street artists, performers, waiters and tourists. (p84)

Pigneto With its noisy market and vibrant bar scene, this hip district is always lively. (p171)

Campo de' Fiori Market-stall holders holler at each other during the day and student drinkers strut their stuff by night. (p90)

Month by Month

January

As New Year celebrations fade, the winter cold digs in. It's a quiet time of year but the winter sales are a welcome diversion.

🛍 Shopping Sales

Running from early January to mid-February, the winter sales offer savings of between 20% and 50%. Action is particularly frenzied around Piazza di Spagna and on Via del Corso.

February

Rome's winter quiet is shattered by high-spirited *carnevale* **celebrations, while romance comes to town for St Valentine's Day (14 February). Restaurants do a roaring trade in tables for two, so book ahead.**

✨ Carnevale Romano

Rome really goes to town for *carnevale,* with leaping horse shows on Piazza del Popolo, costumed parades down Via del Corso, street performers on Piazza Navona, and crowds of kids in fancy dress. Check the schedule at www.carnevale.roma.it.

March

The onset of spring brings blooming flowers, rising temperatures and unpredictable rainfall. Unless Easter falls in late March, the city is fairly subdued and low-season prices still apply.

🏃 Maratona di Roma

Sightseeing becomes sport at Rome's annual marathon. The 42km route starts and finishes near the Colosseum, taking in many of the city's big sights. Details online at www.maratonadiroma.it.

April

April is a great month with lovely, sunny weather, fervent Easter celebrations, a week of free museums, azaleas on the Spanish Steps and Rome's birthday festivities. Expect high-season prices.

✨ Easter

In the capital of the Catholic world, Easter is big business. On Good Friday the pope leads a candlelit procession around the Colosseum. At noon on Easter Sunday he blesses the crowds in St Peter's Square.

✨ Natale di Roma

Rome celebrates its birthday on 21 April with music, historical recreations and fireworks. Events are staged throughout the city but the focus is Campidoglio and Circo Massimo.

✨ Mostra delle Azalee

From mid-April to early May, the Spanish Steps are decorated with 600 vases of blooming, brightly coloured azaleas – a perfect photo opportunity.

May

May is a busy, high-season month. The weather's perfect – it's generally

warm enough to eat outside – and the city is looking gorgeous with blue skies and spring flowers.

☆ Primo Maggio

Hundreds of thousands of fans troop to Piazza di San Giovanni in Laterano for Rome's free May Day rock concert. It's a mostly Italian affair with big-name local performers but you might catch the occasional foreign guest star.

June

Summer has arrived and with it hot weather, school vacations and a full festivals programme. Stages, stalls and open-air bars are set up across the city, creating a laid-back holiday atmosphere.

✷ Estate Romana

Between June and October, Rome's big summer festival involves everything from dance performances and concerts to book fairs, puppet shows and late-night museum openings. Check the website – www.estate_romana.comune.roma.it.

✷ Lungo il Tevere

Nightly crowds converge on the river Tiber for this hugely popular summer-long event. Stalls, clubs, bars, restaurants and dance floors line the river bank as Rome's nightlife goes alfresco.

✷ Isola del Cinema

The Isola Tiberina provides the picturesque backdrop for this open-air film festival, which screens a range of Italian and international films with a focus on independent productions. See www.isoladelcinema.com.

✷ Roma Incontro Il Mondo

Villa Ada is transformed into a colourful multi-ethnic village for this popular annual event. There's a laid-back party vibe and an excellent programme of concerts ranging from Roman rap to jazz and world music. Check www.villaada.org.

✷ Festa dei Santi Pietro e Paolo

On 29 June, Rome celebrates its two patron saints, Peter and Paul, with a mass at St Peter's Basilica and a street fair on Via Ostiense near the Basilica di San Paolo Fuori-le-Mura.

July

Hot summer temperatures make sightseeing a physical endeavour, but come the cool of evening, the city's streets burst into life as locals come out to enjoy summer festivities.

✷ Festa di Noantri

Trastevere celebrates its roots with a raucous street party in the last two weeks of the month. Centred on Piazza Santa Maria in Trastevere, events kick off with a religious procession and continue with much eating, drinking, dancing and praying.

August

Rome melts in the heat as locals flee the city for their summer hols. Many businesses shut down around 15 August but hoteliers offer discounts and there are loads of summer events to enjoy.

✷ Festa della Madonna della Neve

On 5 August, rose petals are showered on celebrants in the Basilica di Santa Maria Maggiore to commemorate a miraculous 4th-century snowfall.

October

Autumn is a good time to visit – the warm weather is holding, Romaeuropa ensures plenty of cultural action and, with the schools back, there are far fewer tourists around.

✷ Romaeuropa

Established international performers join emerging stars at Rome's premier dance and drama festival. Events, staged from late September through to November, range from avant-garde dance performances to installations, multimedia shows, recitals and readings. Get details at http://romaeuropa.net/.

November

Although the wettest month, November has its compensations – low-season prices, excellent jazz concerts and no queues outside the big sights. Autumn is also great for foodies.

✷ Roma Jazz Festival

Jazz masters descend on the Auditorium Parco della Musica for the three-week Roma Jazz Festival (www.romajazzfestival.it). Recent

(Top) Christmas at St Peter's Square (p154)

(Bottom) Historical procession to celebrate the founding of Rome

HENRYK SADURA / GETTY IMAGES ©

GETTY IMAGES ©

performers have included Macy Gray, Joe Jackson and Stefano Bollani, one of Italy's top jazz pianists.

⚝ Festival Internazionale del Film di Roma

Held at the Auditorium Parco della Musica, Rome's film festival rolls out the red carpet for Hollywood hotshots and bigwigs from Italian cinema. Consult the programme at www.roma cinemafest.org.

⚝ Festival Internazionale di Musica e Arte Sacra

Over several days in early November, the Vienna Philharmonic Orchestra and other top ensembles perform a series of classical concerts in Rome's four papal basilicas and other churches. Check the programme on www.festival musicaeartesacra.net.

December

The build up to Christmas is a jolly time. Crowds brave the cold to shop for gifts and enjoy the festive lights in the city centre.

🔒 Piazza Navona Christmas Fair

Rome's most beautiful baroque square becomes a big, brash marketplace as brightly lit market stalls set up shop, selling everything from nativity scenes to stuffed toys and teethcracking *torrone* (nougat).

With Kids

Despite a reputation as a highbrow cultural destination, Rome has a lot to offer kids. Child-specific sights might be thin on the ground, but if you know where to go there's plenty to keep the little 'uns occupied and Mum and Dad happy.

Playing among the ruins of the Roman Forum (p67)

PHILIP AND KAREN SMITH / GETTY IMAGES ©

History for Kids

Colosseum

Everyone wants to see the Colosseum (p62) and it doesn't disappoint, especially if accompanied by tales of bloodthirsty gladiators and hungry lions. For maximum effect prep your kids beforehand with a Rome-based film – perhaps *The Lizzie McGuire Movie* or, for older teenagers, *Gladiator*.

Catacombs

Spook your teens with a trip to the catacombs on Via Appia Antica (p210). These pitch-black tunnels, full of tombs and ancient burial chambers, are fascinating, but not suitable for kids under about seven.

Palazzo Valentini

Parents and older kids will enjoy the multimedia tour of Roman excavations beneath Palazzo Valentini (p121).

Museums for Kids

Explora

Not far from Piazza del Popolo, Explora–Museo dei Bambini di Roma (p229) is a hands-on museum for kids under 12, with interactive displays and, outside, a free play park open to all.

Museo della Civiltà Romana

In EUR, the Museo della Civiltà Romana (p213) has recreations of ancient bridges, forts and monuments, as well as a room-sized model of 4th-century Rome.

Museo delle Cere

Go face to face with popes, rockstars, football players and opera singers at Rome's cheesy wax museum (p123).

Food for Kids

Pizza

Pizza *al taglio* (by the slice) is a godsend for parents. It's cheap (about €1 buys two slices of *pizza bianca* – with salt and olive oil), easy to get hold of (there are hundreds of takeaways across town) and works wonders on flagging spirits.

Gelato

Ice cream is another manna from heaven, served in *coppette* (tubs) or *coni* (cones) with child-friendly flavours: *fragola* (strawberry), *cioccolato* (chocolate) and *bacio* (with hazelnuts).

Run in the Park

When the time comes to let the kids off the leash, head to Villa Borghese (p225), the most central of Rome's main parks. There's plenty of space to run around in – though it's not absolutely car-free – and you can hire family bikes. Other parks include Villa Celimontana (p203) and Villa Torlonia (p230).

Animal Spotting

Animal Sculptures

Get your kids to spot as many animal sculptures as they they can. There are hun-

dreds around town, including an elephant (outside the Chiesa di Santa Maria Sopra Minerva), lions (at the foot of the Cordonata staircase up to Piazza del Campidoglio), bees (in Bernini's fountain just off Piazza Barberini), horses, eagles and, of course, Rome's trademark wolf.

Zoo

In Villa Borghese, the Bioparco isn't cheap, and it's not the best zoo in the world, but after dragging your loved ones to all those churches and museums, it is an option.

A Family Day Out

Ostia Antica

Many of Rome's ancient ruins can be boring for children, but Ostia Antica (p236) is different. Here your kids can run along the ancient town's streets, among shops and up its impressive amphitheatre.

Tivoli

Kids love exploring the gardens at Villa D'Este (p238) with their water-spouting fountains and grim-faced gargoyles. Nearby, the extensive ruins of Villa Adriana (p238) provide ample opportunity for hide and seek.

Seaside

When the heat of the city starts getting to you, escape to the beach (p240). The nearest is at Ostia Lido, but there are nicer ones at Fregene and Santa Marinella. Alternatively, head to Anguillara Sabazia for swimming in Lago Bracciano (p249).

Like a Local

Gregarious and convivial, the Romans enjoy their city. They love hanging out in its piazzas and speeding around the streets in small cars; they like to dress up and they adore going out. They know theirs is a beautiful city, but they're not jealous and everyone is welcome.

Enjoying an evening drink in Trastevere (p181)

Drink Like a Local

Coffee

What tea is for the Brits, coffee is for the Romans, and no day starts without one. As a rule, locals will stop at a bar for a coffee twice a day: in the morning before work, and then again after lunch to ward off any post-prandial drowsiness. During the working week 'going for a coffee' is a quick business that's usually over in a matter of minutes, but at the weekend the pace slackens and the ritual is more leisurely.

To have coffee like a local, ask for *un caffè* (the term *espresso* is rarely used) and drink it standing at the bar. Also never order a cappuccino after lunch. For a taste of Rome's finest head to Caffè Sant'Eustachio (p103) or Caffè Tazza d'Oro (p103) near the Pantheon.

Aperitivo

Hit many of the capital's bars in the early evening and you'll find crowds of animated Romans chatting over cocktails and plates of finger food. The *aperitivo* custom has really taken off in recent years and bars across the city compete to put on the most extravagant buffet displays. Hot bars include Freni e Frizioni (p191) in Trastevere and fashionable Ostiense bar Doppiozeroo (p218).

Cool Neighbourhoods

Trastevere

A picturesque district full of bars, cafes and trattorias, Trastevere (p181) has long been a foreigners' favourite. But Romans love it too, and amid the tourist bustle you'll find some characteristic city haunts. Come early evening for an aperitif, followed by dinner and cool tunes.

Ostiense

With its disused factories, authentic trattorias and university campus, Ostiense (p216) is home to Rome's hottest clubs and hippest bars. But before the nightlife revs up, you can explore several fascinating cultural gems.

GLENN BEANLAND/ GETTY IMAGES ©

Pigneto

Pigneto (p171), a former working-class district southeast of Termini, is now one of the capital's coolest neighbourhoods, a bar-heavy pocket frequented by bohemians, fun seekers and trendsetting urbanites.

Testaccio

Formerly a working-class enclave, Testaccio (p204) retains a genuine neighbourhood feel with its boisterous daily market, traditional Roman trattorias and popular mainstream clubs.

Passeggiata on Via del Corso

The early evening *passeggiata* (evening stroll) is a quintessential Italian experience that's particularly colourful at weekends when families, friends and lovers take to the streets to parade up and down, to see and be seen. In times past, the *passeggiata* provided the perfect setting for young people to eye each other up and flirt, and still today there's plenty of strutting on show.

To partake in this evening spectacle, head to Via del Corso around 6pm and join the crowds for a leisurely stroll, perhaps stopping for an ice cream or to window shop in one of the many flagship stores. Alternatively, grab a seat on the Spanish Steps and watch as the theatrics unfold beneath you on Piazza di Spagna (p113).

Catch Some Culture

Exhibitions

Romans are great exhibition-goers and while the city's big museums are mainly left to out-of-towners, temporary exhibitions are eagerly supported by locals. Top locations include the Scuderie Papali al Quirinale (p123), a beautiful gallery housed in the former stables of the Palazzo del Quirinale, the Complesso del Vittoriano (p76), in the interior of Il Vittoriano, and the beautiful Renaissance Chiostro del Bramante (Bramante Cloisters) (p86).

Auditorium Parco della Musica

Music concerts attract passionate audiences to venues across town, most noticeably the Auditorium Parco della Musica (p233), Rome's principal concert venue and one of Europe's busiest cultural centres.

Football at the Stadio Olimpico

Football is a Roman passion, with support in the city divided between the two local teams: Roma and Lazio. Both play their home games at the Stadio Olimpico (p234), Rome's impressive Olympic stadium, which also stages international rugby matches and rock concerts. If you go to a football game, make sure you get it right – Roma plays in red and yellow and their supporters stand in the *Curva Sud* (South Stand); Lazio plays in sky blue and their fans fill the *Curva Nord* (North Stand).

For Free

Although Rome is an expensive city, you don't have to break the bank to enjoy it. A surprising number of the big sights are free and it costs nothing to stroll the historic streets, piazzas and parks, basking in their extraordinary beauty.

Michelangelo's *Moses*, Basilica di San Pietro in Vincoli (p163)

PAOLO GAETANO ROCCO / GETTY IMAGES ©

Free Art

Feast on fine art in the city's churches and basilicas. They're all free and many contain priceless treasures by big-name artists.

Michelangelo

You'll find sculptures by Michelangelo in the Basilica di San Pietro in Vincoli (p163), Chiesa di Santa Maria Sopra Minerva (p85), and St Peter's Basilica (p138), where his *Pietà* is one of the many masterpieces on display.

Caravaggio

Rome's churches boast an impressive collection of Caravaggio paintings, with famous works in the Chiesa di San Luigi dei Francesi (p86), Chiesa di Sant'Agostino (p90) and Chiesa di Santa Maria del Popolo (p114).

Free Museums & Galleries

Vatican Museums

Home to the Sistine Chapel and kilometre upon kilometre of awesome art, the vast Vatican Museums (p143) are free on the last Sunday of the month.

Museum Discounts

Many of Rome's museums and galleries are free to EU citizens under 18 and over 65. There are also discounts available to anyone between 18 and 24.

Free Monuments

Pantheon

A pagan temple turned church, the Pantheon (p82) is a staggering work of architecture with its record-breaking dome and echoing, marble-clad interior.

Trevi Fountain

You don't have to spend a penny to admire the Trevi Fountain (p115), although if you're like most people you'll throw a coin in to ensure your return to Rome.

Bocca della Verità

According to legend, if you put your hand in the Bocca della Verità (Mouth of Truth p78) and tell a lie it'll bite your hand off.

Spanish Steps

Rising from Piazza di Spagna (p113), the Steps are a popular site for a rest, and as long as you don't eat anything while you're sitting there, you can hang around for as long as you like.

People-Watching on the Piazzas

Hanging out and enjoying the spectacle on Rome's operatic piazzas is a signature Roman experience. Top people-watching spots include Piazza Navona (p84), Campo de' Fiori (p90), scene of a vibrant morning market, and the monumental Piazza del Popolo (p118).

Exploring the Parks

It doesn't cost a thing to enjoy Rome's parks. The most famous is Villa Borgh-ese (p225) but you'll also find pockets of greenery at Villa Torlonia (p230) and Villa Celimontana (p203). Rising behind Trastevere, the Gianicolo Hill (p185) offers superb rooftop views – yours for nothing more than the effort it takes to walk there.

Free (or Nearly Free) Food & Drink

Aperitivo

A good way to snag a meal for the price of a drink is to have an *aperitivo*. Pay for your drink (usually around €8) and feast on pastas, snacks, rice salads and other nibbles from the buffet spread.

Drinking Fountains

To slake your thirst on free natural spring water, fill up at one of the many drinking fountains across town. The water is refreshingly cool and perfectly safe to drink.

Free Festivals & Events

May Day Concert

This massive free concert, held every 1 May on Piazza di San Giovanni in Laterano, attracts hundreds of thousands of fans and Italy's top music acts.

Public Holidays

Rome's public holidays and festivals are a great way of experiencing the city. Summer is a good time with many free events, but there's action year-round: February means Carnevale, while Rome celebrates its birthday, the Natale di Roma, on 21 April with fireworks and historical processions.

Different flavours of gelato on display

 **Eating**

Romans live to eat. Food is a favoured topic of conversation and essential to every social occasion, and cooking with seasonal ingredients is the norm, as it has been for millennia. Over recent decades, the restaurant scene has become increasingly sophisticated, but the city's no-frills, local trattorias still provide some of Rome's most memorable gastronomic experiences.

Roman Cooking

Like many other Italian cuisines, Roman cooking was born of careful use of local ingredients, using cheaper cuts of meat, such as *guanciale* (pig's cheek), and greens that could be gathered wild from the fields. Other local ingredients include olives, olive oil, pulses, cured pork, lamb, offal, vegetables grown in Lazio, *pecorino* (sheep's milk cheese), ricotta, wood-baked bread, pasta and fish. There are certain staple, classic dishes that are served by almost every trattoria and restaurant in Rome.

CLASSIC DISHES

The Roman classics are all comfort foods that are seemingly simple (yet notoriously difficult to prepare well) and remarkably tasty. In the classic Roman comedy *I Soliti Ignoti* (Big Deal on Madonna Street; 1958) inept thieves break through a wall to burgle a safe, find themselves in a kitchen by mistake, and console themselves by cooking *pasta e ceci* (pasta with chickpeas). Other iconic Roman dishes include *carbonara* (pasta with lardons, egg and Parmesan), *alla gricia* (pasta with *guanciale* and *pecorino*), *amatriciana* (invented when a chef from Amatrice added tomatoes to *alla gricia*) and *cacio e pepe* (pasta with cheese and pepper).

ROMAN-JEWISH CUISINE

Most entrenched in culinary tradition is the Jewish Ghetto area, with its hearty Roman-Jewish cuisine. Deep-frying is a staple of *cucina ebraico-romanesca* (Roman-Jewish cooking), which developed between the 16th and 19th centuries when the Jews were confined to the city's ghetto. To add flavour to their limited ingredients – those spurned by the rich, such as courgette (zucchini) flowers – they began to fry everything from mozzarella to *baccalà* (salted cod). Particularly fantastic are the locally grown artichokes, which are flattened out to form a kind of flower shape and then deep-fried and salted. The season to eat these is from February to May, but you will find artichokes out of season too; however, this means they've been imported or frozen.

OFFAL SPECIALITIES

For the heart (and liver and brains) of the *cucina Romana*, head to Testaccio, a traditional working-class district, clustered around the city's former slaughterhouse. In the past, butchers who worked in the city abattoir were often paid in cheap cuts of meat as well as money. The Roman staple *coda alla vaccinara* translates as 'oxtail cooked butcher's style'. This is cooked for hours to create a rich sauce with tender slivers of meat.

A famous Roman dish that's not for the faint-hearted is pasta with *pajata,* made with the entrails of veal calves, considered a delicacy since they contain the mother's congealed milk. If you see the word *coratella* on a menu, it means you'll be eating lights (lungs), kidneys and hearts.

SEAFOOD

Seafood is often excellent in Rome; it's fished locally in Lazio. There are lots of dedicated seafood restaurants, usually high-end places with delicate takes on fish such as skate and tuna.

DESSERT

Dolci (sweets) tend to be the same at every trattoria: usually tiramisu (which means 'pick me up') and panna cotta ('cooked cream', with added sugar and cooled to set). For a traditional Roman *dolce* you should look out for ricotta cakes – a kind of cheese-

NEED TO KNOW

Prices

The pricing here refers to the average cost of a meal that includes *primo* (first course), *secondo* (second course) and *dolce* (dessert), plus a glass of wine. Don't be surprised to see *pane e coperto* (bread and cover charge; €1 to €5 per person) added to your bill.

€	under €25
€€	€25 to €45
€€€	over €45

Opening Hours

➡ Most restaurants open noon to 3pm and 7.30 to 11pm, usually closing one day per week (often Sunday or Monday).

➡ Most eateries close for at least a week in August, but the timing varies from year to year. Some restaurants close for the whole month. It's advisable to ring first in August to check that everyone hasn't gone to the beach.

Etiquette

➡ Dress up when eating out; Italians dress relatively smartly at most meals.

➡ Bite through hanging spaghetti rather than slurping it up.

➡ Pasta is eaten with a fork (not fork and spoon).

➡ It's OK to eat pizza with your hands.

➡ In an Italian home you may *fare la scarpetta* (make a little shoe) with your bread and wipe plates clean of sauces.

➡ If invited to someone's home, traditional gifts are a tray of *dolci* (sweets) from a *pasticceria* (pastry shop), a bottle of wine or flowers.

Tipping

Although service is included, leave a tip: anything from 5% in a pizzeria to 10% in a more upmarket place. At least round up the bill.

cake with chocolate chips or cherries or both – at a local bakery. Many Romans eat at a restaurant and then go elsewhere for a gelato and a coffee to finish off the meal.

Eat as the Romans Do

For *colazione* (breakfast), most Romans head to a bar for a cappuccino and a *cornetto* – a croissant filled with *cioccolato* (chocolate), *marmelata* (jam) or *crema* (custard cream).

The main meal of the day is *pranzo* (lunch), eaten at about 1.30pm. Many shops and businesses close for three to four hours every afternoon to accommodate the meal and siesta that follows. On Sundays *pranzo* is particularly important.

Cena (dinner), eaten any time from about 8.30pm, is usually a simple affair, although this is changing as fewer people make it home for the big lunchtime feast.

A full Italian meal consists of an antipasto (starter), a *primo piatto* (first course), a *secondo piatto* (second course) with an *insalata* (salad) or *contorno* (vegetable side dish), *dolci* (sweets), fruit, coffee and *digestivo* (liqueur). When eating out, however, you can do as most Romans do, and mix and match: order, say, a *primo* followed by an *insalata* or *contorno*.

Vegetarians & Vegans

Panic not, vegetarians, you can eat well in Rome, with a bountiful choice of antipasti, pasta dishes, *insalati, contorni* and pizzas.

Be mindful of hidden ingredients not mentioned on the menu – for example, steer clear of anything that's been stuffed (like courgette flowers, often spiced up with anchovies) or check that it's *senza carne o pesce* (without meat or fish). Note that to many Italians vegetarian means you don't eat red meat.

Vegans are in for a tougher time. Cheese is used universally, so you must specify that you want something *'senza formaggio'* (without cheese). Also remember that *pasta fresca,* which may also turn up in soups, is made with eggs. The safest option is to self-cater or try a dedicated vegetarian restaurant, which will always have some vegan options.

GLUTEN-FREE

Most restaurants offer gluten-free options, as there is a good awareness of celiac disease here. Just say *'Io sono celiaco'* or *'senza glutine'* when you sit down, and usually the waiters will be able to recommend you suitable dishes.

THE CULINARY CALENDAR

According to the culinary calendar (initiated by the Catholic Church to vary the nutrition of its flock), fish is eaten on Friday and *baccalà* (salted cod) is often eaten with *ceci* (chickpeas), usually on Wednesday. Thursday is the day for gnocchi (dumplings). The traditional, heavy Roman recipe uses semolina flour, but you can also find the typical gnocchi with potatoes. Many traditional Roman restaurants still offer dishes according to this calendar.

Where to Eat

Eateries are divided into several categories.

FAST FOOD

A *tavola calda* (hot table) offers cheap, pre-prepared pasta, meat and vegetable dishes. Quality is usually reasonable while atmosphere takes a back seat.

A *rosticceria* sells cooked meats but often has a larger selection of takeaway food. There are also takeaway pizza joints serving pizza *al taglio* (by the slice). When it's good, it's very good.

Other great snack food to look out for are *arancini,* fried rice balls that have fillings such as mozzarella and ham. These originate from Sicily, but are very popular in Rome too, where they're known as *supplì.*

ENOTECHE (WINE BARS)

You can eat well at many *enoteche,* wine bars that usually serve snacks (such as cheeses or cold meats, bruschette and *crostini*) and hot dishes. In this book these are mostly listed in the Drinking sections, but they're usually great places to eat as well.

TRATTORIA, OSTERIA OR RESTAURANT?

Usually for a full meal you'll want a trattoria, an *osteria* (neighbourhood inn), a *ristorante* (restaurant) or a pizzeria.

The differences between the various types of eateries are now fairly blurred. Traditionally, trattorias were family-run places that offered a basic, affordable local menu, while *osterie* usually specialised in one dish and *vino della casa* (house wine). There are still lots of these around. *Ristoranti* offer more choices and smarter service, and are more expensive.

Eating by Neighbourhood

Villa Borghese & Northern Rome
Park cafes and smart, fashionable restaurants (p220)

Vatican City, Borgo & Prati
Sophisticated restaurants, delicious takeaways, heavenly gelaterie (p136)

Tridente, Trevi & the Quirinale
Classy neighbourhood eateries and upmarket cafes (p111)

Centro Storico
Romantic hideaways, old-school trattorias, top pizzerias (p80)

Monti, Esquilino & San Lorenzo
Ethnic eats, cool bars, boho restaurants (p159)

Trastevere & Gianicolo
Touristy but great trattorias, bars and pizzerias (p181)

Ancient Rome
Hidden gems among the tourist traps (p60)

San Giovanni to Testaccio
Traditional Roman cuisine, good cheap eats (p195)

Southern Rome
Trendsetting foodie venues in a hip area (p208)

0   1.4 km
0   1 miles

Ethnic restaurants are more prevalent these days, though in Rome, Italian food remains king.

Aperitivo

Aperitivo is a trend from Milan that's been taken up with gusto in Rome – a buffet of snacks to accompany evening drinks in bars and some restaurants, usually from around 6pm till 9pm, and costing around €5 to €10 for a drink and unlimited platefuls. The younger generation sometimes turn *aperitivo* into a replacement for dinner (but don't tell their parents).

Pizza

Remarkably, pizza was only introduced to Rome post-WWII, by southern immigrants. It caught on. Every Roman's favourite casual meal is the gloriously simple pizza, with Rome's signature wafer-thin bases, covered in fresh, bubbling toppings, slapped down on tables by waiters on a mission. Pizzerias often only open in the evening. Most Romans will precede their pizza with a starter of bruschetta or *fritti* (mixed fried foods, such as zucchini flowers, potato, olives etc) and wash it all down with beer.

For a snack on the run, Rome's *pizza al taglio* places are hard to beat, with toppings loaded onto a thin, crispy, light-as-air, slow-risen bread that verges on the divine.

THE MEANING OF BRUNCH

Many restaurants offer 'brunch' at weekends, but this isn't the breakfast/lunch combination featuring pancakes and eggs that English and American visitors might expect. Brunch in Rome tends to mean a buffet, available from around noon to 3pm.

Markets

Rome's fresh-produce markets are a fabulous feature of the city's foodscape, and most neighbourhoods have their own daily food market. Go to see what's in season and enter the fray with the neighbourhood matriarchs. The markets operate from around 7am to 1.30pm, Monday to Saturday. There are also some excellent farmers markets, mostly taking place at the weekends. The best is at Circo Massimo on Saturday and Sunday.

Rome's most famous markets include the following:

Campo de' Fiori (Map p360 🚌Corso Vittorio Emanuele II) The most picturesque, but also the most expensive. Prices are graded according to the shopper's accent.

Mercato di Circo Massimo (Map p356; www.mercatocircomassimo.it; Via di San Teodoro 74; ⊙9am-6pm Sat, to 4pm Sun; 🚌Via dei Cerchi) Rome's best and most popular farmers market.

Nuovo Mercato Esquilino (Map p376; Via Lamarmora; Ⓜ Vittorio Emanuele) Cheap and the best place to find exotic herbs and spices.

Piazza dell' Unità (Map p368; (🚌Piazza del Risorgimento) Near the Vatican, perfect for stocking up for a picnic.

Piazza San Cosimato (Map p372; 🚌Viale di Trastevere, 🚋Viale di Trastevere) Trastevere's neighbourhood market, still the business with foodstuffs.

Nuovo Mercato di Testaccio (Map p370; Via Galvani; ⊙6am-3pm Mon-Sat; 🚌Via Marmorata) Even if you don't need to buy anything, a trip to Testaccio's daily food market is fun. Occupying a new, purpose-built site, it hums with activity as locals go about their daily shopping, picking and prodding the piles of brightly coloured produce and cheerfully shouting at all and sundry.

Self-Catering

For deli supplies and wine, shop at *alimentari,* which generally open 7am to 1.30pm and 5pm to 8pm daily except Thursday afternoon and Sunday (during the summer months they will often close on Saturday afternoon instead of Thursday). Rome's fresh-produce markets are also a good option. There are plenty of small supermarkets dotted around town.

Conad (Map p376; Stazione Termini)

DeSpar (Via Giustiniani 18b-21)

DeSpar (Map p376; Via Nazionale 212-213)

Carrefour Express (Map p364; Via Vittoria)

Sir (Map p376; Piazza dell'Indipendenza 28)

Todis (Map p372; Via Natale del Grande 24)

A FOODIE'S PERFECT DAY IN ROME

Start your day with a breakfast cappuccino and *cornetto* at **Caffè Tazza d'Oro** (p103), an iconic cafe that serves some of Rome's finest coffee. Then, with a spring in your step, wend your way over to the food market at Campo de' Fiori where you can browse what's in season. If your morning *cornetto* hasn't filled you up, pop into **Forno di Campo de' Fiori** (p100) for some of its amazing pizza *al taglio* (by the slice). You're also close to renowned deli/food store **Roscioli** (p172), whose *forno* (bakery) around the corner is likewise famous for its pizza *al taglio*. It's worth visiting the deli to drink in the mingled scents of this temple of delights, packed with salami, cheese, pastas and condiments. For lunch, make your way to Monti, close to the Colosseum, where you can browse in the Tuscan-products shop, **Podere Vecciano** (p178), which sells wine, marmalade, pesto and more, before eating at **L'Asino d'Oro** (p172), which serves outstanding Umbrian food. It's a difficult call whether to have dessert here or to stroll over to Piazza di Zingari to sample gelato from **Fatamorgana**, with its fresh flavours such as almond and cardamom, or white chocolate and pine nuts. In the afternoon, if you've planned ahead, you can take a cookery course with **Tricolore** (p173) or have a wine-tasting session at **Vino Roma** (p173), both in Monti. After this, you'll still have time to make your way to **Eataly** (p217), the culinary megastore, which not only sells an incredible range of Italian foodstuffs, cookery books and implements, but also contains 19 restaurants and cafes. You could finish off your foodie day by eating at its top-floor fine-dining restaurant, Ristorante Italia, or eat in the heartland of traditional Roman cuisine, Testaccio, at somewhere like **Flavio al Velavevodetto** (p205).

Ice Cream

Eating gelato is as much a part of Roman life as morning coffee – try it and you'll understand why. The city has some of the world's finest ice-cream shops, which use only the finest seasonal ingredients. In these artisanal gelaterie you won't find a strawberry flavour in winter, for example, and ingredients are sourced from where they are reputedly the best: pistachios from Bronte, almonds from Avola, and so on. It's all come a long way since Nero snacked on snow mixed with fruit pulp and honey. A rule of thumb is to check the colour of the pistachio flavour: ochre green is good, bright green is bad.

Most places open from around 8am to 1am, with shorter hours in winter. Prices range from around €1.70 to €3.50 for a *cona* (cone) or *coppetta* (tub or cup).

Seasonal Calendar

Although nowadays you can, of course, get some produce year round, Rome's kitchens still remain true to seasonal freshness.

SPRING

Spring is prime time for lamb, perfect roasted with potatoes – *agnello al forno con patate*. Sometimes it's described as *abbacchio* (Roman dialect for lamb) *scottadito* ('hot enough to burn fingers').

March to April is the finest season for *carciofo alla giudia* (Jewish-style artichoke), when the big, round artichokes from Cerveteri appear on the table (smaller varieties are from Sardinia).

May and June are favourable fishing months, and thus good for cuttlefish and octopus, as well as other seafood.

Grass-green *fave* (broad beans) are eaten after a meal (especially on 1 May), accompanied by some salty *pecorino*.

It's also time to tuck into *risotto con asparagi di bosco* (rice with woodland asparagus), as asparagus comes into its prime.

You'll see two types of courgette on Roman market stalls; the familiar dark-green kind, and the lighter green, fluted *zucchine romanesche* (Roman courgette), usually with the flowers still attached – these orange petals, deep-fried, are a delectable feature of Roman cooking.

This is the time to visit Nemi in the Castelli Romani to eat its famous wild strawberries.

FOOD TOUR

Food Tours Italy (www.eatingitalyfoodtours.com; tours €65; ☉daily) is run by American expat Kenny Dunn and offers informative four-hour tours around Testaccio, with chances to taste delicacies, such as *prosciutto*, along the way, before finishing up with some of Rome's best pizza. There are a maximum of 12 people to a tour.

SUMMER

Tonno (tuna) comes fresh from the seas around Sardinia; *linguine ai frutti di mare* and *risotto alla pescatora* are good light summer dishes.

Summertime is *melanzane* (aubergine or eggplant) time: tuck into them grilled as antipasti or fried and layered with rich tomato sauce in *melanzane alla parmagiana,* or try *melanzane e peperoni stufati* (stuffed aubergine and peppers).

Summer is the season for leafy greens, and Rome even has its own lettuce, the sturdy, flavourful *lattuga romana.*

Tomatoes are at their full-bodied finest – it's the ideal moment for a light *spaghetti al pomodoro* (with fresh tomatoes and basil).

Seductive heaps of *pesche* (peaches) and *albicocche* (apricots) dominate market stalls. Luscious, succulent, fleshy *fichi* (figs) ripen in June, perfect with some salty *prosciutto crudo* (cured ham).

AUTUMN

Alla cacciatora (hunter-style) dishes are sourced from Lazio's hills, with meats such as *cinghiale* (boar) and *lepre* (hare).

Fish is also good in autumn; you could try fried fish from Fiumicino, such as *triglia* (red mullet), or mixed small fish, such as *alici* (anchovies).

Autumn also brings mushrooms – the meaty porcini, *galletti* and *ovuli* – and *broccoletti* (also called *broccolini*), a cross between broccoli and asparagus; it's often served fried with *aglio* (garlic) and *olio* (olive oil). Other autumnal vegetables include cauliflower and *spinaci* (spinach), while aubergine, peppers and tomatoes continue. *Cicoria selvatica* (wild chicory) has dark-green leaves and a bitter taste, and is at its best sautéed with spicy pepper and garlic.

FOOD GLOSSARY

abbacchio al forno – lamb roasted with rosemary and garlic; usually accompanied by rosemary-roasted potatoes

agnello alla cacciatora – lamb 'hunter-style' with onion and fresh tomatoes

baccalà – salted cod, often served deep-fried in the Roman-Jewish tradition

bresaola – wind-dried beef, a feature of Roman-Jewish cuisine; served as a replacement for prosciutto (ham)

bruschette – grilled bread rubbed with garlic, splashed with olive oil and sprinkled with salt, most commonly then topped by tomatoes

bucatini all'amatriciana – thick spaghetti with tomato sauce, onions, pancetta, cheese and chilli; originated in Amatrice, a town east of Rome, as an adaptation of *spaghetti alla gricia*

cacio e pepe – pasta mixed with freshly grated *pecorino romano* (a sharp, salty, sheep's milk cheese), ground black pepper and a dash of olive oil

carciofi alla giudia – deep-fried 'Jewish-style' artichokes; the heart is soft and succulent, the leaves taste like delicious crisps

carciofi alla romana – artichokes boiled with oil, garlic and mint

coda alla vaccinara – beef tail stewed with garlic, parsley, onion, carrots, celery and spices; a dish developed when abattoir workers received the cheapest cuts of meat

fiori di zucca – courgette flowers, usually stuffed with mozzarella and anchovies and fried

frutti di mare – seafood; usually served as a sauce with pasta, comprising tomatoes, clams, mussels and perhaps prawns and calamari

gnocchi alla romana – semolina-based mini-dumplings baked with *ragù* or tomato *sugo*; traditionally served on Thursdays

involtini – thin slices of veal or beef, rolled up with sage or sometimes vegetables and mozzarella

minestra di arzilla con pasta e broccoli – skate soup with pasta and broccoli; Roman-Jewish dish served only at the most traditional restaurants

pasta con lenticchie – popular local dish of pasta with lentils

pasta e ceci – pasta with chickpeas; warms the cockles in winter

pizza bianca – 'white pizza' unique to Rome; a plain pizza brushed with salt, olive oil and often rosemary; can split and fill to make a sandwich

pollo alla romana – chicken cooked in butter, marjoram, garlic, white wine and tomatoes or peppers

polpette al sugo – meatballs served with traditional tomato sauce

porchetta – a hog roasted on a spit with herbs and an abundance of *finocchio selvatico* (wild fennel); the best comes from Ariccia, in the hills south of Rome

ragù – classic Italian meat sauce traditionally made by slowly stewing cuts of meat, or mince, in a rich tomato *sugo*

rigatoni alla pajata – thick ridged pasta tubes with the small intestine of a milk-fed calf or lamb; a Testaccio speciality

saltimbocca alla romana – the deliciously named 'leap in the mouth'; a veal cutlet jazzed up with sparing amounts of prosciutto and sage

spaghetti alla carbonara – sauce of egg, cheese and *guanciale* (cured pig's cheek); the egg is added raw, and stirred into the hot pasta to cook it

spaghetti alla gricia – pasta with *pecorino*, black pepper and pancetta or *guanciale* ;

spaghetti con le vongole – spaghetti with clams and a dash of red chilli to pep things up; sometimes served with tomatoes, sometimes without

stracciatella – humble chicken broth given a lift by the addition of Parmesan and whisked egg

sugo – all-purpose tomato sauce served in many dishes; it's traditionally combined with *basilico* (basil)

supplì – rice balls, like large croquettes; if they contain mozzarella, they're called *supplì a telefono* because when you break one open, the cheese forms a string like a telephone wire between the two halves

trippa alla romana – tripe cooked with potatoes, tomato and mint and sprinkled with *pecorino*; a typical Saturday-in-Rome dish

Fruit-wise, heaping the markets are *uva* (grapes), *pere* (pears) and *meloni* (melon).

Nuts are now in season, and creamy *nocciola* (hazelnut) and *marron* (chestnut) will be adorning ice-cream cones all over the city.

WINTER
Winter is the ideal time to eat dishes with *ceci* (chickpeas) and minestrone, as well as herb-roasted *porchetta di Ariccia* (pork from Ariccia).

Puntarelle ('little points' – Catalonian chicory), a green found only in Lazio, is a delicious, slightly bitter winter green, often tossed with a dressing of anchovy, garlic and olive oil. *Finochio* (fennel) is a favourite winter vegetable, eaten in salads or on its own. *Broccolo romanesco* (Roman broccoli) looks like a cross between broccoli and cauliflower.

Markets are piled high with *aranci* (oranges) and *mandarini* (mandarins), their brilliant orange set off by dark-green leaves.

In February, look out for *frappé* (strips of fried dough sprinkled with sugar), eaten at carnival time.

Food & Wine Courses

Check out the **Città di Gusto** (Map p382; ☑06 551 11 21; www.gamberorosso.it; Via Fermi 161), a six-storey shrine to food created by Italian foodie organisation Gambero Rosso. It has cooking courses starring Rome's top chefs, a wine bar, pizza workshop, cookbook shop and the Teatro del Vino for demonstrations, tastings and lessons.

Cookery writer Diane Seed (*The Top One Hundred Pasta Sauces*) runs her **Roman Kitchen** (Map p360; ☑06 678 5759; www.italiangourmet.com) several times a year from her kitchen in the Palazzo Doria Pamphilj. There are one-, two- and three-day courses (which include a market visit) costing €200 per day.

In Monti you can take a wine-tasting course or a food tour with **Vino Roma** (p173), which has a state-of-the-art tasting studio. There's also the cooking school **Tricolore** (p173) nearby, which offers pizza making and other culinary courses in English and Italian.

Lonely Planet's Top Choices

La Rosetta (p98) Sublime, classy fish restaurant in view of the Pantheon.

Forno di Campo de' Fiori (p100) If angels made pizza by the slice, this is how it'd taste.

Glass Hostaria (p191) Italian cuisine as a creative art in Trastevere.

Open Colonna (p173) Cooking with verve, wit and flair under a glass roof.

L'Asino d'Oro (p172) Fantastic food, stunning value and Umbrian flavours.

Best Roman

Flavio al Velavevodetto (p205)
Da Danilo (p173)
Da Felice (p206)

Best Vegetarian

Margutta Ristorante (p127)

Best Gelato

Il Gelato (p127)
Fatamorgana (p155)
Gelateria del Teatro (p99)
Il Caruso (p130)
Gelarmony (p156)

Best Food Shops

Eataly (p217)
Salumeria Roscioli (p101)
Podere Vecciano (p178)
Volpetti (p207)

Best Creative

Agata e Romeo (p173)
Glass Hostaria (p191)
Metamorfosi (p232)
Open Colonna (p173)
Ditirambo (p101)

Best Pizzerias

Pizzeria Ivo (p190)
Panattoni (p189)
Li Rioni (p204)
Bir & Fud (p190)
Pizzeria Da Remo (p205)

Best Pizza by the Slice

Forno di Campo de' Fiori (p100)
Pizzarium (p157)
Forno Roscioli (p100)
Antico Forno Urbani (p101)
00100 (p205)

Best Value

L'Asino d'Oro (p172)
Casa Coppelle (p97)
Open Colonna (p173)
Flavio al Velavevodetto (p205)
Cacio e Pepe (p156)

Best Settings

Il Palazzetto (p129)
La Veranda de l'Hotel Columbus (p155)
Open Colonna (p173)
Casa Bleve (p100)
Aroma (p205)

Best Regional

Palatium (p128)
L'Asino d'Oro (p172)
Colline Emiliane (p130)
Trattoria Monti (p173)
Mondo Arancina (p156)
Enoteca Provincia Romana (p78)

Best See & Be Seen

Said (p175)
Dal Bolognese (p127)
Settembrini (p157)
Ristorante L'Arcangelo (p157)
Molto (p232)

Best Pastry Shops

Andreotti (p218)
Artigiano Innocenti (p189)
Dolce Maniera (p158)
La Dolceroma (p101)

Best Cheap Trattorias

Da Tonino (p99)
Sergio alle Grotte (p101)
Sora Margherita (p102)
Da Valentino (p172)
Trattoria da Bucatino (p206)

Having a drink at Antica Enoteca (p128)

Drinking & Nightlife

Often the best way to enjoy nightlife in Rome is to wander from restaurant to bar, getting happily lost down picturesque cobbled streets and being serendipitously awestruck by ancient splendour. There's simply no city with better backdrops for a drink: you can savour a Campari overlooking the Roman Forum or sample some artisanal beer while watching the light bounce off baroque fountains.

Rome After Dark

Rome, like most cities, is a collection of districts, each with its own character. Different areas attract differing types of people as night falls. The *centro storico* and Trastevere pull in a mix of locals and tourists. Ostiense and Testaccio are popular with a younger, nightclubbing crowd. Northern Rome spots, such as Parioli and Ponte Milvio, tend towards a right-wing, bourgeois milieu, while places such as San Lorenzo and Pigneto, to the south, are popular with more leftist, alternative types.

The *bella figura* (loosely translated as 'looking good') is important. The majority of locals spend evenings looking beautiful, checking each other out, partaking in gelato, and not getting particularly drunk – that would be unseemly. However, this is changing and certain areas – those popular with a younger crowd – can get rowdy with tipsy teens (for example, Campo de' Fiori and parts of Trastevere).

NEED TO KNOW

Opening Hours

➡ Most cafes: 7.30am to 8pm

➡ Traditional bars: 7.30am to 1am or 2am

➡ Most bars, pubs and *enoteche* (wine bars): lunchtime or 6pm to 2am

➡ Nightclubs: 10pm to 4am

Dress Codes

Romans tend to dress up to go out, and most people will be looking pretty sharp in the smarter clubs and bars in the *centro storico* and Testaccio. However, over in Pigneto and San Lorenzo or at the *centri sociali* (social centres) the look of choice is much more grungy – men without beards may look out of place.

Internet Resources

➡ **Roma 2 Night** (http://2night.it)

➡ **Zero** (http://roma.zero.eu)

Door Policies

Some of the more popular nightclubs have a seemingly whimsical door policy, and men, whether single or in groups, will often find themselves turned away. At many clubs both men and women will have to dress up to get in and fit in.

Although the city is no Berlin or London, there's still plenty of after-dark fun to be had. Up-for-it Romans tend to eat late, then drink at bars before heading off to a club at around 1am. It can be difficult to get around as some of the best nightclubs are far-flung. Despite drink-and-drive rules, most locals drive, which partly explains the alarming road-accident statistics.

Enoteche (Wine Bars)

The *enoteca* was where the old boys from the neighbourhood used to drink rough local wine poured straight from the barrel. Times have changed: nowadays they tend to be sophisticated, if still atmospheric places, offering Italian and international vintages, delicious cheeses and cold cuts.

Bars & Pubs

In recent years beer drinking has really taken off, with some specialised bars and restaurants offering microbrewed beers.

These reflect the seasonality that's so important in Rome – for example, look for winter beers made from chestnuts. Important addresses on the artisanal-beer trail include Ma Che Siete Venuti a Fà (p191) and Open Baladin (p104).

Bars range from regular Italian cafe-bars that have seemingly remained the same for centuries, to chic, carefully styled places made for esoteric cocktails – such as Salotto 42 (p105) – and laid-back, perennially popular haunts – such as Freni e Frizioni (p191) – that have a longevity rarely seen in other cities.

Nightclubs

Rome has a range of nightclubs, mostly in Ostiense and Testaccio, with music policies ranging from lounge and jazz to dancehall and hip-hop. Clubs tend to get busy after midnight, or even after 2am. Often admission is free, but drinks are expensive. Cocktails can cost from €10 to €16, but you can drink much more cheaply in the student clubs of San Lorenzo, Pigneto and the *centri sociali* (social centres).

Centri Sociali

Rome's flip side is a surprising alternative underbelly, centred on left-wing *centri sociali*: grungy squatter arts centres that host live music and contemporary arts events. These centres of anti-establishment counterculture were set up in the 1970s in disused public buildings, such as factories, garages or industrial estates. Back then squatters often battled with police, but nowadays most *centri sociali* have been around long enough to become part of the establishment. However, they still offer Rome's most unusual and alternative nightlife option. They're also a bargain, in accordance with their ethic of accessible culture. The best of these are Brancaleone(p233) and Villaggio Globale (p207).

Rome in Summer (& Winter)

From around mid-June to mid-September, many nightclubs and live-music venues close, some moving to EUR or the beaches at Fregene or Ostia. The area around the Isola Tiberina throngs with life nightly during the Lungo il Tevere...Roma, which sprouts bars, stalls and an open-air cinema.

Be aware that in winter, bars often close earlier in the evening, particularly in areas where the norm is to drink outside.

Listings

For listings check *Trovaroma* (an insert in daily newspaper *La Repubblica*) on Thursday, which has a short English section, or the English-language *Wanted in Rome* magazine, published every second Wednesday.

Gay & Lesbian Rome

There is only a smattering of dedicated clubs and bars in Rome, though many nightclubs host regular gay and lesbian nights. Close to the Colosseum, San Giovanni in Laterano is nicknamed 'gay street' as it has a cluster of a couple of gay bars and businesses. Elsewhere, you usually have to ring a bell to gain entry to Rome's gay bars. However, Rome's pinker side is by no means invisible: there's a Gay Pride march annually in mid-June and the 10-week **Gay Village** (www.gayvillage.it; ☺Jul–mid-Sep), a temporary complex of bars, clubs, cinema and even fitness areas, hosting gigs and club nights, such as **Bears in Rome** (www.bearsinrome.it). It usually takes place in EUR.

For local information, pick up a copy of the monthly magazine *AUT,* which has listings and is published by Circolo Mario Mieli. **AZ Gay** (www.azgay.it) also produces an annual gay guide to Rome, available at tourist kiosks. Lesbians can find out more about the local scene at Coordinamento Lesbiche Italiano (p326), which has a recommended women-only restaurant, Luna e L'Altra (men are allowed at lunchtime).

Most gay venues (bars, clubs and saunas) require you to have an Arcigay (p326) membership card. These cost €15/8 per year/three months and are available from any venue that requires one.

Social Networking

Friends in Rome (www.friendsinrome.com) is a social organisation that offers a chance to mingle with an international crowd – a mix of expats, locals and out-of-towners – and find out about the local social scene. The friendly organisers arrange regular social events, including *aperitivi* evenings and film showings.

Lazio Wines

Lazio wines may not be household names yet, but it's well worth trying some local wines while you're here. Although whites dominate Lazio's production – 95% of the region's Denominazione di Origine Controllata (DOC; the second of Italy's four quality classifications) wines are white – there are a few notable reds as well. To sample Lazio wines, Palatium (p128) and Enoteca Provincia Romana (p78) are the best places to go.

WHITES

Most of the house white in Rome will be from the Castelli Romani area to the southeast of Rome, centred on Frascati and Marino. As Italian wine producers have raised their game to face international competition, so Lazio's winemakers have joined the fray. New production techniques have led to a lighter, drier wine that is beginning to be taken seriously. Frascati Superiore is now an excellent tipple, Castel de Paolis' Vigna Adriana wins plaudits, while the emphatically named Est! Est!! Est!!!, produced by the renowned wine house Falesco, based in Montefiascone on the volcanic banks of Lago Bolsena, is increasingly drinkable.

REDS

Falesco, based in Lazio, also produces the excellent Montiano, blended from merlot grapes. Colacicchi's Torre Ercolana from Anagni is another opulent red, which blends local Cesanese di Affile with cabernet sauvignon and merlot. Velvety, complex and fruity, this is a world-class wine.

Coffee

To do as the Romans do, you have to be precise about your coffee needs. For an espresso (a shot of strong black coffee), ask for *un caffè;* if you want it with a drop of hot/cold milk, order *un caffè macchiato*

ROME'S BEST GAY VENUES & NIGHTS

Hangar (p176) A cruisy, long-standing gay bar that hosts various special nights.

Coming Out (p206) Under the shadow of the Colosseum on what's sometimes nicknamed 'gay street', this popular laid-back bar is more out than most – it spills onto the street and there's no doorbell.

Venus Rising The capital's only lesbian night: last Sunday of the month at **Goa** (p218).

Muccassassina Hosts weekly extravaganzas (www.muccassassina.com)

('stained' coffee) *caldo/freddo*. Long black coffee (as in a weaker, watered-down version) is known as *caffè lungo* (an espresso with more water) or *caffè all'american* (a filter coffee). If you fancy a coffee but one more shot will catapult you through the ceiling, you can drink *orzo*, made from roasted barley but served like coffee.

Then, of course, there's the cappuccino (coffee with frothy milk, served warm rather than hot). If you want it without froth, ask for a *cappuccino senza schiuma;* if you want it hot, ask for it *ben caldo*. Italians drink cappuccino only during the morning and never after meals; to order it after 11.30am would be, well, foreign.

In summer *cappuccino freddo* (iced coffee with milk, usually already sugared), *caffè freddo* (iced espresso) and *granita di caffè* (frozen coffee, usually with cream) top the charts.

A *caffè latte* is a milkier version of the cappuccino with less froth; a *latte macchiato* is even milkier (warmed milk 'stained' with a spot of coffee). A *caffè corretto* is an espresso 'corrected' with a dash of grappa or something similar.

There are two ways to drink coffee in a Roman bar-cafe: you can either take it standing up at the bar, in which case pay first at the till and then, with your receipt, order at the counter; or you can sit down at a table and enjoy waiter service. In the latter case you'll pay up to double what you'd pay at the bar.

Drinking & Nightlife by Neighbourhood

➡ **Centro Storico** Bars and a few clubs, a mix of touristy and sophisticated (p80).

➡ **Trastevere** Everyone's favourite place for a *passeggiata* (evening stroll), with plenty of bars and cafes (p181).

➡ **Testaccio** With a cluster of mainstream clubs, there's something poptastic for most tastes (p206).

➡ **Ostiense** Home to Rome's cooler nightclubs, mostly housed in ex-industrial venues (p218).

➡ **San Lorenzo** Favoured by students; the bars and alternative clubs concentrated here are cheaper than the city centre (p176).

➡ **Pigneto** Bohemian ex-working-class district lined with bars and restaurants and popular with artists and wannabes (p171).

➡ **Ponte Milvio** Top of the pops with Rome's Smart car–driving, designer-clad bank-of-mama-and-papa youth (p232).

Lonely Planet's Top Choices

Ai Tre Scalini (p175) Buzzing *enoteca* that feels as convivial as a pub.

Ma Che Siete Venuti a Fà (p191) Tiny pub that's the heart of Rome's artisanal-beer explosion.

Il Tiaso (p171) Welcoming, cool Pigneto bar with outside tables and regular live music in its tiny gallery.

Caffè Sant'Eustachio (p103) Serves Rome's best coffee, with a secret recipe.

La Scena (p130) Beautiful art deco bar that's perfect for a glass of *prosecco*.

Best Cafes

Caffè Tazza d'Oro (p103)

Caffè della Pace (p104)

Chiostro del Bramante Caffè (p98)

2 Periodico Caffè (p175)

Art Studio Café (p157)

Best for a Lazy Drink

Ombre Rosse (p192)

Caffè della Pace (p104)

La Scena (p130)

Stravinkij Bar (p130)

Fandango Incontro (p105)

Best for Dancing

Circolo degli Artisti (p171)

Goa (p218)

Rashomon (p218)

La Saponeria (p218)

Neo Club (p218)

Best Enoteche

Cavour 313 (p79)

Fafiuché (p175)

Palatium (p128)

Enoteca Provincia Romana (p78)

Best Settings

Chiostro del Bramante Caffè (p98)

Caffè Capitolino (p79)

Il Baretto (p192)

La Scena (p130)

Best Museum Cafes

Caffè Capitolino (p79)

MAXXI (p228)

Auditorium Parco della Musica (p225)

Galleria Nazionale d'Arte Moderna (p225)

Castel Sant'Angelo (p154)

Best Aperitivo

Freni e Frizioni (p191)

La Meschita (p192)

Doppiozeroo (p218)

Necci (p171)

Interior of the Teatro dell'Opera di Roma (p177)

 # Entertainment

Watching the world go by in Rome is often entertainment enough, but don't overlook the local arts and sports scenes. Rome is home to the extraordinary Auditorium Parco della Musica, hosting performances by international artists of all genres. There are also fantastic arts festivals, especially in summer, performances with Roman ruins as a backdrop and football games that split the city asunder.

Music

Rome's abundance of beautiful settings makes it a superb place to catch a concert. Once it was overlooked on the international gig circuit, but these days myriad international stars play in the Eternal City. This artistic revolution is all down to one building: the Auditorium Parco della Musica (p225), a state-of-the-art, Renzo Piano–designed complex that combines architectural innovation with perfect acoustics.

CLASSICAL

Music in Rome is not just about the Auditorium, however. There are concerts by the Accademia Filarmonica Romana at Teatro Olimpico (p233), the Auditorium Conciliazione (p158), Rome's premier classical music venue before the newer Auditorium was opened, is still a force to be reckoned with and the Istituzione Universitaria dei Concerti (p177) holds concerts in the Aula Magna of La Sapienza University.

Free classical concerts are often held in many of Rome's churches, especially at

Easter and around Christmas and New Year; look out for information at Rome's tourist kiosks. The Basilica di San Paolo Fuori le Mura (p168) hosts an important choral mass on 25 January and the hymn *Te Deum* is sung at the Chiesa del Gesù on 31 December.

OPERA

Historically, opera in Rome was long opposed by the papacy, and although the first public opera house opened here in the 17th century, it was only after independence that Rome's opera scene began to develop.

Rome's current opera house, the Teatro dell'Opera di Roma, is a magnificent, grandiose venue, lined in gilt and red, but productions can be a bit hit and miss. The company moves outdoors for the summer season at the ancient Roman Terme di Caracalla, an even more spectacular setting.

You can also see opera in various other outdoor locations: check listings or at the tourist information kiosks for details.

JAZZ, ROCK & POP

Besides the Auditorium Parco della Musica, large concerts also take place at Rome's sports stadiums, including Stadio Olimpico and the racetrack on the Appia Nuova, the Ippodromo La Capannelle.

Jazz is a popular soundtrack for the Eternal City, and there are numerous jazz and blues clubs, including Big Mama, Gregory's, Alexanderplatz, the Charity Café and the Casa del Jazz.

Many bars and nightclubs also host live gigs. San Lorenzo and Pigneto addresses such as Locanda Atlantide, Esc Atelier, Dimmidisi and Circolo degli Artisti host alternative rock and pop acts. Blackmarket, a wine bar in Monti, hosts the acoustic 'Unplugged in Monti'.

In summer, concerts take place in the wonderful setting of Centrale Montemartini, an ex-power station in Ostiense filled with classical sculpture, and at Open Colonna, the glass-roofed restaurant at the Palazzo delle Esposizioni. Other clubs, such as Contestaccio in Testaccio, line up acts from extreme electro to U2 tribute bands. Micca Club, in southern Rome, hosts an eclectic mix, including swing, rockabilly and jazz.

The *centri sociali*, alternative arts centres set up in venues around Rome, are also good places to catch a gig, especially Brancaleone in northern Rome, and Villa-

gio Globale in Testaccio, with music encompassing hip-hop, electro, dubstep, reggae and dancehall.

Dance

Dance is not an art form that receives much patronage in Italy, and the best dancers tend to go abroad to work. But visiting dance companies are often class acts, and they're enthusiastically supported. The Teatro dell'Opera di Roma is home to Rome's official Corps de Ballet and has a ballet season running in tandem with its opera performances. In summer performances are outdoors at the Terme di Caracalla. Rome's Auditorium hosts classical and contemporary dance performances, as well as the Equilibrio Festival della Nuova Danza, in February. The Auditorium Conciliazione is another good place to catch contemporary dance companies. Invito alla Danza is a contemporary dance festival in July that encompasses tango, jazz dance, contemporary and more.

Film

Rome's cinematic heyday was in the 1960s, with Fellini producing films like *La Dolce Vita* and *Roma,* and in the 1970s when the Cinecittà (Film City) studios churned out a feast of spaghetti westerns. Cinecittà is still going, with recent films made here

PLAN YOUR TRIP ENTERTAINMENT

NEED TO KNOW

Internet Resources

➡ **Comune di Roma** (www.comune.roma.it; www.060608.it)

➡ **In Rome Now** (www.inromenow.com)

➡ **Roma Musica** (www.romamusica.it)

➡ **Tutto Teatro** (www.tuttoteatro.com)

Tickets

Tickets for concerts, live music and theatrical performances are widely available across the city. Prices range enormously depending on the venue and artist. Hotels can often reserve tickets for guests, or you can contact the venue or organisation directly – check listings publications for booking details. Otherwise you can try:

Hellò Ticket (☑800 90 70 80; www.helloticket.it)

Orbis (☑06 474 47 76; Piazza dell'Esquilino 37)

including Woody Allen's *To Rome with Love*, but is now mainly used for TV work. The studios, built by Mussolini in 1937, suffered a setback in 2007, when around 3000 sq metres of the complex were destroyed by fire. It started in storage lots for the *Rome* set, though no-one could confirm if Nero was fiddling as it burned. The studios did arise, phoenix-like, from the ashes, but have been hit by competition from cheaper studio alternatives in Eastern Europe.

In 2006, Rome began holding a star-studded international film festival, Festival Internazionale del Film di Roma, which has since taken place every year in November.

Filmgoing is perennially popular, and there are some 80-odd cinemas dotted around the city. Most foreign films are dubbed into Italian; those shown in the original language are indicated in listings by *versione originale* or VO after the title. There are several cinemas that regularly show English versions.

Tickets cost around €8. Afternoon and early evening screenings are generally cheaper, while all tickets are discounted on Wednesday.

Theatre

Rome has a thriving local theatre scene, with more than 80 theatres dotted across town, which include both traditional places and an increasing number of smaller experimental venues. Performances are usually in Italian.

Particularly wonderful are the summer festivals that make use of Rome's archaeological scenery. Performances take place in settings such as Villa Adriana in Tivoli, Ostia Antica's Roman theatre and the Teatro di Marcello. In summer the **Miracle Players** (06 7039 3427; www.miracleplayers.org) perform classic English drama or historical comedy in English next to the

Roman Forum and other open-air locations. Performances are usually free.

Arts Festivals

Rome hosts a marvellous (if shrinking, due to lack of funds) array of arts and cultural festivals, especially during the summer.

Concerti del Tempietto (www.tempietto.it) The ancient Teatro di Marcello (June to September) and the lovely Villa Torlonia (July) form marvellous venues for a summer concert series.

Festival Internazionale di Villa Adriana (06 8024 1281; www.auditorium.com/villaadriana) Concerts, international theatre and dance in the magnificent ruins of the emperor Hadrian's country villa in Tivoli (June to July).

Lungo il Tevere (www.lungoiltevereroma.it) Summer-long festival, with comedy acts, jazz, film, craft stalls and bars, clustered around the banks of Isola Tiberina.

Invito alla Danza (www.invitoalladanza.it) International performers (anything from tango to jazz) in the beautiful parklands of Villa Doria Pamphilj (p188) in July; part of the Estate Romana festival.

Roma Incontra il Mondo (www.villaada.org) This fabulous world music festival takes place lakeside from June to July in the breathtaking setting of Villa Ada, with music from everywhere from Japan to Jamaica.

Spectator Sports

FOOTBALL

In this country of great passions, *il calcio* (football) is one of the greatest, and from September to May, Romans flock to the Stadio Olimpico (p234) to worship or curse their team of choice.

In Rome you're either for A.S. Roma (*giallorossi* – yellow and reds) or Lazio (*biancazzuri* – white and blues), with both

---

CINEMA UNDER THE STARS

There are various atmospheric outdoor summer film festivals; check current listings. The following take place annually.

Isola del Cinema (www.isoladelcinema.com) Independent films in the romantic setting of the Isola Tiberina in summer. This runs in conjunction with the riverside Lungo il Tevere festival.

Notti di Cinema a Piazza Vittorio (www.agisanec.lazio.it) Italian and international releases at two open-air screens in Piazza Vittorio Emanuele II from June to September. Tickets cost €7.

A.S. ROMA VS LAZIO

The Rome derby is one of the football season's highest-profile games. The rivalry between Roma and Lazio is fierce and little love is lost between the fans. If you go to the Stadio Olimpico, make sure you get it right – Roma fans (in deep red with a natty orange/yellow trim) flock to the *Curva Sud* (South Stand), while Lazio supporters (in light blue) stand in the *Curva Nord* (North Stand). If you want to sit on the fence, head to the Tribuna Tevere or Tribuna Monte Mario.

For more details on the clubs, check out www.asroma.it and www.sslazio.it (both in Italian).

teams playing in Serie A (Italy's premier league). Both sides are considered solid, top-level performers, but Lazio has run into problems in recent years, while Roma has seen patchy success. Financial problems have beset both clubs, forcing them to sell top players and rely on one or two star performers. A new Roma stadium is currently being built at Tor di Valle, due to be completed in time for the 2016/17 season.

Lazio's fans traditionally come from the provincial towns outside Rome, while Roma's supporters, known as *romanisti*, are historically working class, from Rome's Jewish community and from Trastevere, Testaccio and Garbatella. Both sets of supporters have an unfortunate controversial minority who have been known to cause trouble at matches.

From September to May there's a game at home for Roma or Lazio almost every weekend and a trip to Rome's football stadium, the Stadio Olimpico, is an unforgettable experience. Note that ticket purchase regulations are far stricter than they used to be. Tickets have to bear the holder's name and passport or ID number, and you must present a photo ID at the turnstiles when entering the stadium. Two tickets are permitted per purchase for Serie A, Coppa Italia and UEFA Champions League games; if you want to buy more, you can, but they will probably not be together. Tickets cost from around €20 to €150. You can buy them from www.ticketone.it, www.listicket.it, from ticket agencies or at one of the A.S. Roma or Lazio stores around the city. To get to the stadium, take metro line A to Ottaviano–San Pietro and then bus 32.

BASKETBALL
Basketball is a popular spectator sport in Rome, though it inspires nothing like the fervour of football. Rome's team, Virtus Roma, plays throughout the winter months at the **Palalottomatica** (☑199 12 88 00; Viale dell'Umanesimo; Ⓜ EUR Palasport) in EUR.

RUGBY UNION
Every time a Six Nations game is played in Rome, the city fills with a swell of foreign spectators, easily discernible by their penchant for amusing hats and beer.

Italy's rugby team, the Azzurri (the Blues), entered the Six Nations tournament in 2000, and has been the competition underdog ever since. However, it has scored some big wins in recent years, with shock wins over France in 2011 and 2013.

The team usually plays home international games at Rome's **Stadio Flaminio** (☑06 3685 7309; www.federugby.it; Viale Maresciallo Pilsudski), but works are currently taking place there, and so games are being staged at the Stadio Olimpico.

TENNIS
Italy's premier tennis tournament, the Italian International Tennis Championships, is one of the most important events on the European tennis circuit. Every May the world's top players meet on the clay courts at the monumental, Fascist-era **Foro Italico** (☑06 3685 8218; Viale del Foro Italico). Tickets can be bought at the Foro Italico each day of the tournament, except for the final days, which are sold out weeks in advance.

EQUESTRIAN EVENTS
Rome's top equestrian event is the **Piazza di Siena showjumping competition** (☑06 3685 8420; www.piazzadisiena.org), an international annual event held in May, gorgeously set in Villa Borghese. An important fixture on the high-society calendar, it attracts a moneyed Anglophile crowd.

Lonely Planet's Top Choices

Auditorium Parco della Musica (p233) An incredible venue hosting an eclectic, must-see programme of music, art and more.

Opera di Roma at Terme di Caracalla (p202) Opera and ballet set against an unforgettable ancient Roman backdrop.

Silvano Toti Globe Theatre (p233) Like the Globe Theatre in London, but with much better weather.

Estate Romana (p26) Great umbrella festival that sees arts events all summer long.

Best Classical Venues

Auditorium Parco della Musica (p233)

Teatro dell'Opera di Roma (p177)

Terme di Caracalla (p202)

Auditorium Conciliazione (p158)

Best for Live Gigs

Circolo degli Artisti (p171)

Villaggio Globale (p207)

Micca Club (p176)

Locanda Atlantide (p176)

Best for Jazz

Alexanderplatz (p158)

Charity Café (p177)

Big Mama (p192)

Gregory's (p131)

Best Theatres

Silvano Toti Globe Theatre (p233)

Ostia Antica (p236)

Teatro Argentina (p105)

Best Festivals

Estate Romana (p26)

Lungo il Tevere (p50)

Concerti del Tempietto (p50)

Roma Incontra il Mondo (p50)

Best Sporting Venues

Foro Italico (p228)

Stadio Olimpico (p234)

Piazza di Siena (p225)

Palalottomatica (p51)

LONELY PLANET / GETTY IMAGES ©

Shoppers on the Via dei Condotti (p119)

Shopping

Rome's shops, studios and boutiques make retail therapy diverting enough to distract you from the incredible cityscape. Wander the backstreets and you'll find yourself glancing into dusty workshops of framers and furniture restorers. Narrow lanes are dotted by jewel-like boutiques and department stores have an old-school glamour. It's not that there are no chain stores in Rome, but the city is still dominated by individual shops.

What to Buy

Italy's reputation for quality is deserved, and Rome is a splendid place to shop for designer clothes, shoes and leather goods. There is also a wonderful array of designers with one-off boutiques, places to buy bespoke shoes, and jewellery and leather goods. Foodstuffs are, of course, the tops, and heavenly temples to gourmet snacks abound – delis, bakeries, *pasticcerie (pastry shops)* and chocolate shops. Homewares are another Italian speciality, and many shops focus on covetable stainless-steel kitchenware and super-sleek interior design.

High Fashion

Big-name designer boutiques gleam in the grid of streets between Piazza di Spagna and Via del Corso. The great Italian and international names are represented here, as well as many more off-beat designers, selling clothes, shoes, accessories and dreams. The immaculately clad high-fashion spine is Via dei Condotti, but there's also lots of high fashion in

NEED TO KNOW

Opening Hours

➡ Most city-centre shops: 9am to 7.30pm (or 10am to 8pm) Monday to Saturday; some close Monday morning

➡ Smaller shops: 9am to 1pm & 3.30 to 7.30pm (or 4 to 8pm) Monday to Saturday

Prices & Sales

Good quality costs money, so to grab a bargain, you should try to time your visit to coincide with the *saldi* (sales). These don't take place as often as in other countries and are a real event as everyone tries to grab a bargain. Winter sales run from early January to mid-February and summer sales from July to early September.

Payment & Receipts

Most shops accept credit cards and many accept travellers cheques. Note that you're required by Italian law to have a *ricevuta* (receipt) for your purchases.

Taxes & Refunds

Non-EU residents who spend more than €155 at shops with a **'Tax Free for Tourists'** (www.taxrefund.it) sticker are entitled to a tax rebate. Fill in a form in the shop and get it stamped by customs as you leave Italy.

Via Borgognona, Via Frattina, Via della Vite and Via del Babuino.

Downsizing a euro or two, Via Nazionale, Via del Corso, Via dei Giubbonari and Via Cola di Rienzo are good for midrange clothing stores, with some enticing small boutiques set amid the chains.

ONE-OFF BOUTIQUES & VINTAGE

Best for cutting-edge designer boutiques and vintage clothes is bohemian Via del Governo Vecchio, running from a small square just off Piazza Navona towards the river. Other places for one-off boutiques are Via del Pellegrino and around Campo de' Fiori. Via del Boschetto, Via Urbana and Via dei Serpenti in the Monti area feature unique designers and jewellery makers. Head to San Lorenzo for edgy arts and crafts; you can preview these at **Made in San Lorenzo** (www.madeinsanlorenzo.it).

Antiques

For antiques, Via dei Coronari, Via Margutta, Via Giulia and Via dei Banchi Vecchi are the best places to look – quality is high, as are the prices.

Artisan Works

Rome's shopping scene has a surprising number of artists and artisans who create their goods on the spot in hidden workshops. There are several places in Tridente where you can get a bag, wallet or belt made to your specifications; in other shops you can commission lamps or embroidery.

Foodstuffs

Rome is deli heaven, of course. Also well worth a visit are Rome's many food markets, where you can buy cheese, salami and other delicious stuff; note there's also the farmers market at Circo Massimo at weekends.

Ecclesiastical

South of the Pantheon, a string of ecclesiastical shops has clerics from all over the world trying out ceremonial capes for their swish factor. If you want an icon or a pair of (glorious!) cardinal's socks (in poppy red or ecclesiastical purple), try Via dei Cestari.

Ghezzi (Map p360; ☑06 686 97 44; Via dei Cestari 32-33) The least daunting of the shops.

Annibale Gammarelli (Map p360; ☑06 680 13 14; www.gammarelli.com; Via di Santa Chiara 34) If nothing but the pope's tailors will do.

Statuaria – Arte Sacra (☑06 679 37 53; www.statuariaartesacra.com; Via Andrea Solario 86, EUR) For a life-sized statue of the Virgin Mary or a host of smaller icons..

Centro Russia Ecumenica il Messaggio dell'Icona (Map p368; ☑06 689 66 37; www.russiaecumenica.it; Borgo Pio 141) Near St Peter's; sells original painted icons, some glinting with real gold leaf.

Lonely Planet's Top Choices

Confetteria Moriondo & Gariglio (p109) A magical-seeming chocolate shop.

Vertecchi (p133) Art emporium with beautiful paper and notebooks.

Lucia Odescalchi (p133) Exotic, work-of-art jewellery housed in a palace.

Armando Rioda (p132) Artisans create luscious handbags at non-designer prices.

Bottega di Marmoraro (p131) Have the motto of your choice carved into a marble slab at this delightful shop.

Best Foodstuffs

Volpetti (p207)

Eataly (p217)

Salumeria Roscioli (p101)

Pio La Torre (p109)

Podere Vecciano (p178)

Best Bookshops

Feltrinelli (p106)

Feltrinelli International (p180)

Almost Corner Bookshop (p193)

Libreria La Gru (p178)

Best Rome Souvenirs

Vertecchi (p133)

Bottega di Marmoraro (p131)

Arion Esposizioni (p178)

A.S. Roma Store (p110)

Best Artisanal

Claudio Sanò (p180)

Bottega di Marmoraro (p131)

Armando Rioda (p132)

Le Artigiane (p105)

Best Clothing

Eleonora (p133)

Luna & l'Altra (p107)

daDADA 52 (p108)

101 (p178)

Best Homewares

C.U.C.I.N.A. (p133)

Leone Limentani (p109)

Retrò (p106)

Spazio Sette (p106)

Best Gifts

Vertecchi (p133)

Fabriano (p132)

C.U.C.I.N.A. (p133)

Officina della Carta (p193)

Best Shoes

Borini (p108)

Fausto Santini (p134)

Danielle (p132)

Barrilà Boutique (p132)

Explore Rome

ROME'S TOP SIGHTS

Neighbourhoods
at a Glance

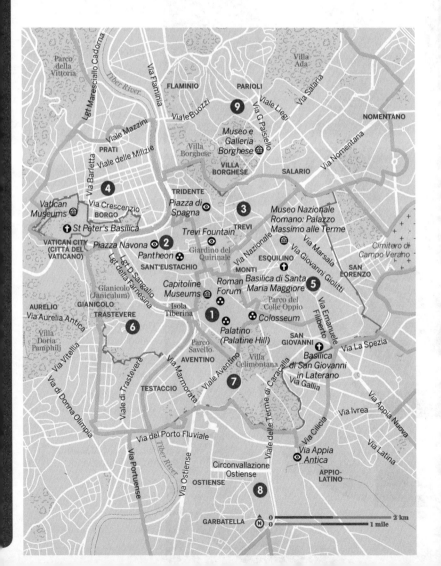

❶ Ancient Rome (p60)

In a city of extraordinary beauty, Rome's ancient heart stands out. It's here that you'll find the great icons of Rome's past: the Colosseum, the Palatino, the forums and Campidoglio (Capitoline Hill). Touristy by day, it's quiet at night with few after-hours attractions.

❷ Centro Storico (p80)

The tangled historic centre is the Rome that many come to see – a heady warren of cobbled alleyways, animated piazzas, Renaissance *palazzi* (mansions), cafes, restaurants and stylish bars. The Pantheon and Piazza Navona are the star turns, but you'll also find a host of monuments, museums and art-laden churches.

❸ Tridente, Trevi & the Quirinale (p111)

Counting the Trevi Fountain and Spanish Steps among its headline sights, this area is glamorous, debonair and touristy. The streets around Piazza di Spagna ooze money with their designer boutiques, fashionable bars and swish hotels; the Trevi Fountain area swarms with overpriced eateries and brassy souvenir shops; and the hilltop Quirinale exudes sober authority.

❹ Vatican City, Borgo & Prati (p136)

Over the river from the historic centre, the Vatican is home to two of Rome's top attractions – St Peter's Basilica and the Vatican Museums (where you'll find the Sistine Chapel) – as well as hundreds of overpriced restaurants and souvenir shops. Nearby, the upmarket residential district of Prati offers excellent accommodation, eating and shopping.

❺ Monti, Esquilino & San Lorenzo (p159)

Centred on transport hub Stazione Termini, this is a large and cosmopolitan district. Hidden behind its busy roads you'll find some amazing churches, one of Rome's best museums (Palazzo Massimo alle Terme), and any number of cool bars and restaurants, mostly in the Monti, San Lorenzo and Pigneto districts.

❻ Trastevere & Gianicolo (p181)

With its picture-perfect lanes, colourful *palazzi* and boho vibe, Trastevere is one of Rome's most vibrant neighbourhoods. Formerly a bastion of working-class independence, it's now a trendy hang-out full of restaurants, cafes, pubs and pizzerias. Behind it, the Gianicolo Hill is a lovely, romantic spot commanding superb views.

❼ San Giovanni to Testaccio (p195)

This sweeping, multifaceted area has something for everyone: medieval churches and monumental basilicas (Basilica di San Giovanni in Laterano above all), towering ruins (Terme di Caracalla) and tranquil parkland (Villa Celimontana). Down by the river, Testaccio is an earthy, workaday district known for its traditional trattorias and thumping nightlife.

❽ Southern Rome (p208)

Boasting a wealth of diversions, from ancient catacombs to futuristic ministries and cutting-edge clubs, this huge region extends to Rome's southern limits. Interest centres on Via Appia Antica, the ancient Appian Way and home to the early Christian catacombs; post-industrial Ostiense, full of clubs and popular eateries; and EUR, a modernistic purpose-built suburb in the extreme south of the city.

❾ Villa Borghese & Northern Rome (p220)

This moneyed part of Rome encompasses the city's most famous park (Villa Borghese) and its most sought-after residential district (Parioli). Concert-goers head to the Auditorium Parco della Musica while art-lovers choose between contemporary exhibitions at MAXXI or baroque marvels at the Museo e Galleria Borghese, one of Rome's best galleries.

Ancient Rome

COLOSSEUM | PALATINO | THE FORUMS | CAMPIDOGLIO | PIAZZA VENEZIA | FORUM BOARIUM

Neighbourhood Top Five

1 Getting your first glimpse of the **Colosseum** (p62). Rome's towering gladiatorial amphitheatre is an architectural masterpiece, the blueprint for many modern stadiums and a stark, spine-tingling reminder of the brutality of ancient times.

2 Exploring the haunting ruins of the **Palatino** (p64), ancient Rome's most exclusive neighbourhood.

3 Coming face to face with centuries of awe-inspiring art at the historic **Capitoline Museums** (p71).

4 Walking up Via Sacra, the once grand thoroughfare of the **Roman Forum** (p67).

5 Surveying the city spread out beneath you from atop **Il Vittoriano** (p76).

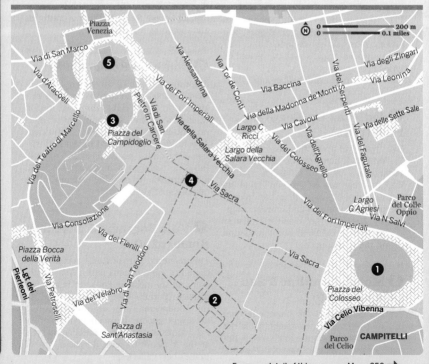

For more detail of this area, see Map p356 ➡

Explore: Ancient Rome

Located to the south of the city centre, this area contains the great ruins of the ancient city, all concentrated within walking distance of each other. They start to get crowded mid-morning and thronged with tourists until mid- to late afternoon, although in peak season they can be busy all day. Apart from the big sights, which you can comfortably cover in a couple of days, there's little in the way of nightlife or after-hours action.

The area has two focal points: the Colosseum to the east and the Campidoglio (Capitoline Hill) to the west. In between lie the forums: the more famous Roman Forum on the left of Via dei Fori Imperiali as you walk up from the Colosseum, and the Imperial Forums on the right. Rising above the Roman Forum is the Palatino, and behind that the Circo Massimo. Continuing northwest from the Circo Massimo brings you to the Forum Boarium, ancient Rome's cattle market and river port, where you'll find the Bocca della Verità, Rome's mythical lie detector.

To explore the area, the obvious starting point is the Colosseum, which is easily accessible by metro. From here you could go directly up to the Roman Forum, but if you go first to the Palatino (your Colosseum ticket covers the Palatino and Roman Forum) you'll get some wonderful views over the forums. From the Palatino enter the Forum and work your way up to Piazza del Campidoglio and the Capitoline Museums. Nearby, the mammoth white Vittoriano is difficult to miss.

Local Life

➡ **Exhibitions** While tourists climb all over Il Vittoriano, locals head inside to catch an exhibition at the Complesso del Vittoriano (p76).

➡ **Celebrations** Join Romans to celebrate the city's birthday, the Natale di Roma, on 21 April. Events and historical re-enactments are held in and around Rome's ancient sights.

➡ **Jogging** Don your trainers and run with the Romans on the Circo Massimo (p74), a popular jogging venue.

Getting There & Away

➡ **Bus** Frequent buses head to Piazza Venezia, including numbers 40, 64, 87, 170, 492, 916 and H.

➡ **Metro** Metro line B has stops at the Colosseum (Colosseo) and Circo Massimo. At Termini follow signs for Line B direzione Laurentina.

Lonely Planet's Top Tip

The big sights in this part of Rome are among the city's most visited. To avoid the worst of the crowds try to visit early morning or in the late afternoon, when it's cooler and the light is much better for taking photos.

Bring bottled water and eats with you as the bars and snack trucks on Via dei Fori Imperiali are a real rip-off.

 Best Places to Eat

➡ Enoteca Provincia Romana (p78)

➡ Cristalli di Zucchero (p78)

➡ Hostaria da Nerone (p78)

For reviews, see p78 ➡

 Best Places to Drink

➡ Cavour 313 (p79)

➡ Caffè Capitolino (p79)

➡ 0,75 (p79)

For reviews, see p79 ➡

Best Lookouts

➡ Il Vittoriano (p76)

➡ Orti Farnesiani, Palatino (p64)

➡ Tabularium, Capitoline Museums (p71)

➡ Cordonata, Piazza del Campidoglio (p75)

For reviews, see p62 ➡

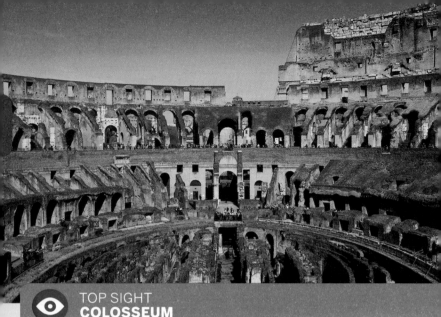

TOP SIGHT
COLOSSEUM

A monument to raw, merciless power, the Colosseum is the most thrilling of Rome's ancient sights. It's not just the amazing completeness of the place, or its size, but the sense of violent history that resonates: it was here that gladiators met in mortal combat and condemned prisoners fought off wild beasts in front of baying, bloodthirsty crowds. Two thousand years on and it's Italy's top tourist attraction, drawing up to five million visitors a year.

Built by Vespasian (r AD 69–79) in the grounds of Nero's vast Domus Aurea complex, the Colosseum was inaugurated in AD 80. To mark the occasion, Vespasian's son and successor Titus (r AD 79–81) staged games that lasted 100 days and nights, during which some 5000 animals were slaughtered. Trajan (r AD 98–117) later topped this, holding a marathon 117-day killing spree involving 9000 gladiators and 10,000 animals.

The 50,000-seat arena was originally known as the Flavian Amphitheatre, and although it was Rome's most fearful arena, it wasn't the biggest – the Circo Massimo could hold up to 250,000 people. The name Colosseum, when introduced in medieval times, was not a reference to its size but to the *Colosso di Nerone,* a giant statue of Nero that stood nearby.

With the fall of the Roman Empire in the 5th century, the Colosseum was abandoned and gradually became overgrown. In the Middle Ages it became a fortress, occupied by two of the city's warrior families, the Frangipani and the Annibaldi. During the Renaissance and baroque era it was used as a quarry for travertine, and marble stripped from it was used in the construction of Palazzo Venezia, Palazzo Barberini and Palazzo Cancelleria, among other buildings. In more recent times pollution and vibrations caused by traffic and the metro have taken a toll. The battle to maintain it is continuous and work is

DON'T MISS...

➡ The stands
➡ The arena
➡ The hypogeum

PRACTICALITIES

➡ Map p356
➡ ✆06 3996 7700
➡ www.coopculture.it
➡ Piazza del Colosseo
➡ adult/reduced incl Roman Forum & Palatino €12/7.50
➡ ⊘8.30am-1hr before sunset
➡ Ⓜ Colosseo

currently underway on a major 2½-year €25 million restoration project, involving a serious clean up of the grime-encrusted walls, the opening up of new areas to the public and the construction of a new visitor centre.

The Exterior
The outer walls have three levels of arches, articulated by Ionic, Doric and Corinthian columns. They were originally covered in travertine, and marble statues once filled the niches on the 2nd and 3rd storeys. The upper level had supports for 240 masts that held up a canvas awning over the arena, shading the spectators from sun and rain. The 80 entrance arches, known as *vomitoria,* allowed the spectators to enter and be seated in a matter of minutes.

The Arena
The arena originally had a wooden floor covered in sand to prevent the combatants from slipping and to soak up the blood. It could also be flooded for mock sea battles. Trapdoors led down to the hypogeum, an underground complex of corridors, cages and lifts that extended beneath the arena floor.

The Seating
The *cavea,* for spectator seating, was divided into three tiers: magistrates and senior officials sat in the lowest tier, wealthy citizens in the middle and the plebs in the highest tier. Women (except for Vestal Virgins) were relegated to the cheapest sections at the top. And as for modern games, tickets were numbered and spectators were assigned a specified seat in a specified sector.

The podium, a broad terrace in front of the tiers of seats, was reserved for emperors, senators and VIPs.

Hypogeum
The hypogeum, along with the top tier, can be visited on guided tours. These cost €8 on top of the normal Colosseum ticket and require advance booking.

The hypogeum extended under the Colosseum's main arena and served as the stadium's backstage area. Here, scenery for the elaborate performances was put together and hoisted up by a complex system of lifts and pulleys. Gladiators would enter the hypogeum directly from the nearby gladiator school and wild animals would be brought in from the 'zoo' on the Celio Hill and kept in cages built into the walls.

BEAT THE QUEUES

The Colosseum gets very busy and long queues are the norm. Buy your ticket from the Palatino entrance (about 250m away at Via di San Gregorio 30) or the Roman Forum entrance (Largo della Salara Vecchia). Alternatively, you could get the Roma Pass, which is valid for three days and a whole host of sites; book your ticket online at www.coopculture.it (booking fee of €1.50). Or you could join an official English-language tour (€5 on top of the regular Colosseum ticket price). Buy tickets at the designated counter, where queues are usually shorter.

Games staged at the Colosseum usually involved gladiators fighting wild animals or each other. But contrary to Hollywood folklore, bouts rarely ended in death as the games' sponsor was required to pay compensation to a gladiator's owner if the gladiator died in action.

TOP SIGHT
PALATINO

Sandwiched between the Roman Forum and the Circo Massimo, the Palatino (Palatine Hill) is an atmospheric area of towering pine trees, majestic ruins and memorable views. According to legend, this is where Romulus and Remus were saved by a wolf and where Romulus founded Rome in 753 BC. Archaeological evidence cannot prove the legend but it has dated human habitation here to the 8th century BC.

As the most central of Rome's seven hills, and because it was close to the Roman Forum, the Palatino was ancient Rome's most exclusive neighbourhood. The emperor Augustus lived here all his life and successive emperors built increasingly opulent palaces. But after Rome's fall, it fell into disrepair and in the Middle Ages churches and castles were built over the ruins. Later, during the Renaissance, wealthy families established gardens on the hill.

Most of the Palatino as it appears today is covered by the ruins of the emperor Domitian's vast complex, which served as the main imperial palace for 300 years. Divided into the Domus Flavia (imperial palace), Domus Augustana (the emperor's private residence) and a *stadio* (stadium), it was built in the 1st century AD.

DON'T MISS...

➡ Stadio
➡ Domus Augustana
➡ Casa di Augusto
➡ Orti Farnesiani

PRACTICALITIES

➡ Map p356
➡ ☎06 3996 7700
➡ www.coopculture.it
➡ Via di San Gregorio 30
➡ adult/reduced incl Colosseum & Roman Forum €12/7.50
➡ ⊙8.30am-1hr before sunset
➡ ⓂColosseo

Stadio

On entering the Palatino from Via di San Gregorio, head uphill until you come to the first recognisable construction, the *stadio*. This sunken area, which was part of the main imperial palace, was used by the emperor for private games. Adjoining the stadium to the south are the impressive remains of a complex built by Septimius Severus, comprising baths (the **Terme di Settimio Severo**) and a palace (the **Domus Severiana**).

Domus Augustana & Domus Flavia

Next to the *stadio* are the ruins of the Domus Augustana, the emperor's private residence. Over two levels, rooms lead off a *peristilio* (garden courtyard) on each floor. You can't get to the lower level, but from above you can see the basin of a fountain and beyond it rooms that were paved with coloured marble.

Over on the other side of the Museo Palatino is the Domus Flavia, the public part of Domitian's palace complex. The Domus was centred on a grand columned peristyle – the grassy area with the base of an octagonal fountain – off which the main halls led. To the north was the emperor's vast throne room (the *aula regia*); to the west, a basilica (used by the emperor to meet his advisers); and to the south, a large banqueting hall, the *triclinium*.

Museo Palatino

The **Museo Palatino** (Map p356; admission incl in Palatino ticket; ⊙8.30am-1hr before sunset; ⓂColosseo) houses a small collection of finds from the Palatino. The downstairs section illustrates the history of the hill from its origins to the Republican age, while upstairs you'll find artefacts from the Imperial age, including a beautiful 1st-century bronze, the Erma di Canefora.

Casa di Livia & Casa di Augusto

Among the best-preserved buildings on the Palatino is the Casa di Livia (closed to the public), northwest of the Domus Flavia. Home to Augustus' wife Livia, it was built around an atrium leading onto what were once frescoed reception rooms. In front is the Casa di Augusto (Map p356; ⊙11am-3.30pm Mon, Wed, Sat & Sun; ⓂColosseo), Augustus' separate residence, which contains superb frescoes in vivid reds, yellows and blues. Entry to the Casa di Augusto is in groups of five.

Criptoportico

Reached from near the Orti Farnesiani, the *criptoportico* is a 128m tunnel where Caligula is said to have been murdered, and which Nero used to connect his Domus Aurea with the Palatino. Lit by a series of windows, it originally boasted elaborate stucco decorations and is now used to stage temporary exhibitions.

Orti Farnesiani

In the northwest corner of the Palatino the Orti Farnesiani are one of Europe's earliest botanical gardens. Named after Cardinal Alessandro Farnese, who had them laid out in the mid-16th century, they boast lovely perfumed hedges and shady pines. Twin pavilions at the garden's northernmost point command breathtaking views over the Roman Forum.

ROMULUS & REMUS

The Palatino is closely associated with the legend of Romulus and Remus. Rome's mythical founders were said to have been brought up here by the shepherd Faustulus after a wolf had saved them from death. From near the Casa di Augusto you can look down into the 8th-century-BC Capanne Romulee (Romulean Huts) where the twins supposedly lived with their adopted father. In 2007 the discovery of a mosaic-covered cave 15m beneath the Domus Augustana reignited interest in the legend. According to some scholars, this was the Lupercale, the cave believed by ancient Romans to be where Romulus and Remus were suckled by a wolf. Others vigorously contested this, and the mystery remains.

The best spot for a picnic is the Vigna Barberini (Barberini Vineyard), near the Orti Farnesiani. It is signposted off the path to the Roman Forum.

PALATINO (PALATINE HILL)

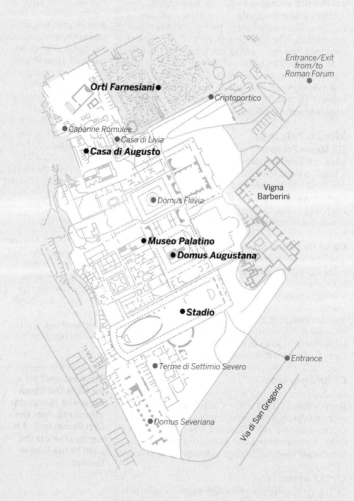

Entrance/Exit
from/to
Roman Forum

Orti Farnesiani●

●Criptoportico

●Capanne Romulee

●Casa di Livia

●**Casa di Augusto**

Vigna
Barberini

●Domus Flavia

●**Museo Palatino**

●**Domus Augustana**

●**Stadio**

●Entrance

●Terme di Settimio Severo

Via di San Gregorio

●Domus Severiana

TOP SIGHT
ROMAN FORUM

Once the beating heart of the ancient world, a grandiose district of marble-clad temples, proud basilicas and vibrant public spaces, the Roman Forum (Foro Romano) is now a collection of impressive but badly labelled ruins that can leave you drained and confused. But if you can set your imagination going, there's something compelling about walking in the footsteps of Julius Caesar and other legendary figures of Roman history.

Originally an Etruscan burial ground, the Forum was first developed in the 7th century BC and expanded over subsequent centuries to become the centre of the Roman Republic. In the Middle Ages it was reduced to pasture land and extensively plundered for its marble. The area was systematically excavated in the 18th and 19th centuries and work continues to this day.

Via Sacra Towards Campidoglio

Entering the Forum from Largo della Salara Vecchia – you can also enter directly from the Palatino – you'll see the **Tempio di Antonino e Faustina** ahead to your left. Erected in AD 141, this was later transformed into a church, so the soaring columns now frame the **Chiesa di San Lorenzo in Miranda**. To your right the **Basilica Fulvia Aemilia** built in 179 BC, was a 100m-long public hall, with a two-storey porticoed facade.

At the end of the short path, you will come to **Via Sacra**, the Forum's main thoroughfare. Over this stands the **Tempio di Giulio Cesare** (Temple of Julius Caesar), built by Augustus in 29 BC on the site of Caesar's cremation. Head right up Via Sacra and you reach

DON'T MISS...

➡ Curia
➡ Arco di Settimio Severo
➡ Tempio di Saturno
➡ Casa delle Vestali
➡ Basilica di Massenzio
➡ Arco di Tito

PRACTICALITIES

➡ Map p356
➡ ☎06 3996 7700
➡ www.coopculture.it
➡ Largo della Salara Vecchia
➡ adult/reduced incl Colosseum & Palatino €12/7.50
➡ ⊘8.30am-1hr before sunset
➡ 🚌Via dei Fori Imperiali

ROMAN FORUM

In ancient times, a forum was a market place, civic centre and religious complex all rolled into one, and the greatest of all was the Roman Forum (Foro Romano). Situated between the Palatino (Palatine Hill), ancient Rome's most exclusive neighbourhood, and the Campidoglio (Capitoline Hill), it was the city's busy, bustling centre. On any given day it teemed with activity. Senators debated affairs of state in the **Curia 1** , shoppers thronged the squares and traffic-free streets, crowds gathered under the **Colonna di Foca 2** to listen to politicians holding forth from the **Rostrum 2** . Elsewhere, lawyers worked the courts in basilicas including the **Basilica di Massenzio 3** , while the Vestal Virgins quietly went about their business in the **Casa delle Vestali 4** . Special occasions were also celebrated in the Forum: religious holidays were marked with ceremonies at temples such as the **Tempio di Saturno 5** and the **Tempio di Castore e Polluce 6** , and military victories were honoured with dramatic processions up Via Sacra and the building of monumental arches like the **Arco di Settimio Severo 7** and the **Arco di Tito 8** .

The ruins you see today are impressive but they can be confusing without a clear picture of what the Forum once looked like. This spread shows the Forum in its heyday, complete with temples, civic buildings and towering monuments to heroes of the Roman Empire.

TOP TIPS

➡ Get grandstand views of the Forum from the Palatino and Campidoglio.

➡ Visit first thing in the morning or late afternoon; crowds are worst between 11am and 2pm.

➡ In summer it gets hot in the Forum and there's little shade, so take a hat and plenty of water.

Colonna di Foca & Rostrum

The free-standing, 13.5m-high Column of Phocas is the Forum's youngest monument, dating to AD 608. Behind it, the Rostrum provided a suitably grandiose platform for pontificating public speakers.

Campidoglio (Capitoline Hill)

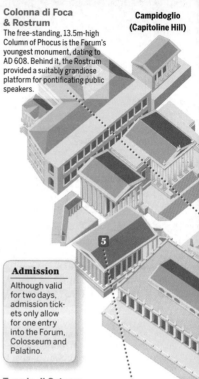

Admission

Although valid for two days, admission tickets only allow for one entry into the Forum, Colosseum and Palatino.

Tempio di Saturno

Ancient Rome's Fort Knox, the Temple of Saturn was the city treasury. In Caesar's day it housed 13 tonnes of gold, 114 tonnes of silver and 30 million sestertii worth of silver coins.

JONATHAN SMITH/GETTY IMAGES©

LONELY PLANET/GETTY IMAGES ©

Tempio di Castore e Polluce

Only three columns of the Temple of Castor and Pollux remain. The temple was dedicated to the Heavenly Twins after they supposedly led the Romans to victory over the Etruscans.

Arco di Settimio Severo

One of the Forum's signature monuments, this imposing triumphal arch commemorates the military victories of Septimius Severus. Relief panels depict his campaigns against the Parthians.

Curia

This big barnlike building was the official seat of the Roman Senate. Most of what you see is a reconstruction, but the interior marble floor dates to the 3rd-century reign of Diocletian.

Basilica di Massenzio

Marvel at the scale of this vast 4th-century basilica. In its original form the central hall was divided into enormous naves; now only part of the northern nave survives.

> **Julius Caesar RIP**
>
> Julius Caesar was cremated on the site where the Tempio di Giulio Cesare now stands.

Via Sacra

Tempio di Giulio Cesare

Casa delle Vestali

White statues line the grassy atrium of what was once the luxurious 50-room home of the Vestal Virgins. The virgins played an important role in Roman religion, serving the goddess Vesta.

Arco di Tito

Said to be the inspiration for the Arc de Triomphe in Paris, the well-preserved Arch of Titus was built by the emperor Domitian to honour his elder brother Titus.

THE VESTAL VIRGINS

Despite privilege and public acclaim, life as a vestal virgin was no bed of roses. Every year, six physically perfect patrician girls between the ages of six and 10 were chosen by lottery to serve Vesta, goddess of hearth and household. Once selected, they faced a 30-year period of chaste servitude at the Tempio di Vesta. During this time their main duty was to ensure that the temple's sacred fire never went out. If it did, the priestess responsible would be flogged. The well-being of the state was thought to depend on the cult of Vesta and on the vestals' chastity. If a priestess were to lose her virginity she risked being buried alive and the offending man being flogged to death.

There are public toilets by the Chiesa di Santa Maria Antiqua.

the **Curia**, the original seat of the Roman Senate. This was rebuilt on various occasions and what you see today is a 1937 reconstruction of the Curia as it looked in the reign of Diocletian (r 284–305).

In front of the Curia, hidden by scaffolding, is the **Lapis Niger**, a large piece of black marble covering what is said to be the tomb of Romulus.

At the end of Via Sacra is the 23m-high **Arco di Settimio Severo** (Arch of Septimius Severus), a triumphal arch dedicated to the emperor and his sons, Caracalla and Geta.

Southwest of the arch, eight granite columns are all that remain of the **Tempio di Saturno** (Temple of Saturn), an important temple that doubled as the state treasury. Behind it are (from north to south): the ruins of the **Tempio della Concordia** (Temple of Concord), the **Tempio di Vespasiano** (Temple of Vespasian and Titus) and the **Portico degli Dei Consenti**.

To the southeast, the **Colonna di Foca** (Column of Phocus) rises above what was once the Forum's main plaza, the **Piazza del Foro**. Looking onto the piazza are the remains of the **Rostrum**, an elaborate podium where Shakespeare had Mark Antony make his famous 'Friends, Romans, countrymen...' monologue, and from which politicians would make speeches.

Tempio di Castore e Polluce & Casa delle Vestali

From the path that runs parallel to Via Sacra, you'll see the stubby ruins of the **Basilica Giulia**, which was begun by Julius Caesar and finished by Augustus. At the end of the basilica, the three columns you see belong to the 5th-century-BC Tempio di Castore e Polluce (Temple of Castor and Pollux). Near the temple, the **Chiesa di Santa Maria Antiqua** is the oldest Christian church in the Forum, and the Casa delle Vestali (House of the Vestal Virgins) was home to the virgins who tended the flame in the adjoining **Tempio di Vesta**.

Via Sacra Towards the Colosseum

Further up Via Sacra past the **Tempio di Romolo** (Temple of Romulus) is the **Basilica di Massenzio**. Started by the emperor Maxentius and finished by Constantine (it's also known as the Basilica di Costantino), it covered an area of approximately 100m by 65m. Continuing, you come to the **Arco di Tito** (Arch of Titus), built in AD 81 to celebrate Vespasian and Titus' victories against Jerusalem.

TOP SIGHT
CAPITOLINE MUSEUMS

The world's oldest national museums, the Capitoline Museums (Musei Capitolini) occupy two stately *palazzi* (mansions) on the Michelangelo-designed Piazza del Campidoglio. Their origins date to 1471, when Pope Sixtus IV donated a number of bronze statues to the city, forming the nucleus of what is now one of Italy's finest collections of classical art. The focus is very much on ancient sculpture, but the museums' picture gallery also boasts some wonderful works, including a number of great Italian and Dutch artists.

Palazzo dei Conservatori – 1st Floor

Before you head up to start on the sculpture collection proper, take a moment to admire the marble body parts littered around the ground-floor **courtyard**. The mammoth head, hand and feet all belonged to a 12m-high statue of Constantine that once stood in the Basilica di Massenzio in the Roman Forum.

Of the permanent sculpture collection on the 1st floor, the Etruscan Lupa Capitolina (Capitoline Wolf) is the most famous piece. Standing in the **Sala della Lupa**, this 5th-century-BC bronze wolf stands over her suckling wards Romulus and Remus, who were added to the composition in 1471. Other crowd-pleasers include the Spinario, a delicate 1st-century-BC bronze of a boy removing a thorn from his foot, in the **Sala dei Trionfi**, and Gian Lorenzo Bernini's *Medusa* bust in the **Sala delle Oche**.

Dominating the light-filled modern wing known as the **Esedra di Marco Aurelio** is an imposing bronze **equestrian statue** of the emperor Marcus Aurelius – the original of the copy that stands in the piazza outside. Here you can also see the foundations of the Temple

DON'T MISS...

- ➡ Lupa Capitolina
- ➡ Spinario
- ➡ *La Buona Ventura*
- ➡ Galata Morente
- ➡ Venere Capitolina

PRACTICALITIES

- ➡ Map p356
- ➡ ☑06 06 08
- ➡ www.museicapitolini.org
- ➡ Piazza del Campidoglio 1
- ➡ adult/reduced €9.50/7.50
- ➡ ⏰9am-8pm Tue-Sun, last admission 7pm
- ➡ 🚇Piazza Venezia

TREATY OF ROME

With its frescoes depicting episodes from ancient Roman history, and two papal statues – one of Urban VIII by Bernini and one of Innocent X by Algardi – the **Sala degli Orazi e Curiazi** provided the suitably grand setting for one of modern Europe's key events. On 25 March 1957, the leaders of Italy, France, West Germany, Belgium, Holland and Luxembourg congregated here to sign the Treaty of Rome and establish the European Economic Community, the precursor of the European Union. The hall has a long history of hosting political movers and shakers. In the late 15th century it was used for the public hearings of the Council of Conservatori (elected magistrates), after whom the *palazzo* is named.

The **Caffè Capitolino**, the museums' elegant cafe, is on the 2nd floor of Palazzo dei Conservatori. Serving coffee, snacks and fine views, it's an excellent spot for a sightseeing time-out.

of Jupiter, one of the ancient city's most important temples that once dominated the Capitoline Hill.

Palazzo dei Conservatori – 2nd Floor

The 2nd floor is given over to the **Pinacoteca**, the museums' picture gallery. Dating to 1749, the gallery's collection is arranged chronologically with works from the Middle Ages through to the 18th century. Each room harbours masterpieces but two stand out: the **Sala Pietro da Cortona**, which features Pietro da Cortona's famous depiction of the *Ratto delle sabine* (Rape of the Sabine Women), and the **Sala di Santa Petronilla**, named after Guercino's huge canvas *Seppellimento di Santa Petronilla* (The Burial of St Petronilla). This airy hall boasts a number of important canvases, including two by Caravaggio: *La Buona Ventura* (The Fortune Teller; 1595), which shows a gypsy pretending to read a young man's hand but actually stealing his ring, and *San Giovanni Battista* (John the Baptist; 1602), a sensual and unusual depiction of the saint.

Tabularium

A tunnel links Palazzo dei Conservatori to Palazzo Nuovo on the other side of the square via the Tabularium, ancient Rome's central archive, beneath Palazzo Senatorio. The tunnel is lined with panels and inscriptions from ancient tombs, but more inspiring are the views over the Roman Forum from the brick-lined Tabularium – make sure you've got your camera to hand.

Palazzo Nuovo

Palazzo Nuovo is crammed to its elegant 17th-century rafters with classical Roman sculpture, including some unforgettable show-stoppers.

From the lobby, where the curly-bearded **Mars** stares ferociously at everyone who passes by, stairs lead up to the main galleries. The first hall you come to, at the head of the stairs, is the **Sala del Galata**. This is where you'll find one of the museums' greatest works – the Galata Morente (Dying Gaul). A Roman copy of a 3rd-century-BC Greek original, this sublime sculpture movingly captures the quiet, resigned anguish of a dying French warrior. The next room, the **Sala del Fauno**, takes its name from the red marble statue of a faun. Another superb figurative piece is the sensual yet demure portrayal of the Venere Capitolina (Capitoline Venus) in the **Gabinetto della Venere**, off the main corridor.

Also worth a look are the busts of philosophers, poets and orators in the **Sala dei Filosofi** – look out for likenesses of Homer, Pythagoras, Socrates and Cicero.

CAPITOLINE MUSEUMS

Ground Floor

First Floor

Palazzo Nuovo

Mars

Piazza del Campidoglio

Main Entrance

Courtyard

stairs

Palazzo dei Conservatori

Palazzo Nuovo

Gabinetto della Venere

stairs

Sala del Galata

Venere Capitolina

Faun

Salone

Galata Morente

Sala dei Filosofi

Sala del Fauno

Sala dei Trionfi

Sala degli Orazi e Curiazi

Spinario

Sala della Lupa

Lupa Capitolina

Sala delle Oche

Medusa

Esedra di Marco Aurelio

Equestrian Statue of Marcus Aurelius

Foundations of Temple of Jupiter

Palazzo dei Conservatori

◉ SIGHTS

◉ Colosseum & Palatino

COLOSSEUM   AMPHITHEATRE
See p62.

ARCO DI COSTANTINO   MONUMENT
(Map p356; MColosseo) On the western side
of the Colosseum, this triumphal arch was
built in 312 to honour the emperor Constantine's victory over rival Maxentius at
the battle of Ponte Milvio (Milvian Bridge).

PALATINO (PALATINE HILL)   RUIN
See p64.

CIRCO MASSIMO   ROMAN SITE
(Map p356; Via del Circo Massimo; MCirco
Massimo) Now little more than a basin of
thinning grass, the Circo Massimo (Circus
Maximus) was ancient Rome's largest stadium, a 250,000-seater capable of holding a
quarter of the city's entire population. The
600m racetrack circled a wooden dividing
island with ornate lap indicators and Egyptian obelisks.

Chariot races were held here as far back
as the 4th century BC, but it wasn't until
Trajan rebuilt it after the AD 64 fire that it
reached its maximum grandeur.

◉ The Forums & Around

Before venturing into the forums, take
a minute to prepare yourself at the **Tourist Information Point** (Via dei Fori Imperiali;
☺9.30am-7pm; ☐Via dei Fori Imperiali), which
has a big plan map of the forums.

ROMAN FORUM   RUINS
See p67.

BASILICA DI SS COSMA
E DAMIANO   BASILICA
(Map p356; Via dei Fori Imperiali; presepio donation €1; ☺9am-1pm & 3-7pm, presepio 10am-1pm
& 3-6pm Fri-Sun; ☐Via dei Fori Imperiali) Backing
onto the Roman Forum, this 6th-century basilica incorporates parts of the **Foro di Vespasiano** and **Tempio di Romolo**, visible at
the end of the nave. The real reasons to visit,
though, are the vibrant 6th-century apse
mosaics, depicting Christ's Second Coming.
Also worth a look is the 18th-century Nea-

politan **presepio** (nativity scene) in a room
off the tranquil 17th-century cloisters.

MERCATI DI TRAIANO MUSEO
DEI FORI IMPERIALI   MUSEUM
(Map p356; ☎06 06 08; www.mercatiditraiano.it;
Via IV Novembre 94; adult/reduced €9.50/7.50;
☺9am-7pm Tue-Sun, last admission 6pm; ☐Via
IV Novembre) This striking museum brings
to life the **Mercati di Traiano**, emperor
Trajan's great 2nd-century market complex,
while also providing a fascinating introduction to the **Imperial Forums** with detailed
explanatory panels and a smattering of archaeological artefacts.

From the main hallway, a lift whisks
you up to the **Torre delle Milizie** (Militia
Tower), a 13th-century red-brick tower, and
the upper levels of the Mercati. These markets, housed in a three-storey semicircular
construction, hosted hundreds of traders
selling everything from oil and vegetables
to flowers, silks and spices. An additional
exhibition entry fee may apply.

CARCERE MAMERTINO   HISTORIC SITE
(Mamertine Prison; Map p356; ☎06 69 89 61;
Clivo Argentario 1; adult €6; ☺9.30am-7pm summer, to 5pm winter, last admission 40min before
close; ☐Via dei Fori Imperiali) At the foot of the
Campidoglio, the Mamertine Prison was
ancient Rome's maximum-security jail. St

LOCAL KNOWLEDGE

BARBARA NAZZARO: ARCHITECT

The Technical Director at the Colosseum, Barbara Nazzaro, explains
what went on in the Colosseum's
hypogeum.

'Gladiators entered the hypogeum
through an underground corridor which
led directly in from the nearby Ludus
Magnus (gladiator school). In side corridors, which stand over a natural spring,
boats were kept. When they wanted
these boats up in the arena they would
let the spring water in and flood the tunnels. Later these passages were used
for winch mechanisms, all of which were
controlled by a single pulley system.
There were about 80 lifts going up to
the arena as well as cages where wild
animals were kept. You can still see the
spaces where the cages were.'

TOP SIGHT
IMPERIAL FORUMS

The Imperial Forums (Fori Imperiali) were constructed between 42 BC and AD 112, but they were largely buried in 1933 when Mussolini built Via dei Fori Imperiali. Excavations have unearthed much of them, but visits are limited to the Mercati di Traiano (Trajan's Markets).

Little recognisable remains of the **Foro di Traiano** (Trajan's Forum), except for some pillars from the **Basilica Ulpia** and the **Colonna di Traiano** (Trajan's Column), whose reliefs celebrate Trajan's military victories over the Dacians.

To the southeast, three temple columns rise from **Foro di Augusto** (Augustus' Forum), now mostly under Via dei Fori Imperiali. The 30m-high wall behind the forum was built to protect it from the frequent fires in the area.

The **Foro di Nerva** (Nerva's Forum) was also buried by Mussolini's road-building, although part of a temple dedicated to Minerva still stands. Originally, it would have connected the Foro di Augusto to the 1st-century **Foro di Vespasiano** (Vespasian's Forum). Over the road, three columns are the most visible remains of the **Foro di Cesare** (Caesar's Forum).

DON'T MISS...

➡ Mercati di Traiano
➡ Colonna di Traiano
➡ Basilica Ulpia

PRACTICALITIES

➡ Map p356
➡ Via dei Fori Imperiali
➡ ▢ Via dei Fori Imperiali

Peter did time here and while imprisoned supposedly created a miraculous stream of water to baptise his jailers. On the bare stone walls you can make out early Christian frescoes depicting Jesus and Sts Peter and Paul. Visits are by guided tour only.

◉ Campidoglio

Rising above the Roman Forum, the Campidoglio (Capitoline Hill) was one of the seven hills on which Rome was founded. At its summit were Rome's two most important temples: one dedicated to Jupiter Capitolinus (a descendant of Jupiter, the Roman equivalent of Zeus) and one to the goddess Juno Moneta (which housed Rome's mint). More than 2000 years on, the hill still wields political clout as seat of Rome's municipal government.

PIAZZA DEL CAMPIDOGLIO   PIAZZA

(Map p356; ▢ Piazza Venezia) Designed by Michelangelo in 1538 and flanked by stately *palazzi*, this elegant hilltop piazza is one of Rome's most beautiful squares. You can reach it from the Roman Forum, but the most dramatic approach is via the **Cordonata**, the graceful staircase that leads up from Piazza d'Ara Coeli.

At the top, the piazza is bordered by three *palazzi*: **Palazzo Nuovo** to the left, **Palazzo Senatorio** straight ahead and **Palazzo dei Conservatori** on the right. Together, Palazzo Nuovo and Palazzo dei Conservatori house the Capitoline Museums, while Palazzo Senatorio is home to Rome's city council.

In the centre, the bronze equestrian **statue of Marcus Aurelius** is a copy. The

❶ POSING CENTURIONS

Outside the Roman Forum and Il Vittoriano, and possibly also the Colosseum, you might find yourself being hailed by costumed Roman soldiers offering to pose for a photo with you. They are not doing this for love and will expect payment. There's no set rate but coins are sufficient, certainly no more than €5 – and that's €5 in total, not per person.

ℹ MAPS & GUIDES

As fascinating as Rome's ruins are, they are not well labelled and it can be hard to know what you're looking at without a map or specialist guide. ATS Italia produces a *Guide to the Fora and the Colosseum* (€6) with a useful map and plan. Electa publishes a number of insightful guides, including guides to the *Colosseum* (€5), the *Foro, Palatine and Colosseum* (€10), and the *Archaeological Guide to Rome* (€15 in English; €12.90 in Italian), available at the Colosseum and Roman Forum bookshops.

original, which dates from the 2nd century AD, is in the Capitoline Museums.

CAPITOLINE MUSEUMS MUSEUM
See p71.

**CHIESA DI SANTA
MARIA IN ARACOELI** CHURCH
(Map p356; Piazza Santa Maria in Aracoeli; ⊘9am-12.30pm & 2.30-5.30pm; 🚇Piazza Venezia) Atop the 14th-century Aracoeli staircase on the highest point of the Campidoglio, this 6th-century Romanesque church boasts an impressive Cosmatesque floor and an important 15th-century fresco by Pinturicchio. But its main claim to fame is a much-loved wooden baby Jesus believed to have healing powers.

In fact, the Jesus doll is a copy. The original, which was supposedly made of wood from the garden of Gethsemane, was pinched in 1994 and never recovered.

The church sits on the site of the Roman temple to Juno Moneta and has long had an association with the nativity. According to legend, it was here that the Tiburtine Sybil told Augustus of the coming birth of Christ.

◉ Piazza Venezia

IL VITTORIANO MONUMENT
(Map p356; Piazza Venezia; ⊘9.30am-5.30pm summer, to 4.30pm winter; 🚇Piazza Venezia) **FREE** Love it or loathe it (as most locals do), you can't ignore the massive mountain of white marble that towers over Piazza Venezia. Known also as the Altare della Patria

(Altar of the Fatherland), it was begun in 1885 to commemorate Italian unification and honour Victor Emmanuel II, Italy's first king and the subject of its vast equestrian statue.

The monument also hosts the **Tomb of the Unknown Soldier** and, inside, the **Museo Centrale del Risorgiment** (Via di San Pietro in Carcere; ⊘9.30am-6.30pm), a free museum documenting Italian unification, and the **Complesso del Vittoriano** (☑06 678 06 64; Via di San Pietro in Carcere; ⊘depends on exhibition), a gallery space that regularly hosts major art exhibitions.

For Rome's best 360-degree views, take the **Roma dal Cielo** (adult/reduced €7/3.50; ⊘9.30am-6.30pm Mon-Thur, to 7.30pm Fri-Sun) lift from the side of the building up to the top of the monument.

ROMAN INSULA RUIN
(Map p356; Piazza Santa Maria in Aracoeli; 🚇Piazza Venezia) At the bottom of the Campidoglio, next to the Aracoeli staircase, are the ruins of a Roman *insula* (apartment block). Only the upper storeys are now visible – the unexcavated ground-floor shops are well below the current road level – but they provide a fascinating if fleeting glimpse into the cramped, squalid conditions that many ancient Romans lived in.

PALAZZO VENEZIA PALACE
(Map p356; Piazza Venezia; 🚇Piazza Venezia) This was the first of Rome's great Renaissance palaces, built between 1455 and 1464. For centuries it served as the embassy of the Venetian Republic, although its best-known resident was Mussolini, who famously made speeches from its balcony. Nowadays, it's home to the **Museo Nazionale del Palazzo Venezia** (Map p356; ☑06 678 01 31; Via del Plebiscito 118; adult/reduced €5/2.50; ⊘8.30am-7.30pm Tue-Sun; 🚇Piazza Venezia) and its eclectic collection of Byzantine and early Renaissance paintings, tapestries and arms.

BASILICA DI SAN MARCO BASILICA
(Map p356; Piazza di San Marco 48; ⊘8.30am-noon & 4-6pm Tue-Sat, 9am-1pm & 4-8pm Sun; 🚇Piazza Venezia) The early 4th-century Basilica di San Marco stands over the house where St Mark the Evangelist is said to have stayed while in Rome. Its main attraction is the golden 9th-century apse mosaic.

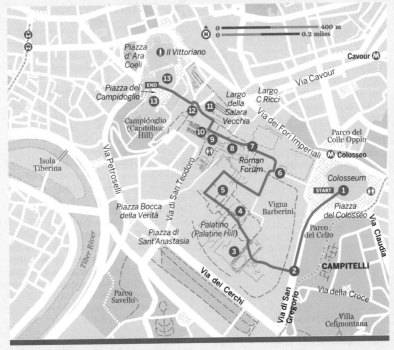

Neighbourhood Walk
Explore the Ruins

Follow in the footsteps of an ancient Roman on this whistle-stop tour of the city's most famous ruins.

Start at the ❶ **Colosseum** (p62), the great gladiatorial arena that more than any other monument encapsulates the drama of the ancient city. From there, follow down Via di San Gregorio to the ❷ **Palatino** (p64), ancient Rome's most sought-after neighbourhood where the emperor lived alongside the cream of imperial society. The ruins here are confusing, but their scale gives some sense of the luxury in which the ancient VIPs liked to live. You can still make out parts of the ❸ **Domus Augustana**, the emperor's private residence, and the ❹ **Domus Flavia**, where he would hold official audiences. From the Domus find your way up to the ❺ **Orti Farnesiani**. These gardens weren't part of the ancient city but give good views over the Roman Forum. Then head down to the Forum, entering near the ❻ **Arco di Tito**, one of the site's great triumphal arches. Beyond this, bear left and pick up ❼ **Via Sacra**, the Forum's main drag. Follow this down and after a few hundred metres you'll come to the ❽ **Casa delle Vestali**, where the legendary Vestal Virgins lived, tending to their duties and guarding their virtue. Beyond the three columns of the ❾ **Tempio di Castore e Polluce**, you'll see a flattened area littered with column bases and brick stumps. This is the ❿ **Basilica Giulia**, where lawyers and magistrates worked in the crowded law courts. Meanwhile, senators debated matters of state at the ⓫ **Curia**, over on the other side of the Forum. From near the Curia, exit the Forum past the ⓬ **Arco di Settimio Severo** and climb the Campidoglio (Capitoline Hill) to the magnificent ⓭ **Capitoline Museums** (p71), whose collection of classical art includes some of the city's finest ancient sculptures.

⊙ Forum Boarium & Around

BOCCA DELLA VERITÀ   MONUMENT

(Map p356; Piazza Bocca della Verità 18; donation €0.50; ☺9.30am-4.50pm winter, to 5.50pm summer; 🚇Piazza Bocca della Verità) A round piece of marble that was once part of an ancient fountain, or possibly an ancient manhole cover, the Bocca della Verità (Mouth of Truth) is one of Rome's most popular curiosities. Legend has it that if you put your hand in the carved mouth and tell a lie, it will bite your hand off.

The mouth lives in the portico of the **Chiesa di Santa Maria in Cosmedin**, one of Rome's most beautiful medieval churches. Originally built in the 8th century, the church was given a major revamp in the 12th century, when the seven-storey bell tower and portico were added and the floor was decorated with Cosmati inlaid marble.

FORUM BOARIUM   ROMAN SITE

(Map p356; Piazza Bocca della Verità; 🚇Piazza Bocca della Verità) Car-choked Piazza Bocca della Verità stands on what was once ancient Rome's cattle market, the Forum Boarium. Opposite the Chiesa di Santa Maria in Cosmedin are two tiny Roman temples dating to the 2nd century BC: the round **Tempio di Ercole Vincitore** and the **Tempio di Portunus**, dedicated to the god of rivers and ports, Portunus.

Just off the piazza, the **Arco di Giano** (Arch of Janus) is a four-sided Roman arch that once covered a crossroads. Beyond it is the medieval **Chiesa di San Giorgio in Velabro** (Via del Velabro 19; ☺10am-12.30pm & 4-6.30pm Tue, Fri & Sat; 🚇Piazza Bocca della Verità), a beautiful church whose original 7th-century portico was destroyed by a Mafia bomb attack in 1993.

 EATING

CRISTALLI DI ZUCCHERO   PASTRIES & CAKES €

(Map p356; Via di San Teodoro 88; pastries from €3.50; ☺7am-8.30pm; 🚇Via dei Cerchi) Pastry cooking becomes high art at this sophisticated *pasticceria* (pastry shop) near the Bocca della Verità. Leave the crowds behind and sneak off to indulge in pastries so perfectly crafted that they'd make fine kitchen decor if they weren't so delicious. Coffee and ice cream are also available.

★ENOTECA PROVINCIA ROMANA   REGIONAL CUISINE €€

(Map p356; ☎06 6994 0273; Foro Traiano 82-4; meals €35, aperitifs from €5; ☺11am-11pm Mon-Sat; 🚇Via dei Fori Imperiali) The best option in the touristy Forum area, this stylish wine-bar-cum-restaurant showcases food from the surrounding Lazio region. There's a full daily menu of pastas and mains, as well as finger foods, wine by the glass and evening aperitifs. Service is friendly and the location overlooking the Colonna di Traiano is wonderfully atmospheric. Lunchtime is busy but it quietens down in the evening.

HOSTARIA DA NERONE   TRATTORIA €€

(Map p356; ☎06 481 79 52; Via delle Terme di Tito; meals €35; ☺lunch & dinner Mon-Sat; Ⓜ Colosseo) This old-school, family-run trattoria near the Colosseum is not the place for a romantic dinner or a special-occasion splurge, but if you're after a good earthy meal after a day's sightseeing, it does the job nicely. Tourists tuck into classic Roman pastas and salads outside, while in the yellowing, woody interior visiting businessmen cut deals over osso buco and tiramisu.

SAN TEODORO   MODERN ITALIAN €€€

(Map p356; ☎06 678 09 33; www.st-teodoro.it; Via dei Fienili 49-50; meals €80; ☺lunch & dinner daily,

---

UNDERGROUND ARTS CENTRE

The sheer depth of Rome's archaeological legacy came to light in December 2012, when archaeologists announced they had finished excavating a 900-seat *athenaeum* (arts centre) some 5m beneath Piazza Venezia. Dating to the 2nd-century reign of Hadrian, the complex is huge, consisting of three 13m-high arched halls where spectators would have relaxed on terraced marble seating to be entertained by poets and philosophers.

The discovery came during tunnelling work on Rome's third metro line, illustrating the difficulties that engineers face as they inch through the city's treasure-laden undersoil.

It is hoped that the site will be open to the public by 2016.

PICNIC PROVISIONS

Trawling through ancient Rome's extensive ruins can be hungry work. But rather than stop off for an overpriced bite in a touristy restaurant, search out **Alimentari Pannella Carmela** (Map p356; Via dei Fienili 61; panini €2; ⊙8.30am-2.30pm & 5-8pm Mon-Fri, 8.30am-2.30pm Sat; ⌨Via Petroselli) for a fresh, cheap *panino*. A small, workaday food store concealed behind a curtain of creeping ivy, it's a lunchtime favourite supplying many local workers with bread rolls, pizza slices, salads and marinated vegetables.

closed Sun winter; ⌨Via Petroselli) Hidden away on a picturesque corner behind the Palatino, San Teodoro is a refined restaurant specialising in modern Roman cuisine and top-end seafood. Sit in the cool, minimalist interior or outside on the covered terrace and enjoy sophisticated creations like pasta with mussels, chicory and orange zest, or lobster with potatoes and baby onions.

relax over a drink or light snack (*panini,* salads and pizza). Although part of the museum complex, you don't need a ticket to come here as it's accessible via an independent entrance on Piazzale Caffarelli.

CAVOUR 313 WINE BAR

(Map p356; www.cavour313.it; Via Cavour 313; ⊙12.30pm-2.45pm & 7.30pm-12.30am, closed Sun summer; MCavour) Close to the Forum, wood-panelled, intimate Cavour 313 attracts everyone from tourists to actors and politicians. Sink into its pub-like cosiness and while away hours over sensational wine (more than 1200 labels) accompanied by cold cuts and cheese (€8 to 12) or a plate of pasta.

0,75 BAR

(Map p356; www.075roma.com; Via dei Cerchi 65; ⊙11am-1.30am; ☎; ⌨Via dei Cerchi) This funky bar on the Circo Massimo is good for a lingering drink, weekend brunch (€15; 11am to 3pm), *aperitivo* (6.30pm onwards) or light lunch (pastas €7 to €8.50, salads €5.50 to €7.50). It's a friendly place with a laid-back vibe, an attractive exposed-brick look and cool tunes. Free wi-fi.

 # DRINKING & NIGHTLIFE

CAFFÈ CAPITOLINO CAFE

(Map p356; Piazzale Caffarelli 4; ⊙9am-7.30pm Tue-Sun; ⌨Piazza Venezia) The charming rooftop cafe of the Capitoline Museums is a good place to rest your aching legs and

 # SHOPPING

MERCATO DI CIRCO MASSIMO MARKET

(Map p356; www.mercatocircomassimo.it; Via di San Teodoro 74; ⊙9am-6pm Sat, to 4pm Sun; ⌨Via dei Cerchi) Rome's best and most popular farmers market.

Centro Storico

PANTHEON | PIAZZA NAVONA | CAMPO DE' FIORI | JEWISH GHETTO | ISOLA TIBERINA | PIAZZA COLONNA

Neighbourhood Top Five

1 Stepping into the **Pantheon** (p82) and feeling the same sense of awe that the ancients must have felt 2000 years ago. The sight of the dome soaring up above you is a genuinely jaw-dropping spectacle.

2 Exploring **Piazza Navona** (p84) and the picturesque streets that surround it.

3 Browsing the fabulous art collection at the **Palazzo e Galleria Doria Pamphilj** (p94).

4 Catching three Caravaggio masterpieces at the **Chiesa di San Luigi dei Francesi** (p86).

5 Escaping the crowds in the shadowy lanes of the **Jewish Ghetto** (p92).

For more detail of this area, see Map p360 and p362 ➡

Explore: Centro Storico

Rome's *centro storico* (historic centre) is made for lei-surely strolling and although you could spend weeks exploring its every corner, you can cover most of the main sights in two or three days. Many people enter the area by bus, getting off at Largo di Torre Argentina, from where it's a short walk up to the Pantheon and beyond that to Rome's political nerve-centre Piazza Colonna. Nearby, on Via del Corso, the Palazzo e Galleria Doria Pamphilj houses one of the capital's finest private art collections. Art is thick on the ground in these parts and many of the centre's churches harbour extraordinary frescoes and sculptures. To the west of the Pantheon, the streets around Piazza Navona, itself one of Rome's great must-see sights, are a magnet for tourists and hip Romans with their bohemian boutiques, cool bars and popular pizzerias.

Over on the other side of Corso Vittorio Emanuele II, the main road that bisects the area, all streets lead to Campo de' Fiori, home to a colourful daily market and hectic late-night drinking scene. From 'il Campo' you can shop your way down to the medieval Jewish Ghetto, a wonderfully atmospheric area of romantic corners, hidden piazzas and authentic eateries.

Local Life

➡ **Piazzas** The restaurants on Piazza Navona and Piazza Rotonda attract a touristy crowd while Campo de' Fiori pulls in boozing students. Locals head to places in the quieter back streets.

➡ **Shopping Strips** Browse retro fashions and second-hand threads on Via del Governo Vecchio; Via dei Giubbonari is good for frocks and heels.

➡ **Aperitif** Young Romans love to meet over an evening *aperitivo* in the bars around Piazza Navona.

Getting There & Away

➡ **Bus** The best way to access the *centro storico*. A whole fleet serves the area from Termini, including Nos 40 and 64, which both stop at Largo di Torre Argentina and continue down Corso Vittorio Emanuele II. From Barberini metro station, bus 116 stops at Corso del Rinascimento (for Piazza Navona), Piazza Farnese and Via Giulia.

➡ **Metro** There are no metro stations in the neighbourhood but it's within walking distance of Barberini, Spagna and Flaminio stations, all on line A.

➡ **Tram** No 8 connects Largo di Torre Argentina with Trastevere.

Lonely Planet's Top Tip

The *centro storico* is the perfect area to ditch your guidebook and go it alone. You'll probably get lost at some point, but don't worry if you do – sooner or later you'll emerge on a main road or find a recognisable landmark.

See masterpieces by the likes of Michelangelo, Raphael, Caravaggio and Bernini for absolutely nothing by visiting the area's churches, which are all free to enter.

CENTRO STORICO

Best Places to Eat

➡ Casa Coppelle (p98)

➡ Ditirambo (p101)

➡ La Rosetta (p98)

➡ Forno Roscioli (p100)

➡ Armando al Pantheon (p98)

For reviews, see p97 ➡

Best Places to Drink

➡ Caffè Sant'Eustachio (p103)

➡ Barnum Cafe (p104)

➡ Open Baladin (p104)

➡ Salotto 42 (p105)

For reviews, see p103 ➡

Best Art Churches

➡ Chiesa di San Luigi dei Francesi (p86)

➡ Chiesa del Gesù (p93)

➡ Chiesa di Sant'Ignazio di Loyola (p97)

➡ Chiesa di Santa Maria Sopra Minerva (p85)

For reviews, see p85 ➡

TOP SIGHT
PANTHEON

Along with the Colosseum, the Pantheon is one of Rome's iconic sights. A striking 2000-year-old temple, now a church, it is the city's best-preserved ancient monument and one of the most influential buildings in the Western world. The greying, pock-marked exterior might look its age, but inside it's a different story, and it's a unique and exhilarating experience to pass through the towering bronze doors and have your vision directed upwards to the breathtaking dome.

DON'T MISS...

➡ The entrance doors
➡ The dome
➡ Raphael's Tomb

PRACTICALITIES

➡ Map p360
➡ Piazza della Rotonda
➡ ⊗8.30am-7.30pm Mon-Sat, 9am-6pm Sun
➡ ▣Largo di Torre Argentina

History

In its current form the Pantheon dates to around AD 120. Originally, Marcus Agrippa, son-in-law of the emperor Augustus, constructed a temple here in 27 BC, but it burnt down in AD 80. Although it was rebuilt by Domitian, it was destroyed for a second time in AD 110 after being struck by lightning. The emperor Hadrian rebuilt it once again, and it's this version that you see today.

Hadrian's temple was dedicated to the classical gods – hence the name Pantheon, a derivation of the Greek words *pan* (all) and *theos* (god) – but in AD 608 it was consecrated as a Christian church in honour of the Madonna and all martyrs after the Byzantine emperor Phocus donated it to Pope Boniface IV. (Its official name is now the Basilica di Santa Maria ad Martyres.) Thanks to this consecration the Pantheon was spared the worst of the medieval plundering that reduced many of Rome's ancient buildings to their bare bones. However, it wasn't totally safe from plundering hands. The gilded-bronze roof tiles were removed and, in the 17th century, the Barberini Pope Urban VIII had the portico's bronze ceiling melted down to make 80 canons for Castel Sant'Angelo and the baldachino over the main altar of St Peter's Basilica.

During the Renaissance the Pantheon was much admired – Brunelleschi used it as inspiration for his Duomo in Florence and Michelangelo studied it before designing the cupola over St Peter's Basilica – and it became an important burial chamber. Today you'll find the tomb of the artist Raphael here, alongside those of kings Vittorio Emanuele II and Umberto I.

Exterior

Originally, the Pantheon was on a raised podium, its entrance facing onto a rectangular porticoed piazza. Nowadays, the dark-grey pitted exterior faces the busy, cafe-lined Piazza della Rotonda. Although it's somewhat the worse for wear, the facade is still an imposing sight. The monumental entrance portico has 16 Corinthian columns, each 13m high and made of Egyptian granite, supporting a triangular pediment. Little remains of the ancient decor, although rivets and holes in the brickwork indicate where the marble-veneer panels were once placed, and the towering 20-tonne bronze doors are 16th-century restorations of the originals.

Interior

Although impressive from outside, it's only when you get inside the Pantheon that you can really appreciate its full size. With light streaming in through the oculus (the 8.7m-diameter hole in the centre of the dome), the cylindrical marble-clad interior seems absolutely vast, an effect that was deliberately designed to cut worshippers down to size in the face of the gods.

Opposite the entrance is the church's main altar, over which hangs a 7th-century icon of the Madonna and Child. To the left (as you look in from the entrance) is the tomb of Raphael, marked by Lorenzetto's 1520 sculpture of the *Madonna del Sasso* (Madonna of the Rock), and next door, the tombs of King Umberto I and Margherita of Savoy. Over on the opposite side of the rotunda is the tomb of King Vittorio Emanuele II.

The Dome

The Pantheon's dome, considered the Romans' most important architectural achievement, is the largest unreinforced concrete dome ever built. Its harmonious appearance is due to a precisely calibrated symmetry – the diameter is equal to the building's interior height of 43.3m. Light enters through the central oculus, which served as a symbolic connection between the temple and the gods as well as an important structural role – it absorbs and redistributes the huge tensile forces. Radiating out from the oculus are five rows of 28 coffers (indented panels). These coffers were originally ornamented but more importantly served to reduce the immense weight of the dome.

THE INSCRIPTION

For centuries the Latin inscription over the Pantheon's entrance led historians to believe that the current temple was Marcus Agrippa's original. Certainly, the wording would suggest so, reading: 'M.AGRIPPA.L.F.COS. TERTIUM.FECIT' or 'Marcus Agrippa, son of Lucius, consul for the third time, built this'. However, excavations in the 19th-century revealed traces of an earlier temple and scholars realised that Hadrian had simply reinstated Agrippa's original inscription over his new temple.

According to the attendants who work at the Pantheon, the question tourists most often ask is: what happens when it rains? The answer is that rain gets in through the open oculus then rainwater drains away through 22 almost-invisible holes in the sloping marble floor.

TOP SIGHT
PIAZZA NAVONA

With its ornate fountains, exuberant baroque *palazzi* (mansions) and pavement cafes, Piazza Navona is central Rome's showcase square. Long a hub of local life, it hosted Rome's main market for close on 300 years, and today attracts a colourful daily circus of street performers, hawkers, artists, tourists, fortune-tellers and pigeons.

DON'T MISS...

➡ Fontana dei Quattro Fiumi

➡ Chiesa di Sant'Agnese in Agone

➡ Palazzo Pamphilj

PRACTICALITIES

➡ Map p360

➡ 🚇Corso del Rinascimento

Stadio di Domiziano

Like many of the city's great landmarks, the piazza sits on the site of an ancient monument, in this case the 1st-century-AD **Stadio di Domiziano** (Map p360; ☑06 06 08; Piazza Tor Sanguigna 13; ☺closed for restoration; 🚇Corso del Rinascimento). This 30,000-seat stadium, remains of which can be seen from the adjacent Piazza Tor Sanguigna, used to host games – the name Navona is a corruption of the Greek word *agon*, meaning public games. Inevitably, though, it fell into disrepair and it wasn't until the 15th century that the crumbling arena was paved over and Rome's central market transferred here from Campidoglio.

Fountains

Of the piazza's three fountains, it's Gian Lorenzo Bernini's high-camp **Fontana dei Quattro Fiumi** (Fountain of the Four Rivers; Map p360) that dominates. Commissioned by Pope Innocent X and completed in 1651, it depicts the Nile, Ganges, Danube and Plate, representing the then-known four continents of the world, and is festooned with a palm tree, lion and horse, and topped by an obelisk. Legend has it that the figure of the Nile is shielding his eyes from the nearby Chiesa di Sant'Agnese in Agone designed by Bernini's hated rival, Francesco Borromini. In truth, it simply indicates that the source of the Nile was unknown at the time the fountain was created.

The **Fontana del Moro** (Map p360) at the southern end of the square was designed by Giacomo della Porta in 1576. Bernini added the Moor holding a dolphin in the mid-17th century, but the surrounding Tritons are 19th-century copies. The 19th-century **Fontana del Nettuno** (Map p360) at the northern end of the piazza depicts Neptune fighting with a sea monster, surrounded by sea nymphs.

Chiesa di Sant'Agnese in Agone

With its stately, yet vibrantly theatrical facade, the **Chiesa di Sant'Agnese in Agone** (Map p360; www.santagneseinagone.org; concerts €10; ☺9.30am-12.30pm & 4-7pm Tue-Sun; 🚇Corso del Rinascimento) is typical of Francesco Borromini's baroque style. The church, which hosts an annual season of classical music concerts, is said to stand on the spot where the virgin martyr Agnes performed a miracle before being killed. According to legend, she was stripped naked by her executioners but miraculously grew her hair to cover her body and preserve her modesty.

Palazzo Pamphilj

The largest building in the square is this elegant baroque *palazzo,* built between 1644 and 1650 by Girolamo Rainaldi and Borromini to celebrate Giovanni Battista Pamphilj's election as Pope Innocent X. Inside there are some impressive frescoes by Pietro da Cortona, but the building, which has been the Brazilian Embassy since 1920, is not open to the general public.

◉ SIGHTS

Bound by the River Tiber and Via del Corso, the *centro storico* is made for aimless wandering. Even without trying you'll come across some of Rome's great sights: the Pantheon, Piazza Navona and Campo de' Fiori, as well as a host of monuments, museums and churches. To the south, the Jewish Ghetto has been home to Rome's Jewish community since the 2nd century BC.

◉ Pantheon & Around

PANTHEON   CHURCH
See p82.

ELEFANTINO   MONUMENT
(Map p360; Piazza della Minerva; ▣Largo di Torre Argentina) Just south of the Pantheon, the Elefantino is a curious and much-loved sculpture of a puzzled elephant carrying a 6th-century-BC Egyptian obelisk. Unveiled in 1667 and designed to glorify Pope Alexander VII, the elephant, symbolising strength and wisdom, was sculpted by Ercole Ferrata to a design by Bernini. The obelisk was taken from the nearby Chiesa di Santa Maria Sopra Minerva.

CHIESA DI SANTA MARIA
SOPRA MINERVA   CHURCH
(Map p360; Piazza della Minerva; ⊙8am-7pm Mon-Fri, 8am-1pm & 3.30-7pm Sat & Sun; ▣Largo di Torre Argentina) Built on the site of an ancient temple to Minerva, the Dominican Chiesa di Santa Maria Sopra Minerva is Rome's only Gothic church. However, little remains of the original 13th-century church and these days the main drawcard is a Michelangelo sculpture and colourful art-rich interior.

Inside, in the **Cappella Carafa** (also called the Cappella della Annunciazione), you'll find two superb 15th-century frescoes by Filippino Lippi and the majestic tomb of Pope Paul IV. Left of the high altar is one of Michelangelo's lesser-known sculptures, *Cristo Risorto* (Christ Bearing the Cross; 1520). An altarpiece of the *Madonna and Child* in the second chapel in the northern transept is attributed to Fra Angelico, the Dominican friar and painter, who is also buried in the church.

The body of St Catherine of Siena, minus her head (which is in Siena), lies under the high altar, and the tombs of two Medici popes, Leo X and Clement VII, are found in the apse.

LARGO DI TORRE ARGENTINA   RUINS
(Map p360; ▣Largo di Torre Argentina) A busy public transport hub, Largo di Torre Argentina is set around the sunken **Area Sacra** (Map p360) and the remains of four Republican-era temples, all built between the 2nd and 4th centuries BC. These ruins, which are among the oldest in the city, are off-limits to humans but home to a thriving population of around 250 stray cats and a volunteer-run **cat sanctuary** (Map p360; www.romancats.com; ⊙noon-6pm daily; ▣Largo di Torre Argentina).

On the piazza's western flank stands Rome's premier theatre, the Teatro Argentina (p105).

MUSEO NAZIONALE ROMANO:
CRYPTA BALBI   MUSEUM
(Map p360; ☑06 3996 7700; http://archeoroma. beniculturali.it/en/museums/national-roman-museum-crypta-balbi; Via delle Botteghe Oscure 31; adult/reduced €7/3.50; ⊙9am-7.45pm Tue-Sun ; ▣Via delle Botteghe Oscure) The least known of the Museo Nazionale Romano's four museums, the Crypta Balbi is built around the ruins of medieval and Renaissance structures, themselves set atop the ancient Teatro di Balbus (13 BC). Duck down into the underground excavations, then examine artefacts taken from the Crypta, as well as items found in the forums and on the Oppio and Celian Hills. For more information on a combined admission ticket, see p168.

◉ Piazza Navona & Around

PIAZZA NAVONA   PIAZZA
See p84.

VIA DEI CORONARI   HISTORIC STREET
(Map p360; ▣Corso del Rinascimento) Named after the *coronari* (rosary-bead sellers) who used to work here, this elegant pedestrian street is famous for its antique shops. A lovely, quiet place for a stroll, it follows the course of the ancient Roman road that connected Piazza Colonna with the River Tiber and was once a popular thoroughfare for pilgrims.

CHIESA DI SANTA MARIA DELLA PACE & CHIOSTRO DEL BRAMANTE
CHURCH, CLOISTER

(Map p360; www.chiostrodelbramante.it; Vicolo dell'Arco della Pace 5; exhibitions adult/reduced €12/10; ⊙church 10am-12.50pm Mon-Wed & Fri, 9am-11.50am Sat, cloister 10am-8pm; ⬚Corso del Rinascimento) Tucked away in the backstreets near Piazza Navona, this small 15th- century church boasts an elaborate porticoed exterior and a celebrated Raphael fresco, *Sibille* (Sibyls; c 1515). Next door, the **Chiostro del Bramante** (Bramante Cloister) is a masterpiece of High Renaissance architectural styling that is now used to stage temporary art exhibitions and cultural events.

The cloister, which you can visit freely by popping up to the first floor shop or cafe, was originally part of the same monastery complex as the Chiesa di Santa Maria della Pace. Its sober, geometric lines and perfectly proportioned spaces provide a marked counterpoint to the church's undulating facade, beautifully encapsulating the Renaissance aesthetic that Bramante did so much to promote.

PASQUINO
MONUMENT

(Map p360; Piazza Pasquino; ⬚Corso Vittorio Emanuele II) This unassuming sculpture is Rome's most famous 'talking statue'. During the 16th century, when there were no safe outlets for dissent, a Vatican tailor named Pasquino began sticking notes to the statue with satirical verses lampooning the church and aristocracy. Soon others joined in and, as the trend spread, talking statues popped up all over town.

Until recently, Romans were still writing messages, known as *pasquinade*, and sticking them to the statue. However, the sculpture is now off-limits and disgruntled Romans are forced to leave their post-it protests on the small noticeboard.

VIA DEL GOVERNO VECCHIO
HISTORIC STREET

(Map p360; ⬚Corso Vittorio Emanuele II) Striking off west from near Piazza Navona, Via del Governo Vecchio is an atmospheric street full of attractive boutiques, popular eateries and vintage clothes shops. The road, once part of the papal processional route that linked the Basilica di San Giovanni in Laterano to St Peter's, acquired its name in 1755 when the pontifical govern-

---

 TOP SIGHT
CHIESA DI SAN LUIGI DEI FRANCESI

Church to Rome's French community since 1589, this opulent baroque bonanza boasts no less than three paintings by Caravaggio. In the Cappella Contarelli, to the left of the main altar, crowds gather to admire the *Vocazione di San Matteo* (The Calling of Saint Matthew), the *Martiro di San Matteo* (The Martyrdom of Saint Matthew) and *San Matteo e l'angelo* (Saint Matthew and the Angel), together known as the St Matthew cycle.

These are among Caravaggio's earliest religious works, painted between 1599 and 1602, but they are inescapably his, featuring down-to-earth realism and stunning use of chiaroscuro (the bold contrast of light and dark). Caravaggio's refusal to adhere to artistic conventions and glorify his religious subjects often landed him in hot water and his first version of *San Matteo e l'angelo*, which depicted St Matthew as a bald, bare-legged peasant, was originally rejected by his outraged patron, Cardinal Matteo Contarelli.

Before you leave the church, take a moment to enjoy Domenichino's faded 17th-century frescoes of St Cecilia in the second chapel on the right. St Cecilia is also depicted in the altarpiece by Guido Reni, a copy of a work by Raphael.

DON'T MISS...

➡ *Vocazione di San Matteo*

➡ *Martiro di San Matteo*

➡ *San Matteo e l'angelo*

* Domenichino's St Cecilia frescoes

PRACTICALITIES

➡ Map p360

➡ Piazza di San Luigi dei Francesi

➡ ⊙10am-12.30pm & 3-7pm, closed Thu afternoon

➡ ⬚Corso del Rinascimento

LEGENDARY CRIMES

On the Ides of March (15 March) 44 BC, Julius Caesar was stabbed to death in the Curia of the Teatro di Pompeo – a vast theatre complex that covered much of what is now the Largo di Torre Argentina (p85). The exact location of the murder scene has always been a mystery but in October 2012 a team of Spanish archaeologists announced that they had found it on the Teatro Argentina side of the Area Sacra. As evidence they pointed to a concrete structure that they believed was a memorial placed on the spot by Augustus, Caesar's heir and successor.

Violent crime is a recurring feature of Rome's long and tortuous history. The city was founded on the back of a murder – Romulus' killing of his twin Remus on the Palatino (p64) – and blood stains many of the city's *palazzi*. One of the city's most notorious crimes took place in Palazzo Cenci (p93) in the Jewish Ghetto. There Beatrice Cenci, a young aristocrat, was driven by years of abuse to murder her tyrannical father. After a long and brutal investigation she and her accomplice, her stepmother Lucrezia, were beheaded on 11 September 1599 in front of a vast and largely sympathetic crowd on Ponte Sant'Angelo (p155).

ment relocated from Palazzo Nardini at No 39 to Palazzo Madama.

The architect Bramante is thought to have lived at No 123.

CHIESA NUOVA CHURCH
(Map p360; Piazza della Chiesa Nuova; ⊘7.30am-noon & 4.30-7.30pm; ⊒Corso Vittorio Emanuele II) Not exactly *nuova* (new) as the name would suggest, this imposing landmark church overlooking Corso Vittorio Emanuele II boasts a fine 17th-century facade and an impressive baroque interior decorated by the likes of Rubens and Pietro da Cortona.

Built in 1575 as part of a complex to house Filippo Neri's Oratorian order, it was originally a large plain church in accordance with Neri's wishes. But when Neri died in 1595 the artists moved in – Rubens painted over the high altar, and Pietro da Cortona decorated the dome, tribune and nave. Neri was canonised in 1622 and is buried in a chapel to the left of the apse.

Next to the church is Borromini's **Oratorio dei Filippini** and behind it is the **Torre dell'Orologio**, a clock tower built to decorate the adjacent convent.

MUSEO DI ROMA MUSEUM
(Map p360; ⊘06 06 08; www.museodiroma.it; entrances Piazza di San Pantaleo 10 & Piazza Navona 2; adult/reduced €8.50/6.50; ⊘10am-8pm Tue-Sun, last admission 7pm; ⊒Corso Vittorio Emanuele II) The baroque Palazzo Braschi houses the Museo di Roma's eclectic collection of paintings, photographs, etchings, clothes and furniture, charting the history of Rome from the Middle Ages to the early

20th century. But as striking as the collection are the palazzo's beautiful frescoed halls, including the extravagant Sala Cinese and the Egyptian-themed Sala Egiziana.

Among the paintings, look out for Raphael's 1511 portrait of Cardinal Alessandro Farnese, the future Pope Paul III.

CHIESA DI SANT'IVO
ALLA SAPIENZA CHURCH
(Map p360; Corso del Rinascimento 40; ⊘9am-12.30pm Sun; ⊒Corso del Rinascimento) Hidden in the porticoed courtyard of **Palazzo della Sapienza**, this tiny church is a masterpiece of baroque architecture. Built by Francesco Borromini between 1642 and 1660, and based on an incredibly complex geometric plan, it combines alternating convex and concave walls with a circular interior topped by a twisted spire.

Palazzo della Sapienza, seat of Rome's university until 1935 and now home to the Italian state archive, is often used to stage temporary exhibitions.

PALAZZO MADAMA PALACE
(Map p360; ⊘06 6706 2430; www.senato.it; Piazza Madama 11; ⊘guided tours 10am-6pm, 1st Sat of month Jul-Sep; ⊒Corso del Rinascimento) **FREE** Seat of the Italian Senate since 1871, the regal Palazzo Madama was originally the 16th-century residence of Giovanni de' Medici, the future Pope Leo X. It was enlarged in the 17th century, when the baroque facade was added together with the decorative frieze, and later provided office space for several pontifical departments.

1. Fontana del Nettuno, Piazza Navona (p84) 2. St Peter's Square (p154) 3. Piazza del Popolo (p118)

Showtime on Rome's Piazzas

From the baroque splendour of Piazza Navona to the clamour of Campo de' Fiori and the majesty of St Peter's Square, Rome's showcase piazzas encapsulate much of the city's beauty, history and drama.

Piazza Navona

In the heart of the historic centre, Piazza Navona (p84) is the picture-perfect Roman square. Graceful baroque *palazzi* (mansions), flamboyant fountains, packed pavement cafes and costumed street artists set the scene for the daily invasion of camera-toting tourists.

St Peter's Square

The awe-inspiring approach to St Peter's Basilica, this monumental piazza (p154) is a masterpiece of 17th-century urban design. The work of Bernini, it's centred on a towering Egyptian obelisk and flanked by two grasping colonnaded arms.

Piazza del Popolo

Neoclassical Piazza del Popolo (p118) is a vast, sweeping spectacle. In centuries past, executions were held here; nowadays crowds gather for political rallies, outdoor concerts or just to hang out.

Piazza del Campidoglio

The centrepiece of the Campidoglio (Capitoline Hill), this Michelangelo-designed piazza (p75) is thought by many to be the city's most beautiful. Surrounded on three sides by *palazzi*, it's home to the Capitoline Museums.

Campo de' Fiori

Campo de' Fiori (p90) is the cousin of the more refined Piazza Navona, with market traders and an unpretentious atmosphere.

Piazza di Spagna

In Rome's swank shopping district, Piazza di Spagna (p113) has long attracted footsore foreigners who come to sit on the Spanish Steps and watch the world go by.

The name 'Madama' is a reference to Margaret of Parma, the illegitimate daughter of the Holy Roman Emperor Charles V, who lived here from 1559 to 1567.

CHIESA DI SANT'AGOSTINO CHURCH

(Map p360; Piazza di Sant'Agostino 80; ⏱7.30am-12.30pm & 4-6.30pm; ▣Corso del Rinascimento) The plain white facade of this early Renaissance church, built in the 15th century and renovated in the late 18th, gives no indication of the impressive art inside. The most famous work is Caravaggio's *Madonna dei Pellegrini* (Madonna of the Pilgrims) but you'll also find a fresco by Raphael and a much-venerated sculpture by Jacopo Sansovino.

The *Madonna del Parto* (Madonna of Childbirth), Sansovino's 1521 statue of the Virgin Mary with baby Jesus, is the subject of much local devotion, particularly by soon-to-be mums who come here to pray for a safe pregnancy. The Madonna also stars in Caravaggio's striking *Madonna dei Pellegrini*, which caused uproar when it was unveiled in 1604, due to its depiction of Mary as barefoot and her two devoted pilgrims as filthy beggars. Painting almost a century before, Raphael provoked no such scandal with his fresco of Isaiah, visible on the third pilaster on the left in the nave.

⦿ Campo de' Fiori & Around

CAMPO DE' FIORI PIAZZA

(Map p360; ▣Corso Vittorio Emanuele II) Noisy, colourful 'Il Campo' is a major focus of Roman life: by day it hosts a much-loved market, while at night it morphs into a raucous open-air pub. For centuries it was the site of public executions and it was here that philosopher monk Giordano Bruno was burned at the stake for heresy in 1600. The spot is today marked by a sinister statue of the hooded monk, created by Ettore Ferrari and unveiled in 1889.

PALAZZO FARNESE PALACE

(Map p360; www.inventerrome.com; Piazza Farnese; admission €5; ⏱guided tours 3pm, 4pm, 5pm Mon, Wed & Fri; ▣Corso Vittorio Emanuele II) Home of the French Embassy, this formidable Renaissance *palazzo*, one of Rome's finest, was started in 1514 by Antonio da Sangallo the Younger, continued

---

⦿ TOP SIGHT **MUSEO NAZIONALE ROMANO: PALAZZO ALTEMPS**

Palazzo Altemps is a beautiful, late-15th-century *palazzo*, housing the best of the Museo Nazionale Romano's classical sculpture and Egyptian collection. Many pieces come from the celebrated Ludovisi collection, amassed by Cardinal Ludovico Ludovisi in the 17th century.

Prize exhibits include the beautiful 5th-century *Trono Ludovisi* (Ludovisi Throne), a carved marble block whose central relief depicts a naked Aphrodite being modestly plucked from the sea. It shares a room with two colossal heads, one of which is the goddess Juno dating from around 600 BC. The wall frieze (about half of which remains) depicts the 10 plagues of Egypt and the Exodus.

Equally affecting is the sculptural group *Galata Suicida* (Gaul's Suicide), a melodramatic depiction of a Gaul knifing himself to death over a dead woman.

The building's baroque frescoes provide an exquisite decorative backdrop. The walls of the **Sala delle Prospettive Dipinte** are decorated with landscapes and hunting scenes seen through trompe l'œil windows. These frescoes were painted for Cardinal Altemps, the rich nephew of Pope Pius IV (r 1560–65) who bought the *palazzo* in the late 16th century. For more information on a combined admission ticket, see p108.

DON'T MISS...

➜ Trono Ludovisi
➜ *Galata Suicida*
➜ Sala delle Prospettive Dipinte

PRACTICALITIES

➜ Map p360
➜ ☏06 3996 7700
➜ http://archeoroma.beniculturali.it
➜ Piazza Sant'Apollinare 44
➜ adult/reduced €7/3.50
➜ ⏱9am-7.45pm Tue-Sun
➜ ▣Corso del Rinascimento

by Michelangelo and finished by Giacomo della Porta. Inside, it boasts a series of sublime frecsoes by Annibale Carracci that are said by some to rival Michelangelo's in the Sistine Chapel.

The frescoes are about to undergo restoration but visits continue. These are by guided tour only (available in English, Italian and French), for which you'll need to book ahead at least a week in advance. Photo ID is required for entry and children under 10 are not admitted.

The twin fountains in the square are enormous granite baths taken from the Terme di Caracalla.

PALAZZO SPADA   PALACE, GALLERY

(Map p360; ☑06 683 24 09; http://galleriaspada. beniculturali.it; Via Capo di Ferro 13; adult/reduced €5/2.50; ⊗8.30am-7.30pm Tue-Sun; ☑Corso Vittorio Emanuele II) With its stuccoed ornamental facade and handsome courtyard, this grand *palazzo* is a fine example of 16th-century Mannerist architecture. Upstairs, a small gallery houses the Spada family art collection with works by Andrea del Sarto, Guido Reni, Guercino and Titian, whilst downstairs Francesco Borromini's famous optical illusion, aka the *Prospettiva* (Perspective), continues to confound visitors.

What appears to be a 25m-long corridor lined with columns leading to a hedge and life-sized statue is, in fact, only 10m long. The sculpture, which was a later addition, is actually hip-height and the columns diminish in size not because of distance but because they actually get shorter. And look closer at that perfect-looking hedge – Borromini didn't trust the gardeners to clip a real hedge precisely enough so he made one of stone.

VIA GIULIA   HISTORIC STREET

(Map p360; ☑Via Giulia) Designed by Bramante in 1508, Via Giulia is one of Rome's most charming roads lined with colourful Renaissance *palazzi* and potted orange trees.

At its southern end, the **Fontana del Mascherone** (Map p362) depicts a 17th-century hippy surprised by water spewing from his mouth. Just beyond it, and spanning the road, is the ivy-clad **Arco Farnese** (Map p360), designed by Michelangelo as part of an ambitious, unfinished project to connect Palazzo Farnese with Villa Farnesina on the opposite side of the Tiber.

Continuing north, on the left, in Via di Sant'Eligio, is the lovely Raphael-designed

ARCO DEGLI ACETARI

For one of Rome's most picture-perfect scenes, head to Via del Pellegrino 19, just off Campo de' Fiori. Here you'll come across a dark archway called the **Arco degli Acetari** (Vinegar-Makers' Arch; Map p360). This in itself isn't especially memorable but if you duck under it you'll emerge onto a tiny medieval square enclosed by rusty orange houses and full of colourful cascading plants. Cats and bicycles litter the cobbles, while overhead washing hangs off pretty flower-lined balconies.

Chiesa di Sant'Eligio degli Orefici (Map p360; ☑06 686 82 60; ⊗by prior reservation only 9am-1pm Mon-Fri; ☑Via Giulia).

MUSEO CRIMINOLOGICO   MUSEUM

(Map p360; ☑06 6889 9442; www.museocriminologico.it; Via del Gonfalone 29; admission €2; ⊗9am-1pm Tue-Sat & 2.30-6.30pm Tue & Thu; ☑Via Giulia) Check out Rome's dark side at this macabre museum of crime. Housed in a 19th-century prison, its gruesome collection runs the gauntlet from torture devices and murder weapons to fake Picassos, confiscated smut and the red cloak of Massimo Titta, the Papal State's official executioner who carried out 516 executions between 1796 and 1865.

CHIESA DI SAN GIOVANNI BATTISTA DEI FIORENTINI   CHURCH

(Map p360; Piazza dell'Oro 2; ⊗7.30am-noon & 5-7pm; ☑Ponte Vittorio Emanuele II) The last resting place of architects Francesco Borromini and Carlo Maderno, this graceful 16th-century church was commissioned by Pope Leo X as a showcase for Florentine artistic talent. Jacopo Sansovino won a competition for its design, which was then executed by Antonio Sangallo the Younger and Giacomo della Porta. Carlo Maderno completed the elongated cupola in 1614, while, inside, the altar is by Borromini.

PALAZZO DELLA CANCELLERIA   PALACE

(Map p360; Piazza della Cancelleria; ☑Corso Vittorio Emanuele II) As impressive an example of Renaissance architecture as you'll find in Rome, this huge *palazzo* was built for Cardinal Raffaele Riario between 1483 and 1513. It was later acquired by the Vatican and became the seat of the Papal Chancellory. It is still Vatican property and nowadays houses the Tribunal of the Roman Rota, the Holy See's highest ecclesiastical court.

It is often used to stage exhibitions and if you get the chance you should nip through to the courtyard to take a peek at Bramante's glorious double loggia.

Incorporated into the palazzo, the 4th-century **Basilica di San Lorenzo in Damaso** (Map p360; ☉7.30am-noon & 4.30-8pm; ☐Corso Vittorio Emanuele II), is one of Rome's oldest churches.

MUSEO BARRACCO DI
SCULTURA ANTICA   MUSEUM

(Map p360; www.museobarracco.it; Corso Vittorio Emanuele II 166; adult/reduced €6.50/5.50; ☉10am-4pm Tue-Sun Oct-May, 3-7pm Tue-Sun Jun-Sep; ☐Corso Vittorio Emanuele II) This charming museum boasts a fascinating collection of early Mediterranean sculpture. You'll find Greek, Etruscan, Roman, Assyrian, Cypriot and Egyptian works, all donated to the state by Baron Giovanni Barracco in 1902.

The *palazzo* housing the museum, known as the Piccolo Farnesina, was built for a French clergyman, Thomas Le Roy, in 1523.

CHIESA DI SANT'ANDREA
DELLA VALLE   CHURCH

(Map p360; Piazza Vidoni 6; ☉7.30am-noon & 4.30-7.30pm Mon-Sat, 7.30am-12.45pm & 4.30-7.45pm Sun; ☐Corso Vittorio Emanuele II) A must for opera fans, this towering 17th-century church is where Giacomo Puccini set the first act of *Tosca*. Its most obvious feature is Carlo Maderno's soaring dome, the highest in Rome after St Peter's Basilica, but its bombastic baroque interior reveals some wonderful frescoes by Mattia Preti, Domenichino and, in the dome, Lanfranco.

Competition between the artists working on the church was fierce and rumour has it that Domenichino once took a saw to Lanfranco's scaffolding, almost killing him in the process.

⊙ Jewish Ghetto

Centred on lively Via Portico d'Ottavia, the Jewish Ghetto is a wonderfully atmospheric area studded with artisans' studios, vintage clothes shops, kosher bakeries and popular trattorias.

ROME'S FAVOURITE FOOT

It doesn't appear on any tourist brochures and you could easily pass by without noticing it. But the **Piè di Marmo** (Map p360) is one of Romans' favourite monuments. A giant marble foot, now on Via di Santo Stefano del Cacco, it started life attached to a statue in a 1st-century temple dedicated to the Egyptian gods Isis and Serapis. Some 1600 years later it cropped up on the street that now bears its name, Via del Piè di Marmo. It was placed in its current position in 1878 to clear the path for King Vittorio Emanuele II's funeral procession to reach the Pantheon.

Rome's Jewish community dates back to the 2nd century BC, making it one of the oldest in Europe. At one point there were as many as 13 synagogues in the city but Titus's defeat of Jewish rebels in Jerusalem in AD 70 changed the status of Rome's Jews from citizen to slave. Confinement to the Ghetto came in 1555 when Pope Paul IV ushered in a period of official intolerance that lasted, on and off, until the 20th century. Ironically, though, confinement meant that Jewish cultural and religious identity survived intact.

MUSEO EBRAICO
DI ROMA   SYNAGOGUE, MUSEUM

(Jewish Museum of Rome; Map p362; ☎06 6840 0661; www.museoebraico.roma.it; Via Catalana; adult/reduced €10/7.50; ☉10am-6.15pm Sun-Thu, 10am-3.15pm Fri mid-Jun–mid-Sep, 10am-4pm Sun-Thu, 9am-1.15pm Fri mid-Sep–mid-Jun; ☐Lungotevere de' Cenci) The historical, cultural and artistic heritage of Rome's Jewish community is chronicled in this small but engrossing museum. Housed in the city's early-20th-century synagogue, Europe's second largest, it presents harrowing reminders of the hardships experienced by the city's Jewry. Exhibits include copies of Pope Paul IV's papal bull confining the Jews to the ghetto and relics from Nazi concentration camps.

PALAZZO CENCI   PALACE

(Map p362; Vicolo dei Cenci; ☉closed to the public; ☐Via Arenula, ☐Via Arenula) A real-life house of horrors, Palazzo Cenci was the scene of one of the 16th century's most infamous crimes, the murder of Francesco Cenci by his long-suffering daughter Beatrice and wife Lucrezia.

Shelley based his tragedy *The Cenci* on the family, and a famous portrait of Beatrice by Guido Reni hangs in the Galleria Nazionale d'Arte Antica – Palazzo Barberini. It shows a sweet-faced young girl with soft eyes and fair hair.

FONTANA DELLE TARTARUGHE   MONUMENT
(Map p362; Piazza Mattei; ⊡Via Arenula, ⊡Via Arenula) This playful much-loved 16th-century fountain depicts four boys gently hoisting tortoises up into a bowl of water. Now covered in scaffolding, it's the subject of a romantic fairy tale which holds that it was created in a single night in 1585.

The story goes that Taddeo Landini crafted it for the Duke of Mattei, who had gambled his fortune away and was on the verge of losing his fiancée. On seeing the fountain, Mattei's future father-in-law was so impressed that he relented and let Mattei marry his daughter. The tortoises were added by Bernini in 1658.

AREA ARCHEOLOGICA DEL TEATRO DI MARCELLO E DEL PORTICO D'OTTAVIA   ARCHAEOLOGICAL SITE
(Map p362; entrances Via del Teatro di Marcello 44 & Via Portico d'Ottavia 29; ⊙9am-7pm summer, 9am-6pm winter; ⊡Via del Teatro di Marcello) **FREE** To the east of the Jewish Ghetto, the **Teatro di Marcello** (Theatre of Marcellus; Map p362) is the star turn of this dusty archaeological area. This 20,000-seat mini-Colosseum was planned by Julius Caesar and completed in 11 BC by Augustus who named it after a favourite nephew, Marcellus. In the 16th century, a *palazzo*, which now contains several exclusive apartments, was built on top of the original structure.

Beyond the theatre, the **Portico d'Ottavia** is the oldest *quadriporto* (four-sided porch) in Rome. The dilapidated columns and fragmented pediment once formed part of a vast rectangular portico, supported by 300 columns, that measured 132m by 119m. Erected by a builder called Octavius in 146 BC, it was rebuilt in 23 BC by Augustus, who kept the name in honour of his sister Octavia. From the Middle Ages until the late 19th century, the portico housed Rome's fish market.

CENTRO STORICO SIGHTS

⊙ TOP SIGHT
CHIESA DEL GESÙ

An imposing example of late-16th-century Counter-Reformation architecture, this is Rome's most important Jesuit church. The facade by Giacomo della Porta is impressive, but it's the awesome gold and marble interior that is the real attraction. The most astounding artwork is the *Trionfo del Nome di Gesù* (Triumph of the Name of Jesus), the swirling, hypnotic fresco by Giovanni Battista Gaulli (aka Il Baciccia), who also painted the cupola frescoes.

Baroque master Andrea Pozzo designed the **Cappella di Sant'Ignazio** in the northern transept. Here you'll find the tomb of Ignatius Loyola, the Spanish soldier and saint who founded the Jesuits in 1540. The altar-tomb is an opulent marble-and-bronze affair with columns encrusted with lapis lazuli. On top, the terrestrial globe, representing the Trinity, is the largest solid piece of lapis lazuli in the world. On either side are sculptures of *Fede che vince l'Idolatria* (Faith Defeats Idolatry) and *Religione che flagella l'Eresia* (Religion Lashing Heresy).

The Spanish saint lived in the church from 1544 until his death in 1556. His private **rooms**, with a masterful trompe l'œil by Andrea del Pozzo, are just to the right of the main church.

DON'T MISS...

➡ The *Trionfo del Nome di Gesù* fresco
➡ Cappella di Sant'Ignazio

PRACTICALITIES

➡ Map p360
➡ www.chiesa-delgesu.org
➡ Piazza del Gesù
➡ rooms admission free
➡ ⊙7am-12.30pm & 4-7.45pm, St Ignatius rooms 4-6pm Mon-Sat, 10am-noon Sun
➡ ⊡Largo di Torre Argentina

TOP SIGHT
PALAZZO E GALLERIA DORIA PAMPHILJ

The grimy exterior of this *palazzo* hides one of Rome's richest private art collections, with works by Raphael, Tintoretto, Brueghel, Titian, Caravaggio, Bernini and Velázquez.

Palazzo Doria Pamphilj dates to the mid-15th century, but its current look was largely the work of the current owners, the Doria Pamphilj family, who acquired it in the 18th century. The Pamphilj's golden age, during which the family collection was started, came during the papacy of one of their own, Innocent X (r 1644–55).

The opulent picture galleries, decorated with frescoed ceilings and gilded mirrors, are hung with floor-to-ceiling paintings. Masterpieces abound, but look out for Titian's *Salomè con la testa del Battista* (Salome with the Head of John the Baptist) and two early Caravaggios: *Riposo durante la fuga in Egitto* (Rest During the Flight into Egypt) and *Maddalene Penitente* (Penitent Magdalen). However, the undisputed star is the Velázquez portrait of an implacable Pope Innocent X, who grumbled that it was 'too real'. Compare it with Gian Lorenzo Bernini's sculptural interpretation of the same subject. The free audioguide, narrated by Jonathan Pamphilj, brings the place alive with family anecdotes and background information.

DON'T MISS...

➡ *Salome con la testa del Battistsa*

➡ *Riposo durante la fuga in Egitto*

➡ *Ritratto di papa Innocenzo X*

PRACTICALITIES

➡ Map p360

➡ ☎06 679 73 23

➡ www.dopart.it

➡ Via del Corso 305

➡ adult/reduced €11/7.50

➡ ⊙9am-7pm, last admission 6pm

➡ 🚇Piazza Venezia

CHIESA DI SAN NICOLA IN CARCERE
CHURCH

(Map p362; ☎347 3811874; www.sotterraneidiroma.it; Via del Teatro di Marcello 46; ⊙10.30am-7pm, excavations to 6pm Mon-Fri, to 5pm Sat & Sun; 🚇Via del Teatro di Marcello) This innocuous-looking 11th-century church harbours some fascinating Roman excavations. Beneath the main church you can poke around the claustrophobic foundations of three Republican-era temples over which the church was built, and the remnants of an Etruscan vegetable market. Marble columns from the temples were incorporated into the church's structure and are still visible today.

Visits, led by local experts from Sotterranei di Roma, are by guided tour only.

◉ Isola Tiberina

One of the world's smallest inhabited islands, the boat-shaped Isola Tiberina (Tiber Island) has been associated with healing since the 3rd century BC, when the Romans adopted the Greek god of healing Asclepius (aka Aesculapius) as their own and erected a temple to him on the island. Today, the island is home to the Ospedale Fatebenefratelli.

To reach the Isola from the Jewish Ghetto, cross Rome's oldest standing bridge, the 62 BC **Ponte Fabricio**. Visible to the south are the remains of the **Ponte Rotto** (Broken Bridge), Ancient Rome's first stone bridge, which was all but swept away in a 1598 flood.

CHIESA DI SAN BARTOLOMEO
CHURCH

(Map p362; ⊙9am-1pm & 3.30-5.30pm Mon-Sat, 9am-1pm Sun; 🚇Lungotevere dei Pierleoni) Built on the ruins of the Roman temple to Aesculapius, the Greek god of healing, the island's 10th-century church is an interesting hybrid of architectural styles: the facade is baroque, as is the richly frescoed ceiling; the belltower is 12th-century Romanesque and the 28 columns that divide the interior naves date to ancient times.

Inside, there's a marble wellhead, which is thought to stand over the spring that provided the temple's healing waters.

◉ Piazza Colonna & Around

PIAZZA COLONNA
PIAZZA

(Map p360; 🚇Via del Corso) Together with Piazza di Montecitorio, this stylish piazza is

Rome's political nerve centre. On its northern flank, the 16th-century **Palazzo Chigi** (Map p360; www.governo.it; Piazza Colonna 370; ⊙guided visits 9am-1pm Sat Oct-May, booking required) **FREE** has been the official residence of Italy's prime minister since 1961. In the centre, the 30m-high **Colonna di Marco Aurelio** (Map p360) was completed in AD 193 to honour Marcus Aurelius' military victories.

The column's vivid reliefs depict scenes from battles against the Germanic tribes (169–73) and, further up, the Sarmatians (174–76). In 1589 Marcus was replaced on the top of the column with a bronze statue of St Paul.

South of the piazza, in **Piazza di Pietra**, is the **Tempio di Adriano** (Map p360). Eleven huge Corinthian columns, now embedded in what used to be Rome's stock exchange, are all that remain of Hadrian's 2nd-century temple.

PALAZZO DI MONTECITORIO　　　PALACE
(Map p360; ☑800 012955; www.camera.it; Piazza di Montecitorio; ⊙guided visits 10.30am-3.30pm, 1st Sun of month; ⬛Via del Corso) **FREE** Home to Italy's Chamber of Deputies, this baroque *palazzo* was built by Bernini in 1653, expanded by Carlo Fontana in the late 17th century, and given an art nouveau facelift in 1918. Visits take in the palazzo's lavish reception rooms and the main chamber where the 630 deputies debate beneath a beautiful art nouveau skyline.

CENTRO STORICO SIGHTS

ROME'S HISTORIC FAMILIES

The Farnese

At home at Palazzo Farnese (p90), the all-powerful Farnese dynasty was one of Renaissance Rome's most celebrated families. Originally landed gentry in northern Lazio, they hit the big time in 1493 when Giulia Farnese became the mistress of Pope Alexander VI. Hardly an official post, it nevertheless gave Alessandro, Giulia's brother, enough influence to secure his election as Pope Paul III (r 1534–49).

The Borghese

Originally from Siena, the Borghese moved to Rome in the 16th century and quickly established themselves in high society. It was Camillo Borghese's election as Pope Paul V (r 1605–21) that opened the family's path to untold wealth. They became one of Rome's leading landowners and Scipione Borghese, Camillo's nephew, established himself as the city's most influential art patron – his collection is now on show in his former residence at the Museo e Galleria Borghese (p222).

The Chigi

Agostino Chigi (1465–1520), one of the richest men in early-16th-century Rome, was the star of the Chigi banking family. A close confidant of Pope Julius II (the man who commissioned Michelangelo to paint the Sistine Chapel), he was celebrated for his lavish entertaining at Villa Farnesina (p188), his palatial residence. Later, the Chigi amassed further fortunes under Pope Alexander VII (r 1655–67), aka Fabio Chigi.

The Barberini

The only one of Rome's great families to have a metro station named after it, the Barberini arrived in Rome in the early 16th century, escaping their native Tuscany and a dangerous rivalry with the Florentine Medici. They settled well and in 1623 Maffeo Barberini was elected Pope Urban VIII, opening the floodgates to the usual round of family appointments and extravagant building projects, including the lavish Palazzo Barberini (p124).

The Borgias

A byword for intrigue and excess, the Spanish Borgias shocked Renaissance Rome with their murderous ambition and unbridled debauchery. The family patriarch, Rodrigo, served as Pope Alexander VI (r 1492–1503), while his two illegitimate children Cesare (said to have been the model for Machiavelli's *Il Principe*) and Lucrezia (a supposed serial poisoner) earned reputations for deviousness and cruelty.

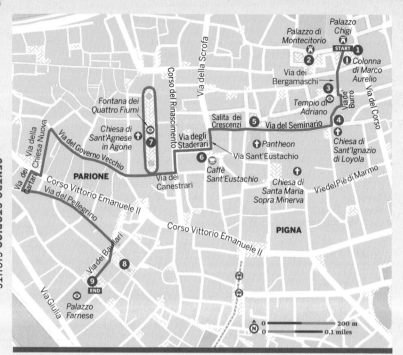

Neighbourhood Walk
Centro Storico Piazzas

START PIAZZA COLONNA
END PIAZZA FARNESE
LENGTH 1.5KM; ALL MORNING

Start in ❶ **Piazza Colonna** (p94), a grand square dominated by the 30m-high Colonna di Marco Aurelio and flanked by Palazzo Chigi, the official residence of the Italian prime minister. Next door, and facing onto ❷ **Piazza di Montecitorio**, is the equally impressive seat of the Chamber of Deputies, Palazzo di Montecitorio. From Piazza Colonna follow Via dei Bergamaschi down to ❸ **Piazza di Pietra**, a refined rectangular space overlooked by the 2nd-century Tempio di Adriano. Continue past the columns down Via de' Burro to ❹ **Piazza di Sant'Ignazio**, a small stagy piazza with a church of the same name. From here, it's a short walk along Via del Seminario to ❺ **Piazza della Rotonda** where the Pantheon needs no introduction.

Leaving the Pantheon, head up Salita dei Crescenzi and then go left along

Via Sant'Eustachio to ❻ **Piazza Sant'Eustachio**. On this small square is the Caffè Sant'Eustachio, a busy cafe serving the best espresso in town. Then follow Via degli Staderari to Corso del Rinascimento, drop a quick left followed by a short right and you're into Rome's showpiece square, ❼ **Piazza Navona** (p84). Here, among the street artists and tourists compare the two giants of Roman baroque – Bernini, creator of the Fontana dei Quattro Fiumi, and Borromini, designer of the Chiesa di Sant'Agnese in Agone.

Exit the piazza and follow on to Via del Governo Vecchio, an atmospheric street lined with fashion boutiques and buzzing eateries. At the end, turn left down Via della Chiesa Nuova to Corso Vittorio Emanuele II, the busy thoroughfare that bisects the historic centre. Cross over and follow Via dei Cartari down to Via del Pellegrino. Follow on to the noisy market square, ❽ **Campo de' Fiori** (p90), and beyond that, the more sober ❾ **Piazza Farnese** overshadowed by the Renaissance Palazzo Farnese.

The **obelisk** (Map p360) outside was brought from Heliopolis in Egypt by Augustus to celebrate victory over Cleopatra and Mark Antony in 30 BC.

CHIESA DI SANT'IGNAZIO
DI LOYOLA   CHURCH
(Map p360; Piazza di Sant'Ignazio; ⊙7.30am-7pm Mon-Sat, 9am-7pm Sun; ▣Via del Corso) Flanking a delightful rococo piazza, this important Jesuit church boasts a Carlo Maderno facade and a celebrated trompe l'œil ceiling fresco by Andrea Pozzo (1642–1709) depicting St Ignatius Loyola being welcomed into paradise by Christ and the Madonna.

For the best views of the fresco, stand on the small yellow spot on the nave floor and look up. The ceiling, which is, in fact, absolutely flat, appears to curve. But walk a little further into the church and the carefully created perspective stops working and the deception becomes clearer.

The church, which was built by the Jesuit architect Orazio Grassi in 1626, flanks **Piazza di Sant'Ignazio**, an exquisite square laid out in 1727 to resemble a stage set. Note the exits into 'the wings' at the northern end and how the undulating surfaces create the illusion of a larger space.

CHIESA DI SAN
LORENZO IN LUCINA   CHURCH
(Map p360; Piazza San Lorenzo in Lucina 16; ⊙8am-8pm; ▣Via del Corso) Little remains of the original 5th-century church that was built here atop an ancient well sacred to Juno. But that shouldn't detract from what is a very pretty church, complete with Romanesque bell tower and a long 12th-century columned portico.

Inside, the otherwise standard baroque decor is elevated by Guido Reni's *Crocifisso* (Crucifixion) above the main altar, and a fine bust by Bernini in the fourth chapel on the southern side. The French painter Nicholas Poussin, who died in 1655, is buried in the church.

✖ EATING

Around Piazza Navona, Campo de' Fiori and the Pantheon you'll find all manner of eateries, including some of the capital's best restaurants (both contemporary and traditional), alongside hundreds of overpriced tourist traps. The atmospheric Jewish Ghetto is famous for its unique Roman-Jewish cuisine.

✖ Pantheon & Around

VICE   GELATO $
(Map p360; www.viceitalia.it; Corso Vittorio Emanuele II 96; cones/tubs from €2; ⊙11am-1am; ▣Largo di Torre Argentina) If you're hot and tired, treat yourself to an ice cream from this cool, contemporary gelateria near the bus stops on Largo di Torre Argentina. Alongside classic flavours such as *nocciola* (hazelnut) and *limone* (lemon), both made from top Italian ingredients, you'll find more creative choices such as the wonderfully decadent blueberry cheesecake.

SAN CRISPINO   GELATO $
(Map p360; Piazza della Maddalena 3; tubs from €2; ⊙noon-12.30am Mon, Wed, Thu & Sun, to 1.30am Fri & Sat; ▣Corso del Rinascimento) A branch of Rome's highly rated San Crispino gelateria, serving fab ice cream made from seasonal natural ingredients.

ENOTECA CORSI   OSTERIA $$
(Map p360; ☏06 679 08 21; www.enotecacorsi. com; Via del Gesù 87; meals €25; ⊙lunch Mon-Sat; ▣Largo di Torre Argentina) Merrily the worse for wear, family-run Corsi is a genuine old-style Roman eatery. The look is rustic – bare wooden tables, paper tablecloths, wine bottles – and the atmosphere one of controlled mayhem. The menu, chalked up on a blackboard, offers no surprises, just honest, homey fare such as *melanzane parmigiana* or roast chicken with potatoes.

ZAZÀ   PIZZA $
(Map p360; ☏06 6880 1357; Piazza Sant'Eustachio 49; pizza slice around €3; ⊙9am-11pm Mon-Sat, to noon Sun; ▣Corso del Rinascimento) Handily sandwiched between Piazza Navona and the Pantheon, this hole-in-the-wall *pizza al taglio* (pizza by the slice) takeaway hits the spot with its tasty, low-cal, organic pizza. It also does home delivery from 4pm to 10pm.

CASA COPPELLE   MODERN ITALIAN $$
(Map p360; ☏06 6889 1707; www.casacoppelle.it; Piazza delle Coppelle 49; meals €35; ⊙lunch and dinner daily; ▣Corso del Rinascimento) Exposed brick walls, books, flowers and subdued lighting set the stage for wonderful French-

inspired food at this intimate, romantic restaurant. There's a full range of starters and pastas but the real tour de force is the steak served with crunchy, thinly sliced potato crisps. Service is quick and attentive. Book ahead.

ARMANDO AL PANTHEON TRATTORIA $$

(Map p360; ☑06 6880 3034; www.armandoalpantheon.it; Salita dei Crescenzi 31; meals €40; ✆closed Sat dinner & Sun & Aug; 🚇Largo di Torre Argentina, 🚇Largo di Torre Argentina) An institution in these parts, wood-panelled Armando is a rare find – a genuine family-run trattoria in the touristy Pantheon area. It's been on the go for more than 50 years and has served its fair share of celebs – philosopher Jean-Paul Sartre and Brazilian footballer Pelè have both eaten here – but the focus remains traditional, earthy Roman food. Reservationss recommended.

OSTERIA SOSTEGNO TRATTORIA $$

(Map p360; ☑06 679 38 42; www.ilsostegno.it; Via delle Colonnele 5; meals €35-40; ✆Tue-Sun; 🚇Largo di Torre Argentina) Follow the green neon arrow to the end of a narrow alley and you'll find this well-kept secret. It's an intimate place, a favourite of journalists and politicians who sneak off here to dine on old-school staples such as *pasta e ceci* (pasta with chickpeas) and *saltimbocca* (sliced veal cooked with wine, ham and sage).

IL BACARO RISTORANTE $$

(Map p360; ☑06 687 25 54; www.ilbacaroroma.com; Via degli Spagnoli 27; lunch €25, dinner €45; 🚇Corso del Rinascimento) Not an easy one to get to, this romantic restaurant is tucked away in the warren of streets north of the Pantheon. Run by an enthusiastic couple, it offers separate lunch and dinner menus with the onus on creative, forward-looking Italian cooking. Summer seating spills out under a vine-covered pergola.

LA ROSETTA SEAFOOD $$$

(Map p360; ☑06 686 10 02; www.larosetta.com; Via della Rosetta 8; meals €90-120; ✆daily, closed 3 weeks Aug; 🚇Corso del Rinascimento) Run by Roman super-chef Massimo Riccioli, La Rosetta is one of the capital's oldest and best-known seafood restaurants. The menu, which makes no compromises for vegetarians or meat-eaters, features a selection of raw and classic fish dishes alongside more elaborate creations. A cheaper lunch menu

is served Monday to Saturday. Bookings are essential.

GREEN T CHINESE $$$

(Map p360; ☑06 679 86 28; www.green-tea.it; Via del Piè di Marmo 28; lunch menus from €9, meals €50; ✆Mon-Sat; 🚇Via del Corso) It's unusual to find good Chinese food in Rome, and this five-room feng shui–designed restaurant is something entirely different: a tearoom and boutique, serving street food, meat and fish dishes, as well as a selection of sushi and dim sum. Save money at lunch by opting for one of the daily fixed-price menus.

✗ Piazza Navona & Around

ALFREDO E ADA TRATTORIA $

(Map p360; ☑06 687 88 42; Via dei Banchi Nuovi 14; meals €20; ✆Tue-Sat; 🚇Corso Vittorio Emanuele II) For a taste of authentic Roman cooking, head to this much-loved trattoria with its wood panelling and spindly, marble-topped tables. It's distinctly no-frills but there's a warm, friendly atmosphere and the traditional Roman food is unpretentious and filling, just like your Italian *nonna* would have cooked it.

BAR DEL FICO TRADITIONAL ITALIAN $

(Map p360; Via della Pace 34-35; meals €15-20; ✆8am-2am daily; 🚇Corso Vittorio Emanuele II) Named after the fig tree which shades the chess-playing old boys outside, Bar del Fico is good any time of the day, from breakfast through to dinner. The big bowls of lunch-time pasta hit the spot nicely and the low-key boho decor – rough wooden floors, tin tables and grey, chipped walls – makes for a relaxed, laid-back ambience.

CHIOSTRO DEL BRAMANTE CAFFÈ CAFE $

(Map p360; www.chiostrodelbramante.it; Vicolo dell'Arco della Pace 5; dishes €10-14; ✆10am-8pm; 🚇; 🚇Corso del Rinascimento) This swish bistro-cafe is beautifully located on the first floor of Bramante's elegant Renaissance cloisters. It's open throughout the day, so you can drink, snack or lunch on salads, baguettes or light pastas, all the while making use of the free wi-fi. Aperitifs are served in the early evening.

ROSTICCERÍ FAST FOOD $

(Map p360; www.rosticceri.com; Corso del Rinascimento 83; snacks from €1.80, mains €5-10;

⊙10am-9pm Mon-Sat, to 3pm Sun; 🚇Corso del Rinascimento) Fast food goes upmarket at this trendy takeaway opposite the Senate. The brainchild of Roman superchef Massimo Riccioli, it offers a wide range of snacks, including gooey, filling *arancini* (fried rice balls), as well as pastas, salads, couscous and main courses. You can eat in, perched on a high stool in the narrow white interior, or take away.

PIZZERIA DA BAFFETTO   PIZZERIA $

(Map p360; ☑06 686 16 17; www.pizzeriabaffetto.it; Via del Governo Vecchio 114; pizzas €6-9; ⊙6.30pm-1am; 🚇Corso Vittorio Emanuele II) For the full-on Roman pizza experience, get down to Baffetto. Not everyone loves this historic pizzeria but if you're up for an experience to remember, meals are raucous, chaotic and fast, and the thin-crust pizzas are spot on. To partake, join the queue and wait to be squeezed in wherever there's room. No credit cards. There's a second Baffetto, **Baffetto 2** (Map p360; Piazza del Teatro di Pompeo 18; ⊙6.30pm-12.30am Mon & Wed-Fri, 12.30-3.30pm & 6.30pm-12.30am Sat & Sun; 🚇Corso Vittorio Emanuele II), near Campo de' Fiori.

GELATERIA DEL TEATRO   GELATO $

(Map p360; Via di San Simone 70; cones & tubs from €2; ⊙11am-11.30pm daily; 🚇Corso del Rinascimento) In a cute alleyway just off pedestrian Via dei Coronari, this lovely little gelateria offers around 40 flavours made from thoughtfully sourced ingredients. There are any number of combos to go for including a delicious Sicilian double of *mandorle* (almonds from the Sicilian town of Avola) and *pistachio* (pistacchio nuts grown at Bronte near Mt Etna).

DA TONINO   TRATTORIA $

(Map p360; Via del Governo Vecchio 18; meals €20; ⊙Mon-Sat; 🚇Corso Vittorio Emanuele II) You'll be hard-pressed to find a cheaper place for a sit-down meal in this neck of central Rome. Unsigned Tonino's might be defiantly low-key with its simple wooden tables and yellowing pictures, but it's almost always packed. Don't expect silver service, or even a menu, just straight-up Roman staples and honest local wine.

FIOCCO DI NEVE   GELATO $

(Map p360; Via del Pantheon 51; cones €2; ⊙daily; 🚇Largo di Torre Argentina) Tiny place, grumpy staff, natural colours – this pocket-size place near the Pantheon has all the hallmarks of a good Roman gelateria. The cream flavours are particularly good as is the house speciality, *affogato di zabaglione al caffè*, a delicious coffee and zabaglione creation.

PIZZERIA LA MONTECARLO   PIZZERIA $

(Map p360; ☑06 686 18 77; www.lamontecarlo.it; Vicolo Savelli 13; pizzas €5.50-9; ⊙Tue-Sun; 🚇Corso Vittorio Emanuele II) La Montecarlo, a historic Roman pizzeria full of raucous charm, draws a mixed crowd of sightseers, locals and even the occasional city celeb. Expect thin, wood-charred pizzas, paper tablecloths, milling queues and turbocharged waiters.

LO ZOZZONE   SANDWICHES $

(Map p360; ☑06 6880 8575; Via del Teatro Pace 32; panini from €6; ⊙Mon-Sat; 🚇Corso del Rinascimento) With a few inside tables and a mile-long menu of *panini*, the affectionately named 'dirty one' is a top spot for a cheap lunchtime bite. The filling *panini* are made with pizza *bianca* and combinations of cured meats, cheeses and vegetables.

GIOLITTI   GELATO $

(Map p360; ☑06 699 12 43; www.giolitti.it; Via degli Uffici del Vicario 40; ⊙7am-1am; 🚇Via del Corso) Rome's most famous gelateria started as a dairy in 1900 and still keeps the hoards happy with succulent sorbets and creamy combinations. Gregory Peck and Audrey Hepburn swung by in *Roman Holiday* and it used to deliver marron glacé to Pope John Paul II. More recently, Barack Obama's daughters stopped off whilst pops was with his G8 chums.

CUL DE SAC   WINE BAR, TRATTORIA $$

(Map p360; ☑06 6880 1094; www.enoteca-culdesac.com; Piazza Pasquino 73; meals €30; ⊙noon-4pm & 6pm-12.30am daily; 🚇Corso Vittorio Emanuele II) A popular little wine bar, just off Piazza Navona, with an always-busy terrace and narrow, bottle-lined interior. Choose from the encyclopedic wine list and ample menu of Gallic-inspired cold cuts, pâtés, cheeses and main courses. Book ahead in the evening.

CAMPANA   TRATTORIA $$

(Map p360; ☑06 687 52 73; www.ristorante-lacampana.com; Vicolo della Campana 18; meals €35-40; ⊙Tue-Sun; 🚇Via di Monte Brianzo) Caravaggio, Goethe and Federico Fellini are among the luminaries who have dined at what is said to be Rome's oldest trattoria, dating back to around 1518. Nowadays,

CENTRO STORICO EATING

locals crowd its two dining rooms to dine on fresh fish and traditional Roman cuisine in a cheerful, pleasantly hectic atmosphere.

DA FRANCESCO
TRATTORIA, PIZZERIA **$$**

(Map p360; ☑06 686 40 09; Piazza del Fico 29; pizzas from €6, meals €35; ☺daily; 🚇Corso Vittorio Emanuele II) The queues outside give the game away. This is a quintessential Roman pizzeria-cum-trattoria with a small bustling interior and a few tables spilling out onto a pretty piazza. The wood-fired pizzas are thin-crust Roman style or there's a menu of pastas and classic meat dishes. No credit cards.

LILLI
TRATTORIA **$$**

(Map p360; ☑06 686 19 16; www.trattorialilli.it; Via Tor di Nona 23; meals €25-30; ☺closed Sun dinner & Mon; 🚇Corso del Rinascimento) Eat like a local at this authentic neighbourhood trattoria on a cobbled cul-de-sac five minutes' walk from Piazza Navona. Few tourists make it here but it still gets busy as local diners dig into honest *casareccia*-style (homestyle) cooking.

LA FOCACCIA
PIZZERIA, TRATTORIA **$$**

(Map p360; ☑06 6880 3312; Via del Pace 11; pizzas from €7, meals €30; ☺11pm-12.30am; 🚇Corso del Rinascimento) Hotfoot it to one of the few outside tables at this unsigned pizzeria, facing the Chiostro del Bramante, or settle for a place in the surprisingly large interior. Kick off with a *supplì* (fried rice croquette) or antipasto of fried zucchini before launching into the main event, Neapolitan-style wood-fired pizza.

CASA BLEVE
WINE BAR, GASTRONOMIC **$$$**

(Map p360; ☑06 686 59 70; www.casableve.it; Via del Teatro Valle 48-49; meals €65; ☺Tue-Sat, closed Aug; 🚇Largo di Torre Argentina) Ideal for a romantic assignation, this stately wine-bar-cum-restaurant dazzles with its column-lined courtyard and stained glass roof. Its wine list, one of the best in town, accompanies hard-to-find cheeses and cold cuts, while in the evening there's a full à la carte menu of creative Italian dishes.

✗ Campo De' Fiori & Around

★I DOLCI DI NONNA VINCENZA
PASTRIES & CAKES **$**

(Map p360; www.dolcinonnavincenza.it; Via Arco del Monte 98a; pastries from €2.50; ☺9am-9pm;

🚇Via Arenula) Although a pastry shop – and a delightful one with old wooden dressers laden with traditional Sicilian cakes and all manner of tempting gift ideas – it's difficult to resist eating here. Next to the shop is a bar area showcasing a heavenly selection of creamy, flaky, puffy pastries, all just lying there waiting to be gobbled down.

FORNO ROSCIOLI
PIZZA, BAKERY **$**

(Map p360; Via dei Chiavari 34; pizza slices from €2, snacks from €1.50; ☺7.30am-8pm Mon-Fri, 7.30am-2.30pm Sat; 🚇Via Arenula) Join the lunchtime crowds at this renowned bakery for a slice of delicious pizza (the *pizza bianca* is legendary), fresh-from-the-oven pastries and hunger-sating *supplì*. There's also a counter serving hot pastas and vegetable side dishes.

FORNO DI CAMPO DE' FIORI
BAKERY **$**

(Map p360; Campo de' Fiori 22; pizza slices about €3; ☺7.30am-2.30pm & 4.45-8pm Mon-Sat; 🚇Corso Vittorio Emanuele II) On Campo de' Fiori, this is one of Rome's best takeaway joints, serving bread, *panini* and delicious straight-from-the-oven *pizza al taglio* (by the slice). Aficionados swear by the pizza *bianca* ('white' pizza with olive oil, rosemary and salt), but the *panini* and pizza *rossa* ('red' pizza with olive oil, tomato and oregano) are just as good.

DAR FILETTARO A SANTA BARBARA
STREET FOOD **$**

(Map p360; Largo dei Librari 88; meals €15-20; ☺5-10.40pm Mon-Sat; 🚇Via Arenula) On a pretty, scooter-strewn piazza, this tiny stuck-in-time institution is a classic Roman *friggitoria* (shop selling fried food). The house speciality is battered *baccalà* (cod) but you can also have crispy fried veggies, such as *puntarella* (chicory) and zucchini flowers.

RENATO E LUISA
MODERN ITALIAN **$$**

(Map p360; ☑06 686 96 60; www.renatoeluisa. it; Via dei Barbieri 25; meals €45; ☺8.30am-12.30pm Tue-Sun; 🚇Largo di Torre Argentina) A favourite among in-the-know Romans, this backstreet trattoria is always packed. Chef Renato takes a creative approach to classic Roman cooking, resulting in dishes that are modern, seasonal and undeniably local. Typical of this approach is his *cacio e pepe e fiori di zucca* (pasta with pecorino cheese, black pepper and courgette flowers).

DITIRAMBO   MODERN ITALIAN **$$**

(Map p360; ☑06 687 16 26; www.ristoranteditirambo.it; Piazza della Cancelleria 72; meals €40; ⊘closed lunch Mon; ☐Corso Vittorio Emanuele II) Hugely popular Ditirambo broke culinary ground when it opened in 1996, marrying the informality of an old-school trattoria with forward-looking, creative cooking. Since then it has performed consistently well and it's still a top spot for seasonal, organic cooking and excellent vegetarian dishes. Book ahead.

GRAPPOLO D'ORO   MODERN ITALIAN **$$**

(Map p360; ☑06 689 70 80; www.hosteriagrappolodoro.it; Piazza della Cancelleria 80; meals €40; ⊘closed Tue & Wed lunch; ☐Corso Vittorio Emanuele II) This informal, welcoming eatery stands out among the sometimes lacklustre options around Campo de' Fiori. The food is creative without being fussy, and includes some timeless favourites such as *baccalà alla romana* (cod with raisins, pinenuts and tomatoes) and *spaghetti alla carbonara*.

SERGIO ALLE GROTTE   TRATTORIA **$$**

(Map p360; ☑06 686 42 93; Vicolo delle Grotte 27; meals €30-35; ⊘Mon-Sat; ☐Via Arenula) A flower's throw from Campo de' Fiori, Sergio's is a textbook Roman trattoria: chequered tablecloths, dodgy wall murals, bustling waiters and steaming plateloads of hearty, down-to-earth pasta and large steaks grilled over hot coals. In the summer there are a few tables outside on the cobbled, ivy-hung lane.

SALUMERIA ROSCIOLI   GASTRONOMIC **$$$**

(Map p362; ☑06 687 52 87; Via dei Giubbonari 21; meals €55; ⊘Mon-Sat; ☐Via Arenula) This

deli-cum-wine-bar-cum-restaurant is a gourmet's paradise. Under the brick arches, you'll find a mouth-watering array of olive oils, conserves, cheeses (around 450 varieties), Spanish and Italian hams, and much, much more. Behind the deli, the chic restaurant serves a menu of sophisticated Italian food and some truly outstanding French and Italian wines.

✖ Jewish Ghetto

ANTICO FORNO URBANI   BAKERY **$**

(Map p362; Piazza Costaguti 31; pizza slices from €2; ⊘7.40am-2.30pm & 5-8.45pm Mon-Fri, 9am-1.30pm Sat & Sun; ☐Via Arenula) Come mid-morning and you'll find this popular Ghetto bakery packed with locals queueing for their mid-morning snack. And once you get a whiff of the yeasty smells wafting off the freshly baked pizzas, breads, biscuits and focaccias, you'll probably want to follow suit. Grab a ticket and wait your turn.

LA DOLCEROMA   BAKERY **$**

(Map p362; www.ladolceroma.com; Via del Portico d'Ottavia 20; pastries from €1; ⊘8am-8pm Tue-Sat, 10am-6.30pm Sun; ☐Via Arenula) Bringing the sweet taste of Vienna (and the US) to the Jewish Ghetto, this well-known bakery specialises in delicious strudel and Sachertorte, as well as rye breads, pastries, cookies, cheesecake and chocolate-fudge brownies. Everything's made on the premises.

BOCCIONE   BAKERY **$**

(Map p362; ☑06 687 86 37; Via del Portico d'Ottavia 1; ⊘8am-7.30pm Sun-Thu, to 3.30pm Fri; ☐Via Arenula) This tiny, unsigned Jewish

---

LOCAL KNOWLEDGE

KOSHER ROME

If you want to eat kosher in Rome head to Via del Portico d'Ottavia, the main strip on the Jewish Ghetto. Lined with trattorias and restaurants specialising in kosher food and Roman-Jewish cuisine, it's a lively hangout, especially on hot summer nights when diners crowd the many sidewalk tables. For a taste of typical Ghetto cooking, try the landmark **Giggetto al Portico d'Ottavia** (Map p362; ☑06 686 11 05; www. giggettoalportico.it; Via del Portico d'Ottavia 21a; meals €40; ⊘Tue-Sun; ☐Via Arenula), or, at No 16, **Nonna Betta** (Map p362; ☑06 6880 6263; www.nonnabetta.it; Via del Portico d'Ottavia 16; €30-35; ⊘noon-4pm & 6-11pm, closed Fri dinner & Sat lunch; ☐Via Arenula), a small tunnel of a trattoria serving traditional kosher food and local staples such as *carciofi alla guidia* (crisp fried artichokes). Further down the road, the unmarked **Gelateria** (Map p362; Via del Portico d'Ottavia 1b; tubs €2-5, cones from €3; ⊘9am-10pm Sun-Fri, to midnight summer; ☐Via Arenula) at has a small but tasty selection of kosher ice cream, including some ripe fruit flavours.

bakery is where the locals come to buy their special occasion *dolci* (cakes and pastries). The burnished cakes are bursting with fruit and sultanas, and specialities include ricotta cake with chocolate flakes and cherries, and *mostacciolo romano* (a kind of sweet biscuit) – all served by authentically grumpy, elderly ladies.

ALBERTO PICA   GELATO $

(Map p362; Via della Seggiola; cones/tubs from €1.50; ☺8.30am-2am; 🚇Via Arenula) It looks nothing special but this old-fashioned bar is famous for its ice cream. In summer, it offers flavours such as *fragoline di bosco* (wild strawberry) and *petali di rosa* (rose petal), but rice flavours are specialities year-round (resembling frozen rice pudding).

SORA MARGHERITA   TRATTORIA $$

(Map p362; ☎06 687 42 16; Piazza delle Cinque Scole 30; meals €30-35; ☺closed dinner Tue & Thu, all day Sun; 🚇Via Arenula) No-frills Sora Margherita started as a cheap kitchen for hungry locals, but word has spread and it's now a popular lunchtime haunt of everyone from local workers to slumming uptowners. Expect dog-eat-dog queues, a rowdy Roman atmosphere and classic Roman dishes such as *gnocchi al sugo* (gnocchi in tomato sauce) and *fegato* (liver). Service is prompt and you're expected to be likewise.

LA TAVERNA
DEGLI AMICI   TRADITIONAL ITALIAN $$$

(Map p362; ☎06 6992 0637; Piazza Margana 37; meals €50; ☺closed Sun dinner & Mon; 🚇Piazza Venezia) A smart trattoria in a delightful medieval setting, the Taverna sits on a pretty ivy-draped piazza on the edge of the Jewish Ghetto. It serves consistent classics such as *saltimbocca alla romana* ('leap in the mouth' veal with sage), plus delicious seafood and homemade desserts. There's also an excellent wine list.

VECCHIA ROMA   TRADITIONAL ITALIAN $$$

(Map p362; ☎06 686 46 04; www.ristorantevecchiaroma.com; Piazza Campitelli 18; meals €60; ☺Thu-Tue, closed 3 weeks Aug; 🚇Via del Teatro di Marcello) This old-fashioned restaurant is the very picture of formal elegance with chandeliers, gilt-framed oil paintings and impeccably groomed, white-jacketed waiters. Outside, a candlelit terrace looks onto a picture book cobbled piazza. But it's not all show and the food is excellent with tasty salads, seafood antipasti and top-drawer pastas.

PIPERNO   TRADITIONAL ITALIAN $$$

(Map p362; ☎06 6880 6629; www.ristorante-piperno.it; Via Monte de' Cenci 9; meals €50-55; ☺closed Mon & Sun dinner; 🚇Via Arenula) This historic restaurant is tucked away in a quiet corner of the Jewish Ghetto. It's formal without being stuffy, a wood-panelled restaurant of the old school, where white-clad waiters serve wonderful deep-fried *filetti di baccalà* (cod fillets) and *tagliolini alla pescatora* (long ribbon pasta with seafood). To finish, try the delicious *palle del Nonno* ('grandpa's balls' or ricotta and chocolate puffs). Booking recommended.

✖ Isola Tiberina

SORA LELLA   TRADITIONAL ITALIAN $$$

(Map p362; ☎06 686 16 01; www.soralella.com; Via Ponte Quattro Capi 16; meals €60; ☺daily; 🚇Lungotevere dei Cenci) This long-standing family-run restaurant enjoys a memorable setting in a tower on the Tiber's tiny island. Named after a much-loved Roman actress (the owner's mother), it serves a classic Roman menu spiced up with some wonderful fish dishes – try the *tagliolini alla maniera der capitano pescatore* (spaghetti-like pasta with clams, mussels, squid, shrimp and tomatoes).

✖ Piazza Colonna & Around

PIZZERIA AL LEONCINO   PIZZERIA $

(Map p360; ☎06 686 77 57; Via del Leoncino 28; pizzas from €6; ☺closed Wed & lunch Sat & Sun; 🚇Via del Corso) Some places just never change and this boisterous neighbourhood pizzeria is one of them. A bastion of budget eating in an otherwise expensive area, it has a wood-fired oven, two small rooms and gruff waiters who efficiently serve bruschettas, excellent Roman-style pizza and ice-cold beer. Cash only.

MATRICIANELLA   TRATTORIA $$

(Map p360; ☎06 683 21 00; www.matricianella.it; Via del Leone 2/4; meals €40; ☺Mon-Sat; 🚇Via del Corso) With its gingham tablecloths, chintzy murals and fading prints, this model trattoria is loved for its traditional Roman cuisine. You'll find all the usual menu stalwarts as well as some great Roman-Jewish dishes. Romans go crazy for the fried antipasti, the artichoke *alla giudia* (fried, Jewish style) and the meatballs. Booking is essential.

GINO TRATTORIA **$$**
(Map p360; ☏06 687 34 34; Vicolo Rosini 4; meals €30; ☉Mon-Sat; 🚇Via del Corso) Hidden down a narrow lane close to parliament, Gino's is perennially packed with gossiping journalists and politicians. Join the right honourables for well-executed staples such as *rigotoni alla gricia (*pasta with cured pig's cheek) and meatballs, served under hanging garlic and gaudily painted murals. No credit cards.

OSTERIA DELL'INGEGNO MODERN ITALIAN **$$**
(Map p360; ☏06 678 06 62; Piazza di Pietra 45; meals €45; ☉Mon-Sat; 🚇Via del Corso) Not far from the Italian parliament, this boho-chic restaurant and wine bar is much frequented by politicians and their glamorous entourages. Sit down to wine by the glass, American-style breakfasts, large salads and creative pastas in the intimate art-filled interior or, better still, on the charming piazza outside. *Aperitivo* is served every evening from 5pm.

GRAN CAFFÈ LA CAFFETTIERA CAFE
(Map p360; Piazza di Pietra 65; ☉7am-9pm Mon-Sat, from 8am Sun; 🚇Via del Corso) This stately, art deco cafe is famous for its Neapolitan cakes – try the *sfogliatelle* (a flaky pastry stuffed with ricotta and pieces of candied fruit) for something sweet, or the *rustici* (cheese-and-tomato-filled pastry puffs) for something savoury.

🍷 DRINKING & NIGHTLIFE

The *centro storico* is home to a couple of nightlife centres: the area around Piazza Navona, with a number of elegant bars and clubs catering to the beautiful, rich and stylish (and sometimes all three); then the rowdier area around Campo de' Fiori, where the crowd is younger and the drinking is heavier. This is where people tend to congregate after football games and foreign students head out on the booze. The *centro storico* also harbours many of Rome's best cafes.

📍 Pantheon & Around

CAFFÈ SANT'EUSTACHIO CAFE
(Map p360; Piazza Sant'Eustachio 82; ☉8.30am-1am Sun-Thu, to 1.30am Fri, to 2am Sat; 🚇Corso del Rinascimento) This small, unassuming cafe, generally three deep at the bar, is famous for its *gran caffè*, said by many to be the best coffee in town. Created by beating the first drops of espresso and several teaspoons of sugar into a frothy paste, then adding the rest of the coffee, it's superbly smooth and guaranteed to put some zing into your sightseeing.

⭐**CAFFÈ TAZZA D'ORO** CAFE
(Map p360; www.tazzadorocoffeeshop.com; Via degli Orfani 84; ☉7am-8pm; 🚇Via del Corso) A busy, stand-up bar with polished wood and brass fittings, this is one of Rome's best coffee houses. Its espresso hits the mark perfectly and there's a range of delicious coffee concoctions, including a refreshing *granita di caffè*, (a crushed-ice coffee drink served with whipped cream). There's also a small shop selling teas, coffee and coffee-related paraphernalia.

📍 Piazza Navona & Around

ETABLÌ BAR, RISTORANTE
(Map p360; ☏06 9761 6694; www.etabli.it; Vicolo delle Vacche 9a; ☉6.30pm-1am Mon-Wed, to 2am Thu-Sat; 🚇Corso del Rinascimento) Housed in a lofty 17th-century *palazzo,* Etablì is a rustic-chic lounge bar and restaurant where Roman beauties drop by to chat over cocktails, snack on tapas, and indulge in *aperitivo*. It's laid-back and good-looking, with occasional jam sessions and original French country decor – think wrought-iron fittings, comfy armchairs and a crackling fireplace. Restaurant meals average about €40.

CIRCUS BAR
(Map p360; www.circusroma.it; Via della Vetrina 15; ☉10am-2am; 🚇Corso del Rinascimento) A great little cafe-bar, tucked around the corner from Piazza Navona. It's a funky, informal place popular with American students from the nearby school where you can drink and catch up on the news from home – wi-fi is free and there are international newspapers to read. Regular events

are staged, ranging from retro celebrations of '90s Britpop to themed aperitif nights.

LES AFFICHES
BAR

(Map p360; Via Santa Maria dell'Anima 52; ☺6pm-2am; ⬜Corso del Rinascimento) Excellent cocktails, vintage Parisian ambience and late-night closing (2am) ensure a cool crowd of laid-back locals at this trendy watering hole. *Aperitivo* is served from 7.30pm, although unfortunately there's no help-yourself bar buffet.

EMPORIO ALLA PACE
CAFE

(Map p360; Via della Pace 28; ☺6am-midnight Mon & Tue, to 2am Wed-Sat, 8am-2am Sun; ⬜Corso del Rinaascimento) Students sitting solo with a book, lunching ladies, gossiping friends, tourists, priests, Romans. This retro-hip bookshop-cafe caters to a mixed crowd throughout the day, serving cappuccino and cornettos in the morning, *panini* and pastas at lunch, cocktails and midnight beers in the evening.

CAFFÈ DELLA PACE
CAFE

(Map p360; www.caffedellapace.it; Via della Pace 5; ☺9am-3am Tue-Sun, 4pm-3am Mon; ⬜Corso del Rinascimento) Live the *dolce vita* at this perennially fashionable art nouveau cafe. Inside it's all gilt and mismatched wooden tables; outside stylishly dressed drinkers strike poses over their Camparis against a backdrop of cascading ivy. The perfect people-watching spot.

📍 Campo de' Fiori & Around

★BARNUM CAFE
CAFE

(Map p360; www.barnumcafe.com; Via del Pellegrino 87; ☺9.30am-2am Tue-Sat, to 9pm Mon; ⬜Corso Vittorio Emanuele II) A relaxed, friendly spot to check your email over a freshly squeezed orange juice or spend a pleasant hour reading a newspaper on one of the tatty old armchairs in the white bare-brick interior. If you like tunes with your drinks, stop by on Tuesday evening for the DJ-accompanied Sounds Good aperitif (from 7pm).

OPEN BALADIN
BAR

(Map p362; www.openbaladinroma.it; Via degli Specchi 6; ☺12pm-2am; 🚇Via Arenula) A hip lounge bar near Campo de' Fiori, Open Baladin is a leading light in Rome's thriving beer scene. With more than 40 beers on tap and up to 100 bottled brews, many produced by artisanal microbreweries, it's a great place for buffs of the brown stuff. There's also a decent food menu with *panini*, burgers and daily specials.

IL GOCCETTO
WINE BAR

(Map p360; Via dei Banchi Vecchi 14; ☺11.30am-2pm Tue & Sat & 6.30pm-midnight Mon-Sat, closed Aug; ⬜Corso Vittorio Emanuele II) Should anyone decide to make an Italian version of *Cheers*, they should set it at this wood-panelled *vino e olio* (wine and oil) shop, where a colourful cast of regulars finish each other's sentences, banter with the owners and work their way through an 800-strong wine list. Eavesdrop over plates of prized north Italian cheese and salami.

L'ANGOLO DIVINO
WINE BAR

(Map p360; www.angolodivino.it; Via dei Balestrari 12; ☺10am-3pm & 5pm-2am Tue-Sat, 6pm-2am Sun; ⬜Corso Vittorio Emanuele II) A hop and a skip from Campo de' Fiori, this is a warm, woody, bottle-filled wine bar. It's an oasis of genteel calm, with a carefully selected wine list, mostly Italian but a few French and New World labels, and a small menu of hot and cold dishes.

CAFFÈ FARNESE
CAFE

(Map p360; Via dei Baullari 106; ☺7.30am-8pm, to late summer; ⬜Corso Vittorio Emanuele II) On a street between Campo de' Fiori and Piazza Farnese, this unassuming cafe is a top people-watching pad, ideal for whiling away the early afternoon hours. It also does a very fine espresso.

VINERIA REGGIO
WINE BAR

(Map p360; www.vineriareggio.com; Campo de' Fiori 15; ☺8.30am-2am Mon-Sat; ⬜Corso Vittorio Emanuele II) The pick of the bars and cafes on Campo de' Fiori, this has a cosy, bottle-lined interior and outside tables. Busy from lunchtime onwards, it attracts tourists and *fighi* (cool) Romans like bees to a honeypot. Wine by the glass from €3.50 and snacks from €3.

📍 Jewish Ghetto

BARTARUGA
BAR

(Map p362; www.bartaruga.com; Piazza Mattei 9; ☺6pm-1am Tue-Thu, to 2am Fri & Sat, to midnight Sun; 🚇Via Arenula) A high-camp blast of baroque and art deco, this velvet-lined, chandelier-slung bar is a theatrical choice beloved of VIPs, theatre darlings and bohemians. Outside, a few humble wooden tables face the Jewish Ghetto's much-loved turtle fountain, the Fontana delle Tartarughe. The soundtrack is lounge and jazzy, the mood laid-back and chatty. No credit cards.

🍷 Piazza Colonna & Around

SALOTTO 42 BAR
(Map p360; www.salotto42.it; Piazza di Pietra 42; ☺10am-2am Tue-Sat, to midnight Sun & Mon; 🚇Via del Corso) On a picturesque piazza, facing the columns of the Temple of Hadrian, this is a hip, glamorous lounge bar, complete with vintage armchairs, suede sofas and a collection of two-tonne design books. Come for the daily lunch buffet or to hang out with the beautiful people over an aperitif.

CIAMPINI CAFE
(Map p360; Piazza di San Lorenzo in Lucina 29; ☺7.30am-8.30pm Mon-Sat, to midnight summer; 🚇Via del Corso) An elegant old cafe on graceful, traffic-free Piazza di San Lorenzo in Lucina, this is an ideal place for an alfresco coffee with the neighbourhood's well-heeled locals. Sit outside and enjoy the scenery over a creamy cappuccino or tip-top gelato. There's also a full food menu of salads, sandwiches, pastas and mains.

FANDANGO INCONTRO BAR, BOOKSHOP
(Map p360; www.fandangoincontro.it; Via dei Prefetti 22; ☺10am-9pm Tue-Sun; 🚇Via del Corso) This relaxed bookshop-bar is run by Fandango, an Italian film producer and publisher. It's a big, airy affair, often used to host cultural events, where you can sift through comics and discuss art house cinema over an evening aperitif.

☆ ENTERTAINMENT

LA MAISON CLUB
(Map p360; Vicolo dei Granari 4; 🚇Corso del Rinascimento) A dressy disco in the heart of the historic centre, La Maison pulls a see-and-be-seen crowd, who flirt and frolic to a soundtrack of poppy tunes and commercial house. It's smooth, mainstream and exclusive, yet more fun than you might expect.

TEATRO ARGENTINA THEATRE
(Map p360; ☎06 684 00 03 11; www.teatrodiroma.net; Largo di Torre Argentina 52; tickets €12-27; 🚇Largo di Torre Argentina) Rome's top theatre is one of the two official homes of the Teatro di Roma; the other is the Teatro India in the southern suburbs. Founded in 1732, it retains its original frescoed ceiling and a grand gilt-and-velvet auditorium. Rossini's *Barber of Seville* premiered here and today it stages a wide-ranging programme of drama (mostly in Italian) and high-profile dance performances.

TEATRO VALLE THEATRE
(Map p360; www.teatrovalleoccupato.it; Via del Teatro Valle 21; 🚇Largo di Torre Argentina) One of Rome's historic stages, this perfectly proportioned 18th-century theatre is where Pirandello's *Six Characters in Search of an Author* premiered in 1921. Since 2011 it has been occupied by a group of theatre workers protesting against privatisation plans, but it still stages events ranging from film retrospectives to open rehearsals. Check the website for upcoming events.

TEATRO DELL'OROLOGIO THEATRE
(Map p360; ☎06 687 55 50; www.teatrorologio.it; Via dei Filippini 17a; 🚇Corso Vittorio Emanuele II) A well-known experimental theatre, the Orologio offers a varied programme of contemporary and classic works, with occasional performances in English.

ENGLISH THEATRE OF ROME THEATRE
(Map p360; ☎06 444 13 75; www.rometheatre.com; Piazza Monte Vecchio 5, Teatro L'Arciliuto; tickets €15; 🚇Corso del Rinascimento) The English Theatre of Rome stages a mix of contemporary and classic plays, comedies and bilingual productions at the Teatro L'Arciliuto near Piazza Navona.

🛍 SHOPPING

🛍 Pantheon & Around

LE ARTIGIANE ARTISANAL
(Map p360; www.leartigiane.it; Via di Torre Argentina 72; ☺10am-7.30pm; 🚇Largo di Torre Argentina) A space for local artisans to showcase their wares, this eclectic shop is the result of an ongoing project to sustain and promote Italy's artisanal traditions. It's a

browser's dream selling an eclectic range of handmade clothes, costume jewellery, design objects and lamps.

SPAZIO SETTE   HOMEWARE

(Map p360; www.spaziosette.com; Via dei Barbieri 7; ⊘10am-7.30pm Tue-Sun, 3.30-7.30pm Mon; ᐧLargo di Torre Argentina) Even if you don't buy any of the designer homeware at Spazio Sette, it's worth popping in to see the sharp modern furniture set against 17th-century frescoes. Formerly home to a cardinal, the *palazzo* now houses a three-floor shop full of quality furniture, kitchenware, tableware and gifts.

STILO FETTI   PENS

(Map p360; www.stilofetti.it; Via degli Orfani 82; ⊘9am-1pm Tue-Sat & 3.30-7.30pm Mon-Sat; ᐧVia del Corso) Technology might have largely done for fountain pens but they still make excellent gifts, and this old-fashioned family-run pen shop, on the go since 1893, has a wonderful selection. All styles are covered and many top brands are represented, from Parker to Mont Blanc and Graf von Faber-Castell.

FELTRINELLI   BOOKS

(Map p360; www.lafeltrinelli.it; Largo di Torre Argentina 11; ⊘9am-9pm Mon-Fri, to 10pm Sat, 10am-9pm Sun; ᐧLargo di Torre Argentina) Italy's most famous bookseller (and publisher) has shops across the capital. This one has a wide range of books (in Italian) on art, photography, cinema and history, as well as an extensive selection of Italian literature and travel guides in various languages, including English. You'll also find CDs, DVDs and a range of stationery products.

ALBERTA GLOVES   ACCESSORIES

(Map p360; Corso Vittorio Emanuele II 18; ⊘10am-6.30pm; ᐧLargo di Torre Argentina) From elbow-length silk gloves for a grand premiere to crochet for first communions; from tan-coloured driving mitts to kinky black numbers; from fur-lined kid to polkadots, this tiny shop has gloves for every conceivable occasion. Scarves and woolly hats too.

ᐧ Piazza Navona & Around

SBU   CLOTHING

(Map p360; www.sbu.it; Via di San Pantaleo 68-69; ⊘10am-7.30pm Mon-Sat; ᐧCorso Vittorio Emanuele II) The flagship store of hip jeans brand, SBU, aka Strategic Business Unit, occupies a 19th-century workshop near Piazza Navona, complete with cast-iron columns, wooden racks and a hidden backyard. Pride of place goes to the jeans, superbly cut from top-end Japanese denim, but you can also pick up street-cool shirts, jackets, hats, sweaters and T-shirts.

TEMPI MODERNI   FASHION, JEWELLERY

(Map p360; Via del Governo Vecchio 108; ⊘9am-1.30pm & 3-8pm Mon-Sat; ᐧCorso Vittorio Emanuele II) Bart Simpson ties and Ferragaomo fashions sit side by side at this kooky curiosity shop. It's packed with vintage costume jewellery, Bakelite pieces from the '20s and '30s, art nouveau and art deco trinkets, pop art bangles, 19th-century resin brooches and pieces by couturiers such as Chanel, Dior and Balenciaga.

RETRÒ   DESIGN

(Map p360; www.retrodesign.it; Piazza del Fico 20; ⊘11am-1pm Tue-Sat & 4-8pm Mon-Sat; ᐧCorso del Rinascimento) Design buffs, prepare to swoon over the rainbow rows of sexy retro glassware, Bakelite jewellery, pop art carpets, vintage furniture and iconic chairs by the likes of Italian design great Giò Ponti and influential French designer Pierre Paulin.

OFFICINA PROFUMO FARMACEUTICA DI SANTA MARIA NOVELLA   COSMETICS

(Map p360; Corso del Rinascimento 47; ⊘10am-7.30pm Mon-Sat; ᐧCorso del Rinascimento) The Roman branch of one of Italy's oldest pharmacies, this bewitching, aromatic shop stocks natural perfumes and cosmetics as well as herbal infusions, tea and pot pourri, all carefully shelved in wooden cabinets under a giant Murano-glass chandelier. The original pharmacy was founded in Florence in 1612 by the Dominican monks of Santa Maria Novella, and many of its cosmetics are based on 17th-century herbal recipes.

NARDECCHIA   ART

(Map p360; Piazza Navona 25; ⊘10am-1pm Tue-Sat & 4.30-7.30pm Mon-Sat; ᐧCorso del Rinascimento) You'll be inviting people to see your etchings after a visit to this historic Piazza Navona shop. Famed for its antique prints, Nardecchia sells everything from 18th-century etchings by Giovanni Battista Piranesi to more affordable 19th-century panoramas. Bank on at least €120 for a small framed print.

CUADROS ROMA DESIGN
(Map p360; www.cuadrosroma.com; Vicolo della Campanella 39; ⊘11.30am-7.30pm Mon-Sat; █Corso Vittorio Emanuele II) Interior design made easy. That's the thinking behind this arty shop and its collection of fashionable modern wallpaper, floor stickers and self-adhesive wall tattoos. The designs are sharp, fresh and original, and prices easy on the pocket.

LUNA & L'ALTRA FASHION
(Map p360; Piazza Pasquino 76; ⊘10am-2pm Tue-Sat & 3.30-7.30pm Mon-Sat; █Corso Vittorio Emanuele II) A must-stop on any Roman fashion trail, this is one of a number of independent boutiques on and around Via del Governo Vecchio. In its austere, gallery-like interior, clothes and accessories by hip designers Issey Miyake, Marc Le Bihaan, Jean Paul Gaultier and Yohji Yamamoto are exhibited in reverential style.

ALDO FEFÈ ARTISANAL
(Map p360; Via della Stelletta 20b; ⊘Mon-Sat; █Corso del Rinascimento) Started by the owner's father in 1932, this tiny, arched workshop produces beautifully handpainted paper. Products include little chests of drawers, leather-bound notebooks (€28), writing paper, picture frames and beautiful photo albums (€33). You can also buy Florentine wrapping paper and calligraphic pens.

ZOUZOU FASHION
(Map p360; www.zouzou.it; Vicolo della Cancelleria 9a; ⊘11am-7.30pm Tue-Sat, 2-7.30pm Mon; █Corso Vittorio Emanuele II) Spice up your Roman romance with a trip to this upmarket erotic boutique just off Via del Governo Vecchio. Set up like a Victorian boudoir with crimson walls and corseted mannequins, it has a range of lingerie, toiletries and toys that's sure to bring out the bad girl in every *signora.*

VESTITI USATI CINZIA VINTAGE
(Map p360; Via del Governo Vecchio 45; ⊘10am-8pm Mon-Sat, 2-8pm Sun; █Corso Vittorio Emanuele II) Cinzia remains one of the best vintage shops on Via del Governo Vecchio, owned by a former costume designer. There are jackets (in leather, denim, corduroy and linen), stagy cocktail dresses, screen-printed T-shirts, retro skirts and suede coats, as well as designer sunglasses and colourful bags.

OMERO E CECILIA VINTAGE
(Map p360; Via del Governo Vecchio 110; █Corso Vittorio Emanuele II) A wonderful tunnel of a place stashed full of second-hand leather bags, '70s velvet coats, tweed jackets, '60s Italian dresses, old Burberry trench coats and so on. It's a browser's heaven.

AI MONASTERI COSMETICS
(Map p360; www.emonasteri.it; Corso del Rinascimento 72; ⊘4.30-7.30pm Mon, Wed & Fri; █Corso del Rinascimento) This apothecary-like, wonderfully scented shop sells herbal essences, spirits, soaps, balms and liqueurs, all created by monks across Italy. You can stock up on everything from sage toothpaste to rose shampoo, cherry brandy and elixirs for happiness (€13) and love (€20), though quite why monks are expert at this is anyone's guess.

CASALI ART
(Map p360; Via dei Coronari 115; ⊘10am-1pm Mon-Sat & 3.30-7.30pm Sat; █Corso del Rinascimento) On Via dei Coronari, a lovely pedestrian street lined by antique shops, Casali deals in old prints, many delicately hand-coloured. The shop is small but the choice is not, ranging from 16th-century botanical manuscripts to postcard prints of Rome.

BERTÈ TOYS
(Map p360; Piazza Navona 107-111; ⊘9.30am-1pm Tue-Sat & 3.30-7.30pm Mon-Sat; █Corso del Rinascimento) On Piazza Navona, this is one of Rome's great toy shops, an emporium specialising in wooden dolls and puppets, but with a great mishmash of other stuff, from tractors to pushchairs, doll houses and tea sets. Perfect for pre-/post-sightseeing bribes.

COMICS BAZAR ANTIQUES
(Map p360; Via dei Banchi Vecchi 127-128; ⊘9.30am-7.30pm, closed Mon morning & Sun; █Corso Vittorio Emanuele II) Not a comic in sight – this treasure-trove is crammed to its rafters with antiques. Wade through the lamps that hang like jungle creepers and peruse old dolls, framed prints and furniture dating from the 19th century to the 1940s, including pieces by the 19th-century Viennese designer Thonet. You might even find the shopkeeper hidden away among it all.

CITTÀ DEL SOLE TOYS
(Map p360; www.cittadelsole.it; Via della Scrofa 65; ⊘10am-7.30pm Tue-Sat, 3.30-7.30pm Mon;

CENTRO STORICO SHOPPING

Corso del Rinascimento) Città del Sole is a parent's dream, a treasure-trove of imaginative toys created to stretch the growing mind rather than numb it. From well-crafted wooden trains to insect investigation kits, here you'll find toys to keep your children occupied for hours.

LE TELE DI CARLOTTA
ARTISANAL

(Map p360; Via dei Coronari 228; ☉10.30am-1pm & 3.30-7pm; ☐Corso del Rinascimento) This tiny little sewing box of a shop is a delicate concoction of hand-embroidered napkins, bags and antique pieces of jewellery, ranging from 19th century to 1930s. You can have pieces embroidered on request, if you have enough time in Rome. Heirlooms in the making.

AL SOGNO
TOYS

(Map p360; www.alsogno.net; Piazza Navona 53; ☉10am-8pm, to 10pm summer; ☐Corso del Rinascimento) Just by looking at its elaborate, elegant window displays you know that Al Sogno is more than your average toy shop. Inside is a wonderland of puppets, trolls, fairies, fake Roman weapons, dolls and stuffed animals. The don't-touch atmosphere is best suited to well-behaved little darlings.

☐ Campo De' Fiori & Around

★IBIZ – ARTIGIANATO IN CUOIO
ACCESSORIES

(Map p360; Via dei Chiavari 39; ☉9.30am-7.30pm Mon-Sat; ☐Corso Vittorio Emanuele II) In their diminutive workshop, Elisa Nepi and her father craft exquisite, well-priced leather goods, including wallets, bags, belts and sandals, in simple but classy designs and myriad colours. With €70 you should be able to pick up a purse, whilst satchels cost around €200.

★RACHELE
CLOTHING

(Map p360; Vicolo del Bollo 6; ☉10.30am-2pm & 3.30-7.30pm Tue-Sat; ☐Corso Vittorio Emanuele II) Mums looking to update their kids' (under 12s) wardrobe would do well to look up Rachele in her delightful little workshop. With everything from hats and mitts to romper suits and jackets, all brightly coloured and all handmade, this sort of shop

is a dying breed. Most items are around the €40 to €50 mark.

ARSENALE
CLOTHING

(Map p360; www.patriziapieroni.it; Via del Pellegrino 172; ☉10am-7.30pm Tue-Sat, 3.30-7.30pm Mon; ☐Corso Vittorio Emanuele II) Arsenale, the atelier of Roman designer Patrizia Pieroni, is a watchword with female fashionistas. Its virgin-white space marries urban minimalism with heavy, rustic fittings to create a clean, contemporary showcase for her beautifully made clothes in rich, luscious fabrics.

LIBRERIA DEL VIAGGIATORE
BOOKS

(Map p360; Via del Pellegrino 78; ☉10am-2pm Tue-Sat & 4-7.20pm Mon-Sat; ☐Corso Vittorio Emanuele II) If Rome is only a stop on your Grand Tour, this beguiling old-fashioned travel bookshop is a must. Small but world-encompassing, it's crammed with guides and travel literature in various languages and has a huge range of maps, including hiking maps.

MONDELLO OTTICA
EYEWEAR

(Map p360; www.mondelloottica.it; Via del Pellegrino 98; ☉10am-1.30pm & 4-7.30pm Tue-Sat ; ☐Corso Vittorio Emanuele II) If you're in Rome, you need shades. And this is the place to look. Known for its hip window displays, often produced by contemporary artists, Mondello Ottica is a sparkling white temple of sunglasses with frames by leading designers, including Anne et Valentin, l.a.Eyeworks, Cutler and Gross, and Theo. Prescription glasses can be ready on the same day.

BORINI
SHOES

(Map p362; Via dei Pettinari 86-87; ☉9am-1pm Tue-Sat & 3.30-7.30pm Mon-Sat; ☐Via Arenula) Don't be fooled by the piles of boxes and the discount, workaday look – those in the know pile into this seemingly down-at-heel shop, run by the Borinis since 1940, for the latest foot fashions. Whatever is 'in' this season, Borini will have it, at reasonable prices and in every delicious hue.

DADADA 52
CLOTHING

(Map p360; www.dadada.eu; Via dei Giubbonari 52; ☉11am-2pm & 2.30-7.30pm Mon, 10am-7.30pm Tue-Sat, 11am-7.30pm Sun; ☐Via Arenula) Every young Roman fashionista makes a stop at daDADA, for its funky cocktail dresses, bright print summer frocks, eclectic coats and colourful hats. Prices start at around

€100 but many items are north of €200. There's a second **branch** (Map p364; ☑06 6813 9162; www.dadada.eu; Via del Corso 500; ⓂFlaminio or Spagna) at Via del Corso 500.

ETHIC   CLOTHING
(Map p362; www.3ndlab.com; Piazza Cairoli 11; ☻10.30am-7.30pm Tue-Sat, 11.30am-7.30pm Sun & Mon; 🚇Via Arenula) This hint-of-boho place is an Italian clothing chain, with retro-influenced, bold designs and its own line of girls' fashions. Clothes come in interesting colours, fabrics and designs, and everything is reasonably priced. There are six other branches across town.

LOCO   SHOES
(Map p360; Via dei Baullari 22; ☻10.30am-8pm Tue-Sat, 3.30-8pm Mon; 🚇Corso Vittorio Emanuele II) Sneaker fetishists should hotfoot it to Loco for the very latest in big-statement trainers. It's a small shop, but full of attitude, with an interesting collection of original sneakers (for boys and girls), boots and pumps by international and Italian designers. Also bags and costume jewellery.

POSTO ITALIANO   SHOES
(Map p360; www.postoitaliano.com; Via dei Giubbonari 37a; ☻10am-8pm Mon-Sat, 11.30am-7.30pm Sun; 🚇Via Arenula) Small, unmarked Posto Italiano has an always-beguiling collection of fashionable, accessible and highly wearable women's shoes. With its wood-beamed ceiling and dripping chandelier, it's

---

LOCAL KNOWLEDGE

HELP FIGHT THE MAFIA

To look at it there's nothing special about **Pio La Torre** (Map p360; www.liberaterra.it; Via dei Prefetti 23; ☻10am-1pm & 3.30-7.30pm Mon-Sat; 🚇Via del Corso), a small, unpretentious food store near Piazza del Parlamento. But shop here and you're making a small but concrete contribution to the fight against the mafia. All the gastro goodies on sale, including organic olive oils, pastas, honeys and wine, are produced on land confiscated from organised crime outfits. The shop is part of a countrywide chain called *I Sapori e I Saperi della Legalità* (The Taste and Awareness of Legality) which distributes food produced on ex-mafia terrain.

---

a handsome showcase for emerging Italian designers and more established brands.

🔒 Jewish Ghetto

LEONE LIMENTANI   KITCHENWARE
(Map p362; www.limentani.com; Via del Portico d'Ottavia 47; ☻9am-1pm & 3.30-7pm Mon-Fri, 10am-8pm Sat; 🚇Via Arenula) Family-run for seven generations, this well-stocked basement store has a huge, rambling choice of kitchenware and tableware, expensive porcelain and knick-knacks, crockery, cutlery and crystal, many by top brands and all at bargain prices.

🔒 Piazza Colonna & Around

★CONFETTERIA MORIONDO
& GARIGLIO   CHOCOLATE
(Map p360; Via del Piè di Marmo 21-22; ☻9am-7.30pm Mon-Sat; 🚇Via del Corso) Roman poet Trilussa was so smitten with this historic chocolate shop – established by the Torinese confectioners to the royal house of Savoy – that he dedicated several sonnets in its honour. Many of the handmade chocolates and bonbons, laid out in ceremonial splendour in glass cabinets set against dark crimson walls, are still made to 19th-century recipes.

TARTARUGHE   CLOTHING
(Map p360; www.letartarughe.eu; Via del Piè di Marmo 17; ☻10am-7.30pm Tue-Sat, 12-7.30pm Mon; 🚇Via del Corso) Designer Susanna Liso's elegant designs adorn this, her stylish, white-walled boutique. Her clothes, which include wonderful, multicoloured knit dresses, strikingly cut jackets, coats, and trousers, play on classic styles but add a vibrant, modern touch. She also has novel accessories in stone, glass and perspex.

BARTOLUCCI   TOYS
(Map p360; www.bartolucci.com; Via dei Pastini 98; 🚇Via del Corso) It's difficult to resist going into this magical toy shop where everything is crafted out of wood. It's guarded by a cycling Pinocchio and a full-sized motorbike, and within are all manner of ticking clocks, rocking horses, planes and more Pinocchios than you'll have ever seen in your life.

DAVIDE CENCI
CLOTHING

(Map p360; www.davidecenci.com; Via di Campo Marzio 1-7; ☺10.30am-7.30pm Tue-Sat & 3.30-7.30pm Mon; 🚇Via del Corso) For that discreet old-money look – think blazers, brogues, tweed and flannels – head to Davide Cenci, an old-school outfitter's that has been dressing Rome's finest since 1926. It carries a selection of impeccable Italian and international labels (Ralph Lauren, Tod's, Hogan, Ballantyne, Pucci) as well as its own house brand.

A.S. ROMA STORE
SPORTS

(Map p360; Piazza Colonna 360; ☺10am-7.30pm Mon-Sat, 10.30am-7pm Sun; 🚇Via del Corso) An official club store of A.S. Roma, one of Rome's two top-flight football teams. There's an extensive array of Roma-branded kit, including replica shirts, caps, T-shirts, scarves, hoodies, keyrings and a whole lot more. You can also buy match tickets between 10am and 6pm.

DE SANCTIS
ARTISANAL

(Map p360; www.desanctis1890.com; Piazza di Pietra 24; ☺10am-1.30pm & 3-7.30pm Mon-Sat, closed Tue morning; 🚇Via del Corso) De Sanctis – in business since 1890 – is full of impressive Italian ceramics from Sicily and Tuscany, with sunbursts of colour decorating candleholders, vases, tiles, urns and plates. If your purchases are too heavy to carry, they ship all over the world.

Tridente, Trevi & the Quirinale

PIAZZA DEL POPOLO | WEST OF VIA DEL CORSO | PIAZZA DI SPAGNA | TREVI FOUNTAIN | QUIRINALE | PIAZZA BARBERINI | VIA VENETO

Neighbourhood Top Five

1 People watching, photosnapping and daydreaming on the **Spanish Steps** (p113), with a view down the glittering backbone of the Tridente district, designer-store-lined Via dei Condotti.

2 Gazing at the Caravaggio masterpieces in **Chiesa di Santa Maria del Popolo** (p114).

3 Visiting the **Trevi Fountain** (p115) late in the evening, when the crowds have ebbed away.

4 Hearing a concert in the Cortona-designed chapel after a Sunday visit to the **Palazzo del Quirinale** (p123).

5 Seeing **Palazzo Barberini's** (p124) architectural treasures and wealth of masterpieces.

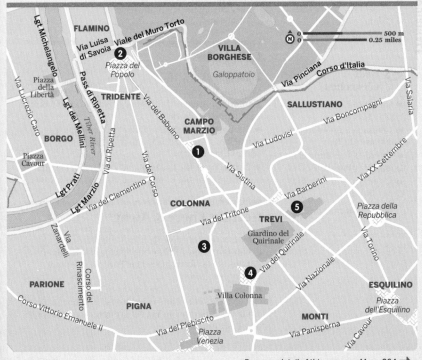

For more detail of this area, see Map p364 ➡

Lonely Planet's Top Tip

Note that local churches are usually locked up for two to three hours over lunch, so if you want to visit the interiors, time your visit for the morning or late afternoon.

Best Places to Eat

➡ Palatium (p128)
➡ Nino (p129)
➡ Babette (p127)
➡ Colline Emiliane (p130)
➡ Il Gelato (p127)

For reviews, see p126 ➡

Best Places to Drink

➡ La Scena (p130)
➡ Stravinkij Bar – Hotel de Russie (p130)
➡ Canova Tadolini (p131)
➡ Ciampini 2 (p131)

For reviews, see p130 ➡

Best Churches

➡ Chiesa di Santa Maria del Popolo (p114)
➡ Chiesa di Sant'Andrea al Quirinale (p122)
➡ Chiesa di San Carlo alle Quattro Fontane (p122)
➡ Chiesa di Santa Maria della Vittoria (p122)

For reviews, see p118 ➡

Explore: Tridente, Trevi & the Quirinale

Tridente is Rome's most glamorous district, full of designer boutiques, fashionable bars and swish hotels. However, it's not just about shopping, dining and drinking. The area also contains the splendid and vast neoclassical showpiece, Piazza del Popolo; the Spanish Steps; the Museo dell'Ara Pacis, a controversial modern museum designed by US architect Richard Meier; and several masterpiece-packed churches. To see all the sights here, factoring in some window shopping, would take around half a day to a day, and it's all easily walkable – a short walk from the *centro storico* or Piazza Venezia – and easily accessible from the Spagna and Flaminio metro stations.

Alongside Tridente, the Roman hill of Quirinale is home to the extraordinary Trevi Fountain and the imposing presidential Palazzo del Quirinale, as well as important churches by the twin masters of Roman baroque, Gian Lorenzo Bernini and Francesco Borromini. Other artistic hot spots in the area include the lavish Galleria Colonna and the Galleria Nazionale d'Arte Antica – Palazzo Barberini, a fabulous gallery containing works by a who's who of Renaissance and baroque artists. To see all this at leisure you'll need several days. The Trevi and Quirinale's principal gateway is the Barberini metro stop.

Busy during the day, both Tridente and the Quirinale are sleepy after dark.

Local Life

➡ **Ambling** Imagine yourself as part of *Roman Holiday* along the laid-back, cobbled and ivy-draped Via Margutta, and enjoy the upscale neighbourhood feel of this distinctive district.
➡ **Shopping** Commission yourself a handmade bag, a unique lamp or a marble motto from one of the area's artisanal shops.
➡ **Coffee** Do as the locals do and grab a caffeine hit, propping up the bar at one of the district's iconic cafes.

Getting There & Away

➡ **Metro** The Trevi and Quirinale areas are closest to Barberini metro stop, while Spagna and Flaminio stations are perfectly placed for Tridente. All three stops are on line A.
➡ **Bus** Numerous buses run down to Piazza Barberini or along Via Veneto, and many stop at the southern end of Via del Corso and on Via del Tritone, ideal for a foray into Tridente.

TOP SIGHT
PIAZZA DI SPAGNA & THE SPANISH STEPS

The Piazza di Spagna and the Spanish Steps (Scalinata della Trinità dei Monti) are the focal point of the Tridente district, and most visitors will settle down here to take stock at some point. The area has been a magnet for foreigners since the 1800s. When Dickens visited in the 19th century he reported that 'these steps are the great place of resort for the artists' "models"... The first time I went up there, I could not conceive why the faces seemed familiar to me... I soon found that we had made acquaintance, and improved it, for several years, on the walls of various Exhibition Galleries.'

DON'T MISS...

➡ The view from the top of the Spanish Steps

➡ Barcaccia

PRACTICALITIES

➡ Map p364

➡ Ⓜ Spagna

The Piazza di Spagna was named after the Spanish Embassy to the Holy See, although the staircase, designed by the Italian Francesco de Sanctis and built in 1725 with a legacy from the French, leads to the French Chiesa della Trinità dei Monti. In the late 1700s the area was much loved by English visitors on the Grand Tour and was known to locals as *er ghetto de l'inglesi* (the English ghetto). Keats lived for a short time in an apartment overlooking the Spanish Steps, and died here of tuberculosis at the age of 25. The rooms are now a museum devoted to the Romantics, especially Keats.

At the foot of the steps, the fountain of a sinking boat, the **Barcaccia** (1627), is believed to be by Pietro Bernini, father of the more famous Gian Lorenzo. It's fed from a low-pressure aqueduct, hence the low-key nature of the central fountain. Bees and suns decorate the structure, symbols of the commissioning Barbarini family. Opposite, Via dei Condotti is Rome's most exclusive shopping street, glittering with big-name designers such as Gucci, Bulgari and Prada.

To the southeast of the piazza, adjacent Piazza Mignanelli is dominated by the Colonna dell'Immacolata, built in 1857 to celebrate Pope Pius IX's declaration of the Immaculate Conception.

TOP SIGHT
CHIESA DI SANTA MARIA DEL POPOLO

A magnificent repository of art, this is one of Rome's earliest and richest Renaissance churches. Artists including Pinturicchio worked on the building in the 15th century, while Bramante and Bernini added later architectural elements. The lavish chapels, decorated by Caravaggio, Bernini, Raphael and others, were commissioned by local noble families.

DON'T MISS...

➡ Caravaggio's paintings in the Cerasi Chapel

➡ Raphael and Bernini's work in the Chigi Chapel

PRACTICALITIES

➡ Map p364
➡ Piazza del Popolo
➡ ⊙7.30am–noon & 4-7pm
➡ Ⓜ Flaminio

The Church

The first chapel was built here in 1099, over the tombs of the Domiti family, to exorcise the ghost of Nero, who was secretly buried on this spot and whose malicious spirit was thought to haunt the area. Some 400 years later, in 1472, it was given a major overhaul by Pope Sixtus IV. Pinturicchio was called in to decorate the pope's family chapel, the Cappella Delle Rovere, and to paint a series of frescoes on the apse, itself designed by Bramante. Also in the apse are Rome's first stained-glass windows, crafted by Frenchman Guillaume de Marcillat in the early 16th century. The altar houses the 13th-century painting Madonna del Popolo, and the altarpiece of the Assumption is by Annibale Carracci.

The former Augustinian convent adjoining the church hosted Martin Luther during his month-long mission here in 1511, and now houses the Genio di Leonardo da Vinci exhibition (p118).

Chigi Chapel

Raphael designed the Cappella Chigi, dedicated to his patron Agostino Chigi, but never lived to see it completed. Bernini finished the job for him more than 100 years later, contributing statues of Daniel and Habakkuk to the altarpiece, which was built by Sebastiano del Piombo. The most famous feature is the 17th-century mosaic of a kneeling skeleton, placed there to remind the living of the inevitable.

Cerasi Chapel

The church's dazzling highlight is the Cappella Cerasi with its two works by Caravaggio: the *Conversione di San Paolo* (Conversion of St Paul) and the *Crocifissione di San Pietro* (Crucifixion of St Peter). Both are exquisitely spotlit via the artist's use of light and shade. The latter is frighteningly realistic: the artist used perspective to emphasise the weight of the cross as it's turned upside down, and St Peter's facial expression as he is upturned is heartrendingly human; sorrowful rather than afraid.

Della Rovere Chapel

The frescoes in the lunettes and the Nativity above the altar in this chapel were painted by Pinturicchio in the 15th century. They show delicate, graceful figures; restrained, elaborate, classically allusive decoration; and gold motifs.

TOP SIGHT
TREVI FOUNTAIN

Fontana di Trevi is a baroque extravaganza that almost fills an entire piazza. The foaming masterpiece is famous as the place where Anita Ekberg cavorted in a ballgown in Fellini's *La Dolce Vita* (1960).

The flamboyant baroque ensemble was designed by Nicola Salvi in 1732 and depicts Neptune's chariot being led by Tritons with sea horses – one wild, one docile – representing the moods of the sea. The water still comes from the Aqua Virgo, an underground aqueduct that is over 2000 years old, built by General Agrippa under Augustus and which brings water from the Salone springs around 19 km away. The name Trevi refers to the *tre vie* (three roads) that converge at the fountain.

To the eastern side of the fountain is a large round stone urn. The story goes that Salvi, during the construction of the fountain, was harassed by a barber, who had his shop to the east of the fountain and who was critical of the work in progress. Thus the sculptor added this urn in order to block this irritating critic.

The famous tradition (since the film *Three Coins in the Fountain*) is to toss a coin into the fountain, thus ensuring your return to Rome. Around €3000 is thrown into the Trevi on an average day. This money is collected daily and goes to the Catholic charity Caritas, with their yield increasing significantly since the crackdown on criminal elements extracting the money for themselves.

In 2012, Karl Lagerfeld announced that Fendi would fund a much-needed €2.18m restoration of the fountain. This is one of the latest trends in Italian fashion: saving monuments that the Italian government cannot afford to repair or maintain (in return for some free advertising on hoardings as the restoration takes place, and plaques commemorating their assistance).

DON'T MISS...

➡ The contrasting seahorses, or moods of the sea.

➡ Throwing a coin or three into the fountain.

PRACTICALITIES

➡ Map p364

➡ Piazza di Trevi

➡ Ⓜ Barberini

Il Tridente

The three streets that radiate south from Piazza del Popolo cut straight to the heart of ancient Rome. Historian and presenter Dan Cruickshank explained the appeal of 'Il Tridente' to *Lonely Planet Traveller* magazine.

Rome is one of the few capital cities whose heart is still girdled by long sections of defensive wall. But what makes Rome different from other great walled cities is its gates. These mighty and majestic works remain portals between different worlds.

For me, most exciting and in many ways perfect, is the Porta del Popolo on the northern tip of the city centre. Perfect not because of its design but because it is the perfect way to enter the magic domain of Rome. Outside the gate all is movement and space: wide modern roads and, to the east, the beautiful gardens of the Villa Borghese.

Pass through the gate, which until the mid-19th century was the main point of entry to the city for travellers, and the heart of Rome opens before you. From the south side of this oval radiate three long, straight streets – the famed Il Tridente – offering heroic and breathtaking vistas through the chaotic fabric of the city.

Via del Babuino

The Via del Babuino is named after an ancient statue that since the 16th century has lolled halfway along its length and is deemed to be so ugly that it's called babuino, the baboon. In the past Romans let off steam by 'talking' through these statues, on which were hung satirical verses that mocked the ruling elite of the city.

1. Piazza del Popolo (p118) at the start of Via del Corso 2. Via del Corso at sunset 3. Detail of the Trevi Fountain (p115)

Via del Corso

Running almost due south from Piazza del Popolo is the Via del Corso. It cuts laser-like through the very heart of the city, following the course of the 2200-year-old Via Flaminia, the route along which the legions marched heading north and along which they returned, proclaiming Rome's glory. Go to the east, along Via delle Muratte, and you suddenly find yourself in front of the triumphal façade and fresh waters of the Trevi Fountain, which still manages to rise above the hordes of tourists that engulf it.

Via di Ripetta

The third spoke of the Piazza del Popolo's Il Tridente is the Via di Ripetta, heading southeast, towards the River Tiber and on to the sacred city of the Vatican. The Via di Ripetta also leads to my favourite Rome, the Rome where the past and the present coexist in a most dramatic and intimate manner: narrow rows of artisan shops nestling within the shadow of a rearing palazzo; a mighty church juxtaposed in dramatic contrast with cramped alleys; swirling patterns of eager pedestrians and scooters throbbing and revving as they weave through the city.

◉ SIGHTS

The **Piazza del Popolo**, the **Spanish Steps**, the **Trevi Fountain**, Rome's most fashionable district, **Palazzo Barberini** and a sprinkling of **Caravaggios**...it's all a hop and a skip from **Villa Borghese** when you're in need of a breather. This area is one of Rome's richest, in terms of cuisine, art and culture (as well as hard cash) and offers an embarrassment of treasures for the visitor.

◉ Piazza del Popolo & Around

CHIESA DI SANTA MARIA DEL POPOLO CHURCH
See p114.

PINCIO HILL GARDENS PARK
(Map p364; MFlaminio) Overlooking Piazza del Popolo, the 19th-century Pincio Hill is named after the Pinci family, who owned this part of Rome in the 4th century. It's quite a climb up from the piazza, but at the top you're rewarded with lovely views over

to St Peter's and the Gianicolo Hill. From the gardens you can strike out to explore Villa Borghese or head up to the Chiesa della Trinità dei Monti at the top of the Spanish Steps.

IL GENIO DI LEONARDO DA VINCI EXHIBITION
(Map p364; ☎06 3600 4224; Piazza del Popolo 12; admission €7; ☻9.30am-8pm; MFlaminio) This small exhibition has working models of some of Leonardo da Vinci's remarkable inventions. It's fascinating to see his futuristic visions and some of the models are interactive (it could be a handy child-pleaser), but it feels overpriced for what it is.

◉ West of Via del Corso

MUSEO DELL'ARA PACIS MUSEUM
(Map p364; ☎06 06 08; http://en.arapacis. it; Lungotevere in Augusta; adult/reduced €8.50/6.50; ☻9am-7pm Tue-Sun, last admission 6pm; MFlaminio) Many Romans detest Richard Meier's minimalist glass-and-marble pavilion (the first modern construction in Rome's historic centre since WWII). Inside is the less-controversial Ara Pacis Augustae

---

◉ TOP SIGHT
PIAZZA DEL POPOLO

For centuries the site of public executions (the last was in 1826), this public space was laid out in 1538 to provide a grandiose entrance to what was then Rome's main northern gateway. Via Flaminia connected the city with the north from here. The piazza has been remodelled several times since, most significantly by Giuseppe Valadier in 1823, who created the gaping ellipse we see today.

In the centre, the 36m-high **obelisk** was brought by Augustus from Heliopolis, in ancient Egypt, and originally stood in Circo Massimo. To the east is the viewpoint of the Pincio Hill Gardens. This is not one of Rome's original seven hills, as it lay outside the original city boundary – it was included within the city from the 3rd century.

Guarding the piazza's southern end are Carlo Rainaldi's twin 17th-century baroque churches, **Chiesa di Santa Maria dei Miracoli** and **Chiesa di Santa Maria in Montesanto**, while over on the northern flank is the **Porta del Popolo**, created by Bernini in 1655 to celebrate Queen Christina of Sweden's defection to Catholicism. Beside the gate is the treasure-trove of art that is Chiesa di Santa Maria del Popolo.

DON'T MISS...
➡ The obelisk
➡ The view from the Pincio Hill Gardens

PRACTICALITIES
➡ Map p364
➡ MFlaminio

ROME'S VERSAILLES

If Napoleon had had his way, the Palazzo del Quirinale would have been Rome's Versailles. Journalist and author Corrado Augias explains:

'Napoleon actually chose Rome as his second capital after Paris. He wanted Versailles at Paris and the Palazzo del Quirinale – incidentally, Rome's greatest and most beautiful palace – in Rome. He set artists and architects to prepare it for him and sent down furniture from Paris. In the end he never came and when he was defeated in 1815 the popes took the *palazzo* back for themselves.'

(Altar of Peace), Augustus' great monument to peace. One of the most important works of ancient Roman sculpture, the vast marble altar (it measures 11.6m by 10.6m by 3.6m) was completed in 13 BC.

It was originally positioned near Piazza San Lorenzo in Lucina, slightly to the southeast of its current site. The location was calculated so that on Augustus' birthday the shadow of a huge sundial on Campus Martius would fall directly on it. Over the centuries the altar fell victim to Rome's avid art collectors, and panels ended up in the Medici collection, the Vatican and the Louvre. However, in 1936 Mussolini unearthed the remaining parts and decided to reassemble them in the present location.

Of the reliefs, the most important depicts Augustus at the head of a procession, followed by priests, the general Marcus Agrippa and the entire imperial family.

Mayor Gianni Alemanno promised on his election in 2008 to have the unpopular monument pulled down. However, such plans have been modified, and instead the wall dividing the busy Lungotevere Augusta from Piazza Augusto Imperatore – which has been criticised for obscuring the baroque facade of the church of San Rocco all'Augusteo – is to be dismantled. The vast sum of €1.4 million was set aside for this, but the work shows no sign of being taken to fruition.

MAUSOLEO DI AUGUSTO   MONUMENT
(Map p364; Piazza Augusto Imperatore; ⊒Piazza Augusto Imperatore) This mausoleum was built in 28 BC and is the last resting place of Augustus, who was buried here in AD 14,

and his favourite nephew and heir Marcellus. Mussolini had it restored in 1936 with an eye to being buried here himself.

Once one of ancient Rome's most imposing monuments, it's now an unkempt mound of earth, smelly and surrounded by unsightly fences. Work is apparently ongoing, though it's proceeding at a slow pace.

◉ Piazza di Spagna & Around

PIAZZA DI SPAGNA & THE SPANISH STEPS   PIAZZA
See p113.

★KEATS-SHELLEY HOUSE   MUSEUM
(Map p364; ☑06 678 42 35; www.keats-shelley-house.org; Piazza di Spagna 26; adult/reduced €4.50/3.50; ⊙10am-1pm & 2-6pm Mon-Fri, 11am-2pm & 3-6pm Sat; ⓂSpagna) The Keats-Shelley House is where Romantic poet John Keats died of tuberculosis at the age of 25, in February 1821. A year later, fellow poet Percy Bysshe Shelley drowned off the coast of Tuscany. The house is now a small museum crammed with memorabilia relating to the poets and their colleagues Mary Shelley and Lord Byron.

Keats had come to Rome in 1820, on an obviously unsuccessful trip to try to improve his health in the Italian climate. There are interesting regular talks and tours in English and Italian (free with your ticket), and occasional creative writing workshops – check the website for details.

VIA DEI CONDOTTI   STREET
(Map p364; ⓂSpagna) High-rolling shoppers and window-dreamers take note, this is Rome's smartest shopping strip. At the eastern end, near Piazza di Spagna, Caffè Greco (p131) was a favourite meeting point of 18th- and 19th-century writers. Other top shopping streets in the area include **Via Frattina**, **Via della Croce**, **Via delle Carrozze** and **Via del Babuino**.

GALLERIA D'ARTE MODERNA   GALLERY
(Map p364; ☑06 06 08; www.galleriaartemodernaroma.it; Via F Crispi 24; adult/reduced €6.50/5.50; ⊙10am-6pm Tue-Sun; ⓂBarberini) Housed in an 18th-century Carmelite convent, this interesting collection of art and sculpture from the 20th century was reopened in 2011 after a lengthy closure. There are works on three floors, as well

TRIDENTE, TREVI & THE QUIRINALE SIGHTS

BERNINI VS BORROMINI

Born within a year of each other, the two giants of Roman baroque hated each other with a vengeance. Gian Lorenzo Bernini (1598–1680), suave, self-confident and politically adept, was the polar opposite of his great rival Francesco Borromini (1599–1677), a solitary and peculiar man who often argued with clients. His passion for architecture was a matter of life and death: once he caught a man disfiguring some pieces of stone while he was working on rebuilding San Giovanni in Laterano and had him beaten so fiercely that he later died of his injuries (Borromini received a papal pardon).

Their paths first crossed at St Peter's Basilica. Borromini, who had been working as an assistant to Carlo Maderno, a distant relative and the basilica's lead architect, was furious when Bernini was appointed to take over the project on Maderno's death. Nevertheless, he stayed on as Bernini's chief assistant and actually contributed to the design of the baldachin – a work for which Bernini took full public credit. To make matters worse, Bernini was later appointed chief architect on Palazzo Barberini, again in the wake of Maderno, and again to Borromini's disgust.

Over the course of the next 45 years, the two geniuses competed for commissions and public acclaim. Bernini flourished under the Barberini pope Urban VIII (r 1623–44) and Borromini under his Pamphilj successor Innocent X (r 1644–1655), but all the while their loathing simmered. Borromini accused Bernini of profiting from his (Borromini's) talents while Bernini claimed that Borromini 'had been sent to destroy architecture'. Certainly, both had very different views on architecture: for Bernini it was all about portraying an experience to elicit an emotional response, while Borromini favoured a more geometrical approach, manipulating classical forms to create dynamic, vibrant spaces.

Of the two, Bernini is generally reckoned to have had the better of the rivalry. His genius was rarely questioned and when he died he was widely regarded as one of Europe's greatest artists. Borromini, in contrast, struggled to win popular and critical support and after a life of depression committed suicide in 1677.

as in the cloister (amid the orange trees). Highlights include Gerolamo Masini's voluptuous, boho-looking neoclassical *Cleopatra*, Giovanni Prini's elegant *Lovers* (1909–13), and de Chirico's painting *Gladiators in Combat* (1930–34).

Views of Rome, painted by Francesco Trombadori and Riccardo Francalancia in the 1950s, are interesting for how they make Villa Borghese and the Colosseum resemble outposts of EUR (the Mussolini-built neoclassical suburb). Upstairs there is also a rich collection of still lifes, including works by Giorgio Morandi.

CHIESA DELLA TRINITÀ DEI MONTI CHURCH

(Map p364; Piazza Trinità dei Monti; ☺6am-8pm Tue-Sun; MSpagna) Looming over the Spanish Steps, this landmark church was commissioned by King Louis XII of France and consecrated in 1585. Apart from the great views from outside, it boasts some wonderful frescoes by Daniele da Volterra. His *Deposizione* (Deposition), in the second chapel on the left, is regarded as a masterpiece of mannerist painting.

If you don't fancy climbing the steep steps, there's a lift up from Spagna metro station.

MUSEO MISSIONARIO DI PROPAGANDA FIDE MUSEUM

(Map p364; ☎06 6988 0266; Via di Propaganda 1; admission €8; ☺2.30-6pm Mon, Wed & Fri; MSpagna) Rome's 'propogation of the faith' museum is housed in a 17th-century baroque masterpiece designed by Gian Lorenzo Bernini and Francesco Borromini, and is an opportunity to peer into Bernini's wooden, Hogwarts-reminiscent library, with its ceiling carved with Barberini bees; and Borromini's Chapel of the Magi, where the theme of the wise mens' epiphany acts as an allegory for converts to Christianity.

This little-visited museum also has an eclectic collection of items brought back from overseas missions, such as paintings of Japanese life in the 1930s and a Canova portrait of Ezzelino Romano, and some of the extraordinary gifts the pope has received over the years.

PALAZZO VALENTINI   ARCHAEOLOGICAL SITE

(Map p364; ☑06 3 28 10; www.palazzovalentini.it; Via IV Novembre 119a; adult/reduced €10/8, advance booking fee €1.50; ⊘9.30am-5.30pm Wed-Mon; ⓜSpagna) Underneath a grand mansion that's been the seat of the Province of Rome since 1873 lie the archaeological remains of several lavish ancient Roman houses; the excavated fragments have been turned into a fascinating multimedia 'experience'. Tours are every 30 minutes, but alternate between Italian, English and French. Book well ahead online or by phone, especially during holiday periods.

The visit takes you on a virtual tour of the dwellings, complete with sound effects, vividly projected frescoes and glimpses of ancient life as it might have been lived in the area around the buildings. It's genuinely thrilling and great for older kids. A newly excavated area allows you to visit the remains of a great public building, with columns built from huge Egyptian granite blocks, underground close to Trajan's Column. There are also displays that vividly illuminate the history of Trajan's military campaign and allow a close-up look at the column's bas-reliefs and the story they tell.

CASA DI GOETHE   MUSEUM

(Map p364; ☑06 3265 0412; www.casadigoethe.it; Via del Corso 18; adult/reduced €5/3; ⊘10am-6pm Tue-Sun; ⓜFlaminio) A gathering place for German intellectuals, the Via del Corso apartment where Johann Wolfgang von Goethe enjoyed a happy Italian sojourn (despite complaining of the noisy neighbours) from 1786 to 1788 is now a lovingly maintained museum. Exhibits include documents and some fascinating drawings and etchings. With advance permission, ardent fans can use the library which is full of first editions. There are free guided tours in Italian at 11am on Sundays.

VILLA MEDICI   PALACE

(Map p364; ☑06 6 76 11; www.villamedici.it; Viale Trinità dei Monti 1; gardens adult/reduced €9/7, Wed tour including cardinal's apartments €11/9; ⊘10.30am-12.30pm & 2-5.30pm Tue-Sun; ⓜSpagna) This striking Renaissance palace was built for Cardinal Ricci da Montepulciano in 1540, but Ferdinando dei Medici bought it in 1576. It remained in Medici hands until 1801, when Napoleon acquired

TRIDENTE, TREVI & THE QUIRINALE SIGHTS

◉ TOP SIGHT
GALLERIA COLONNA

The only part of **Palazzo Colonna** open to the public, this thrillingly opulent gallery houses the Colonna family's small but stunning private art collection. The polished yellow columns represent the 'Colonna' (which also means column) of the family name.

The purpose-built gallery (constructed by Antonio del Grande from 1654 to 1665) has six rooms crowned by fantastical ceiling frescoes, all dedicated to Marcantonio Colonna, the family's greatest ancestor, who defeated the Turks at the naval Battle of Lepanto in 1571. Works by Giovanni Coli and Filippo Gherardi in the Great Hall, Sebastiano Ricci in the Landscapes Room and Giuseppe Bartolomeo Chiari in the Throne Room all commemorate his efforts. Note also the cannonball lodged in the gallery's marble stairs, a vivid reminder of the 1849 siege of Rome.

The art on display features a fine array of 16th- to 18th-century paintings, the highlight of which is Annibale Carracci's vivid *Mangiafagioli* (The Beaneater).

From January 2013, the palace opened three additional rooms to the public: the Yellow, Tapestry, and Embroidery rooms.

DON'T MISS...

➡ Fantastic ceiling frescoes

➡ Annibale Carracci's *Mangiafagioli*

PRACTICALITIES

➡ Map p364

➡ ☑06 678 43 50

➡ www.galleria colonna.it

➡ Via della Pilotta 17

➡ adult/reduced €12/10

➡ ⊘9am-1.15pm Sat, closed Aug

➡ ☐Via IV Novembre

it and gave it to the French Academy. There are regular tours of the landscaped **gardens**, and the villa often hosts art exhibitions.

The villa's most famous resident was Galileo, who was imprisoned here between 1630 and 1633 during his trial for heresy, though Keith Richards and Anita Pallenberg stayed here in the 1960s.

◎ Trevi Fountain to the Quirinale

TREVI FOUNTAIN FOUNTAIN

See p115.

PIAZZA DEL QUIRINALE PIAZZA

(Map p364; **M**Barberini) A wonderful spot to enjoy a glowing Roman sunset, this piazza marks the summit of the Quirinale hill. The central **obelisk** was moved here from the Mausoleo di Augusto in 1786 and is flanked by 5.5m statues of **Castor** and **Pollux** reining in a couple of rearing horses.

If you're in the neighbourhood on a Sunday you can catch the weekly changing of the guard (6pm in summer, 4pm the rest of the year).

CHIESA DI SANTA MARIA DELLA VITTORIA CHURCH

(Via XX Settembre 17; ⊘7am-noon & 3.30-7pm; **M**Repubblica) This modest church is an unlikely setting for an extraordinary work of art – Bernini's extravagant and sexually charged *Santa Teresa trafitta dall'amore di Dio* (Ecstasy of St Teresa). This daring sculpture depicts Teresa, engulfed in the folds of a flowing cloak, floating in ecstasy on a cloud while a teasing angel pierces her repeatedly with a golden arrow.

Watching from two side balconies are a number of figures, including Cardinal Federico Cornaro, for whom the chapel was built. It's a stunning work, bathed in soft natural light from a concealed window. Go in the afternoon for the best effect.

CHIESA DI SANT'ANDREA AL QUIRINALE CHURCH

(Map p364; Via del Quirinale 29; ⊘8.30am-noon & 2.30-6pm winter, 9am-noon & 3-6pm summer; **Q**Via Nazionale) It's said that in his old age Bernini liked to come and enjoy the peace of this late-17th-century church, regarded by many as one of his greatest. Faced with severe space limitations, he managed to produce a sense of grandeur by designing an elliptical floor plan with a series of chapels opening onto the central area.

The opulent interior, decorated with polychrome marble, stucco and gilding, was a favourite of Pope Alexander VII while in residence at the Palazzo del Quirinale.

CHIESA DI SAN CARLO ALLE QUATTRO FONTANE CHURCH

(Map p364; Via del Quirinale 23; ⊘10am-1pm & 3-6pm Mon-Fri, 10am-1pm Sat, noon-1pm Sun; **Q**Via Nazionale) It might not look it, with its grubby facade and traffic-choked location, but this tiny church is a masterpiece of Roman baroque. It was Borromini's first church and bears all the hallmarks of his genius. The elegant curves of the facade, the play of convex and concave surfaces,

---

MIRACULOUS MADONNAS

Overlooking Vicolo delle Bollette, a tiny lane near the Trevi Fountain, there's a small, simple painting of the Virgin Mary. This is the *Madonna della Pietà*, one of the most famous of Rome's *madonnelle* (small madonnas). There are estimated to be around 730 of these roadside madonnas in Rome's historic centre, most placed on street corners or outside historic *palazzi* (mansions). Many were added in the 16th and 17th centuries, but their origins date to pagan times when votive wall shrines were set up at street corners to honour the Lares, household spirits believed to protect passersby. When Christianity emerged in the 4th century AD, these shrines were simply rededicated to the religion's new icons.

The subject of much popular devotion, they are shrouded in myth. The most famous legend dates to 1796 when news of a French invasion is said to have caused 36 *madonnelle*, including the *Madonna della Pietà*, to move their eyes and some even to cry. A papal commission set up to investigate subsequently declared 26 madonnas to be officially miraculous.

As well as food for the soul, the madonnas also provided a valuable public service. Until street lamps were introduced in the 19th century, the candles and lamps that lit up the images were the city's only source of street lighting.

TOP SIGHT
PALAZZO DEL QUIRINALE

Overlooking the high-up Piazza del Quirinale is the imposing presidential palace, formerly the papal summer residence, open to the public on Sundays.

The immense Palazzo del Quirinale served as the papal summer residence for almost three centuries until the keys were begrudgingly handed over to Italy's new king in 1870. Since 1948, it has been the home of the Presidente della Repubblica, Italy's head of state.

Pope Gregory XIII (r 1572–85) originally chose the site and over the next 150 years the top architects of the day worked on it, including Bernini, Domenico Fontana and Carlo Maderno.

On the other side of the piazza, the palace's former stables, the **Scuderie Papali al Quirinale** (Map p364; ☑06 3996 7500; www.scuderiequirinale.it; Via XXIV Maggio 16; tickets around €12; ⊘depends on exhibition), is now a magnificent space that hosts art exhibitions; recent shows have included Titian and Augusto (commemorating 2000 years since the emperor's death).

DON'T MISS...

➡ Sunday concerts held in the chapel designed by Carlo Maderno

➡ Splendid exhibitions in the former stables, the Scuderie Papali

PRACTICALITIES

➡ Map p364

➡ ☑06 4 69 91

➡ www.quirinale.it

➡ admission €5

➡ ⊘8am-noon Sun mid-Sep–Jun

➡ Ⓜ Barberini

TRIDENTE, TREVI & THE QUIRINALE SIGHTS

and the dome illuminated by hidden windows, all combine to transform a minuscule space into a light, airy interior.

The church, completed in 1641, stands at the road intersection known as the **Quattro Fontane**, after the late-16th-century fountains on its four corners, representing Fidelity, Strength and the rivers Arno and Tiber.

BASILICA DEI SANTI APOSTOLI   CHURCH
(Map p364; Piazza dei Santissimi Apostoli; ⊘7am-noon & 4-7pm; ▣Via IV Novembre) This much-altered 6th-century church is dedicated to the apostles James and Philip, whose relics are in the crypt. Its most obvious attraction is the portico with its Renaissance arches and the two-tier facade topped by 13 towering figures. Inside, the flashy baroque interior was completed in 1714 by Carlo and Francesco Fontana. Highlights include the ceiling frescoes by Baciccia and Antonio Canova's grandiose tomb of Pope Clement XIV.

Surrounding the basilica are two imposing baroque *palazzi* (mansions): at the end of the square, **Palazzo Balestra** which was given to James Stuart, the Old Pretender, in 1719 by Pope Clement XI, and opposite, **Palazzo Odelschalchi**, with its impressive Bernini facade.

CITTÀ DELL'ACQUA   ARCHAEOLOGICAL SITE
(Map p364; www.archeodomani.com; Vicolo del Puttarello 25; adult/reduced €3/1; ⊘11am-5.30pm Wed-Fri, 11am-7pm Sat & Sun; Ⓜ Barberini) The little-known excavations of Vicus Caprarius (the name of the ancient street), include a Roman house and a Hadrian-era cistern that connected with the Aqua Virgo cistern. Eight metres deep, they lie just a few paces from the eternal hubbub of the Trevi Fountain – the spring waters that once fed these waterworks now gush forth from the fountain.

This is a chance to appreciate the many layers that lie beneath present-day Rome; mosaics and decorations discovered during the excavations are displayed in a small museum.

MUSEO DELLE CERE   MUSEUM
(Map p364; ☑06 679 64 82; www.museodellecereroma.com; Piazza dei Santissimi Apostoli 67; adult/reduced €9/7; ⊘9am-9pm; ▣Via IV Novembre) Rome's waxwork museum is said to have the world's third-largest collection, which comprises more than 250

⊙ TOP SIGHT GALLERIA NAZIONALE D'ARTE ANTICA – PALAZZO BARBERINI

The sumptuous Palazzo Barberini is an architectural feast before you even consider the National Art Collection that it houses. This huge baroque palace was commissioned by Urban VIII to celebrate the Barberini family's rise to papal power. Many high-profile architects worked on it, including rivals Bernini and Borromini; the former contributed a large squared staircase, the latter a helicoidal one.

The palace houses part of the Galleria Nazionale d'Arte Antica and has many beautifully painted ceilings, most spectacular of which is the ceiling of the 1st floor main salon, the *Triumph of Divine Providence* by Pietro da Cortona. Amid the collection, don't miss Hans Holbein's famous portrait of a pugnacious Henry VIII, Filippo Lippi's luminous *Annunciazione e due devoti*, and works by Tintoretto, Titian, Bernini and Caravaggio.

Another must-see is Raphael's *La fornarina* (The Baker's Girl), a portrait of the artist's mistress. She apparently proved such a distraction that Raphael failed to complete commissions.

DON'T MISS...

➡ Pietro da Cortona's painted ceiling
➡ Raphael's *La fornarina*
➡ Works by Caravaggio

PRACTICALITIES

➡ Map p364
➡ ☑06 3 28 10
➡ www.gebart.it
➡ Via delle Quattro Fontane 13
➡ adult/reduced €7/3.50, with Palazzo Corsini €9/4.50
➡ ⊙8.30am-7pm Tue-Sun
➡ Ⓜ Barberini

---

figures, ranging from Barack Obama to Snow White, plus plentiful popes, poets, politicians, musicians and murderers. You can also visit the laboratory where the waxworks are created.

⊙ Piazza Barberini & Via Veneto

PIAZZA BARBERINI PIAZZA
(Map p364; Ⓜ Barberini) More a traffic thoroughfare than a place to linger, this noisy square is named after the Barberini family, one of Rome's great dynastic clans. In the centre, the Bernini-designed **Fontana del Tritone** (Fountain of the Triton) depicts the sea-god Triton blowing a stream of water from a conch while seated in a large scallop shell supported by four dolphins. Bernini also crafted the **Fontana delle Api** (Fountain of the Bees) in the northeastern corner, again for the Barberini family, whose crest featured three bees in flight.

CONVENTO DEI CAPPUCCINI MUSEUM
(Map p364; ☑06 487 11 85; Via Vittorio Veneto 27; adult/reduced €6/4; ⊙9am-7pm; Ⓜ Barberini)

This church and convent complex has recently gained an interesting multimedia museum telling the story of the Capuchin order of monks, including a work attributed to Caravaggio: *St Francis in Meditation*. The main attraction, however, is the extraordinary **Capuchin cemetery** that lies below, where everything from the picture frames to the light fittings is made of human bones.

Between 1528 and 1870 the resident Capuchin monks used the bones of 4000 of their departed brothers to create this mesmerising, macabre memento mori (reminder of death). There's an arch crafted from hundreds of skulls, vertebrae used as fleurs-de-lys and light fixtures made of femurs. Happy holidays!

VIA VITTORIO VENETO STREET
(Map p364; Ⓜ Barberini) Curving up from Piazza Barberini to Villa Borghese, Via Vittorio Veneto is the spiritual home of *la dolce vita* – the Rome of the swinging '50s and '60s that was epitomised in Fellini's eponymous film. However, the atmosphere of Fellini's Rome has long gone and the street

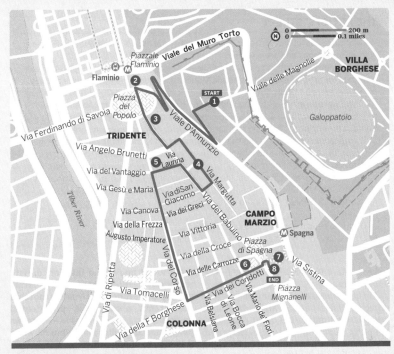

🏃 Neighbourhood Walk
Literary Footsteps

START PINCIO HILL GARDENS
END KEATS-SHELLEY HOUSE
LENGTH 1KM; TWO HOURS

This walk explores the literary haunts, both real and fictional, which speckle the lovely Tridente district.

Begin your walk in **1 Pincio Hill Gardens** (p118), where Henry James' Daisy Miller walked with Frederick Winterborne. Then make your way downhill to Piazza del Popolo, and visit the church of **2 Santa Maria del Popolo** (p114). Dan Brown's *Angels and Demons* made use of this remarkable church in its convoluted plot.

From here it's merely a few steps to **3 Hotel de Russie** (p259), favoured by the artistic avant garde in the early 20th century. Jean Cocteau stayed here with Picasso, and wrote a letter home in which he described plucking oranges from outside his window.

Running parallel to Via del Babuino is **4 Via Margutta** (p126). Famous for its artistic and cinematic connections, this picturesque cobbled street was where Truman Capote wrote his short story *Lola* about a raven who lived with him at his apartment. Fellini, Picasso, Stravinsky and Puccini all lived here at some point, and Gregory Peck's character in *Roman Holiday* had his apartment here.

Next make your way to Via del Corso, to see the **5 Casa di Goethe** (p121), where Goethe had a whale of a time from 1786 to 1788. Head down Via del Corso then turn left up into Via dei Condotti, stopping for some refreshment at **6 Caffè Greco** (p131), a former haunt of Casanova, Goethe, Keats, Byron and Shelley. Leaving here, you're almost at the **7 Spanish Steps** (p113), which Dickens described in his *Pictures from Italy* with some amusement, seeing the characterful artists' models waiting to be hired here. Just south of the steps is the apartments where Keats died of tuberculosis, aged just 25. The **8 Keats-Shelley House** (p119) is now a small museum devoted to the Romantic poets.

THE ARTISTS' STREET

Via Margutta has long been associated with art and artists, and today it is still lined with antique shops and art galleries.

'The street's reputation goes back to the 16th century, when it was declared a tax-free zone for artists,' explains Valentina Moncada, owner of the eponymous **gallery** at Via Margutta 54 (Map p364).

'If you were an artist and a resident, you paid no taxes, so artists came from all over Europe. Also, there was Villa Medici nearby and all the winners of the Prix de Rome (a prestigious French art scholarship) would often come down here.'

By the late 1800s, the studio that Valentina's family had established in the mid-19th century had grown into a popular meeting point for visiting artists, writers and musicians. Valentina notes 'A string of important musicians visited, including all the Italian opera greats – Puccini, Verdi, Mascagni – as well as the composers Wagner, Liszt and Debussy. The Italian futurists also held their first meetings here and in 1917 Picasso worked here; he met his wife, Olga, in the courtyard of number 54.'

Of the street's more recent residents, the most famous is film director Federico Fellini, who lived at number 110 with his wife Giulietta Masina until his death in 1993.

today, while still impressive, has the feel of a tourist trap.

Luxury hotels occupy many of the towering streetside *palazzi*, and waistcoated waiters stand on the tree-lined pavement, tempting passers-by into their overpriced restaurants. The huge building on the right as you walk up is the US embassy.

GAGOSIAN GALLERY   GALLERY
(Map p364; ☑06 4208 6498; www.gagosian.com; Via Francesco Crispi 16; ◉10.30am-7pm Tue-Sat; MBarberini) **FREE** Since it opened in 2007, the Rome branch of Larry Gagosian's contemporary art empire has hosted the big names of modern art: Cy Twombly, Damien Hirst and Lawrence Weiner, to name a few. The gallery is housed in a stylishly converted 1920s bank, and was designed by Roman architect Firouz Galdo and Englishman Caruso St John.

Always worth a look, exhibitions are housed in a dramatic, airy 750-sq-metre area and the building is fronted by a theatrical neoclassical colonnaded facade.

✖ EATING

Rome's designer shopping district may be fashionista heaven, but it retains a neighbourhood feel, albeit a particularly wealthy one. Lots of classy eateries are sandwiched between the boutiques.You have to take care choosing a restaurant around the Trevi Fountain, as there are a lot of unexciting just-for-tourists restaurants. But gems still sparkle among the stones, with some notable restaurants around the presidential palace and parliament – Italian politicians are a discerning bunch when it comes to dining out.

✖ Piazza del Popolo & Around

AL GRAN SASSO   TRATTORIA €
(Map p364; ☑06 321 48 83; www.trattoriaal-gransasso.com; Via di Ripetta 32; mains €13; ◉lunch & dinner Sun-Fri; MFlaminio) The perfect lunchtime spot, this is a classic, dyed-in-the-wool trattoria serving filling portions of old-school country cooking. It's a relaxed place with a welcoming vibe, garish murals on the walls (strangely, often a good sign) and tasty, value-for-money food. The fried dishes are especially good and there's fresh fish on Tuesdays and Fridays.

BUCCONE   WINE BAR €
(Map p364; ☑06 361 21 54; Via di Ripetta 19; meals €20; ◉12.30-2.30pm Mon-Sat; MFlaminio) Step in, under the faded gilt and mirrored sign, and you'll feel as though you've gone back in time. Once a coach house, then a tavern, this building became Buccone in the 1960s, furnished with 19th-century antiques and lined with around a thousand Italian wines. It's perfect for a light meal, with salads, cured meats, cheeses and *torta* (cakes).

PIZZA RÉ
PIZZERIA €€

(Map p364; ☑06 321 14 68; Via di Ripetta 14; pizzas €7-10; ☺noon-midnight; ⓜFlaminio) Part of a chain, but a good one, this popular pizzeria offers Neapolitan-style pizzas, with thick doughy bases and delicious, diverse toppings. The salads are fresh and the antipasti is great – try the fried things or the *mozzarella fresca di bufala e prosciutto San Daniele* (buffalo mozzarella with San Daniele dry-cured ham).

EDY
TRATTORIA €€

(Map p364; ☑06 3600 1738; Vicolo del Babuino 4; meals €45; ☺Mon-Sat; ⓜSpagna) This classy neighbourhood restaurant's high-ceilinged, intimate interior is peppered with paintings. Despite the tourist-central location, it caters to mainly Italian clientele; the food, such as *linguine al broccoletti*, is delicious. In nice weather there are a few tables outside on the cobbled street.

BUCA DI RIPETTA
TRADITIONAL ITALIAN €€

(Map p364; ☑06 321 93 91; Via di Ripetta 36; meals €45; ⓜFlaminio) Popular with actors and directors from the district, who know a good thing when they see it, this foodie destination offers robust Roman cuisine. Try the *zuppa rustica con crostini do pane aromatizzati* (country-style soup with rosemary-scented bread) or the *matolino do latte al forno alle erbe con patate* (baked suckling pork with potatoes) and you'll be fuelled either for more sightseeing or for a lie down.

MARGUTTA RISTORANTE
VEGETARIAN €€

(Map p364; ☑06 678 60 33; Via Margutta 118; meals €45; ☑; ⓜSpagna, Flaminio) Vegetarian restaurants in Rome are rarer than parking spaces, and this airy art gallery–restaurant is an unusually chic way to eat your greens. Dishes are excellent and most produce is organic, with offerings such as artichoke hearts with potato cubes and smoked provolone cheese. Best value is the Saturday and Sunday buffet brunch (€25).

There's an impressive wine list and staff are friendly and bilingual. It also offers a seven-course vegan menu (€50).

BABETTE
ITALIAN €€€

(Map p364; ☑06 321 15 59; Via Margutta 1; meals €55; ☺closed Jan & Aug; ☑; ⓜSpagna, Flaminio) Babette is run by two sisters who used to produce a fashion magazine, which accounts for its effortlessly chic *Fried Green Tomatoes*-style interior of exposed brick walls and vintage painted signs. You're in for a feast too, as the cooking is delicious, with a sophisticated, creative French twist (think *tortiglioni* with courgette and pistachio pesto).

The lunch buffet (€10 Tuesday to Friday, €25 weekends) is a good deal. There's seating out in the small, modern courtyard.

DAL BOLOGNESE
TRADITIONAL ITALIAN €€€

(Map p364; ☑06 361 14 26; Piazza del Popolo 1; meals €90; ☺Tue-Sun, closed Aug; ⓜFlaminio) The moneyed and models mingle at this historically chic restaurant. Dine inside, surrounded by wood panelling and exotic flowers, or outside, people-watching with views over Piazza del Popolo. As the name suggests, Emilia-Romagna dishes are the name of the game; everything is good, but try the tortellini in soup, tagliatelle with *ragú*, or the damn fine fillet steak.

✖ West of Via del Corso

★IL GELATO
GELATO €

(Map p364; Piazza Monte d'Oro 91; from €2; ☐Via del Corso) Claudio Torcè, the artisanal, all-

---

ROME'S OPTICAL ILLUSIONS

Aptly for such a theatrical city, Rome contains some magical visual tricks. Overlooking Piazza del Popolo, there are the seemingly twin churches: constructed to look identical while occupying different-sized sites. Then, there's Borromini's perspective-defying corridor at Palazzo Spada (p91), Andrea Pozzo's amazing trompe l'œil at the Chiesa di Sant'Ignazio di Loyola (p97) and the secret keyhole view from Piazza dei Cavalieri di Malta (p204). Strangest of all is the view of St Peter's dome from Via Piccolomini near Villa Doria Pamphilj (p188). Here the dome looms, filling the space at the end of the road, framed by trees. But the really curious thing is that as you move towards the cupola it seems to get smaller rather than larger as the view widens.

natural, superbly creative gelato maker, has revolutionised the ice-cream scene in Rome. Seek this place out to try out his glorious range of imaginative flavours. These range from eight different types of chocolate to more curious creations such as celery, wasabi, or gorgonzola with pear. You can ask to taste before committing to a whole cup/cone.

'GUSTO
RISTORANTE €

(Map p364; ☎06 322 62 73; Piazza Augusto Imperatore 9; pizzas €7-10; ⃞Via del Corso) Once a mould-breaking warehouse-style gastronomic complex – all exposed-brickwork and industrial chic – 'Gusto is still buzzing after all these years. It's a great place to sit on the terrace, but it's more about the atmosphere and location than the Neapolitan-style pizzas or the upmarket restaurant fare, which receives mixed reports. There are several more offshoots dotted around the square, including an *osteria/formaggeria* and cafe. Service can be slow.

✗ Piazza di Spagna & Around

PASTICCIO
FAST FOOD €

(Map p364; Via della Croce; pasta €4; ⃝1-3pm Mon-Sat; ⃝Spagna) A great find in this pricey 'hood, Pasticcio is a pasta shop that serves up two choices of pasta at lunch time. It's fast food, Italian style – fresh pasta with tasty sauces, with wine and water included. There's not much room so you'll have to nab a chair while you can and eat up quickly. This is better than taking away, however, as if you do, you'll miss out on your drink and your pasta will get cold.

GINA
CAFE €

(Map p364; ☎06 678 02 51; Via San Sebastianello 7a; snacks €10-15; ⃝11am-8pm; ⃝Spagna) Around the corner from the Spanish Steps, this is an ideal place to drop once you've shopped. Comfy white seats are strewn with powder-blue cushions, and it gets packed by a Prada-clad crowd, gossiping and flirting over sophisticated salads and perfect *panini*. You can also order a €40/60 regular/deluxe picnic-for-two to take up to Villa Borghese.

POMPI
DESSERTS €

(Map p364; Via della Croce 82) Rome's most famous vendor of tiramisu has opened a central Rome shop, so you no longer have to trek to its Re di Roma branch to sample the deliciously yolky yet light-as-air dessert. As well as classic, it comes in pistachio and strawberry flavours.

You can eat it on the spot or buy frozen portions that will keep for a few hours until you're ready to tuck into it. They also sell ice cream.

★PALATIUM
WINE BAR €€

(Map p364; ☎06 692 02 132; Via Frattina 94; meals €45; ⃝11am-11pm Mon-Sat, closed Aug; ⃞Via del Corso) A rich showcase of regional bounty, run by the Lazio Regional Food Authority, this sleek, ground-breaking wine bar serves excellent local specialities, such as *porchetta* (pork roasted with herbs), artisan cheese and delicious salami, as well as an impressive array of Lazio wines (try lesser-known drops such as Aleatico). *Aperitivo* is a good bet, too. One-course meals are priced at a tempting €14.

ANTICA ENOTECA
WINE BAR €€

(Map p364; ☎06 679 08 96; Via della Croce 76b; meals €45; ⃝noon-midnight; ⃝Spagna) Near the Spanish Steps, locals and tourists alike prop up the 19th-century wooden bar, or sit at outside tables or in the tastefully distressed interior, sampling wines by the glass, snacking on antipasti and ordering well-priced soul food such as seasonal soups, pasta and polenta.

DA PIETRO
OSTERIA €€

(Map p364; ☎06 320 88 16; http://hostariadapietro.com; Via Gesù e Maria 18; meals around €45; ⃝lunch & dinner Mon-Sat, closed Aug; ⃝Spagna) This is an appealing small Roman *osteria*, occupying several narrow rooms, with patterned tiled floors, arched exposed-stone ceilings, and cheery red tablecloths. Expect robust local cuisine, with dishes such as *saltimbocca alla romana* (veal with prosciutto and sage) or *melanzane alla parmigiana* (layered aubergine with tomato and ham).

FIASCHETTERIA BELTRAMME
TRATTORIA €€

(Map p364; Via della Croce 39; meals €45; ⃝Spagna) With a tiny, dark interior whose walls are covered in paintings and sketches right up to the high ceilings, Fiaschetteria (meaning 'wine-sellers') is a discreet, intimate, stuck-in-time place with a short menu and no telephone. Expect fashionistas with appetites digging into traditional Roman dishes (*pasta e ceci* and so on).

OTELLO ALLA CONCORDIA TRATTORIA €€
(Map p364; ☑06 679 11 78; Via della Croce 81; meals €45; ⊗12.30-3pm & 7.30-11pm Mon-Sat; ⓜSpagna) A perennial favourite with both tourists and locals, Otello is a haven near the Spanish Steps. Outside seating is in the vine-covered courtyard of an 18th-century *palazzo,* where, if you're lucky, you can dine in the shadow of the wisteria-covered pergola.

IL PALAZZETTO MODERN ITALIAN €€€
(Map p364; ☑06 699 341 000; Via del Bottino 8; meals €75; ⊗Tue-Sun, closed Aug; ⓜSpagna) Despite its sumptuous deep-red interior, this restaurant's spangling jewel is the sun-trap shaded terrace hidden at the top of the Spanish Steps. It's perfect for a glass of *prosecco* (sparkling wine) and a salad or pasta dish on a sunny day or, for more formal dining, there is a wow-factor tasting menu. The *palazzo* also houses a wine academy and it's open as a wine bar from 4pm.

NINO TUSCAN €€€
(Map p364; ☑06 679 56 76; Via Borgognona 11; meals €65; ⊗12.30-3pm & 7.30-11pm Mon-Sat; ⓜSpagna) With a look of wrought-iron chandeliers, polished dark wood and white tablecloths that has worked since it opened in 1934, Nino is enduringly popular with the rich and famous. Waiters can be brusque if you're not on the A-list, but the food is good hearty fare, including memorable steaks and Tuscan bean soup.

GINGER ORGANIC €€€
(Map p364; ☑06 9603 6390; www.ginger.roma.it; Via Borgognona 43-44; meals €50; ⊗10am-midnight; ⓜSpagna) 🍃 Perfecto for the ladies-who-lunch crowd, this chic, buzzy, white-tiled, high-ceilinged place feels a bit NYC and proffers all-day dining, with a focus on organic dishes including some unusual ingredients such as quinoa. There are salads, pricey gourmet sandwiches, pasta dishes, smoothies and shakes.

OSTERIA MARGUTTA TRATTORIA €€€
(Map p364; ☑06 323 10 25; www.osteriamargutta.it; Via Margutta 82; meals €70; ⊗12.30-3pm & 7.30-11pm Mon-Sat; ⓜSpagna) Theatrical Osteria Margutta is colourful inside and out: inside combines blue glass, rich reds and fringed lampshades, while outside it's flowers and ivy (snap up a terrace table in summer). Plaques on the chairs testify to the famous thespian bums they have supported. The menu combines classic and regional dishes; desserts are homemade and there's a top wine list.

✖ Trevi Fountain to the Quirinale

DA MICHELE PIZZERIA €
(Map p364; ☑349 2525347; Via dell'Umiltà 31; pizza slices from €3; ⊗8am-5pm Mon-Fri, to 8pm summer; 🚇Via del Corso) A handy address in the Spagna district: buy your fresh, light and crispy pizza *al taglio* (by the slice), and you'll have a delicious fast lunch. It's all kosher, so meat and cheese are not mixed.

ALICE PIZZA PIZZERIA €
(Map p364; www.alicepizza.it; Via San Basilio 56; pizza slices from €3; ⊗8am-3pm Mon-Sat) This hole-in-the-wall pizza *al taglio* place is busy with local workers, tempted in by an enticing range of toppings that proffer something outside the norm, with combinations that might include Emmental and courgette, or aubergine with chilli. There are a couple of seats inside, but they'll only serve as a brief perch.

ANTICO FORNO FAST FOOD €
(Map p364; ☑06 679 28 66; Via delle Muratte 8; panini €3.50; ⊗7am-9pm; 🚇Via del Tritone) A mini-supermarket opposite the Trevi Fountain, this busy place has a well-stocked deli counter where you can choose a filling for your freshly baked *panino* or *pizza bianca,* plus an impressive selection of focaccia and pizza.

BACCANO BRASSERIE €€
(Map p364; www.baccanoroma.com; Via delle Muratte 23; meals €45; ⊗8.30am-2am) This is one of a new breed of restaurant-cafe-bars that are open all day. It serves breakfasts (eggs Benedict, etc) if you're hankering after more than a coffee and *cornetto,* then lunch, dinner, burgers, club sandwiches, cocktails, *aperitivi* – you name it, they've got it covered. The look is polished wood, vintage Parisian glamour combined with 1990s NYC chic, ceilings are high and there are cosy booths to settle into.

VINERIA CHIANTI WINE BAR €€€
(Map p364; ☑06 678 75 50; Via del Lavatore 81-82; meals €55; ⊗12.30-3.30pm & 7-11.30pm; 🚇Via del Tritone) This pretty ivy-clad wine

bar is bottle-lined inside, with watch-the-world-go-by streetside seating in summer. Cuisine is Tuscan, so the beef is particularly good, but it also serves up imaginative salads and pizza in the evenings.

LE TAMERICI
SEAFOOD €€€

(Map p364; ☑06 6920 0700; Vicolo Scavolino 79; meals €75; ⊗7.30-11pm Mon-Sat, closed Aug; ☑Via del Tritone) Tucked-away Le Tamerici impresses with its wine list and range of *digestivi*, as well as with its classy food, including light-as-air homemade pasta. The two intimate rooms with bleached-wood beamed ceilings are a suitably discreet place to settle for an epicurean lunch.

Piazza Barberini & Via Veneto

IL CARUSO
GELATO €

(Via Collina 15; ⊗noon-9pm; ☑Termini) Spot Il Caruso by the gelato-licking hordes outside. This best-kept-secret artisanal gelateria only does a few strictly seasonal flavours, but they're created to perfection. Try the incredibly creamy pistachio. It also offers two types of *panna*: the usual whipped cream or the verging-on-sublime *zabaglione* (egg and marsala custard) combined with whipped cream.

SAN CRISPINO
GELATO €

(Map p364; ☑06 679 39 24; Via della Panetteria 42; ice cream from €2.30; ⊗noon-12.30am Mon, Wed, Thu & Sun, 11am-1.30am Fri & Sat; ☑Barberini) Once considered Rome's finest gelato, but there are now plenty more contenders for that artisanal crown. It's still worth tucking into, though service tends to be a bit po-faced and servings a little small. The delicate, strictly natural and seasonal flavours are served only in tubs (cups) – cones would detract from the taste.

★COLLINE EMILIANE
EMILIA-ROMAGNA €€

(Map p364; ☑06 481 75 38; Via degli Avignonesi 22; meals €45; ⊗12.45-2.45pm Tue-Sun & 7.30-10.45pm Tue-Sat, closed Aug; ☑Barberini) This welcoming restaurant just off Piazza Barberini flies the flag for Emilia-Romagna, the well-fed Italian province that has blessed the world with Parmesan, balsamic vinegar, bolognese sauce and Parma ham. This is a consistently excellent place to eat; there are delicious meats, homemade pasta

and rich *ragù*. Try to save room for dessert, too.

SANTOPADRE
ROMAN €€

(☑06 474 54 05; Via Collina 18; meals €45; ⊗dinner Mon-Sat; ☑Termini) Plastered with photos of horses and jockeys, this little neighbourhood restaurant is a local favourite that's been cooking up Roman faves such as *pasta alla gricia* (pasta with pancetta and onion), *involtini* (rolls of finely sliced beef) and *trippa alla romana* (Roman-style tripe) since 1946. The antipasti is delicious – think delicate marinated vegetables and melt-in-the-mouth meatballs.

AL MORO
ITALIAN €€€

(Map p364; ☑06 678 34 96; Vicolo delle Bollette 13; meals around €50; ⊗1-3.30pm & 8-11.30pm Mon-Sat; ☑Via del Corso) This one-time Fellini haunt feels like a step back in time with its picture-gallery dining rooms, Liberty wall lamps, cantankerous buttoned-up waiters and old-money regulars. Join faux royals for soothing classics like *cicoria al brodo* (chicory in broth) or melt-in-your-mouth veal liver with crusty sage and butter.

🍷 DRINKING & NIGHTLIFE

🍸 Piazza del Popolo & Around

LA SCENA
BAR

(Map p364; Via della Penna 22; ⊗noon-3am; ☑Flaminio) Part of the art deco Hotel Locarno, this bar has a lovely, faded Agatha Christie–era feel, and a greenery-shaded outdoor terrace bedecked in wrought-iron furniture. A glass of *prosecco* costs from €5.

STRAVINKIJ BAR – HOTEL DE RUSSIE
BAR

(Map p364; ☑06 328 88 70; Via del Babuino 9; ⊗9am-1am; ☑Flaminio) Can't afford to stay at the celeb-magnet Hotel de Russie? Then splash out on a drink at its swish bar. There are sofas inside, but best is a sunny drink in the courtyard, with sunshaded tables overlooked by terraced gardens. Impossibly romantic in the best *dolce vita* style, it's perfect for a cocktail (€20) and some posh snacks.

ROSATI CAFE

(Map p364; ☑06 322 58 59; Piazza del Popolo 5; ⏱7.30am-11.30pm; ⓂFlaminio) Rosati, over-looking the vast disc of Piazza del Popolo, was once the hang-out of the left-wing chattering classes. Authors Italo Calvino and Alberto Moravia used to drink here while their right-wing counterparts went to the **Canova** (Map p364; ☑06 361 22 31; Piazza del Popolo 16; ⏱8am-midnight) across the square. Today, tourists are the main clientele, and the views are as good as ever.

Piazza di Spagna & Around

CANOVA TADOLINI CAFE

(Map p364; ☑06 3211 0702; Via del Babuino 150a/b; ⏱9am-10.30pm Mon-Sat; ⓂSpagna) In 1818 sculptor Canova signed a contract for this studio that agreed it would be forever preserved for sculpture. The place is still stuffed with statues and it's a unique experience to sit among the great maquettes and sup an upmarket tea or knock back some wine and snacks.

CAFFÈ GRECO CAFE

(Map p364; ☑06 679 17 00; Via dei Condotti 86; ⏱9am-8pm; ⓂSpagna) Caffè Greco opened in 1760 and is still working the look: penguin waiters, red flock and age-spotted gilt mirrors. Casanova, Goethe, Wagner, Keats, Byron, Shelley and Baudelaire were all once regulars. Now there are fewer artists and lovers and more shoppers and tourists. Prices reflect this, unless you do as the locals do and have a drink at the bar.

CIAMPINI 2 CAFE

(Map p364; ☑06 6813 5108; Viale Trinità dei Monti; ⏱8am-9pm May-Oct; ⓂSpagna) Hidden away a short walk from the top of the Spanish Steps towards the Pincio Hill Gardens, this graceful cafe has a garden-party vibe, with green wooden latticework surrounding the outside tables. There are lovely views over the back-streets behind Spagna, and the ice cream is renowned (particularly the truffle).

Piazza Barberini & Via Veneto

MOMA CAFE

(Map p364; ☑06 4201 1798; Via di San Basilio; ⏱7am-11pm Mon-Sat, closed Aug; ⓂBarberini)

Molto trendy: this cafe-restaurant is a find. It's sleekly sexy and popular with workers from nearby offices. There's a small stand-up cafe downstairs, with a nice little deck outside where you can linger longer over coffee and delicious *dolcetti*. Upstairs is a recommended *cucina creativa* (creative cuisine) restaurant (meals €65).

☆ ENTERTAINMENT

GREGORY'S LIVE MUSIC

(Map p364; ☑06 679 63 86; www.gregorysjazz. com; Via Gregoriana 54d; ⏱7pm-2am Tue-Sun Sep-Jun; ⓂBarberini, Spagna) If Gregory's were a tone of voice, it'd be husky. Unwind in the downstairs bar, then unwind some more on squashy sofas upstairs to some slinky live jazz and swing, with quality local performers. Gregory's is a popular hang-out for local musicians.

TEATRO QUIRINO THEATRE

(Map p364; ☑06 679 45 85; www.teatroquirino. it; Via delle Vergini 7; 🚇Via del Tritone) Within splashing distance of the Trevi Fountain, this grand 19th-century theatre produces the odd new work and a stream of well-known classics – expect to see works (in Italian) by Arthur Miller, Tennessee Williams, Shakespeare, Seneca and Luigi Pirandello.

TEATRO SISTINA THEATRE

(Map p364; ☑06 420 07 11; www.ilsistina.com; Via Sistina 129; ⓂBarberini) Big-budget theatre spectaculars, musicals, concerts and comic star turns are the staples of the Sistina's ever-conservative, ever-popular repertoire.

SHOPPING

Piazza del Popolo & Around

BOTTEGA DI MARMORARO ARTISANAL

(Map p364; Via Margutta 53b; ⓂFlaminio) A particularly charismatic hole-in-the-wall shop lined with marble carvings, where you can get marble tablets engraved with any inscription you like (€15). Peer inside at lunchtime and you might see the *marmoraro* cooking a pot of tripe for his lunch on the open log fire.

TRIDENTE, TREVI & THE QUIRINALE ENTERTAINMENT

DANIELLE SHOES

(Map p364; ☑06 679 24 67; Via Frattina 85a; ⓂSpagna) If you're female and in need of an Italian shoe fix, this is an essential stop on your itinerary. It sells both classic and fashionable styles – foxy heels, boots and ballet pumps – at extremely reasonable prices. Shoes are soft leather and come in myriad colours.

ARMANDO RIODA ARTISANAL

(Map p364; Via Belsiana 90; ⊙9am-1pm & 4-8pm Mon-Sat; ⓂSpagna) Climb the well-worn stairs to this workshop, show them your design, choose from the softest leathers and you will shortly be the proud owner of a handmade, designer-style bag, wallet, belt or briefcase. Bags cost €200 to €250 and take around a week to make. Don't rely on them posting overseas; readers have found this a frustrating experience.

FABRIANO ARTS & CRAFTS

(Map p364; ☑06 3260 0361; www.fabrianoboutique.com; Via del Babuino 173; ⊙10am-8pm; ⓂFlaminio, Spagna) Fabriano makes stationery sexy, with deeply desirable leather-bound diaries, funky notebooks and products embossed with street maps of Rome. It's perfect for picking up a gift, with other items including beautifully made leather key rings (€10) and quirky paper jewellery by local designers.

BARRILÀ BOUTIQUE SHOES

(Map p364; Via del Babuino 34; ⊙10am-8pm; ⓂFlaminio, Spagna) For classic, handmade Italian women's shoes that won't crack the credit card, head to Barrilà. This boutique stocks myriad styles in soft leather. From the window they all look a bit traditional, but you're bound to find something you'll like in the jam-packed interior.

ALINARI ANTIQUES, BOOKS

(Map p364; ☑06 679 29 23; Via Alibert 16; ⓂSpagna) This is the oldest photographic business in the world. The Florentine Alinari brothers founded their enterprise in 1852 and produced more than a million plate-glass negatives in their lifetimes. At their Rome shop you can buy beautiful prints of their work depicting the city in the 19th century, as well as some meaty coffee-table books on photography.

ANIMALIER E OLTRE ANTIQUES

(Map p364; ☑06 320 82 82; Via Margutta 47; ⓂSpagna) This basement appears to be full

SPAS IN ROME

The admission charge of €45 is a bargain when you consider that the glamorous and gorgeous day spa **Hotel de Russie Wellness Zone** (Map p364; ☑06 3288 8820; www.hotelderussie.it; Via del Babuino 9; ⊙7am-10pm; ⓂFlaminio) is not only in one of Rome's best hotels, but that there is also the exceedingly remote possibility of bumping into Brad Pitt in the Turkish bath, sauna or gym. Treatments are also available, including shiatsu and deep-tissue massage; a 50-minute massage costs around €95.

of the cast-offs of an eccentric, aristocratic family, with bric-a-brac, curios, antiques and unique furniture. Wrought-iron furniture and leather sofas sit alongside a selection of animal-shaped antiques that includes reproductions of 19th-century French *animalier* sculptures.

DISCOUNT DELL'ALTA MODA CLOTHING

(Map p364; ☑06 361 37 96; Via Gesù e Maria 14; ⓂFlaminio, Spagna) Discount dell'Alta Moda sells big names, such as Dolce & Gabbana and Gucci, at knock-down prices (around 50% off). It's well worth a rummage.

🏠 West of Via del Corso

MERCATO DELLE STAMPE MARKET

(Map p364; Largo della Fontanella di Borghese; ⊙7am-1pm Mon-Sat; 🚌Piazza Augusto Imperatore) The Mercato delle Stampe (Print Market) is well worth a look if you're a fan of vintage books and old prints. Squirrel through the permanent stalls and among the tired posters and dusty back editions, and you might turn up some interesting music scores, architectural engravings or chromolithographs of Rome.

L'OLFATTORIO PERFUME

(Map p364; ☑06 361 23 25; Via di Ripetta 34; ⊙10.30am-7.30pm Mon-Sat; ⓂFlaminio) This is like an *enoteca* (wine bar), but with perfume instead of drinks: scents are concocted by names such as Artisan Parfumeur, Diptyque, Les Parfums de Rosine and Coudray. The assistants will guide you through different combinations of scents to work out your ideal fragrance. Exclusive perfumes are available to buy. Smellings are free but you should book ahead.

TOD'S   SHOES
(Map p364; ☎06 6821 0066; Via della Fontanella di Borghese 56; Ⓜ Via del Corso) Tod's trademark is its rubber-studded loafers (the idea was to reduce those pesky driving scuffs), perfect weekend footwear for kicking back at your country estate.

🏠 Piazza di Spagna & Around

VERTECCHI ART   ART
(Map p364; Via della Croce 70; ☺3.30-7.30pm Mon, 10am-7.30pm Tue-Sat; Ⓜ Spagna) Ideal for last-minute gift buying, this large paperware and art shop has beautiful printed paper, cards and envelopes that will inspire you to bring back the art of letter writing, plus an amazing choice of notebooks, art stuff and trinkets.

LUCIA ODESCALCHI   JEWELLERY
(Map p364; ☎06 6992 5506; Piazza Santissimi Apostoli 81, Palazzo Odescalchi; Ⓜ Spagna) If you're looking for a unique piece of statement jewellery that will make an outfit, this is the place to head. Housed in the evocative archives of the family *palazzo*, the avant-garde pieces often have an almost medieval beauty, and run from incredible polished steel and chain mail to pieces created out of pearls and fossils. Beautiful. Prices start at around €140.

ARTIGIANI PELLETTIERI –
MARCO PELLE/DI CLEMENTE   ARTISANAL
(Map p364; ☎06 361 34 02; Via Vittoria 15, int 2; Ⓜ Spagna) Ring the bell at this unassuming doorway and hurry up flights of stairs to a family-run leather workshop that feels like it hasn't changed for decades. The elderly artisans create belts (€70 to €100), watch straps (€40 to €90), bags, picture frames, travel cases and other elegant stuff. You can take along a buckle or watch to which you want a belt or strap fitted.

C.U.C.I.N.A.   KITCHENWARE
(Map p364; ☎06 679 12 75; Via Mario de' Fiori 65; Ⓜ Spagna) If you need a foodie gadget, C.U.C.I.N.A. is the place. Make your own *cucina* (kitchen) look the part with the designerware from this famous shop, with myriad devices you'll decide you simply must have, from jelly moulds to garlic presses.

ELEONORA   CLOTHING
(Map p364; ☎06 6919 0554; Via del Babuino 97; ☺10am-7.30pm Mon-Sat, 11am-7.30pm Sun; Ⓜ Spagna) The brash exterior disguises a Tridente hot spot; venture into this Tardis-like shop and you'll find that its finger is on the pulse, with a very classy selection of designers, including Dolce & Gabbana, Fendi, Missoni, Marc Jacobs and Sergio Rossi.

FURLA   ACCESSORIES
(Map p364; ☎06 6920 0363; Piazza di Spagna 22; ☺10am-8pm Mon-Sat, 10.30am-8pm Sun; Ⓜ Spagna) Simple, good-quality bags in soft leather and a brilliant array of colours is why the handbagging hordes keep flocking to Furla, where all sorts of accessories, from sunglasses to shoes, are made. There are many other branches dotted across Rome.

SERMONETA   ACCESSORIES
(Map p364; ☎06 679 19 60; Piazza di Spagna 61; Ⓜ Spagna) Buying leather gloves in Rome is a rite of passage for some, and its most famous glove-seller is the place to do it. Choose from a kaleidoscopic range of quality leather and suede gloves lined with silk and cashmere. An expert assistant will size up your hand in a glance. Just don't expect them to crack a smile.

ANGLO-AMERICAN
BOOKSHOP   BOOKS
(Map p364; ☎06 679 52 22; Via della Vite 102; Ⓜ Spagna) Particularly good for university reference books, the Anglo-American is well stocked and well known. It has an excellent range of literature, travel guides, children's books and maps, and if it hasn't got the book you want, the staff will order it for you.

BATTISTONI   CLOTHING
(Map p364; www.battistoni.com; Via dei Condotti 60; ☺3-7pm Mon, 10am-7pm Tue-Sat; Ⓜ Spagna) Battistoni has been a Roman institution since 1946 and offers the ultimate classic Italian tailoring, incredibly elegant and exquisitely cut (off the peg, but the shop tailors to fit). The beautiful store looks onto a courtyard and is adorned with paintings and photographs of immaculate Battistoni-clad celebs, from Bill Clinton to Richard Gere. A men's suit costs a heart-racing €1600.

TRIDENTE, TREVI & THE QUIRINALE SHOPPING

LOCAL KNOWLEDGE

BIG HAIR

For a touch of Italian va va voom, Roman ladies know where to go: **Sergio Valente** (Map p364; 06 6477 0041; www.sergiovalente.it; 2nd floor, Via del Babuino 107; Mon-Sat; Spagna), who has tended the hair of the likes of Sophia Loren. His family-run, 2nd-floor salon is adorned with photos of Sr Valente with Valentino, Helen Mirren and Pope John Paul (not sure whether he had a blow dry), and you're greeted by two pristine poodles. It's less expensive than you might expect: €27 for a for a blow dry, €20 to €25 for a manicure and €30 to €40 for a pedicure.

FENDI CLOTHING

(Map p364; 06 69 66 61; Largo Goldoni 420; 10am-7.30pm Mon-Sat, 11am-2pm & 3-7pm Sun; Spagna) A temple to subtly blinging accessories, this multistorey art deco building is the Fendi mothership: this is the global headquarters, as the brand was born in Rome. Fendi is particularly famous for its products made of leather and (more controversially) fur.

FOCACCI FOOD

(Map p364; 06 679 12 28; Via della Croce 43; 8am-8pm Mon-Fri, 8am-3pm Sat; Spagna) One of several smashing delis along this pretty street, this is the place to buy cheese, cold cuts, smoked fish, caviar, pasta, olive oil and wine.

FRATELLI FABBI FOOD

(Map p364; 06 679 06 12; Via della Croce 27; 8am-7.30pm Mon-Sat; Spagna) A small but flavour-packed delicatessen, this is a good place to pick up all sorts of Italian delicacies – fine cured meats, buffalo mozzarella from Campania, *parmigiano reggiano*, olive oil, *porchetta* from Ariccia – as well as Iranian caviar.

BULGARI JEWELLERY

(Map p364; 06 679 38 76; Via dei Condotti 10; 10am-5pm Tue-Sat, 11am-7pm Sun & Mon; Spagna) If you have to ask the price, you can't afford it. Sumptuous window displays mean you can admire the world's finest jewellery without spending a *centesimo*.

FAUSTO SANTINI SHOES

(Map p364; 06 678 41 14; Via Frattina 120; 11am-7.30pm Mon, 10am-7.30pm Tue-Sat, 11am-2pm & 3-7pm Sun; Spagna) Rome's best-known shoe designer, Fausto Santini is famous for his beguilingly simple, architectural shoe designs, with beautiful boots and shoes made from butter-soft leather. Colours are beautiful, the quality impeccable. Seek out the end-of-line discount shop (p178) if this looks out of your price range.

Trevi Fountain to the Quirinale

VIGANO ACCESSORIES

(Map p364; 06 679 51 47; Via Marco Minghetti; Via del Corso) Piled high with head candy, Vigano opened in 1873 and sells top hats, bowlers and deerstalkers, as well as hacking jackets, to a princely clientele, as if nothing much has changed since it first opened its doors. The hours are quintessentially Roman, too – they open when they feel like it.

LIBRERIA GIUNTI AL PUNTO BOOKS

(Map p364; 06 6994 1045; www.giuntialpunto.it; Piazza dei Santissimi Apostoli 59-65; 9.30am-7.30pm Mon-Sat; Piazza Venezia) The 'Straight to the Point' children's bookshop is an ideal place to distract your kids. Large, colourful and well stocked, it has thousands of titles in Italian and a selection of books in French, Spanish, German and English, as well as a good range of toys, from Play-Doh to puzzles.

LA RINASCENTE DEPARTMENT STORE

(Map p364; 06 679 76 91; Galleria Alberto Sordi, Piazza Colonna; 10am-9pm; Via del Corso) La Rinascente is a stately, upmarket department store, with a particularly buzzing cosmetics department, all amid art nouveau interiors.

GALLERIA ALBERTO SORDI SHOPPING CENTRE

(Map p364; Piazza Colonna; 10am-10pm; Via del Corso) This elegant stained-glass arcade appeared in Alberto Sordi's 1973 classic, *Polvere di Stelle*, and has since been renamed for Rome's favourite actor, who died in 2003. It's a serene place to browse stores such as Zara and Feltrinelli, and there's an airy cafe ideal for a quick coffee break.

⌂ Piazza Barberini & Via Veneto

UNDERGROUND   MARKET

(Map p364; ☏06 3600 5345; Via Francesco Crispi 96, Ludovisi underground car park; ☉3-8pm Sat & 10.30am-7.30pm Sun, 2nd weekend of the month Sep-Jun; ⓜBarberini) Monthly market held underground in a car park near Villa Borghese. There are more than 150 stalls selling everything from antiques and collectables to clothes and toys.

Vatican City, Borgo & Prati

VATICAN CITY | BORGO | PRATI | AURELIO

Neighbourhood Top Five

1 Gazing heavenwards at Michelangelo's cinematic ceiling frescoes in the **Sistine Chapel** (p143). See God pointing his finger at Adam and pinch yourself that you're looking at the original painting, not a dime-a-dozen poster copy.

2 Being blown away by the super-sized opulence of **St Peter's Basilica** (p138).

3 Trying to line up the columns on **St Peter's Square** (p154) – it is possible.

4 Revelling in the wonderful rooftop views from **Castel Sant'Angelo** (p154).

5 Marvelling at the vibrant colours of the fabulously frescoed **Stanze di Raffaello** (p143).

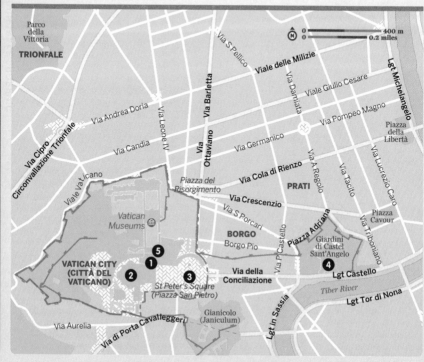

For more detail of this area, see Map p368 ➡

Explore: Vatican City, Borgo & Prati

The Vatican, the world's smallest sovereign state (a mere 0.44 sq km), is a few hundred metres west of the Tiber. Centred on the domed bulk of St Peter's Basilica, it boasts some of Italy's most celebrated masterpieces, many housed in the vast Vatican Museums.

You will need at least a morning to do justice to the Vatican Museums. The highlight here is the Michelangelo-decorated Sistine Chapel, but there's enough art on display to keep you busy for years. If you're with a tour guide, or if you can join a tour group, you can pass directly from the Sistine Chapel through to St Peter's Basilica; otherwise you'll have to walk around and approach from St Peter's Square, itself one of the Vatican's most dramatic sights. Once finished in the basilica, you'll probably be ready for a break. There are few good eating options in the Vatican itself, but the graceful residential district of Prati is full of excellent trattorias, takeaways and restaurants.

Between the Vatican and the river lies the cobbled, medieval district of the Borgo. The big sight here is Castel Sant'Angelo, the big drum-shaped castle overlooking the river.

Local Life

→ **Fast Food** Rather than having a full-length midday meal, local office workers tend to grab a snack from the many excellent takeaways in Prati. Join them and lunch on *pizza al taglio* (pizza by the slice) and gelato.

→ **Shopping Strips** Spearing off Piazza del Risorgimento, Via Cola di Rienzo is lined with busy department stores.

→ **Live Music** Join the locals for sweet melodies at Alexanderplatz (p158), Rome's top jazz joint. Another favourite venue is the basement pub Fonclea (p158).

Getting There & Away

→ **Bus** From Termini, bus 40 is the quickest bus to the Vatican – it'll drop you off near Castel Sant'Angelo. You can also take bus 64, which runs a similar route but stops more often. Bus 492 runs to Piazza del Risorgimento from Stazione Tiburtina, passing through Piazza Barberini and the *centro storico* (historic centre).

→ **Metro** Take metro line A to Ottaviano–San Pietro. From the station, signs direct you to St Peter's.

Lonely Planet's Top Tip

Be wary of the touts around Ottaviano metro station selling queue-jumping tours of the Vatican Museums. Many of these are not authorised and the tours they offer cost more than those sold by the museums' online ticket office or by the Vatican-sponsored Roma Cristiana (www.operaro-manapellegrinaggi.org).

Note that if you want to attend Easter or Christmas mass at St Peter's you have to book tickets through the Prefettura della Casa Pontificia (www.vatican.va).

 Best Places to Eat

→ Fatamorgana (p155)

→ Pizzarium (p157)

→ Romeo (p156)

→ Osteria dell'Angelo (p156)

→ Ristorante L'Arcangelo (p157)

For reviews, see p155 →

Best Places to Drink

→ Alexanderplatz (p158)

→ Passaguai (p157)

→ Art Studio Café (p157)

→ Fonclea (p158)

For reviews, see p157 →

 Best Overground & Underground

→ Dome of St Peter's Basilica (p138)

→ Terrace of Castel Sant'Angelo (p154)

→ St Peter's tomb (p142)

→ Vatican Grottoes (p138)

For reviews, see p138 →

VATICAN CITY, BORGO & PRATI

TOP SIGHT
ST PETER'S BASILICA

In a city of outstanding churches, none can hold a candle to St Peter's Basilica (Basilica di San Pietro), Italy's largest, richest and most spectacular church. A monument to centuries of artistic genius, it contains some magnificent works of art, including three of Italy's most celebrated masterpieces: Michelangelo's *Pietà*, his breathtaking dome and Bernini's *baldachin* (canopy) over the papal altar.

Note that the basilica gets very busy so expect queues in peak periods. Also, strict dress codes are enforced: no shorts, miniskirts or bare shoulders.

DON'T MISS...

➡ *Pietà*
➡ Statue of St Peter
➡ The dome
➡ The baldachin
➡ Cattedra di San Pietro
➡ Vatican Grottoes

PRACTICALITIES

➡ Map p368
➡ www.vatican.va
➡ St Peter's Square
➡ ⊙7am-7pm Apr-Sep, to 6.30pm Oct-Mar
➡ ⓂOttaviano–San Pietro

History

The original St Peter's – which lies beneath the current basilica – was commissioned by the emperor Constantine and built around 349 on the site where St Peter is said to have been buried. But like many medieval churches, it eventually fell into disrepair and it wasn't until the mid-15th century that efforts were made to restore it, first by Pope Nicholas V and then, rather more successfully, by Julius II. In 1506 Bramante came up with a design for a basilica based on a Greek-cross plan, with four equal arms and a huge central dome. It was an audacious plan and when building eventually began, Bramante attracted fierce criticism for destroying the old basilica and many of its Byzantine mosaics and frescoes.

On Bramante's death in 1514, construction work ground to a halt as architects, including Raphael and Antonio da Sangallo, tried to modify his original plans. But little progress was made and it wasn't until Michelangelo took over in 1547 at the age of 72 that the situation changed. Michelangelo simplified Bramante's plans and drew up designs for what was to become his greatest architectural achievement, the dome. He never lived to see it built, though, and it was left to Giacomo della Porta and Domenico Fontana to finish it in 1590.

With the dome in place, Carlo Maderno inherited the project in 1605. He designed the monumental facade and lengthened the nave towards the piazza.

The Facade

Built between 1608 and 1612, Carlo Maderno's immense facade is 48m high and 118.6m wide. Eight 27m-high columns support the upper attic on which 13 statues stand, representing Christ the Redeemer, St John the Baptist and the 11 apostles. The central balcony is known as the **Loggia della Benedizione**, and it's from here that the pope delivers his *Urbi et Orbi* blessing at Christmas and Easter.

Behind the facade is the grand atrium, through which you pass to enter the basilica. Note the first door on the right, the **Porta Santa** (Holy Door), which is opened only in Jubilee Years.

Interior – Right Nave

At the beginning of the right aisle, Michelangelo's hauntingly beautiful **Pietà** sits in its own chapel behind a panel of bullet-proof glass. Sculpted when the artist was a little-known 25-year-old (in 1499), it's the only work he ever signed – his signature is etched into the sash across the Madonna's breast.

Nearby, the **red porphyry disk** on the floor inside the main door marks the spot where Charlemagne and later Holy Roman emperors were crowned by the pope.

Paying tribute to a woman whose reputation was far from holy, Carlo Fontana's gilt and bronze **monument to Queen Christina of Sweden** is dedicated to the Swedish monarch who converted to Catholicism in 1655. You'll see it on a pillar just beyond the *Pietà*.

Moving down the aisle you come to the **Cappella di San Sebastiano**, home of Pope John Paul II's tomb, and the **Cappella del Santissimo Sacramento**, a small chapel decorated in sumptuous baroque style. The iron grille was designed by Borromini; the gilt bronze ciborium above the altar is by Bernini; and the altarpiece, *The Trinity,* is by Pietro da Cortona.

Just beyond the chapel, the grandiose **monument to Gregory XIII** sits near the **Cappella Gregoriana**, built by Gregory XIII from designs by Michelangelo. The outstanding work here is the 12th-century fresco of the *Madonna del Soccorso* (Madonna of Succour), which was moved from the original basilica in 1578.

Much of the right-hand transept is roped off but from outside you can still see the **monument to Clement XIII**, one of Antonio Canova's most famous works.

CHRISTINA, QUEEN OF SWEDEN

Famously portrayed by Greta Garbo in the 1933 film *Queen Christina*, the Swedish monarch is one of just three women buried in St Peter's Basilica – the other two are Queen Charlotte of Cyprus, a minor 15th-century royal, and Agnesina Colonna, a 16th-century Italian aristocrat. Christina earned her place by abdicating the Swedish throne and converting to Catholicism in 1655. As Europe's most high-profile convert, she became a Vatican favourite and spent much of her later life in Rome, where she enjoyed fame as a brilliant patron of the arts. Her active private life was the subject of much salacious gossip, and rumours abounded of affairs with courtiers and acquaintances of both sexes.

Free English-language tours of the basilica are run from the Centro Servizi Pellegrini e Turisti, at 9.45am on Tuesday and Thursday and at 2.15pm every afternoon between Monday and Friday.

ST PETER'S BASILICA

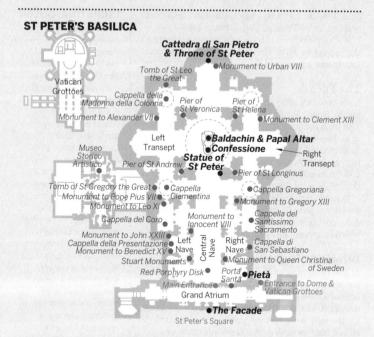

Interior – Central Nave

Dominating the centre of the basilica is Bernini's 29m-high **baldachin**. Supported by four spiral columns and made with bronze taken from the Pantheon, it stands over the papal altar, also known as the Altar of the Confession, which itself sits on the site of St Peter's grave. The pope is the only priest permitted to serve at the high altar. In front, the elaborate **Confessione**, built by Carlo Maderno, is where St Peter was originally buried.

Above the baldachin, Michelangelo's **dome** rises to a height of 119m. Based on Brunelleschi's cupola in Florence, this towering masterpiece is supported by four stone **piers** that rise around the papal altar. They are named after the saints whose statues adorn their Bernini-designed niches – Longinus, Helena, Veronica and Andrew – and decorated with reliefs depicting the *Reliquie Maggiori* (Major Relics): the lance of St Longinus, which he used to pierce Christ's side; the cloth of St Veronica, which bears a miraculous image of Christ; and a piece of the True Cross, collected by St Helena.

At the base of the **Pier of St Longinus**, to the right as you face the papal altar, is a much-loved bronze **statue of St Peter**, whose right foot has been worn down by centuries of caresses. It is believed to be a 13th-century work by Arnolfo di Cambio. On the Feast Day of St Peter and St Paul (29 June), the statue is dressed in papal robes.

Behind the altar in the tribune at the end of the basilica, the **throne of St Peter** (1665) is the centrepiece of Bernini's extraordinary **Cattedra di San Pietro**. In the middle of the elaborate gilded-bronze throne, supported by statues of Sts Augustine, Ambrose, Athanasius and John Chrysostom, is a wooden seat, which was once thought to have been St Peter's but in fact dates to the 9th century. Above, rays of yellow light shine through a gaudy window, framed by a gilded

The baldachin in St Peter's Basilica

mass of golden angels and in whose central pane flies a dove (representing the Holy Spirit).

To the right of the throne, Bernini's **monument to Urban VIII** depicts the pope flanked by the figures of Charity and Justice.

Interior – Left Nave

In the roped-off left transept behind the **Pier of St Veronica**, the **Cappella della Madonna della Colonna** takes its name from the image of the Madonna that once adorned the old basilica but now stares out from Giacomo della Porta's marble altar. To its right, above the **tomb of St Leo the Great**, is a particularly fine relief by the baroque sculptor Alessandro Algardi. Opposite it, under the next arch, is Bernini's last work in the basilica, the **monument to Alexander VII**.

About halfway down the left aisle, the cupola of the **Cappella Clementina** is named after Clement VIII (d 1605), who had Giacomo della Porta decorate it for the Jubilee of 1600. Beneath the altar is the **tomb of St Gregory the Great** and, above it, a mosaic representing the *Miracolo di San Giorgio* (Miracle of St George), inspired by a work of Andrea Sacchi. To the left is a classical **monument to Pope Pius VII** by Thorvaldsen.

In the next arch, Alessandro Algardi's 16th-century **monument to Leo XI** depicts the bearded Medici pope seemingly weighed down by the weight of the job. Beyond it, the richly decorated **Cappella del Coro** was created by Giovanni Battista Ricci to

Contrary to popular opinion, St Peter's Basilica is not the world's largest church – the Basilica of Our Lady of Peace in Yamoussoukro on the Ivory Coast is bigger. Bronze floor plates in the central aisle indicate the respective sizes of the 14 next-largest churches.

designs by Giacomo della Porta; Bernini designed the elegant choir stalls. The **monument to Innocent VIII** by Antonio Pollaiuolo (in the next aisle arch) is a recreation of a monument from the old basilica.

Continuing back towards the front of the basilica, the **Cappella della Presentazione** contains two of St Peter's most modern works: a black relief **monument to John XXIII** by Emilio Greco, and a **monument to Benedict XV** by Pietro Canonica. Under the next arch are the so-called **Stuart monuments**. On the right is the monument to Clementina Sobieska, wife of James Stuart, by Filippo Barigioni, and on the left is Canova's vaguely erotic monument to the last three members of the Stuart clan, the pretenders to the English throne who died in exile in Rome.

Dome

To climb the dome look for the entrance to the right of the basilica. You can walk the 551 steps to the top or take a small lift halfway up and then follow on foot for the last 320 steps. Either way, it's a steep, long, narrow climb that's not recommended for sufferers of claustrophobia or vertigo. Make it to the top, though, and you're rewarded with stunning rooftop views from a lofty perch 120m above St Peter's Square.

Museo Storico Artistico

Accessed from halfway down the left nave, the **Museo Storico Artistico** (Treasury of St Peter's; adult/reduced €6/4; ⊘8am-7pm Apr-Sep, 8am-6.15pm Oct-Mar) sparkles with sacred relics and priceless artefacts. Highlights include a tabernacle by Donatello; the Colonna Santa, a 4th-century Byzantine column from the earlier church; the 6th-century Crux Vaticana (Vatican Cross), a jewel-encrusted crucifix presented by the emperor Justinian II to the original basilica; and the massive 15th-century bronze tomb of Sixtus IV by Pollaiuolo.

Tomb of St Peter

Excavations beneath the basilica have uncovered part of the original church and what archaeologists believe is the **tomb of St Peter** (admission €13, over 15s only; ⊘by reservation only). In 1942, the bones of an elderly, well-built man were found in a box hidden behind a wall covered by pilgrims' graffiti. After more than 30 years of forensic examination, in 1976, Pope Paul VI declared the bones to be those of St Peter.

The excavations can be visited only on a 90-minute guided tour. To book a spot email your request to the **Ufficio Scavi** (scavi@fsp.va) as far in advance as possible.

Vatican Grottoes

Extending beneath the basilica, the **Vatican Grottoes** (admission free; ⊘8am-6pm Apr-Sep, 8am-5.30pm Oct-Mar) were created during the construction of the current basilica in the late 16th century as a burial place for popes. You'll see the tombs and sarcophagi of many popes as well as several huge columns from the original 4th-century basilica.

RUSSELL MOUNTFORD / GETTY IMAGES ©

TOP SIGHT
VATICAN MUSEUMS

Visiting the Vatican Museums is a thrilling and unforgettable experience. With some 7km of exhibitions and more masterpieces than many small countries, this vast museum complex, housed in the 5.5-hectare Palazzo Apostolico Vaticano, contains one of the world's greatest art collections. You'll never manage to cover the whole collection in one go – it's said that if you spent one minute on every exhibit it would take you 12 years to see everything – so it pays to be selective.

Vatican Library

Founded by Nicholas V in 1450, the Biblioteca Apostolica Vaticana contains more than 1.5 million volumes, including illuminated manuscripts, early printed books, prints and drawings.

Pinacoteca

Often overlooked by visitors, the papal picture gallery was founded by Pope Pius XI in 1932. Its collection comprises 460 paintings dating from the 11th to 19th centuries, with works by Giotto, Fra Angelico, Filippo Lippi, Guido Reni, Guercino, Nicholas Poussin, Van Dyck and Pietro da Cortona.

Look out for Raphael's *Madonna di Foligno* (Madonna of Folignano) and his last painting, *La Trasfigurazione* (Transfiguration), which was completed by his students after he died in 1520. Other highlights include Giotto's *Polittico Stefaneschi* (Stefaneschi Triptych), Giovanni Bellini's *Pietà*, Leonardo da Vinci's unfinished *San Gerolamo* (St Jerome) and Caravaggio's *Deposizione* (Deposition from the Cross).

DON'T MISS...

→ Sistine Chapel
→ Stanze di Raffaello
→ Apollo Belvedere and Laocoön, Museo Pio-Clementino
→ *La Trasfigurazione*, Pinacoteca

PRACTICALITIES

→ Map p368
→ ☎06 6988 4676
→ http://mv.vatican.va
→ Viale Vaticano
→ adult/reduced €16/8, admission free last Sun of month
→ ⊙9am-6pm Mon-Sat, last admission 4pm, 9am-2pm last Sun of month, last admission 12.30pm
→ Ⓜ Ottaviano–San Pietro

continued on p150

Museum Tour
Vatican Museums

Follow this tour to see the museums' greatest hits, culminating in the Sistine Chapel. Once you've passed through the entrance complex, head up the escalator. At the top, nip out to the terrace for views over St Peter's dome and the Vatican Gardens. Re-enter and go into the **1 Cortile della Pigna**, named after the huge Augustan-era bronze pine cone. Cross the courtyard and enter the long corridor that is the **2 Museo Chiaramonti**. Continue left, up the stairs, to the Museo Pio-Clementino, home of the Vatican's finest classical statuary. Follow the flow of people through to the **3 Cortile Ottagono** (Octagonal Courtyard), where you'll find two celebrated masterpieces: the Laocoön and Apollo Belvedere. Continue on through a series of rooms, each more impressive than the last – the **4 Sala degli Animali** (Animal Room), the **5 Sala delle Muse** (Room of the Muses), famous for the Torso

Belvedere, and the **6 Sala Rotonda** (Round Room), centred on a vast red basin. From the **7 Sala Croce Greca** (Greek Cross Room), stairs lead up to the **8 Galleria dei Candelabri** (Gallery of the Candelabra), the first of three galleries along a lengthy corridor. Then you are funnelled through the **9 Galleria degli Arazzi** (Tapestry Gallery) and onto the **10 Galleria delle Carte Geografiche** (Map Gallery), a 120m-long hall hung with huge topographical maps. At the end of the corridor, carry on through the **11 Sala Sobieski** to the **12 Sala di Costantino**, the first of the four Stanze di Raffaello (Raphael Rooms). The others are the **13 Stanza d'Eliodoro**, the **14 Stanza della Segnatura**, featuring Raphael's superlative *La Scuola di Atene*, and the **15 Stanza dell'Incendio di Borgo**. Anywhere else these magnificent frescoed chambers would be the star attraction, but here they're the warm-up for the grand finale, the **16 Sistine Chapel**.

VATICAN MUSEUMS

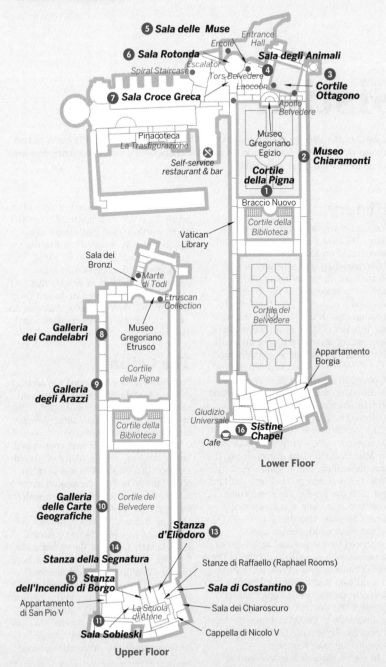

5 *Sala delle Muse*

Ercole

Entrance Hall

6 *Sala Rotonda*

Escalator

Spiral Staircase

Tors Belvedere

Sala degli Animali **4**

Laocoön

3

7 *Sala Croce Greca*

Cortile Ottagono

Apollo Belvedere

Pinacoteca La Trasfigurazione

Museo Gregoriano Egizio

Museo Chiaramonti **2**

Self-service restaurant & bar

Cortile della Pigna **1**

Braccio Nuovo

Cortile della Biblioteca

Vatican Library

Sala dei Bronzi

Marte di Todi

Etruscan Collection

Cortile del Belvedere

Galleria dei Candelabri **8**

Museo Gregoriano Etrusco

Cortile della Pigna

Galleria degli Arazzi **9**

Cortile della Biblioteca

Appartamento Borgia

Giudizio Universale

Sala di Costantino **12**

Sistine Chapel **16**

Cafe

Lower Floor

Galleria delle Carte Geografiche **10**

Cortile del Belvedere

Stanza d'Eliodoro **13**

Stanza della Segnatura **14**

Stanze di Raffaello (Raphael Rooms)

15 **Stanza dell'Incendio di Borgo**

Appartamento di San Pio V

La Scuola di Atene

Sala dei Chiaroscuro

11

Sala Sobieski

Cappella di Nicolo V

Upper Floor

VATICAN CITY, BORGO & PRATI VATICAN MUSEUMS

Sistine Chapel

The jewel in the Vatican crown, the Sistine Chapel (*Cappella Sistina*) is home to two of the world's most famous works of art – Michelangelo's ceiling frescoes and his *Giudizio Universale* (Last Judgment).

History

The chapel was originally built for Pope Sixtus IV, after whom it is named, and consecrated on 15 August 1483. It's a big, barn-like structure, measuring 40.2m long, 13.4m wide and 20.7m high – the same size as the Temple of Solomon – and even pre-Michelangelo it would have been impressive. Its walls had frescoes painted by a crack team of Renaissance artists, including Botticelli, Ghirlandaio, Pinturicchio, Perugino and Luca Signorelli, the vaulted ceiling was coloured to resemble a blue sky with golden stars, and the floor had an inlaid polychrome marble pattern.

However, apart from the wall frescoes and floor, little remains of the original decor, which was sacrificed to make way for Michelangelo's two masterpieces. The first, the ceiling, was commissioned by Pope Julius II and painted between 1508 and 1512; the second, the spectacular *Giudizio Universale*, was completed almost 30 years later in 1541.

Both were controversial works influenced by the political ambitions of the popes who commissioned them. The ceiling came as part of Julius II's drive to transform Rome into the Church's showcase capital, while Pope Paul III intended the *Giudizio Universale* to serve as a warning to Catholics to toe the line during the Reformation, which was then sweeping through Europe.

In recent years debate has centred on the chapel's multi-million dollar restoration, which finished in 1999 after nearly 20 years. In removing almost 450 years' worth of dust and candle soot, restorers finally revealed the frescoes in their original technicolour glory. But some critics claimed that they also removed a layer of varnish that Michelangelo had added to darken them and enhance their shadows. Whatever the truth, the Sistine Chapel remains a truly spectacular sight.

The Ceiling

The Sistine Chapel provided the greatest challenge of Michelangelo's career, and painting the 800-sq-metre vaulted ceiling at a height of more than 20m pushed him to the limits of his genius.

When Pope Julius II first approached him – some say on the advice of his chief architect, Bramante, who was keen for Michelangelo to fail – he was reluctant to accept. He regarded himself as a sculptor and had had virtually no experience painting frescoes. However, Julius was determined and in 1508 he persuaded Michelangelo to accept the commission for a fee of 3000 ducats (more or less €1.5 to €2 million in today's money).

Originally, Pope Julius wanted Michelangelo to paint the twelve apostles and a series of decorative architectural elements. But the artist rejected this and came up with a much more complex design to cover the entire ceiling based

1. Ceiling of the Sistine Chapel by Michelangelo

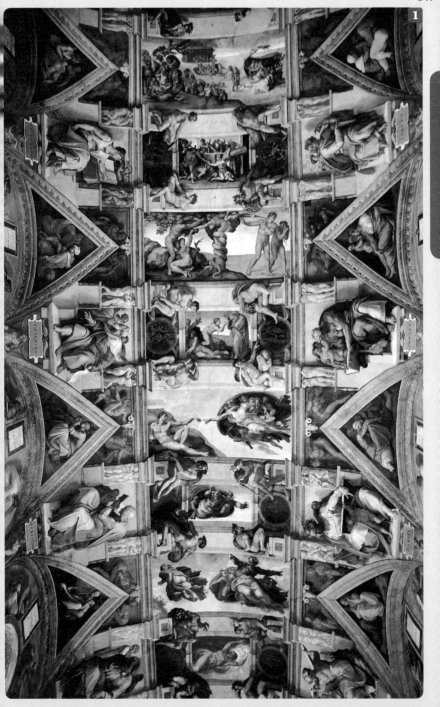

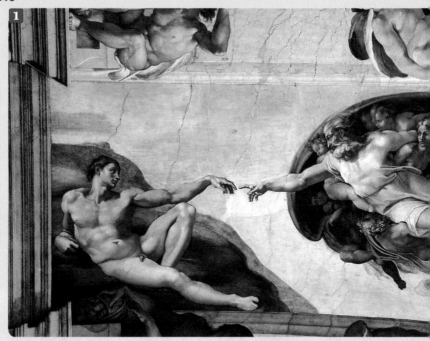

on stories from the book of Genesis. And it's this that you see today.

The Ignudi

The focus of the ceiling frescoes are the nine central panels, but set around them are 20 athletic male nudes, known as *ignudi*. These muscle-bound models caused a scandal when they were first revealed and today art historians are still divided over their meaning – some claim they are angels, others say that they represent Michelangelo's neo-Platonic vision of ideal man.

Wall Frescoes

If you can tear your eyes from the Michelangelos, the Sistine Chapel also boasts some superb wall frescoes. These formed part of the original chapel decoration and were painted between 1481 and 1482 by a team of Renaissance artists, including Botticelli, Ghirlandaio, Pinturicchio, Perugino and Luca Signorelli. They represent events in the lives of Moses (to the left, looking at the *Giudizio Universale*) and Christ (to the right).

Giudizio Universale (Last Judgment)

Michelangelo's second stint in the Sistine Chapel, from 1535 to 1541, resulted in the *Giudizio Universale* (Last Judgment), his highly charged depiction of Christ's

HEAVENLY BLUE

One of the striking features of the *Giudizio Universale* is the amount of ultramarine blue in the painting – in contrast with the ceiling frescoes which don't have any. In the 16th century, blue paint was made from the hugely expensive stone lapis lazuli, and artists were reluctant to use it unless someone else was paying. In the case of the *Giudizio Universale*, the pope picked up the tab for all of Michelangelo's materials; on the ceiling, however, the artist had to cover his own expenses and so used less costly colours.

1. Detail of Michelangelo's *Creation of Adam* fresco **2.** Section of *The Last Judgment* fresco by Michelangelo

second coming on the 200-sq-metre western wall.

The project, which was commissioned by Pope Clement VII and encouraged by his successor Paul III, was controversial from the start. Critics were outraged when Michelangelo destroyed two Perugino frescoes when preparing the wall – it had to be replastered so that it tilted inwards to protect it from dust – and when it was unveiled in 1541, its dramatic, swirling mass of 391 predominantly naked bodies provoked outrage. So fierce were feelings that the Church's top brass, meeting at the 1564 Council of Trent, ordered the nudity to be covered up. The task fell to Daniele da Volterra, one of Michelangelo's students, who added fig leaves and loincloths to 41 nudes, earning himself the nickname *il braghettone* (the breeches maker).

For his part Michelangelo rejected the criticism. He even got his own back on one of his loudest critics, Biagio de Cesena, the papal master of ceremonies, by depicting him as Minos, judge of the underworld, with donkey ears and a snake wrapped around him.

Another famous figure is St Bartholomew, just beneath Christ, holding his own flayed skin. The face in the skin is said to be a self-portrait of Michelangelo, its anguished look reflecting the artist's tormented faith.

MYTHS DEBUNKED

It's often said that Michelangelo worked alone. He didn't. Throughout the job, he employed a steady stream of assistants to help with the plasterwork (producing frescoes involves painting directly onto wet plaster).

Another popular myth is that Michelangelo painted lying down, as portrayed by Charlton Heston in the film *The Agony and the Ecstasy*. In fact, Michelangelo designed a curved scaffolding system that allowed him to work standing up, albeit in an awkward backward-leaning position.

JUMP THE QUEUE

Here's how to jump the ticket queue. Book tickets at the museums' online ticket office (http://biglietteriamusei.vatican.va/musei/tickets/do; €4 booking fee). On payment, you'll receive email confirmation, which you should print and present, along with valid ID, at the museum entrance. You can also book guided tours (adult/reduced €32/24) online. Alternatively, book a tour with a reputable guide. Time your visit: Tuesday and Thursday are the quietest days; Wednesday morning is also good, as everyone is at the pope's weekly audience; afternoon is better than the morning; and avoid Monday, when many other museums are shut.

On the whole, exhibits are not well labelled, so consider hiring an audioguide (€7) or buying the excellent *Guide to the Vatican Museums and City* (€12). The museums are well equipped for visitors with disabilities, and wheelchairs are available free of charge from the Special Permits desk in the entrance hall. They can also be reserved by emailing accoglienza. musei@scv.va. Strollers can be taken into the museums.

continued from p143

Museo Gregoriano Egizio

Founded by Pope Gregory XVI in 1839, the Egyptian museum contains pieces taken from Egypt in ancient Roman times. The collection is small, but there are fascinating exhibits, including the *Trono di Rameses II,* part of a statue of the seated king, vividly painted sarcophagi from about 1000 BC, and a couple of macabre mummies.

Museo Chiaramonti

This museum is effectively the long corridor that runs down the lower east side of the Belvedere Palace. Its walls are lined with thousands of statues representing everything from immortal gods to playful cherubs and ugly Roman patricians. Near the end of the hall, off to the right, is the **Braccio Nuovo** (New Wing), which contains a famous sculpture of Augustus and a statue depicting the Nile as a reclining god covered by 16 babies.

Museo Pio-Clementino

This spectacular museum contains some of the Vatican Museums' finest classical statuary, including the peerless Apollo Belvedere and the 1st-century-BC Laocoön, both in the **Cortile Ottagono** (Octagonal Courtyard).

Before you go into the courtyard, take a moment to admire the 1st-century Apoxyomenos, one of the earliest known sculptures to depict a figure with a raised arm.

To the left as you enter the courtyard, the Apollo Belvedere is a Roman 2nd-century copy of a 4th-century-BC Greek bronze. A beautifully proportioned representation of the sun god Apollo, it's considered one of the great masterpieces of classical sculpture. Nearby, the Laocoön depicts a muscular Trojan priest and his two sons in mortal struggle with two sea serpents.

Back inside the museum, the **Sala degli Animali** is filled with sculptures of all sorts of creatures and some magnificent 4th-century mosaics. Continuing through the *sala* (room), you come to the **Galleria delle Statue**, which has several important classical pieces; the **Sala delle Buste**, which contains hundreds of Roman busts; and the **Gabinetto delle Maschere**, named after the floor mosaics of theatrical masks. To the east, the **Sala delle Muse** (Room of the Muses) is centred on the Torso Belvedere, another of the museum's must-sees. A fragment of a muscular Greek sculpture from the 1st century BC, it was found in Campo de' Fiori and used by Michelangelo as a model for his *ignudi* (male nudes) in the Sistine Chapel.

SISTINE CHAPEL CEILING

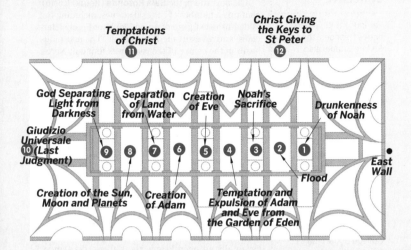

Temptations of Christ ⑪

Christ Giving the Keys to St Peter ⑫

God Separating Light from Darkness

Separation of Land from Water

Creation of Eve

Noah's Sacrifice

Drunkenness of Noah

Giudizio Universale ⑩ **(Last Judgment)**

⑨ ⑧ ⑦ ⑥ ⑤ ④ ③ ② ①

East Wall

Flood

Creation of the Sun, Moon and Planets

Creation of Adam

Temptation and Expulsion of Adam and Eve from the Garden of Eden

VATICAN CITY, BORGO & PRATI VATICAN MUSEUMS

🏃 Museum Tour
Sistine Chapel

LENGTH MINIMUM 30 MINUTES

As you enter the chapel, it's difficult not to be rooted to the spot, but for the best views head over to the far (east) wall and the chapel's main entrance.

Michelangelo's ceiling design – which took him four years to complete – covers the entire 800-sq-metre surface. With painted architectural features and a colourful cast of biblical figures, it centres on nine central panels depicting the Creation, Adam and Eve, the Fall, and the plight of Noah.

As you look up from the east wall the first panel is the ❶ **Drunkenness of Noah**, followed by the ❷ **Flood** and ❸ **Noah's Sacrifice**. Next, the ❹ **Temptation and Expulsion of Adam and Eve from the Garden of Eden** famously depicts Adam and Eve being sent packing after accepting the forbidden fruit from Satan, represented by a snake with the body of a woman coiled around a tree. The ❺ **Creation of Eve** is then followed by the ❻ **Creation of Adam**.

This, one of the most famous images in Western art, shows a bearded God pointing his finger at Adam, thus bringing him to life. Completing the sequence are the ❼ **Separation of Land from Water**; the ❽ **Creation of the Sun, Moon and Planets**; and ❾ **God Separating Light from Darkness**, featuring a fearsome God reaching out to touch the sun.

Straight ahead of you on the west wall is Michelangelo's mesmeric ❿ **Giudizio Universale** (Last Judgment), showing Christ (in the centre near the top) passing sentence over the souls of the dead as they are torn from their graves. The saved get to stay up in heaven (in the upper right), the damned are sent down to face the demons in hell (in the bottom right).

The chapel's side walls also feature stunning Renaissance frescoes, representing events in the lives of Moses (to your left) and Christ (to the right). Look out for Botticelli's ⑪ **Temptations of Christ** and Perugino's ⑫ **Christ Giving the Keys to St Peter**.

CONCLAVE

Famous for its Renaissance frescoes, the Sistine Chapel also plays an important religious function as the place where the papal conclave meets to elect a new pope. Dating to 1274, give or take a few modifications, the rules of the voting procedure are explicit: between 15 and 20 days after the death of a pope (or retirement as in the case of Benedict XVI, who resigned in February 2013), the entire College of Cardinals (comprising all cardinals under the age of 80) is locked in the Sistine Chapel to elect a new pontiff. Four secret ballots are held a day until a two-thirds majority has been secured. News of the election is then communicated by the emission of white smoke through a specially erected chimney.

The need to protect the frescoes and cool the cardinals during the conclave means that the Sistine Chapel is one of the few places in the Vatican Museums with air-conditioning.

The next room, the **Sala Rotonda** (Round Room), contains a number of colossal statues, including the gilded-bronze figure of an odd-looking Ercole (Hercules) and an exquisite floor mosaic. The enormous basin in the centre of the room was found at Nero's Domus Aurea and is made out of a single piece of red porphyry stone.

Museo Gregoriano Etrusco

On the upper level of the Belvedere (off the 18th-century Simonetti staircase), the Museo Gregoriano Etrusco contains artefacts unearthed in the Etruscan tombs of northern Lazio, and a collection of Greek vases and Roman antiquities. Of particular interest is the Marte di Todi (Mars of Todi), a full-length bronze statue of a warrior dating from the 4th century BC, in the **Sala dei Bronzi**.

Galleria dei Candelabri & Galleria degli Arazzi

Originally an open loggia, the Galleria dei Candelabri is packed with classical sculpture and several elegantly carved marble candelabras that give the gallery its name. The corridor continues through to the Galleria degli Arazzi (Tapestry Gallery) and its 10 huge tapestries. The best tapestries, on the left, were woven in Brussels in the 16th century.

Galleria delle Carte Geografiche & Sala Sobieski

One of the unsung heroes of the Vatican Museums, the 120m-long Map Gallery is hung with 40 huge topographical maps. These were created between 1580 and 1583 for Pope Gregory XIII based on drafts by Ignazio Danti, a leading cartographer of his day.

Beyond the gallery is the **Appartamento di San Pio V**, with some interesting Flemish tapestries, and the **Sala Sobieski**, named after an enormous 19th-century painting depicting the victory of the Polish King John III Sobieski over the Turks in 1683.

Stanze di Raffaello

Even in the shadow of the Sistine Chapel, the Stanze di Raffaello (Raphael Rooms) stand out. The four rooms were part of Pope Julius II's private apartment and in 1508 he commissioned the relatively unknown 25-year-old Raphael to decorate them. The resulting frescoes cemented Raphael's reputation, establishing him as a rising star.

But while they carry his name, not all the rooms were completed by Raphael: he painted the Stanza della Segnatura (Study) and Stanza d'Eliodoro (Waiting Room), while the Stanza dell'Incendio di

THE VATICAN: A POTTED HISTORY

Established under the terms of the 1929 Lateran Treaty, the Vatican is the modern vestige of the Papal States, the papal fiefdom that ruled Rome and much of central Italy until Italian unification in 1861. It's an independent nation and as such has a head of state (the pope) and government, as well as its own postal service and army – the nattily dressed Swiss Guards.

The Vatican's association with Christianity dates to the 1st century when St Peter was crucified upside down in Nero's Circus (roughly where St Peter's Square now stands). To commemorate this, the emperor Constantine commissioned a basilica to be built on the site where the saint was buried.

For centuries, St Peter's Basilica stood at the centre of a densely populated quarter, but it wasn't until the 12th century that the Palazzo Apostolico Vaticano was built. Like much of the Vatican, this fell into disrepair during the exile of the papacy to Avignon (1305–78) and the Great Schism (the period between 1378 and 1417 when rival popes ruled in Rome and Avignon).

Life returned to the Vatican in the 15th and 16th centuries when a series of ambitious Renaissance popes revamped St Peter's and modernised the Palazzo Apostolico Vaticano. The baroque 17th century saw further transformations, most notably the laying of St Peter's Square.

Borgo (Dining Room) and Sala di Costantino (Reception Room) were decorated by students following his designs.

The first room you come to, the **Sala di Costantino**, was finished by Giulio Romano in 1525, five years after Raphael's death. It features the huge *Battaglia di Costantino contro Maxentius* (Battle of the Milvian Bridge), which depicts the victory of Constantine, Rome's first Christian emperor, over his rival Maxentius.

Leading off the *sala* are two rooms that are not traditionally counted as Raphael Rooms: the **Sala dei Chiaroscuri**, featuring a Raphael-designed ceiling, and the **Cappella di Niccolò V**, Pope Nicholas V's private chapel. This tiny chapel, which is often closed to the public, features a superb cycle of frescoes by Fra Angelico.

The **Stanza d'Eliodoro**, which was used for private audiences, was painted between 1512 and 1514. It takes its name from the *Cacciata d'Eliodoro* (Expulsion of Heliodorus from the Temple), an allegorical work referring to Pope Julius II's policy of forcing foreign powers off Church lands. To the right of it is the *Messa di Bolsena* (Mass of Bolsena), showing Julius II paying homage to the relic of a 13th-century miracle at the lake town of Bolsena. Next is the *Incontro di Leone Magno con Attila* (Encounter of Leo the Great with Attila) by Raphael and his school, and, on the fourth wall, the *Liberazione di San Pietro* (Liberation of St Peter), one of Raphael's most brilliant works, which illustrates the artist's masterful depiction of light.

The **Stanza della Segnatura**, Pope Julius' study and library, was the first room that Raphael painted, and it's here that you'll find his great masterpiece, *La Scuola di Atene* (The School of Athens), featuring philosophers and scholars gathered around Plato and Aristotle. The seated figure in front of the steps is believed to be Michelangelo, while the figure of Plato is said to be a portrait of Leonardo da Vinci, and Euclide (the bald man bending over) is Bramante. Raphael also included a self-portrait in the lower right corner (he's the second figure from the right in the black hat). Opposite is *La Disputa del Sacramento* (Disputation on the Sacrament), also by Raphael.

The most famous work of the **Stanza dell'Incendio di Borgo** is the *Incendio di Borgo* (Fire in the Borgo), which depicts Leo IV extinguishing a fire by making the sign of the cross. The ceiling was painted by Raphael's master, Perugino.

From the Raphael Rooms, stairs lead to the **Appartamento Borgia** and the Vatican's collection of modern religious art.

◉ SIGHTS

Boasting priceless treasures at every turn, the Vatican is home to some of Rome's most popular sights. The Vatican Museums and St Peter's Basilica are the star attractions, but Castel Sant'Angelo, one of the city's most recognisable landmarks, is also well worth a visit. For details of companies offering guided tours of the Vatican Museums and St Peter's Basilica, see p323.

◉ Vatican City

ST PETER'S BASILICA   BASILICA
See p138.

ST PETER'S SQUARE   PIAZZA
(Piazza San Pietro; Map p368; ⓂOttaviano–San Pietro) Overlooked by St Peter's Basilica, the Vatican's central square was laid out between 1656 and 1667 to a design by Gian Lorenzo Bernini. Seen from above, it resembles a giant keyhole with two semicircular colonnades, each consisting of four rows of Doric columns, encircling a giant ellipse that straightens out to funnel believers into the basilica.

The effect was deliberate – Bernini described the colonnades as representing 'the motherly arms of the church'. However, the

---

SEPARATE ENTRANCES
It's a common misunderstanding, but many people think that St Peter's Basilica, the Vatican Museums and the Sistine Chapel share a single entrance. They do not. The entrance to St Peter's Basilica is on St Peter's Square – join the queue on the piazza's northern flank; the entrance to the Vatican Museums is on Viale Vaticano – follow the Vatican walls westwards from Piazza del Risorgimento. The Sistine Chapel is part of the Vatican Museums complex and can only be accessed through the museums.

You can, in theory, pass from the Sistine Chapel through to St Peter's Basilica, although officially this short cut is reserved for groups with a guide. You can not, however, go in the opposite direction, from St Peter's straight to the Sistine Chapel.

---

piazza's modern approach is very different to how Bernini originally envisaged it. His idea was to have the piazza open up before visitors as they emerged from the jumble of narrow streets that originally surrounded the area. Mussolini, however, spoiled the effect when he had much of the Borgo district razed to the ground and the monumental Via della Conciliazione built.

The scale of the piazza is dazzling: at its largest it measures 340m by 240m; there are 284 columns and, on top of the colonnades, 140 saints. In the midst of all this the pope seems very small as he delivers his weekly address at noon on Sunday.

The 25m obelisk in the centre was brought to Rome by Caligula from Heliopolis in Egypt and later used by Nero as a turning post for the chariot races in his circus.

VATICAN MUSEUMS   MUSEUM
See p143.

VATICAN GARDENS   GARDEN
(Map p368; http://biglietteriamusei.vatican.va; adult/reduced incl Vatican Museums €32/24; ☺by reservation only; ⓂOttaviano–San Pietro) Up to half of the Vatican is covered by the perfectly manicured Vatican Gardens, which contain fortifications, grottoes, monuments and fountains dating from the 9th century to the present day. Visits are by two-hour guided tour only, for which you'll need to book at least a week in advance.

◉ Borgo

Overshadowed by Castel Sant'Angelo, this quarter retains a low-key medieval charm despite the batteries of restaurants, hotels and pizzerias.

CASTEL SANT'ANGELO   MUSEUM
(Map p368; ☎06 681 91 11; Lungotevere Castello 50; adult/reduced €8.50/6; ☺9am-7.30pm Tue-Sun, last admission 6.30pm; ◻Piazza Pia) With its chunky round keep, this castle is an instantly recognisable landmark. Built as a mausoleum for the emperor Hadrian, it was converted into a papal fortress in the 6th century and named after an angelic vision that Pope Gregory the Great had in 590. Nowadays, it houses an eclectic collection of paintings, sculpture, military memorabilia and medieval firearms.

Many of these weapons were used by soldiers fighting to protect the castle, which,

At 11am on Wednesday, the pope addresses his flock at the Vatican (in July and August in Castel Gandolfo near Rome). For details of how to apply for free tickets, see the Vatican website (www.vatican.va/various/prefettura/index_en.html).

When he is in Rome, the pope blesses the crowd in St Peter's Square on Sunday at noon. No tickets are required.

thanks to a secret 13th-century passageway to the Vatican (the Passetto di Borgo), provided sanctuary to many popes in times of danger. Most famously, Pope Clemente VI holed up here during the 1527 sack of Rome.

The castle's upper floors are filled with lavishly decorated Renaissance interiors, including, on the 4th floor, the beautifully frescoed Sala Paolina. Two storeys further up, the terrace, immortalised by Puccini in his opera *Tosca*, offers great views over Rome.

Additional fees may be charged during temporary exhibitions.

PONTE SANT'ANGELO   BRIDGE
(Map p360; 🚇Piazza Pia) The emperor Hadrian built the Ponte Sant'Angelo in 136 to provide an approach to his mausoleum, but it was Bernini who brought it to life with his angel sculptures in the 17th century. The three central arches of the bridge are part of the original structure; the end arches were restored and enlarged in 1892–94 during the construction of the Lungotevere embankments.

**COMPLESSO MONUMENTALE
SANTO SPIRITO IN SAXIA**   HISTORIC BUILDING
(Map p368; 📞06 6835 2433; www.giubilarte.it; Borgo Santo Spirito 1; 🚇Lungotevere in Sassia) Originally an 8th-century lodging for Saxon pilgrims, this ancient hospital complex was established by Pope Innocent III in the late 12th century. Three hundred years later Sixtus IV added an octagonal courtyard and two vast frescoed halls, known collectively as the Corsia Sistina (Sistine Ward).

The complex is currently undergoing restoration and guided visits have been indefinitely suspended.

**MUSEO STORICO NAZIONALE
DELL'ARTE SANITARIA**   MUSEUM
(Map p368; 📞06 689 30 51; Lungotevere in Sassia 3; group visits only, admission €7; ⊙by reservation; 🚇Lungotevere in Sassia) Next to the Pronto Soccorso department of the Ospedale Santo Spirito, this medical museum has a ghoulish collection of surgical instruments, macabre curiosities and anatomical models.

EATING

Beware, hungry travellers: there are unholy numbers of overpriced, tourist traps around the Vatican and St Peter's. A better bet is nearby Prati, which has lots of excellent eateries catering to the lawyers and media bods who work in the area.

Vatican City

OLD BRIDGE   GELATO €
(Map p368; www.oldbridgelateria.com; Viale dei Bastioni di Michelangelo 5; cones from €1.50; ⊙9am-2am daily; 🚇Piazza del Risorgimento, 🚇Piazza del Risorgimento) Ideal for a pre- or post-Vatican pick-me-up, this tiny ice-cream parlour has been cheerfully dishing up huge portions of delicious gelato for over 20 years. Alongside all the traditional flavours, there are also yoghurts and refreshing sorbets.

Borgo

LA VERANDA   GASTRONOMIC €€€
(Map p368; 📞06 687 29 73; www.laveranda.net; Borgo Santo Spirito 73; meals €70, brunch €13-24; ⊙Tue-Sun; 🚇Piazza Pia) Dine in romantic splendour under Pinturicchio frescoes in the loggia of the 15th-century Palazzo della Rovere. In line with the setting, dishes use superb Italian ingredients and are accompanied by top-quality Italian and international wines. To enjoy the atmosphere for a snip of the regular price, stop by for brunch, served between 11.30am and 3pm every Sunday.

Prati

★FATAMORGANA   GELATO €
(Map p368; www.gelateriafatamorgana.it; Via Bettolo 7; ice cream from €2; ⊙noon-11pm;

Ⓜ Ottaviano–San Pietro) It's some way off the beaten track, but you won't regret searching out this superb gelateria, one of the city's finest. As well as all the classic flavours there are some wonderfully original creations, such as a mouth-wateringly good *agrumi* (citrus fruit) and a strange but delicious *basilico, miele e noci* (basil, honey and hazelnuts).

GELARMONY
GELATO €

(Map p368; Via Marcantonio Colonna 34; ice cream from €1.50; ☺10am-late; Ⓜ Lepanto) This fab Sicilian gelateria is the ideal place for a lunchtime dessert, a mid-afternoon treat, an evening fancy – in fact, anything at any time. Alongside 60 flavours of ice cream, there's a devilish selection of creamy sweets, including to-die-for *cannoli*.

MONDO ARANCINA
SICILIAN, FAST FOOD €

(Map p368; Via Marcantonio Colonna 38; arancini from €2.50; ☺10am-late; Ⓜ Lepanto) All sunny yellow ceramics, cheerful crowds and tantalising deep-fried snacks, this bustling takeaway brings a little corner of Sicily to Rome. Star of the show are the classic fist-sized *arancini,* fried rice balls stuffed with a range of fillers, from classic *ragù* to more exotic fare such as truffle risotto and quail's eggs.

FRANCHI
DELI €

(Map p368; ☏06 687 46 51; Via Cola di Rienzo 198; snacks from €1.20; ☺9am-8.30pm Mon-Sat; 🚇 Via Cola di Rienzo) One of Rome's historic delicatessens, Franchi is great for a swift bite or to stock up on stuff to take home. White-jacketed assistants work with practised dexterity slicing hams, cutting cheese, weighing olives and preparing *panini,* to take away or eat at stand-up tables.

CACIO E PEPE
TRATTORIA €

(Map p368; ☏06 321 72 68; Via Avezzana 11; meals €25; ☺closed Sat dinner & Sun; 🚇 Piazza Giuseppe Mazzini) A local institution, this humble trattoria is as authentic as it gets with a menu of traditional Roman dishes, a spartan interior and no-frills service. If you can find a free seat at one of the gingham-clad tables splayed across the pavement, keep it simple with *cacio e pepe* followed by *pollo alla cacciatora* ('hunter's chicken').

HOSTARIA-PIZZERIA
GIACOMELLI
PIZZERIA €

(Map p368; ☏06 372 59 10; Via Emilio Faà di Bruno 25; meals €15-20; ☺Tue-Sat; Ⓜ Ottaviano–San Pietro) This old-school neighbourhood pizzeria has diners queuing around the block for thin and crispy Roman pizzas. The decor is nothing fancy, but the reliably good food, from the *crostini* to the spicy *diavola* pizza, has locals voting with their feet. No credit cards.

VELAVEVODETTO
AI QUIRITI
TRADITIONAL ITALIAN €€

(Map p368; ☏06 3600 0009; www.ristoranteve-lavevodetto.it; Piazza dei Quiriti 5; meals €35; ☺daily; Ⓜ Lepanto) Since it opened in spring 2012, this Prati newcomer has won over locals with its unpretentious earthy food, honest prices and welcoming service. The menu reads like a directory of Roman staples, and while it's all pretty good, standout choices include *polpette di bollito* (fried meatballs) and *carciofi fritti* (fried artichokes).

OSTERIA DELL'ANGELO
TRATTORIA €€

(Map p368; ☏06 372 94 70; Via Bettolo 24; set menu €25; ☺lunch Tue-Fri, dinner Mon-Sat; Ⓜ Ottaviano–San Pietro) Laid-back and informal, this hugely popular neighbourhood trattoria (reservations are a must) is a great place to try genuine local cuisine. The set menu features a mixed antipasti, a robust Roman-style pasta and a choice of hearty mains with a side dish. To finish off, you're offered lightly spiced biscuits to dunk in sweet dessert wine.

ROMEO
PIZZERIA, RISTORANTE €€

(Map p368; ☏06 3211 0120; www.romeo.roma.it; Via Silla 26a; pizza slices €3.50, meals €35-40; ☺9am-midnight Mon-Sat; Ⓜ Ottaviano–San Pietro) One of the new breed of multipurpose gastro outfits that has sprung up across the city, Romeo serves everything from freshly prepared *panini* to fabulous *pizza al taglio* and full restaurant meals. The look is contemporary chic with black walls and sprouting tubular lights; the food is a mix of classic Italian fare and forward-looking international creations.

HOSTARIA DINO E TONY
TRATTORIA €€

(Map p368; ☏06 3973 3284; Via Leone IV 60; meals €30; ☺Mon-Sat, closed Aug; Ⓜ Ottaviano–San Pietro) Something of a rarity, Dino e Tony is an authentic trattoria in the Vatican area. Kick off with the monumental antipasto, a minor meal in its own right, before plunging into its signature dish, *rigatoni all'amatriciana* (pasta tubes with pancetta, chilli and tomato sauce). No credit cards.

DEL FRATE   WINE BAR €€

(Map p368; ☑06 323 64 37; www.enotecadelfrate.
it; Via degli Scipioni 122; meals €40; ⊘Mon-Sat;
MOttaviano–San Pietro) Locals love this upmarket wine bar with its simple wooden
tables and high-ceilinged, brick-arched
rooms. There's a formidable wine and cheese
list, with everything from *burrata* (like
mozzarella but filled with a buttery cream)
to gorgonzola, and a small but refined menu
of tartars, salads and fresh pastas.

DAL TOSCANO   TUSCAN €€

(Map p368; ☑06 3972 5717; www.ristorantedalto-
scano.it; Via Germanico 58-60; meals €45; ⊘Tue-
Sun; MOttaviano–San Pietro) Dal Toscano is
one for the traditionalists: an old-fashioned
ristorante that serves top-notch Tuscan
meats. Start with the hand-cut *prosciutto*
before attempting the colossal chargrilled
bistecca alla fiorentina (T-bone steak).
You'll need to book.

PIZZERIA AMALFI   PIZZERIA €€

(Map p368; ☑06 3973 3165; Via dei Gracchi 12;
pizzas from €6, mains from €25; ⊘lunch & dinner
daily; MOttaviano–San Pietro) While Roman
pizzas are thin and crispy, Neapolitan pizzas are thicker and more doughy. And
that's what you get at this brassy, brightly
coloured pizzeria-cum-restaurant. If pizza
doesn't appeal, there's a decent range of
grilled meats, pastas, salads and fish dishes.
Note that there's a second branch across the
road at Via dei Gracchi 5.

SHANTI   INDIAN, PAKISTANI €€

(Map p368; ☑06 324 49 22; www.ristoranteshanti.
com; Via Fabio Massimo 68; meals €30; ⊘lunch &
dinner daily; MOttaviano–San Pietro) When you
need a change from pizza and pasta, this
dependable Indian and Pakistani restaurant
serves up delicately spiced dishes in a handsome, softly lit setting. Alongside tandooris,
curries, dhals and naans, there are three set
menus – vegetarian (€20), meat (€23) or fish
(€26) – offering good value for money.

**RISTORANTE
L'ARCANGELO**   GASTRONOMIC €€€

(Map p368; ☑06 321 09 92; Via Belli 59-61; meals
€60, tasting menu €50; ⊘closed lunch Sat &
Sun; ☐Piazza Cavour) Frequented by politicians and local celebs, this smart restaurant enjoys a stellar reputation with local
gourmets. The highlights for many are the
classic Roman staples such as carbonara
and gnocchi, but there's also a tempting
choice of innovative modern dishes. The

wine list is also top draw, with some interesting Italian labels.

SETTEMBRINI   CAFE, MODERN ITALIAN €€€

(Map p368; ☑06 323 26 17; www.viasettembrini.
it; cafe Via Settembrini 21, restaurant Via Settembrini 25; aperitivi €8, restaurant meals €60; ⊘cafe
7am-1am daily, restaurant lunch & dinner Mon-Fri,
dinner Sat; ☐Piazza Giuseppe Mazzini) All labels,
suits and lipstick, this fashionable watering
hole is a hot foodie fixture. Join the sharply
dressed darlings for bar snacks, a light lunch
or evening *aperitivo* at the cafe, or make an
occasion of it and dine on creative Italian
cuisine at the smart restaurant next door.

✗ Aurelio

⭐**PIZZARIUM**   PIZZERIA €

(Map p368; Via della Meloria 43; pizza slices from
€3; ⊘11am-9pm Mon-Sat; MCipro–Musei Vaticani) A gourmet revelation masquerading
as an unassuming takeaway, hard-to-find
Pizzarium serves some of Rome's best sliced
pizza. Served on a wooden chopping board,
its perfect crust is topped with original, in-
tensely flavoured ingredients. There's also
a daily selection of *supplì* (crunchy rice croquettes), juices and chilled beers.

⊖ DRINKING &
⚲ NIGHTLIFE

**The quiet area around the Vatican
harbours a few charming wine bars and
cafes. For nightlife there are a couple of
live-music venues, including Italy's best
jazz club.**

⚑ Prati

PASSAGUAI   WINE BAR

(Map p368; www.passaguai.it; Via Leto 1; ⊘10am-
2am Mon-Sat; ☎; ☐Piazza del Risorgimento) A
small, cavelike basement wine bar, Passaguai has a few outdoor tables on a quiet
street and feels pleasingly off-the-radar. It
boasts a good wine list and a range of artisanal beers, and the food – think cheese
and cold cuts – is tasty, too. Free wi-fi.

ART STUDIO CAFÉ   CAFE

(Map p368; www.artstudiocafe.it; Via dei Gracchi 187a; MLepanto) A cafe, exhibition space
and craft school all in one, this bright and

breezy spot serves one of Prati's most popular aperitifs. It's also good for a light lunch – something like chicken couscous or fresh salad – or restorative mid-afternoon tea.

MAKASAR
TEAROOM, WINE BAR

(Map p368; www.makasar.it; Via Plauto 33; ⊗10am-1.30pm & 4.30pm-1am Tue-Sat, 5pm-midnight Sun; ⬛Piazza del Risorgimento) Recharge your batteries with a quiet drink at this oasis of bookish tranquillity. Pick your tipple from the nine-page tea menu or opt for an Italian wine and sit back in the bottle-lined interior whilst poring over a lavish art book.

ENTERTAINMENT

ALEXANDERPLATZ
JAZZ

(Map p368; ☑06 3974 2171; www.alexanderplatz.it; Via Ostia 9; ⊗concerts 9.45pm Sun-Thu, 10.30pm Fri & Sat; ⓂOttaviano–San Pietro) Small and intimate, Rome's top jazz joint attracts top Italian and international performers and a respectful, cosmopolitan crowd. Book a table if you want to dine to the tunes.

FONCLEA
LIVE MUSIC

(Map p368; ☑06 689 63 02; www.fonclea.it; Via Crescenzio 82a; ⊗7pm-2am Sep-May; ⬛Piazza del Risorgimento) Fonclea is a great little pub venue, serving up nightly gigs and sounds ranging from jazz and soul to funk, rockabilly and gospel (concerts start at around 9.30pm). Get in the mood with a drink during happy hour (7pm to 8.30pm daily). From June to August, Fonclea moves to a riverside site under the Ponte Palatino on the Tiber.

AUDITORIUM CONCILIAZIONE
THEATRE

(Map p368; ☑06 3281 0333; www.auditorium conciliazione.it; Via della Conciliazione 4; ⬛Piazza

---

LOCAL KNOWLEDGE

SNACK HEAVEN

There are hundreds of bars, cafes and takeaways in the Prati area, but for a quick, cheap bite nowhere beats **Dolce Maniera** (Map p368; Via Barletta 27; ⊗24hr; ⓂOttaviano–San Pietro), an unmarked basement bakery that serves freshly made *cornetti* (croissants) for €0.30, as well as slabs of pizza, *panini* and an indulgent array of cakes.

Pia) On the main approach road to St Peter's Basilica, this auditorium plays host to performances of the Orchestra Sinfonica Roma (www.orchestrasinfonicadiroma.it) as well as other classical and contemporary concerts, dance spectacles, film screenings and exhibitions.

TEATRO GHIONE
THEATRE

(Map p368; ☑06 637 22 94; www.teatroghione.it; Via delle Fornaci 37; ⬛Via di Porta Cavalleggeri) A former cinema, the Teatro Ghione is a popular theatre near St Peter's that offers a varied program of classic and modern plays, concerts and musicals, staging anything from Pirandello to Oscar Wilde and Chopin to Sarah Kane.

SHOPPING

CASTRONI
FOOD

(Map p368; www.castronicoladirienzo.com; Via Cola di Rienzo 196; ⊗8am-8pm Mon-Sat; ⬛Via Cola di Rienzo) This Aladdin's cave is stuffed with gourmet treats. Towering shelves groan under the weight of vinegars, truffles, olive oils, pastas, dried mushrooms and all sorts of sweets and chocolates. For desperate expats there's Vegemite, salad cream and baked beans, and for thirsty shoppers there's a good in-store cafe.

C.U.C.I.N.A.
KITCHENWARE

(Map p368; www.cucinastore.com; Via Gioachino Belli 21; ⊗10am-7.30pm Mon-Sat; ⬛Piazza Cavour) If you're into cooking as much for the gear as the food, you'll enjoy this cool kitchenware shop. A branch of the capital's C.U.C.I.N.A. chain, it stocks all sorts of sexy pots and pans, designer cutlery, gourmet gadgets, wine glasses and a full range of fashionable cooking apparel.

OUTLET GENTE
CLOTHING

(Map p368; ☑06 689 26 72; Via Cola di Rienzo 246; ⊗10am-7.30pm Tue-Sat, 3.30-7.30pm Mon & Sun; ⬛Via Cola di Rienzo) This basement outlet of the Gente fashion chain sells everything from Prada loafers to Miu Miu threads at markdowns of up to 50%.

ANGELO DI NEPI
CLOTHING

(Map p368; www.angelodinepi.it; Via Cola di Rienzo 267; ⬛Via Cola di Rienzo) Roman designer Nepi adores strong colours, and combines Italian cuts and styles with rich fabrics to make you as pretty as a peacock.

Monti, Esquilino & San Lorenzo

MONTI | ESQUILINO | PIAZZA DELLA REPUBBLICA | SAN LORENZO

Neighbourhood Top Five

1 Visiting the **Palazzo Massimo alle Terme** (p161), with its incredible frescoes from imperial Rome.

2 Lingering at wine bars and pottering around the bohemian-chic neighbourhood of **Monti** (p165).

3 Hobnobbing with the bohos in **Pigneto** (p171), the iconic working-class district immortalised by Pasolini.

4 Taking in the splendours of **Basilica di Santa Maria Maggiore** (p162).

5 Admiring Michelangelo's mighty Moses-with-horns at the **Basilica di San Pietro in Vincoli** (p163).

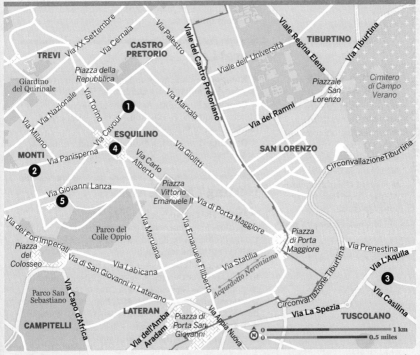

For more detail of this area, see Map p375 and p376 ➡

Lonely Planet's Top Tip

Don't neglect to visit the oft-overlooked patriarchal Basilica di San Lorenzo Fuori le Mura (p169) – it's starkly beautiful.

Best Places to Eat

➡ L'Asino d'Oro (p172)
➡ Open Colonna (p173)
➡ Panella l'Arte del Pane (p172)
➡ Trattoria Monti (p173)

For reviews, see p170 ➡

Best Places to Drink

➡ Ai Tre Scalini (p175)
➡ Micca Club (p176)
➡ 2 Periodico Caffè (p175)
➡ La Bottega del Caffè (p175)
➡ Il Tiaso (p171)

For reviews, see p175 ➡

Best Works of Art

➡ Frescoes at Palazzo Massimo alle Terme (p161)
➡ Michelangelo's colossal *Moses* (p163)
➡ Fuga's 13th-century facade mosaics (p162)
➡ Richard Meier's modernist Chiesa Dio Padre Misericordioso (p169)

For reviews, see p161 ➡

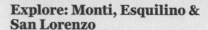

Explore: Monti, Esquilino & San Lorenzo

Esquilino is one of Rome's seven hills, and the area encompasses the sometimes scruffy area around Stazione Termini and Piazza Vittorio Emanuele II. It is also home to some fantastic sights, including some of Rome's finest medieval churches, and the Museo Nazionale Romano: Palazzo Massimo alle Terme, which displays stunning classical art.

Heading downhill, Monti was the ancient city's notorious Suburra slum – a red-light district and the childhood home of Julius Caesar – but is now a charming neighbourhood of inviting eateries, shops and *enoteche* (wine bars). You could say Monti is Rome's Greenwich Village, and, as if to put the seal on its accelerating gentrification, Woody Allen filmed parts of *To Rome with Love* here in 2011.

San Lorenzo is a lively student quarter east of Termini, home to a beautiful, little-visited patriarchal basilica. It was the area most damaged by Allied bombing during WWII, ironic given the area's vehemently anti-Fascist politics. By day the area feels hungover, a grid of graffitied streets that nonetheless harbour some gemlike boutiques, but after dark it shows its true colours as a student nightlife haunt; it's also home to some excellent restaurants.

A quick tram ride southeast, Pigneto is even more bohemian, the Roman equivalent of London's Shoreditch. House prices are rising and its bars and funky offbeat shops attract a regular crowd of artists and fashion-conscious urbanites.

Local Life

➡ **Hang-outs** While away an hour or so at Monti's La Bottega del Caffè (p175), watching the world go by.
➡ **Shopping** Find exotic foodstuffs at the Nuovo Mercato Esquilino (p180), Rome's most eclectic food market, next to Piazza Vittorio Emanuele II.
➡ **Drinking** Have a drink amid artists and wannabes on the buzzing street of Via del Pigneto, (p171).

Getting There & Away

➡ **Metro** The Cavour metro stop (line B) is most convenient for Monti, while the Termini (lines A and B), Castro Pretorio (line B) and Vittorio Emanuele (line A) stations are useful for Esquilino.
➡ **Bus** Termini is the city's main bus hub, connected to places all over the city. Access Monti from buses stopping on Via Nazionale or Via Cavour. San Lorenzo is served by buses 71, 140 and 492; Pigneto is served by buses 81, 810 and 105, and night bus n12.
➡ **Tram** This is an easy way to access San Lorenzo (tram 3) or Pigneto (trams 5, 14 or 19).

 TOP SIGHT **MUSEO NAZIONALE ROMANO: PALAZZO MASSIMO ALLE TERME**

One of Rome's finest museums, this light-filled treasure trove is packed with spectacular classical art yet remains off the beaten track. It's not to be missed.

The ground and 1st floors are devoted to sculpture, examining imperial portraiture as propaganda and including some breathtaking works of art, including the 2nd-century-BC Greek bronzes, the Boxer and the Prince, a crouching Aphrodite from Villa Adriana, the 2nd-century-BC Sleeping Hermaphrodite, and the idealized vision of the Discus Thrower. Also fascinating are the elaborate bronze fittings that belonged to Caligula's ceremonial ships.

The sensational frescoes on the 2nd floor are the undoubted highlight of the museum. They include scenes from nature, mythology, domestic and sensual life, using rich, vivid and expensive colours.

The showstopper is the decoration covering an entire room from Villa Livia, one of the homes of Augustus' wife Livia Drusilla. The frescoes depict a paradisaical garden full of a wild tangle of roses, violets, pomegranates, irises and camomile under a deep-blue sky. These decorated a summer *triclinium*, a large living and dining area built half underground to provide protection from the heat. The new display includes special lighting that mimics the modulation of daylight and highlights the richness of the millennia-old colours.

In the basement, the unexciting-sounding coin collection is far more absorbing than you might expect, tracing the Roman Empire's propaganda offensive via coinage. There's also jewellery dating back several millennia that looks as good as new, and the disturbing remains of mummified eight-year-old girl.

DON'T MISS...

➡ The Boxer
➡ Sleeping Hermaphrodite
➡ Frescoes from Villa Livia

PRACTICALITIES

➡ Map p376
➡ ☎06 3996 7700
➡ www.coopculture.it
➡ Largo di Villa Peretti 1
➡ adult/reduced €7/3.50
➡ ⊙9am-7.45pm Tue-Sun
➡ Ⓜ Termini

TOP SIGHT
BASILICA DI SANTA MARIA MAGGIORE

One of Rome's four patriarchal basilicas, this monumental church stands on the summit of the Esquilino Hill, on the spot where snow is said to have fallen in the summer of AD 358. To commemorate the event, every year on 5 August thousands of white petals are released from the basilica's coffered ceiling.

Outside, the 18.78m-high column came from the basilica of Massenzio in the Roman Forum. The church exterior is decorated by 13th-century mosaics, protected by a baroque porch. The 75m belfry, the highest in Rome, is 14th-century Romanesque.

The great interior retains its 5th-century structure, as well as the original mosaics in the triumphal arch and nave. The central image in the apse, signed by Jacopo Torriti, dates from the 13th century.

Twelfth-century Cosmati paving covers the nave floor. The baldachin over the high altar practically squirms with gilt cherubs; the altar itself is a porphyry sarcophagus, said to contain the relics of St Matthew and other martyrs. Gian Lorenzo Bernini and his father Pietro are buried to the right of the altar.

Don't miss the upper loggia, the extraordinary creation of Ferdinando Fuga, where you'll get a closer look at the 13th-century mosaics, created by Filippo Rusuti. You'll also see Bernini's baroque helical staircase.

DON'T MISS...

➡ The loggia
➡ Cosmatesque floor
➡ Jacopo Torriti apse mosaics

PRACTICALITIES

➡ Map p376
➡ Piazza Santa Maria Maggiore
➡ basilica free, museum €3, loggia €2
➡ ⊙7am-7pm, museum & loggia 9.30am-6.30pm
➡ 🚇Piazza Santa Maria Maggiore

◉ TOP SIGHT
BASILICA DI SAN PIETRO IN VINCOLI

Pilgrims and art lovers flock to this 5th-century church for two reasons: to marvel at Michelangelo's macho sculpture of Moses and to see the chains that bound St Peter when he was imprisoned in the Carcere Mamertino.

St Peter's Shackles

The church was built in the 5th century specially to house these shackles, which had been sent to Constantinople after the saint's death but were later returned as relics. They arrived in two pieces; legend has it that when they were reunited, they miraculously joined together. They are now displayed under the altar.

Michelangelo's *Moses*

To the right of the altar, Michelangelo's colossal *Moses* (1505) forms the centrepiece of Pope Julius II's unfinished tomb. On either side of the prophet are statues of Leah and Rachel, probably completed by Michelangelo's students. Moses, who sports a magnificent waist-length beard and two small horns sticking out of his head, has been studied for centuries, most famously by Sigmund Freud in a 1914 essay, *The Moses of Michelangelo*. The horns were inspired by a mistranslation of a biblical passage: where the original said that rays of light issued from Moses' face, the translator wrote 'horns'. Michelangelo was aware of the mistake, but he gave Moses horns anyway.

Despite the tomb's imposing scale, it was never completed – Michelangelo originally envisaged 40 statues but he got sidetracked by the Sistine Chapel, and Pope Julius was buried in St Peter's Basilica.

DON'T MISS...

➡ Michelangelo's *Moses*

➡ St Peter's chains

PRACTICALITIES

➡ Map p376

➡ Piazza di San Pietro in Vincoli 4a

➡ ⊗8am-12.30pm & 3-7pm Apr-Sep, to 6pm Oct-Mar

➡ Ⓜ Cavour

◉ SIGHTS

The sometimes scruffy district of Esquilino is lined by grand 19th-century buildings. It might not be Rome's prettiest district, but it's studded with some stupendous art and museums, including one of Rome's finest patriarchal basilicas in Santa Maria Maggiore, Michelangelo's *Moses* at San Pietro in Vincoli, and two masterpiece-packed outposts of the Museo Nazionale Romano.

◉ Esquilino

BASILICA DI SANTA MARIA MAGGIORE
BASILICA

See p162.

BASILICA DI SAN PIETRO IN VINCOLI
BASILICA

See p163.

DOMUS AUREA
ARCHAEOLOGICAL SITE

(Map p376; ☑06 3996 7700; www.coopculture.it; Viale della Domus Aurea; ⊘closed for restoration; ⓂColosseo) A monumental exercise in vanity, the Domus Aurea (Golden House) was Nero's great gift to himself. Built after the fire of AD 64 and named after the gold that covered its facade, it was a huge complex covering up to a third of the city, but it's estimated that only around 20% remains of the original complex.

Nero's successors attempted to raze all trace of his megalomania. Vespasian drained Nero's ornamental lake and in, a highly symbolic gesture, built the Colosseum in its place. Domitian built a palace on the Palatino, while Hadrian, after having sacked Nero's palace, entombed it in earth and constructed a baths complex. The baths were abandoned by the 6th century; it is this area that is being excavated. It has been frequently closed for repairs following flooding and was last open in 2010.

During the Renaissance, artists (including Ghirlandaio, Perugino and Raphael) lowered themselves into the ruins in order to study the frescoed grottoes and to doodle on the walls.

MUSEO NAZIONALE D'ARTE ORIENTALE
MUSEUM

(Map p376; ☑06 4697 4832; www.museorientale. beniculturali.it; Via Merulana 248; adult/reduced €6/3; ⊘9am-2pm Tue, Wed & Fri, 9am-7.30pm Thu, Sat & Sun; ⓂVittorio Emanuele) This little-known but impressive collection is housed in the 19th-century Palazzo Brancaccio. The collection includes 5th-century-BC Iranian glassware, items from the ancient settlement of Swat in Pakistan, 12th-century homewares from Afghanistan, engraved ritual vessels from China dating to 800 to 900 BC, and Ming porcelain figures.

CHIESA DI SANTA CROCE IN GERUSALEMME
CHURCH

(Map p375; www.santacroceroma.it; Piazza di Santa Croce in Gerusalemme 12; ⊘7am-12.45pm & 3.30-7.30pm; ☑Piazza di Porta Maggiore) One of Rome's seven pilgrimage churches, the Chiesa di Santa Croce was founded in 320 by St Helena, mother of the emperor Constantine, in the grounds of her palace. It takes its name from the Christian relics here – including a piece of Christ's cross and St Thomas' doubting finger – that St Helena brought to Rome from Jerusalem, housed in a chapel to the left of the altar.

Of particular note are the lovely 15th-century Renaissance apse frescoes representing the legends of Christ's cross, showing from where the wood came and how it was turned into the cross.

In 2011, the monks who lived in the adjoining monastery were ousted by Pope Benedict XVI following accusations of financial mismanagement and lifestyles that were deemed unsuitable for monks.

CHIESA DI SANTA PUDENZIANA
CHURCH

(Map p376; www.stpudenziana.org; Via Urbana 160; ⊘8.30am-noon & 3-6pm; ⓂCavour) The church of Rome's Filipino community contains a sparkling 4th-century apse mosaic, the oldest of its kind in the city. An enthroned Christ is flanked by two female figures who are crowning St Peter and St Paul; on either side of them are the apostles dressed as Roman senators. Unfortunately, you can only see 10 of the original 12 apostles, as a barbarous 16th-century facelift lopped off two and amputated the legs of the others.

CHIESA DI SANTA PRASSEDE
CHURCH

(Map p376; Via Santa Prassede 9a; ⊘7.30am-noon & 4-6.30pm; ☑Piazza Santa Maria Maggiore) Famous for its brilliant mosaics, this 9th-century church is dedicated to St Praxedes, an early Christian heroine who hid Christians fleeing persecution and buried those she couldn't save in a well. The position of the well is now marked by a marble disc on the floor of the nave.

The mosaics, produced by artists whom Pope Paschal I had brought in specially from Byzantium, bear all the hallmarks of their eastern creators, with bold gold backgrounds and a marked Christian symbolism. The apse mosaics depict Christ flanked by Sts Peter, Pudentiana and Zeno on the right, and Paul, Praxedes and Pope Paschal on the left. All the figures have golden halos except for Paschal, whose head is shadowed by a blue nimbus to indicate that he was still alive at the time. Further treasures await in the heavily mosaiced **Cappella di San Zenone**, including a piece of the column to which Christ was tied when he was flogged, brought back from Jerusalem – it's in the glass case on the right.

CHIESA DI SAN MARTINO
AI MONTI   CHURCH
(Map p376; Viale del Monte Oppio 28; ⊘9am-noon & 4.30-7pm; ⓂCavour) This was already a place of worship in the 3rd century, when Christians would meet in what was then the home of a Roman named Equitius. In the 4th century, after Christianity was legalised, a church was constructed, later rebuilt in the 6th and 9th centuries. It was then completely transformed by Filippo Gagliardi in the 1650s.

LOCAL KNOWLEDGE

VILLA ALDOBRANDINI

If you're in need of a breather around Via Nazionale or are in search of somewhere for a picnic, then take Via Mazzarino off the main road and walk up the steps, past 2nd-century ruins, where you'll find a graceful, sculpture-dotted garden (open dawn until dusk), with gravelled paths and tranquil lawns, raised around 10m above street level. These are the grounds of **Villa Aldobrandini** (Map p376), overlooked by the house built here in the 16th century by Cardinal Pietro Aldobrandini to hold his extensive art collection. Today the villa is closed to the public and houses the headquarters of an international law institute.

It's of particular interest for Gagliardi's frescoes showing the Basilica di San Giovanni in Laterano before it was rebuilt in the mid-17th century and St Peter's Basilica before it assumed its present 16th-century look. Remnants of the more distant past include the ancient Corinthian columns dividing the nave and aisles.

CHIESA DI SANTA LUCIA IN SELCI   CHURCH
(Map p376; Via in Selci 82; ⊘8am-noon & 2-6pm; ⓂCavour) The small Chiesa di Santa Lucia in Selci is a convent church devoted to the 4th-century martyr St Lucy. It dates to some time before the 8th century, but was reconstructed by Carlo Maderno in the 16th century, who kept it within the then monastery, hence the lack of a facade. It was later restored by Borromini in the 17th century.

PIAZZA VITTORIO EMANUELE II   PIAZZA
(Map p376) Laid out in the late 19th century as the centrepiece of an upmarket residential district, Rome's biggest square is a grassy expanse with a down-at-heel feel, surrounded by speeding traffic, porticoes and bargain stores. Within the fenced-off central section are the ruins of **Trofei di Mario** once a fountain at the end of an aqueduct.

In the northern corner, the **Chiesa di Sant'Eusebio** is popular with pet owners, who bring their companions to be blessed on St Anthony's feast day (17 January).

The square itself hosts cultural festivals throughout the year and an outdoor film festival in the summer.

PORTA MAGGIORE   MONUMENT
(Map p375; Piazza di Porta Maggiore; 🚋Porta Maggiore) Porta Maggiore was built by Claudius in AD 52. Then, as now, it was a major road junction under which passed the two main southbound roads, Via Prenestina and Via Labicana (modern-day Via Casilina). The arch supported two aqueducts – the Acqua Claudia and the Acqua Aniene Nuova – and was later incorporated into the Aurelian Wall.

MUSEO STORICO
DELLA LIBERAZIONE   MUSEUM
(Map p375; ☎06 700 38 66; www.viatasso.eu; Via Tasso 145; ⊘9.30am-12.30pm Tue-Sun & 3.30-7.30pm Tue, Thu & Fri; ⓂManzoni) **FREE** Now a small, chilling museum, Via Tasso 145 was the headquarters of the German SS during the Nazi occupation of Rome (1943–44).

Rome's Churches

Rome is a feast, and whatever your faith, it's impossible not to be awestruck by its riches. Nowhere will you be able to visit such a splendid array and wealth of ecclesiastic architecture, from the stark simplicity of Basilica di Santa Sabina (p203) and the tiny perfection of Bramante's Tempietto (p185) to the awe-inspiring grandeur of St Peter's Basilica (the world's greatest church; p138) and the Sistine Chapel (p146), Rome's other inspirational pilgrimage sites include huge edifices such as the basilicas of San Lorenzo Fuori le Mura (p169), Santa Maria Maggiore (p162), San Giovanni in Laterano (p197) and the Chiesa di Santa Croce in Gerusalemme (p164).

PAOLO CORDELLI / GETTY IMAGES ©

1. The courtyard garden of Basilica di San Paolo Fuori le Mura (p216) 2. Basilica di Santa Maria in Trastevere (p183) 3. A glimpse of the dome of Basilica di Santa Maria Maggiore (p162)

Ancient Architecture

Whether they're baroque, medieval or Renaissance, many churches also feature a form of recycling that's uniquely Roman, integrating leftover architectural elements from imperial Rome. For example, you'll see ancient columns in Santa Maria in Trastevere (p183), and the famous ancient manhole, the Bocca della Verità, in the beautiful medieval Chiesa di Santa Maria in Cosmedin (p78). Taking the idea to the limit, the mesmerising Pantheon (p82) is an entire Roman temple converted into a church.

Divine Art

Rome's churches, which dot almost every street corner, also serve as free art galleries, bedecked in gold, inlay-work, mosaic and carvings. The wealth of the Roman Catholic church has benefited from centuries of virtuoso artists, architects and artisans who descended here to create their finest and most heavenly works in the glorification of God. Without paying a cent, anyone can wander in off the street to see this glut of masterpieces, including works by Michelangelo (in San Pietro in Vincoli, p163, and St Peter's Basilica), Caravaggio (in Santa Maria del Popolo, p114, and San Luigi dei Francesi, p86) and Bernini (in Santa Maria della Vittoria, p122).

ⓘ COMBINED TICKET

Note that the ticket (adult/reduced €7/3.50, when there's an exhibition €10/6.50) for the Crypta Balbi and Palazzo Altemps (Centro Storico), Palazzo Massimo, Terme di Diocleziano, and Aula Ottagona combines admission for all five sites but is only valid for three days, so plan accordingly. Another worthwhile investment could be an Archaeologia Card (€23; valid 7 days), which covers these sights as well as the Colosseum, Palatino, Terme di Caracalla, Villa dei Quintilli and Cecilia Metella. It's available at any of the above.

Members of the Resistance were interrogated, tortured and imprisoned in the cells and you can still see graffiti scrawled on the walls by condemned prisoners.

Exhibits, which include photos, documents and improvised weapons, chart the events of the occupation, covering the persecution of the Jews, the underground resistance and the Fosse Ardeatina massacre.

◉ Piazza della Repubblica & Around

MUSEO NAZIONALE ROMANO: PALAZZO MASSIMO ALLE TERME   MUSEUM
See p161.

MUSEO NAZIONALE ROMANO: TERME DI DIOCLEZIANO   MUSEUM
(Map p376; ☏06 3996 7700; www.coopculture.it; Viale Enrico de Nicola 78; adult/reduced €7/3.50; ◷9am-7.30pm Tue-Sun; MTermini) The Terme di Diocleziano was ancient Rome's largest bath complex, covering about 13 hectares and with a capacity for 3000 people. Today its ruins constitute part of the impressive Museo Nazionale Romano, which supplies fascinating insight into the structure of Roman society through memorial inscriptions and other artefacts. Outside, the vast, elegant cloister was constructed from drawings by Michelangelo.

It's lined with classical sarcophagi, headless statues and huge sculptured animal heads, thought to have come from the Foro di Traiano.

Elsewhere in the museum, look out for exhibits relating to cults and the development of Christianity and Judaism. Upstairs there are exhibits of tomb objects dating from the 11th to 9th centuries BC, including jewellery and amphora.

As you wander the museum, you'll see glimpses of the original complex, which was completed in the early 4th century as a state-of-the-art combination of baths, libraries, concert halls and gardens – the Aula Ottagona and Basilica di Santa Maria degli Angeli buildings were also once part of this enormous endeavour. It fell into disrepair after the aqueduct that fed the baths was destroyed by invaders in about AD 536.

AULA OTTAGONA   ARCHAEOLOGICAL SITE
(Map p376; Piazza della Repubblica; adult/reduced €7/3.50; ◷9am-7pm Tue-Sun; MRepubblica) The Octagonal Hall was part of the ancient structure of the Terme di Diocleziano, and today form a beautiful vaulted space that houses temporary exhibitions, often of sculpture.

BASILICA DI SANTA MARIA DEGLI ANGELI   BASILICA
(Map p376; www.santamariadegliangeliroma.it; Piazza della Repubblica; ◷7am-8.30pm Mon-Sat, to 7.30pm Sun; MRepubblica) This hulking basilica occupies what was once the central hall of Diocletian's baths complex. It was originally designed by Michelangelo, but only the great vaulted ceiling remains from his plans.

CHIESA DI SAN PAOLO ENTRO LE MURA   CHURCH
(Map p376; www.stpaulsrome.it; cnr Via Nazionale & Via Napoli; ◷9.30am-4.30pm Mon-Fri; ▣Via Nazionale) With its stripy neo-Gothic exterior, Rome's American Episcopal church has some unusual 19th-century mosaics, designed by the Birmingham-born artist Edward Burne-Jones. In his representation of *The Church on Earth,* St Ambrose (on the extreme right of the centre group) has JP Morgan's face, and General Garibaldi and Abraham Lincoln (wearing a green tunic) are among the warriors.

PALAZZO DELLE ESPOSIZIONI   CULTURAL CENTRE
(Map p376; ☏06 3996 7500; www.palazzoesposizioni.it; Via Nazionale 194; ◷10am-8pm Tue-Thu & Sun, 10am-10.30pm Fri & Sat; ▣Via Nazionale) This huge neoclassical palace was built in 1882 as an exhibition centre, though it has since served as HQ for the Italian Communist Par-

ty, a mess hall for Allied servicemen, a polling station and even a public toilet. Nowadays it's a splendid cultural hub, with cathedral-scale exhibition spaces hosting blockbuster art exhibitions and sleekly designed art labs, as well as a bookshop and cafe.

The building also hosts everything from multimedia events to concert performances, film screenings and conferences, and has an excellent glass-roofed restaurant that proffers a bargain buffet lunch (€15).

PIAZZA DELLA REPUBBLICA PIAZZA
(Map p376; MRepubblica) Flanked by grand 19th-century neoclassical colonnades, this landmark piazza was laid out as part of Rome's post-unification makeover. It follows the lines of the semicircular *exedra* (benched portico) of Diocletian's baths complex and was originally known as Piazza Esedra.

In the centre, the **Fontana delle Naiadi** aroused puritanical ire when it was unveiled by architect Mario Rutelli in 1901. The nudity of the four naiads (water nymphs), who surround the central figure of Glaucus wrestling a fish, was considered too provocative – how Italy has changed! Each reclines on a creature symbolising water in a different form: a water snake (rivers), a swan (lakes), a lizard (streams) and a sea horse (oceans).

◉ San Lorenzo & Beyond

★**BASILICA DI SAN LORENZO FUORI LE MURA** BASILICA
(Map p375; www.basilicasanlorenzo.it; Piazzale San Lorenzo; ⊗8am-noon & 4-7pm; ⦂Piazzale del Verano) This is one of Rome's four patriarchal basilicas and is an atmospheric, tranquil edifice that's starker than many of the city's grand churches, a fact that only adds to its breathtaking beauty. It was the only one of Rome's major churches to have suffered bomb damage in WWII, and is a hotchpotch of rebuilds and restorations, yet still feels harmonious.

St Lawrence was burned to death in AD 258, and Constantine had the original basilica constructed in the 4th century over his burial place, which was rebuilt 200 years later. Subsequently, a nearby 5th-century church dedicated to the Virgin Mary was incorporated into the building, resulting in the church you see today. The nave, portico and much of the decoration date to the 13th century.

Highlights are the Cosmati floor and the frescoed portico, depicting events from St Lawrence's life. The remains of St Lawrence and St Stephen are in the church crypt beneath the high altar. A pretty barrel-vaulted cloister contains inscriptions and sarcophagi and leads to the Catacombe di Santa Ciriaca, where St Lawrence was initially buried.

CIMITERO DI CAMPO VERANO CEMETERY
(Map p375; ☑06 4923 6349; www.cimiteridi-roma.it; Piazzale del Verano; ⊗7.30am-6pm Apr-Sep, 7.30am-5pm Oct-Mar; ⦂Piazzale del Verano) The city's largest cemetery dates to the Napoleonic occupation of Rome between 1804 and 1814, when all the city's dead had to be buried outside the city walls. Between the 1830s and the 1980s virtually all Catholics who died in Rome (with the exception of popes, cardinals and royalty) were buried here. If you're in the area it's worth a look but try to avoid 2 November (All Souls' Day), when thousands of Romans flock to the cemetery to leave flowers on the tombs of loved ones.

PASTIFICIO CERERE GALLERY
(Map p375; ☑06 4470 3912; www.pastificiocer-ere.com; Via degli Ausoni 7; ⊗3-7pm Mon-Fri; ⦂Via Tiburtina) An elegant former pasta

MONTI, ESQUILINO & SAN LORENZO SIGHTS

WORTH A DETOUR

CHIESA DIO PADRE MISERICORDIOSO

Rome's minimalist **church** (www.diopadremisericordioso.it; Via Francesco Tovaglieri 147; ⊗7.30am-12.30pm & 4-7.30pm; ⦂Via Francesco Tovaglieri), set in the suburbs, this beautiful white Richard Meier creation has a remarkable and appropriate purity. Built out of white concrete, stucco, gleaming travertine and 976 sq metres of glass, it is an exercise in dazzling lightness, making use of the play of light both inside and out.

The structure is flanked on one side by three graduated concrete, sail-like shells, while on the other side a four-storey atrium connects the church with a community centre.

PIGNETO & AROUND

Pigneto is emerging as Rome's nuovo-hip district, a rapid metamorphosis from the working-class quarter it has been for decades. However, it has long been part of the Roman artistic consciousness, immortalised by film-maker Pasolini, who used to hang out at Necci and filmed *Accattone* (1961) here. There's a small-town feel, with decaying low-rise houses and graffiti-covered narrow streets. The action is on Via del Pigneto: it's largely pedestrianised with a busy food market by day; bars spread across the street at night. To reach here, take a tram from Termini to Via Prenestina.

Eating

I Porchettoni (Map p375; Via del Pigneto; meals around €25; ☐Via Prenestina) A lively trestle table–style place where you can feast on *porchetta* (pork roasted with herbs), mozzarella, earthy cured meats and simple pastas, without hefting all the way to Frascati – the small town outside Rome where people traditionally eat like this. It's rough and ready, full of studenty types, and with blown-up photos of post-war Pigneto adorning the walls.

Osteria Qui se Magna! (☐06 27 48 03; Via del Pigneto 307; meals €25; ☺Mon-Sat; ☐Via Prenestina) A small, simple place adorned with gingham paper tablecloths and with a couple of outside tables, here you can eat heavenly, hearty, home-cooked food, such as *carciofi con patata* (artichokes with potatoes).

Necci (☐06 9760 1552; www.necci1924.com; Via Fanfulla da Lodi 68; meals around €35; ☺8am-1am daily; ☎; ☐Via Prenestina) To start your exploration of this bar-studded area, try the iconic Necci, which opened as an ice-cream parlour in 1924 and later became a favourite of director Pier Paolo Pasolini. After a devastating fire in 2009, it was given a retro-infused makeover; now under the stewardship of English chef Ben Hirst, it serves up sophisticated Italian cooking to an eclectic crowd of all ages, with a lovely, leafy garden-terrace (ideal for families).

Primo (Map p375; ☐06 701 38 27; www.primoalpigneto.it; Via del Pigneto 46; meals around €40; ☺7.30pm-2am Tue-Sat, Sun lunch; ☎; ☐Via Prenestina) Flagship of the Pigneto scene, Primo is still buzzing after several years, with outdoor tables and a vaguely industrial brasserie-style interior. Service is slow, though.

Pigneto Quarantuno (Map p375; ☐06 7039 9483; Via del Pigneto 41; meals €50; ☺6pm-2am Tue-Sun; ☐Via Prenestina) New kid on the block, this is a chic addition to the eating

factory that hung up its spaghetti racks in 1960 after 55 years of business, this is now a hub of Rome's contemporary art scene, with regular shows in the building's gallery and courtyards.

The Pastificio came to prominence in the 1980s as home of the Nuova Scuola Romana (New Roman School), a group of six artists who are still here, alongside a new generation that includes Maurizio Savini, famous for his pink chewing-gum sculptures.

✕ EATING

Monti, conveniently just north of the Colosseum if you're looking for somewhere nearby, has some wonderful eating choices and is an increasingly chic destination. An ancient slum,

it's one of Rome's most interesting districts, with intimate bars, wine bars, restaurants and boutiques.

In the busy, hotel-packed district around Stazione Termini it's harder to find good eateries, but there are some notable classic trattorias, restaurants and artisanal gelaterie; this area also contains Rome's best ethnic eats.

✕ Monti

CIURI CIURI   PASTRIES & CAKES €
(Map p376; ☐06 4544 4548; Via Leonina 18; snacks around €3; ☺8.30am-midnight Sun-Thu, to 2am Fri & Sat; ⓜCavour) Oh *yes*…what's not to love about a Sicilian ice-cream and pastry shop? Pop by for delectable home-made sweets such as freshly filled *cannoli*

scene, proffering delicious Roman classics such as *cacio e pepe* as well as grilled steak and *baccalà* (cod).

Drinking

Il Tiaso (Map p375; ☑06 4547 4625; www.iltiaso.com; Via Perugia 20; ☎; ⚬Circonvallazione Casilina) Think living room with zebra-print chairs, walls of indie art, Lou Reed biographies shelved between wine bottles, and 30-something owner Gabriele playing his latest New York Dolls album to neo-beatnik chicks, corduroy professors and the odd neighbourhood dog. Well-priced wine, an intimate chilled vibe, and regular live music, with eclectic bands squeezed onto the bar's tiny gallery. *Aperitivo* costs €3.

Vini e Olii (Map p375; Via del Pigneto 18; ⚬Circonvallazione Casilina) Forget the other bars that line Pigneto's main pedestrianised drag, with their scattered outside tables and styled interiors. This is where the locals head. This traditional 'wine and oil' shop has sold cheap beer and wine for over 70 years, though not so much oil these days. It's outside seating only.

Entertainment

Circolo degli Artisti (Map p375; ☑06 7030 5684; www.circoloartisti.it; Via Casilina Vecchia 42; ☾7pm-2am Tue-Thu, to 4.30am Fri-Sun; ⚬Ponte Casilino) Circolo is one of Rome's best nights out, serving up a fine menu of fun: there's Screamadelica, with Italy's alternative music oracle Fabio Luzzietti. Regular gigs feature international alternative stars: think the Ravenettes to Patti Smith. The large garden area is ideal for chilling out. Sunday is vintage market day.

Forte Fanfulla (www.fanfulla.org; Via Fanfulla da Lodi 5; ⚬Circonvallazione Casilina) This cultural association is all vintage chic and left-leaning punters. There are regular live indie, jazz, reggae and rock gigs, plus vintage sales, jam sessions, art-house films, documentaries and poetry readings.

Shopping

Iosselliani (Map p375; Via del Pigneto 39; ☾4-10pm Tue-Sun; ⚬Circonvallazione Casilina) Beautiful exotic jewellery that is the work of the artistic partnership of Roberta Paolucci and Paolo Giacomelli.

(ricotta-filled tubes), *cassata* and *pasticini di mandorla* (almond pastries), all available in bite-sized versions. It's not all sweet: there are also excellent freshly made *arancine* (fried rice balls) and other snacks. Eat in or out.

FORNO DA MILVIO
PIZZERIA €
(Map p376; ☑06 4893 0145; Via dei Serpenti 7; pizza slices from around €3; ☾6.30am-10pm; ⓂCavour) A small pizza *al taglio* (by the slice) place that's always busy and serves up a great range of pizza. It's a fast-and-tasty option when you want a cheap lunch in the Colosseum/Monti area. Eat in or take away.

I MONTICIANI
CAFE €
(Map p376; Via Panisperna; meals around €20; ☾7am-11pm Mon-Sat; ⓂCavour) Full of local workers on their coffee or lunch break, this appealingly unpretentious Argentinian-Italian–owned cafe has a range of home-cooked pasta dishes available all day, plus homemade cakes, fresh salads and juices, and desserts made on the premises, including crème brûlée.

SWEETY ROME
CAFE €
(Map p376; ☑06 752 49 50; Via Milano 48; cupcakes from €3; ☾8am-7pm Mon-Fri, 10.30am-8pm Sat & Sun, closed Jul & Aug; ⓂCavour) This is an unusual proposition in Rome: delectable cupcakes (including an irresistible red velvet option), all topped with a swirl of beautiful creamy icing. Sweety Rome also proffers a great Sunday brunch , plus hearty breakfasts featuring pancakes, eggs and muffins for those tiring of the cafe and *cornetto* combination.

MONTI, ESQUILINO & SAN LORENZO EATING

★ **L'ASINO D'ORO** MODERN ITALIAN €€

(Map p376; ✆06 4891 3832; Via del Boschetto 73; meals €45; Ⓜ Cavour) This fabulous restaurant has been transplanted from Orvieto and its Umbrian origins resonate in Lucio Sforza's delicious, exceptional cooking. It's unfussy yet innovative, with dishes featuring lots of flavourful contrasts, such as slow-roasted rabbit in a rich berry sauce and desserts that linger long after that last crumb. For such excellent food, this intimate, informal yet classy place is one of Rome's best deals, especially for the set lunch.

DA VALENTINO TRATTORIA €€

(Map p376; ✆06 488 06 43; Via del Boschetto; meals €30; Ⓢ Mon-Sat; Ⓜ Cavour) The vintage 1930s sign outside says 'Birra Peroni', and inside the lovely old-fashioned feel indicates that not much has changed here for years, with black-and-white photographs on the walls, white tablecloths and tiled floors. Come here when you're in the mood for grilled *scamorza* (a type of Italian cheese, similar to mozzarella), as this is the main focus of the menu, with myriad variations: served with tomato and rocket, tomato and gorgonzola, cheese and artichokes, grilled meats, hamburgers and so on.

LA CARBONARA TRATTORIA €€

(Map p376; ✆06 482 51 76; Via Panisperna 214; meals €40; Ⓢ Mon-Sat; Ⓜ Cavour) On the go since 1906, this busy restaurant was favoured by the infamous Ragazzi di Panisperna (named after the street), the group of young physicists, including Enrico Fermi, who made discoveries in the field of nuclear physics that led to the construction of the first atomic bomb. The waiters are brusque, the place crackles with energy and the interior is covered in graffiti – tradition dictates that diners should leave their mark in a message on the wall. The speciality is the eponymous carbonara.

URBANA 47 MODERN ITALIAN €€

(Map p376; ✆06 4788 4006; Via Urbana 47; meals €45; Ⓜ Cavour) Opened by the owners of a vintage furniture store, this urbane, informal restaurant is filled with retro furnishings that are all for sale. Chef Alessandro Miotto operates the '0km' rule (as much as possible), meaning that most things you eat here will be sourced from Lazio. Attracts a chic crowd.

✗ **Esquilino**

PANELLA L'ARTE DEL PANE BAKERY, CAFE €

(Map p376; ✆06 487 24 35; Via Merulana 54; pizza slices around €3; Ⓢ noon-midnight Mon-Sat, 10am-4pm Sun Mar-Oct; Ⓜ Vittorio Emanuele) With a sumptuous array of pizza *al taglio, supplì* (fried rice balls), focaccia and fried croquettes, this is a sublime quick lunch stop, where you can sip a glass of chilled *prosecco* while eying up gastronomic souvenirs from the deli.

ROSCIOLI PIZZERIA €

(Map p376; Via Buonarroti 48; pizza €3; Ⓢ 7.30am-8pm Mon-Thu, to 9pm Fri & Sat; Ⓜ Vittorio Emanuele) Off-the-track branch of this splendid deli-bakery-pizzeria, with delish pizza *al taglio*, pasta dishes and other goodies that make it ideal for a swift lunch or picnic stock-up. It's on a road leading off Piazza Vittorio Emanuele II.

GAINN KOREAN €

(Map p376; ✆06 4436 0160; Via dei Mille 18; meals around €20; Ⓢ lunch & dinner Mon-Sat; Ⓜ Termini) A serene choice close to Rome's main train station, where you'll get a warm, friendly welcome, and dishes come with an array of enticing little salads and pickles, known as kimchi. The diners here are mainly Korean and Chinese – perhaps it's slightly spicy for many Italian palates – and the good food makes for a refreshing change if you're hankering after something non-Italian.

PALAZZO DEL FREDDO DI GIOVANNI FASSI GELATO €

(Map p375; ✆06 446 47 40; www.palazzodelfreddo.it; Via Principe Eugenio 65; ice cream from €2; Ⓢ noon-12.30am Sat, 10am-midnight Sun, noon-midnight Tue-Thu Mar-Oct, noon-10pm Tue-Thu, to midnight Fri & Sat, 10am-10pm Sun Nov-Feb; Ⓜ Vittorio Emanuele) A great back-in-time barn of a place, sprinkled with marble tabletops and vintage gelato-making machinery, Fassi is a classic Rome experience, specialising in flavours such as *riso* (rice), pistachio and *nocciola* (hazelnut). The granita, served with dollops of cream, deserves special mention.

INDIAN FAST FOOD INDIAN €

(Map p376; ✆06 446 07 92; Via Mamiani 11; curries €5.50-7.50; Ⓢ 11am-10.30pm; Ⓜ Vittorio Emanuele) Formica tables, Hindi hits, neon lights, chapatti and naan, lip-smacking samosas and bhajis, and a simple selection of main curry dishes: you could almost imagine yourself in India when you're feasting at this authentic joint.

TRATTORIA MONTI   RISTORANTE €€

(Map p376; ☎06 446 65 73; Via di San Vito 13a; meals €45; ⊙12.45-2.45pm Tue-Sun, 7.45-11pm Tue-Sat, closed Aug; Ⓜ Vittorio Emanuele) The Camerucci family runs this elegant brick-arched place, proffering top-notch traditional cooking from the Marches region. There are wonderful *fritti* (fried things), delicate pastas and ingredients such as *pecorino di fossa* (sheep's cheese aged in caves), goose, swordfish and truffles. Try the egg-yolk *tortelli* pasta. Desserts are delectable, including apple pie with *zabaglione*. Word has spread, so book ahead.

DA DANILO   TRATTORIA €€

(Map p376; ☎06 482 51 76; Via Petrarca 13; meals €45; ⊙lunch Tue-Sat, dinner Mon-Sat; Ⓜ Vittorio Emanuele) Ideal if you're looking for a fine robust meal, this upmarket version of the classic neighbourhood trattoria offers icons of Roman cooking in a rustic, eternal-Roman-trattoria atmosphere. It's renowned for its *cacio e pepe* and *carbonara*.

TRIMANI   WINE BAR €€

(Map p376; ☎06 446 96 30; Via Cernaia 37b; meals €45; ⊙11.30am-3pm & 5.30-11pm Mon-Sat; Ⓜ or Ⓡ Termini) Part of the Trimani family's wine empire (their shop just around the corner stocks about 4000 international labels), this is an unpretentious yet highly professional *enoteca*, with knowledgeable, multilingual staff. It's Rome's biggest wine bar and has a vast selection of Italian regional wines as well as an ever-changing food menu – tuck into local salami and cheese or fresh oysters.

AGATA E ROMEO   MODERN ITALIAN €€€

(Map p376; ☎06 446 61 15; Via Carlo Alberto 45; meals €120; ⊙Mon-Fri; Ⓜ Vittorio Emanuele) This elegant, restrained place was one of Rome's gastronomic pioneers and still holds its own as one of the city's most gourmet takes on Roman cuisine. Chef Agata Parisella prepares the menus and runs the kitchen, offering creative uses of Roman traditions; husband Romeo curates the wine cellar; and daughter Maria Antonietta chooses the cheeses. Bookings essential.

WINE-TASTING & COOKING COURSES

There are two very special gastronomic and oenophilic addresses in Monti. The first is **Tricolore** (Map p376; www.tricoloremonti.it; Via Urbana 126), with a specially designed cookery-teaching kitchen, where you can take classes in Italian or English. It runs pizza-making courses (€45/80 1½/3 hours) in English on Tuesday and Thursday. The second is **Vino Roma** (Map p376; ☎328 4874497; www.vinoroma.com; Via in Selci 84/G; €50 for 2 hour tastings per person), whose knowledgeable sommelier Hande Leimer guides novices and experts in wine tasting in beautifully appointed 1000-year-old cellars and a chic tasting studio. Tastings are in English, but German, Japanese, Italian and Turkish sessions are available on request. It also runs three-hour food tours (€80). Book online.

✗ Piazza della Repubblica & Around

DOOZO   JAPANESE €€

(Map p376; ☎06 481 56 55; Via Palermo 51; lunch €15-20, dinner €35-45; ⊙12.30-3pm & 7.30-11pm Tue-Sat, 7.30-10.30pm Sun, tea 4-7pm Tue-Sat; Ⓡ Via Nazionale) Doozo (meaning 'welcome') is a spacious, Zen restaurant-bookshop and gallery that offers tofu, sushi, *soba* (buckwheat noodle) soup and other Japanese delicacies, plus beer and green tea in wonderfully serene surroundings. It's a little oasis, particularly the shady courtyard garden.

★ OPEN COLONNA   MODERN ITALIAN €€€

(Map p376; ☎06 4782 2641; www.antonellocolonna.it; Via Milano 9a; meals €20-80; ⊙noon-midnight Tue-Sat, lunch Sun; ❄; Ⓡ Via Nazionale) Spectacularly set at the back of Palazzo delle Esposizioni, superchef Antonello Colonna's superb restaurant is tucked onto a mezzanine floor under an extraordinary glass roof. The cuisine is new Roman: innovative takes on traditional dishes, cooked with wit and flair. The best thing? There's a more basic but still delectable fixed two-course lunch for €16, and Saturday

LOCAL KNOWLEDGE

EATING IN ROME

Rome resident Elizabeth Minchilli, a prolific food journalist and blogger (www.elizabethminchilliinrome.com), shares some top tips:

I always suggest going first to the markets to see what's fresh, because so much has to do with what's seasonal. Besides the regular city markets, there are also weekend farmers markets, including one at Circus Maximus.

You should try *pizza bianca* (white pizza), which is typical Roman street food. There is always a discussion about who has the best. Most people cite the **Forno di Campo de' Fiori** (p100), but I prefer **Roscioli** (p172) for *pizza bianca*. If you want pizza with red sauce, go to **Antico Forno Urbani** (p101). You won't find any foreigners there, it's all Italians. The *pizza rossa* is very thin, covered with just a little bit of tomato sauce, really caramelised and fantastic.

In the last few years Rome has been having this renaissance of pizza makers. The king of pizza is Gabriele Bonci; people come from all over the world to have his pizza, so it's well worth going to **Pizzarium** (p157) if you're near the Vatican.

Another thing to try is ice cream. You'll pass lots of places with huge fluffy mounds: ignore those and try and look for the artisanal gelato makers. Again, seasonal is always good, so you'll get strawberry in the summer, chestnut in the winter. For example, over near Piazza Navona is **Gelateria del Teatro** (p99).

One of my favourite restaurants is **L'Asino d'Oro** (p172), which has a really affordable lunch menu. I'd also recommend **Settembrini** (p157), **Campana** (p100), which is very old-fashioned, and I also love **Giggetto in the Ghetto**. It has really great *carciofi alla giudia* (deep-fried artichokes). While you're in the Ghetto, stop at the Jewish bakery **Boccione** (p102) to get the *pizza ebraica* (Jewish pizza), a sort of dried-fruit cake; it weighs a ton, but it's delicious!

The latest trend in Rome is for large restaurant-cafe-bar complexes that are open for all-day dining, including **Porto Fluviale** (p218), **Romeo** (p156), and **Baccano** (p129). Plus there's the amazing **Eataly** (p217), where you can eat at many different restaurants and buy excellent Italian food produce.

And finally, Rome's beer scene is still booming, and at places like **Open Baladin** (p104) you can try lots of different craft beers on tap.

and Sunday brunch is €30, served in the dramatic, glass-ceilinged hall, with a terrace for sunny days.

✗ San Lorenzo & Beyond

In San Lorenzo, the vibrant boho student area east of Termini, you'll find an enticing mix of trendy restaurants and dirt-cheap pizzerias.

FORMULA UNO   PIZZERIA €

(Map p375; ☏06 445 38 66; Via degli Equi 13; pizzas from €6; ⊕6.30pm-1.30am Mon-Sat; ⛁Via Tiburtina, ⛁Via dei Reti) This basic, historic San Lorenzo pizzeria is as adrenaline-fuelled as its name: waiters zoom around under whirring fans, delivering tomato-loaded bruschetta, fried courgette flowers, *supplì al telefono* and bubbling thin-crust pizza to eternal crowds of feasting students.

POMMIDORO   TRATTORIA €€

(Map p375; ☏06 445 26 92; Piazza dei Sanniti 44; meals €35; ⊕Mon-Sat, closed Aug; ⛁Via Tiburtina) Throughout San Lorenzo's metamorphosis from down-at-heel working-class district to down-at-heel student enclave, Pommidoro has remained the same. It was a favourite of controversial film director Pasolini and contemporary celebs stop by, but it's an unpretentious place with superb-quality traditional food, specialising in grilled meats.

TRAM TRAM   TRATTORIA €€

(Map p375; ☏06 49 04 16; www.tramtram.it; Via dei Reti 44; meals around €40; ⊕12.30-3.30pm & 7.30-11.30pm Tue-Sun; ⛁Via Tiburtina) This trendy yet old-style lace-curtained trattoria takes its name from the trams that rattle past outside. It's a family-run concern whose menu is an unusual mix of Roman and Pugliese (southern Italian) dishes, featuring taste sensations such as *tiella riso, patate, cozze* (baked rice dish with rice, potatoes and mussels). Book ahead.

SAID
MODERN ITALIAN €€

(Map p375; ☎06 446 92 04; Via Tiburtina 135; meals €50; ☒Via Tiburtina, ☒Via dei Reti) Said is one of San Lorenzo's chicest haunts, housed in a 1920s chocolate factory. It includes a glorious chocolate shop, selling delights such as Japanese pink-tea pralines, and a stylish restaurant-bar, all cosy urban chic, with battered sofas, industrial antiques and creative cuisine.

SUSHIKO
JAPANESE €€

(Map p375; ☎06 4434 0948; Via degli Irpini 8; sushi menus from €40; ☺1-2.30pm Tue-Sat & 8pm-midnight Mon-Sat; ☒Via Tiburtina) This nondescript San Lorenzo lane is an unlikely place to find Rome's best sushi, but here it is, with the freshest fish served up as sushi and sashimi, plus rolls, tempura and teppanyaki. It's tiny, with only 24 covers, so book ahead. A set menu makes better financial sense than à la carte.

🍷 DRINKING & NIGHTLIFE

The Monti area, north of the Colosseum, is splendid for an *aperitivo*, meal or after-dark drinks, and is dotted with charming bars, *enoteche* (wine bars), and even a jazz club. If you want to keep it real, head down to San Lorenzo, the student district, a centre for grungy pubs, bars, clubs and some surprisingly chic restaurants. Less studenty but still with a gritty feel is the happening boho nightlife district of Pigneto.

🍷 Monti

AI TRE SCALINI
WINE BAR

(Map p376; Via Panisperna 251; ☺12.30pm-1am Mon-Fri, 6pm-1am Sat & Sun; ☒Cavour) The Three Steps is always packed, with crowds spilling out into the street. Apart from a tasty choice of wines, it sells the damn fine Menabrea beer, brewed in northern Italy. You can also tuck into a heart-warming array of cheeses, salami and dishes such as *polpette al sugo* (meatballs with sauce; €7).

FAFIUCHÉ
WINE BAR

(Map p376; ☎06 699 09 68; www.fafiuche.it; Via della Madonna dei Monti 28; ☺5.30pm-1am Mon-Sat; ☒Cavour) Fafiuché means 'light-hearted

fun' in the Piedmontese dialect, and this place lives up to its name. The narrow, bottle-lined warm-orange space exudes charm: come here to enjoy wine and artisanal beers, eat delicious dishes originating from Puglia to Piedmont, or buy delectable foodstuffs. *Aperitivo* is from 6.30pm to 9pm.

2 PERIODICO CAFFÈ
CAFE

(Map p376; Via Leonina 77; ☺9am-1am Tue-Thu, to 2am Fri-Sun; ☒Cavour) This cafe has a funky laid-back vibe, with its mismatched vintage furniture, fairylights in jam jars and personable bar staff. It's the kind of place you might find in Shoreditch (London) or the Marais (Paris), but what's uniquely Italian is the cuisine, coffee and delicious little extras such as lavender-scented More Bianche biscuits.

LA BOTTEGA DEL CAFFÈ
CAFE

(Map p376; Piazza Madonna dei Monti 5; ☺8am-2am; ☒Cavour) Ideal for frittering away any balmy section of the day, this appealing cafe-bar, named after a comedy by Carlo Goldoni, has greenery-screened tables out on the pretty Piazza Madonna dei Monti. As well as drinks, it serves snacks, from simple pizzas to cheeses and salamis.

LA BARRIQUE
WINE BAR

(Map p376; Via del Boschetto 41b; ☺noon-2am Mon-Sat; ☒Cavour) Bottle-lined Barrique has expanded and added a full kitchen. This always appealing *enoteca* is now a more spacious place to hang out and sample excellent French, Italian and German wines; the meat skewers and pasta dishes make a great accompaniment. There's also regular live jazz and blues.

CASA CLEMENTINA
BAR

(Map p376; Via Clementina 9; ☺5pm-2am Tue-Sun) Styled like a vintage magazine home-design photo shoot, this self-consciously cool *casa* ('house') feels rather like hanging out in a stranger's apartment with a bunch of easy-on-the-eye hipsters. There's *aperitivo* and regular DJ nights. And now that you've had a drink, live the lifestyle: everything on view is for sale.

AL VINO AL VINO
WINE BAR

(Map p376; Via dei Serpenti 19; ☺6pm-1am, shop open all day; ☒Cavour) A rustic *enoteca* that's a favourite with the locals, mixing ceramic tabletops and contemporary paintings, this is an attractive spot to linger over a fine collection of wines, particularly *passiti* (sweet wines). The other speciality is *distillati* – grappa, whisky and so on – and there are snacks to help it all go down, including some Sicilian delicacies.

BOHEMIEN   BAR

(Map p376; Via degli Zingari 36; ☺6pm-2am Wed-Sun; MCavour) This little bar lives up to its name; it feels like something you might stumble on in Left Bank Paris. It's small, with mismatched chairs and tables and an eclectic crowd drinking wine by the glass, tea and coffee.

ICE CLUB   BAR

(Map p376; www.iceclubroma.it; Via Madonna dei Monti 18; ☺6pm-2am; MColosseo) Novelty value is what the Ice Club is all about. Pay €15 (you get a free vodka cocktail served in a glass made of ice), put on a thermal cloak and mittens, and enter the bar, in which everything is made of ice (temperature: -5˚C). Most people won't chill here for long – the record is held by a Russian (four hours).

🍷 Esquilino

BAR ZEST AT THE RADISSON BLU ES.   BAR

(Map p376; Via Filippo Turati 171; ☺9am-1am; 🖵Via Cavour) In need of a cocktail in the Termini district? Pop up to the 7th-floor bar at the slinkily designed Radisson Blu Es. Waiters are cute, chairs are by Jasper Morrison, views are through plate-glass and there's a sexy rooftop pool to look at. A glass of *prosecco* costs €9 and there are light meals and snacks (plus a children's menu).

CASTRONI   CAFE

(Map p376; Via Nazionale 7; ☺7.30am-8pm Mon-Sat, 9.30am-8pm Sun; 🖵Via Cavour) This gourmet shop sells foodstuffs from all over the world. Although this branch doesn't have as large a range as that on Via Cola di Rienzo, it still has the fab cafe, which has great coffee, *panini* and other snacks, and you can stand at the bar or sit at a few booth tables.

FIDDLER'S ELBOW   PUB

(Map p376; Via dell'Olmata 43; ☺5pm-2am; 🖵Via Cavour) Near the Basilica di Santa Maria Maggiore, the granddaddy of Rome's Irish pubs sticks to the formula that has served it so well over the last 25 years or so: Guin-

ness, darts, crisps and big games, attracting a mix of Romans, expats and tourists. There's live traditional music on Tuesdays and Wednesdays, plus open-mic nights on Thursdays.

FINNEGANS   PUB

(Map p376; www.finneganpub.com; Via Leonina 66; MCavour) At first glance this seems like an identikit Irish pub, but look closer and the craic here has Italian twists – the clientele are well-groomed expats and Romans, and you can order Bellinis as well as Guinness. It's Irish-run and shows all the big football and rugby games, and there's occasional live music.

DRUID'S DEN   PUB

(Map p376; Via San Martino ai Monti 28; ☺5pm-1.30am; MCavour) When in Rome...do as the Romans do and head to an Irish pub. The Druid's Den attracts a cheerful crowd of young expats and Roman Anglophiles. The atmosphere is convivial, the walls are wood-panelled, Celtic paraphernalia is everywhere, Guinness is on tap and it shows all the big games.

HANGAR   NIGHTCLUB

(Map p376; www.hangaronline.it; Via in Selci 69; ☺10.30pm-2.30am Wed-Mon, closed 3 weeks Aug; MCavour) A gay landmark since 1984, Hangar is friendly and welcoming, with a cruisey vibe. It attracts locals and out-of-towners, with porn nights on Monday and strippers on Thursday. Feeling frisky? Head to the dark room.

🍷 San Lorenzo & Beyond

MICCA CLUB   NIGHTCLUB, LIVE MUSIC

(Map p375; www.miccaclub.com; Via Pietra Micca 7a; ☺7pm-2am Mon, Tue & Thu-Sat, from 6pm Sun; MVittorio Emanuele) At eclectic Micca, pop art and jelly-bright lighting fills ancient, cathedral-like arched cellars, and there are regular burlesque, drag, swing and rockabilly nights, plus loads of live gigs. There's *aperitivo* nightly until 10pm, and an admission charge if a gig's on and at the weekend. Register online for discounts.

LOCANDA ATLANTIDE   NIGHTCLUB, LIVE MUSIC

(Map p375; ☏06 4470 4540; www.locandatlantide.it; Via dei Lucani 22b; ☺9pm-2am Oct-Jun; MVia Tiburtina, 🖵Scalo San Lorenzo) Come, tickle Rome's grungy underbelly. Descend through a door in a graffiti-covered wall into this cavernous basement dive, packed to the rafters with studenty, alternative crowds and featuring everything from experimental theatre to DJ-spun electro music. It's good to know that punk is not dead.

SOLEA
BAR

(Map p375; ☎328 9252925; Via dei Latini 51; ⊗9am-2am; ⓜVia Tiburtina, ⓡ Scalo San Lorenzo) With vintage sofas and chairs, and cushions on the floor, this slightly grungy place has the look of a chill-out room in a gone-to-seed mansion, and is full of lounging San Lorenzo dudes drinking mean mojitos. Fun.

PEOPLE
BAR, CAFE

(Map p375; ☎06 445 44 25; Via degli Aurunci 42; ⊗7am-2am; ⓡVia dei Reti) On the corner of San Lorenzo's most happening piazza, this is a relaxed place for a drink, snack or meal (it does good salads). The interior is airy, with warm orange walls and brick arches, and there are some outdoor tables as well as occasional live music.

DIMMIDISÌ
NIGHTCLUB

(Map p375; ☎06 446 18 55; http://dimmidisiclub.org; Via dei Volsci 126B; ⊗6pm-2am Thu-Mon Sep-May; ⓡVia dei Reti, ⓜVia Tiburtina) The intimate, small-scale 'Tell Me Yes' proffers a wide range of off-beat nights, from reggae to the *taranta* music of southern Italy. There are regular DJs and it's a good place to see live bands.

ESC ATELIER
NIGHTCLUB

(Map p375; www.escatelier.net; Via dei Volsci 159; ⊗11pm-4am; ⓜVia Tiburtina, ⓡVia dei Reti) This left-wing alternative arts centre hosts live gigs and club nights: expect electronica DJ sets featuring live sax, discussions, exhibitions, political events and more. Admission and drinks are cheap.

VICIOUS CLUB
NIGHTCLUB

(Map p375; ☎06 7020 1599; Via Achille Grandi 3a; admission varies; ⊗10pm-4.30am Thu-Sat, to 4am Sun; ⓡRoma Lazialì) Vicious, formerly the landmark gay Max's Bar, has been reborn as a gay-friendly club that welcomes all to dance and chatter to a soundtrack of electro, no-wave, deep techno, glam indie, and deep house. It's small enough to feel intimate; try Alchemy every Saturday, featuring DJs such as Claudio Fabrianesi.

ENTERTAINMENT

TEATRO DELL'OPERA DI ROMA
OPERA

(Map p376; ☎06 481 70 03; www.operaroma.it; Piazza Beniamino Gigli; ballet €12-80; opera €17-150; ⊗box office 9am-5pm Mon-Sat, 9am-1.30pm Sun; ⓜRepubblica) Built in 1880, the plush and gilt interior of Rome's premier opera house is a stunning surprise after the Fascist-era exterior (which was revamped in the 1920s). This theatre has an impressive history: it premiered Puccini's *Tosca* and Maria Callas once sang here. Contemporary productions don't always match the splendour of the setting, but you may get lucky.

CHARITY CAFÉ
LIVE MUSIC

(Map p376; ☎06 4782 5881; www.charitycafe.it; Via Panisperna 68; ⊗6pm-2am Tue-Sun; ⓜCavour) Think narrow space, spindly tables, dim lighting and a laid-back vibe: this is a place to snuggle down and listen to some slinky live jazz. Civilised, relaxed, untouristy and very Monti. Gigs usually take place from 9.30pm (Thursday to Saturday), with live music and *aperitivo* on Sundays from 6pm.

UNPLUGGED IN MONTI
LIVE MUSIC

(Map p376; www.black-market.it; Via Panisperna 101; admission €5-10; ⊗Sep-May; ⓜCavour) In a slightly shady corner of Monti, a small bar called Black Market hosts acoustic indie and folk gigs, presented by the Italian music webzine IndieForBunnies. It's rather like sitting in someone's front room. To attend, you'll need free membership, which you can obtain at the door or via the website. In the summer, gigs move outside (various venues, check online).

ISTITUZIONE UNIVERSITARIA DEI CONCERTI
LIVE MUSIC

(IUC; Map p375; ☎06 361 00 51; www.concertiiuc.it; Piazzale Aldo Moro 5; ⓜCastro Pretorio) The

---

RADISSON BLU ES.

This swish, cutting-edge hotel (p262) close to Termini has a sexy rooftop pool open to nonguests for around €55 per day, with a 50% discount for children (under 3 years old free). A cocktail bar and restaurant are located alongside.

MONTI, ESQUILINO & SAN LORENZO ENTERTAINMENT

IUC organises a season of concerts in the Aula Magna of La Sapienza University, including many visiting international artists and orchestras. Performances cover a wide range of musical genres, including baroque, classical, contemporary and jazz.

TEATRO AMBRA JOVINELLI
THEATRE

(Map p375; ☑06 8308 2620; www.ambrajovinelli.org; Via G Pepe 43-47; ⓂVittorio Emanuele) A home from home for many famous Italian comics, the Ambra Jovinelli is a historic venue for alternative comedians and satirists. Between government-bashing, the theatre hosts productions of classics, musicals, opera, new works and the odd concert.

 # SHOPPING

Monti

TINA SONDERGAARD
CLOTHING

(Map p376; ☑06 9799 0565; Via del Boschetto 1D; ⓒ3-7.30pm Mon, 10.30am-1pm & 1.30-7.30pm Tue-Sat, closed Aug; ⓂCavour) Sublimely cut and whimsically retro-esque, these handmade threads are a hit with female fashion cognoscenti, including Italian rock star Carmen Consoli and the city's theatre and TV crowd. Each piece is a limited edition and new creations hit the racks every week.

LA BOTTEGA DEL CIOCCOLATO
FOOD

(Map p376; ☑06 482 14 73; Via Leonina 82; ⓒ9.30am-7.30pm Oct-Aug; ⓂCavour) Run by the younger generation of Moriondo & Gariglio is a magical world of scarlet walls and old-fashioned glass cabinets set into black wood, with irresistible smells wafting in from the kitchen and rows of lovingly homemade chocolates on display.

PODERE VECCIANO
FOOD

(Map p376; ☑06 4891 3812; Via dei Serpenti 33; ⓒ10am-8pm; ⓂCavour) Selling produce from its Tuscan farm, this shop is a great place to pick up presents, such as different varieties of pesto, honey and marmalade, selected wines, olive oil–based cosmetics and beautiful olive wood chopping boards. There's even an olive tree growing in the middle of the shop.

101
CLOTHING

(Map p376; Via Urbana; ⓒ10am-1.30pm & 2-8pm; ⓂCavour) The collection at this individual boutique might include gossamer-light jumpers, broad-brimmed hats, chain-mail earrings and silk dresses: it's always worth a look to discover a special something.

LIBRERIA LA GRU
BOOKS

(Map p376; ☑334 9013091; Via del Boschetto 20; ⓒ5-8pm Mon, 11am-2.30pm & 4-8pm Tue-Sat; ⓂCavour) A lovely small vintage bookshop, with a careful selection of rare books and first editions, beautifully presented.

FABIO PICCIONI
JEWELLERY

(Map p376; ☑06 474 16 97; Via del Boschetto 148; ⓒ10.30am-1pm Tue-Sat, 2-8pm Mon-Sat; ⓂCavour) A sparkling Aladdin's cave of decadent, one-of-a-kind costume jewellery; artisan Fabio Piccioni recycles old trinkets to create remarkable art deco–inspired jewellery.

ABITO
CLOTHING

(Map p376; ☑06 488 10 17; abito61.blogspot.co.uk; Via Panisperna 61; ⓒ10.30am-8pm Mon-Sat, noon-8pm Sun; ⓂCavour) Wilma Silvestre designs elegant clothes with a difference. Choose from the draped, chic, laid-back styles on the rack, and you can have one made up just for you in a day or just a few hours – customise the fabric and the colour. There's usually one guest designer's clothes also being sold at the shop, and there are occasional vintage sales downstairs.

FAUSTO SANTINI OUTLET
SHOES

(Map p376; ☑06 488 09 34; Via Cavour 106; ⓂCavour) Close to the Basilica di Santa Maria Maggiore, this store sells end-of-line and discounted Fausto Santini boots, shoes and bags, and is well worth a look for bargain signature architectural designs in butter-soft leather at a fraction of the retail price. Sizes are limited, however.

Esquilino

ARION ESPOSIZIONI
BOOKS

(Map p376; ☑06 4891 3361; Via Milano 15-17; ⓒ10am-8pm Mon-Thu & Sun, 10am-10.30pm Fri & Sat; ⓓVia Nazionale) In cool, gleaming white rooms designed by Firouz Galdo, Arion Esposizioni – the bookshop attached to Palazzo delle Esposizioni – is just made for browsing. There are books on art,

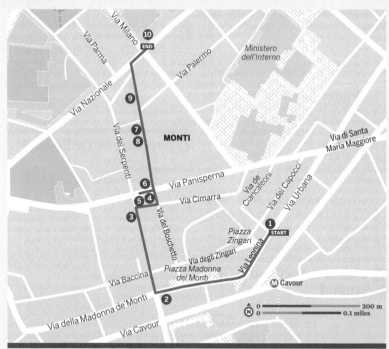

Neighbourhood Walk
Monti Shopping

START 101
END ARION ESPOSIZIONI
LENGTH 1KM; TWO HOURS

This walk visits the shopping highlights of the Monti district, once a Roman slum and today home to appealing wine bars, restaurants and unique boutiques.

First stop is **①101** (p178), to get the chic-casual Roman look (for women). Then walk down to Piazza Madonna dei Monti, the district's picturesque hub. Just past the piazza is **②La Bottega del Cioccolato** (p178), filled with enticing rows of handmade chocolates. In the run-up to Christmas, Easter and Valentine's Day, the shop is dominated by beautifully presented, appropriately themed sweets. Then turn and walk up Via dei Serpenti and on your left is **③Podere Vecciano** (p178), selling delectable Tuscan foodstuffs.

Walking northwards up to the junction with Via Cimarra, turn right, then left into Via del Boschetto. The first shop you'll see

is the glinting treasure trove **④Fabio Piccioni** (p178), filled with vintage, recreated costume jewellery. Tear yourself away and settle down for a drink and a snack around the corner at **⑤Ai Tre Scalini** (p175), everyone's favourite Monti wine bar. A few paces away back on Via del Boschetto is the individual women's tailoring of **⑥Tina Sondergaard** (p178). Amble further up the street and you'll find the tiny **⑦Libreria La Gru** (p178), selling vintage books and first editions, while a little further up is **⑧Archivia** (Via del Boschetto 15/A), a gem of a shop featuring unusual homewares such as silver cutlery with twig-shaped handles. A few steps away is **⑨Perlei** (Via del Boschetto 35), with handmade modernist jewellery. For your last stop, cross busy Via Nazionale and dive into the tempting book-lined **⑩Arion Esposizioni** (p178), a great place to browse books on art and Rome as well as curious objects of design; its entrance is to the side of the magnificent Palazzo delle Esposizioni.

architecture and photography, DVDs, CDs, vinyl, children's books and gifts for the design-lover in your life.

MAS
DEPARTMENT STORE

(Map p376; ✆06 446 80 78; Via dello Statuto 11; ⊙9am-12.45pm & 3.45-7.45pm; Ⓜ Vittorio Emanuele) Glorious MAS (Magazzino allo Statuto) is a multistorey temple of didn't-know-I-needed-it, cheap-as-chips practical goods, thermal vests, bags, watches, pants and the kitchen sink, all piled high and at bargain prices. You can pick up a hat here for a couple of euros or a pair of silk pyjamas for €5.

NUOVO MERCATO ESQUILINO
MARKET

(Map p376; Via Lamarmora; Ⓜ Vittorio Emanuele) Cheap and the best place to find exotic herbs and spices.

🛍 Piazza della Repubblica & Around

FELTRINELLI INTERNATIONAL
BOOKS

(Map p376; ✆06 482 78 78; Via VE Orlando 84; ⊙9am-8pm Mon-Sat, 10.30am-1.30pm & 4-8pm Sun; Ⓜ Repubblica) The international branch of Italy's ubiquitous bookseller has a splendid collection of books in English, Spanish, French, German and Portuguese. You'll find everything from recent bestsellers to dictionaries, travel guides, DVDs and an excellent assortment of maps.

IBS.IT
BOOKS

(Map p376; Via Nazionale 254-255; ⊙9am-8pm Mon-Sat, 10am-1.30pm & 4-8pm Sun; 📶; Ⓜ Repubblica) IBS.it, on three floors, has a good range of Italian literature, reference books and travel guides, as well as CDs, half-priced books (general-fiction paperbacks), a cheery children's section and a few books in English and French.

🛍 San Lorenzo & Beyond

LA GRANDE OFFICINA
JEWELLERY

(Map p375; ✆06 445 03 48; lagrandeofficina-gioielli.blogspot.co.uk; Via dei Sabelli 165B; ⊙1-7.30pm Mon 11am-7.30pm, Tue-Fri; 🚆 Via Tiburtina) Under dusty workshop lamps, husband-and-wife team Giancarlo Genco and Daniela Ronchetti turn everything from old clock parts and Japanese fans into beautiful work-of-art jewellery. Head here for something truly unique.

CLAUDIO SANÒ
ARTISANAL

(Map p375; ✆06 446 92 84; www.claudiosano.it; Largo degli Osci 67A; ⊙10am-1pm & 4.30-8pm Mon-Sat; 🚆 Via Tiburtina) Claudio Sanò creates gleaming moulded works of art in leather that are beautiful, witty and surreal, such as a briefcase with a keyhole through it, another with a bite taken out of it and a handbag in the shape of a fish. They're not cheap, but masterpieces seldom are.

Trastevere & Gianicolo

EAST OF VIALE DI TRASTEVERE | WEST OF VIALE DI TRASTEVERE | GIANICOLO

Neighbourhood Top Five

1 Discovering the Piazza di Santa Maria in Trastevere and visiting its beautiful **church** (p103), with its exquisite interior and exterior mosaics.

2 Exploring the lavishly ornate **Palazzo Corsini** (p184) and settling down to gaze at Caravaggio's sensual, youthful depiction of St John the Baptist.

3 Visiting the nuns' choir of the **Basilica di Santa Cecilia in Trastevere** (p184) to see the Cavallini fresco.

4 Feeling as if you're soaring over Rome: the views from **Gianicolo Hill** (p185).

5 Enjoying the fantastical Raphael frescoes of **Villa Farnesina** (p188).

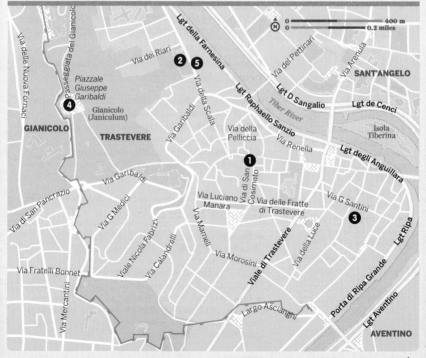

For more detail of this area, see Map p372 ➡

Lonely Planet's Top Tip

Time your visit to Santa Cecilia for between 10am and 2.30pm Monday to Saturday, so that you can gain entrance to the hushed convent next door to see the Cavallini fresco.

Best Places to Eat

➡ Glass Hostaria (p109)
➡ La Gensola (p189)
➡ Le Mani in Pasta (p189)
➡ Fatamorgana (p189)

For reviews, see p189 ➡

🍺 Best Places to Drink

➡ Ma Che Siete Venuti a Fà (p191)
➡ Bar San Calisto (p191)
➡ Freni e Frizioni (p191)
➡ Ombre Rosse (p192)
➡ Bar Stuzzichini (p192)

For reviews, see p191 ➡

⊙ Best Works of Art

➡ Basilica di Santa Maria in Trastevere (p183)
➡ Stefano Maderno's sculpture in the Basilica di Santa Cecilia in Trastevere (p184)
➡ Frescoes in Villa Farnesina (p188)
➡ Caravaggios in Galleria Nazionale d'Arte Antica di Palazzo Corsini (p184)

For reviews, see p183 ➡

Explore: Trastevere & Gianicolo

Trastevere is one of Rome's most vivacious neighbourhoods, an outdoor circus of ochre and butterscotch *palazzi* (mansions), ivy-clad facades and photogenic cobbled lanes, peopled with a bohemian and eclectic cast of tourists, travellers, students and street sellers. The bohos and original Romans might be increasingly rubbing shoulders with wealthy expats and American students from the local John Cabot University, as rental prices in this most beguiling district go through the roof, but Trastevere still retains its distinct, very Roman character. The very name means 'across the Tiber' *(tras tevere)*, emphasising the sense of difference.

The area is ideal for aimless, contented wandering, home cooking in local trattorias and an evening drink to watch the world go by: it's one of Rome's most happening districts after dark, especially on summer evenings. There are also some beautiful sights here: glittering Basilica di Santa Maria in Trastevere is one of Rome's most charming churches, Villa Farnesina contains superb frescoes by Raphael and others, and exquisitely frescoed Palazzo Corsini is home to a dazzling, almost forgotten-feeling art collection. Close by are the tranquil botanical gardens, and you can hike up Gianicolo (Janiculum Hill) to see Rome laid out before you like a dome-punctuated patchwork. Don't neglect to see Bramante's perfect little Tempietto on your way up. To the east, Basilica di Santa Cecilia in Trastevere is the resting place of St Cecilia, patron saint of music, with a wonderful, hidden Cavallini fresco.

Local Life

➡ **Drinking** A coffee or a *sambuca con la mosca* ('with a fly' – coffee bean) at Bar San Calisto (p191).
➡ **Passeggiata** An evening stroll to see and be seen, with a stop for an ice cream.
➡ **Football** Trastevere is a Roma supporters' stronghold: come a big game, the air of excitement is palpable.

Getting There & Away

➡ **Tram** From Largo di Torre Argentina tram 8 runs along Viale di Trastevere, ending up at Villa Doria Pamphilj. Tram 3 also stops at the southern end of Viale di Trastevere, connecting with Testaccio (Via Marmorata), Colosseo, San Giovanni and Villa Borghese.
➡ **Bus** From Termini, bus H runs to Viale di Trastevere, while bus 780 runs from Piazza Venezia. For Gianicolo, if you don't fancy the steep steps from Via G Mameli, take bus 870 from Piazza delle Rovere.

TOP SIGHT
BASILICA DI SANTA MARIA IN TRASTEVERE

This glittering church is said to be the oldest church in Rome dedicated to the Virgin Mary. Its facade is decorated with a beautiful medieval mosaic depicting Mary feeding Jesus surrounded by 10 women bearing lamps. Two are veiled and hold extinguished lamps, symbolising widowhood, while the lit lamps of the others represent their virginity.

A Fountain of Oil

The church was first constructed in the early 3rd century over the spot where, according to legend, a fountain of oil miraculously sprang from the ground. Its current Romanesque form is the result of a 12th-century revamp. The portico was added by Carlo Fontana in 1702, with its balustrade decorated by four popes.

Mosaics

Inside it's the golden 12th-century mosaics that stand out. In the apse, look out for the dazzling depiction of Christ and his mother flanked by various saints and, on the far left, Pope Innocent II holding a model of the church. Beneath this is a series of six mosaics by Pietro Cavallini (c 1291) illustrating the life of the Virgin.

Columns, Ceiling & Cosmati

Note the 21 Roman columns, some plundered from the Terme di Caracalla, the wooden ceiling designed in 1617 by Domenichino and, on the right of the altar, a spiralling Cosmati candlestick, on the exact spot where the oil fountain is said to have sprung. The Cappella Avila is also worth a look for its stunning 17th-century dome. The spiralling Cosmatesque floor was relaid in the 1870s, a recreation of the 13th-century original.

DON'T MISS...

➡ Facade mosaics
➡ 13th-century Cavallini mosaics in the apse
➡ Ancient Roman granite columns

PRACTICALITIES

➡ Map p372
➡ Piazza Santa Maria in Trastevere
➡ ☉7.30am-9pm
➡ ▢or ▢Viale di Trastevere

◉ SIGHTS

Trastevere is dotted with exquisite churches and artworks, yet some of its most memorable sights are picturesque glimpses down narrow, ochre-and-orange-shaded lanes that will make you catch your breath.

◉ East of Viale di Trastevere

CHIESA DI SAN FRANCESCO D'ASSISI A RIPA
CHURCH

(Map p372; Piazza San Francesco d'Assisi 88; ☻7.30am-noon & 2-7.30pm; 🚌or 🚊Viale di Trastevere) St Francis is said to have stayed here in the 13th century, and you can still see the rock that he used as a pillow and his crucifix in his cell. Rebuilt several times, the church's current incarnation dates from the 1680s. It contains one of Bernini's most daring works, the *Beata Ludovica Albertoni* (Blessed Ludovica Albertoni; 1674), a work of highly charged sexual ambiguity.

It shows Ludovica, a Franciscan nun, in a state of rapture as she reclines, eyes shut, mouth open, one hand touching her breast.

The 17th-century church also contains impressive 18th-century Rospigliosi and Pallavici sculptural monuments.

◉ West of Viale di Trastevere

BASILICA DI SANTA MARIA IN TRASTEVERE
CHURCH

See p183.

GALLERIA LORCAN O'NEILL
ART GALLERY

(☏06 6889 2980; www.lorcanoneill.com; Via degli Orti d'Alibert 1E; ☻noon-8pm Mon-Fri, 2-8pm Sat; 🚌Lungotevere Gianicolense) Kick-started by a London art dealer and set in a converted stable, this is one of Rome's most respected private galleries, bringing edgy international names to the city – think Tracey Emin and Max Rental – as well as displaying local talent such as Luigi Ontani and Pietro Ruffo.

GALLERIA NAZIONALE D'ARTE ANTICA DI PALAZZO CORSINI
ART GALLERY

(Map p372; ☏06 6880 2323; galleriacorsini. beniculturali.it/; Via della Lungara 10; adult/reduced €5/2.50, integrated ticket including Pal-

---

TOP SIGHT **BASILICA DI SANTA CECILIA IN TRASTEVERE**

This church, with its serene courtyard, remarkable frescoes by Pietro Cavallini, and ancient Roman excavations beneath the building, is the last resting place of St Cecilia, the patron saint of music.

This basilica stands on the site of an earlier 5th-century church, itself built over the ancient Roman house where it's believed Cecilia was martyred in AD 230. You can visit the network of excavated houses that lie beneath the church. Below the altar, Stefano Maderno's delicate sculpture shows exactly how Cecilia's miraculously preserved body was apparently found when it was unearthed in the Catacombe di San Callisto in 1599.

In the right-hand nave the Cappella del Caldarium, complete with two works by Guido Reni, marks the spot where the saint was allegedly tortured.

But the basilica's hidden wonder is Cavallini's spectacular 13th-century fresco, showing a section of his *Last Judgement*, in the nuns' choir. Much of this late medieval masterwork was lost during the remodelling of the church in the 18th century, but what remains gives an idea of its splendour.

DON'T MISS...

➡ Cavallini's *Last Judgement* fresco
➡ Maderno's sculpture
➡ Excavated buildings

PRACTICALITIES

➡ Map p372
➡ Piazza di Santa Cecilia
➡ basilica free, fresco & crypt each €2.50
➡ ☻basilica & crypt 9.30am-2.30pm & 4-7.30pm, fresco 10am-2.30pm Mon-Sat
➡ 🚌or 🚊Viale di Trastevere

azzo Barberini €9/4.50; ◷8.30am-7.30pm Tue-Sun; 🚇Lgt della Farnesina, 🚇Viale di Trastevere) Once home to Queen Christina of Sweden, whose richly frescoed bedroom witnessed a stready stream of male and female lovers, 16th-century Palazzo Corsini houses part of Italy's national art collection. The highlights include Caravaggio's mesmerising *San Giovanni Battista* (St John the Baptist), Rubens' *Testa di Vecchio* (Head of an Old Man) and Fra Angelico's Corsini Triptych, plus works by Poussin, Reni and Van Dyck.

PIAZZA SANTA MARIA IN TRASTEVERE
PIAZZA

(Map p372; Viale di Trastevere; 🚇or 🚇Viale di Trastevere) Trastevere's focal square is a prime people-watching spot. By day it's full of mums with strollers, chatting locals and guidebook-toting tourists; by night it's the domain of foreign students, young Romans and out-of-towners, all out for a good time. The fountain in the centre of the square is of Roman origin and was restored by Carlo Fontana in 1692.

MUSEO DI ROMA IN TRASTEVERE
MUSEUM

(Map p372; ☎06 8205 9127; www.museodiromaintrastevere.it; Piazza Sant'Egidio 1b; adult/reduced €6.50/5.50; ◷10am-8pm Tue-Sun; 🚇or 🚇Viale di Trastevere) Housed in a 17th-century Carmelite convent, this museum hosts excellent temporary photography exhibitions that are usually worth the price of admission alone. Upstairs the permanent collection contains a selection of 19th-century watercolours depicting Rome, life-size dioramas showing 19th-century Roman life, temporary Rome-related exhibitions, and *Stanza di Trilussa,* an installation relating to the famous Roman poet.

PORTA SETTIMIANA
MONUMENT

(Map p372; 🚇Lgt della Farnesina, Piazza Trilussa) Resembling a crenellated keep, Porta Settimiana marks the start of Via della Lungara, the 16th-century road that connects Trastevere with the Borgo. It was built in 1498 by Pope Alexander VI over a small passageway in the Aurelian Wall and later altered by Pope Pius VI in 1798.

From Porta Settimiana, Via Santa Dorotea leads to Piazza Trilussa, a popular evening hang-out, and Ponte Sisto, which connects with the *centro storico.*

◉ Gianicolo

Today a tranquil and leafy area that combines Rome's finest views, embassies, monuments, piazzas, Rome's botanical gardens and some beautiful architecture, it's difficult to imagine today that in 1849 the Gianicolo was the scene of fierce and bloody fighting. A makeshift army under Giuseppe Garibaldi defended Rome against French troops sent to restore papal rule. The hill today is dotted by monuments to the Italian hero and his army – Garibaldi is commemorated with a massive monument in Piazzale Giuseppe Garibaldi, while his Brazilian-born wife, Anita, has her own equestrian monument about 200m away in Piazzale Anita Garibaldi; she died shortly after the siege from malaria, together with their unborn child.

The Gianicolo is a superb viewpoint with sweeping panoramas over Rome's rooftops, and has several summer-only bars that are blessed with thrilling views. There are also regular children's puppet shows on the hill, a long-standing tradition.

ORTO BOTANICO
GARDEN

(Map p372; ☎06 499 17 107; Largo Cristina di Svezia 24; adult/reduced €8/4; ◷9am-6.30pm Mon-Sat Apr–mid-Oct, 9am-5.30pm Mon-Sat mid-Oct–Mar; 🚇Lgt della Farnesina, Piazza Trilussa) Formerly the private grounds of Palazzo Corsini, Rome's 12-hectare botanical gardens are a little-known, slightly neglected-feeling gem and a great place to unwind in a tree-shaded expanse covering the steep slopes of the Gianicolo, though the admission charge is unfortunately also a bit steep.

Plants have been cultivated here since the 13th century. However, in their present form, the gardens were established in 1883, when the grounds of Palazzo Corsini were given to the University of Rome. They now contain up to 8000 species, including some of Europe's rarest plants. You'll find a Japanese garden and some impressive bamboo, and a collection of cacti in a glasshouse.

TEMPIETTO DI BRAMANTE & CHIESA DI SAN PIETRO IN MONTORIO
CHURCH

(Map p372; www.sanpietroinmontorio.it; Piazza San Pietro in Montorio 2; ◷8.30am-noon, also 3-4pm Tue-Sun; 🚇Via Garibaldi) Considered the first great building of the High Renaissance, Bramante's sublime Tempietto is in the courtyard of the Chiesa di San Pietro

Rome Street Life

As in many sunny countries, much of life in Rome is played out on the street. In the morning, you can watch the city slowly wake up. Shop shutters are cranked open, rubbish collectors do the rounds, restaurants set out their tables: Rome is readying itself for its close-up.

Day to Night

During the next phase, the fruit and veg markets in every *rione* (neighbourhood) will swell with people, with a predominance of matriarchs wheeling grocery trolleys and showing a reckless disregard for queuing (to a degree that many English travellers may find painful).

Throughout the day, people come and go on Rome's piazzas and public spaces.

In Campo de' Fiori (p90), there's a busy food market during the day, then the character of the piazza changes towards the evening when its bars become busy, taking over corners of the square. Pedestrianised Via del Pigneto (p171), to Rome's northeast, follows a similar trajectory: market in the morning, bars and cafes creating a party atmosphere in the evening. In the historic centre, locals and tourists gather to rest and people-watch on the Spanish Steps (p113), but these empty as night falls. Day or evening, the stadium-sized Piazza Navona (p84) ebbs and flows with people-watching entertainment.

La Passeggiata

In the early evening, the *passeggiata* (an early evening stroll) is an important

1. Dinner in the *centro storico* (p80) **2.** Daily market at the Campo de' Fiori (p90) **3.** Lots of ice-cream flavours at a gelateria

part of Roman life, as it is elsewhere in Italy. Locals will usually dress up before heading out. Like many other parts of everyday life, such as coffee-drinking, Italians have elevated a seemingly simple practice into something special.

Romans will usually head to the area that's most convenient for them. Trastevere (p181) tends to be a broader mix of tourists and young people. Villa Borghese (p225) and the Pincio Hill Gardens (p118) attract more families and are more tranquil. Via del Corso is popular among younger window-shoppers, while Rome's smartest shopping strip, Via dei Condotti (p119), attracts a mix of ages. In summer, there's the Lungo il Tevere festival (p26) on Isola Tiberina, and stalls along the

riverside create a new area for early evening wanders.

Many people out on the stroll will opt, instead of paying €5 or so to sit and drink at a bar, to stop for a more affordable gelato, which they can eat on their way. In summer, you'll see lots of people enjoying *grattachecca* – flavoured, crushed ice – along the banks of the Tiber.

The *bella figura* ('beautiful figure', better explained as 'keeping up appearances') is important here, and the *passeggiata* is as much about checking everyone else out as it is about enjoying the atmosphere. The *passeggiata* reaches its height in summer, as 5pm or 6pm is when the heat of the day subsides. There's not much else to do, so why not head out into the street?

TOP SIGHT
VILLA FARNESINA

Villa Farnesina was built in the early 16th century for Agostino Chigi, the immensely wealthy papal banker. Such was his largesse, that at his banquets, he'd encourage his guests to throw their solid gold plates out of the window once they'd finished (little did they know that servants would stand beneath the windows to catch them in nets). The house was bought by Cardinal Alessandro Farnese in 1577, hence its name.

This 16th-century villa is a classic Renaissance design featuring awe-inspiring frescoes by Sebastiano del Piombo, Raphael and the villa's original architect, Baldassare Peruzzi, formerly Bramante's assistant.

The most famous frescoes are in the Loggia of Cupid and Psyche on the ground floor, attributed to Raphael, who also painted the *Trionfo di Galatea* (Triumph of Galatea) depicting a beautiful sea nymph. The vaulted ceiling of the room is covered with astrological scenes that depict the constellations of the stars at the time of Agostino Chigi's birth.

On the 1st floor, Peruzzi's dazzling frescoes in the Salone delle Prospettive are a superb illusionary perspective of a marble colonnade and panorama of 16th-century Rome.

DON'T MISS...

➡ Frescoes by Sebastiano del Piombo
➡ Raphael-attributed loggia decoration
➡ Peruzzi's panorama in the Salone delle Prospettive

PRACTICALITIES

➡ Map p372
➡ ☑06 6802 7268
➡ Via della Lungara 230
➡ adult/reduced €5/4
➡ ⊙9am-5pm Mon & Sat, 10am-2pm Tue-Fri, 9am-5pm 2nd Sun of month
➡ ▣Lgt della Farnesina, ▣Viale di Trastevere

---

in Montorio, on the spot where St Peter is said to have been crucified. It's a small building, but its classically inspired design and ideal proportions epitomise the Renaissance *zeitgeist*.

It has a circular interior surrounded by 16 columns and topped by a classical frieze, elegant balustrade and proportionally perfect dome. More than a century later, in 1628, Bernini added a staircase. Bernini also contributed a chapel to the adjacent church, the last resting place of Beatrice Cenci, an Italian noblewoman who helped murder her abusive father in the 16th century, and subsquently was tried and beheaded on Ponte Sant'Angelo.

It's quite a climb uphill, but you're rewarded by the views. To cheat, take bus 870 from Via Paola just off Corso Vittorio Emanuele II near the Tiber.

MUSEO DELLA REPUBBLICA ROMANA E DELLA MEMORIA GARIBALDINA   MUSEUM
(Map p372; ☑06 06 08; http://en.museodella repubblicaromana.it; Largo di Porta San Pancrazio; adult/reduced €6.50/5.50; ⊙10am-2pm Tue-Fri, 10am-6pm Sat & Sun; ▣Passeggiata del Gianicolo) Housed in the 19th-century Porta San Pan-

crazio, which played a major role in the desperate defence of Rome against the French led by Giuseppe Garibaldi. This small museum gives the background to Garibaldi and his followers, and their role in Italian history, featuring vivid dioramas and artefacts including Garibaldi's red shirt.

FONTANA DELL'ACQUA PAOLA   FOUNTAIN
(Map p372; Via Garibaldi; ▣Via Garibaldi) Just up from the Chiesa di San Pietro in Montorio, this monumental white fountain was built in 1612 to celebrate the restoration of a 2nd-century aqueduct that supplied (and still supplies) water from Lago di Bracciano, 35km to the north of Rome. Four of the fountain's six pink-stone columns came from the facade of the old St Peter's Basilica, while much of the marble was pillaged from the Roman Forum. Originally the fountain had five small basins, but these were replaced by a large granite basin, added by Carlo Fontana, in 1690.

VILLA DORIA PAMPHILJ   PARK
(⊙dawn-dusk; ▣Via di San Pancrazio) Rome's largest park is a great place to escape the relentless city noise. Once a vast private es-

tate, it was laid out around 1650 for Prince Camillo Pamphilj, nephew of Pope Innocent X. At its centre is the prince's summer residence, the **Casino del Belrespiro**, and its manicured gardens and citrus trees. It's now used for official government functions.

EATING

Traditionally working-class and poor, nowadays chic and pricey, picturesque Trastevere is packed with restaurants, trattorias, cafes and pizzerias. The better places dot the maze of side streets, and it pays to be selective, as many of the restaurants are bog-standard tourist traps. But it's not just tourists here – Romans like to eat in Trastevere too.

✖ East of Viale di Trastevere

ARTIGIANO INNOCENTI   BAKERY €
(Map p372; ☑06 580 39 26; Via delle Luce 21; ⊗8am-8pm Mon-Sat, 9.30am-2pm Sun; 🚊or 🚊Viale di Trastevere) It's at reassuring spots like this that you can feel that the world never changes, in some corners at least. Here you can buy light-as-air *crostate*, and stock up on biscuits such as *brutti ma buoni* (ugly but good).

PANATTONI   PIZZERIA €
(Map p372; ☑06 580 09 19; Viale di Trastevere 53; pizzas €6.50-9; ⊗6.30pm-1am Thu-Tue; 🚊or 🚊Viale di Trastevere) Panattoni is nicknamed *l'obitorio* (the morgue) because of its marble-slab tabletops. Thankfully the similarity stops there. This is one of Trastevere's liveliest pizzerias, with paper-thin pizzas, a clattering buzz, testy waiters, streetside seating and fried starters (specialities are *supplì* (fried rice balls) and *baccalà*).

BRASSERIE 4:20   RESTAURANT €
(☑06 5831 0737; Via Portuense 82; meals around €20; ⊗7pm-2am Sun-Wed, to 4am Thu-Sat; 🚊Piazza di Porta Portese) Rome's passion for artisanal beer shows no sign of abating, and this characterful brick-arched place, with kegs outside and a cool neon sign, not only has myriad rare draught beers (plus beers on tap by Revelation Cat), but also takes the concept one step further: many of its dishes are beer-based (how about some tiramistout!). There are also good burgers, if you're in a burger-and-beer mood.

★LA GENSOLA   SICILIAN €€
(Map p372; ☑06 581 63 12; Piazza della Gensola 15; meals €45; ⊗closed Sun mid-Jun–mid-Sep; 🚊or 🚊Viale di Trastevere) This tranquil, classy yet unpretentious trattoria thrills foodies with delicious food that has a Sicilian slant and emphasis on seafood, including an excellent tuna tartare, linguine with fresh anchovies and divine *zuccherini* (tiny fish) with fresh mint. The set menu costs €41.

LE MANI IN PASTA   ITALIAN €€
(Map p372; ☑06 581 60 17; Via dei Genovesi 37; meals €45; ⊗lunch & dinner Tue-Sun; 🚊Viale di Trastevere) Popular and lively, this rustic, snug place has arched ceilings and an open kitchen that serves up delicious fresh pasta dishes such as *fettucine con ricotta e pancetta*. The grilled meats are great, too.

DA TEO   TRATTORIA €€
(Map p372; ☑06 581 83 85; Piazza dei Ponziani 7; meals around €40; ⊗1-3pm & 8-11.30pm Mon-Sat; 🚊Viale di Trastevere) Tucked away on the quieter side of Trastevere, Da Teo gets packed out with locals dining on its steaming platefuls of Roman standards, such as *cacio e pepe* or fried lamb chops. It's great to eat out on the small piazza when the weather suits. Book ahead.

DA ENZO   TRATTORIA €€
(Map p372; ☑06 581 83 55; www.daenzoal29.com; Via dei Vascellari 29; meals €35; ⊗Mon-Sat; 🚊or 🚊 Viale di Trastevere) This snug dining room with warm yellow walls serves up seasonally based Roman meals, such as spaghetti with clams and mussels or grilled lamb cutlets. There's a tiny terrace on the quintessential Trastevere cobbled street.

✖ West of Viale di Trastevere

★FATAMORGANA   GELATO€
(Map p372; Via Roma Libera 11, Piazza San Cosimato; ⊗1-11.30pm winter, 11.30am-midnight summer; 🚊Viale di Trastevere) One of several Fatamorgana shops across Rome, this is one of the finest among the city's new gourmet gelatarie. Maria Agnese Spagnuolo uses the best natural ingredients to produce the classics, such as pistachio, as well as creative and unusual combinations such

LOCAL KNOWLEDGE

GRATTACHECCA

It's summertime, the living is easy, and Romans like nothing better in the sultry evening heat than to amble down to the river and partake of some *grattachecca* (crushed ice covered in fruit and syrup). It's the ideal way to cool down and there are kiosks along the riverbank satisfying this very Roman need; try **Sora Mirella Caffè** (Map p372; grattachecca €3-6; ⊘11am-3am May-Sep), next to Ponte Cestio.

as Thumbelina (walnuts, rose petals and violet flowers).

DA AUGUSTO
TRATTORIA €

(Map p372; ☑06 580 37 98; Piazza de' Renzi 15; meals €25; ⊘lunch & dinner; 🚊Viale di Trastevere) For a Trastevere feast, plonk yourself at one of Augusto's rickety tables, either inside or out on the small piazza, and prepare to enjoy some mamma-style cooking. The gruff waiters dish out hearty platefuls of *rigatoni all'amatriciana* and *stracciatella* (clear broth with egg and Parmesan) among a host of Roman classics. Be prepared to queue. Cash only.

CIURI CIURI
SICILIAN €

(Map p372; ☑06 9521 6082; www.ciuri-ciuri. it; Piazza San Cosimato 49b; snacks around €3; ⊘10.30am-midnight) A splendid Sicilian cafe selling cakes (the *cannoli* – pastry tubes filled with ricotta – are filled for you then and there), creamy artisanal ice cream and delicious savoury snacks, including freshly made *arancini* (fried rice balls with various fillings such as *ragù* or mozzarella and ham).

FIOR DI LUNA
GELATO €

(Map p372; ☑06 6456 1314; Via della Lungaretta 96; gelato from €1.70; ⊘noon-11pm Tue-Sun winter, to 2am summer, open daily Dec; 🚊or 🚊Viale di Trastevere) This busy little hub serves up handmade ice cream and sorbet – it's made in small batches and only uses natural, seasonal ingredients, such as hazelnuts from Tonda and pistachios from Bronte.

PIZZERIA IVO
PIZZERIA €

(Map p372; ☑06 581 70 82; Via San Francesco a Ripa 158; pizzas around €7; ⊘Wed-Mon; 🚊or 🚊Viale di Trastevere) One of Trastevere's most famous pizzerias, Ivo has been slinging pizzas for some 40 years, and still the hungry come. With the TV on in the corner and the tables full (a few outside on the cobbled street), Ivo is a noisy and vibrant place, and the waiters fit the gruff-and-fast stereotype.

FORNO LA RENELLA
BAKERY €

(Map p372; ☑06 581 72 65; Via del Moro 15-16; pizza slices from €2.50; ⊘7am-2am Tue-Sat, to 10pm Sun & Mon; 🚊Piazza Trilussa) The wood-fired ovens at this historical Trastevere bakery have been going for decades, producing a delicious daily batch of pizza, bread and biscuits. Piled-high toppings (and fillings) vary seasonally. It's popular with everyone from skinheads with big dogs to elderly ladies with little dogs.

DA OLINDO
TRATTORIA €

(Map p372; ☑06 581 88 35; Vicolo della Scala 8; meals €25; ⊘dinner Mon-Sat; 🚊Viale di Trastevere) This is your classic family affair; the menu is short, cuisine robust, portions are huge, and the atmosphere is lively. Expect *baccalà con patate* on Fridays and gnocchi on Thursdays, but other dishes – such as *coniglio all cacciatore* (rabbit, hunter-style) or *polpette al sugo* (meatballs in sauce) – whichever day you like.

SISINI
PIZZERIA €

(Map p372; Via San Francesco a Ripa 137; pizza & pasta from €2, supplì €1.10; ⊘9am-10.30pm Mon-Sat, closed Aug; 🚊or 🚊Viale di Trastevere) Locals love this fast-food takeaway joint (the sign outside says 'Supplì'), serving up fresh *pizza al taglio* (pizza by the slice) and different pasta and risotto dishes served in plastic boxes. It's also worth sampling the *supplì* and roast chicken.

BIR & FUD
PIZZERIA €

(Map p372; Via Benedetta 23; meals €25; ⊘7.30pm-midnight, to 2am Fri & Sat; 🚊or 🚊Viale di Trastevere) This orange-and-terracotta, vaulted pizzeria wins plaudits for its organic take on pizzas, *crostini* and fried things (potato, pumpkin etc) and has a microbrewery on site, so serves seasonable tipples such as Birrificio Troll Palanfrina (winter only, made from chestnuts).

VALZANI
PASTRIES & CAKES €

(Map p372; ☑06 580 37 92; Via del Moro 37; cakes €3; ⊘ 3-8pm Mon & Tue, 10am-8pm Wed-Sun, closed Jul & Aug; 🚊or 🚊Piazza Sonnino) The speciality of this glorious, stuck-in-time cake shop, opened in 1925 and not redecorated since, is the legendary *torta sacher*, the favourite cake of Roman film director Nanni Moretti. But there are also chocolate-covered *mostaccioli* (biscuits), Roman *pangiallo* (honey, nuts and dried fruit – typical for Christmas) and Roman *torrone* (nougat).

DAR POETA   PIZZERIA €

(Map p372; ☏06 588 05 16; Vicolo del Bologna 46; pizzas from €6; ⊙lunch & dinner; 🚇Piazza Trilussa) Dar Poeta, a cheery pizzeria hidden away in an atmospheric side street, proffers hearty pizzas in a buzzing atmosphere. The base is somewhere between wafer-thin Roman and Neapolitan comfort food. There are a couple of outdoor tables, and it's famous for its ricotta and Nutella calzone, though pizza followed by this may leave you feeling a little doughy.

MERIDIONALE   ITALIAN €€

(Map p372; www.meridionaletrastevere.com; Via dei Fienaroli; meals €35, Sunday buffet €15; ⊙dinner Tue-Sun, lunch Sat & Sun) Formerly retro-styled Il Boom, this hidden-away, arched-ceilinged restaurant has a new owner and chef and now specialises in southern Italian cooking, with dishes such as spaghetti with squid and cherry tomatoes. The appealing interior has a shabby chic vibe, with its faded newspaper wallpaper, and glass domes over the desserts. There's a buffet lunch on Sunday.

LA BOTTICELLA   TRATTORIA €€

(Map p372; ☏06 581 47 38; Vicolo del Leopardo 39a; meals €45; ⊙daily; 🚇Piazza Trilussa) On a quiet Trastevere backstreet, La Botticella offers pure Roman cooking, outside under the lines of flapping washing, or inside in the picture-lined salon. Menu stalwarts include tripe and *rigatoni alla paiata* (pasta with calf's intestines), but there are less demanding dishes, such as an excellent *spaghetti all'amatriciana*.

GLASS HOSTARIA   MODERN ITALIAN €€€

(Map p372; ☏06 5833 5903; Vicolo del Cinque 58; meals €80; ⊙from 8pm Tue-Sun; 🚇Piazza Trilussa) Trastevere's foremost foodie address, the Glass is a modernist-styled, sophisticated setting with cooking to match. Chef Cristina Bowerman creates inventive, delicate dishes that combine fresh ingredients and traditional elements to delight and surprise the palate. There are tasting menus at €70 and €90.

PARIS   RISTORANTE €€€

(Map p372; ☏06 581 53 78; www.ristoranteparis. it; Piazza San Calisto 7a; meals €55; ⊙Tue-Sat, lunch only Sun; 🚇or 🚋 Viale di Trastevere) An old-school Roman restaurant set in a 17th-century building, with seats out on the piazza, Paris (named for its founder, not the French capital) is the best place outside the Ghetto to sample Roman-Jewish cuisine, such as delicate *fritto misto con baccalà* (deep-fried vegetables with salt cod) and *carciofi alla giudia*. There's a sunshaded terrace.

🍷⚓ DRINKING & NIGHTLIFE

Trastevere is one of the city's most popular areas to wander, drink and decide what to do afterwards. Foreign visitors love it, as do those who love foreign visitors, but it's also a local haunt. The streets in summer are packed, with stalls, bars spilling into the street, and a carnival atmosphere – it's even a bit overcrowded and won't be to everyone's taste.

MA CHE SIETE VENUTI A FÀ   PUB

(Map p372; Via Benedetta 25; ⊙11am-2am; 🚇Piazza Trilussa) This pint-sized pub – whose name, a football chant, translates politely as 'What did you come here for?'– is a beer-buff's paradise, packing a huge number of on-tap craft beers or obscure bottled tipples into its tiny interior.

BAR SAN CALISTO   CAFE

(Map p372; ☏06 589 56 78; Piazza San Calisto 3-5; ⊙6am-2am Mon-Sat; 🚇or 🚋 Viale di Trastevere,) Those in the know head to the down-at-heel 'Sanca' for its basic, stuck-in-time atmosphere and cheap prices. It attracts everyone from drug dealers, intellectuals and pseudo-intellectuals to keeping-it-real Romans, alcoholics and American students. It's famous for its chocolate – drunk hot with cream in winter, eaten as ice cream in summer. Try the *sambuca con la mosca* ('with a fly' – raw coffee beans).

FRENI E FRIZIONI   BAR

(Map p372; ☏06 5833 4210; www.freniefrizioni. com; Via del Politeama 4-6; ⊙6.30pm-2am; 🚇Piazza Trilussa) The young dudes' favourite cool Trastevere bar, this was a garage in a former life, hence its name ('brakes and clutches'). The arty crowd flocks here to slurp well-priced drinks (especially mojitos), feast on the good-value *aperitivo* (7pm to 10pm) and spill into the piazza.

OMBRE ROSSE
BAR

(Map p372; ☑06 588 41 55; Piazza Sant'Egidio 12; ⊘8am-2am Mon-Sat, 11am-2am Sun; ⊒Piazza Trilussa) A seminal Trastevere hang-out; grab a table on the terrace and watch the world go by amid a clientele ranging from elderly Italian wide boys to wide-eyed tourists. A €0.50 beer costs €5. Tunes are slinky and there's live music (jazz, blues, world) on Thursday evenings from September to April.

LA MESCHITA
WINE BAR

(Map p372; ☑06 5833 3920; Piazza Trilussa 41; ⊒Piazza Trilussa) This tiny bar inside the entrance to upmarket restaurant Enoteca Ferrara serves delectable *aperitivo* and has a wide range of wines by the glass, from €7. Fancy an intimate tête-à-tête, with fine wines and yummy snacks? This is your place.

BAR LE CINQUE
BAR

(Map p372; Vicolo del Cinque 5; ⊘6.30am-2am Mon-Sat; ⊒or ⊒Piazza Sonnino) There's no sign outside, and it looks like a run-down ordinary bar, but this is a long-standing Trastevere favourite and always has a small crowd clustered around outside; they're here for the pivotal location, easygoing vibe and cheap drinks.

LIBRERIA DEL CINEMA
CAFE

(Map p372; ☑06 581 77 24; Via dei Fienaroli 31d; ⊘4-10pm Mon-Fri, 4-11pm Sat, 2-9pm Sun; ⊒or ⊒Piazza Sonnino) OK, it's a bookshop and cafe, but it's filed here as a tranquil coffee-and-snack pit stop. There's *aperitivo* from 7pm. And, of course, you can browse

---

> ### SUMMER DRINKS ON THE GIANICOLO
>
> From June to September, the **Gianicolo 150** (Map p372; www.gianicolo150.it; Piazzale Giuseppe Garibaldi; ⊘7pm-2am) opens an outdoor 'street art cafe', run by the cool cats who are responsible for the uber-chic **Salotto 42** (p105). It's an outdoor living room set on Gianicolo Hill, with sofas draped with pretty people, plus even prettier views over Rome.

---

the fab cinematic book, DVD and poster collection, too.

🍷 Gianicolo

BAR STUZZICHINI
BAR

(Map p372; Piazzale Garibaldi; ⊘7.30am-1am; ⊒Passeggiata del Gianicolo) This little kiosk nestles on the top of Gianicolo, and serves up coffees and drinks, including cocktails (€6). There are a few tables to perch at and the views are unmatchable. On New Year's Eve it opens all night.

IL BARRETTO
BAR

(Map p372; ☑06 5836 5422; Via Garibaldi 27; ⊘6am-2am Mon-Sat, 5pm-2am Sun; ⊒or ⊒Piazza Sonnino) Venture a little way up the Gianicolo, up a steep flight of steps from Trastevere. Go on, it's so worth it: you'll discover this well-kept-secret cocktail bar. The basslines are meaty, the bar staff hip, the interior mixes vintage with pop art, and it's genuinely cool.

☆ ENTERTAINMENT

BIG MAMA
BLUES

(Map p372; ☑06 581 25 51; www.bigmama.it; Vicolo San Francesco a Ripa 18; ⊘9pm-1.30am, shows 10.30pm Thu-Sat, closed Jun-Sep; ⊒or ⊒Viale di Trastevere) To wallow in the Eternal City blues, there's only one place to go – this cramped Trastevere basement, which also hosts jazz, funk, soul and R&B.

LETTERE CAFFÈ GALLERY
LIVE MUSIC

(Map p372; ☑06 9727 0991; www.letterecaffe.org; Vicolo San Francesco a Ripa 100/101; ⊘7pm-2am, closed mid-Aug–mid-Sep; ⊒Piazza Trilussa) Like books? Poetry? Blues and jazz? Then you'll love this place – a clutter of bar stools and books, where there are regular live gigs, poetry slams, comedy and gay nights, plus DJ sets playing indie and new wave. There's vegetarian *aperitivo* from 7pm to 9pm nightly (€5).

ANFITEATRO DEL TASSO
THEATRE

(Map p372; ☑06 575 08 27; www.anfiteatroquerciadeltasso.com; Passagiata del Gianicolo; tickets €18; ⊘Jul & Aug; ⊒Piazza Garibaldi) The setting is extraordinary: an amphitheatre overlooking Rome's rooftops that was built over 300 years ago. The productions are ex-

LOCAL KNOWLEDGE

GETTING MARRIED IN ROME

A city as romantic as Rome attracts many foreigners to get married here. Civic weddings take place at the town hall, which is on the Campidoglio (p75), while, for churches, you're spoilt for choice. But where do you start to organise your wedding in Rome? Italo-American events planner Barbara Lessona (www.barbaralessona.com) lives in Rome, and specialises in helping plan weddings for foreigners:

'Having the event in the Eternal City makes it special before you even start with anything else. Things to consider are the location (somewhere uniquely Roman), having the reception somewhere not far from the church or city hall (considering the traffic), and using trusted recommendations for florists, catering and so on. There's so much choice. For example, it's a wonderful experience to get married on one of Rome's seven hills, for the views and there are great venues at places such as the Gianicolo. In addition, believe it or not, churches such as the Chiesa di San Luigi dei Francesi (p86), with its beautiful Caravaggio paintings, may be used for the ceremony, and just opposite is the Palazzo Patrizi, with its exquisite painting collections and red-velvet interiors. In terms of budget, meals can range from 50 to €200 per person, and you can rent a venue from €2000, a beautiful ancient *palazzo* from €4500, or alternatively book a restaurant where you don't pay the rental charge but a special wedding menu will start from around €110 per head.'

traordinary, too, for different reasons, featuring hammy turns in Greek and Roman comedy and the odd 18th-century drama.

TEATRO VASCELLO THEATRE
(✆06 588 10 21; www.teatrovascello.it; Via Giacinto Carini 72, Monteverde; ☐Via Giacinto Carini) Left-field in vibe and location, this independent, fringe theatre stages interesting, cutting-edge new work, including avant-garde dance, multimedia events and works by emerging playwrights.

ALCAZAR CINEMA CINEMA
(Map p372; ✆06 588 00 99; Via Merry del Val 14; ☐or ☐Viale di Trastevere) An old-style cinema with plush red seats, occasionally shows films in their original language with Italian subtitles.

NUOVO SACHER CINEMA
(Map p372; ✆06 581 81 16; www.sacherfilm.eu; Largo Ascianghi 1; ☐or ☐Viale di Trastevere) Owned by cult Roman film director Nanni Moretti, this small, red-velvet-seated place s the place to catch the latest European art-house offering, with regular screenings of films in their original language.

🛍 SHOPPING

PORTA PORTESE FLEA MARKET MARKET
(Map p372; Piazza Porta Portese; ☐7am-1pm Sun; ☐or ☐Viale di Trastevere) To see another side of Rome, head to this mammoth flea market. With thousands of stalls selling everything from rare books and fell-off-a-lorry bikes to Peruvian shawls and MP3 players, it's crazily busy and a lot of fun. Keep your valuables safe and wear your haggling hat.

ROMA-STORE PERFUME
(Map p372; ✆06 581 87 89; Via della Lungaretta 63; ☐10am-8pm; ☐or ☐Viale di Trastevere) With no sign, Roma-Store is an enchanting perfume shop crammed full of deliciously enticing bottles of scent, including lots of less usual brands such as Serge Lutens and Etat Libre d'Orange.

OFFICINA DELLA CARTA GIFTS
(Map p372; ✆06 589 55 57; Via Benedetta 26b; ☐10.30am-7.30pm; ☐Piazza Trilussa) A perfect present pit stop, this tiny workshop produces attractive hand-painted paper-bound boxes, photo albums, recipe books, notepads, photo frames and diaries.

ALMOST CORNER BOOKSHOP BOOKS
(Map p372; ✆06 583 69 42; Via del Moro 45; ☐10am-1.30pm & 2.30-8pm Mon-Sat, 11am-1.30pm & 2.30-8pm Sun; ☐Piazza Trilussa) This is how a bookshop should look: a crammed haven full of rip-roaring reads, with every millimetre of wall space containing English-language books (including children's) and travel guides. There's an excellent selection of contemporary novels

and bestsellers as well as more obscure titles.

LA CRAVATTA SU MISURA ACCESSORIES

(Map p372; ☑06 890 69 41; Via Santa Cecilia 12; ☺10am-7pm Mon-Sat) With ties draped over the wooden furniture, this inviting shop resembles the study of an absent-minded professor. But don't be fooled: these guys know their ties. Only the finest Italian silks and English wools are used in neckwear made to customers' specifications. At a push, a tie can be ready in a few hours.

POLVERE DI TEMPO SOUVENIRS

(Map p372; ☑06 588 07 04; Via del Moro 59; ☐Piazza Trilussa) This intriguing shop is a good place to pick up gifts; take your pick from lovingly crafted hourglasses, globes and pill boxes, based on 16th- to 18th-century

designs, as well as jewellery and leather-bound books.

SCALA QUATTORODICI
CLOTHING CLOTHING

(Map p372; Villa della Scala 13-14; ☺10am-1.30pm & 4-8pm Tue-Sat, 4-8pm Mon; ☐Piazza Trilussa) Make yourself over à la Audrey Hepburn with these classically tailored clothes in beautiful fabrics – either made-to-measure or off-the-peg. Pricey (a frock will set you back €600 plus) but oh so worth it.

BARTOLUCCI TOYS

(Map p372; ☑06 589 52 39; Via della Scala 71; ☺11.30am-9.30pm Mon-Thu, to midnight Fri-Sun; ☐Viale di Trastevere) Purveyors of wooden Pinocchio-themed toys, from moving clocks to coat pegs, all of which may be personalised with the recipient's name.

San Giovanni to Testaccio

SAN GIOVANNI | CELIO | AVENTINO | TESTACCIO

Neighbourhood Top Five

1 Facing up to the overpowering splendour of the monumental **Basilica di San Giovanni in Laterano** (p197). You'll feel very small as you explore the echoing baroque interior of Rome's oldest Christian basilica.

2 Going underground through layers of history at the **Basilica di San Clemente** (p199).

3 Being over-awed by the towering ruins of the **Terme di Caracalla** (p202).

4 Enjoying a quiet moment in the tranquil **Basilica di Santa Sabina** (p203).

5 Looking through the keyhole of the **Priorato dei Cavalieri di Malta** (p204).

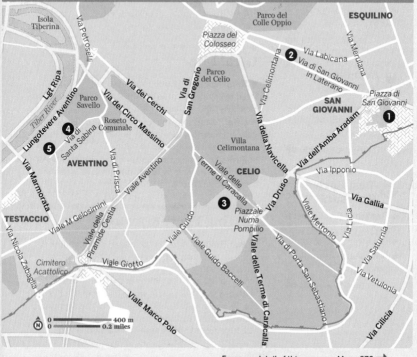

For more detail of this area, see Map p370 ➡

Lonely Planet's Top Tip

If you like opera, check www.operaroma.it for details of summer performances at the Terme di Caracalla. Also, if you visit the Terme di Caracalla, note that the admission ticket includes access to two other sites: the Mausoleo di Cecilia Metella and the Villa dei Quintili. Both these are some distance from the Terme – the Mausoleo on Via Appia Antica and Villa dei Quintili on Via Appia Nuova – and require a bus journey to reach.

Best Places to Eat

➡ Flavio al Velavevodetto (p205)

➡ Li Rioni (p204)

➡ Aroma (p205)

➡ Checchino dal 1887 (p206)

For reviews, see p204 ➡

Best Places to Drink

➡ Il Pentagrappolo (p206)

➡ L'Oasi della Birra (p206)

➡ Linari (p206)

For reviews, see p206 ➡

Best Buried Treasures

➡ Basilica di San Clemente (p199)

➡ Case Romane (p202)

➡ Mithraeum, Terme di Caracalla (p202)

For reviews, see p199 ➡

Explore: San Giovanni to Testaccio

Encompassing two of Rome's seven hills, this oft-overlooked part of town offers everything from barn-storming basilicas and medieval churches to ancient ruins, busy markets and hip clubs. The area can easily be divided into two separate patches: San Giovanni and the Celio; and Aventino and Testaccio. A day in each is sufficient to cover the main sights.

Start off at the landmark Basilica di San Giovanni in Laterano, the focal point of the largely residential San Giovanni neighbourhood. It's easily accessible by metro and quite magnificent, both inside and out. Once you've explored the cathedral and surrounding piazza, head down Via di San Giovanni in Laterano towards the Colosseum. Near the bottom, the Basilica di San Clemente is a fascinating church with some thrilling underground ruins. From there, you can walk across to the Celio, the green hill that rises south of the Colosseum. There's not a lot to see but the graceful Villa Celimontana park is a great place to escape the crowds. Further south, the ruins of the Terme di Caracalla are one of the neighbourhood's highlights, easily on a par with anything in the city.

Further west, on the banks of the Tiber, the once working-class area of Testaccio is a bastion of old-school Roman cuisine with a number of excellent trattorias and a popular nightlife district. Rising above it, the Aventino boasts a number of wonderful medieval churches and one of Rome's great curiosities – the famous keyhole view of St Peter's dome.

Local Life

➡ **Romance** Local Lotharios out to impress their loved ones take them to enjoy the views from the Parco Savello (p203) on the Aventino.

➡ **Offal** Testaccio is the spiritual home of 'blood-and-guts' Roman cooking, and its popular trattorias and restaurants are the place to try it.

➡ **Parks** You'll often see locals relaxing with a book or going for a leisurely lunchtime stroll in Villa Celimontana (p203).

Getting There & Away

➡ **Bus** Useful bus routes include 85 and 87, both of which stop near the Basilica di San Giovanni in Laterano; 714, which serves San Giovanni and the Terme di Caracalla; and 175, which runs to the Aventino.

➡ **Metro** San Giovanni is accessible by metro line A. For Testaccio take line B to Piramide. The Aventino is walkable from Testaccio and Circo Massimo (line B), although from Circo Massimo it's a bit of a hike.

TOP SIGHT
BASILICA DI SAN GIOVANNI IN LATERANO

For 1000 years this monumental cathedral was the most important church in Christendom. Commissioned by the emperor Constantine in the fourth century, it was the first Christian basilica to be built in Rome and, until the 14th century, was the pope's main place of worship. The Vatican still has extraterritorial authority over it, despite it being Rome's official cathedral and the pope's seat as Bishop of Rome.

The oldest of Rome's four papal basilicas (the others are St Peter's, the Basilica di San Paolo Fuori le Mura and the Basilica di Santa Maria Maggiore), it was constructed during the building boom that followed Constantine's accession to power in 312, and consecrated by Pope Sylvester I in 324. From then until 1309, when the papacy moved to Avignon, it was the principal pontifical church, and the adjacent Palazzo Laterano was the pope's official residence. Both buildings fell into disrepair during the papacy's French interlude, and when Pope Gregory XI returned to Rome in 1377 he preferred to decamp to the fortified Vatican rather than stay in the official papal digs.

Over the course of its long history, the basilica has been vandalised by invading barbarians and twice destroyed by fire. It was rebuilt each time and the basilica you see today is a culmination of several comprehensive makeovers.

DON'T MISS...

➡ Monument to Pope Sylvester II
➡ The baldachin
➡ The cloister

PRACTICALITIES

➡ Map p370
➡ Piazza di San Giovanni in Laterano 4
➡ basilica free, cloister €3
➡ ⊙7am-6.30pm, cloister 9am-6pm
➡ Ⓜ San Giovanni

The Facade

Surmounted by fifteen 7m-high statues – Christ with St John the Baptist, John the Evangelist and the 12 Apostles – Alessandro Galilei's monumental white facade is a mid-18th-century work of late-baroque classicism, designed to convey the infinite authority of the Church. Behind the colossal columns, there are five sets of doors into the basilica from the portico. The central **bronze doors** were moved here from the Curia in the Roman

BASILICA LEGENDS

Legend holds that if a pregnant woman touches the basilica's main bronze doors she will give birth to a boy. Inside, on the second pilaster in the right-hand nave, is a monument to Pope Sylvester II (r 999–1003) which is said to sweat and creak when the death of a pope is imminent. Outside on the western side of the cloister, four columns support a slab of marble that medieval Christians believed represented the height of Jesus. A similar story surrounds a piece of porphyry on which it's said Roman soldiers threw lots to win the robes of the crucified Christ.

French President, François Hollande, holds the title 'Protocanonico d'onore del capitolo della basilica lateranense' or 'honorary canon of the Basilica of St John in Lateran'. The title has been granted to France's kings and presidents since 1604 when king Henri IV earned it after donating a generous sum to the Lateran chapter, the ecclesiastical body responsible for the Basilica.

Forum while, on the far right, the carved **Holy Door** is only opened in Jubilee years.

The Interior

The interior has been revamped on numerous occasions, although it owes much of its present look to Francesco Borromini, who was called in by Pope Innocent X to decorate it for the 1650 Jubilee. Divided into a central nave and four minor aisles, it's a breathtaking sight, measuring 130m (length) by 55.6m (width) by 30m (height). Up above, the spectacular gilt **ceiling** was created at different times, but the central section, which is set around Pope Pius IV's carved coat of arms, dates to the 1560s. Beneath your feet, the beautiful inlaid mosaic **floor** was laid down by Pope Martin V in 1425.

The central nave is lined with 18th-century sculptures of the apostles, each 4.6m high and each set in a heroic pose in its own dramatic niche. At the head of the nave, the pointed Gothic **baldachin** that rises over the papal altar is one of the few features that survived Borromini's 17th-century facelift. It's a dramatic work, set atop four columns and decorated with pictures of Jesus, the Virgin Mary and the saints. Up top, behind a grille are the remaining relics of the heads of St Peter and St Paul. In front of the altar, a double staircase leads down to the **confessio**, which houses the Renaissance tomb of Pope Martin V.

Behind the altar, the massive apse is decorated with sparkling mosaics, parts of which date to the 4th century, but most of which were added in the 19th century.

The Cloister

To the left of the altar, the beautiful **cloister** (Map p370; admission €3, with audioguide €5; ⊗9am-6pm) was built by the Vassalletto family in the 13th century. It's a lovely, peaceful place with graceful Cosmatesque twisted columns set around a central garden. These columns were once completely covered with inlaid marble mosaics, remnants of which can still be seen. Lining the ambulatories are marble fragments of the original basilica, including the remains of a 5th-century papal throne and inscriptions of two papal bulls.

⊙ SIGHTS

⊙ San Giovanni

BASILICA DI SAN GIOVANNI IN LATERANO
BASILICA

See p197.

PALAZZO LATERANO
PALACE

(Map p370; Piazza San Giovanni in Laterano; Ⓜ San Giovanni) Flanking Piazza San Giovanni in Laterano, itself dominated by Rome's oldest and tallest **obelisk** (Map p370), is Domenico Fontana's 16th-century Palazzo Laterano. Part of the original 4th-century complex of the Basilica di San Giovanni, it was the official papal residence until the papacy moved to the Vatican in 1377, and today houses offices of the diocese of Rome.

BATTISTERO
CHAPEL

(Baptistry; Map p370; Piazza San Giovanni in Laterano; ⊙7am-12.30pm & 4-7pm; Ⓜ San Giovanni) Around the corner from the Basilica di San Giovanni in Laterano is the fascinating octagonal *battistero* (baptistry). Built by Constantine in the 4th century, it served as the prototype for later Christian churches and bell towers. The chief interest, apart from the architecture, is the decorative mosaics, some of which date back to the 5th century.

SCALA SANTA & SANCTA SANCTORUM
CHAPEL

(Map p370; Piazza di San Giovanni in Laterano 14; Scala/Sancta free/€3.50; ⊙Scala 6.15am-noon & 3.30-6.30pm summer, 6.15am-noon & 3-6pm winter, Sancta Sanctorum 9.30am-noon & 3-5pm, closed Wed am & Sun year-round; Ⓜ San Giovanni) Brought to Rome by St Helena in the 4th century, the **Scala Santa** is said to be the staircase that Jesus walked up in Pontius Pilate's palace in Jerusalem. Pilgrims consider it sacred and climb it on their knees, saying a prayer on each of the 28 steps. At the top, the richly frescoed **Sancta Sanctorum** (Holy of Holies) was formerly the pope's private chapel.

Behind the Scala building you'll see what appears to be a cut-off cross-section of a building, adorned with a showy gold mosaic. This is the **Triclinium Leoninum** (Map p370), an 18th-century reconstruction of the end wall of the banqueting hall in the original Palazzo Laterano.

⊙ TOP SIGHT
BASILICA DI SAN CLEMENTE

This fascinating basilica provides a vivid glimpse into Rome's multilayered past: a 12th-century basilica built atop a 4th-century church, which, in turn, stands over a 2nd-century pagan temple and 1st-century Roman house. Beneath everything are foundations dating to the Roman Republic.

The medieval church features a marvellous 12th-century apse mosaic depicting the *Trionfo della Croce* (Triumph of the Cross), with 12 doves symbolising the apostles, and the Madonna and St John the Baptist standing on either side of the cross. Also impressive are Masolino's 15th-century Renaissance frescoes in the Chapel of St Catherine, which depict a crucifixion scene and episodes from the life of St Catherine.

Steps lead down to the 4th-century *basilica inferiore*, mostly destroyed by Norman invaders in 1084, but with some faded 11th-century frescoes illustrating the life of San Clemente. Follow down another level and you'll find yourself walking an ancient lane leading to the Roman house and a dark temple of Mithras, which contains an altar depicting the god slaying a bull. Beneath it all, you can hear the eerie sound of a subterranean river, running through a Roman Republic–era drain.

DON'T MISS...
➡ *Trionfo della Croce*
➡ Chapel of St Catherine
➡ Basilica Inferiore
➡ Temple of Mithras

PRACTICALITIES
➡ Map p370
➡ www.basilicasan clemente.com
➡ Via di San Giovanni in Laterano
➡ church/excavations free/€5
➡ ⊙9am-12.30pm & 3-6pm Mon-Sat, noon-6pm Sun
➡ Ⓜ Colosseo

Rome at the Movies

Rome's local film industry took off in the 1950s, but the city has long served as an inspiration to film-makers, while its films have helped cement the legend of Rome.

Most iconic are *Roman Holiday* (1953) and Federico Fellini's *La Dolce Vita* (The Sweet Life; 1960), starring Marcello Mastroianni, which saw Anita Ekberg splash into cinematic history via the Trevi Fountain. Fellini's *Roma* (1972) is an impressionistic collage, part autobiography, and part riff on contemporary Rome, which features an unforgettable Vatican fashion show with roller-skating prelates swirling red, satin robes and fierce nuns wearing headdresses with giant wings. *Three Coins in the Fountain* (1954) was a cheesy romance that spawned a great song and the tradition of tossing coins into the Trevi Fountain.

More recently Rome has looked bewitchingly beautiful, if surreal, in Peter Greenaway's *Belly of an Architect* (1987), which opens with a dinner party scene set in Piazza della Rotonda. Anthony Minghella's psychological thriller *The Talented Mr Ripley* (1999) uses Rome as a backdrop for the chilling tale of Matt Damon taking over Jude Law's charmed life. The touching, atmospheric *Pranzo di Ferragosto* (Midsummer Lunch; 2008) is a portrait of a middle-aged man unable to join Rome's mass summer exodus, while Rome in its guise as political powerhouse is seen in Paolo Sorrentino's brilliant *Il Divo* (The Master; 2008), about controversial politician Giulio Andreotti, starring Toni Servillo.

1. Trevi Fountain (p115) seen in *La Dolce Vita* **2.** Bocca della Verità (p78) from *Roman Holiday* **3.** Via dei Condotti leading up to the Spanish Steps (p113) featured in *The Talented Mr Ripley*

Characters bounced between locations in *Angels & Demons* (2009), based on the book by Dan Brown, while the postcard-pretty *Eat, Pray, Love* (2010) starred Julia Roberts and various Italian stereotypes. Nanni Morretti's *Habemus Papum* (2011) tells the pertinent tale of a French cardinal (Michel Piccoli) who refuses to accept his election as pope and escapes to spend time in the ordinary life of Rome. Woody Allen's *To Rome with Love* (2012), a light comedy starring Penelope Cruz, Alec Baldwin, Roberto Benigni, and Woody himself, told four linked stories set against (some might say) a cloyingly cliched vision of the city and its inhabitants.

For a grittier perspective, see the neo-realist films of the 1940s and '50s, such as *The Bicycle Thieves* (1948), which ranges from the desolate outskirts of the city to the bicycle market that still exists at Porta Portese. Other iconic films of this era include *Roma Città Aperta* (Rome, Open City; 1945; Roberto Rossellini) and Pier Paolo Pasolini's *Accattone* (The Scrounger; 1961), where the eponymous pimp hangs out in Necci, in Pigneto, long before the hipsters arrived.

TOP 5 ROME MOVIES

➡ *Roman Holiday* (1953)

➡ *La Dolce Vita* (The Sweet Life; 1960)

➡ *Roma, Città Aperta* (Rome, Open City; 1945)

➡ *Pranzo di Ferragosto* (Midsummer Lunch; 2008)

➡ *Il Divo* (The Master; 2008)

TOP SIGHT
TERME DI CARACALLA

The remnants of the emperor Caracalla's vast baths complex are among Rome's most awe-inspiring ruins. Inaugurated in 216, the original 10-hectare complex comprised baths, gymnasiums, libraries, shops and gardens. Between 6000 and 8000 people were thought to pass through everyday while, underground, hundreds of slaves sweated in 9.5km of tunnels, tending to the intricate plumbing systems.

The baths remained in continuous use until 537, when the Visigoths smashed their way into Rome and cut off its water supply. Excavations of the site in the 16th and 17th centuries unearthed a number of important sculptures, many of which found their way into the Farnese family art collection.

Most of the ruins are what's left of the central bath house. This was a huge rectangular edifice, centred on the *frigidarium* (cold room), where bathers would stop after spells in the warmer *tepidarium* and before that the dome-capped *caldaria* (hot room). Underground, you can visit the tunnels and a recently opened temple (Mithraeum), dedicated to the Persian god Mithras.

In summer the ruins are used to stage spectacular opera performances.

DON'T MISS...

➡ Frigidarium
➡ Caldaria
➡ Mithraeum

PRACTICALITIES

➡ Map p370
➡ ☑06 3996 7700
➡ www.coopculture.it
➡ Viale delle Terme di Caracalla 52
➡ adult/reduced €7/4
➡ ☺9am to 1hr before sunset Tue-Sun, 9am-2pm Mon
➡ ⬛Viale delle Terme di Caracalla

◉ Celio

BASILICA DI SS QUATTRO CORONATI
BASILICA

(Map p370; Via dei Santissimi Quattro Coronati 20; ☺Basilica 6.15am-8pm Mon-Sat, 6.45am-12.30pm & 3-7.30pm Sun, Cappella di San Silvestro & cloisters 9.30am-noon & 4.30-6pm Mon-Sat, 9-10.40am & 4-6pm Sun; ⬛Via Labicana) This brooding fortified church is best known for its well-preserved 13th-century frescoes. In the Cappella di San Silvestro, these depict the story of the Donation of Constantine, a notorious forged document with which the emperor Constantine ceded control of Rome and the Western Roman Empire to the papacy.

Dating to the 6th century, the basilica took on its present form in the 12th-century after the original was destroyed by Normans in 1084. Its name – the Basilica of the Four Crowned Martyrs – is a reference to four Christian sculptors who were killed by the emperor Diocletian for refusing to make a statue of a pagan god. Still today it's revered by stone-cutters and masons.

Also of interest are the beautiful 13th-century cloisters off the northern aisle (ring the bell for admission).

BASILICA DI SS GIOVANNI E PAOLO & CASE ROMANE
BASILICA, ROMAN SITE

(Map p370; Piazza di SS Giovanni e Paolo; ☺8.30am-noon & 3.30-6pm Mon-Thu; ⓂColosseo or Circo Massimo) While there's little of interest at this much-tweaked 4th-century church, the Roman houses that lie beneath it are fascinating. According to tradition, the apostles John and Paul lived in the **Case Romane** (Map p370; ☑06 7045 4544; www.caseromane.it; adult/reduced/child €6/4/free; ☺10am-1pm & 3-6pm Thu-Mon; ⓂColosseo or Circo Massimo) before they were beheaded by Constantine's anti-Christian successor, Julian.

In fact, there's no direct evidence for this, although research has revealed that the houses were used for Christian worship. There are more than 20 rooms, many of them richly decorated. Entry is to the side of the church on Clivo di Scauro.

CHIESA DI SAN GREGORIO MAGNO
CHURCH

(Map p370; Piazza di San Gregorio 1; ☺9am-1pm & 3.30-7pm, Cappella di Sant'Andrea 9.30am-12.30pm Tue, Thu, Sat & Sun; ⓂColosseo or Circo Massimo) Ring the bell for admission to this landmark church, which stands on the site where Pope Gregory is said to have dispatched St Augustine to convert the British. Originally, it was the pope's family home but in 575 he converted it into a monastery. It was rebuilt in the 17th century and the interior was given a baroque facelift a century later.

Inside, look out for a stately 1st-century-BC marble throne said to have been St Gregory's personal perch. Outside, the **Cappella di Sant'Andrea** is the most interesting of three small chapels, with frescoes by Domenichino, Guido Reni and Giovanni Lanfranco.

VILLA CELIMONTANA   PARK
(Map p370; ☉7am-sunset; 🚊Via della Navicella) With its lawns and colourful flower beds, this leafy walled park is a wonderful place to escape the crowds and enjoy a summer picnic. At its centre is a 16th-century villa that was once owned by the Mattei family but now houses the Italian Geographical Society.

CHIESA DI SANTO
STEFANO ROTONDO   CHURCH
(Map p370; www.santo-stefano-rotondo.it; Via di Santo Stefano Rotondo 7; ☉9.30am-12.30pm Tue-Sun & 2-5pm Tue-Sat winter, 9.30am-12.30pm & 3-6pm Tue-Sun summer; 🚊Via della Navicella) 'Such a panorama of horror and butchery no man could imagine in his sleep, though he were to eat a whole pig, raw, for supper.' So wrote Charles Dickens after seeing the 16th-century frescoes that circle this otherwise tranquil church. The X-rated images – and they really are pretty graphic – depict the many tortures suffered by the early Christian martyrs.

The church, one of Rome's oldest, dates to the late 5th century, although it was subsequently altered in the 12th and 15th centuries.

⊙ Aventino & Around

PARCO SAVELLO   PARK
(Map p370; Via di Santa Sabina; ☉7am-6pm Oct-Feb, to 8pm Mar & Sep, to 9pm Apr-Aug; 🚊Lungotevere Aventino) Known to Romans as the *Giardino degli Aranci* (Orange Garden), this pocket-sized park is a romantic haven. Grab a perch at the small panoramic terrace and watch the sun set over the Tiber and St Peter's dome. In summer, theatre performances are sometimes staged among the perfumed orange trees.

SAN GIOVANNI TO TESTACCIO SIGHTS

TOP SIGHT
BASILICA DI SANTA SABINA

This magnificent, solemn basilica was founded by Peter of Illyria in around AD 422. It was enlarged in the 9th century and again in 1216, just before it was given to the newly founded Dominican order – look out for the mosaic tombstone of Muñoz de Zamora, one of the order's founding fathers, in the nave floor. A 20th-century restoration returned it to its original austere look.

One of the few surviving 4th-century elements are the basilica's cypress-wood doors on the church's left flank. They feature 18 carved panels depicting biblical events, including one of the oldest Crucifixion scenes in existence. It's quite hard to make out in the top left, but it depicts Jesus and the two thieves although, strangely, not their crosses.

Inside, the three naves are separated by 24 custom-made Corinthian columns which support an arcade decorated with a faded red-and-green frieze. Light streams in from high nave windows that were added in the 9th century, along with the carved choir, pulpit and bishop's throne.

Behind the church is a garden and a meditative 13th-century cloister, where St Dominic is said to have planted Italy's first ever orange tree.

DON'T MISS...

➡ The cypress-wood doors

➡ Tombstone of Muñoz de Zamora

PRACTICALITIES

➡ Map p370

➡ ☏06 5 79 41

➡ Piazza Pietro d'Illiria 1

➡ ☉8.15am-12.30pm & 3.30-6pm

➡ 🚊Lungotevere Aventino

SUBTERRANEAN CULT

The cult of Mithraism was hugely popular with the ancient Roman military. According to its mythology, Mithras, a young, handsome god, was ordered to slay a wild bull by the Sun. As the bull died, it gave life, its blood causing wheat and other plants to grow. In Mithraic iconography, a serpent and dog are usually shown attacking the bull to try to prevent this, while a scorpion attacks its testicles. Mithraic temples, known as Mithraeums, were almost always in underground locations or caves, reflecting their belief that caverns represented the cosmos. In the Mithraeums, devotees underwent complex processes of initiation, and ate bread and water as a representation of the body and the blood of the bull. Sound familiar? The early Christians thought so too, and were fervently against the cult, feeling its practices were too close to their own.

PIAZZA DEI CAVALIERI DI MALTA   PIAZZA

(Via di Santa Sabina; 🚇Lungotevere Aventino) Named after the *Cavalieri di Malta* (Knights of Malta), who have their Roman headquarters here, in the **Priorato dei Cavalieri di Malta**, this ornate cypress-shaded square is famous for its secret view. Look through the keyhole in the Priorato's main door and you'll see the dome of St Peter's Basilica perfectly aligned at the end of a hedge-lined avenue.

◉ Testaccio

CIMITERO ACATTOLICO
PER GLI STRANIERI   CEMETERY

(Map p370; Via Caio Cestio 5; voluntary donation €3; ☉9am-5pm Mon-Sat, to 1pm Sun; 🚇Piramide) Despite the roads that surround it, Rome's 'non-Catholic' Cemetery is a surprisingly tranquil place. Percy Bysshe Shelley wrote: 'It might make one in love with death to think that one should be buried in so sweet a place.' And so he was, along with fellow poet John Keats and a host of luminaries, including Antonio Gramsci, founder of the Italian Communist Party.

PIRAMIDE DI CAIO CESTIO   LANDMARK

(Map p370; 🚇Piramide) Sticking out like, well, an Egyptian pyramid, this distinctive landmark stands in the Aurelian Wall at the side of a massive traffic junction. A 36m-high marble-and-brick tomb, it was built for Gaius Cestius, a 1st-century-BC magistrate, and some 200 years later was incorporated into the Aurelian fortification near Porta San Paolo. The surrounding area is today known as Piramide.

MONTE TESTACCIO   HISTORICAL SITE

(Map p370; ☎06 06 08; Via Nicola Zabaglia 24, cnr Via Galvani; adult/reduced €4/3 plus cost of tour; ☉group visits by guided tour only; 🚇Via Marmorata) Right in the heart of the Testaccio neighbourhood, Monte Testaccio, aka Monte dei Cocci, is an artificial grass-covered hill made almost entirely of smashed amphorae.

Between the 2nd century BC and the 3rd century AD, Testaccio was Rome's river port. Supplies of wine, oil and grain were transported here in huge terracotta amphorae, which, once emptied, were dumped in the river. But when the Tiber became almost unnavigable as a consequence, the pots were smashed and the pieces stacked methodically in a pile, which over time grew into a large hill – Monte Testaccio.

MACRO TESTACCIO   GALLERY

(Map p370; ☎06 06 08; www.macro.roma.museum; Piazza Orazio Giustiniani 4; adult/reduced €6/4; ☉4pm-10pm Tue-Sun; 🚇Via Marmorata) Housed in Rome's ex-slaughterhouse, MACRO Testaccio (the second of MACRO's two exhibition spaces) serves up contemporary art in two cavernous industrial halls. Note that the gallery opens only when there is an exhibition on – check the website for details.

✕ EATING

✕ San Giovanni

LI RIONI   PIZZERIA €

(Map p370; ☎06 7045 0605; Via dei SS Quattro Coronati 24; pizzas €8; ☉Thu-Tue, closed Aug; 🚇Colosseo) Locals swear by Li Rioni, arriving for the second sitting around 9pm after the tourists have left. A classic neighbourhood pizzeria, it buzzes most nights as diners squeeze into the cosy interior –

cheerfully set up as a Roman street scene – and tuck into wood-fired thin-crust pizzas and crispy *supplì* (fried rice croquettes).

CAFFÈ PROPAGANDA
BISTRO €€

(Map p370; www.caffepropaganda.it; Via Claudia 15; meals €40; ⊘noon-2am daily; ⓂColosseo) Opened to much fanfare in late 2011, this boho Parisian-inspired bistro has quickly established itself on the city's foodie map. It's a good-looking place with a striking zinc bar, 5m-high ceilings, bric-a-brac on the white-tiled walls, and a menu that covers all the bases, with everything from cocktails and coffee to traditional Roman pastas, steaks and delicious handmade *dolci*.

TAVERNA DEI QUARANTA
TRATTORIA €€

(Map p370; ☑06 700 05 50; www.tavernadeiquaranta.com; Via Claudia 24; meals €25-30; ⊘Mon-Sat; ⓂColosseo) Tasty traditional food, honest prices, near the Colosseum but off the beaten track – there's a lot to like about this laid-back, family-run trattoria. There are no great surprises on the menu but daily specials add variety and all the desserts are homemade – always a good sign.

IL BOCCONCINO
TRATTORIA €€

(Map p370; ☑06 7707 9175; www.ilbocconcino.com; Via Ostilia 23; meals €30-35; ⊘Thu-Tue, closed Aug; ⓂColosseo) An old-school Roman trattoria good for lunch after a morning at the Colosseum. With its gingham tablecloths, outdoor seating and cosy interior it looks like all the other eateries in this touristy neighbourhood but it stands out for its excellent pastas and imaginative meat and fish mains.

AROMA
GASTRONOMIC €€€

(Map p370; ☑06 9761 5109; www.palazzomanfredi.com; Palazzo Manfredi, Via Labicana 125; tasting menu €125; ⓂColosseo) If you're one for a romantic dinner, the rooftop restaurant of the five-star Palazzo Manfredi hotel offers unforgettable 'marry-me' views over the Colosseum and food that rises to the occasion. Overseeing the kitchen is chef Giuseppe Di Iorio, whose brand of luxurious, forward-thinking Italian cuisine has won widespread applause from critics and diners alike.

✕ Testaccio

00100 PIZZA
PIZZERIA €

(Map p370; www.00100pizza.com; Via G Branca 88; pizza slices from €3, trapizzini from €3.50;

⊘noon-11pm; ⓠVia Marmorata) A pocket-size pizzeria, this is one of a select group of Roman takeaways with culinary ambitions. As well as pizzas topped with unusual combos such as potato, sausage and beer, you can snack on *supplì* and *trapizzini*, small cones of pizza stuffed with fillers such as *polpette al sugo* (meatballs in tomato sauce) or *seppie con i piselli* (cuttlefish with peas).

PIZZERIA DA REMO
PIZZERIA €

(Map p370; ☑06 574 62 70; Piazza Santa Maria Liberatrice 44; pizzas from €5.50; ⊘7pm-1am Mon-Sat; ⓠVia Marmorata) Pizzeria Da Remo is one of the city's most popular pizzerias, its spartan interior always crowded with noisy diners. The pizzas are thin Roman classics with toppings loaded onto the crisp, charred base. Place your order by ticking your choices on a sheet of paper slapped down by an overstretched waiter. Expect to queue.

VOLPETTI PIÙ
CAFETERIA €

(Map p370; Via Volta 8; mains €8; ⊘10.30am-3.30pm & 5.30-9.30pm Mon-Sat; ⓠVia Marmorata) One of the few places in town where you can sit down for a full meal for less than €20, Volpetti Più is a sumptuous *tavola calda* (canteen-style buffet) offering an opulent choice of pizza, pasta, soup, meat, vegetables and fried nibbles.

FLAVIO AL VELAVEVODETTO
TRATTORIA €€

(Map p370; ☑06 574 41 94; www.flavioalvelavevodetto.it; Via di Monte Testaccio 97-99; meals €30-35; ⊘closed Sat lunch & Sun summer; ⓠVia Marmorata) This welcoming eatery is the sort of place that gives Roman trattorias a good name. Housed in a rustic Pompeian-red villa, complete with intimate

---

ⓘ MENU DECODER

The hallmark of an authentic Roman menu is the presence of offal. The Roman love of nose-to-tail eating arose in Testaccio around the city abattoir, and many of the area's trattorias still serve traditional offal-based dishes. So whether you want to avoid it or try it, look out for *pajata* (veal's intestines), *trippa* (tripe), *coda alla vaccinara* (oxtail), *coratella* (heart, lung and liver), *animelle* (sweetbreads), *testarella* (head), *lingua* (tongue), *zampe* (trotters).

covered courtyard and an open-air terrace, it specialises in earthy, no-nonsense Italian food, prepared with skill and served in mountainous portions. Expect homemade pastas seasoned with veggies and *guanciale* (bacon made from pig's cheek), and uncomplicated meaty mains.

DA FELICE REGIONAL CUISINE €€

(Map p370; ☑06 574 68 00; www.feliceatestac cio.com; Via Mastro Giorgio 29; meals €35-40; ⊗lunch & dinner daily; 🚇Via Marmorata) Foodies swear by this local stalwart, famous for its traditional Roman cuisine. The menu follows a classic weekly timetable with *tonnarelli cacio e pepe* (square-shaped spaghetti with *pecorino* Romano cheese and black pepper) on Tuesdays, *coda alla vaccinara* (oxtail) on Thursdays and pasta *in brodo d'arzilla* (pasta in fish ray broth) on Fridays. Reservations essential.

TRATTORIA DA BUCATINO TRATTORIA €€

(Map p370; ☑06 574 68 86; Via Luca della Robbia 84; meals €30-35; ⊗Tue-Sun; 🚇Via Marmorata) This laid-back neighbourhood trattoria is hugely popular. Ask for a table upstairs and dig into their trademark *bucatini all'amatriciana* and other typical Roman dishes.

CHECCHINO DAL 1887 REGIONAL CUISINE €€€

(Map p370; ☑06 574 63 18; www.checchino -dal-1887.com; Via di Monte Testaccio 30; meals €60; ⊗Tue-Sat, closed Aug; 🚇Via Marmorata) A pig's whisker from the city's former slaughterhouse, Checchino is one of the grander restaurants specialising in the *quinto quarto* (fifth quarter – or insides of the animal). Signature dishes include *coda all vaccinara* (oxtail stew) and *rigatoni alla gricia* (pasta tubes with pecorino cheese, black pepper and pancetta).

🍷 DRINKING & NIGHTLIFE

🍷 San Giovanni

IL PENTAGRAPPOLO WINE BAR

(Map p370; Via Celimontana 21b; ⊗noon-3pm & 6pm-1am Tue-Fri, 6pm-1am Sat & Sun; MColosseo) This relaxed, star-vaulted wine bar

GAY STREET

The bottom end of Via di San Giovanni di Laterano, the sloping street that runs from the Basilica di San Giovanni in Laterano to near the Colosseum is a favourite haunt of Rome's gay community. Not so much during the day but in the evening bars such as **Coming Out** and **My Bar** (Map p370; Via di San Giovanni in Laterano 12; ⊗9am-2am; MColosseo) burst into life, attracting large crowds of mainly gay men.

is the perfect antidote to sightseeing overload. Join the mellow crowd to sip on wine (choose from about 15 wines by the glass) and chat over piano tunes or live jazz. There's also lunch and a daily aperitif from 6pm.

COMING OUT BAR

(Map p370; www.comingout.it; Via di San Giovanni in Laterano 8; ⊗10.30am-2am; MColosseo) On warm evenings, with lively crowds on the street and the Colosseum as a backdrop, there are few finer places to sip than this friendly, gay bar. It's open all day but at its best in the evening when the the atmosphere warms up courtesy of regular DJ acts.

🍷 Testaccio

L'OASI DELLA BIRRA BAR

(Map p370; ☑06 574 61 22; Piazza Testaccio 41; ⊗5pm-1am Mon-Thu & Sun, to 2am Fri & Sat; 🚇Via Marmorata) Underneath the Palombi bottle shop, this popular cellar bar is exactly what it says it is – an Oasis of Beer. With everything from Teutonic heavyweights to boutique brews, as well as an ample wine list, aperitif buffet (from 5pm) and a menu of cheeses, cold cuts, stews and the like, it's ideal for an evening of dedicated carousing.

LINARI CAFE

(Map p370; Via Nicola Zabaglia 9; ⊗7am-11pm Wed-Mon; 🚇Via Marmorata) An authentic neighbourhood hang-out, Linari has the busy clatter of a good bar, with excellent pastries, splendid coffee and plenty of barside banter. There are some outside tables, ideal for a cheap lunch (pastas and main courses €5.50/6.50), but you'll have to arm-wrestle the neighbourhood ladies to get one.

IL SEME E LA FOGLIA BAR

(Map p370; Via Galvani 18; ☺8am-2am Mon-Sat, 6pm-2am Sun; ☐Via Marmorata) Frequented by students during the day, this innocuous bar on the edge of Testaccio's nightlife strip is a popular pre-clubbing stop. Groups of dressed-up clubbers gather here to decide their next move and grab a beer in the tiny, tangerine interior.

 ## ENTERTAINMENT

☆ Testaccio

CONTESTACCIO CLUB, LIVE MUSIC

(Map p370; www.contestaccio.com; Via di Monte Testaccio 65b; ☺7pm-5am Tue-Sun, closed end Jun–mid-Sep; ☐Via Marmorata) With an under-the-stars terrace and cool, arched interior, ConteStaccio is one of the top venues on the Testaccio clubbing strip. Daily gigs by emerging groups set the tone, spanning indie, rock, acoustic, funk and electronic. Admission is usually free with cocktails costing around €8.

VILLAGGIO GLOBALE CLUB, LIVE MUSIC

(Map p370; www.ecn.org/villaggioglobale/joomla; Via Monte del Cocci 22; ☐Via Marmorata) For a warehouse-party vibe, head to this historic *centro sociale* (an ex-squat turned cultural centre) occupying the city's graffiti-sprayed former slaughterhouse. Entrance is cheap, the beer flows and there's plenty of music action with live DJ sets and gigs, mostly techno, dancehall, reggae, dubstep and drum 'n' bass.

L'ALIBI CLUB

(Map p370; www.lalibi.it; Via di Monte Testaccio 44; ☺11.30pm-5am Thu-Sun; ☐Via Marmorata) Rome's best-known gay club, L'Alibi does high-camp with style, putting on kitsch shows and playing sultry, soulful house to a mixed gay and straight crowd. It's spread over three floors and if the sweaty atmosphere in the dance halls gets too much, head up to the huge summer roof terrace. Thursday nights are big with the ever-popular Gloss party featuring drag shows, buff dancers and mainstream tunes.

 # SHOPPING

VOLPETTI FOOD & DRINK

(Map p370; www.volpetti.com; Via Marmorata 47; ☺8am-2pm & 5-8.15pm Mon-Sat; ☐Via Marmorata) This superstocked deli, considered by many the best in town, is an Aladdin's cave of gourmet treasures. Helpful staff will guide you through the extensive selection of smelly cheeses, homemade pastas, olive oils, vinegars, cured meats, veggie pies, wines and grappas. You can also order online.

CALZATURE BOCCANERA SHOES

(Map p370; Via Luca della Robbia 36; ☺9.30am-1.30pm Tue-Sat & 3.30-7.30pm Mon-Sat; ☐Via Marmorata) Testaccio goes glam at this old-fashioned shoe shop. It's lined with just-off-the-runway men's and ladies' footwear from names such as Fendi, Ferragamo, Prada, D&G and Gucci, as well as bags, belts and leather accessories. It's particularly tempting during the sales.

NUOVO MERCATO DI TESTACCIO MARKET

(Map p370; Via Galvani; ☺6am-3pm Mon-Sat; ☐Via Marmorata) Even if you don't need to buy anything, a trip to Testaccio's daily food market is fun. Occupying a new, purpose-built site, it hums with activity as locals go about their daily shopping, picking and prodding the piles of brightly coloured produce and cheerfully shouting at all and sundry.

SOUL FOOD MUSIC

(Map p370; Via di San Giovanni in Laterano 192; ☺10.30am-1.30pm & 3.30-8pm Tue-Sat; ⓂColosseo) Run by Hate Records (www.haterecords.com), Soul Food presents rare, vintage vinyl by the rack-load with an eclectic selection of rock, punk, '60s garage, jazz, rockabilly and glam. Retro-design T-shirts, fanzines and other groupie clobber complete the offering. Almost next door is sister shop, **Junk Food** (Map p370; Via di San Giovanni in Laterano 188; ☺10.30am-1.30pm Tue-Sat & 3.30-8pm Mon-Sat; ⓂColosseo), specialising in records and cassettes for less than €10.

VIA SANNIO MARKET

(Map p370; ☺8am-1pm Mon-Sat; ⓂSan Giovanni) This market in the shadow of the Aurelian Walls is awash with wardrobe staples. It has a good assortment of new and vintage clothes, shoes at bargain prices, and a good range of jeans and leather jackets.

Southern Rome

VIA APPIA ANTICA | OSTIENSE | SAN PAOLO | GARBATELLA

Neighbourhood Top Five

1 Walking or cycling along the **Via Appia Antica** (p210), tracing the route of a thousand ancient Roman footsteps.

2 Exploring Rome's Christian burial catacombs, such as the **Catacombe di San Sebastiano** (p211).

3 Wandering around the ingenious location for the overflow from the Capitoline Museums: **Centrale Montemartini** (p216).

4 Buying, eating and dreaming about food at **Eataly** (p217).

5 Feeling dwarfed by the majesty of **San Paolo Fuori Le Mura** (p216).

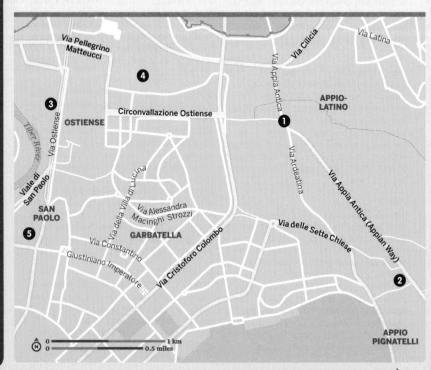

For more detail of this area, see Map p382 ➡

Explore Southern Rome

Southern Rome is a sprawling neighbourhood that comprises four distinct areas: the Via Appia Antica, famous for its catacombs; trendy Via Ostiense; picturesque Garbatella; and EUR, Mussolini's futuristic building development. It's all quite spread out, but public transport connections are good.

Heading southeast from Porta San Sebastiano, Via Appia Antica (the Appian Way) is one of the world's oldest roads and a much-prized Roman address. It's a beautiful part of town, with crumbling ruins set amid pea-green fields and towering umbrella pines.

To the west, Via Ostiense presents a very different picture. Busy and traffic-clogged, it runs through one of the capital's hippest districts. Disused factories and warehouses harbour restaurants, pubs, clubs and bars, and the huge Eataly, a restaurant and Italian foodstuffs complex, opened here in 2012. Planned redevelopments for the ex-Mercati Generali as a 'City of Youth' – comprising leisure, cultural and office space and designed by Rem Koolhaas – are still on the table, but will upgrade the neighbourhood even further if they ever come to fruition.

Ostiense also harbours a couple of gem-like sights: Centrale Montemartini, a disused power plant housing superb classical statuary, and Basilica di San Paolo Fuori le Mura, the world's third-largest church. Over the road, the character-filled Garbatella district merits exploration for its original architecture, while further south, EUR is a world apart. Built by Mussolini as a showcase for his Fascist regime, it's a fascinating, Orwellian quarter of wide boulevards and linear buildings.

Local Life

➡ **Eating** Feel the buzz around the massive new Eataly.

➡ **Clubbing** Some of Rome's coolest clubs are clustered around Via Ostiense.

➡ **Cycling** Escape from the frenetic city centre along the beautiful Appian Way.

Getting There & Away

➡ **Metro** Metro line B runs to Piramide, Garbatella, Basilica San Paolo, EUR Palasport and EUR Fermi.

➡ **Bus** There are bus connections to Porta San Sebastiano (118, 218 and 714), Via Ostiense (23 and 716) and Via Appia Antica (118, 660, and 218). The 118 bus is the best for access to the pedestrianised section.

➡ **Archeobus** If you're spending the day here and want to see several sights, the hop-on hop-off Archeobus (€12) departs from Termini every hour.

Lonely Planet's Top Tip

On Sunday, the first section of Appia Antica is supposedly traffic free. On other days bear in mind that the first section, stretching 1km from Porta San Sebastiano, is not at all pleasant to walk along and even on Sundays there are still vehicles zooming along this stretch. The most atmospheric part of the road is from the Tempio di Romolo to the Via Appia Nuova junction; this section is almost entirely traffic free every day.

If you're not planning to visit lots of sights, take the local bus rather than buying an Archeobus ticket.

Best Places to Eat

➡ Eataly (p217)
➡ Trattoria Priscilla (p217)
➡ Andreotti (p218)
➡ Estrobar (p218)

For reviews, see p217

Best Places to Drink

➡ Porto Fluviale (p218)
➡ Doppiozeroo (p218)
➡ Neo Club (p218)
➡ Rashomon (p218)

For reviews, see p218 ➡

Best Entertainment

➡ La Casa del Jazz (p219)
➡ XS Live (p219)
➡ Caffè Letterario (p219)
➡ Piscina delle Rose (p213)

For reviews, see p219

SOUTHERN ROME

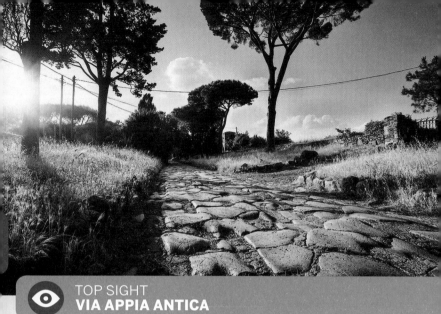

TOP SIGHT
VIA APPIA ANTICA

Heading southeast from Porta San Sebastiano, the Appian Way was known to the Romans as the *regina viarum* (queen of roads). Named after Appius Claudius Caecus, who laid the first 90km section in 312 BC, it was extended in 190 BC to reach Brindisi, some 540km away on the southern Adriatic coast. Flanked by some of the city's most exclusive private villas, as well as Roman tombs, the long cobbled road is a great place for a walk or cycle.

The Appia Antica, peaceful today, resounds with history: it's where Spartacus and 6000 of his slave rebels were crucified in 71 BC, and around it lie 300km of underground tunnels carved out of soft tufa rock, used as burial chambers by the early Christians. Corpses were wrapped in simple white sheets and usually placed in rectangular niches carved into the walls, which were then closed with marble or terracotta slabs. You can't visit all 300km, but three major catacombs (San Callisto, San Sebastiano and Santa Domitilla) are open for guided exploration.

If you're planning on really doing the sights, think about buying the Appia Antica Card (p325). Near the start of the road, the Appia Antica Regional Park Information Point is very informative. You can buy a map of the park here and hire bikes (per hour/day €3/10) and electric bikes (€6/20). Child-sized bikes aren't available, but child seats (up to 20kg) are; book these in advance as there are not many available. The park run tours in English, Spanish and German, which have to be booked by email at least two weeks before your arrival.

DON'T MISS...

➡ The catacombs
➡ Cycling along the Appia
➡ Villa dei Quintilli

PRACTICALITIES

➡ Map p382
➡ 🖉 06 512 63 14
➡ www.parcoappia antica.it
➡ ⊙ Information Point 9.30am-1pm & 2-5pm Mon-Fri, 9.30am-5pm Sat & Sun, to 5.30pm Aug, to 6.30pm Apr-Oct
➡ 🚇 Via Appia Antica

TOP SIGHT
BASILICA & CATACOMBE DI SAN SEBASTIANO

The most famous of the catacombs, these contain frescoes, stucco work, epigraphs and also several immaculately preserved mausoleums. The catacombs extend for more than 12 kilometres and are divided into three levels, three-, nine- and 12-metres deep. They once harboured more than 65,000 tombs.

Basilica

The 4th-century **basilica** (Map p382; Via Appia Antica 136; ☻8am-1pm & 2-5.30pm daily) that was built here by the emperor Constantine was mostly destroyed by Saracen raids in the 9th century, and the church you see today mainly dates from the reconstruction initiated by Cardinal Borghese in the 17th century. It is dedicated to St Sebastian, who was martyred and buried here in the late 3rd century. In 826, his body was transferred to St Peter's for safekeeping, but he was re-interred here in the 12th century. In the Capella delle Reliquie you'll find one of the arrows used to kill him and the column to which he was tied. On the other side of the church is a marble slab with Jesus' footprints.

Catacombs

A warren of tunnels that lie beneath the church and beyond, the Catacombe di San Sebastiano were the first catacombs to be so called, the name deriving from the Greek *kata* (near) and *kymbas* (cavity), because they were located near a cave. During the persecution of Christians by the emperor Vespasian from AD 258, it's believed that the catacombs were used as a safe haven for the remains of St Peter and St Paul and became a popular pilgrimage site. A plastered wall is covered with hundreds of invocations, engraved by worshippers in the 3rd and 4th centuries, featuring personalised entreaties such as 'Peter and Paul, pray for Victor'. However, it may be the case that the remains were never kept here, and the catacombs simply served as a focus for worship during those difficult times.

Mausoleums

Within the catacombs there are three beautifully preserved, decorated mausoleums. Each of the monumental facades feature a door, above which are inscribed symbols and the names of the owners. The first mausoleum belonged to Marcus Clodius Ermete, while the second one is named 'of the innocentiores', which is thought to have been the name of an association. During the 3rd century the area was filled in to build a place of pilgrimage where visitors could come to honour St Peter and St Paul, which is why the delicate stucco has remained so immaculately well preserved.

DON'T MISS...

➡ Graffiti to St Peter & St Paul

➡ Mausoleums

➡ Basilica di San Sebastiano

PRACTICALITIES

➡ Map p382

➡ ☎06 785 03 50

➡ www.catacombe. org

➡ Via Appia Antica 136

➡ adult/reduced €8/4

➡ ☻10am-5pm Mon-Sat, closed Dec

➡ 🚌Via Appia Antica

⊙ SIGHTS

The awe-inspiring Appian Way stretches south of Rome, dotted by Roman ruins above and riddled with catacombs below.

⊙ Via Appia Antica

CATACOMBE DI SAN SEBASTIANO
CATACOMBS

See p211.

VILLA DI MASSENZIO
RUIN

(Map p382; ☑06 780 13 24; www.villadimassen zio.it; Via Appia Antica 153; adult/reduced €5/4; ⊙9am-4pm Tue-Sat; 🚍Via Appia Antica) The outstanding feature of Maxentius' enormous 4th-century palace complex is the **Circo di Massenzio** (Map p382), Rome's best-preserved ancient racetrack – you can still make out the starting stalls used for chariot races. The 10,000-seat arena was built by Maxentius around 309, but he died before ever seeing a race here.

Above the arena are the ruins of Maxentius' imperial residence, most of which are covered by weeds. Near the racetrack, the **Mausoleo di Romolo** (Map p382), also known as the Tombo di Romolo, was built by Maxentius for his son Romulus. The huge mausoleum was originally crowned with a large dome and surrounded by an imposing colonnade, in part still visible.

MAUSOLEO DI CECILIA METELLA
RUIN

(Map p382; ☑06 3996 7700; www.coopculture. it; Via Appia Antica 161; admission incl Terme di Caracalla & Villa dei Quintili adult/reduced €7/4; ⊙9am to 1hr before sunset Tue-Sun; 🚍Via Appia Antica) Dating to the 1st century BC, this great drum of a mausoleum encloses a burial chamber (built for the daughter of the consul Quintus Metellus Creticus), now roofless. The walls are made of travertine and the interior is decorated with a sculpted frieze featuring Gaelic shields, ox skulls and festoons.

In the 14th century it was converted into a fort by the Caetani family, who used to frighten passing traffic into paying a toll.

VILLA DEI QUINTILI
RUIN

(☑06 3996 7700; www.coopculture.it; Via Appia Nuova 1092; adult/reduced incl Terme di Caracalla & Mausoleo di Cecilia Metella €7/4; ⊙9am to 1hr before sunset Tue-Sun; 🚍Via Appia Nuova) Set on lush green fields, this vast 2nd-century villa was the luxurious abode of two brothers who were consuls under the emperor Marcus Aurelius. Alas, the villa's splendour was to be the brothers' downfall – in a fit of jealousy, the emperor Commodus had them both killed, taking over the villa for himself.

The highlight is the well-preserved baths complex with a pool, *caldarium* (hot room) and *frigidarium* (cold room).

CATACOMBE DI SAN CALLISTO
CATACOMBS

(Map p382; ☑06 513 01 51; www.catacombe.roma. it; Via Appia Antica 110 & 126; adult/reduced €8/5; ⊙9am-noon & 2-5pm, closed Wed mid-Jan–mid-Feb; 🚍Via Appia Antica) These are the largest and busiest of Rome's catacombs. Founded at the end of the 2nd century and named after Pope Calixtus I, they became the official cemetery of the newly established Roman Church. In the 20km of tunnels explored to date, archaeologists have found the tombs of 500,000 people and seven popes who were martyred in the 3rd century.

The patron saint of music, St Cecilia, was also buried here, though her body was later removed to the Basilica di Santa Cecilia in Trastevere. When her body was exhumed in 1599, more than a thousand years after her death, it was apparently perfectly preserved, as depicted in Stefano Maderno's softly contoured sculpture, a replica of which is here.

MAUSOLEO DELLE FOSSE ARDEATINE
MONUMENT

(Map p382; ☑06 513 67 42; Via Ardeatina 174; ⊙8.15am-3.30pm Mon-Fri, to 4.30pm Sat & Sun; 🚍Via Appia Antica) **FREE** This moving mausoleum is dedicated to the victims of Rome's worst WWII atrocity. Buried here, outside the Ardeatine Caves, are 335 Italians shot by the Nazis on 24 March 1944. Follow-

ⓘ ACCESS TO VILLA DEI QUINTILI

The entrance to the Villa dei Quintili on the Appia Antica is only open at weekends from March to September. Otherwise, you'll need to use the other main entrance on the Via Appia Nuova, most easily accessible via buses 664 and 665.

ing the massacre, ordered in reprisal for a partisan attack, the Germans used mines to explode sections of the caves and bury the bodies. After the war, the bodies were exhumed, identified and reburied in a mass grave, now marked by a huge concrete slab and sculptures.

The site also has a tiny museum dedicated to the Italian Resistance (doors close 15 minutes before the rest of the site).

CATACOMBE DI SANTA DOMITILLA CATACOMBS

(Map p382; ☎06 511 03 42; www.domitilla.info; Via delle Sette Chiese 283; adult/reduced €8/5; ☺9am-noon & 2-5pm Wed-Mon, closed Jan; ⓠVia Appia Antica) Among Rome's largest and oldest, these wonderful catacombs stretch for about 18km. They were established on the private burial ground of Flavia Domitilla, niece of the emperor Domitian and a member of the wealthy Flavian family.

They contain Christian wall paintings and the haunting underground **Chiesa di SS Nereus e Achilleus**, a 4th-century church dedicated to two Roman soldiers martyred by Diocletian.

CHIESA DEL DOMINE QUO VADIS? CHURCH

(Map p382; Via Appia Antica 51; ☺8am-6.30pm Mon-Fri, 8.15am-6.45pm Sat & Sun winter, to 7.30pm summer; ⓠVia Appia Antica) This pint-sized church marks the spot where St Peter, fleeing Rome, met a vision of Jesus going the other way. When Peter asked: *'Domine, quo vadis?'* (Lord, where are you going?), Jesus replied, *'Venio Roman iterum crucifigi'* (I am coming to Rome to be crucified again). Reluctantly deciding to join him, Peter tramped back into town where he was arrested and executed.

In the aisle are copies of Christ's footprints; the originals are in the Basilica di San Sebastiano.

EUR

One of the few planned developments in Rome's history, EUR was built for an international exhibition in 1942. Although war intervened and the exhibition never took place, the name stuck – Esposizione Universale di Roma (Roman Universal Exhibition) or EUR. There are a few museums but the area's interest lies in its spectacular rationalist architecture. It's unique, if not on a particularly human scale, and the style is beautifully expressed in a number of distinctive *palazzi* (mansions), including the iconic **Palazzo della Civiltà del Lavoro** (Quadrato della Concordia; Ⓜ EUR Magliana), dubbed the Square Colosseum. The Palace of the Workers is EUR's architectural icon, a rationalist masterpiece clad in gleaming white travertine. Designed by Giovanni Guerrini, Ernesto Bruno La Padula and Mario Romano, and built between 1938 and 1943, it consists of six rows of nine arches, rising to a height of 50m.

Elsewhere, other monumentalist architecture includes the **Chiesa Santi Pietro e Paolo** (Piazzale Santi Pietro e Paolo), the **Palazzetto dello Sport** (Piazzale dello Sport) and the wonderful **Palazzo dei Congressi** (Piazza JF Kennedy). Massimiliano Fuksas' cutting-edge Nuvola ('cloud') congress centre is the most recent dramatic architectural addition to the area. A steel and Teflon cloud is suspended by steel cables in a glass box – it was inspired by a cloud-gazing daydream and is an extraordinary building whose interior resembles tangled Meccano.

The **Museo della Civiltà Romana** (☎06 06 08; Piazza G Agnelli 10; adult/reduced €7.50/5.50, incl Museo Astronomico & Planetario €9.50/7.50; ☺9am-2pm Tue-Sun; Ⓜ EUR Fermi) is a possible kid-pleaser, founded by Mussolini in 1937 to glorify imperial Rome. A hulking place, its displays include many small-scale models of Roman weaponry, a giant-scale re-creation of 4th-century Rome and plaster casts of the Colonno di Traiano. The **Museo Astronomico & Planetario** (☎06 06 08; www.planetarioroma.it; adult/child €7.50/5.50, incl Museo Civiltà Romana €9.50/7.50; ☺9am-2pm Tue-Fri, to 7pm Sat & Sun, shorter hours Jul & Aug) has shows that will appeal to older children, but in Italian only.

Also in EUR is Rome's largest public swimming pool, **Piscina delle Rose** (☎06 5422 0333; www.piscinadellerose.it; Viale America 20; admission from €8; ☺10am-10pm Mon-Fri, 9am-7pm Sat & Sun mid-May–Sep; underground rail EUR Palasport). It gets crowded, so arrive early to grab a deck chair.

Roman Catacombs

Ancient Roman law forbade burying the dead within the city walls, for reasons of hygiene. Rome's persecuted Christian community didn't have their own cemeteries, so in the 2nd century AD they began to build an extensive network of subterranean burial grounds outside the city.

The tombs were dug by specialised gravediggers, who tunnelled out the galleries. Bodies were wrapped in simple shrouds and then either placed individually in carved-out niches, called *loculi*, or in larger family tombs. Many tombs were marked with elaborate decorations, from frescoes to stucco work, which remain remarkably well preserved. A great many tombs discovered here bear touching inscriptions, such as the following: 'Apuleia Crysopolis, who lived for 7 years, 2 months; (her) parents made (this) for their dearest daughter'.

Symbolism

An almost secretive language of symbols had evolved to represent elements of the Christian faith. Since many early Christians could not read and write, these symbols served as both a secret code and a means to communicate among the illiterate. The most common of the symbols include the fish, the Greek word for which is *ichthys*, standing for Iesous Christos Theou Yios Soter (Jesus Christ, son of God, Saviour). The anchor, which also appears regularly, symbolises the belief in Christ as a safe haven, a comforting thought in times of persecution. It's thought, too, that this was again an example of Greek wordplay: *ankura* resembling *en kuriol*, which

1. Crypt of the Popes, Catacombe di San Callisto (p212) **2.** Catacombe di San Sebastiano (p211) **3.** Detail from 4th-century carving in Catacombe di Santa Domitilla (p213)

means 'in the Lord'. A dove with an olive branch in the beak is a reference to the biblical dove, meaning salvation.

Abandonment

The catacombs began to be abandoned as early as 313, when Constantine issued the Milan decree of religious tolerance and Christians were thus able to bury their dead in churchyards.

In about 800, after frequent incursions by invaders, the bodies of the martyrs and first popes were transferred to the basilicas inside the city walls for safe keeping. The catacombs were abandoned and by the Middle Ages many had been forgotten.

Since the 19th century, more than 30 catacombs have been uncovered in the area. The warren of tunnels are fascinating to explore, and sections of three sets of catacombs are accessible via guided tour. Unless you're passionate about catacombs, visiting one set will be sufficient.

TOP 5 CATACOMB READS

➡ *The Roman Catacombs*, by James Spencer Northcote (1859)

➡ *Tombs and Catacombs of the Appian Way: History of Cremation*, by Olinto L Spadoni (1892)

➡ *Valeria, the Martyr of the Catacombs*, by WH Withrow (1892)

➡ *Christian Rome: Past and Present: Early Christian Rome Catacombs and Basilicas*, by Philippe Pergola (2002)

➡ *The Roman Catacombs*, by Maurus Wolter (2010)

PORTA SAN SEBASTIANO　　　MUSEUM

(Map p382; ☑06 7047 5284; www.museodellemuraroma.it; Via di Porta San Sebastiano 18; adult/reduced €5/4; ☺9am-2pm Tue-Sun; ☐Porta San Sebastiano) Marking the start of Via Appia Antica, the 5th-century Porta San Sebastiano is the largest of the gates in the Aurelian Wall. During WWII, the Fascist Party secretary Ettore Muti lived here; today it houses the modest Museo delle Mure, which offers the chance to walk along the top of the walls for around 50m as well as displaying their history.

The gate was originally known as Porta Appia but took on its current name in honour of the thousands of pilgrims who passed under it on their way to the Catacombe di San Sebastiano.

⊙ Ostiense, San Paolo & Garbatella

Heading south from Stazione Roma-Ostia, Via Ostiense encompasses converted warehouses, clubs and hidden sights. The area is now home to the biggest news story (apart from the new Pope) to happen to Rome in recent years: Eataly, a temple to Italian foodstuffs.

CAPITOLINE MUSEUMS AT CENTRALE MONTEMARTINI　　　MUSEUM

(Map p382; ☑06 06 08; www.centralemontemartini.org; Via Ostiense 106; adult/reduced €6.50/5.50, incl Capitoline Museums €14/12, valid 7 days; ☺9am-7pm Tue-Sun; ☐Via Ostiense) Housed in a former power station, this fabulous outpost of the Capitoline Museums (Musei Capitolini) boldly juxtaposes classical sculpture against diesel engines and giant furnaces. The collection's highlights are in the **Sala Caldaia**, where ancient statuary strike poses around the giant furnace. Beautiful pieces include the *Fanciulla Seduta* (Seated Girl) and the *Musa Polimnia* (The Muse Polyhymnia) and there are also some exquisite mosaics.

QUARTIERE GARBATELLA　　　DISTRICT

(Ⓜ Garbatella) A favourite location for TV and film-makers, Quartiere Garbatella is an atmospheric, idiosyncratic district. It was originally conceived as a workers' residential quarter, but in the 1920s the Fascists hijacked the project and used the area to house people who'd been dis-

---

⊙ TOP SIGHT
BASILICA DI SAN PAOLO FUORI LE MURA

The world's third-largest church and the biggest in Rome after St Peter's, the magnificent, little-visited basilica of St Paul's stands on the site where St Paul was buried after being decapitated in AD 67. Built by Constantine in the 4th century, it was largely destroyed by fire in 1823; much of what you see today is a 19th-century reconstruction.

Not everything was decimated in the fire, however; many treasures survived, including the 5th-century triumphal arch, with its heavily restored mosaics, and the Gothic marble tabernacle over the high altar. Arnolfo di Cambio designed this around 1285, together with another artist, possibly Pietro Cavallini.

Doom-mongers should check out the papal portraits beneath the nave windows. Every pope since St Peter is represented and legend has it that when there is no room for the next portrait, the world will fall.

The stunning 13th-century Cosmati mosaic work in the **cloisters** (Map p382) of the adjacent Benedictine abbey also survived the 1823 fire.

DON'T MISS...

➡ 5th-century triumphal arch and mosaics
➡ Papal portraits
➡ Cloister

PRACTICALITIES

➡ Map p382
➡ www.abbaziasanpaolo.net
➡ Via Ostiense 190
➡ cloisters €4
➡ ☺7am-6.30pm
➡ Ⓜ San Paolo

EATALY

Surrounded by a gritty urbanscape of former factories and warehouses, Rome's gleaming **Eataly** (Map p382; ☑06 9027 9201; www.roma.eataly.it; Air Terminal Ostiense, Piazzale XII Ottobre 1492; ⊙shop 10am-midnight, restaurants noon-11.30pm) is the largest venue for this international chain devoted entirely to artisanal Italian food. The enormous mall-like (and somewhat confusing) store rises above the district of Ostiense, at once out of place and perfectly situated. The building was converted from the nearly derelict Air Terminal Ostiense, an art deco–influenced edifice built in the late 1980s and designed by Spanish architect Julio Lafuente.

The shop is full of books, cookery implements and foodstuffs from all over the country, and is also home to 19 cafes and restaurants, including a *panini* (sandwich) bar, a *gelateria* (ice-cream seller), *friggitoria* (traditional Roman fried food), a restaurant specialising in Lazio-sourced vegetables (serving salads, minestrone, etc), a slow-food *rosticceria* (for roasted meats) and the fine-dining Ristorante Italia on the uppermost floor, headed by chef Gianluca Esposito.

Depending on your tolerance for department stores and malls, the experience will either leave you exhilarated or with a bit of a headache. However, there are some first-class, good-value eating options here. The pizza (thick-crust, Neapolitan style) and pasta (try the gnocchi) restaurant serves up excellent-quality meals, and the 1st-floor microbrewery is a splendid place to sample craft beers. The complex is about a 10-minute walk from Piramide metro station. There's also a large car park (free for one hour, then €1.50 per hour) next to the building.

placed by construction work in the city. Many people were moved into *alberghi suburbani* (suburban hotels), big housing blocks designed by Innocenzo Sabbatini, the leading light of the 'Roman School' of architecture. The most famous, **Albergo Rosso** (Map p382; Piazza Michele da Carbonara), is typical of the style. Other trademark buildings are the **Scuola Cesare Battisti** (Map p382) on Piazza Damiano Sauli and **Teatro Palladium** on Piazza Bartolomeo Romano.

✖ EATING

The increasingly fashionable southern neighbourhoods of Ostiense and Garbatella feature some excellent restaurants, including those in Ostiense's new Eataly complex. You can also eat well in a rural setting close to Via Appia Antica.

✖ Via Appia Antica

TRATTORIA PRISCILLA   TRATTORIA €€
(Map p382; ☑06 513 63 79; Via Appia Antica 68; meals €35; ⊙Mon-Sat, lunch Sun; ☐Via Appia Antica) Set in a 16th-century former stable,

this intimate family-run trattoria has been feeding hungry travellers along the Appian Way for more than a hundred years, serving up traditional *cucina Romana,* so think *carbonara, amatriciana* and *cacio e pepe.*

RISTORANTE CECILIA METELLA   TRADITIONAL ITALIAN €€
(Map p382; ☑06 511 02 13; Via Appia Antica 125; meals €45; ⊙Tue-Sun; ☐Via Appia Antica) Near the catacombs of San Callisto, the outside seating at Cecilia Metella is great, set on a low hill under a vine canopy and with glimpses of the jewel-green countryside. The interior has a wedding-function vibe, but food is reasonable – the grilled meats are recommended.

L'ARCHEOLOGIA   ITALIAN €€€
(Map p382; ☑06 788 04 94; www.larcheologia.it; Via Appia Antica 139; meals around €50; ⊙12.30-3pm & 8-11pm Wed-Mon; ☐Via Appia Antica) This baronial-esque dining den – complete with elaborate flower arrangements, velvet drapes and Europe's oldest wisteria in the garden – is a safe bet for authentic regional grub and is a hit with perfectly preened Italian families out for Sunday lunch. The *spaghetti primavera* (spaghetti with zucchini, fresh tomato, basil and prawns) is sublime and service friendly.

✖ Ostiense, San Paolo & Garbatella

ANDREOTTI
PASTRIES & CAKES €

(Map p382; ☎06 575 07 73; Via Ostiense 54; ☉7.30am-9.30pm daily; ☒Via Ostiense) Film director and Ostiense local Ferzan Ozpetek is such a fan of the pastries here he's known to cast them in his films. They're all stars, from the fragrant almond biscotti and buttery *crostate* (tarts) to the piles of golden *sfogliatelle romane* (ricotta-filled pastries). There's even a supporting cast of savoury gems such as *frittini* (fried canapés) and cute-as-a-button *bruschettine* (mini bruschetta).

ESTROBAR
ITALIAN €€

(Map p382; ☎06 5728 9141; www.estrobar. com; Via Pellegrino Matteucci 20; meals €40; ☉lunch Mon-Fri, dinner Mon-Sat; ☒Via Ostiense) Designer denizens head to this slinky restaurant-bar-gallery to deconstruct the tales of Claudio di Carlo over a bottle of Brut or a *cocktail benessere* (fruit- or veggie-based cocktail). Fuelling the cultured conversations are chef Francesco Bonanni's Italo-fusion flavours – from sake and soy beef *carpaccio* (raw beef) to a spicy chocolate tart – and a wine list of 200 Italian drops.

PORTO FLUVIALE
TRATTORIA, PIZZERIA €€

(Map p382; ☎06 574 31 99; www.portofluviale. com; Via del Porto Fluviale 22; meals €30; ☉bar 10.30am-2am daily, restaurant lunch & dinner; ⓂPiramide) A hip new restaurant in the industrial-chic vein, Porto Fluviale is a great space and a good place to go with families: it's lively, spacious and fairly good value. Although the pizzas, pasta and roasted meats are nothing out of the ordinary – good, but not great – there's a buzz about the place and you may need to book.

🍷 DRINKING & NIGHTLIFE

The ex-industrial area of Ostiense is fertile clubbing land, with its many warehouses, workshops and factories given a new lease of life as pockets of nightlife nirvana. This is where Rome's serious clubbers lose countless hours worshipping at the shrines of electro, nu-house, nu-funk and all sorts of other eclectica.

DOPPIOZEROO
BAR

(Map p382; ☎06 5730 1961; doppiozeroo.com; Via Ostiense 68; ☉7am-2am Mon-Sat; ⓂPiramide) This easygoing bar was once a bakery, hence the name ('double zero' is a type of flour). But today the sleek, modern interior attracts hungry, trendy Romans like bees to honey, especially for the famously lavish, dinnertastic *aperitivo* between 6.30pm and 9pm. There's a buffet lunch on Saturday and Sunday, and DJs every Thursday.

PORTO FLUVIALE
BAR

(Map p382; ☎06 574 31 99; www.portofluviale. com; Via del Porto Fluviale 22; ☉10.30am-2am; ⓂPiramide) A large bar in a converted factory, this has an ex-industrial, shabby chic look – dark-green walls and a brickwork floor – and is a relaxing, appealing place for morning coffee, *aperitivo* or an evening drink to a soundtrack of plinky jazz. In line with Rome's current love of artisanal brews, they serve their own Porto Fluviale craft beer (medium €4).

NEO CLUB
NIGHTCLUB

(Map p382; Via degli Argonauti 18; ☉11pm-4am Fri & Sat; ⓂGarbatella) This small, dark two-level club has an underground feel and is one of the funkiest choices in the zone, featuring a dancetastic mish-mash of breakbeat, techno and old-skool house.

GOA
NIGHTCLUB

(Map p382; ☎06 574 82 77; www.goaclub.com; Via Libetta 13; ☉11.30pm-4.30am Thu-Sat; ⓂGarbatella) Goa is Rome's serious super-club, with international names, ethnic-styling, a fashion-forward crowd, podium dancers and heavies on the door. Look out for the regular lesbian night, Venus Rising (www. venusrising.com).

LA SAPONERIA
NIGHTCLUB

(Map p382; ☎06 574 69 99; Via degli Argonauti 20; ☉11pm-4.30am Tue-Sun Oct-May; ⓂGarbatella) Formerly a soap factory, nowadays La Saponeria is a cool space that's all exposed-brick and white walls and brain-twisting light shows. It lathers up the punters with guest DJs spinning everything from nu-house to nu-funk, minimal techno, dance, hip-hop and 1950s retro.

RASHOMON
NIGHTCLUB

(Map p382; www.rashomonclub.com; Via degli Argonauti 16; ☉11pm-4am Fri & Sat Oct-May; ⓂGarbatella) Rashomon is sweaty, not posey, and

where to head when you want to dance your ass off. Shake it to a music lovers' feast of the sound of the underground: especially house, techno and electronica.

RISING LOVE   NIGHTCLUB
(Map p382; ☑339 4270672; www.risinglove.net; Via delle Conce 14; ⊘11pm-4am Thu-Sat Oct-May; Ⓜ Piramide) For those who like their electro, techno, funky groove and an underground vibe, this industrial-styled, arty cultural association will tick all the boxes. Guest DJs as well as local talent get the crowd rocking and there are regular special nights.

PLANET ROMA   NIGHTCLUB
(Map p382; ☑06 574 78 26; www.planetroma. com; Via del Commercio 36; ⊘varies; Ⓜ Piramide) Formerly Alpheus, Planet Roma is one of Rome's largest clubs, getting its freak on to an eclectic array of sounds in its four rooms, from live jazz gigs to Latino nights. Glam, a mixed gay and lesbian night, rocks out to house and pop on Saturdays.

 ENTERTAINMENT

LA CASA DEL JAZZ   LIVE MUSIC
(Map p382; ☑06 70 47 31; www.casajazz.it; Viale di Porta Ardeatina 55; admission €5-10; ⊘7pm-midnight; Ⓜ Piramide) In the middle of a 2500-sq-metre park in the southern suburbs, the Casa del Jazz is housed in a three-storey 1920s villa that once belonged to a Mafia boss. When he was caught, the Comune di Roma (Rome Council) converted it into a jazz-fuelled complex, with a 150-

seat auditorium, rehearsal rooms, cafe and restaurant. Some events are free.

XS LIVE   LIVE MUSIC
(Map p382; ☑06 5730 5102; www.xsliveroma. com; Via Libetta 13; ⊘11.30pm-4am Thu-Sun Sep-May; Ⓜ Garbatella) The former club-bar-restaurant complex Distillerie Clandestine has been reborn as a rocking live music and club venue, hosting regular gigs. Big names playing here in recent times range from Peter Doherty to Jefferson Starship, and club nights range from nostalgic Beatles-themed trips to electro odysseys.

CAFFÈ LETTERARIO   ARTS CENTRE
(Map p382; ☑340 3067460, 06 5730 2842; www.caffeletterarioroma.it; Via Ostiense 83, 95; ⊘varies; ⓆVia Ostiense) Caffè Letterario is an intellectual hang-out housed in the funky converted, postindustrial space of a former garage. It combines designer looks, a bookshop, gallery, performance space and lounge bar. There are regular live gigs, ranging from Italian gypsy music to Indian dance. Check the website for upcoming events.

TEATRO INDIA   THEATRE
(Map p382; ☑06 8400 0311; www.teatrodiroma. net; Lungotevere dei Papareschi; tickets €10-30; ⓆVia Enrico Fermi) Inaugurated in 1999 in the post-industrial landscape of Rome's southern suburbs, the India is the younger sister of Teatro Argentina. It's a stark modern space in a converted industrial building, a fitting setting for its cutting-edge programme, with a calendar of international and Italian works.

Villa Borghese & Northern Rome

VILLA BORGHESE | FLAMINIO | SALARIO | NOMENTANA | PARIOLI

Neighbourhood Top Five

1 Getting to grips with genius at the lavish **Museo e Galleria Borghese** (p222). Gian Lorenzo Bernini's sculptures are the star of the show, but look out for Antonio Canova's racy depiction of the voluptuous Paolina Bonaparte.

2 Strolling the leafy lanes of Rome's most famous park, **Villa Borghese** (p225).

3 Catching a world-class concert at the **Auditorium Parco della Musica** (p233).

4 Applauding the sophistication of Etruscan art at the **Museo Nazionale Etrusco di Villa Giulia** (p228).

5 Going face to face with the greats of modern art at the **Galleria Nazionale d'Arte Moderna** (p225).

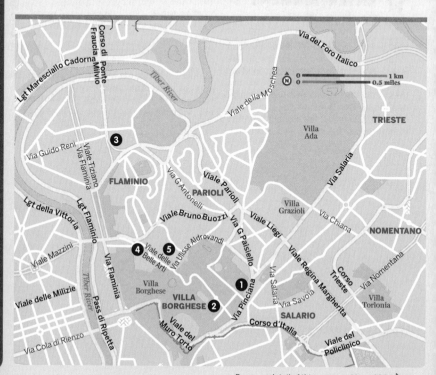

For more detail of this area, see Map p380 ➡

Explore Villa Borghese & Northern Rome

Although less packed with traditional sights than elsewhere, this large swath of northern Rome is well worth investigating. The obvious starting point is Villa Borghese, an attractive park counting the city's zoo, its largest modern art gallery and a stunning Etruscan museum among its myriad attractions. But its pièce de résistance is the Museo e Galleria Borghese, one of Rome's top art galleries. The park is easily explored on foot.

From Piazzale Flaminio, a tram heads up Via Flaminia to two of Rome's most important modern buildings: Renzo Piano's extraordinary Auditorium Parco della Musica and Zaha Hadid's contemporary art gallery, MAXXI. Continue up the road and you come to Ponte Milvio, a handsome footbridge and scene of an ancient Roman battle. Over the river and to the west, the Stadio Olimpico is Rome's impressive football stadium.

Over on the eastern side of Villa Borghese, Via Salaria, the old Roman *sale* (salt) road, is now the heart of a smart residential and business district. To the north, the vast Villa Ada park expands northwards while, to the south, Via Nomentana traverses acres of housing as it heads out of town. On Via Nomentana, Villa Torlonia is a captivating park, and the Basilica di Sant'Agnese fuori le Mura claims Rome's oldest Christian mosaic.

Local Life

➡ **Concerts & Events** Romans are avid supporters of concerts at the Auditorium Parco della Musica (p233). Also check for events at the MAXXI and MACRO art galleries.

➡ **Parks** Tourists tend to stop at Villa Borghese, but locals often head to Villa Torlonia (p230) and Villa Ada (p229).

➡ **Hang-outs** The bars and eateries on Piazzale Ponte Milvio are a favourite of lunching locals and a young drinking crowd.

Getting There & Away

➡ **Bus** Buses 116, 52 and 53 head up to Villa Borghese from Via Vittorio Veneto near Barberini metro station. There are regular buses along Via Nomentana and Via Salaria.

➡ **Metro** To get to Villa Borghese by metro, follow the signs up from Spagna station (line A).

➡ **Tram** Tram 2 trundles up Via Flaminia from Piazzale Flaminio; tram 3 connects Piazza Thorvaldsen with San Lorenzo, San Giovanni and Testaccio.

Lonely Planet's Top Tip

Be sure to book your visit to the Museo e Galleria Borghese. It only takes a quick phone call and you won't get in without a reservation, which would be a real shame.

Many of the museums and galleries around Villa Borghese and Northern Rome have lovely cafes, ideal for a recuperative coffee or small snack.

✖ Best Places to Eat

➡ Metamorfosi (p232)
➡ Bar Pompi (p231)
➡ Molto (p232)
➡ Pasticceria Cavaletti (p232)
➡ Ensô (p231)

For reviews, see p231 ➡

🍷 Best Places to Drink

➡ Chioscetto di Ponte Milvio (p232)
➡ Brancaleone (p233)
➡ Lanificio 159 (p233)

For reviews, see p232 ➡

◉ Best Museums & Galleries

➡ Museo e Galleria Borghese (p222)
➡ Museo Nazionale Etrusco di Villa Giulia (p228)
➡ Galleria Nazionale d'Arte Moderna (p225)
➡ MAXXI (p228)
➡ MACRO (p229)

For reviews, see p222 ➡

VILLA BORGHESE & NORTHERN ROME

TOP SIGHT
MUSEO E GALLERIA BORGHESE

If you have time, or inclination, for only one art gallery in Rome, make it this one. Housing the 'queen of all private art collections', it provides the perfect introduction to Renaissance and baroque art without ever being overwhelming. To limit numbers, visitors are admitted at two-hourly intervals, so you'll need to call to prebook and then enter at an allotted entry time – but trust us, it's worth it.

The collection, which includes works by Caravaggio, Bernini, Botticelli and Raphael, was formed by Cardinal Scipione Borghese (1579–1633) after whom the museum is named.

The Villa

Known as the Casino Borghese, the villa was originally built by Cardinal Scipione to house his immense art collection. However, it owes its current neoclassical look to a comprehensive 18th-century facelift carried out by Prince Marcantonio Borghese, a direct descendant of the cardinal. But while the villa remained intact, the collection did not. Much of the antique statuary was carted off to the Louvre in the early 19th century, and other pieces were gradually sold off. In 1902 the Italian State bought the Casino, but it wasn't until 1997 that the collection was finally put on public display.

The villa is divided into two parts: the ground-floor museum, with its superb sculptures, intricate Roman floor mosaics and hypnotic trompe l'œil frescoes; and the upstairs picture gallery.

DON'T MISS

➡ *Ratto di Proserpina*

➡ *Venere Vincitrice*

➡ *Ragazzo col Canestro di Frutta*

➡ *La Deposizione di Cristo*

➡ *Amor Sacro e Amor Profano*

PRACTICALITIES

➡ Map p380

➡ 📞06 3 28 10

➡ www.galleriaborghese.it

➡ Piazzale del Museo Borghese 5

➡ adult/reduced €9/4.50, plus €2 booking fee and possible exhibition supplement

➡ 🕙9am-7pm Tue-Sun, pre-booking necessary

➡ 🚌Via Pinciana

Ground Floor

The **entrance hall** features 4th-century floor mosaics of fighting gladiators and a 2nd-century Satiro Combattente (Fighting Satyr). High on the wall is a gravity-defying bas-relief of a horse and rider falling into the void by Pietro Bernini (Gian Lorenzo's father).

Sala I is centred on Antonio Canova's daring depiction of Napoleon's sister, Paolina Bonaparte Borghese, reclining topless as *Venere Vincitrice* (Venus Victrix; 1805–08). Apparently Paolina had quite a reputation and tales abounded of her shocking behaviour. When asked how she could have posed almost naked, she's said to have replied that it wasn't cold.

But it's Gian Lorenzo Bernini's spectacular sculptures that really steal the show. Just look at Daphne's hands morphing into leaves in *Apollo e Dafne* (1622–25) in **Sala III**, or Pluto's hand pressing into Persephone's thigh in the *Ratto di Proserpina* (Rape of Proserpina; 1621–22) in **Sala IV**.

Caravaggio dominates **Sala VIII**. You'll see a dissipated *Bacchino malato* (Sick Bacchus; 1593–94), the strangely beautiful *La Madonna dei Palafrenieri* (Madonna of the Palafrenieri; 1605–06), and *San Giovanni Battista* (St John the Baptist; 1609–10), probably his last work. There's also the much-loved *Ragazzo col Canestro di Frutta* (Boy with a Basket of Fruit; 1593–95) and dramatic *Davide con la Testa di Golia* (David with the Head of Goliath; 1609–10): Goliath's head is said to be a self-portrait.

Picture Gallery

With works representing the best of the Tuscan, Venetian, Umbrian and northern European schools, the upstairs picture gallery offers a wonderful snapshot of Renaissance art.

In **Sala IX** don't miss Raphael's extraordinary *La Deposizione di Cristo* (The Deposition; 1507), and his charming *Dama con Liocorno* (Lady with a Unicorn; 1506). Also see the superb *Adorazione del Bambino* (Adoration of the Christ Child; 1499) by Fra Bartolomeo and Perugino's *Madonna col Bambino* (Madonna and Child; early 16th century).

Next door, Correggio's *Danäe* (1530–31) shares wall space with a willowy Venus, as portrayed by Cranach in his *Venere e Amore che Reca Il Favo do Miele* (Venus and Cupid with Honeycomb; 1531).

Moving on, **Sala XIV** boasts two self-portraits by Bernini, and **Sala XVIII** contains two significant works by Rubens: *Compianto su Cristo morto* (The Deposition; 1603) and *Susanna e I Vecchioni* (Susanna and the Elders; 1605–07).

To finish off, Titian's early masterpiece, *Amor Sacro e Amor Profano* (Sacred and Profane Love; 1514), is the star turn of **Sala XX** and one of the collection's most prized works.

CARDINAL SCIPIONE BORGHESE

Cardinal Scipione Caffarelli Borghese (1576–1633) was one of the most influential figures in Rome's baroque art world. Blessed with wealth, power and position – he was made a cardinal at age 26 by his uncle Pope Paul V – he sponsored the greatest artists of the day, including contemporaries Caravaggio, Bernini, Domenichino, Guido Reni and Pieter Paul Rubens. Yet while he promoted the artists he didn't always see eye to eye with them and he was quite prepared to play dirty to get his hands on their works: he had the fashionable painter Cavaliere d'Arpino flung into jail in order to confiscate his canvases and had Domenichino arrested to force him to surrender *La Caccia di Diana* (The Hunt of Diana).

For a coffee or bite to eat, exit the museum and head to the Cinecaffè (p231), near Villa Borghese's southern entrance.

VILLA BORGHESE & NORTHERN ROME MUSEO E GALLERIA BORGHESE

GALLERIA BORGHESE

Services and Amenities Level (Basement)

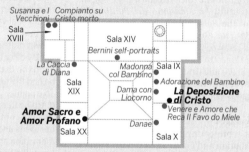

First Floor

Ground Floor

⊙ SIGHTS

This large and attractive area boasts several fascinating sights, including one of the city's best art galleries, a cutting-edge cultural centre and a couple of contemporary museums. In the midst of everything, Villa Borghese park provides a welcome escape from the bustle of the city centre.

⊙ Villa Borghese & Around

| MUSEO E GALLERIA BORGHESE | MUSEUM |

See p222.

| VILLA BORGHESE | PARK |

(Map p380; entrances at Piazzale San Paolo del Brasile, Piazzale Flaminio, Via Pinciana, Largo Pablo Picasso; ⊙dawn-dusk; 🚇Porta Pinciana) Locals, lovers, tourists, joggers – no one can resist the lure of Rome's most celebrated park. Originally the estate of Cardinal Scipione Borghese's 17th-century residence, it covers about 80 hectares and boasts various museums and galleries, as well as the 18th-century **Giardino del Lago** (Map p380) and **Piazza di Siena** (Map p380), an amphitheatre used for Rome's top equestrian event in May.

Film buffs should head to the area around the Piazzale San Paolo del Brasile entrance, where the **Casa del Cinema** (p233) hosts regular film events, and the **Cinema dei Piccoli** (Map p380; ☑06 855 34 85; www.cinemadeipiccoli.it; Viale delle Pineta 15; tickets €5 weekdays, €5.50-6 weekends; 🚇Porta Pinciana) is the world's smallest cinema.

Bike hire is available at various points in the park, including Largo Pablo Picasso, for about €5/15 per hour/day.

| BIOPARCO | ZOO |

(Map p380; ☑06 360 82 11; www.bioparco.it; Viale del Giardino Zoologico 1; adult/child over 1m & under 12yr/child under 1m €14/12/free; ⊙9.30am-6pm Apr-Oct, to 5pm Nov-Mar; 🚇Bioparco) A

ℹ AVOID MONDAYS

Monday is not a good day to explore Villa Borghese. Sure, you can walk the park, but all of the museums and galleries are shut – they open Tuesday through to Sunday.

tried and tested kid-pleaser, Rome's zoo hosts a predictable collection of animals on a far-from-inspiring 18-hectare site. Quite frankly there are better ways to pass your time, but if your kids are driving you bonkers, it's a thought.

| MUSEO CARLO BILOTTI | ART GALLERY |

(Map p380; ☑06 06 08; www.museocarlobilotti.it; Viale Fiorello La Guardia; adult/reduced €8/7; ⊙10am-4pm Tue-Fri Oct-May, 1-7pm Tue-Fri Jun-Sep, 10am-7pm Sat & Sun year-round; 🚇Porta Pinciana) The art collection of billionaire cosmetics magnate Carlo Bilotti is stylishly housed in the Orangery of Villa Borghese. It's a small collection, but it's interesting and well presented with explanatory panels in English and Italian. Paintings range from a Warhol portrait of Bilotti's wife and daughter to 18 works by Giorgio de Chirico (1888–1978), one of Italy's most important 20th-century artists.

| GALLERIA NAZIONALE
D'ARTE MODERNA | ART GALLERY |

(Map p380; ☑06 3229 8221; www.gnam.beniculturali.it; Viale delle Belle Arti 131, disabled entrance Via Gramsci 71; adult/reduced €8/4, plus possible exhibition supplement; ⊙8.30am-7.30pm Tue-Sun; 🚇Piazza Thorvaldsen) Housed in a vast belle époque palace, this oft-overlooked gallery of modern and contemporary art is definitely worth a visit. Its collection runs the gamut from neoclassical romantic sculpture to abstract expressionism with works by many of the most important exponents of 19th- and 20th-century art.

There are canvases by the *macchiaioli* (the Italian Impressionists) and futurists Boccioni and Balla, as well as several impressive sculptures by Canova and major works by Modigliani and De Chirico. International artists are also represented, with works by Degas, Cézanne, Kandinsky, Klimt, Mondrian, Pollock and Henry Moore.

⊙ Flaminio

| AUDITORIUM PARCO
DELLA MUSICA | CULTURAL CENTRE |

(Map p380; ☑06 8024 1281; www.auditorium.com; Viale Pietro de Coubertin 10; guided tours adult/reduced €9/7; ⊙11am-8pm Mon-Sat, 10am-6pm Sat & Sun; 🚇shuttle bus M from Stazione Termini after 5pm, 🚇Viale Tiziano) The hub of Rome's thriving cultural scene, the Auditorium is the capital's premier concert

THE ART ARCHIVE / ALAMY ©

1. *Boy with a Basket of Fruit* by Caravaggio **2.** *Sacred and Profane Love* by Titian **3.** Paolina Bonaparte as *Venere Vincitrice* (Venus Victrix) by Canova **4.** Bernini's *Ratto di Proserpina* (Rape of Proserpina)

ALINARI VIA GETTY IMAGES ©

Treasures of the Museo e Galleria Borghese

Housed in a lavishly decorated 17th-century palace, the Museo e Galleria Borghese (p222) boasts some of the city's finest art treasures. Chief among them are sensational sculptures by Gian Lorenzo Bernini but there are also important works by major Renaissance and baroque artists.

Ratto di Proserpina

One of Bernini's greatest sculptures, *The Rape of Prosperina* portrays Pluto, god of the underworld, abducting Proserpina (Persephone). A work of supreme virtuosity, it shows the artist's ability to craft emotion out of cold, hard marble.

Apollo e Dafne

Bernini was only 24 when he started work on this life-size representation of the nymph Daphne turning into a laurel tree to escape the clutches of Apollo.

Venere Vincitrice

Antonio Canova's depiction of a curvaceous Paolina Bonaparte as the goddess Venus Victrix (Venus Victorious) is typical of his elegant, mildly erotic neoclassical style.

Ragazzo col Canestro di Frutta

One of Caravaggio's early works, *Boy with a Basket of Fruit* reveals stylistic techniques that became his trademarks: realism and the use of chiaroscuro to focus attention on the central figures.

Amor Sacro e Amor Profano

Titian's *Sacred and Profane Love* is a celebration of heavenly love (the nude) and earthly love (the clothed figure).

La Deposizione di Cristo

Raphael's Renaissance masterpiece, *The Deposition* was originally an altarpiece. Its composition, inspired by ancient Roman tomb reliefs, shows the artist's unsurpassed ability to paint large groups of people.

complex and one of Europe's most popular arts centres, hosting a year-round calendar of events. Designed by superstar architect Renzo Piano and inaugurated in 2002, it's a truly audacious work of architecture consisting of three grey pod-like concert halls set round a 3000-seat amphitheatre.

Guided tours (minimum of 10 people) cover the concert halls, amphitheatre (known as the *cavea*) and enormous foyer area, which is itself home to a small archaeology museum and stages temporary exhibitions. Tours depart hourly between 11.30am and 4.30pm Saturday and Sunday, and by arrangement from Monday to Friday.

MUSEO NAZIONALE DELLE
ARTI DEL XXI SECOLO (MAXXI) ART GALLERY

(Map p380; ☏06 3996 7350; www.fondazione-maxxi.it; Via Guido Reni 4A; adult/reduced €11/8; ⊗11am-7pm Tue-Fri & Sun, to 10pm Sat; ☐Viale Tiziano) More than the exhibitions, the real highlight of Rome's flagship contemporary art gallery is Zaha Hadid's stunning building, universally hailed as a triumph of modern architecture. Housed in a former barracks, it's impressive inside and out. The multilayered geometric facade faces onto a landscaped courtyard and gives on to a cavernous light-filled interior full of snaking walkways, suspended staircases, glass, cement and steel.

There's no set route between the exhibition spaces but it's fascinating to follow the sweeping ramps as they curve around the walls. The gallery has a small permanent collection but more interesting are the temporary exhibitions and installations – check the website for details.

PONTE MILVIO BRIDGE

(Map p380; ☐Ponte Milvio) A pretty pedestrian footbridge, Ponte Milvio is best known as the site of the ancient Battle of the Milvian Bridge. It was first built in 109 BC to carry Via Flaminia over the Tiber and survived intact until 1849, when Garibaldi's troops blew it up to stop advancing French soldiers. Pope Pius IX had it rebuilt a year later.

On the northern end of the bridge, the tower **Torretta Valadier** is sometimes used to stage art exhibitions.

FORO ITALICO SPORTS CENTRE

(Map p380; Viale del Foro Italico; ☐Piazzale della Farnesina) At the foot of **Monte Mario**,

---

TOP SIGHT **MUSEO NAZIONALE ETRUSCO DI VILLA GIULIA**

Italy's finest collection of Etruscan treasures is considerately presented in Villa Giulia, Pope Julius III's elegant Renaissance palace, and the nearby **Villa Poniatowski** (Map p380).

There are thousands of exhibits, many of which came from burial tombs in the surrounding Lazio region, ranging from domestic utensils and terracotta vases to extraordinary bronze figurines, black *bucchero* tableware and dazzling jewellery.

Must-sees include a polychrome terracotta statue of an armless Apollo, from the Etruscan town of Veio, just north of Rome, and the Euphronios Krater, a celebrated Greek vase that was returned to Italy in 2008 after a 30-year tug of war between the Italian government and New York's Metropolitan Museum of Art. But perhaps the museum's most famous piece is the 6th-century-BC Sarcofago degli Sposi (Sarcophagus of the Betrothed). This astonishing work, originally unearthed in 400 broken pieces in a tomb in Cerveteri, depicts a husband and wife reclining on a stone banqueting couch. And although called a sarcophagus, it was actually designed as an elaborate urn to hold the couple's ashes.

DON'T MISS

➡ Sarcofago degli Sposi

➡ Apollo di Veio

➡ Euphronios Krater

PRACTICALITIES

➡ Map p380

➡ ☏06 322 65 71

➡ www.villagiulia.beniculturali.it

➡ Piazzale di Villa Giulia

➡ adult/reduced €8/4

➡ ⊗Villa Giulia 8.30am-7.30pm Tue-Sun, Villa Poniatowski 9am-1.45pm Tue-Sat

➡ ☐Via delle Belle Arti

THE BATTLE OF THE MILVIAN BRIDGE

Constantine's defeat of Maxentius at the Battle of the Milvian Bridge on 28 October 312 is one of the most celebrated victories in Roman history.

The battle came as the culmination of a complex seven-year power struggle for control of the Western Roman Empire. Constantine and his vastly outnumbered army approached Rome from the north along Via Flaminia, meeting Maxentius' forces on the northern bank of the Tiber. Fighting was short and bloody, leaving Maxentius dead, his army in tatters and the path to Rome and empire unopposed.

But while this is historically significant, the real reason for the battle's mythical status is the Christian legend that surrounds it. According to the Roman historian Lactantius, Constantine dreamt a message telling him to paint a Christian symbol on his troops' shields. A second historian, Eusebius, provides a more dramatic account, recounting how on the eve of the battle Constantine saw a cross in the sky, accompanied by the words, 'In this sign, conquer.' Whatever the case, the reality is that Constantine won a resounding victory and in so doing set the seeds for the spread of Christianity in the Roman world.

the Foro Italico is a grandiose Fascist-era sports complex, centred on the **Stadio Olimpico** (p234), Rome's 70,000-seat football stadium. Most people pass through en route to the football, but if you're interested in Fascist architecture, it's worth a look.

Designed by the architect Enrico Del Debbio, it remains much as it was originally conceived. A 17m-high marble **obelisk**, inscribed with the words 'Mussolini Dux', stands at the beginning of a broad avenue leading down to the **Stadio dei Marmi** (Map p380), a running track surrounded by 60 marble nudes and the Stadio Olimpico.

EXPLORA – MUSEO DEI
BAMBINI DI ROMA   MUSEUM
(Map p380; ☏06 361 37 76; www.mdbr.it; Via Flaminia 82; adult/child 1-3yr €7/3; ⊗entrance 10am, noon, 3pm, 5pm Tue-Sun; MFlaminio) Rome's only dedicated kids' museum, Explora is aimed at the under-12s. It's set up as a miniature town where children can play at being grown-ups and with everything from a supermarket to a fire engine, it's a hands-on, feet-on, full-on experience that your nippers will love. Outside there's also a free play park open to all.

Booking is advisable on weekdays and essential at weekends.

⊙ Salario

MUSEO D'ARTE CONTEMPORANEA
DI ROMA (MACRO)   ART GALLERY
(Map p380; ☏06 06 08; www.macro.roma.museum; Via Nizza 138, cnr Via Cagliari; adult/reduced €11.50/9.50; ⊗11am-7pm Tue-Fri & Sun, to 10pm Sat; ⊠Via Nizza) Along with MAXXI, this is Rome's most important contemporary art gallery. Exhibits, which include works by all of Italy's important post-WWII artists, are displayed in what was once a brewery. The sexy black-and-red interior retains much of the building's original structure but sports a sophisticated steel-and-glass finish thanks to a revamp by French architect Odile Decq.

CATACOMBE DI PRISCILLA   CATACOMBS
(Map p380; ☏06 8620 6272; www.catacombe-priscilla.com; Via Salaria 430; guided visit adult/reduced €8/5; ⊗8.30am-noon & 2.30-5pm Tue-Sun; ⊠Via Salaria) In the early Christian period, these creepy catacombs were something of a high-society burial ground, known as the Queen of Catacombs. Seven popes and various martyrs were buried in the 13km of tunnels between 309 and 555. They retain a lot of their original decoration, including the oldest-ever image of the Madonna, a scratchy fresco dating to the early 3rd century.

VILLA ADA   PARK
(Map p380; entrances at Via Salaria & Via Ponte Salario; ⊠Via Salaria) Once the private property of King Vittorio Emanuele III, Villa Ada is a big rambling park with shady paths, lakes, lawns and woods. It's popular with locals and explodes to life in summer when outdoor concerts are staged during the Roma Incontro il Mondo festival.

VILLA BORGHESE & NORTHERN ROME SIGHTS

QUARTIERE COPPEDÈ

Hidden among the elegant *palazzi* (mansions) that flank Viale Regina Margherita is the **Quartiere Coppedè** (Map p380; 🚇Viale Regina Margherita), a tiny pocket of fairy-tale buildings and monuments. Tuscan turrets, Liberty sculptures, Moorish arches, Gothic gargoyles, frescoed facades and palm-fringed gardens are all squeezed in to create a truly mesmerising pastiche of architectural styles and influences. The mind behind the madness belonged to a little-known Florentine architect, Gino Coppedè, who designed and built the quarter between 1913 and 1926.

Highlights include the **Fontana delle Rane** (Map p380; Fountain of the Frogs) in Piazza Mincio, a modern take on the better known Fontana delle Tartarughe in the Jewish Ghetto.

The neighbourhood is best entered from the corner of Via Tagliamento and Via Dora.

◉ Nomentana

PORTA PIA   LANDMARK

(Map p380; Piazzale Porta Pia; 🚇Via XX Settembre) Michelangelo's last architectural work, this imposing crenellated structure stands near the ruins of the Porta Nomentana, one of the original gates of the ancient Aurelian walls. Bitter street fighting took place here in 1870 as Italian troops breached the adjacent walls to wrest the city from the pope and claim it for the nascent kingdom of Italy.

VILLA TORLONIA   PARK

(Map p380; Via Nomentana 70; ⊙7am-7.30pm Oct-Mar, to 8.30pm Apr-Sep; 🚇Via Nomentana) Full of towering pine trees, atmospheric palms and scattered villas, this splendid 19th-century park once belonged to Prince Giovanni Torlonia (1756–1829), a powerful banker and landowner. His large neoclassical villa, the **Casino dei Principi**, later became the Mussolini family home (1925–43) and, towards the end of WWII, Allied headquarters (1944–47). These days it's used to stage temporary exhibitions.

MUSEI DI VILLA TORLONIA   MUSEUM

(Map p380; ☑06 06 08; www.museivillatorlonia. it; Via Nomentana 70; Casino Nobile, Casina delle Civitte & exhibition adult/reduced €10/8, Casino Nobile & exhibition adult/reduced €8/7, Casina delle Civitte adult/reduced €5/4; ⊙9am-7pm Tue-Sun; 🚇Via Nomentana) Housed in three villas – Casino Nobile, Casina delle Civitte and Casino dei Principi – this museum boasts an eclectic collection of art, sculpture, furniture and stained glass.

The main ticket office is just inside the Via Nomentana entrance to the park.

With its oversized neoclassical facade – designed by Giuseppe Valadier – **Casino Nobile** (Map p380) makes quite an impression. In the luxuriously decorated interior you can admire the Torlonia family's fine collection of sculpture, period furniture and paintings.

To the northeast, the much smaller **Casina delle Civitte** (Map p380) is a bizarre mix of Swiss cottage, Gothic castle and twee farmhouse decorated in art nouveau style. Built between 1840 and 1930, it is now a museum dedicated to stained glass with designs and sketches, decorative tiles, parquet floors and woodwork.

Casino dei Principi (Map p380), which houses the archive of the Scuola Romana school of art, is used to stage temporary exhibitions.

BASILICA DI SANT'AGNESE FUORI LE MURA & MAUSOLEO DI SANTA COSTANZA   CHURCH, CATACOMBS

(www.santagnese.org; Via Nomentana 349; basilica & mausoleum free, catacombs guided visit adult/reduced €8/5; ⊙basilica 7.30am-noon & 4-7.30pm, mausoleum & catacombs 9am-noon Mon-Sat & 4-6pm daily, catacombs closed Nov; 🚇Via Nomentana) Although a bit of a hike, it's well worth searching out this intriguing medieval religious complex, comprising the **Basilica di Sant'Agnese Fuori le Mura** and the 4th-century **Mausoleo di Santa Costanza**, home to some of the oldest mosaics in Christendom.

In the 7th-century basilica look out for the golden apse mosaic depicting St Agnes with the signs of her martyrhood – a flame and sword, standing on the flames that failed to kill her. According to tradition, the 13-year-old Agnes was sentenced to be burnt at the stake, but when the flames failed to kill her she was beheaded on Piazza Navona and buried in the **catacombs** beneath this church.

Across the convent courtyard is the Mausoleo di Santa Costanza. This squat circular building has a dome supported by 12 pairs of granite columns and a vaulted ambulatory decorated with beautiful 4th-century mosaics.

EATING

Rome's wealthy northern suburbs are speckled with fine restaurants, and there's a cluster around the happening district of Ponte Milvio.

✕ Villa Borghese & Around

SERENELLA   PIZZERIA €

(Map p380; Via Salaria 70; pizza slices from €1.50; ⊗9am-7pm; ⬜Via Salaria) It's a bit out of the way, unless you're walking from Villa Borghese to MACRO, but this innocuous-looking pizza takeaway is a top pit stop. It claims to use natural yeast in its pizza bases, which might or might not explain why the pizza *bianca* is so good – light, crispy and delicately salted.

CAFFÈ DELLE ARTI   CAFE, RISTORANTE €€

(Map p380; ☑06 3265 1236; www.caffedellearti-roma.it; Via Gramsci 73; meal €45; ⊗closed Sun dinner & Mon; ⬜Piazza Thorvaldsen) The cafe-cum-restaurant of the Galleria Nazionale d'Arte Moderna (p225) sits in neoclassical splendour in a leafy corner of Villa Borghese. An elegant venue, it's at its best on sultry summer evenings when you sit on the terrace and revel in the refined romantic atmosphere over coffee, cocktails or a full à la carte dinner.

CINECAFFÈ   CAFE €€

(Map p380; www.cinecaffe.it; Casina delle Rose, Largo Marcello Mastroianni 1; aperitif €6, snacks from €2.50, salads €9; ⊗9am-7pm; ⬜Porta Pinciana) Part of the Casa del Cinema (p233) complex, this slick modern cafe is one of the few places to get a decent bite in Villa Borghese. Stop by for a morning coffee or claim a table on the sunny terrace for an alfresco salad or choice pasta dish. Snacks and *panini* are also available and brunch is served at weekends.

✕ Flaminio

★BAR POMPI   PASTRIES & CAKES €

(Map p380; Via Cassia 8; tiramisu €3.50; ⊗7am-midnight Mon, Wed-Thu & Sun, 7.30am-1am Fri & Sat, 4pm-midnight Tue; ⬜Ponte Milvio) Just behind happening Piazzale Ponte Milvio on the northern side of the Tiber, this small bar is worth searching out for its sensational tiramisu. Alongside the classic coffee, liqueur and cocoa flavour, it comes in three other forms – strawberry, pistachio, and banana and nutella – all of which merit your full attention.

IL GIANFORNAIO   BAKERY €

(Map p380; Largo Maresciallo Diaz 16; pizza slice €3.50; ⊗7.30am-9pm Mon-Sat; ⬜Ponte Milvio) A popular local bakery that does a fantastic range of sweet and savoury snacks – think strudels, *cornettos* (Italian croissants) and excellent crispy pizza slices – as well as pasta and meat dishes.

PALLOTTA   PIZZERIA €

(Map p380; ☑06 333 42 45; Piazzale Ponte Milvio 23; meals €15-20, pizzas €6; ⊗Thu-Tue; ⬜Ponte Milvio) Run by the Pallotta family for generations, this is an archetypal old-school pizzeria. It serves great pizzas, plus the usual fried starters and barbecued meats in an atmospheric leafy garden. A bastion of unpretentious quality, it gets very busy, so it's always best to book.

ENSÔ   JAPANESE €€

(Map p380; ☑06 3322 1175; Piazzale Ponte Milvio 33; lunch menus €8-15, sushi/sashimi from €5/8; ⊗Tues-Sun; ⬜Ponte Milvio) If the daily diet of pasta and pizza is beginning to wear thin, this relaxed Japanese restaurant is a welcome change. There's sushi and sashimi, as well as a selection of curries, all served promptly and with a smile. The lunchtime menus are particularly good value.

RED   MODERN ITALIAN €€€

(Map p380; ☑06 8069 1630; www.redrestaurant.roma.it; Viale Pietro de Coubertin 30; lunch menu €18 Mon-Sat, €20 Sun, dinner €45-50; ⊗9am-2am daily; ⬜Viale Tiziano, shuttle bus M from Stazione Termini after 5pm) The fashionable restaurant-bar of the Auditorium Parco della Musica is a glamorous, loungey place. Open from breakfast to late, it dishes up an abundant lunch spread as well as a popular *aperitivo* and a formal evening menu of creative Italian fare.

PASTICCERIA CAVALETTI

There are no shortage of *pasticcerie* (pastry shops) in Rome, but few can compare to the **Pasticceria Cavaletti** (Via Nemorense 179; ⊙9am-7.30pm Wed-Mon; ⊟Via Nemorense). Locals claim it makes the best *millefoglie* in town and restaurants come here to stock up on their *dolci*. And while it's a bit of a hike to get to, you won't regret the effort as you reward yourself with one of its magnificent creamy concoctions.

✗ Parioli

LA SCALA AI PARIOLI　　TRADITIONAL ITALIAN €€

(Map p380; ☑06 808 44 63; Viale dei Parioli 79d; meals €40; ⊙Thu-Tue; ⊟Viale Parioli) This landmark restaurant on Parioli's main strip is defiantly old-school. The warm, woody dining hall and traditional menu provide sanctuary for its many regulars who stop by for filling meals of classic Roman pastas, fresh fish and grilled meat. Particularly appetising is the tempting antipasto buffet.

METAMORFOSI　　　GASTRONOMIC €€€

(Map p380; ☑06 807 68 39; www.metamorfosiroma.it; Via Giovanni Antonelli 30-32; tasting menus €70/80/100, lunch menus €35/45; ⊙lunch Mon-Fri, dinner Mon-Sat; ⊟Via Giovanni Antonelli) The restaurant of Colombian chef Roy Caceres is one of the hottest dining tickets in town, offering sophisticated contemporary cuisine and a chic but informal setting. The decor is clinical minimalism and the food innovative without ever being overly pretentious. Various tasting menus are available, including two cheaper lunch options, costing €35 for two 'creations' and €45 for three. Reservations required.

MOLTO　　　　RISTORANTE €€€

(Map p380; ☑06 808 29 00; www.moltoitaliano.it; Viale dei Parioli 122; meals €50; ⊙daily; ⊟Viale Parioli) Fashionable and quietly glamorous, Molto is a Parioli favourite. The discreet entrance gives onto an elegant, modern interior and open-air terrace, while the menu ranges from fail-safe pastas to more decadent truffle-flavoured dishes and succulent roast meats. Service is professional and there's a thoughtful wine list of Italian labels.

✗ Over the River

AL SETTIMO GELO　　　　GELATO €

(Map p380; www.alsettimogelo.it; Via Vodice 21a; ⊙10-8pm Mon-Sat winter, to 11pm summer, 11.30am-2pm & 3.30-8pm Sun; ⊟Piazza Giuseppe Mazzini) The name's a play on 'seventh heaven' and it's not a far-fetched title for this excellent gelateria whose devotion to creativity and natural ingredients is all too evident. Taste for yourself and order an *Iranian*, a house speciality made with rosewater, pistachio and saffron.

DRINKING & NIGHTLIFE

Many of the galleries and museums in this area have excellent on-site cafes. Otherwise, the drinking scene is centred on Piazzale Ponte Milvio, a popular hangout for north Rome's young well-to-do crowd.

⛾ Flaminio

CHIOSCHETTO DI PONTE MILVIO　　BAR

(Map p380; Ponte Milvio 44; ⊙6pm-2am Apr-Oct; ⊟Ponte Milvio) A local landmark, this tiny green kiosk next to the Ponte Milvio bridge has been open since the 1920s and is perennially popular, with lots of pavement tables. It might look like a shack – in fact, it is a shack – but the mojitos are the business and they do an excellent thirst-quenching *grattachecca* (a chipped ice drink flavoured with fruit syrup).

⛾ Salario

PIPER CLUB　　　　NIGHTCLUB

(Map p380; www.piperclub.it; Via Tagliamento 9; ⊙11pm-4am; ⊟Viale Regina Margherita) Keeping Rome in the groove since 1965, Piper just keeps on going. Very popular with young partygoers from the wealthy Parioli district – particularly on Friday nights – it's primarily a disco but it also hosts funky theme nights and stages some great gigs. Previous performers have included White Lies, Nitin Sawney, Babyshambles and Pete Yorn.

VILLA BORGHESE & NORTHERN ROME DRINKING & NIGHTLIFE

Nomentana

BRANCALEONE NIGHTCLUB
(www.brancaleone.eu; Via Levanna 11; ⊘Oct-Jun; 🚋Via Nomentana) In the outlying Montesacro district, this former *centro sociale* is one of Rome's top clubs, attracting blockbuster DJs and a young alternative crowd. Everything from house and hip-hop to drum n bass, reggae and electronica is on the menu, and there's a regular calendar of events and one-off evenings. Check the website for details.

LANIFICIO 159 NIGHTCLUB
(www.lanificio159.com; Via Pietralata 159a; ⊘varies; 🚋Via Val Brembana) Occupying an ex-wool factory overlooking a nature reserve in Rome's northeastern suburbs, this cool underground venue hosts live gigs and hot clubbing action, led by Rome's top crews including L-Ektrica and Female Cut. More reserved events are also staged, such as Sunday markets, exhibitions and aperitifs. Bank on at least €7 for entry to club nights.

 ENTERTAINMENT

**AUDITORIUM PARCO
DELLA MUSICA** CONCERT VENUE
(Map p380; ☑06 8024 1281; www.auditorium. com; Viale Pietro de Coubertin 30; 🚋shuttle bus M from Stazione Termini, 🚋Viale Tiziano) Rome's main concert venue, this state-of-the-art modernist complex combines architectural innovation with perfect acoustics. Designed by Renzo Piano, its three concert halls and 3000-seat open-air arena host everything from classical music concerts to tango exhibitions, book readings and film screenings.

The auditorium is also home to Rome's top orchestra, the world-class **Orchestra dell' Accademia Nazionale di Santa Cecilia** (www.santacecilia.it).

To get to the auditorium, take tram 2 from Piazzale Flaminio or bus M from Stazione Termini, which departs every 15 minutes between 5pm and the end of the last performance.

TEATRO OLIMPICO THEATRE
(Map p380; ☑06 326 59 91; www.teatroolimpico. it; Piazza Gentile da Fabriano 17; 🚋Piazza Mancini, 🚋Piazza Mancini) The Teatro Olimpico

is home to the **Accademia Filarmonica Roman** (Map p380; www.filarmonicaromana. org), one of Rome's major classical music organisations whose past members have included Rossini, Donizetti and Verdi. The theatre offers a varied programme that concentrates on classical and chamber music, but also features opera, ballet and contemporary multimedia events.

CASA DEL CINEMA CINEMA
(Map p380; ☑06 06 08; www.casadelcinema.it; Largo Marcello Mastroianni 1; 🚋Porta Pinciana) In Villa Borghese, the Casa del Cinema comprises two exhibition spaces, three projection halls, an outdoor theatre and a popular cafe. It screens everything from documentaries to shorts, indie flicks and arthouse classics (sometimes in their original language), and hosts a regular programme of film-related events and book presentations.

SILVANO TOTI GLOBE THEATRE THEATRE
(Map p380; ☑06 06 08; www.globetheatreroma. com; Largo Aqua Felix, Villa Borghese; 🚋Piazzale Brasile) Like London's Globe Theatre with better weather, this open-air Elizabethan theatre in the middle of Villa Borghese serves up Shakespeare (mostly in Italian but with the occasional performance in English) from June to September. Tickets start at €10 for a place in the stalls, rising to €23.

🛍 **SHOPPING**

LIBRERIA L'ARGONAUTA BOOKS
(Map p380; www.librerialargonauta.com; Via Reggio Emilia 89; ⊘10am-8pm Tue-Sat, 4-8pm Mon winter, 10am-8pm Mon-Fri summer; 🚋Via Nizza) Off the main tourist trail, this travel bookshop is a lovely place to browse. The serene atmosphere and shelves of travel literature, guides, maps and photo tomes can easily spark daydreams of far-off places. Staff are friendly and happy to let you drift around the world in peace.

BULZONI WINE
(Map p380; www.enotecabulzoni.it; Viale Parioli 36; ⊘8.30am-2pm, 4.30-8.30pm; 🚋Viale Parioli) The knowledgeable folk at this historic wine shop have been supplying the local burghers with wine and bubbly since 1929. Alongside wine, liqueur and champagne,

FOOTBALL IN ROME

Watching a game of football (or rugby) at Rome's **Stadio Olimpico** (Map p380; ☑06 3685 7520; Viale dei Gladiatori 2, Foro Italico) is an unforgettable experience, although you'll have to keep your wits about you as crowd trouble is not unheard of.

Throughout the season (September to May), there's a game most Sundays involving one of the city's two teams: **A.S. Roma**, known as the *giallorossi* (yellow and reds; www. asroma.it), or **Lazio**, the *biancazzuri* (white and blues; www.sslazio.it). Ticket prices start at €16 and can be bought at Lottomatica (lottery centres), the stadium, ticket agencies, www.listicket.it or one of the many Roma or Lazio stores around the city.

there's also a carefully curated selection of organic olive oils and gastro nibbles. You can even get *panini* made up.

FRANCESCA VILLA
JEWELLERY

(Map p380; ☑06 9357 2898; www.francescavilla. it; Via Mercalli 13; ☺by appointment; ☐Via Giovanni Antonelli) For a very special gift, consider a one-off creation by jewellery designer Francesca Villa. Her speciality is a 'Diary of a Journey', a personalised piece crafted to incorporate an object or keepsake that you've picked up on your travels.

MAXXI
BOOKS

(Map p380; www.fondazionemaxxi.it; Via Guido Reni 2f; ☺11am-7pm Tue-Fri & Sun, to 10pm Sat; ☐Viale Tiziano) The bookshop of the MAXXI art museum is in a cool white space over the courtyard from the main gallery. Its collection is small but specialised with an excellent selection of books on modern art, architecture and design. You can also pick up exhibition catalogues.

NOTEBOOK
BOOKS, MUSIC

(Map p380; www.notebookauditorium.it; Viale Pietro de Coubertin 30; ☺10am-8pm, closed Aug; ☐Viale Tiziano, ☐Viale Tiziano) Part of the Auditorium Parco della Musica complex, this attractive modern shop offers a sizeable collection of art, film, music, design and travel books (mostly in Italian), as well as CDs, DVDs and Auditorium merchandise. Not surprisingly, it's particularly good for classical music.

BAGHEERA
SHOES, ACCESSORIES

(Map p380; www.bagheeraboutique.com; ☺9.30am-1pm Tue-Sat & 3.30-7.30pm Mon-Sat; ☐Piazza Euclide) This modish boutique on Piazza Euclide has long been a local go-to for fashionable footwear. The selection is small but up-to-the-minute with ladies shoes, bags and accessories by big-name international designers.

ANTICAGLIE A PONTE MILVIO
MARKET

(Map p380; Piazzale Ponte Milvio; ☺9am-8pm 1st & 2nd Sun of month, closed Aug; ☐Ponte Milvio) The 2nd-century-BC Ponte Milvio is the scene of a great monthly antique market along the riverbank. On the first and second Sunday of every month up to 200 stalls spring up laden with antiques, objets d'art, vintage clothes, period furniture and all manner of collectable clobber.

ANTIQUARIATO IN PIAZZA VERDI
MARKET

(Map p380; Piazza Verdi; ☺9am-sunset 4th Sun of month; ☐Via Paisiello) Stalls piled high with antiques and arty bric-a-brac take over the imposing Piazza Verdi for this popular flea market.

GOODY MUSIC
MUSIC

(Map p380; Via Cesare Beccaria 2; ☺10am-2pm & 3.30-8pm Mon-Sat; Ⓜ Flaminio) This is where DJs go to stock up on tunes, with a trainspotting collection of hip-hop, nu-jazz, deep and funky house, hardstyle and rare grooves, on vinyl and CD. Staff are knowledgeable, and you can also buy equipment and T-shirts.

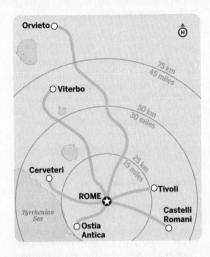

Day Trips from Rome

Ostia Antica p236
Wander through complete streets, gape at Roman toilets and see an original Roman menu at the ancient port of Ostia Antica, whose preservation in places matches that of Pompeii.

Tivoli p237
This hilltop town is home to two Unesco World Heritage sites: Villa Adriana, the mammoth country estate of the emperor Hadrian, and 16th-century Villa d'Este, with its fantastical gardens featuring musical fountains.

Castelli Romani p239
Studding the hills to the south of Rome are 13 hilltop towns that have long been a green escape for Romans.

Cerveteri & Tarquinia p244
The exquisite tombs and fantastic museums of these once important Etruscan centres provide a window into a mysterious ancient world.

Viterbo p245
A medieval gem, graceful Viterbo evokes its 13th-century golden age, and is also famous for its health-imbuing hot springs.

Orvieto p249
This gorgeous hilltop Umbrian town is an easy and rewarding day trip.

Ostia Antica

Explore

Half a day or more would be ideal to explore the impressive remains of Ostia Antica. This ancient Roman city was a busy working port until 42 AD, and the ruins are substantial and well preserved. The main thoroughfare, the **Decumanus Maximus**, runs over 1km from the city's entrance (the Porta Romana) to the Porta Marina, which originally led to the sea, and it's still the main drag. The site gets busy at weekends, but is usually empty during the week.

The Best...
➡ **Sight** Thermopolium
➡ **Place to Eat** Ristorante Cipriani

Top Tip

Bring a picnic or time your visit so that you can eat at one of the restaurants in the town, as the canteen-style cafe on site can get busy.

Getting There & Away
➡ **Car** Take Via del Mare, parallel to Via Ostiense, and follow the signs for the *scavi* (ruins).

➡ **Train** From Rome, take metro line B to Piramide, then the Ostia Lido train (half-hourly) from Stazione Porta San Paolo, getting off at Ostia Antica. The trip is covered by the standard BIT tickets.

Need to Know
➡ **Location** 25km southwest of Rome

◉ SIGHTS

Founded in the 4th century BC, Ostia (named for the mouth or *ostium* of the Tiber) became a great port and later a strategic centre for defence and trade, with a population of around 50,000, of whom 17,000 were slaves, mostly from Turkey, Egypt and the middle East. In the 5th century AD barbarian invasions and the outbreak of malaria led to its abandonment followed by its slow burial – up to the 2nd-

floor level – in river silt, hence its survival. Pope Gregory IV re-established the town in the 9th century.

RUINS RUIN

(✆06 5635 2830; www.ostiaantica.info; Viale dei Romagnoli 717; adult/reduced €6.5/3.75; ☺8.30am-7.15pm Tue-Sun summer, to 6pm Mar, to 5pm Nov-Feb, last admission 1hr before closing) Ostia was a busy working port until it began to decline in the 3rd century AD, and the town was made up of restaurants, laundries, shops, houses and public meeting places.

On both sides of the main thoroughfare, **Decumanus Maximus**, are networks of narrow streets lined by buildings.

At one stage, Ostia had 20 baths complexes, including the **Terme di Foro** – these were equipped with a roomful of stone toilets (the *forica*) that remain largely intact. Pivot-holes show that the entrances had revolving doors and there are 20 marble seats that remain intact. Water flowed along channels in front of the seats, into which the user would dip a sponge on a stick to clean themselves.

The most impressive mosaics on site are at the huge **Terme di Nettuno**, which occupied a whole block and date from Hadrian's renovation of the port. Make sure you climb the elevated platform and look at the three enormous mosaics here, including Neptune driving his seahorse chariot, surrounded by sea monsters, mermaids and mermen. In an adjacent room is a mosaic with Neptune's wife, Amphitrite, on a hippocampus, accompanied by Hymenaeus – the god of weddings – and tritons. In the centre of the complex are the remains of a large arcaded courtyard called the Palaestra, in which athletes used to train. There's an impressive mosaic depicting boxing and wrestling.

Next to the Nettuno baths is a good-sized **amphitheatre**, built by Agrippa and later enlarged to hold 4000 people. Stucco is still visible in the entrance hall. In late antiquity, the orchestra could be flooded to present watery tableaux. By climbing to the top of the amphitheatre and looking over the site, you'll get a good idea of the original layout of the port and how it would have functioned.

Behind the amphitheatre is the **Piazzale delle Corporazioni** (Forum of the Corporations), the offices of Ostia's merchant guilds, which sport well-preserved mosaics depicting the different interests of each business. The pictures represent dolphins, ships, the lighthouse at Portus (the older nearby settlement) and the grain trade, and the symbols here indicate just how international the nature of business in Ostia was. Both Latin and Greek graffiti has been discovered on the walls of the city.

The **Forum**, the main square of Ostia, is dominated by the huge Capitolium. Built by Hadrian, this was a temple dedicated to the main Roman deities, the Capitoline triad (Jupiter, Juno and Minerva).

Nearby is another of the site's highlights: the **Thermopolium**, an ancient cafe. Check out the bar counter, surmounted by a frescoed menu, the kitchen and the small courtyard, where customers would have sat next to the fountain and relaxed with a drink.

CASTELLO DI GIULIO II   CASTLE
(☑06 5635 8044; Piazza della Rocca; ⊘free guided tours 11am Thu, 11am & noon Sun) Near the entrance to the excavations is this imposing castle, an impressive example of 15th-century military architecture, which lost its purpose when a freak flood changed the course of the river, making the location less accessible.

✖ EATING

RISTORANTE CIPRIANI   RESTAURANT €
(☑06 5635 2956; meals €25; ⊘lunch Thu-Tue, dinner Mon, Tue, Thu-Sun) If it's sunny enough to eat outside, this location can't be beat; dine on *cucina Romana*, with dishes such as *pasta alla' Gricia* (with lardons and onion) and *cacio e pepe* (with cheese and pepper), while seated in a cobbled street in the old *borgo* by the castle. They do a bargain menu at €10.

RISTORANTE MONUMENTO   RESTAURANT €€
(☑06 565 00 21; Piazza Umberto I 8; meals €25; ⊘lunch & dinner Tue-Sun) Close to the ruins, this has a history stretching back to the 19th century, when it used to serve the men working on reclaiming the local marshlands. It specialises in homemade pasta and fish and has a traditional interior decked with vintage black-and-white photos.

Tivoli

Explore

For millennia, the hilltop town of Tivoli has been a summer escape for rich Romans, as amply demonstrated by its two historic hedonistic playgrounds, both Unesco World Heritage sites. Villa Adriana was the mammoth country estate of the emperor Hadrian, and the 16th-century Villa d'Este is a wonder of the High Renaissance. You can visit both in a day, though you'll have to start early.

The Best...

➡ **Sight** Villa Adriana's Maritime Theatre (p238)
➡ **Place to Eat** Sibilla (p239)

Top Tip

Take a picnic or organise your day to eat in Tivoli town before heading over to Villa Adriana (a short bus ride out of town).

Getting There & Away

➡ **Bus** Tivoli is 30km east of Rome and is accessible by Cotral bus from outside the Ponte Mammolo station on metro line B (€2.20, every 15 minutes, 50 minutes). It's best to buy a 3-Zone BIRG ticket (€8), which will cover you for the whole day.

The easiest way to visit both sites is to visit the Villa D'Este first, as it is close to Tivoli town centre. Then take the bus back towards Ponte Mammolo from Largo Garibaldi, asking the driver to stop close to Villa Adriana. After visiting the villa, you can then catch the bus (€2.20, every 15 minutes, 50 minutes) on to Ponte Mammolo.

Note that traffic is usually heavy on the route, so it's likely to take longer than the official times quoted here.

➡ **Car** Take either Via Tiburtina (SS5) or the faster Rome–L'Aquila autostrada (A24).
➡ **Train** From Stazione Tiburtina (€2.60, 40 minutes to one hour 20 minutes, at least hourly).

Need to Know

➡ **Location** 30km east of Rome
➡ **Tourist Office** On Piazza Garibaldi, where the bus arrives

◉ SIGHTS

VILLA ADRIANA
ARCHAEOLOGICAL SITE

(☎06 3996 7900; www.villaadriana.beniculturali. it; adult/reduced €8/4, plus possible exhibition supplement, car park €3; ☺9am to 1hr before sunset) Emperor Hadrian's summer residence **Villa Adriana**, 5km outside Tivoli, set new standards of luxury when it was built between AD 118 and 134 – a remarkable feat given the excesses of the Roman Empire. Consider hiring an audioguide (€5), which gives a helpful overview. Bring a picnic lunch or eat in Tivoli town.

A model near the entrance gives you an idea of the scale of the original complex, which you'll need several hours to explore.

A great traveller and enthusiastic architect, Hadrian personally designed much of the complex, taking inspiration from buildings he'd seen around the world. The **pecile**, a large porticoed pool area where the emperor used to stroll after lunch, was a reproduction of a building in Athens. Similarly, another highlight of the site, the **canopo**, is a copy of the sanctuary of Serapis in the Egyptian town of Canopus, with a long canal of water enclosed by a colonnade. The Serapaeum providing a backdrop for the pool was an outdoor summer dining room, where Hadrian would hold banquets.

To the east of the pecile is one of the highlights, Hadrian's private retreat, the **Teatro Marittimo**. Built on an island in an artificial pool, it was originally a minivilla accessible only by swing bridges, which the emperor would have raised when he felt like a dip. Nearby, the fish pond is encircled by an underground gallery where Hadrian liked to wander.

Don't neglect to take a short walk to the isolated tower of Rocca Bruna. You can walk up to the top of this for a wonderful belvedere (viewpoint) over the site and the hills beyond. Hadrian doubtless also enjoyed the view from here.

There are also several magnificent bath complexes, barracks and more, and a museum with the latest discoveries from ongoing excavations (often closed).

VILLA D'ESTE
VILLA, GARDENS

(☎0774 331 20 70; www.villadestetivoli.info; Piazza Trento; adult/reduced €8.50/4, plus possible exhibition supplement; ☺8.30am to 1hr before sunset Tue-Sun) In Tivoli's hilltop centre, the steeply terraced gardens of Villa d'Este are a superlative example of a High Renaissance garden, dotted by fantastical fountains all powered by gravity alone. The villa was once a Benedictine convent, converted by Lucrezia Borgia's son, Cardinal Ippolito d'Este, into a pleasure palace in 1550.

From 1865 to 1886 it was home to Franz Liszt and inspired his compositions 'To the Cypresses of the Villa d'Este' and 'The Fountains of the Villa d'Este'.

The rich mannerist frescoes of the villa interior merit a glance, but it's the garden that you're here for: water-spouting gargoyles and elaborate avenues lined with deep-green, knotty cypresses. One fountain (designed by Gian Lorenzo Bernini) used its water pressure to play an organ concealed in the top part of its structure, which plays regularly throughout the day. Another highlight is the 130m-long path of the Hundred Fountains, which joins the Fountain of Tivoli to the Fountain of Rome.

The villa is a two-minute walk north from Largo Garibaldi. Picnics are forbidden, but there's a stylish cafe.

VILLA GREGORIANA
PARK

(☎06 3996 7701; www.villagregoriana.it; Piazza Tempio di Vesta; adult/child €5/2.50; ☺10am-6.30pm Tue-Sun summer, to 2.30pm Tue-Sat, to 4pm Sun winter) In 1826 the Aniene river overflowed its banks, carrying away houses in the flood waters. As a result, Pope Gregory XVI ordered the river to be diverted through a tunnel, creating a magnificent waterfall over a steep gorge, crashing down 120m to the bottom of the canyon, known as the Cascata Grande (Great Waterfall). The architects used the old riverbed, the gorge and the thickly wooded setting, full of caves, ravines and archaeological fragments, to create the park of Villa Gregoriana.

✖ EATING

DA PIPPO
FAST FOOD €

(Via San Valerio 2; Sandwich €7.50) Pippo is famous for his huge (one will feed two), good value, tasty *panini*, filled with fresh ingredients; spot it by the queues of hungry day-tripping Romans. Particularly recommended is the Zingaresca, which combines mozzarella, rocket, parmesan, speck and oil, and takes around 30 minutes to prepare. Take away and eat your *panino* on one of the lush Tivoli estates.

SUBIACO & ST BENEDICT

St Benedict is generally regarded as the father of Western monasticism. Fleeing the vice that had so disgusted him as a student in Rome, he sought the gloom of the grotto to meditate and pray. During this time he attracted a large local following that eventually provoked the ire of his fellow friars and forced him onto the road.

Remote-feeling and dramatic, Subiaco is carved into the rock above the saint's former humble cave and well worth the trip to see its wonderful monasteries and impressive abbey, with breathtaking views across the biblical-seeming countryside. Apart from its stunning setting, described by Petrarch as 'the edge of Paradise', the **Monastery of St Benedict** (☑0774 8 50 39; www.benedettini-subiaco.org; ⊘9am-12.30pm & 3-6pm) is adorned with rich 13th- to 15th-century frescoes. Halfway down the hill from St Benedict is the **Monastery of St Scholastica** (☑0774 8 55 69; www. benedettini-subiaco.org; ⊘9.30am-12.15pm & 3.30-6.15pm), the only one of the 13 monasteries built by St Benedict still standing in the Valley of the Amiene. It has a restaurant offering reasonably priced set menus.

To reach Subiaco, you can take a bus direct from Viale Mazzini in Tivoli (one hour, hourly). To get here from Rome, take a Cotral bus to Subiaco's Piazza Falcone (1¼ hours, every 15 to 30 minutes Monday to Friday, less frequently at weekends) from Ponte Mammolo on metro line B. The bus stops a little way from the Monastery of St Scholastica – it's a 3km scenic, if demanding, uphill walk. Buy a 3-zone BIRG ticket (€8) to cover your journey there and back.

SIBILLA
RESTAURANT €€

(☑0774 33 52 81; Via della Sibilla 50; meals €45; ⊘May-Sep) Chef Adriano Baldassare, who studied under Antonello Colonna, serves up exciting creative cuisine that combines Roman traditions with innovation at this impressive restaurant, which has a glorious setting beside two impressive Roman temples, with views over the slopes of Villa Gregoriana. The food lives up to the view, there's an extensive wine list and it's less expensive than you would expect.

TRATTORIA DEL FALCONE
TRATTORIA €€

(☑0774 31 23 58; Via del Trevio 34; meals €45; ⊘Wed-Mon) In Tivoli town, this is a cheerful, family-run trattoria with exposed stone walls that's been serving up classic pasta, meat and fish dishes since 1918. It is popular with both tourists and locals.

Castelli Romani

Explore

About 20km south of Rome, the Colli Albani (Alban hills) and their 13 towns are collectively known as the Castelli Romani. For millennia they've provided Romans with a green refuge on hot summer weekends. The most famous towns are Castel Gandolfo, where the pope has his summer residence; Frascati, renowned for its wine; lakeside Nemi, with its small museum; and Grottaferrata, which has a fine abbey. The other towns are Monte Porzio Catone, Montecompatri, Rocca Priora, Colonna, Rocca di Papa, Marino, Albano Laziale, Ariccia and Genzano.

The Best...

➡ **Sight** Lago Albano (p241)
➡ **Place to Eat** Cacciani (p241)
➡ **Place to Drink** The town of Frascati (p240)

Top Tip

In Frascati, wander around until you find a place serving fresh local wine and *porchetta*, and settle down for a simple feast (preferably at trestle tables out on a cobbled street).

If you want to visit several towns but don't have your own transport, the easiest two to see in a day are Frascati and Castel Gandolfo, as there is a bus linking the two.

Getting There & Away

➡ **Car** For Frascati and Grottaferrata take Via Tuscolana (SS215); for Castel Gandolfo and Albano Laziale take Via Appia Nuova

ROME'S BEST SEASIDE ESCAPES

Before you pack your bucket and spade, be warned that most beach stretches near Rome are occupied by *stabilimenti* (private beach clubs), so you'll need to pay a fee and rent an umbrella and bed for the day (usually around €10-15 per person), or otherwise be limited to the tiny scraps of remaining public beach.

The easiest stretch of seaside to reach from Rome is **Ostia Lido**, around 30km southwest, accessible via a half-hourly train from Stazione Porta San Paolo. It has a good atmosphere in summer, as it's thronged with people. It is a fun place to sit in the sun and eat ice cream, but few people would dream of swimming here – the water's too darn dirty. Film buffs should note that controversial director Pasolini was killed on this beach, run over by his own car.

More chic, and with no morbid history, is the Fellini-favoured **Fregene**, around 39km west of Rome, backed by tall pine forest. However, it also gets crowded and the water quality is only marginally better. Regular Cotral buses (€2.80, one hour) run here from Cornelia metro stop.

A longer trip away, around 60km northwest, are the appealing (rammed in summer, but great off season) **Santa Severa** (train from Termini, Ostiense, or Trastevere, from €3.60, 45 to 60 minutes), overlooked by a castle, and lovely **Santa Marinella** (train from Termini or San Pietro, €4.60, one hour).

And finally, for the best sand-and-sea that's still a worthwhile day trip, try **Sperlonga**, 116km south of Rome (€6.90, 70 minutes to two hours by train from Termini, at least hourly), which has a beautiful crescent of white-sand beach backed by tangled dark greenery and a pretty town. The train takes you to Fondi, from where it's a short bus trip.

Alternatively, you could head out of Rome for a swim in one of Lazio's lakes: Lago Albano or Lago Bracciano (p249).

(SS7) south, following signs for Ciampino Airport.

➡ **Train** There are buses to Frascati, but the best way to reach it is by train from Stazione Termini (€2.10, 30 minutes, hourly Monday to Saturday, every two hours Sunday). Castel Gandolfo is best reached by train from Rome's Stazione Termini (€2.10, 45 minutes). It's not possible to catch a train between Frascati and Castel Gandolfo.

Getting Around

➡ **Bus** To get from Frascati to Grottaferrata (€1.10, 15 minutes, every 30 to 40 minutes), catch a Cotral bus from Piazza Marconi. Buses also leave from here to Genzano di Roma (€1.10, 45 minutes, about hourly); from where you can catch another bus to Nemi (€1.10, 10 minutes, about hourly). There are buses from Frascati's Piazza Marconi to Castel Gandolfo (€1.10, 30 minutes).

Need to Know

➡ **Location** 20km southeast of Rome

➡ **Tourist Office** (☑06 9401 5378; Piazza Marconi, Frascati; ⊙8am-8pm Mon-Fri 10am-8pm Sat & Sun)

⊙ SIGHTS

FRASCATI   TOWN

A villa perches over the town above ornamental gardens, its flat-fronted facade like an expensive stage set. This is the 16th-century **Villa Aldobrandini**, designed by Giacomo della Porta and built by Carlo Maderno; it's closed to the public, but you can visit the impressive **garden** (Via Cardinal Massai 18; ⊙9am-5.30pm Mon-Fri) . A fine example of early Italian baroque design, the palace is the focal point, set dramatically into the wooded hill. Water features in the garden were designed by Orazio Olivieri, though many of the fountains no longer function.

Also worth a visit in Frascati, sharing the stable building with the tourist office, is the **Museo Tuscolano** (☑06 941 71 95; admission €7; ⊙10am-6pm Tue-Fri, to 7pm Sat & Sun) with artfully lit republican and imperial artefacts and interesting models of Tuscolo villas.

However, villas and views are all very well, but most people come to Frascati for the food and fresh white wine. You can pick up a *porchetta panini* (sandwich made of pork roasted with herbs) from one of the stands that do a brisk weekend trade around Piazza del Mercato, or head to the cantinas that dot the town, which sell jugs of wine and snacks.

TUSCULUM   RUIN

FREE If you have a car, head up to the ruins of ancient **Tusculum**. All that remains of this once-imposing 4th-century-BC town is a small amphitheatre, a crumbling villa and a small stretch of road leading up to the city, but it's a lovely spot for a walk and the views are stupendous.

GROTTAFERRATA ABBEY   CHURCH

(Abbazia; ☐06 945 93 09; www.abbaziagreca.it; Viale San Nilo; ⊙7am-12.30pm & 3.30pm to one hour before sunset) Another trip that requires you to have your own transport is **Grottaferrata**, where there's a 15th-century **abbey**, founded in 1004. It's the last remaining example of the Byzantine-Greek monasteries that once dotted medieval Italy. The church interior resembles an incense-perfumed jewellery box and Mass is very atmospheric. The congregation of Greek monks wear distinctive flat-topped black caps.

CASTEL GANDOLFO   TOWN

Continuing southwest brings you to **Castel Gandolfo**, an impressive, dome-capped hilltop *borgo* (small village) overlooking Lago di Albano. This is the pope's summer residence, which, although closed to the public, still attracts hordes of tourists to the impressive town square. The small town is a very pretty place for a wander, with views opening out across the lake below.

LAGO ALBANO   LAKE

Close to Castel Gandolfo, this great azure expanse is simply glorious for a summer swim, and cafes and boating-hire places dot its banks. Filling two volcanic craters, the lake is about 3.5km by 2.3km.

NEMI   TOWN

The town of Nemi is perched high above Lago di Nemi, the smaller of the two volcanic lakes in the Castelli Romani. This area was the centre of a cult to the goddess Diana in ancient times and a favourite holiday spot of the emperor Caligula. Today it's a popular getaway from Rome and famous for its wild strawberries, best eaten in the early summer. There's a great little museum here, the **Museo delle Navi Romani** (Via Diana 15; ⊙currently closed for renovation) on the shore of the lake. This was built

by Mussolini to house two incredibly preserved wooden Roman boats, dating from Caligula's reign, that were discovered and salvaged from the lake in 1932. These were tragically destroyed by fire in 1944 – what you see now are scale models.

✗ EATING & DRINKING

The Frascati area is famous for its white wine and there are plenty of places where you can try local varieties. In Frascati itself, most fun are the town's famous rough-and-ready *cantinas*, which usually sell *porchetta*, olives, salami and cheese to go with jugs of the fresh young white wine. You can also pick up a *porchetta panini* from one of the stands that do a brisk weekend trade around the town's Piazza del Mercato.

HOSTERIA SAN ROCCO   OSTERIA €

(☐06 9428 2786; www.hosteriasanrocco.com; Via Cadorna 1; meals around €25; ⊙lunch & dinner) To try a typical *fraschette* (osteria that traditionally served only *porchetta* and wine) head to Frascati's 'Da Trinca', as it's nicknamed by locals. It serves up traditional dishes such as *spaghetti alla gricia* (with pecorino cheese and cured pork jowl) and *saltimbocca* (veal topped with prosciutto), as well as a fine array of antipasti.

CACCIANI   RESTAURANT €€€

(☐06 942 03 78; Via Armando Diaz 13; meals €50; ⊙Tue-Sat) Frascati's smartest and most renowned restaurant is Cacciani, with fine food and a graceful terrace. The menu offers some modern creative dishes, but it's the regional staples such as *spaghetti cacio e pepe* (with pecorino cheese and pepper) that really stand out. There's also a weighty wine list and a lovely terrace with twinkling views of Rome.

ANTICO RISTORANTE
PAGNANELLI   RESTAURANT €€€

(☐06 936 00 04; www.pagnanelli.it; Via Antonio Gramsci 4, Castel Gandolfo; meals €70) A few hundred yards from the hotel of the same name and a short walk from the centre of Castel Gandolfo, this greenery-laden restaurant is a great place for a romantic meal. It's no casual trattoria, erring on the formal and touristy side, but the views over the deep blue chasm of Lago Albano can't be beat.

Meet the Etruscans

In the 1920s, DH Lawrence spent several years living in Italy. He became fascinated by Etruria, the sophisticated civilisation that developed from around 800BC in what is today Tuscany and Lazio, and suggested in his book *Etruscan Places*: 'Italy today is far more Etruscan in its pulse, than Roman: and will always be so.'

A Great Civilisation

The Etruscans have a mysterious reputation, and yet much of their handiwork still survives, mainly discovered in lavish cemeteries, which you can visit in Lazio at Cerveteri and Tarquinia. Cerveteri is an entire town of tombs; the tombs at Tarquinia are lined with breathtaking paintings. The Etruscans were master sailors, soldiers, architects, metalworkers, and artists, and you can see many artefacts at museums in Rome, Cerveteri, Tarquinia and Viterbo.

Mining the mineral-rich hills around Tuscany for tin and copper, and Elba for iron ore, they traded metals with the Greeks and the Phoenicians, becoming exceedingly prosperous. This wealth meant they were able to commission artists from Greece; more ancient Greek pottery has been discovered in Etruscan tombs than in Greece itself.

Where Did They Come From?

This question has fascinated historians ever since the 5th century BC when Herotodus wrote that they came from Lydia, escaping famine in what is now Turkey. It was later proposed that the Etruscans were a pre-Indo-European native race, and archaeological and linguistic evidence supports this theory.

1. The Etruscan necropolis of Banditaccia (p245), Cerveteri **2.** Detail from a fresco on an Etruscan tomb, Tarquinia (p244) **3.** Sarcophagus of the Spouses, Cerveteri (p244)

However, in 2007, DNA tests seemed to support the idea that they came from north-west Asia, and so the controversy continues.

According to legend, Rome's first king, Romulus, was Etruscan and a family of Etruscans, the Tarquins, were also the last dynastic rulers of Rome. Their influence continued: Augustus had 19 Etruscan families (the old, established aristocracy) backing him as late as the end of the 1st century AD. Claudius' first wife was Etruscan, and the emperor himself wrote a 20-volume history of the Etruscans, though this has completely disappeared.

The Mystery of the Etruscans

Part of the mystery surrounding Etruria is that no literature remains nor any historical chronicles – only tomb inscriptions or votive offerings. Written evidence of Etruscan culture largely comes from contemporary Greek and Roman commentary – much of which was unsurprisingly (as their rivals) negative, painting them as a decadent people. It's been theorised that their literature was destroyed by the Romans, ashamed of their former dominance.

However, it's perhaps also misleading to talk about the Etruscans as if they were a nation. Although the discovery of warrior graves shows that military status was important, unlike the Romans, the Etruscans didn't fight together as a block. Evidence shows that, like the Greek city-state, each town operated independently, making its own alliances. Perhaps DH Lawrence was correct in suggesting that Italy is less Roman than Etruscan: even today, this relatively new country is enduringly a collection of distinct regions.

 **SLEEPING**

HOTEL PAGNANELLI LUCIA HOTEL €
(📞06 936 14 22; www.albergopagnanelli.it; Via A Gramsci 2, Castel Gandolfo; s/d from €80/100) A modest two-star hotel perched high above Lago Albano; rooms have wrought-iron beds and lake views.

Cerveteri

Explore

A town was established here around 9th century BC and just outside Cerveteri lies the only architectural reminder of what was a great Etruscan city: an extraordinary, Unesco-listed Etruscan burial complex, a haunting necropolis set around a grid of streets. Spend the morning wandering around the curious townscape-of-the-dead, where you almost expect to see hobbits pop out of the grassy mounds, then lunch in the appealing small town centre, before completing your day with a visit to Cerveteri's fascinating Etruscan museum.

The Best...

➡ **Sight** Necropoli di Banditaccia
➡ **Place to Eat** Antica Locanda le Ginestre

Top Tip

Don't miss Cerveteri's Etruscan museum, which provides context for the tombs and brings the ancient era to life.

Getting There & Away

➡ **Bus** Take the Cotral bus (€3.90, 55 minutes, half-hourly) from outside the Cornelia metro stop on metro line A.

WORTH A DETOUR

TARQUINIA

Tarquinia is entirely different from Cerveteri, yet equally breathtaking. Here lies the world's most remarkable collection of pre-classical painting, with a huge complex of tombs that are vivid with detail and colour. Modern-day Tarquinia, with its narrow cobbled streets, perfectly preserved walled city and graceful buildings, merits a visit in any case, especially for its fantastic Etruscan museum.

On the edge of Tarquinia's *centro storico* lies the **Museo Nazionale Tarquiniese** (📞0766 85 60 36; Via Cavour 1; admission €6, incl Necropoli di Monterozzi €8; ⏰8.30am-7.30pm Tue-Sun) housed in the exquisite 15th-century Palazzo Vitelleschi, a fabulous palace centred around a courtyard. Highlights of its collection are a breathtaking terracotta frieze of winged horses (the Cavalli Alati) and, on the upper floors, several frescoed tombs that have been transported here in their entirety, full of incredibly vibrant paintings.

To see Tarquinia's famous painted tombs in situ, head for the **necropolis** (📞06 3996 7150; adult/child €6/3, incl museum €8/4; ⏰8.30am to 1hr before sunset Tue-Sun), located 1.5km from town. To get here, either take bus D (€0.60, nine daily) from outside the tourist office or walk – head up Corso Vittorio Emanuele, turn right into Via Porta Tarquinia and follow straight into Via Ripagretta.

This site is unlike Cerveteri in that the parts of the tombs above ground have been destroyed, and the treasures beneath are now protected by functional little corrugated huts. However, it's what lies beneath the ground that is important.

Of the 6000 tombs that have been excavated since 1489, 19 are currently open to the public, including the Tomba della Caccia e della Pesca, the richly decorated Tomba dei Leopardi and the Tomba della Fustigazione with its erotic depiction of a little friendly S&M. The tombs made the news in 2013, when paleography professor Carlo Tedeschi presented his study of graffiti in the Tomb of Bartoccini, which indicates the Knights Templar took part in sexual rituals here in the Middle Ages.

To reach Tarquinia from Cerveteri, take one of the regular Cotral buses from Piazza A Moro to Ladispoli railway station (six minutes), then take a train to Tarquinia (€3.50, 35 minutes, hourly). Returning to Rome from Tarquinia, there are trains direct to Termini (€6.90, one hour 20 minutes, half-hourly).

Buses leave Cerveteri for Rome from the main square. Bus G runs hourly (roughly) between the main square and the Necropoli (€0.60, five minutes).

➡ **Car** Take either Via Aurelia (SS1) or the Civitavecchia autostrada (A12) and exit at Cerveteri–Ladispoli.

....

Need to Know

➡ **Location** 35km northwest of Rome

➡ **Tourist Office** (☑06 9955 2637; Piazza Aldo Moro; ☺9.30am-12.30pm Mon-Sat, 10am-1pm Sun Nov-Feb, 9.30am-12.30pm & 5-7pm daily Mar-Oct)

◉ SIGHTS

Cerveteri, or Kysry to the Etruscans and Caere to Latin speakers, was one of the most important commercial centres in the Mediterranean from the 7th to the 5th centuries BC. However, most of the city was built of wood; hence there is nothing left. Only the necropolis, carved underground, gives an indication of how splendid the Etruscan city must have been.

As Roman power grew, so Cerveteri's fortunes faded, and in 358 BC the city was annexed by Rome. After the fall of the Roman Empire, the spread of malaria and repeated Saracen invasions caused further decline. In the 13th century there was a mass exodus from the city to the nearby town of Ceri, and Caere became Caere Vetus (Old Caere), from which its current name derives. The early 19th century saw the first tentative archaeological explorations in the area, and in 1911 systematic excavations began in earnest.

NECROPOLI DI BANDITACCIA   NECROPOLIS
(☑06 3996 7150; Via del Necropoli; admission adult/reduced €6/3, incl museum €8/4; ☺8.30am to 1hr before sunset) This 10-hectare necropolis is laid out as an afterlife townscape, with streets, squares and terraces of tombs. Some of the major tombs, including the 6th-century-BC **Tomba dei Rilievi**, are decorated with painted reliefs. Recent additions include a worthwhile 3D film about the Etruscans and some stunning 3D installations in several tombs that reconstruct the frescoes and funerary items that were once kept here.

The most common type of tomb construction is the tumulus, a circular structure cut into the earth and topped by a cumulus – a topping of turf. The favoured

subject matter for the tomb frescoes is mostly endearingly domestic, featuring cooking implements and other household items as well as figures from the underworld.

MUSEO NAZIONALE DI CERVETERI   MUSEUM
(Piazza Santa Maria; admission adult/reduced €6/3, incl necropolis €8/4; ☺8.30am-5.30pm Tue-Sun) In Cerveteri's medieval town centre is this splendid museum, where treasures taken from the tombs help to bring the dead to life – figuratively, at least.

✗ EATING

ANTICA LOCANDA LE GINESTRE   RESTAURANT €€
(☑06 994 33 65; www.anticalocandaleginestre. com; Piazza Santa Maria 5; meals €40; ☺Tue-Sun) This top-notch family-run Cerveteri restaurant offers delicious food, prepared with organically grown local produce and served in the elegant dining room or flower-filled courtyard garden. Book ahead.

Viterbo

....

Explore

Viterbo makes a good base for exploring Lazio's rugged north, or it can be visited on a day trip – there are plenty of sights within the town, whose pretty *centro storico* is compact and walkable. It's well worth spending the whole day out here, perhaps visiting some of the city's surrounding sights, such as the local hot springs or beautiful Lago Bolsena.

....

The Best...

➡ **Sight** Palazzo dei Priori (p247)

➡ **Place to Eat** Ristorante Enoteca la Torre (p248)

➡ **Place to Drink** Gran Caffè Schenardi (p248)

....

Top Tip

The most hassle-free way to reach Viterbo is by train, as journeys by bus can get snarled in traffic.

Viterbo

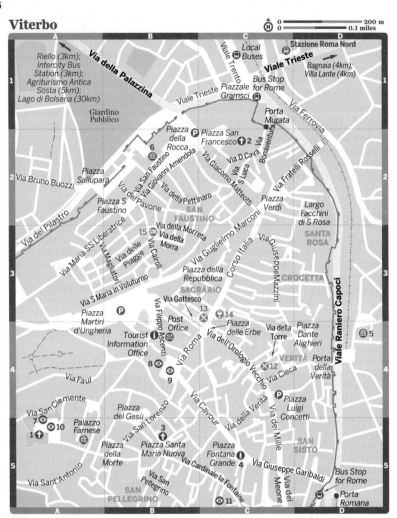

Getting There & Away

➤ **Bus** From Rome, Cotral buses (€5, every 30 minutes) depart from the Saxa Rubra station on the Ferrovia Roma-Nord train line. Catch the train (standard BIT) to Saxa Rubra from Piazzale Flaminio (just north of Piazza del Popolo). Viterbo is covered by a 5-zone 5 BIRG ticket (€12). In Viterbo, ensure you get off at Porta Romana, not the intercity bus station at Riello, which is a few kilometres northwest of the town. Returning to Rome, take the bus from the Porta Romana or Piazzale Gramsci stops.

➤ **Car** Take Via Cassia (SS2). Once in Viterbo, for parking try either Piazza Martiri d'Ungheria or Piazza della Rocca.

➤ **Train** Trains depart hourly from Monday to Saturday and every two hours on Sundays from Rome's Ostiense station (get off at Viterbo Porta Romana). The journey takes 1½ to two hours and costs €5 one way.

Need to Know

➤ **Location** 105km northwest of Rome
➤ **Tourist Office** (☎0761 32 59 92; www. provincia.vt.it; Via Filippo Ascenzi 4; ⊗9am-noon Mon-Fri & 3-4.30pm Tue & Thu)

Viterbo

⊙ SIGHTS

Founded by the Etruscans and eventually taken over by Rome, Viterbo developed into an important medieval centre and in the 13th century became the residence of the popes. Papal elections were held in the Gothic Palazzo dei Papi, where in 1271 the entire college of cardinals was briefly imprisoned. The story goes that after three years of deliberation the cardinals still hadn't elected a new pope. Mad with frustration, the Viterbesi locked the dithering priests in a turreted hall and starved them into electing Pope Gregory X.

Apart from its historical appeal, Viterbo is famous for its therapeutic hot springs. The best known is the sulphurous Bulicame pool, mentioned by Dante in the *Divine Comedy.*

PALAZZO DEI PRIORI — PALACE
(Piazza del Plebiscito; ⊙9am-1pm & 3-6pm Mon-Sat, 10am-1pm & 3-6pm Sun) FREE The elegant Renaissance Piazza del Plebiscito is dominated by this imposing palace. Now home to the town council, it's worth venturing inside for the 16th-century frescoes that colourfully depict Viterbo's ancient origins – the finest are in the Sala Regia on the 1st floor. Outside, the elegant courtyard and fountain were added two centuries after the *palazzo* was built in 1460.

PIAZZA SAN LORENZO — PIAZZA
For an idea of how rich Viterbo once was, head southwest to **Piazza San Lorenzo**, the medieval city's religious heart. It was here that the cardinals came to vote for their popes and pray in the 12th-century **Cattedrale di San Lorenzo**. Built originally to a simple Romanesque design, it owes its current Gothic look to a 14th-century makeover; damage by Allied bombs in WWII meant the roof and nave had to be rebuilt.

MUSEO DEL COLLE DEL DUOMO — MUSEUM
(Piazza San Lorenzo; adult/reduced incl guided visit to Palazzo dei Papi, Sala del Conclave & Loggia €7/5; ⊙10am-1pm & 3-8pm Tue-Sun, to 6pm winter, to 8pm Aug) Next door to the cathedral, this museum displays a small collection of religious artefacts, including a reliquary said to contain the chin of John the Baptist.

CHIESA DI SANTA MARIA NUOVA — CHURCH
(Piazza Santa Maria Nuova; ⊙7am-7pm) This 11th-century Romanesque church, the oldest in Viterbo, was restored to its original form after bomb damage in WWII. The cloisters are particularly lovely and are believed to date from an earlier period.

PIAZZA SAN PELLEGRINO — PIAZZA
South of here lies the remarkably well-preserved medieval quarter. Wander down Via San Pellegrino with its low-slung arches and claustrophobic grey houses to this pint-sized and picturesque square.

MUSEO NAZIONALE ETRUSCO — MUSEUM
(☎0761 32 59 29; Piazza della Rocca; adult/reduced €6/3; ⊙8.30am-7.30pm Tue-Sun) For a shot of Etruscan culture head to this museum, which evokes the Etruscan lifestyle via reconstructions, as well as exhibiting artefacts found locally, the highlight being the entire 'tomb of the chariot' discovered in Ischia di Castro. It's all housed in the Albornaz fortress by the town's northern entrance.

CHIESA DI SAN FRANCESCO — CHURCH
(Piazza San Francesco; ⊙8am-6.30pm) A short walk away from Museo Nazionale

DAY TRIPS FROM ROME VITERBO

248

WORTH A DETOUR

LAGO DI BOLSENA

Surrounded by lush rolling countryside a few kilometres short of the regional border with Umbria, Lago di Bolsena is the largest and northernmost of Lazio's lakes. The lake's main town is Bolsena, a charming, low-key place that, despite a heavy hotel presence, retains its medieval character.

Like many Italian towns, Bolsena has its own miracle story. In 1263 a priest who had been tormented by doubts about the veracity of transubstantiation (the transformation of wine and bread into the blood and body of Christ) was saying Mass when he noticed blood dripping from the bread he was blessing. The bloodstained cloth in which he wrapped the bread may be seen in Orvieto's cathedral, which was built to commemorate the miracle.

In the medieval centre is the 11th-century **Basilica di Santa Cristina** (⏏0761 79 90 67; www.basilicasantacristina.it; Piazza Santa Cristina; ⏲7.15am-12.30pm & 3.30-7.30pm summer, to 5.30pm winter, catacombs 9.30am-noon & 3.30-6.30pm) where you'll find four stones stained with miraculous blood. The church is named for the martyr, who was daughter of the local prefect and who was tortured and finally killed for her faith – her story is re-enacted annually on 23 and 24 July. Beneath the basilica are a series of **catacombs**, where the young saint (aged only 12) was buried. They are also noteworthy for the number of tombs that are still sealed.

Etrusco is this Gothic church, which contains the tombs of two popes: Clement IV (d 1268) and Adrian V (d 1276). Both are attractively decorated, particularly that of Adrian, which features Cosmati work (multicoloured marble and glass mosaics set into stone and white marble).

MUSEO CIVICO
MUSEUM

(⏏0761 34 82 75; Piazza Crispi; admission €3.10; ⏲9am-6pm Tue-Sun Oct-Mar, to 7pm Apr-Sep) On the other side of town, this museum is housed in the cloister and nunnery adjoining Santa Maria della Verità. It features more Etruscan goodies, as well as curious fake Etruscan antiquities created in the 15th century by Annius of Viterbo, a monk and forger trying to give Viterbo extra kudos. There's also an art gallery, the highlight of which is Sebastiano del Piombo's *Pietà*.

FONTANA GRANDE
FOUNTAIN

In its eponymous piazza, the 'Big Fountain' lives up to its name and is also the oldest of Viterbo's Gothic fountains.

VILLA LANTE
PALACE

For a High Renaissance spectacle, head to the wonderful Villa Lante, 4km northeast of Viterbo at Bagnaia. This mannerist drama of terraces, water cascades and gaily waving statues forms part of the bucolic **park** (⏏0761 28 80 08; admission adult/reduced €5/2.50; ⏲8.30am to 1hr before sunset

Tue-Sun) that surrounds the 16th-century villa. To get to Bagnaia from Viterbo, take the bus from Viale Trieste (€1.10).

 EATING & DRINKING

GRAN CAFFÈ SCHENARDI
CAFE €

(⏏0761 34 58 60; Corso Italia 11-13) The Schenardi has been operating since 1818 and the wonderfully ornate interior looks like it hasn't changed much since, though the coffee and cakes are nothing out of the ordinary.

RISTORANTE TRE RE
TRATTORIA €€

(⏏0761 30 46 19; Via Gattesco 3; meals €35; ⏲Fri-Wed) This historical trattoria dishes up steaming plates of tasty local specialities and seasonally driven dishes. None is more typical than the *pollo alla viterbese*, excellent roast chicken stuffed with spiced potato and green olives.

RISTORANTE ENOTECA LA TORRE
RESTAURANT €€€

(⏏0761 22 64 67; www.enotecalatorrevt.com; Via della Torre 5; meals €80; ⏲lunch & dinner Mon & Thu-Sat, lunch only Sun) This is Viterbo's best restaurant: chef Danilo Ciavattini cooks beautifully presented creative cuisine, using fresh seasonal produce; his work is complemented by that of sommelier Luigi Picca. There's a tasting menu at €80.

🛏 SLEEPING

TUSCIA HOTEL   HOTEL €

(📞0761 34 44 00; www.tusciahotel.com; Via Cairoli 41; s €40-64, d €62-82; ❄) The best of the city's midrange options, this central, spick-and-span three-star place is leagues ahead of the competition in cleanliness and comfort. The rooms here are large, light and kitted out with satellite TV; nine rooms have air-con. There's a sunny roof terrace.

AGRITURISMO ANTICA SOSTA   AGRITURISMO €

(📞0761 25 13 69; www.agriturismoanticasosta.it; SS Cassia Nord; s/d €40/65, restaurant meals €35; ❄🔊) This mansion, set in pea-green countryside, is five kilometres from Viterbo on SS Cassia Nord, with spacious, simple rooms and a delicious restaurant, serving scrumptious dishes such as *strozzapreti con salsiccia, porcini e pancetta* ('priest-strangler' pasta with sausage, porcini mushrooms and cured ham).

Orvieto

Explore

Crowning a steep hill, beautiful medieval Orvieto is dominated by its awe-inspiring humbug-striped *duomo* (cathedral). Unsurprisingly, it's a tourist honeypot and gets crowded, particularly in summer. But don't let that deter you. This is a wonderful place to wander and makes a perfect and easily accessible day trip from Rome.

The Best...

➡ **Sight** Duomo (p250)
➡ **Place to Eat** Ristorante la Pergola (p250)
➡ **Place to Drink** Caffè Clandestino (p251)

Top Tip

Stay overnight to experience the atmosphere of the town once all the day trippers have ebbed away.

Getting There & Away

➡ **Bus** From Rome, buses depart from Stazione Tiburtina (€8, 1½ hours, 3.15pm Monday to Saturday, 9pm Sunday). Bargagli runs daily buses to Rome (8.10am Monday to Saturday, 7.10pm Sunday).

➡ **Car** The city is on the A1 north–south autostrada. There's plenty of parking space in Piazza Cahen and in several designated areas outside the old city walls.

➡ **Train** Trains depart from Rome's Stazione Termini (from €7.50, 60 to 80 minutes, about hourly). Take the funicular up to Piazza Cahen at the eastern end of the old town, then a shuttle bus (which fills up very quickly) to the Piazza del Duomo. If you can, opt for the very pleasant 20-minute walk uphill.

Need to Know

➡ **Location** 120km northwest of Rome
➡ **Tourist Office** (📞0763 34 17 72; info@iat.orvieto.tr.it; Piazza Duomo 24; ◷8.15am-1.50pm & 4-7pm Mon-Fri, 10am-1pm & 3-6pm Sat, Sun & holidays)

DAY TRIPS FROM ROME ORVIETO

WORTH A DETOUR

LAGO BRACCIANO & AROUND

Lovely Bracciano lies 32km northwest of Rome, and is the second largest of the volcanic lakes in the region. It's a beautiful blue expanse of 57.5 sq km, with picturesque towns dotted around its edge. At **Bracciano** itself, you can visit the 15th-century **Castello Odescalchi** (📞06 9980 2379; www.odescalchi.it; Via Gregorio VII 368; €7.50/5; ◷10am-noon & 3-6pm daily summer, shorter hours in winter), with its small museum. A particularly good base is **Anguillara Sabazia**, a charming small medieval town. It's possible to swim in the lake from the small gravelly beach in the town. If you'd like to stay, **Domus Anguillara** (📞06 996 83 96; www.domusangularia.com; Piazza del Comune 7; d €60-75) is a charming small B&B with three rooms, lovely owners and stunning lake views. If you have your own transport, the restaurant **Iotto** (📞06 904 17 46; Corso Vittorio Emanuele 96; meals around €35), in nearby Campagnano di Roma, is a fabulous place to eat, with particularly good fried dishes. Anguillara (55 minutes) and Bracciano (one hour) are accessible via train from Roma Ostiense (€2.60, half-hourly).

◉ SIGHTS

Perched precariously on a cliff made of the area's tufa stone, Orvieto also houses an important collection of Etruscan artefacts besides its magnificent cathedral. The cliff beneath is riddled with a fascinating series of ancient underground caves.

There's a pleasant, tranquil walk around Orvieto's walls (5km) – pick up a map at the tourist office, where you can also enquire about wine tours in the Umbrian countryside.

DUOMO   CATHEDRAL

(www.opsm.it; Piazza Duomo; admission €3, €5 including Cappella di S Brizio, Palazzi Papali, & Chiesa S Agostino; ☺9.30am-7pm Apr-Sep, 10am-5pm Wed-Mon Mar & Oct, 10am-1pm & 2-5pm Wed-Mon Nov-Feb) Orvieto's magnificent humbug-striped Duomo was commissioned in 1290 to celebrate the Miracle of Bolsena, but it took 30 years to plan and three centuries to complete. The great bronze doors, the work of Emilio Greco, were added in the 1960s.

In the **Capella di San Brizio** to the right of the altar, Luca Signorelli's fresco cycle, *Il Giudizio Universale* (The Last Judgment), shimmers with life. Signorelli began work on the series in 1499. It is said to have inspired Michelangelo's work in the Sistine Chapel.

The **Capella del Corporale** (Chapel of the Body) houses the blood-stained altar linen from Bolsena and features frescoes by Ugolino di Prete Ilario that depict the miracle.

MODO   MUSEUM

(Museale dell'Opera del Duomo di Orvieto; ☑0763 34 24 77; Piazza Duomo; €4, includes Palazzi Papali & Chiesa S Agostino; ☺9.30am-7pm summer, 9.30am-1pm & 3-5pm Wed-Mon winter) Housed in the former papal palaces, MODO contains a fine collection of religious relics, as well as Etruscan antiquities and paintings by artists such as Arnolfo di Cambio and the three Pisanos: Andrea, Nino and Giovanni.

PALAZZO PAPALI   MUSEUM

(Piazza Duomo) In the **Papal Palace**, you can see one of Italy's most important collections of Etruscan archaeological artefacts in both the **Museo Archeologico Nazionale** (☑0763 34 10 39; adult/reduced €3/1.50;

☺8.30am-7.30pm) and the more interesting **Museo Claudio Faina e Civico** (☑0763 34 15 11; www.museofaina.it; adult/reduced €8/5; ☺9.30am-6pm Apr-Sep, 10am-5pm Tue-Sun Oct-Mar). The latter also contains some significant Greek ceramic works, mostly found near Piazza Cahen in tombs dating to the 6th century BC.

TORRE DEL MORO   HISTORIC BUILDING

(Moor's Tower; ☑0763 34 45 67; Corso Cavour 87; adult/reduced €3/2; ☺10am-8pm May-Aug, 10am-7pm Mar, Apr, Sep & Oct, 10.30am-1pm & 2.30-5pm Nov-Feb) From the Piazza Duomo, head northwest along Via del Duomo to Corso Cavour and the 13th-century Torre del Moro. Climb all 250 steps for sweeping views of the city.

ORVIETO UNDERGROUND   HISTORIC SITE

(☑0763 34 48 91; www.orvietounderground.it; Parco delle Grotte; adult/reduced €6/5; ☺tours 11am, 12.15pm, 4pm & 5.15pm daily) The coolest place in Orvieto – literally – this series of 440 caves has been used for millennia by locals for various purposes, including as WWII bomb shelters, refrigerators, wells and, during many a pesky Roman or barbarian siege, as dovecotes to trap the usual one-course dinner: pigeon (still seen on local restaurant menus as *palombo*). Tours (with English-speaking guides) leave from in front of the tourist office.

✕ EATING & DRINKING

CANTINA FORESI   WINE BAR €

(☑0763 34 16 11; Piazza Duomo 2; snacks from €4.50; ☺9am-8pm) This family-run *enoteca* and cafe serves up *panini* and sausages, washed down with dozens of local wines from the ancient cellar.

RISTORANTE LA PERGOLA   RESTAURANT €€

(☑0763 34 30 65; Via dei Magoni 9b; meals €40; ☺Thu-Tue) Intimate and elegant, with a conservatory at the back, this serves great Umbrian cuisine, with plenty of truffles and 'hunter-style' chicken, lamb and boar dishes, all in a warm, welcoming atmosphere.

TRATTORIA DELL'ORSO   TRATTORIA €€

(☑0763 34 16 42; Via della Misericordia 18; meals €32; ☺Wed-Sun) As the owner of Orvieto's oldest restaurant, Gabriele sees no need for such modern fancies as written menus,

NAPLES & POMPEII

With a frenzy of baroque buildings, bellowing baristas, a Unesco-listed old city centre and the extraordinary sights of Pompeii, all overlooked by the menacingly beautiful volcano Vesuvius, Naples has a magnetic allure, and it's eminently possible to take a day trip here from Rome.

While you're there, some unmissable sights include Giuseppe Sanmartino's superlative *Cristo velato* (Veiled Christ) in the **Cappella Sansevero** (☑081 551 84 70; www.museosansevero.it; Via Francesco de Sanctis 19; adult/reduced €7/5; ☉10am-5.40pm Mon & Wed-Sat, to 1.10pm Sun; ▣Dante); the ancient artefacts of the **Museo Archeologico Nazionale** (☑081 44 01 66; Piazza Museo Nazionale 19; admission €8; ☉9am-7.30pm Wed-Mon; ▣Museo, Piazza Cavour); opera at the lavish **Teatro San Carlo** (☑081 797 24 68; www.teatrosancarlo.it; Via San Carlo 98; guided tour adult/reduced €6/3; ☉guided tours every hour from 10.30am-4.30pm Mon-Sat, to 12.30pm Sun, morning tours only Jan & Feb; ▣R2 to Piazza Treiste e Trento); Caravaggio, Warhol and regal excess at the epic **Palazzo Reale di Capodimonte** (☑081 749 91 11; www.polomusealenapoli.beniculturali.it/museo_cp/cp_info.html; Parco di Capodimonte; museum adult/reduced €7.50/3.75; park admission free; ☉museum 8.30am-7.30pm Thu-Tue, last entry 1hr before closing; park 7am-8pm daily); and a subterranean otherworld of ancient frescoes and burial sites at the lovingly restored **Catacomba di San Gennaro** (☑081 744 37 14; www.catacombedinapoli.it; Via Tondo di Capodimonte 13; adult/reduced €8/5; ☉1hr tours every hour 10am-5pm Mon-Sat, to 1pm Sun).

However, your first stop is likely to be **Pompeii** (☑081 857 53 47; www.pompeiisites.org; Via Marina, enter through Porta Marina; €10; ☉Apr-Oct 8:30am-7:30pm; Nov-Mar to 5pm, last entry: Apr-Oct 6pm; Nov-Mar 3:30pm), victim of the world's most famous volcano disaster. Highlights include the Villa dei Misteri, with its wonderful frescoes, the Lupanare (an ancient brothel), and the moving Garden of the Fugitives, with its huddled bodies preserved in ash. Reach the site via train to Pompei-Scavi-Villa dei Misteri from Naples (35 minutes), or by SITA bus from near Naples Stazione Centrale.

Naples is famous for its glorious pizza; sample it at **Brandi** (☑081 41 69 28; Salita S Anna di Palazzo 1; ☉Wed-Mon; ▣R2 to Piazza Treiste e Trento), or try sublime *fritti* (deep-fried snacks) at **Friggitoria Vomero** (☑081 578 31 30; Via Cimarosa 44; snacks from €0.20; ☉9.30am-2.30pm & 5-9.30pm Mon-Fri, to 11pm Sat; ▣Centrale to Fuga).

There are regular high-speed trains to/from Rome Termini (from €39; 70 minutes).

---

instead reeling off the day's dishes at you as you walk in the door. Go with his recommendations – perhaps the *zuppa di farro* followed by fettuccine with porcini – as he knows what he's talking about. And be prepared to take your time.

CAFFÈ CLANDESTINO — CAFE
(☑0763 34 08 68; Corso Cavour 40; snacks from €3) This cafe-bar has a lively buzz, high ceilings, good coffee, nice snacks and brasserie-style meals, as well as a few outside tables where you can sit with the sun on your face and regular live music tucked into a relatively small space. What more could you want?

🛏 SLEEPING

HOTEL MAITANI — HOTEL €
(☑0763 34 20 11; www.hotelmaitani.com; Via Lorenzo Maitani 5; s/d €79/130, breakfast €10; 🖥) Polished parquet floors, sober antique furnishings and cathedral views (in some rooms) are a winning combination at this thoughtful hotel.

B&B VALENTINA — B&B €
(☑0763 34 16 07; www.bandbvalentina.com; Via Vivaria 7; s €40-70, d €50-130, tr €70-130) On a cobbled alley, Valentina offers casually elegant, spacious rooms, some with kitchen facilities, and also has a couple of apartments available.

DAY TRIPS FROM ROME ORVIETO

Sleeping

From opulent five-star palaces to chic boutique hotels, family-run pensions, B&Bs, hostels and convents, Rome has accommodation to please everyone, from the fussiest prince to the most impecunious nun. But while there's plenty of choice, rates are universally high and you'll need to book early to get the best deal.

Rates & Payment

Although Rome doesn't have a low season as such, the majority of hotels offer discounts from November to March (excluding the Christmas and New Year period) and from mid-July through August. Expect to pay top whack in spring (April to June) and autumn (September and October) and over the main holiday periods (Christmas, New Year and Easter). Nowadays, the rates that many hotels apply change on a daily basis and can often vary enormously depending on demand, season and booking method (online, through an agency etc). Where possible, we've given prices for the low-season minimum and high-season maximum, unless there's a single year-round price. Most midrange and top-end hotels accept credit cards. Budget places might, but it's always best to check in advance. Many smaller places offer discounts of up to 10% for payment in cash.

Getting There

Most tourist areas are a bus ride or metro journey away from Stazione Termini. If you come by car, be warned that much of the city centre is a ZTL (limited traffic zone) and off-limits to unauthorised traffic – see the Transport chapter, p318, for more details. Note also that there is a terrible lack of on-site parking facilities in the city centre, though your hotel should be able to direct you to a private garage. Street parking is not recommended.

Pensions & Hotels

The bulk of accommodation in Rome consists of *pensioni* (pensions) and *alberghi* (hotels).

A *pensione* is a small, family-run hotel or guesthouse. In Rome they are generally housed in converted apartments. Rooms tend to be simple and although most come with a private bathroom, those that don't will usually have a basin and bidet.

Hotels are bigger and more expensive than *pensioni,* but at the cheaper end of the market there's often little difference between the two. All hotels are rated from one to five stars, although this rating relates to facilities only and gives no indication of value, comfort, atmosphere or friendliness. Most hotels in Rome's city centre tend to be three-star and up. As a rule, a room in a three-star hotel will come with a hairdryer, minibar (or fridge), safe and air-conditioning. Many will also have satellite TV and internet connection.

A common complaint in Rome is that hotel rooms are small. This is especially true in the *centro storico* (historic centre) and Trastevere, where many hotels are housed in centuries-old *palazzi* (mansions). Similarly, a spacious lift is a rare find, particularly in older *palazzi,* and you'll seldom find one that can accommodate more than one average-sized person with luggage.

Breakfast in cheaper hotels is rarely worth setting the alarm for, so, if you have the option, save a few euros and pop into a bar for a coffee and *cornetto* (croissant).

B&Bs & Guesthouses

Alongside the hundreds of traditional B&Bs (private homes offering a room or two to paying guests), Rome has a large number of boutique-style guesthouses that offer chic, upmarket accommodation at midrange to top-end prices. Note also that breakfast in a Roman B&B is usually a combination of bread rolls, croissants, ham and cheese.

Hostels

Rome's hostels cater to everyone from backpackers to budget-minded families. Many hostels offer traditional dorms as well as smart hotel-style rooms (singles, doubles, even family rooms) with private bathrooms. Curfews are generally a thing of the past and some places even have a 24-hour reception. Many hostels don't accept prior reservations for dorm beds, so arrive after 10am and it's first come, first served.

For information on Rome and Italy's official Hostelling International hostels, contact the **Italian Youth Hostel Association** (Associazione Italiana Alberghi per la Gioventù; Map p376; ☑06 487 11 52; www.aighostels.com; Via Cavour 44).

Religious Institutions

Unsurprisingly, Rome is well furnished with religious institutions, many of which offer cheap(ish) rooms for the night. Bear in mind, though, that many have strict curfews and that the accommodation, while spotlessly clean, tends to be short on frills. Also, while there are a number of centrally located options, many convents are situated out of the centre, typically in the districts north and west of the Vatican. Book well in advance.

Rental Accommodation

For longer stays, renting an apartment might well work out cheaper than an extended hotel sojourn. Bank on spending about €900 per month for a studio apartment or a small one-bedroom place. For longer-term stays, you will probably have to pay bills plus a condominium charge for building maintenance. A room in a shared apartment will cost from €600 per month, plus bills. You'll usually be asked to pay a deposit equal to one or two months' rent and the first month in advance.

Accommodation Websites

The Comune di Roma's **tourist information line** (☑06 06 08; www.060608.it; ☺9am-9pm) has an extensive list of B&Bs, rentals and hotels. Prices are quoted for many places but are not always up to date.

HOTELS

You can consult a list of author-reviewed accommodation options on Lonely Planet's website (hotels.lonelyplanet.com) and book directly online.

For a mini-apartment in a hotel block, go online at www.060608.it and click on Hospitality, Sleeping, Apartment Hotels. Some hotels also offer apartment rental.

B&BS

These agencies offer online booking:
➡ **Bed & Breakfast Association of Rome** (Map p382; www.b-b.rm.it) Lists B&Bs and short-term apartment rentals.
➡ **Bed & Breakfast Italia** (www.bbitalia.it) Rome's longest-established B&B network.
➡ **Cross Pollinate** (www.cross-pollinate. com) Has B&Bs, private apartments and guesthouses.

RELIGIOUS INSTITUTIONS

Santa Susanna (www.santasusanna.org/com ingToRome/convents.html) provides a useful list of religious institutions which also offer accommodation.

RENTAL ACCOMMODATION

Useful rental resources:
➡ **Accommodations Rome** (www. accomodationsrome.com)
➡ **Flat in Rome** (www.flatinrome.it)
➡ **Leisure in Rome** (www.leisureinrome.com)
➡ **Rental in Rome** (www.rentalinrome.com)
➡ **Sleep in Italy** (www.sleepinitaly.com)

SLEEPING

NEED TO KNOW

Price Ranges
These price ranges are for rooms with a private bathroom, and unless otherwise stated include breakfast. The following price indicators apply for a high-season double room:

€	under €120
€€	€120 to €250
€€€	€250 and up

Reservations
➡ Always try to book ahead, especially if coming in high season or for a major religious festival.

➡ Ask for a *camera matrimoniale* for a room with a double bed; a *camera doppia* (literally 'double room') has twin beds.

➡ There's a **hotel reservation service** (Map p376; ☑06 699 10 00; booking fee €3; ☉7am-10pm) next to the tourist office at Stazione Termini.

Checking In & Out
➡ Checkout is usually between 10am and noon. In hostels it's around 9am.

➡ Some guesthouses and B&Bs require you to arrange a time to check in.

➡ If you're going to arrive late, mention this when you book your room.

Lonely Planet's Top Choices

Babuino 181 (p259) Chic luxury on top shopping street.

Arco del Lauro (p262) Minimalist comfort in Trastevere B&B.

Beehive (p260) This place puts the boutique into hostel accommodation.

Hotel Villa Mangili (p264) A charming postcard-pretty villa.

Best by Budget

€
Athea Inn (p264) Designer comfort at budget prices.

Beehive (p260) Classy hostel near Termini.

Hotel Panda (p258) A budget bastion in a pricey shopping district.

Arco del Lauro (p262) A cool bolthole in happening Trastevere.

€€
Hotel Villa Mangili (p264) Delightful villa in an exclusive neighbourhood.

Daphne Inn (p258) Boutique hotel with superlative service.

€€€
Babuino 181 (p259) Bask in understated luxury.

Donna Camilla Savelli (p263) Five-star accommodation in a former convent.

Villa Laetitia (p260) Gorgeous riverside villa with fabulous Fendi decor.

Best for Location

Albergo Abruzzi (p257) Wake up opposite the Pantheon.

Teatropace 33 (p257) A short hop from Piazza Navona.

Hotel Scalinata di Spagna (p258) At the top of the Spanish Steps.

Casa di Santa Brigida (p257) A convent overlooking Piazza Farnese.

Best for Romance

Donna Camilla Savelli (p263) Court your loved one at this ex-convent classic.

Hotel Sant'Anselmo (p264) Escape to this beautiful Liberty-style villa.

Hotel Locarno (p259) Star in your own romance at this art-deco gem.

Where to Stay

Neighbourhood	For	Against
Ancient Rome	Close to major sights such as Colosseum, Roman Forum and Capitoline Museums; quiet at night.	Not cheap and has few budget options; restaurants tend to be touristy.
Centro Storico	Most atmospheric part of Rome with everything on your doorstep – Pantheon, Piazza Navona, restaurants, bars and shops.	Most expensive part of town; few budget options; can be noisy.
Tridente, Trevi & the Quirinale	Good for Spanish Steps, Trevi Fountain and designer shopping; excellent mid-range to top-end options; good transport links.	Decidedly upmarket area with prices to match; subdued after dark.
Vatican City, Borgo & Prati	Near St Peter's Basilica and Vatican Museums; decent range of accommodation; some excellent shops and restaurants; on the metro.	Expensive near St Peter's; not much nightlife; sells out quickly for religious holidays.
Monti, Esquilino & San Lorenzo	Lots of budget accommodation around Stazione Termini; some top eating options in Monti and good nightlife in San Lorenzo; good transport links.	Some dodgy streets in Termini area, which is not Rome's most characterful.
Trastevere & Gianicolo	Gorgeous, atmospheric area; party vibe with hundreds of bars, cafes, restaurants and trattorias; some interesting sights.	Very noisy, particularly on summer nights; expensive; hotel rooms often small.
San Giovanni to Testaccio	More authentic than many central areas, with good eating and drinking options; Aventino is a quiet, romantic area, Testaccio a top nightlife district.	Few options available and away from San Giovanni not many big sights.
Southern Rome	Trendy area with cool clubs and bars; on metro line B.	Few sights; disused factories give an industrial feel that's not for everyone.
Villa Borghese & Northern Rome	Largely residential area good for the Auditorium and some top museums; generally quiet after dark.	Out of the centre; few budget choices.

🛏 Ancient Rome

HOTEL NERVA
HOTEL €€

(Map p356; ☎06 678 18 35; www.hotelnerva. com; Via Tor de' Conti 3; s €50-149, d €69-229; ❄🛜; MCavour) Cheerful and family-run, the Nerva is tucked away on a narrow road behind the Imperial Forums. A small place, it manages to squeeze 22 carpeted rooms onto its three floors as well as plenty of Roman paraphernalia. At the time of research, some rooms were about to be refurbished.

CAESAR HOUSE
HOTEL €€

(Map p356; ☎06 679 26 74; www.caesarhouse. com; Via Cavour 310; s €150-200, d €160-260; ❄🛜; MCavour) Quiet and friendly, yet in the thick of it on Via Cavour, this is a small hotel in a renovated apartment. Its public areas are polished and modern, while the six guest rooms feature tiled floors, soothing colours and four-poster beds.

FORTY SEVEN
BOUTIQUE HOTEL €€€

(Map p356; ☎06 678 78 16; www.fortysevenho tel.com; Via Petroselli 47; r €170-300; ❄🛜; 🚇Via Petroselli) This classy retreat sits at the back of the Roman Forum near the Bocca della Verità. Its plain grey facade opens onto a bright modern interior, full of sunshine and sharply designed guest rooms. There's also a panoramic rooftop restaurant (open to everyone, meals about €60), while in the basement you can sweat away your troubles in the gym and Turkish bath.

HOTEL FORUM
HOTEL €€€

(Map p356; ☎06 679 24 46; www.hotelforum. com; Via Tor de' Conti 25; r €180-350; ❄🛜; MCavour) The stately Forum offers formal elegance and stunning views. From the rooftop restaurant, you can look down on a sea of ancient ruins stretching from the Campidoglio to the Colosseum. Inside, the look is old world, with antiques and leather armchairs, wood-panelling and dangling chandeliers.

🛏 Centro Storico

ALBERGO DEL SOLE
PENSION €

(Map p360; ☎06 687 94 46; www.solealbiscione. it; Via del Biscione 76; s €70-100, d €100-145, tr €120-180; ❄🛜; 🚇Corso Vittorio Emanuele II) One of the few budget options in the historic centre, this is said to be the oldest hotel in Rome, dating back to 1462. There's nothing special about the functional rooms but there's a pleasant 2nd-floor roof terrace, and the location near Campo de' Fiori is excellent. No credit cards and no breakfast.

HOTEL DUE TORRI
HOTEL €€

(Map p360; ☎06 6880 6956; www.hotelduetorri roma.com; Vicolo del Leonetto 23; s €80-150, d €140-230; ❄🛜; 🚇Via di Monte Brianzo) The Hotel Due Torri has always offered discretion – first as a residence for cardinals, then as a brothel, and now as a refined hotel. The look is classic, with period furniture, gilt-framed mirrors and parquet floors, and while rooms aren't huge they're bright and comfortable.

DIMORA DEGLI DEI
BOUTIQUE HOTEL €€

(Map p360; ☎06 6819 3267; www.pantheondi moradeglidei.com; Via del Seminario 87; r €120-200; ❄🛜; 🚇Largo di Torre Argentina) Location and discreet style are the selling points of this elegant hideaway only metres from the Pantheon. On the 1st floor of a centuries-old *palazzo* are six spacious, high-ceilinged rooms, each named after a Roman god and each tastefully furnished.

HOTEL TAX

Everyone overnighting in Rome has to pay a room-occupancy tax on top of their regular accommodation bill. This amounts to:

➡ €1 per person per night for a maximum of five days in campsites

➡ €2 per person per night for a maximum of 10 days in *agriturismi* (farmstay accommodation), B&Bs, guesthouses, convents, monasteries and one-, two- and three-star hotels

➡ €3 per person per night for a maximum of 10 days in four- and five-star hotels

The tax is applicable to anyone who is not a resident in Rome. Prices quoted in this chapter do not include the tax.

SLEEPING CENTRO STORICO

RELAIS PALAZZO TAVERNA
BOUTIQUE HOTEL €€

(Map p360; ☎06 2039 8064; www.relaispalazzo
taverna.com; Via dei Gabrielli 92; s €80-150, d
€100-210, tr €120-240; ❄☎; ᐧCorso del Rinascimento) Housed in a 15th-century *palazzo*,
this boutique hotel is superbly located off
a cobbled pedestrian-only street. Its six
rooms cut a stylish dash with white wood-
beamed ceilings, funky wallpaper and dark
parquet.

HOTEL FONTANELLA BORGHESE
HOTEL €€

(Map p360; ☎06 6880 9504; www.fontanella
borghese.com; Largo Fontanella Borghese 84; s
€90-130, d €120-190; ❄☎; ᐧVia del Corso) This
friendly three-star sits on the 2nd floor of an
imposing aristocratic palace, once owned by
the powerful Borghese family. From reception, carpeted corridors lead off to smart,
classically designed rooms furnished with
period-style furniture, honey-tinted parquet
and the occasional chandelier.

TEATROPACE 33
HOTEL €€

(Map p360; ☎06 687 90 75; www.hotelteatro
pace.com; Via del Teatro Pace 33; s €80-150, d
€130-270; ❄☎; ᐧCorso del Rinascimento) Near
Piazza Navona, this welcoming three-star is
a classy choice with 23 beautifully appointed
rooms decorated with parquet, damask curtains and exposed wood beams. There's no
lift, just a monumental 17th-century stone
staircase and a porter to carry your bags.

CASA DI SANTA BRIGIDA
RELIGIOUS ACCOMMODATION €€

(Map p360; ☎06 6889 2596; www.brigidine.org;
Piazza Farnese 96, entrance Via di Monserrato 54;
s/d €120/200; ❄☎; ᐧCorso Vittorio Emanuele
II) Named after the Swedish St Brigid who
died here in 1373, this tranquil convent enjoys a superb location overlooking Piazza
Farnese. Rooms are simple, clean and decidedly low-tech – entertainment here is
limited to a piano in the communal room,
a small library and views from the roof
terrace.

CASA BANZO
B&B €€

(Map p362; ☎06 683 39 09; www.casabanzo.it;
Piazza del Monte di Pietà 30; r €100-135, apt €180-
220; ❄; ᐧVia Arenula) Not an easy place to
find (there's no sign), Casa Banzo has seven
simply decorated rooms and two ground-
floor apartments in a 16th-century *palazzo*
near Campo de' Fiori. The facilities are
modest and rooms are a little dark, but the

fantastic location, monumental setting and
polite staff more than make up for it.

HOTEL TEATRO DI POMPEO
HOTEL €€

(Map p360; ☎06 6830 0170; www.hotelteatrodi
pompeo.it; Largo del Pallaro 8; s €100-165, d €120-
220; ❄@☎; ᐧCorso Vittorio Emanuele II) Built
on top of a 1st-century BC theatre (now
the breakfast room), this charming hotel
is tucked away behind Campo de' Fiori.
Rooms boast a classic old-fashioned feel
with polished wood bedsteads and terracotta floor tiles. The best rooms, on the 3rd
floor, have sloping wood-beamed ceilings.

HOTEL NAVONA
HOTEL €€

(Map p360; ☎06 6821 1392; www.hotelnavona.
com; Via dei Sediari 8; s €60-170, d €60-260; ❄☎;
ᐧCorso del Rinascimento) The Navona has a
good range of rooms spread over several
floors of a 15th-century *palazzo* near Piazza
Navona. Those on the reception floor feature gilt-framed decor and antique furniture, while upstairs you'll find modern grey
and silvers and mosaic-tiled bathrooms.
Breakfast is €10 extra.

ARGENTINA RESIDENZA
BOUTIQUE HOTEL €€

(Map p360; ☎06 6819 3267; www.argentinaresi
denza.com; Via di Torre Argentina 47; r €120-200;
❄☎; ᐧLargo di Torre Argentina) Escape the
hustle of Largo di Torre Argentina and relax in the comfort of this quiet boutique hotel. On the 3rd floor of a towering *palazzo*,
rooms are tastefully furnished in discreet
modern style. Breakfast costs €10 extra.

★ HOTEL CAMPO DE' FIORI
BOUTIQUE HOTEL €€€

(Map p360; ☎06 687 48 86; www.hotelcampo
defiori.com; Via del Biscione 6; r & apt €90-600;
❄@☎; ᐧCorso Vittorio Emanuele II) This rakish four-star has got the lot – sexy decor, an
enviable location, professional staff and a
panoramic roof terrace. Rooms are individually decorated but they all feel delightfully
decadent with boldly coloured walls, low
wooden ceilings, gilt mirrors and restored
bric-a-brac. The hotel also has 13 apartments, ideal for families.

ALBERGO ABRUZZI
HOTEL €€€

(Map p360; ☎06 679 20 21; www.hotelabruzzi.it;
Piazza della Rotonda 69; s €110-200, d €120-340;
❄☎; ᐧLargo di Torre Argentina) This popular
three-star hotel enjoys one of Rome's premier locations, bang opposite the Pantheon.
But while it's a friendly place and the rooms

are comfortable, it's a tight squeeze and late-night noise can be a problem.

🛏 Tridente, Trevi & the Quirinale

HOTEL PANDA   PENSION €

(Map p364; 📞06 678 01 79; www.hotelpanda.it; Via della Croce 35; s €65-80, d €85-108, tr €120-140, q €180; 🛜; MSpagna) Only 50m from the Spanish Steps, in an area where a bargain is a Bulgari watch bought at the sales, the friendly, efficient Panda is an anomaly: a budget pension and a splendid one. The clean rooms are smallish but nicely furnished, and there are several triples with a bed on a cosy mezzanine. Air-con costs €6 per night. Book well ahead.

LA PICCOLA MAISON   B&B €

(Map p364; 📞06 4201 6331; www.lapiccola maison.com; Via dei Cappuccini 30; s €50-180, d €70-200; ❄🛜; MVittorio Emanuele II) The excellent Piccola Maison is housed in a 19th-century building in a great location close to Piazza Barberini, and has pleasingly plain, neutrally decorated rooms and thoughtful staff. It's a great deal.

OKAPI ROOMS   HOTEL €

(Map p364; 📞06 3260 9815; www.okapirooms.it; Via della Penna 57; s €65-80, d €85-120, tr €110-140, q €120-180; ❄🛜; MFlaminio) Twenty-room Okapi occupies a townhouse in a great location close to Piazza del Popolo. Rooms are simple, small, airy affairs with cream walls, terracotta floors and double glazing. Some are decorated with ancient-style carvings, and several have small terraces. Bathrooms are tiny but sparkling clean.

HOTEL ERCOLI   PENSION €

(📞06 474 54 54; www.hotelercoli.com; Via Collina 48; s €50-80, d €75-100; ❄🛜; 🖥Via Piave) Old-fashioned and friendly, the 3rd-floor Ercoli (there's an elderly cage lift) is a straight-up *pensione*, renovated a couple of years back. It's popular with foreign students. The 14 rooms are functional rather than memorable, but they're all sparkling clean with tiled floors. Breakfast is included and the air-con works.

DAPHNE INN   BOUTIQUE HOTEL €€

(Map p364; 📞06 8745 0086; www.daphne-rome. com; Via di San Basilio 55; s €110-180, d €140-230, without bathroom s €70-130, d €90-160; ❄🛜;

MBarberini) Daphne is a gem, run by an American-Italian couple. The chic, sleek, comfortable rooms come in various shapes and sizes but the overall look is minimalist, modern-hued in earthy tones. The English-speaking staff are exceedingly helpful. There is another **branch** (Map p364; Via degli Avignonesi 20) just a few streets away.

CROSSING CONDOTTI   GUESTHOUSE €€

(Map p364; 📞06 6992 0633; www.crossingcon dotti.com; Via Mario de' Fiori 28; r €190-320; ❄🛜; MSpagna) A five-room place, this is one of Rome's breed of upmarket guesthouses, where all the fittings, linen and comforts are top of the range, and the pretty though not large rooms have lots of character and antique furnishings. There's also a well-stocked kitchen with drinks and a Nespresso machine.

GREGORIANA   HOTEL €€

(Map p364; 📞06 679 42 69; www.hotelgregori ana.it; Via Gregoriana 18; s €120-270, d €180-270; ❄; MSpagna) This low-key, polished art-deco hotel is fantastically set behind the Spanish Steps. Beds have beautiful, circular maple-wood headboards, snow-white linen and lots of gleaming rosewood. Staff are friendly and unpretentious.

CENCI   B&B €€

(Map p364; 📞340 3556788; www.cencibedand breakfast.it; Vicolo Scavolino 61; d €140-170; ❄@🛜; MBarberini) There are only three rooms, so the early birds will snag this cool place with contemporary decor in warm hues that complement the high ceilings and sunny rooms. It is virtually atop the Trevi Fountain. Minimum three nights' stay.

HOTEL SCALINATA DI SPAGNA   HOTEL €€

(Map p364; 📞06 6994 0896; www.hotelscali nata.com; Piazza della Trinità dei Monti 17; d €110-190; ❄@🛜; MSpagna) Given its location – perched alongside the Spanish Steps – the Scalinata is surprisingly modestly priced. An informal and friendly place, it's something of a warren, with a great roof terrace and low corridors leading off to smallish, old-fashioned yet romantic rooms. Book early for a room with a view.

HOTEL MOZART   HOTEL €€

(Map p364; 📞06 3600 1915; www.hotelmozart. com; Via dei Greci 23b; r €120-260; ❄@🛜; MSpagna) A credit-card's flourish from Via del Corso, the Mozart has classic, immaculate rooms, decorated in dove greys, eggshell blues, golden yellows and rosy pinks, with comfortable beds, gleaming linen and polished wooden furniture; deluxe rooms have jacuzzis and small terraces. It also administers the Vivaldi Luxury Suites and several apartments nearby.

HOTEL BAROCCO   HOTEL €€

(Map p364; ✆06 487 20 01; www.hotelbarocco. com; Piazza Barberini 9; d €170-290; ※@হ; ⓂBarberini) Very central, this well-run, welcoming 41-room hotel overlooking Piazza Barberini (the pricier rooms have views) has a classic feel, with rooms featuring oil paintings, spotless linen, gentle colour schemes and fabric-covered walls. Breakfast is ample and served in a wood-panelled room.

HOTEL LOCARNO   HOTEL €€

(Map p364; ✆06 361 08 41; www.hotellocarno. com; Via della Penna 22; s €90-140, d €100-180; ※@হ; ⓂFlaminio) With its ivy-clad exterior, stained-glass doors and rattling cage lift, the Locarno is an art-deco classic – the kind of place Hercule Poirot might stay at if he were in town. Many rooms have silk wallpaper and period furniture, occasionally in need of renovation, but full of period charm. There's a roof garden, a restaurant and an atmospheric bar.

HOTEL MODIGLIANI   HOTEL €€

(Map p364; ✆06 4281 5226; www.hotelmodi gliani.com; Via della Purificazione 42; s €100-180, d €110-200; ※হ; ⓂBarberini) Run by an artistic couple, the Modigliani is all about attention to detail and customer service. The 23 dove-grey rooms are spacious and light, and the best ones have views and balconies, either outside or over the quiet internal courtyard garden.

★BABUINO 181   BOUTIQUE HOTEL €€€

(Map p364; ✆06 3229 5295; www.romeluxury suites.com/babuino; Via del Babuino 181; r €180-780; ※হ) A beautifully renovated old *palazzo*, Babuino offers discreet luxury, with great attention to detail, a sleek roof terrace and modern, chic rooms with touches such as a Nespresso machine and fluffy bathrobes. A new annexe across the street has added more suites and rooms that continue the theme of understated elegance.

PORTRAIT SUITES   BOUTIQUE HOTEL €€€

(Map p364; ✆06 6938 0742; www.portraitsuites. com; Via Bocca di Leone 23; r €450-650; ※হ;

Ⓜ Flaminio) Owned by the Ferragamo family, this is an exclusive residence with 14 exquisite suites and not huge but opulent-feeling studios across six floors in an elegant townhouse, plus a dreamy 360-degree roof terrace and made-in-heaven staff. There's no restaurant, but you can have meals delivered. Breakfast is served in your room or on the terrace.

HOTEL DE RUSSIE   HOTEL €€€

(Map p364; ✆06 32 88 81; www.hotelderussie.it; Via del Babuino 9; d €460-690; ※@; ⓂFlaminio) The historic de Russie is almost on Piazza del Popolo, and has exquisite terraced gardens. The decor is softly luxurious in many shades of grey, and the rooms offer state-of-the-art entertainment systems, massive mosaic-tiled bathrooms and all the luxuries. There's a lovely courtyard bar.

HASSLER VILLA MEDICI   HOTEL €€€

(Map p364; ✆06 69 93 40; www.hotelhassler roma.com; Piazza della Trinità dei Monti 6; d €370-700; ※@হ; ⓂSpagna) Surmounting the Spanish Steps, the Hassler has been recently renovated but remains a byword for old-school luxury. A long line of VIPs have stayed here, enjoying the ravishing views and sumptuous hospitality. The Michelin-starred restaurant Imàgo has a great city view. Under the same management is nearby boutique Il Palazzetto (Map p364; ✆06 699 341 000; www.ilpalazzettoroma.com; Vicolo del Bottino 8), with views over the Spanish Steps.

🛏 Vatican City, Borgo & Prati

HOTEL SAN PIETRINO   HOTEL €

(Map p368; ✆06 370 01 32; www.sanpietrino.it; Via Bettolo 43; s €45-75, d €55-112, without bathroom s €35-55, d €45-85; ※@হ; ⓂOttaviano–San Pietro) Within easy walking distance of St Peter's, San Pietrino is an excellent budget choice. Its cosy rooms are characterful and prettily decorated with terracotta-tiled floors and the occasional statue. There's no breakfast but a drinks machine can supply emergency coffee.

BIBI E ROMEO'S   B&B €

(Map p368; ✆346 9656937; www.bberomeo. com; Via Andrea Doria 36; s €50-80, d €60-130, tr €90-130, q €100-150; ※হ; ⓂOttaviano–San Pietro) Up from a broad cafe-lined avenue,

SLEEPING VATICAN CITY, BORGO & PRATI

this excellent B&B offers a warm welcome and smart, modern rooms themed after four writers – Neruda, Pessoa, Terzani and Santagostino. There's a kitchen for guest use (with microwave and fridge), and the owners are a mine of local information.

COLORS HOTEL
HOTEL €

(Map p368; 📞06 687 40 30; www.colorshotel. com; Via Boezio 31; s €35-90, d €45-125; ❄️🖥️; 🚇Via Cola di Rienzo) Popular with young travellers, this is a bright budget hotel with smart, vibrantly coloured rooms spread over three floors (no lift though). There are also cheaper rooms with shared bathrooms and, from June to August, dorms (€12 to €35 per person) for guests under 38.

CASA DI ACCOGLIENZA PAOLO VI
RELIGIOUS ACCOMMODATION €

(Map p368; 📞06 390 91 41; www.casapaolosesto. it; Viale Vaticano 92; s €35-40, d €65-70, tr €83-88; ❄️🖥️; 🚇Ottaviano–San Pietro) This tranquil, palm-shaded convent is ideally positioned for the Vatican Museums. The resident nuns keep everything ship-shape and the 21 small, sunny rooms are clean as a pin, if slightly institutional in feel. No breakfast.

HOTEL BRAMANTE
HOTEL €€

(Map p368; 📞06 6880 6426; www.hotelbra mante.com; Vicolo delle Palline 24-25; s €100-160, d €140-240, tr €170-250, q €175-260; ❄️🖥️; 🚇Piazza del Risorgimento) Tucked away in an alleyway under the Vatican walls, the Bramante exudes country-house charm with its cosy internal courtyard and quietly elegant rooms – think rugs, wood-beamed ceilings and antiques. It's housed in the 16th-century building where architect Domenico Fontana once lived.

HOTEL FLORIDA
HOTEL €€

(Map p368; 📞06 324 18 72; www.hotelflorida roma.it; Via Cola di Rienzo 243; s €40-150, d €50-170, tr €65-200, q €80-210; ❄️🖥️; 🚇Via Cola di Rienzo) This friendly two-star on Prati's main shopping strip is housed on the 1st floor of a lofty townhouse. It's nothing flash but the modern rooms are a decent size and come with en suite designer bathrooms. Breakfast is optional at €5.

HOTEL GIUGGIOLI
HOTEL €€

(Map p368; 📞06 3600 5389; www.hotelgiuggio lirome.com; Via Germanico 198; s €60-140, d €70-180; ❄️🖥️; 🚇Lepanto) The pick of several hotels in the same building, the 1st-floor

Giuggioli offers nine dapper, pearl-grey rooms with a minimum of furniture and large, comfortable beds. Three floors up, the Giuggioli's sister hotel, the Hotel dei Quiriti, has more old-fashioned rooms for the same price.

★VILLA LAETITIA
BOUTIQUE HOTEL €€€

(📞06 322 67 76; www.villalaetitia.com; Lungotevere delle Armi 22; r from €190; ❄️🖥️; 🚇Lepanto) A stunning boutique hotel in a graceful riverside villa owned by the famous Fendi fashion family. The 14 gorgeous rooms are all individually decorated – particularly impressive is the Crystal Room with its perspex furniture, and the Garden Room with its original Picasso – and each comes with its own kitchen facilities. Breakfast is not included.

🛏️ Monti, Esquilino & San Lorenzo

★BEEHIVE
HOSTEL €

(Map p376; 📞06 4470 4553; www.the-beehive. com; Via Marghera 8; dm €25-30, s €50-60, d €90-100, without bathroom s €40-50, d €80-90, tr €95-105; ❄️🖥️; 🚇Termini) 🍃 More boutique-chic than backpacker crash pad, the Beehive is one of the best hostels in town. Run by a southern-Californian couple, it's an oasis of style with original artworks on the walls, funky modular furniture and a vegetarian cafe (room prices don't include breakfast). Beds are in a spotless, eight-person mixed dorm or in one of six private double rooms, all with fans; private rooms now have aircon too (€10 per night). Book ahead.

HOTEL DOLOMITI
HOTEL €

(Map p376; 📞06 495 72 56; www.hotel-dolomiti. it; Via San Martino della Battaglia 11; s €45-100, d €60-160, extra person €20-35; ❄️@🖥️; 🚇Castro Pretorio) Welcoming, family-run Dolomiti has rooms on the 4th floor of an apartment block. The rooms are colour-coordinated with cream walls, cherry-wood furniture, rich-red fabrics and prints of chubby-cheeked cherubs. The same family manages the similar Hotel Lachea two floors below. The combined reception is on the 1st floor.

NICOLAS INN
B&B €

(Map p376; 📞06 9761 8483; www.nicolasinn. com; Via Cavour 295, 1st fl; s €95-160, d €100-180; ❄️🖥️; 🚇Cavour) This sunny B&B is on noisy Via Cavour. Run by a welcoming young couple, it has four big guest rooms, each of which boasts homely furnishings with wrought-iron beds, colourful pictures and a large bathroom. For such a central place it's remarkably quiet, and has a long line of satisfied customers. No children under five.

HOTEL GIULIANA
HOTEL €

(Map p376; ✆06 488 07 95; www.hotelgiuliana.com; Via Agostino de Pretis 70; s €60-85, d €80-140; ✳; Ⓜ Termini) A cosy little hotel, run by a jolly Londoner and her daughter, the Giuliana ticks all the right boxes. Rooms, divided into standard and superior, are dapper; the location, near Via Nazionale, is convenient; and the service is cheery and efficient.

ABERDEEN HOTEL
HOTEL €

(Map p376; ✆06 482 39 20; www.hotelaberdeen.it; Via Firenze 48; s €57-82, d €71-110; ✳ @; Ⓜ Repubblica) This sparkling three-star is a decent, easygoing hotel in a well-connected, central location. The spacious rooms feature chequered floors, comfy beds and spotless mint-green bathrooms. Buffet breakfast is served under a charming, coffered wood ceiling, and the staff are cheerful, cordial and helpful.

HOTEL CERVIA
PENSION €

(Map p376; ✆06 49 10 57; www.hotelcerviaroma.com; Via Palestro 55; s €35-70, d €50-90, without bathroom s €20-35, d €40-65; ☎; Ⓜ Castro Pretorio) Considerately run by two friendly, multilingual sisters, the Cervia is a welcoming and good-value place. Children are welcome, with free cots available on request. Wi-fi is downstairs only. They offer dorm beds (€15 to €20) from July to August, but it's worth asking at other times of year.

WELROME HOTEL
HOTEL €

(Map p376; ✆06 4782 4343; www.welrome.it; Via Calatafimi 15-19; d/tr/q €110/148/187; ✳ ☎; Ⓜ Termini) Not only does Mary de Rosa take huge pride in her small, spotless hotel, but she will also enthusiastically point out the cheapest places to eat, tell you where not to waste your time and suggest what's good to do. Families should go for the large room named after Piazza di Spagna; a cot is provided at no extra charge.

PAPA GERMANO
HOTEL €

(Map p376; ✆06 48 69 19; www.hotelpapagermano.it; Via Calatafimi 14a; dm €18-30, d €60-110, without bathroom s €50-65, d €60-90; ✳ @ ☎; Ⓜ Termini) Easygoing and popular, Papa Germano is a budget stalwart. There are various sleeping options, ranging from four-person dorms to private rooms with or without bathrooms. It has a family-run feel, the decor is plain and fairly smart, and all rooms are scrupulously clean.

ALESSANDRO PALACE HOSTEL
HOSTEL €

(Map p376; ✆06 446 19 58; www.hostelsalessandro.com; Via Vicenza 42; dm €19-35, d €70-120, tr €95-120; ✳ @ ☎; Ⓜ Castro Pretorio) This long-standing, well-kept favourite offers spick-and-span, terracotta-floored doubles and triples, as well as dorms sleeping from four to eight, all with cheery bedspreads. Every room has its own bathroom with hairdryer. There's a basement bar and it runs local tours.

ALBERGO GIUSTI
RELIGIOUS ACCOMMODATION €

(Map p376; ✆06 7045 3462; http://hotelgiusti.com/en/enhome.html; Via Giusti 5; s/d €50/90; ✳ @; Ⓜ Vittorio Emanuele II) This spartan, spotless bed-and-breakfast is a great deal and feels very safe, if lacking in character and frills. It's run by the sisters of Sant'Anna in a convent in the side streets near the Basilica di Santa Maria Maggiore. Rooms are salmon-pink or institutional mint-green, and a few have small balconies.

HOTEL & HOSTEL DES ARTISTES
HOTEL €

(Map p376; ✆06 445 43 65; www.hoteldesartistes.com; Via Villafranca 20; dm €12-23, s €34-114, d €39-160, tr €80-120, q €100-140; ✳ @; Ⓜ Castro Pretorio) The wide range of rooms here (including triples and family rooms) are decked out in wood and gold, with faux-antique furniture and rich reds, gilt lamps and terracotta or tiled floors, and have decent bathrooms. Offers discounts for longer stays and/or cash payment.

HOTEL ARTORIUS
HOTEL €€

(Map p376; ✆06 482 11 96; www.hotelartoriusrome.com; Via del Boschetto 13; d €130-185; ✳ @ ☎; Ⓜ Cavour) The art-deco-flavoured lobby looks promising, and the rest delivers too in this 10-room Monti hotel with a family-run feel. Rooms are simple and plain – not large but perfectly comfortable – and one (room 109) has a terrace.

DUCA D'ALBA
HOTEL €€

(Map p376; ✆06 48 44 71; www.hotelducadalba.com; Via Leonina 14; r €70-200; ✳ ☎; Ⓜ Cavour)

This appealing four-star hotel in the Monti district has small but charming rooms: most have fabric-covered or handpainted walls, wood-beamed ceilings, big flat-screeen TVs and sleek button-studded headboards.

RESIDENZA CELLINI
GUESTHOUSE €€

(Map p376; ✆06 4782 5204; www.residenzace llini.it; Via Modena 5; d €120-240, tr €150-260; ❀@🛜; Ⓜ Repubblica) With grown-up furnishings featuring potted palms, polished wood, pale-yellow walls, oil paintings and a hint of chintz, this charming, family-run place on a quiet road parallel to Via Nazionale offers spacious, elegant rooms, all with satellite TV and jacuzzi or hydro-massage shower. There's a sunny flower-surrounded terrace for summer breakfasts.

66 IMPERIAL INN
B&B €€

(Map p376; ✆06 482 56 48; www.66imperialinn. com; Via del Viminale 66; s €80-180, d €80-210; ❀🛜; 🚊Via Nazionale) This smart B&B is a cut above, with frescoed hallways and chic and funky rooms that combine designer wallpapers, brilliant silks and gleaming white linen. Rooms also have high ceilings and are airy, comfortable and quiet. The bathrooms are spotless and the jacuzzi showers are a treat. Book ahead.

TARGET INN
GUESTHOUSE €€

(Map p376; ✆06 474 53 99; www.targetinn.com; Via Modena 5, 3rd fl; s €100-150, d €140-170, ste €160-170; ❀@🛜; Ⓜ Repubblica) Sleek, minimalist Target has only seven rooms, featuring high ceilings, red-leather furniture, gleaming white walls, abstract art, black wardrobes and traditional parquet floors. Families should go for the junior suite, which sleeps four.

HOTEL COLUMBIA
HOTEL €€

(Map p376; ✆06 488 35 09; www.hotelcolumbia. com; Via del Viminale 15; d €140-220; ❀@🛜; Ⓜ Termini or Repubblica) In a workaday area sandwiched between Rome's brutalist (on the outside) Opera House and Stazione Termini, the friendly Columbia sports a polished look with beamed or exposed stone ceilings. The white-walled rooms are bright and surprisingly full of character – some have beautiful Murano crystal chandeliers. Breakfast is served on the pretty roof terrace in summer.

HOTEL OCEANIA
HOTEL €€

(Map p376; ✆06 482 46 96; www.hoteloceania. it; Via Firenze 38; s/d €140/180; @🛜; Ⓜ Repubblica) The homely, quaint Oceania is a welcome break from the bustle of the streets five floors below. It's an intimate, old-fashioned hotel, with 34 rooms that have fabric-covered walls and heavy curtains, wooden furnishings and brightly tiled bathrooms. Book early.

RADISSON BLU ES.
HOTEL €€

(Map p376; ✆06 44 48 41; www.radissonblu /eshotel-rome; Via Filippo Turati 171; d €130-250; ❀@🏊; Ⓜ Vittorio Emanuele II) The location may not be the best, unless proximity to Stazione Termini is a must, but the Radisson Blu Es. is a popular choice with business travellers and design-conscious customers who appreciate the sci-fi decor and hi-tech gadgetry; standard rooms verge on the silly, with their central bathroom cubes. The rooftop pool is a plus, and the bar alongside it serves swell cocktails.

★VILLA SPALLETTI TRIVELLI
HOTEL €€€

(Map p376; ✆06 4890 7934; www.villaspalletti.it; Via Piacenza 4; r €450-530; ❀@🛜; Ⓜ Spagna) With 12 rooms in a glorious mansion in central Rome, Villa Spalletti Trivelli has upped the ante for luxurious stays in the capital. Rooms are soberly and elegantly decorated, overlooking the gardens of the Quirinale or the estate's Italian garden. The overall feel is that of staying in the stately home of some aristocratic friends.

🛏 Trastevere & Gianicolo

★ARCO DEL LAURO
B&B €

(Map p372; ✆9am-2pm 06 9784 0350, mobile 346 2443212; www.arcodellauro.it; Via Arco de' Tolomei 27; s €75-125, d €95-145; ❀@🛜; 🚊Viale di Trastevere, 🚊Viale di Trastevere) Through a large stone arch and on a narrow cobbled street, this fab six-room B&B in an ancient *palazzo* is a find, offering gleaming white rooms that combine rustic charm with minimalist simplicity. The largest has a high wood-beamed ceiling. Beds are comfortable, showers are powerful and the owners are eager to please. Book well ahead.

SUITES TRASTEVERE
B&B €

(✆347 0744086; www.trastevere.bbsuites.com; Viale di Trastevere 248; s €70-105, d €80-160; ❀🛜; 🚊Viale di Trastevere, 🚊Viale di Trastevere)

On the 4th floor of a honey-hued *palazzo* on the wide main drag and tramway running from Trastevere: you'll know you're in Rome in this friendly, popular B&B – each room is dramatically frescoed with local sights, such as the Colosseum and the Pantheon.

LA FORESTERIA ORSA MAGGIORE   HOSTEL €
(Map p372; ☑06 689 37 53; www.casainter nazionaledelledonne.org; Via San Francesco di Sales 1a, 2nd fl; dm €26-42, s €55-75, d €110-150, without bathroom s €36-55, d €72-100; @⊕; ⬚Piazza Trilussa) A lesbian-friendly, women-only guesthouse (boys aged 12 or younger are welcome) in a lovely 16th-century convent, close to the river. It is run by the Casa Internazionale delle Donne (International Women's House) and offers safe and well-priced accommodation in a quiet corner of Trastevere. The 13 simple rooms sleep two, four, eight or nine, and some have views onto the attractive internal garden. There's a minimum two-night stay, and a 3am curfew. It's wheelchair-accessible.

RESIDENZA ARCO DE' TOLOMEI   HOTEL €€
(Map p372; ☑06 5832 0819; www.bbarcodei tolomei.com; Via Arco de' Tolomei 27; d €140-200; ⊕⊕; ⬚Piazza Sonnino, ⬚Piazza Sonnino) This gorgeous place is decorated with polished antiques and rich contrasting chintzes that make the interiors feel like a country cottage. It's a lovely place to stay, and the owners are friendly and helpful.

BUONANOTTE GARIBALDI   GUESTHOUSE €€
(Map p372; ☑06 5833 0733; www.buonanotte garibaldi.com; Via Garibaldi 83; r €180-280; ⊕@⊕; ⬚Piazza Sonnino, ⬚Piazza Sonnino) With only three rooms, this is a haven, an upmarket B&B in a divinely pretty inner-city villa, set around a courtyard. The rooms – themed Green, Orange and Blue – are beautifully decorated, and works of art and sculpture are all over the place – this is artist Luisa Longo's house. Pick of the rooms is Blue, upstairs, which opens onto a greenery-shaded terrace.

HOTEL SANTA MARIA   HOTEL €€
(Map p372; ☑06 589 46 26; www.hotelsantama ria.info; Vicolo del Piede 2; s €115-190, d €140-260; ⊛@⊕; ⬚Piazza Sonnino, ⬚Piazza Son-nino) Walk along the ivy-lined approach and you'll enter a tranquil haven. Surrounding a spacious modern cloister (a former convent site), shaded by orange trees, rooms are cool and comfortable, with slightly fussy decor and terracotta floors. There are some larger family rooms. Staff are helpful and professional, and there's access for people with a disability. There are deals offered for longer stays in summer. Its smaller sister is **Residenza Santa Maria** (Map p372; ☑06 5833 5103; www.residenzasantamaria.com; Via dell'Arco di San Calisto 20), located a few streets away.

VILLA DELLA FONTE   B&B €€
(Map p372; ☑06 580 37 97; www.villafonte.com; Via della Fonte dell'Olio 8; s €110-145, d €135-180; ⊛⊕; ⬚Viale di Trastevere, ⬚Viale di Trastevere) A lovely terracotta-hued, ivy-shrouded gem, Villa della Fonte is a romantic choice, occupying a 17th-century building in a street off Piazza Santa Maria in Trastevere. It has only five rooms, all of which are simply decorated but have pretty outlooks, good bathrooms and comfortable beds. The sunny garden terrace (for breakfast in warm weather) is a plus.

★DONNA CAMILLA SAVELLI   HOTEL €€€
(Map p372; ☑06 58 88 61; www.hoteldonna camillasavelli.com; Via Garibaldi 27; d €180-345; ⊛@⊕; ⬚Viale di Trastevere, ⬚Viale di Traste-vere) If you have the cash, stay here, in a converted convent that was designed by baroque genius Borromini. It's been beautifully updated; muted colours complement the serene concave and convex curves of the architecture, and service is excellent. The pricier of the 78 rooms overlook the lovely cloister garden or have views of Rome, and are decorated with antiques, but the cheaper ones are still very lovely.

BARTER FOR A B&B

Money is not the only currency. Some of Rome's B&B owners are now offering stays in return for services provided or even goods supplied. To investigate further, you can check out www.barattobb.it – unfortunately only in Italian – which lists B&Bs participating in this exchange scheme and what they'll accept in lieu of payment, be it English lessons, home repairs or even jewellery.

🛏 San Giovanni to Testaccio

★ATHEA INN
B&B €

(Map p370; ☑06 9893 2666; www.atheainn. com; Via dei Conciatori 9; r €70-110; MPiramide) Within walking distance of Testaccio's bars, clubs and restaurants, this hidden B&B offers superb value for money. Its three light-filled rooms, on the 5th floor of a workaday apartment block, sport a clean, modish look with white walls, lilac touches and tasteful modern furniture. Each also has a small individual terrace, ideal for sitting out on sultry summer nights.

HOTEL ROMANCE
HOTEL €€

(Map p370; ☑06 8929 5106; www.hotelromance. it; Via Marco Aurelio 37a; s €70-140, d €70-200; ❄🀢; MColosseo) An excellent location near the Colosseum and a warm welcome from the English-speaking owner await at this family-run three-star. It has quiet, comfy rooms decorated in traditional Roman style and views over the lush garden of the next-door *carabinieri* station.

★HOTEL SANT'ANSELMO
HOTEL €€€

(Map p370; ☑06 57 00 57; www.aventinohotels. com; Piazza Sant'Anselmo 2; s €130-265, d €150-290; ❄@; 🚌Via Marmorata) A ravishing romantic hideaway set amid the terracotta villas and umbrella pines of the elegant Aventino district. Its rooms are not the biggest but they are stylish, marrying four-poster beds, polished marble and dripping chandeliers with modern touches and contemporary colours. A few also have terraces offering views over southern Rome.

🛏 Southern Rome

TWINCITIES HOSTEL
HOSTEL €

(Map p382; ☑334 9491461; www.twincitieshostel.it; Viale Leonardo da Vinci 223 ; dm €10-21, s €21-40, d €19-48; MSan Paolo) This hostel is outside the centre and about a 20-minute metro ride from Rome's main sights. However, it's homely and a good choice if you fancy staying in a Roman suburb to get a feel for ordinary local life. Rooms are small and the showers somewhat cramped and erratic, but it's welcoming and inexpensive, and there's a small kitchen.

HOTEL ABITART
HOTEL €€

(Map p382; ☑06 454 31 91; www.abitarthotel. com; Via Matteucci; d €85-140; MPiramide, 🚋Ostiense) If you'd like to stay in the on-the-up Ostiense area, the Abitart is funkily decorated, with a pop-arty feel, and close to some good restaurants. Despite the area's new lease of life, you'll pass through a scrappy, noisy district on the way to Pyramide Metro.

🛏 Villa Borghese & Northern Rome

★HOTEL VILLA MANGILI
BOUTIQUE HOTEL €€

(Map p380; ☑06 321 71 30; www.hotelvilla mangili.it; Via Giuseppe Mangili 31; s €130-180, d €150-200; ❄🀢; 🚌Viale Bruno Buozzi) Housed in a glorious early 20th-century villa, this gracious three-star offers a stylish retreat in the heart of the exclusive Parioli neighbourhood. Its 12 individually styled rooms are good looking, and the intimate, shady garden is a wonderful place for a cool drink at the end of a hard day.

CASA MONTANI
GUESTHOUSE €€

(Map p380; ☑06 3260 0421; www.casamontani. com; Piazzale Flaminio 9; d from €140; ❄@🀢; MFlaminio) A lovely, upmarket guesthouse with just five rooms. All are slightly different but the overall look is contemporary cool with grey colour schemes, modern parquet, custom-made furniture and modern art. The largest, the junior suite, also enjoys views over to Porta del Popolo.

Understand Rome

Rome Today

As Italy's political hub, Rome has been at the centre of the country's recent political and economic upheavals. A nationwide austerity drive led by technocrat PM Mario Monti caused tensions on the city's streets and protest voting in the ballot box, while spending cuts have given rise to a new trend for cultural sponsorship. Over the river in the Vatican, scandal and in-fighting culminated in the first papal resignation in 600 years.

Best on Film

Roma Città Aperta (Rome Open City; 1945) A neo-realist study of desperation in Nazi-occupied Rome.

Dear Diary (1994) Cult director Nanni Moretti scoots around a semi-deserted Rome.

The Talented Mr Ripley (1999) Murderous intrigue on Piazza di Spagna and in other Italian locations.

To Rome with Love (2012) Woody Allen's saccharine homage to the Eternal City.

Roman Holiday (1953) Gregory Peck, Audrey Hepburn, a Vespa and *dolce vita* romance.

Best in Print

The Secrets of Rome: Love & Death in the Eternal City (Corrado Augias; 2007) Journalist Augias muses on little-known historical episodes.

Rome (Robert Hughes; 2012) A personal portrait of the city by straight-talking Australian art critic.

Imperium (Robert Harris; 2006) Fictional biography of Cicero by bestselling Brit author.

Michelangelo & the Pope's Ceiling (Ross King; 2003) Fascinating account of the painting of the Sistine Chapel.

Roman Tales (Alberto Moravia; 1954) Short stories set in Rome's poorest neighbourhoods.

Election Fever & Punk Politics

In 2013 election fever broke out across the city. Within the space of a few months Romans were called to vote for a new president, a new regional governor and a new mayor.

Predictably, the outcome of the general election was dramatic, if not decisive. The result was a political deadlock which dragged on for two months until Enrico Letta, a moderate from the centre-left Partito Democratico (PD; Democratic Party), was able to cobble together a cross-party coalition government. More than the result, though, the big story from the elections was the emergence of Beppe Grillo, a charismatic former comedian, as a political force. His antipolitical 5 Star Movement polled 25% of the vote, leading commentators to hail the birth of 'punk politics'.

Berlusconi's performance also stunned many. When *il Cavaliere* was booed from office in late 2011 amid political and economic chaos, everyone gave him up for dead. But he returned to the public stage in early 2013 and took almost a third of the national vote, despite a prison sentence hanging over him (in October 2012 he had been sentenced to a year for tax fraud) and standing trial for having sex with an underage prostitute.

While Berlusconi's 'bunga bunga' parties were the talk of town in 2011, in 2012 it was the turn of Lazio's right-wing regional government to provide the scandal. Reports of a masked toga party, allegedly paid for with public funds, sparked a major political furore that eventually led to the resignation of governor Renata Polverini. Taking her place was the victor of the 2013 regional election, Nicola Zingaretti, brother of a famous TV star and a member of the centre-left PD.

At the time of writing, the city has yet to vote in the mayoral elections in which incumbent Gianni Alemanno is seeking re-election.

Vatican Drama

The Vatican was thrust into the spotlight in February 2013 when Pope Benedict XVI broke a 600-year-old taboo and announced his resignation. Rumours of rifts within the Roman Curia (the Catholic Church's governing body) had long been circulating, but not even experienced Vatican-watchers were prepared for such devastating news. The 85-year-old pontiff (the first pope to step down since Gregory XII in 1415) explained his decision, saying that he no longer had the strength for the job.

Benedict's papacy (2005–13) had been a rocky one, overshadowed by child sexual abuse scandals and clerical in-fighting. In a particularly dramatic episode, dubbed Vatileaks, the pope's personal butler was imprisoned for stealing documents from his boss's desk and leaking them to an Italian journalist. The butler, Paolo Gabriele, defended himself saying he had been acting to root out 'evil and corruption' within the Church.

But all such talk was put on hold in late March as huge crowds on St Peter's Square cheered the election of Benedict's successor. Taking the name Francis, the Argentinian cardinal Jorge Mario Bergoglio became the first Jesuit to be elected pope and the first non-European since the 8th century.

Austerity, Culture & Fashion

Italy's well-publicised economic woes have caused headaches in Rome as well as boardrooms across the eurozone. But while the politicians strive to balance the books, Rome's citizens have faced increased taxes and cuts in services. Tensions came to a head in November 2012 when thousands took to the streets to protest, resulting in clashes between police and a small minority of demonstrators.

Austerity cut-backs have also affected the city's ability to maintain its high-profile monuments. To make up for budget shortfalls, mayor Gianni Alemanno has courted private investment and in recent years has struck deals with two of Italy's best-known fashion firms. Tod's, the luxury shoemaker, has agreed to finance a major restoration of the Colosseum costing €25 million, while Fendi has signed up to fund a €2.5 million makeover of the Trevi Fountain.

Tourism Thrives

Surprisingly, though, all this political and economic turmoil has not adversely affected tourism, a mainstay of the Roman economy, and the number of visitors continues to grow. According to figures released by the Comune di Roma, 2012 was a bumper year with 11.9 million arrivals registered, a record for recent times.

if Rome were 100 people

52 drive a car
27 use public transport
15 ride a scooter
6 travel on foot

nationality
(% of population)

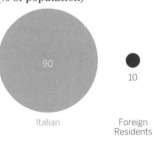

90
Italian

10
Foreign Residents

population per sq km

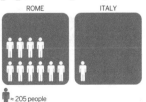

ROME   ITALY

= 205 people

History

Rome's history spans three millennia, from the classical myths of vengeful gods to the follies of Roman emperors, from Renaissance excess to swaggering 20th-century fascism. Emperors, popes and dictators have come and gone, playing out their ambitions and conspiring for their place in history. Everywhere you go in this remarkable city, you're surrounded by the past. Martial ruins, Renaissance *palazzi* and flamboyant baroque basilicas all have tales to tell – of family feuding, historic upheavals, artistic rivalries, intrigues and dark passions.

Ancient Rome, the Myth

As much a mythical construct as a historical reality, ancient Rome's image has been carefully nurtured throughout history. Intellectuals, artists and architects have sought inspiration from this skilfully constructed legend, while political and religious rulers have invoked it to legitimise their authority and serve their political ends.

**Historical
Reads**

....

*Rome: The
Biography of a
City (Christopher
Hibbert)*

....

*The Families Who
Made Rome: A
History and a
Guide (Anthony
Majanlahti)*

....

*Absolute Mon-
archs (John Julius
Norwich)*

Imperial Spin Doctors

Rome's original mythmakers were the first emperors. Eager to reinforce the city's status as *caput mundi* (capital of the world), they turned to writers such as Virgil, Ovid and Livy to create an official Roman history. These authors, while adept at weaving epic narratives, were less interested in the rigours of historical research and frequently presented myth as reality. In the *Aeneid,* Virgil brazenly draws on Greek legends and stories to tell the tale of Aeneas, a Trojan prince who arrives in Italy and establishes Rome's founding dynasty. Similarly, Livy, a writer celebrated for his monumental history of the Roman Republic, makes liberal use of mythology to fill the gaps in his historical narrative.

Ancient Rome's rulers were sophisticated masters of spin; under their tutelage, art, architecture and elaborate public ceremony were employed to perpetuate the image of Rome as an invincible and divinely sanctioned power. Monuments such as the Ara Pacis, the Colonna di Traiano and the Arco di Costantino celebrated imperial glories, while gladiatorial games highlighted the Romans' physical superiority.

TIMELINE	753 BC	509 BC	146 BC
	According to legend, this is the year Romulus kills his twin brother Remus and founds Rome. Evidence exists of an 8th-century settlement on the Palatino.	On the death of the king Tarquinius Superbus, the Roman Republic is founded, giving birth to the acronym SPQR (Senatus Populusque Romanus; the Senate and People of Rome).	Carthage is razed to the ground at the end of the Third Punic War and mainland Greece is conquered by rampant legionaries. Rome becomes undisputed master of the Mediterranean.

The Colosseum, the Roman Forum and the Pantheon were not only supremely sophisticated feats of engineering, they were also impregnable symbols of Rome's eternal might.

The Past as Inspiration

During the Renaissance, a period in which ancient Rome was hailed as the high point of Western civilisation, these symbols inspired a whole generation of artists and architects. Bramante, Michelangelo and Raphael modelled their work on classical precedents as they helped rebuild Rome as the capital of the Catholic Church.

But more than anyone, it was Italy's 20th-century fascist dictator, Benito Mussolini, who invoked the glories of ancient Rome. Mussolini spared no effort in his attempts to identify his fascist regime with imperial Rome – he made Rome's traditional birthday, 21 April, an official fascist holiday, he printed stamps with images of ancient Roman emperors and he commissioned archaeological digs to unearth further proof of Roman might. His idealisation of the Roman Empire underpinned much of his colonialist ideology.

Nowadays, the myth of Rome is used less as a rallying cry and more as an advertising tool – and with some success. However cynical and world-weary you are, it's difficult to deny the thrill of seeing the Colosseum for the first time or of visiting the Palatino, the hill where Romulus is said to have founded the city.

Legacy of an Empire

Rising out of the bloodstained remnants of the Roman Republic, the Roman Empire was the Western world's first great superpower. At its zenith under the emperor Trajan (r AD 98–117), it extended from Britannia in the north to North Africa in the south, from Hispania (Spain) in the west to Palestina (Palestine) and Syria in the east. Rome itself had more than 1.5 million inhabitants and the city sparkled with the trappings of imperial splendour: marble temples, public baths, theatres, circuses and libraries. Decline eventually set in during the 3rd century; by the latter half of the 5th century, Rome was in barbarian hands.

Europe Divided

The empire's most immediate legacy was the division of Europe into east and west. In AD 285 the emperor Diocletian, prompted by widespread disquiet across the empire, split the Roman Empire into eastern and western halves – the west centred on Rome, and the east on Byzantium (later called Constantinople) – in a move that was to have far-reaching consequences. In the west, the fall of the Western Roman

---

Ancient Rome on Screen

Spartacus (1960; Stanley Kubrick)

Quo Vadis (1951; Mervyn LeRoy)

Gladiator (2000; Ridley Scott)

I, Claudius (1976; BBC)

Rome (2005–07; HBO)

HISTORY LEGACY OF AN EMPIRE

Virgil (70 BC–19 BC), real name Publius Vergilius Maro, was born near the northern Italian town of Mantua to a wealthy family. He studied in Cremona, Milan, Rome and Naples, before becoming Rome's best-known classical poet. His most famous works are the *Eclogues*, *Georgics* and the *Aeneid*.

73–71 BC	49 BC	15 March, 44 BC	AD 14
Spartacus leads a slave revolt against dictator Cornelius Sulla. Defeat is inevitable; punishment is brutal. Spartacus and 6000 followers are crucified along Via Appia Antica.	*'Alea iacta est'* ('The die is cast'). Julius Caesar leads his army across the River Rubicon and marches on Rome. In the ensuing civil war, Caesar defeats rival Pompey.	On the Ides of March, soon after Julius Caesar is proclaimed dictator for life, he is stabbed to death in the Teatro di Pompeo (on modern-day Largo di Torre Argentina).	Augustus dies after 41 years as Rome's first emperor. His reign is successful, unlike those of his mad successors Tiberius and Caligula, who go down in history for their cruelty.

The Roman Empire

Greatest extent of Roman Empire (AD 116)
Present-day international boundaries

Empire in AD 476 paved the way for the emergence of the Holy Roman Empire and the Papal States, while in the east, Roman (later Byzantine) rule continued until 1453 when the empire was finally conquered by rampaging Ottoman armies.

Democracy & the Rule of Law

In broader cultural terms, Roman innovations in language, law, government, art, architecture, engineering and public administration remain relevant to this day.

One of the Romans' most striking contributions to modern society was democratic government. Democracy had first appeared in Athens, in the 5th century BC but it was the Romans, with their genius for organisation, who took it to another level. Under the Roman Republic (509–47 BC), the Roman population was divided into two categories: the Senate and the Roman people. Both held clearly defined responsibilities. The people, through three assembly bodies – the Centuriate Assembly, the Tribal Assembly and the Council of the People – voted on all new laws and elected two annual tribunes who had the power of veto in the Senate. The Senate, for its part, elected and advised two annual consuls who acted as political and military leaders. It also controlled the Republic's purse strings and, in times of grave peril, could nominate a dictator for a six-month period.

You'll see the letters SPQR everywhere in Rome. They were adopted during the Roman Republic and stand for Senatus Populusque Romanus (the Senate and People of Rome).

64	67	80	285
Rome is ravaged by a huge fire that burns for five and a half days. Some blame Nero, although he was in Anzio when the conflagration broke out.	St Peter and St Paul become martyrs as Nero massacres Rome's Christians. The persecution is a thinly disguised ploy to win back popularity after the great fire of 64 AD.	The 50,000-seat Flavian Amphitheatre, better known as the Colosseum, is inaugurated by the emperor Titus. Five thousand animals are slaughtered in the 100-day opening games.	To control anarchy within the Roman Empire, Diocletian splits it into two. The eastern half is later incorporated into the Byzantine Empire; the western half falls to the barbarians.

This system worked pretty well for the duration of the Republic, and remained more or less intact during the empire – at least on paper. In practice, the Senate assumed the assemblies' legislative powers and the emperor claimed power of veto over the Senate, a move that pretty much gave him complete command.

The observance of law was an important element in Roman society. As far back as the 5th century BC, the Republic had a bill of rights, known as the Twelve Tables. This remained the foundation stone of Rome's legal system until the emperor Justinian (r 527–65) produced his mammoth *Corpus Iurus Civilis* (Body of Civil Law) in 529. This not only codified all existing laws, but also included a systematic treatise on legal philosophy. In particular, it introduced a distinction between *ius civilis* (civil law – laws particular to a state), *ius gentium* (law of nations – laws established and shared by states) and *ius naturale* (natural law – laws concerning male-female relationships and matrimony).

Latin

But more than the laws themselves, Rome's greatest legacy to the legal profession was the Latin language. Latin was the lingua franca of the Roman Empire and was later adopted by the Catholic Church, a major reason for its survival. It is still one of the Vatican's official languages and until the second Vatican Council (1962–65) it was the only language in which Catholic Mass could be said. As the basis for modern Romance languages such as Italian, French and Spanish, it provides the linguistic roots of many modern words.

Roman Roads

And just as many words lead to Latin, so all roads lead to Rome. The ancient Romans were the master engineers of their day and their ability to travel quickly was an important factor in their power to rule. The queen of all ancient roads was Via Appia Antica, which connected Rome with the southern Adriatic port of Brindisi. Via Appia survives to this day, as do many of the other consular roads: Via Aurelia, Via Cassia, Via Flaminia and Via Salaria are among the most important.

Christianity & Papal Power

For much of its history Rome has been ruled by the pope and today the Vatican still wields immense influence over the city.

The ancient Romans were remarkably tolerant of foreign religions. They themselves worshipped a cosmopolitan pantheon of gods, ranging from household spirits and former emperors to deities appropriated from Greek mythology (Jupiter, Juno, Neptune, Minerva etc). Religious

---

Via Appia Antica is named after Appius Claudius Caecus, the Roman censor who initiated its construction in 312 BC. He also built Rome's first aqueduct, the Aqua Appia, which brought in water from the Sabine Hills.

Historical Sites

Palatino

Largo di Torre Argentina

Capitoline Hill

Roman Forum

Castel Sant'Angelo

Chiesa del Gesù

Palazzo Venezia

313

A year after his victory at the Battle of the Milvian Bridge, the emperor Constantine issues the Edict of Milan, officially establishing religious tolerance and ending Christian persecution.

476

The fall of Romulus Augustulus marks the end of the Western Empire. This had been on the cards for years: in 410 the Goths sacked Rome; in 455 the Vandals followed suit.

JONATHAN SMITH / GETTY IMAGES ©

Arco di Constantino commemorates the Battle of the Milvian Bridge

ROMULUS & REMUS, ROME'S LEGENDARY TWINS

The most famous of Rome's many legends is the story of Romulus and Remus, and the foundation of the city on 21 April 753 BC.

According to myth, Romulus and Remus were the children of Rhea Silva, a vestal virgin, and Mars, god of war. While still babies they were set adrift on the Tiber to escape a death penalty imposed by their great-uncle Amulius, who at the time was battling with their grandfather Numitor for control of Alba Longa. However, they were discovered near the Palatino by a she-wolf, who suckled them until a shepherd, Faustulus, found and raised them.

Years later the twins decided to found a city on the site where they'd originally been saved. They didn't know where this was, so they consulted the omens. Remus, on the Aventino, saw six vultures; his brother over on the Palatino saw 12. The meaning was clear and Romulus began building, much to the outrage of his brother. The two subsequently argued and Romulus killed Remus.

Romulus continued building and soon had a city. To populate it he created a refuge on the Campidoglio, Aventino, Celio and Quirinale Hills, to which a ragtag population of criminals, ex-slaves and outlaws soon decamped. However, the city still needed women. Romulus therefore invited everyone in the surrounding country to celebrate the Festival of Consus (21 August). As the spectators watched the festival games, Romulus and his men pounced and abducted all the women, an act that went down in history as the Rape of the Sabine Women.

The patron saints of Rome, Peter and Paul, were both executed during Nero's persecution of the Christians between 64 and 68. Paul, who as a Roman citizen was entitled to a quick death, was beheaded, while Peter was crucified upside down on the Vatican Hill.

cults were also popular – the Egyptian gods Isis and Serapis enjoyed a mass following, as did Mithras, a heroic saviour-god of vaguely Persian origin, who was worshipped by male-only devotees in underground temples.

Emergence of Christianity

Christianity entered this religious cocktail in the 1st century AD, sweeping in from Judaea, a Roman province in what is now Israel and the West Bank. Its early days were marred by persecution, most notably under Nero (r 54–68), but it slowly caught on, thanks to its popular message of heavenly reward and the evangelising efforts of Saints Peter and Paul. However, it was the conversion of the the emperor Constantine (r 306–37) that really set Christianity on the path to European domination. In 313 Constantine issued the Edict of Milan, officially legalising Christianity, and later, in 378, Theodosius (r 379–95) made Christianity Rome's state religion. By this time, the Church had developed a sophisticated organisational structure based on five major sees: Rome, Constantinople, Alexandria, Antioch and Jerusalem. At the outset, each

754	800	1084	1300
Pope Stephen II and Pepin, king of the Franks, cut a deal resulting in the creation of the Papal States. The papacy is to rule Rome until Italian unification.	Pope Leo III crowns Pepin's son, Charlemagne, Holy Roman Emperor during Christmas mass at St Peter's Basilica. A red disk in the basilica marks the spot where it happened.	Rome is sacked by a Norman army after Pope Gregory VII invites them in to help him against the besieging forces of the Holy Roman Emperor Henry IV.	Pope Boniface VIII proclaims Rome's first ever Jubilee, offering a full pardon to anyone who makes the pilgrimage to the city. Up to 200,000 people are said to have come.

bishopric carried equal weight, but in subsequent years Rome emerged as the senior party. The reasons for this were partly political – Rome was the wealthy capital of the Roman Empire – and partly religious – early Christian doctrine held that St Peter, founder of the Roman Church, had been sanctioned by Christ to lead the universal Church.

Papal Control

But while Rome had control of Christianity, the Church had yet to conquer Rome. This it did in the dark days that followed the fall of the Roman Empire. And although no one person can take credit for this, Pope Gregory the Great (r 590–604) did more than most to lay the groundwork. A leader of considerable foresight, he won many friends by supplying free bread to Rome's starving citizens and restoring the city's water supply. He also stood up to the menacing Lombards, who presented a very real threat to the city.

It was this threat that pushed the papacy into an alliance with the Frankish kings, an alliance that resulted in the creation of the two great powers of medieval Europe: the Papal States and the Holy Roman Empire. In Rome, the battle between these two superpowers translated into endless feuding between the city's baronial families and frequent attempts by the French to claim the papacy for their own. This political and military fighting eventually culminated in the papacy transferring to the French city of Avignon between 1309 and 1377, and the Great Schism (1378–1417), a period in which the Catholic world was headed by two popes, one in Rome and one in Avignon.

Longest-Serving Popes

St Peter (30–67)

Pius XI (1846–78)

John Paul II (1978–2005)

Leo XIII (1878–1903)

Pius Vi (1775–99)

HISTORY CHRISTIANITY & PAPAL POWER

DONATION OF CONSTANTINE

The most famous forgery in medieval history, the Donation of Constantine is a document in which the Roman emperor Constantine purportedly grants Pope Sylvester I (r 314–35) and his successors control of Rome and the Western Roman Empire, as well as primacy over the holy sees of Antioch, Alexandria, Constantinople, Jerusalem and all the world's churches.

No one is exactly sure when the document was written but the consensus is that it dates to the mid- or late 8th century. Certainly this fits with the widespread theory that the author was a Roman cleric, possibly working with the knowledge of Pope Stephen II (r 752–57).

For centuries the donation was accepted as genuine and used by popes to justify their territorial claims. But in 1440 the Italian philosopher Lorenzo Valla proved that it was a forgery. By analysing the Latin used in the document he was able to show that it was inconsistent with the Latin used in the 4th century.

1309	1347	1378–1417	1506
Fighting between French-backed pretenders to the papacy and Roman nobility ends in Pope Clement V transferring to Avignon. Only in 1377 does Pope Gregory XI return to Rome.	Cola di Rienzo, a local notary, declares himself dictator of Rome. Surprisingly, he's welcomed by the people; less surprisingly he's later driven out of town by the hostile aristocracy.	Squabbling between factions in the Catholic Church leads to the Great Schism. The pope rules in Rome while the alternative antipope sits in Avignon.	Pope Julius II employs 150 Swiss mercenaries to protect him. The 100-strong Swiss Guard, all practising Catholics from Switzerland, are still responsible for the pope's personal safety.

A WHO'S WHO OF ROMAN EMPERORS

Of the 250 or so emperors of the Roman Empire, only a few were truly heroic. Here we highlight 10 of the best, worst and completely mad.

➡ **Augustus (27 BC–AD 14)** Rome's first emperor. Ushers in a period of peace and security; the arts flourish and many monuments are built, including the Ara Pacis and Pantheon.

➡ **Caligula (37–41)** Emperor number three after Augustus and Tiberius. Remains popular until illness leads to the depraved behaviour for which he is famous. Is murdered by his bodyguards on the Palatino.

➡ **Claudius (41–54)** Expands the Roman Empire and conquers Britain. Is eventually poisoned, probably at the instigation of Agrippina, his wife and Nero's mother.

➡ **Nero (54–68)** Initially rules well but later slips into insanity – he has his mother murdered, persecutes the Christians and attempts to turn half the city into a palace, the Domus Aurea. He is eventually forced into suicide.

➡ **Vespasian (69–79)** First of the Flavian dynasty, he imposes peace and cleans up the imperial finances. His greatest legacy is the Colosseum.

➡ **Trajan (98–117)** Conquers the east and rules over the empire at its zenith. Back home he revamps Rome's city centre, adding a forum, marketplace and column, all of which still stand.

➡ **Hadrian (117–38)** Puts an end to imperial expansion and constructs walls to mark the empire's borders. He rebuilds the Pantheon and has one of the ancient world's greatest villas built at Tivoli.

➡ **Aurelian (270–75)** Does much to control the rebellion that sweeps the empire at the end of the 3rd century. Starts construction of the city walls that bear his name.

➡ **Diocletian (284–305)** Splits the empire into eastern and western halves in 285. Launches a savage persecution of the Christians as he struggles to control the empire's eastern reaches.

➡ **Constantine I (306–37)** Although based in Byzantium (later renamed Constantinople in his honour), he legalises Christianity and embarks on a church-building spree in Rome.

As both religious and temporal leaders, Rome's popes wielded influence well beyond their military capacity. For much of the medieval period, the Church held a virtual monopoly on Europe's reading material (mostly religious scripts written in Latin) and was the authority on virtually every aspect of human knowledge. All innovations in science, philosophy and literature had to be cleared by the Church's hawkish scholars, who were constantly on the lookout for heresy.

1508

Michelangelo starts painting the Sistine Chapel, while down the hall Raphael begins to decorate Pope Julius II's private apartments, better known as the Stanze di Raffaello (Raphael Rooms).

1527

Pope Clement VII takes refuge in Castel Sant'Angelo as Rome is overrun by troops loyal to Charles V, king of Spain and Holy Roman Emperor.

LONELY PLANET / GETTY IMAGES ©

Ponte Sant'Angelo leading to the Castel Sant'Angelo (p154)

Modern Influence

Almost a thousand years on and the Church is still a major influence on modern Italian life. Its rigid stance on social and ethical issues such as abortion, same-sex marriage and euthanasia informs much public debate, often with highly divisive results. A famous case in point was a right-to-die case in 2008 that saw the Vatican try to block a High Court decision allowing doctors to cease treatment of a long-term coma-patient.

The relationship between the Church and Italy's modern political establishment has been a fact of life since the founding of the Italian Republic in 1946. For much of the First Republic (1946–94), the Vatican was closely associated with the Christian Democrat party (DC, *Democrazia Cristiana*), Italy's most powerful party and an ardent opponent of communism. At the same time, the Church, keen to weed communism out of the political landscape, played its part by threatening to excommunicate anyone who voted for Italy's Communist Party (PCI, *Partito Comunista Italiano*).

Today, no one political party has a monopoly on Church favour, and politicians across the spectrum tread warily around Catholic sensibilities. But this reverence isn't limited to the purely political sphere; it also informs much press reporting and even law enforcement. In September 2008, Rome's public prosecutor threatened to prosecute a comedian for comments made against the pope, invoking the 1929 Lateran Treaty under which it is a criminal offence to 'offend the honour' of the pope and Italian president. The charge, which ignited a heated debate on censorship and the right to free speech, was eventually dropped by the Italian justice minister.

The pope's personal kingdom, the Papal States were established in the 8th century after the Frankish King Pepin drove the Lombards out of northern Italy and donated large tracts of territory to Pope Stephen II. At the height of their power, the States encompassed Rome and much of central Italy.

Renaissance – a New Beginning

Bridging the gap between the Middle Ages and the modern age, the Renaissance (*Rinascimento* in Italian) was a far-reaching intellectual, artistic and cultural movement. It emerged in 14th-century Florence but quickly spread to Rome, where it gave rise to one of the greatest makeovers the city had ever seen.

Humanism & Rebuilding

The movement's intellectual cornerstone was humanism, a philosophy that focused on the central role of humanity within the universe. This was a major break from the medieval world view, which had placed God at the centre of everything. It was not antireligious, though. Many humanist scholars were priests and most of Rome's great works of Renaissance art were commissioned by the Church. In fact, it was one of the

1540	1555	1626	1632
Pope Paul III officially recognises the Society of Jesus, aka the Jesuits. The order is founded by Ignatius de Loyola, who spends his last days in the Chiesa del Gesù.	As fear pervades Counter-Reformation Rome, Pope Paul IV confines the city's Jews to the area known as the Jewish Ghetto. Official intolerance continues on and off until the 20th century.	After more than 150 years of construction, St Peter's Basilica is consecrated. The hulking basilica remains the largest church in the world until well into the 20th century.	Galileo Galilei is summoned to appear before the Inquisition. He is forced to renounce his belief that the earth revolves around the sun and is exiled to Florence.

INQUISITION

The Roman Inquisition was set up in the 16th century to counter the threat of Protestantism. It was responsible for prosecuting people accused of heresy, blasphemy, immorality and witchcraft, and although it did order executions, it often imposed lighter punishments such as fines and the recital of prayers.

most celebrated humanist scholars of the 15th century, Pope Nicholas V (r 1447–84), who is generally considered the harbinger of the Roman Renaissance.

When Nicholas became pope in 1447, Rome was not in a good state. Centuries of medieval feuding had reduced the city to a semideserted battleground, and the city's bedraggled population lived in constant fear of plague, famine and flooding (the Tiber regularly broke its banks). In political terms, the papacy was recovering from the trauma of the Great Schism and attempting to face down Muslim encroachment in the east.

It was against this background that Nicholas decided to rebuild Rome as a showcase of Church power. To finance his plans, he declared 1450 a Jubilee year, a tried and tested way of raising funds by attracting hundreds of thousands of pilgrims to the city (in a Jubilee year anyone who comes to Rome and confesses receives a full papal pardon).

Over the course of the next 80 years or so, Rome underwent a complete overhaul. Pope Sixtus IV (r 1471–84) had the Sistine Chapel built and, in 1471, gave the people of Rome a selection of bronzes that became the first exhibits of the Capitoline Museums. Julius II (r 1503–13) laid Via del Corso and Via Giulia, and ordered Bramante to rebuild St Peter's Basilica. Michelangelo frescoed the Sistine Chapel and designed the dome of St Peter's, while Raphael inspired a whole generation of painters with his masterful grasp of perspective.

The Sack of Rome & Protestant Protest

But outside Rome an ill wind was blowing. The main source of trouble was the longstanding conflict between the Holy Roman Empire, led by the Spanish Charles V, and the Italian city states. This simmering tension came to a head in 1527 when Rome was invaded by Charles' marauding army and ransacked as Pope Clement VII (r 1523–34) hid in Castel Sant'Angelo. The sack of Rome, regarded by most historians as the nail in the coffin of the Roman Renaissance, was a hugely traumatic event. It left the papacy reeling and gave rise to the view that the Church had been greatly weakened by its own moral shortcomings. That the Church was corrupt was well known, and it was with considerable public support that Martin Luther pinned his famous 95 Theses to a church door in Wittenberg in 1517, thus sparking off the Protestant Reformation.

The Counter-Reformation

The Catholic reaction to the Reformation was all-out. The Counter-Reformation was marked by a second wave of artistic and architectural ac-

1656–67	1798	1870	1885
Gian Lorenzo Bernini lays out St Peter's Square for Pope Alexander VII. Bernini, along with his great rival Francesco Borromini, are the leading exponents of Roman baroque.	Napoleon marches into Rome, forcing Pope Pius VI to flee. A republic is announced, but it doesn't last long and in 1801 Pius VI's successor Pius VII returns to Rome.	Nine years after Italian unification, Rome's city walls are breached at Porta Pia and Pope Pius IX is forced to cede the city to Italy. Rome becomes the Italian capital.	To celebrate Italian unification and honour Italy's first king, Vittorio Emanuele II, construction work begins on Il Vittoriano, the mountainous monument dominating Piazza Venezia.

tivity, as the Church once again turned to bricks and mortar to restore its authority. But in contrast to the Renaissance, the Counter-Reformation was a period of persecution and official intolerance. With the full blessing of Pope Paul III, Ignatius Loyola founded the Jesuits in 1540, and two years later the Holy Office was set up as the Church's final appeals court for trials prosecuted by the Inquisition. In 1559 the Church published the *Index Librorum Prohibitorum* (Index of Prohibited Books) and began to persecute intellectuals and freethinkers. Galileo Galilei (1564–1642) was forced to renounce his assertion of the Copernican astronomical system, which held that the earth moved around the sun. He was summoned by the Inquisition to Rome in 1632 and exiled to Florence for the rest of his life. Giordano Bruno (1548–1600), a freethinking Dominican monk, fared worse. Arrested in Venice in 1592, he was burned at the stake eight years later in Campo de' Fiori. The spot is today marked by a sinister statue.

Despite, or perhaps because of, the Church's policy of zero tolerance, the Counter-Reformation was largely successful in re-establishing papal prestige. And in this sense it can be seen as the natural finale to the Renaissance that Nicholas V had kicked off in 1450. From being a rural backwater with a population of around 20,000 in the mid-15th century, Rome had grown to become one of Europe's great 17th-century cities, home to Christendom's most spectacular churches and a population of some 100,000 people.

Power & Corruption

The exercise of power has long gone hand in hand with corruption. And no one enjoyed greater power than Rome's ancient emperors and Renaissance popes.

Caligula

Of all Rome's cruel and insane leaders, few are as notorious as Caligula. A byword for depravity, he was hailed as a saviour when as a 25 year-old he inherited the empire from his hated great-uncle Tiberius in AD 37.

Their optimism was to prove ill-founded. After a bout of serious illness, Caligula began showing disturbing signs of mental instability. He made his senators worship him as a deity and infamously tried to make his horse, Incitatus, a senator. He was accused of all sorts of perversions and progressively alienated himself from all those around him. By AD 41 his Praetorian Guard had had enough and on 24 January its leader, Cassius Chaerea, stabbed him to death.

Emperors' Hall of Shame

Caligula (r 37–41)

Nero (r 54–68)

Commodus (r 180–92)

Caracalla (r 211–17)

Elagabalus (r 218–24)

1922	1929	1946	1957
Some 40,000 fascists march on Rome. King Vittorio Emanuele III, worried about the possibility of civil war, invites the 39-year-old Mussolini to form a government.	Keen to appease the Church, Mussolini signs the Lateran Treaty, creating the state of the Vatican City. To celebrate, Via della Conciliazione is bulldozed through the medieval Borgo.	The republic is born after Italians vote to abolish the monarchy. Two years later, on 1 January 1948, the Italian constitution becomes law.	Leaders of Italy, France, West Germany, Belgium, Holland and Luxembourg sign the Treaty of Rome establishing the European Economic Community.

Papal Foibles

Debauchery on such a scale was rare in the Renaissance papacy, but corruption was no stranger to the corridors of ecclesiastical power. It was not uncommon for popes to father illegitimate children and nepotism was rife. The Borgia pope Alexander VI (r 1492–1503) fathered two illegitimate children with the first of his two high-profile mistresses. The second mistress, Giulia Farnese, was the sister of the cardinal who was later to become Pope Paul III (r 1534–59), himself no stranger to earthly pleasures. When not persecuting heretics during the Counter-Reformation, the Farnese pontiff managed to sire four children.

Tangentopoli

Corruption has also featured in modern Italian politics, most famously during the 1990s *Tangentopoli* (Kickback City) scandal. Against a backdrop of steady economic growth, the controversy broke in Milan in 1992 when a routine corruption case – accepting bribes in exchange for public works contracts – blew up into a nationwide crusade against corruption.

Led by the 'reluctant hero', magistrate Antonio di Pietro, the *Mani Pulite* (Clean Hands) investigations exposed a political and business system riddled with corruption. Politicians, public officials and business people were investigated and for once no one was spared, not even the powerful Bettino Craxi (prime minister between 1983 and 1989), who rather than face a trial in Italy fled to Tunisia in 1993. He was subsequently convicted in absentia on corruption charges and died in self-imposed exile in January 2000.

Tangentopoli left Italy's entire establishment in shock, and as the economy faltered – high unemployment and inflation combined with a huge national debt and an extremely unstable lira – the stage was set for the next act in Italy's turbulent political history.

Chief among the actors were Francesco Rutelli, a suave media-savvy operator who oversaw a successful citywide cleanup as mayor of Rome (1993–2001), and the larger-than-life media magnate Silvio Berlusconi, whose three terms as prime minister (1994, 2000–06 and 2008–11) were dogged by controversy and scandal.

The First Tourists

As a religious centre Rome has long attracted millions of pilgrims. In 1300 Pope Boniface VIII proclaimed the first Jubilee Year, with the promise of a full pardon for anyone who made the pilgrimage to St Peter's Basilica and the Basilica di San Giovanni in Laterano. Hundreds of thousands came and the Church basked in popular glory. In 2000 some

THE BORGIAS

The Borgias, led by family patriarch Rodrigo, aka Pope Alexander VI (r 1492–1503), were one of Renaissance Rome's most notorious families. Machiavelli is said to have modelled *Il Principe* (The Prince) on Rodrigo's son, Cesare, while his daughter, Lucrezia, earned a reputation as a femme fatale with a penchant for poisoning her enemies.

1960
Rome stages the Olympic Games while Federico Fellini makes *La Dolce Vita* in Cinecittà film studios. Meanwhile Stanley Kubrick is using Cinecittà to film his Roman epic, *Spartacus*.

1968
Widespread student unrest results in mass protests across Italy. In Rome, students clash with police at La Sapienza's architecture faculty, an event remembered as the Battle of Valle Giulia.

Cinecittà film studios

NEIL SETCHFIELD / GETTY IMAGES ©

24 million visitors poured into the city for Pope John Paul II's Jubilee. However, it was in the late 18th and early 19th centuries that Rome's reputation as a tourist destination was born.

Gentlemen Visitors & Romantic Poets

The Grand Tour, the 18th-century version of the gap year, was considered an educational rite of passage for wealthy young men from northern Europe, and Britain in particular. In the 19th century it became fashionable for young ladies to travel, chaperoned by spinster aunts, but in the late 1700s the tour was largely a male preserve.

The overland journey through France and into Italy followed the medieval pilgrim route, entering Italy via the St Bernard Pass and descending the west coast before cutting in to Florence and then on to Rome. After a sojourn in the capital, tourists would venture down to Naples, where the newly discovered ruins of Pompeii and Herculaneum were causing much excitement, before heading up to Venice.

Rome, enjoying a rare period of peace, was perfectly set up for this English invasion. The city was basking in the aftermath of the 17th-century baroque building boom, and a craze for all things classical was sweeping Europe. Rome's papal authorities were also crying out for money after their excesses had left the city coffers bare, reducing much of the population to abject poverty.

Thousands came, including Goethe, who stopped off to write his travelogue *Italian Journey* (1817), as well as Byron, Shelley and Keats, who all fuelled their romantic sensibilities in the city's vibrant streets. So many English people stayed around Piazza di Spagna that locals christened the area *er ghetto de l'inglesi* (the English ghetto). Trade in antiquities flourished and local artists did a roaring business producing etchings for souvenir-hungry visitors.

Artistically, rococo was the rage of the moment. The Spanish Steps, built between 1723 and 1726, proved a major hit with tourists, as did the exuberant Trevi Fountain.

The Ghosts of Fascism

Rome's fascist history is a highly charged subject. In recent years historians on both sides of the political spectrum have accused each other of recasting the past to suit their views: left-wing historians have accused their right-wing counterparts of glossing over the more unpleasant aspects of Mussolini's regime, while right-wingers have attacked their left-wing colleagues of whitewashing the facts to perpetuate a simplified myth of anti-fascism.

In his 1818 work *Childe Harold's Pilgrimage,* the English poet Lord Byron quotes the words of the 8th-century monk Bede: 'While stands the Coliseum, Rome shall stand; When falls the Coliseum, Rome shall fall! And when Rome falls – the World.'

1978	1992–93	1999	2000
Former PM Aldo Moro is kidnapped and shot by a cell of the extreme left-wing *Brigate Rosse* (Red Brigades) during Italy's *anni di piombo* (years of lead).	A nationwide anti-corruption crusade, *Mani Pulitei* (Clean Hands), shakes the political and business establishment. Many high-profile figures are arrested.	After 20 years, the Sistine Chapel restoration is finally completed. The Michelangelo frescoes have never looked so vibrant, leading some critics to question the restorers' methods.	Pilgrims pour into Rome from all over the world to celebrate the Catholic Church's Jubilee year. A highpoint is a mass attended by two million people at Tor Vergata university.

Mussolini

Benito Mussolini was born in 1883 in Forlì, a small town in Emilia-Romagna. As a young man he was an active member of the Italian Socialist Party, but service in WWI and Italy's subsequent descent into chaos led to a change of heart, and in 1919 he founded the Italian Fascist Party. Calling for rights for war veterans, law and order, and a strong nation, the party won support from disillusioned soldiers, many of whom joined the squads of Blackshirts that Mussolini used to intimidate his political enemies.

In 1921 Mussolini was elected to the Chamber of Deputies. His parliamentary support was limited but on 28 October 1922 he marched on Rome with 40,000 black-shirted followers. The march was largely symbolic but it had the desired effect. Fearful of civil war between the fascists and socialists, King Vittorio Emanuele III invited Mussolini to form a government. His first government was a coalition of fascists, nationalists and liberals, but victory in the 1924 elections left him much better placed to consolidate his personal power, and by the end of 1925 he had seized complete control of Italy. In order to silence the Church he signed the Lateran Treaty in 1929, which made Catholicism the state religion and recognised the sovereignty of the Vatican State.

On the home front, Mussolini embarked on a huge building program: Via dei Fori Imperiali and Via della Conciliazione were laid out; parks were opened on the Oppio Hill and at Villa Celimontana; the Imperial Forums and the temples at Largo di Torre Argentina were excavated; and the monumental Foro Italico sports complex and EUR were built. Abroad, Mussolini invaded Abyssinia (now Ethiopia) in 1935 and sided with Hitler in 1936. In 1940, from the balcony of Palazzo Venezia, he announced Italy's entry into WWII to a vast, cheering crowd. The good humour didn't last, as Rome suffered, first at the hands of its own fascist regime, then, after Mussolini was ousted in 1943, at the hands of the Nazis. Rome was liberated from German occupation on 4 June 1944.

The Post-War Period

But defeat in WWII didn't kill off Italian fascism and in 1946 hardline Mussolini supporters founded the *Movimento Sociale Italiano* (MSI; Italian Social Movement). For close on 50 years this overtly fascist party participated in mainstream Italian politics, while on the other side of the spectrum the *Partito Comunista Italiano* (PCI; Italian Communist Party) grew into Western Europe's largest communist party. The MSI was finally dissolved in 1994, when Gianfranco Fini rebranded it as the

No stranger to controversy, Berlusconi caused international outrage in January 2012 when he publicly defended Italy's former fascist dictator Mussolini on Holocaust Memorial Day.

2001	2002	2005	2008
Charismatic media tycoon Silvio Berlusconi becomes prime minister for the second time. His first term in 1994 was a short-lived affair; his second lasts the full five-year course.	On 1 January, the euro becomes legal tender in Italy and 11 other European countries. Critics later blame the single currency for the country's economic woes.	Pope John Paul II dies after 27 years on the papal throne. He is replaced by his long-standing ally Josef Ratzinger, who takes the name Benedict XVI.	Gianni Alemanno, a former member of the neo-fascist party MSI (Movimento Sociale Italiano), sweeps to victory in Rome's mayoral elections. The news makes headlines across the world.

post-fascist *Alleanza Nazionale* (AN; National Alliance). AN remained an important political player until it was incorporated into Silvio Berlusconi's *Popolo della Libertà* party in 2009.

Outside the political mainstream, fascism (along with communism) was a driving force of the domestic terrorism that rocked Italy during the *anni di piombo* (years of lead), between the late 1960s and early 1980s. In these years, terrorist groups emerged on both sides of the ideological spectrum, giving rise to a spate of politically inspired violence. Most famously, the communist *Brigate Rosse* (Red Brigades) kidnapped and killed former prime minister Aldo Moro in 1978, and the neo-fascist Armed Revolutionary Nuclei bombed Bologna train station in 1980, killing 85 people and leaving up to 200 injured.

BERLUSCONI, ITALY'S MEDIA KING

Since 1994 Silvio Berlusconi has dominated Italian political and public life like a modern-day colossus. A colourful, charismatic and highly divisive character, he has served three terms as PM and is one of the country's richest men, with a fortune that US business magazine *Forbes* puts at US$5.9 billion. His business empire spans the media, advertising, insurance, food, construction and sport.

For much of his controversial political career, he has been criticised for his hold over Italy's media and, in particular, for his control of the nation's TV output. Italian TV is dominated by two networks – RAI, the Rome-based state broadcaster, and Mediaset, Italy's largest private media company – and Berlusconi has major interests in both camps. This 'conflict of interest' has long aroused debate, both inside and outside Italy.

More recently, attention has turned to Berlusconi's courtroom battles. Over the years he has faced several trials, mostly due to business-related corruption and fraud offences, but until he was sentenced to four years' imprisonment (later cut to a year) for tax fraud in October 2012, he had never been convicted. He is currently appealing the sentence.

His most famous trial, however, arose out of the so-called 'Rubygate' scandal. This erupted in early 2011 when it was alleged that Berlusconi had had sex with an under-age exotic dancer called Ruby Rubacuore and then pressured police into releasing her when she was arrested on an unrelated theft charge. After a police investigation he was formally charged and trial proceedings, which continue today, began in April 2011.

Yet for all his trials and tribulations, Berlusconi continues to seduce the Italian electorate. When he resigned as PM in late 2011, commentators wrote him off as a spent force. But they were wrong: after a bravura campaign performance in the run-up to the 2013 general election, he took almost a third of the total vote.

2008–09	2011	2011	2012
Berlusconi bounces back for a third term as PM after a two-year spell in opposition. In 2009 he hosts the G8 summit in the earthquake-shattered city of L'Aquila.	On 1 May, hundreds of thousands of pilgrims gather in St Peter's Square to witness the beatification of Pope John Paul II. The ceremony is the last step before sainthood.	PM Berlusconi resigns on 12 November as Italy's debt crisis threatens to spiral out of control. He is replaced by economist Mario Monti.	On 31 October, the Church's top brass meet in the Sistine Chapel to celebrate the 500th anniversary of Michelangelo's ceiling frescoes.

Genoese come-dian Beppe Grillo hit the political big time when his 5 Star Movement took a quarter of the vote in the February 2013 election. A charismatic rabble-rouser with a savage turn of phrase, Grillo articulated the anger felt by many Italians against the coun-try's pampered political elite.

The 2000s

Fascism once again hit the headlines in April 2008 when Gianni Ale-manno, an ex-MSI activist and member of AN, was elected mayor of Rome. As mayor he has strived to distance himself from his far-right past and until fairly recently his first term was marked more by stand-ard political controversy (in 2010 he was drawn into a scandal about nepotistic job appointments to a city bus company) and austerity-driven cut-backs than ideological battles.

However in late 2012, an increase in right-wing militancy led to violent clashes between police and *Blocco Studensco*, a youth group associated with the city's neo-fascist CasaPound movement. Then, in November 2012, a group of English first soccer fans – in town to support Tot-tenham Hotspur, a team with a large Jewish following – were attacked by masked assailants, stoking fears of an increase in anti-Semitism. Alemanno immediately condemned the attack and urged the police to find the culprits.

2012	2013	2013	2013
The Vatileaks scandal breaks when the pope's personal butler leaks documents to the press purporting to expose corruption and in-fighting within the Holy See.	On 11 February, 85-year-old Pope Benedict XVI shocks the world by announcing his resignation. He is the first pope to resign since Gregory XII in 1415.	Italy's general election results in a stalemate as neither left nor right emerge victorious. The real winner is comedian Beppe Grillo whose 5 Star Movement lands 25% of the vote.	Argentinian cardinal Jorge Mario Bergoglio becomes the first Jesuit to be elected pope, taking the papal name Francis in honour of St Francis of Assisi.

The Arts

Rome's turbulent history and magical cityscape have long provided inspiration for painters, sculptors, film-makers, writers and musicians. The great classical works of Roman antiquity fuelled the imagination of Renaissance artists; Counter-Reformation persecution led to baroque art and popular street satire; the trauma of Mussolini and WWII found expression in neo-realist cinema. More recently, the tough economic climate has led to spending cuts but the setbacks are borne and Rome's arts scene continues to thrive.

Painting & Sculpture

Home to some of the Western world's most recognisable art, Rome is a visual feast. Its churches alone contain more masterpieces than many mid-size countries and the city's galleries are laden with works by world-famous artists.

Etruscan Groundwork

Laying the groundwork for much later Roman art, the Etruscans placed great importance on their funerary rites and they developed sepulchral decoration into a highly sophisticated art form. Elaborate stone sarcophagi were often embellished with a reclining figure or a couple, typically depicted with a haunting, enigmatic smile. A stunning example is the *Sarcofago degli Sposi* (Sarcophagus of the Betrothed) in the Museo Nazionale Etrusco di Villa Giulia. Underground funerary vaults, such as those unearthed at Tarquinia, were further enlivened with bright, exuberant frescoes. These frequently represented festivals or scenes from everyday life, with stylised figures shown dancing or playing musical instruments, often with little birds or animals in the background.

The Etruscans were also noted for their bronze work and filigree jewellery. Bronze ore was abundant and was used to craft everything from chariots to candelabras, bowls and polished mirrors. One of Rome's most iconic sculptures, the 5th-century-BC Lupa Capitolina (Capitoline Wolf), now in the Capitoline Museums, is, in fact, an Etruscan bronze. Etruscan jewellery was unrivalled throughout the Mediterranean and goldsmiths produced elaborate pieces using sophisticated filigree and granulation techniques that were only rediscovered in the 20th century.

For Italy's best collection of Etruscan art, head to the Museo Nazionale Etrusco di Villa Giulia; to see Etruscan treasures in situ head out of town to Cerveteri and Tarquinia.

Roman Developments

In art, as in architecture, the ancient Romans borrowed heavily from the Etruscans and Greeks. In terms of decorative art, the Roman use of floor mosaics and wall paintings was derived from Etruscan funerary decoration. By the 1st century BC, floor mosaics were a popular form of home decor. Typical themes included landscapes, still lifes, geometric patterns and depictions of gods. Later, as production and artistic techniques

The best surviving examples of Etruscan frescoes are found in Tarquinia where up to 6000 tombs have been discovered. Particularly graphic are the erotic paintings in the *Tomba della Fustigazione* (Tomb of the Flogging).

improved, mosaics were displayed on walls and in public buildings and places of worship. In the Museo Nazionale Romano: Palazzo Massimo alle Terme, you'll find some spectacular wall mosaics from Nero's villa in Anzio, as well as a series of superb 1st-century-BC frescoes from Villa Livia, one of the homes of Livia Drusilla, Augustus' wife.

Sculpture

Sculpture was an important element of Roman art and was largely influenced by Greek styles. In fact, early Roman sculptures were often made by Greek artists or were, at best, copies of imported Greek works. They were largely concerned with the male physique and generally depicted visions of male beauty in mythical settings – the Apollo Belvedere and the Laocoön in the Vatican Museums' Museo Pio-Clementino are classic examples.

However, over time differences began to emerge between Greek and Roman styles. Roman sculpture lost its obsession with form and began to focus on accurate representation, mainly in the form of sculptural portraits. Browse the collections of the Museo Palatino or the Museo Nazionale Romano: Palazzo Massimo alle Terme and you'll be struck by how lifelike – and often ugly – so many of the marble faces are.

In terms of function, Greek art was all about beauty, harmony and dramatic expression, while Roman art was highly propagandistic. From the time of Augustus (r 27 BC–AD 14), art was increasingly used to serve the state, and artists came to be regarded as little more than state functionaries. This new narrative art often took the form of relief decoration recounting the story of great military victories. The Colonna di Traiano and Ara Pacis are two stunning examples of the genre.

Early Christian Art

The earliest Christian art in Rome are the traces of biblical frescoes in the Catacombe di Priscilla on Via Salaria and the Catacombe di San Sebastiano on Via Appia Antica. These, and other early works, are full of stock images: Lazarus being raised from the dead, Jesus as the good shepherd, the first Christian saints. Symbols also abound: the dove representing peace and happiness, the anchor or trident symbolising the cross, fish in reference to an acrostic from the ancient Greek word for fish (Ichthys) which spells out Jesus Christ, Son of God, Saviour.

Mosaics

With the legalisation of Christianity in the 4th century, these images began to move into the public arena, appearing in mosaics across the city. Mosaic work was the principal artistic endeavour of early Christian Rome and mosaics adorn many of the churches built in this period. Stunning examples include the 4th-century apse mosaic in the Chiesa di Santa Pudenziana, the wonderful mosaics in the vaulted ambulatory of the Mausoleo di Santa Costanza and the 5th-century works in the Basilica di Santa Maria Maggiore.

Eastern influences became much more pronounced between the 7th and 9th centuries, when Byzantine styles swept in from the east, leading to a brighter, golden look. The best examples in Rome are in the Basilica di Santa Maria in Trastevere and the Chiesa di Santa Prassede, a small 9th-century church built in honour of an early Christian heroine.

The Renaissance

Originating in late-14th-century Florence, the Renaissance had already made its mark in Tuscany and Venice before it arrived in Rome in the latter half of the 15th century.

THE ARTS PAINTING & SCULPTURE

Dramatically ensconced in a Richard Meier–designed pavilion, the Ara Pacis is a key work of ancient Roman sculpture. The vast marble altar is covered with detailed reliefs, including one showing Augustus with his family.

One of the greatest artists of the Middle Ages was Pietro Cavallini (c 1240–1330), a Roman-born painter and mosaic designer. Little is known about his life but his most famous work is the *Giudizio Universale* (Last Judgment) fresco in the Chiesa di Santa Cecilia in Trastevere.

ROME'S TOP ART CHURCHES

➡ **St Peter's Basilica** Michelangelo's divine *Pietà* is just one of the many masterpieces on display at the Vatican's showcase basilica.

➡ **Basilica di San Pietro in Vincoli** Moses stands as the muscular centrepiece of Michelangelo's unfinished tomb of Pope Julius II.

➡ **Chiesa di San Luigi dei Francesi** Frescoes by Domenichino are outshone by three Caravaggio canvases depicting the life and death of St Matthew.

➡ **Chiesa di Santa Maria del Popolo** A veritable gallery with frescoes by Pinturicchio, a Raphael-designed chapel, and two paintings by Caravaggio.

➡ **Chiesa di Santa Maria della Vittoria** The church's innocuous exterior gives no clues that this is home to Bernini's extraordinary *Santa Teresa traffita dall'amore di Dio* (Ecstasy of St Teresa).

➡ **Chiesa di Santa Prassede** The Cappella di San Zenone features some of Rome's most brilliant Byzantine mosaics.

➡ **Chiesa del Gesù** Feast your eyes on the magnificent fresco *Trionfo del Nome di Gesù* (Triumph of the Name of Jesus) at Rome's top Jesuit church.

➡ **Basilica di Santa Maria Maggiore** Admire beautiful Cosmati flooring and, high up in the triumphal arch, wonderful 5th-century mosaics.

➡ **Chiesa di Santa Maria Sopra Minerva** Rome's only Gothic church boasts its own Michelangelo, a sculpture of *Cristo Risorto* (Christ Bearing the Cross).

➡ **Chiesa di Sant'Agostino** Houses the *Madonna dei Pellegrini* (*Madonna di Loreto*: Madonna of the Pilgrims), one of Caravaggio's most controversial paintings, and a fresco by Raphael.

But over the next few decades it was to have a profound impact on the city as the top artists of the day were summoned to decorate the many new buildings going up around town.

Michelangelo & the Sistine Chapel

Rome's most celebrated works of Renaissance art are Michelangelo's paintings in the Sistine Chapel: the ceiling frescoes, painted between 1508 and 1512, and the *Giudizio Universale* (Last Judgment), which he worked on between 1536 and 1541. Regarded as the high point of Western artistic achievement, these two works completely outshine the chapel's wall paintings, themselves masterpieces of 15th-century fresco art painted by Pietro Vannucci (Perugino; 1446–1523), Sandro Botticelli (1445–1510), Domenico Ghirlandaio (1449–94), Cosimo Rosselli (1439–1507), Luca Signorelli (c 1445–1523) and Bernadino di Betto (Pinturicchio; 1454–1513).

Michelangelo Buanarroti (1475–1564), born near Arrezzo in Tuscany, was the embodiment of the Renaissance spirit. A painter, sculptor, architect and occasional poet, he, more than any other artist of the era, left an indelible mark on the Eternal City. The Sistine Chapel, his *Pietà* in St Peter's Basilica, sculptures in the city's churches – his masterpieces are legion and they remain city highlights to this day.

Michelangelo and Raphael didn't get on. Despite this, Raphael felt compelled to honour his elder after sneaking into the Sistine Chapel to look at Michelangelo's half-finished ceiling frescoes. He was so impressed with what he saw that he painted Michelangelo into his masterpiece *La Scuola di Atene*.

The Human Form

The human form was central to much Renaissance art, and Michelangelo and Leonardo da Vinci famously studied human anatomy to perfect their representations. Underlying this trend was the humanist philosophy, the intellectual foundation stone of the Renaissance, which held man to be central to the God-created universe and beauty to represent a deep inner virtue.

SAINTS GLOSSARY

As befits the world's Catholic capital, Rome is overrun by saints. Roads are named after them, churches commemorate them and paintings portray them in all their righteous glory. Here we list some of the big-name *santi* (saints) you'll come across in Rome.

➡ **Sant'Agnese** (d 305, b Rome) Patron saint of virgins and Girl Scouts, St Agnes died a martyr at the age of 13. According to tradition, she was beheaded on Piazza Navona.

➡ **Santa Cecilia** (2nd century, b Rome) A popular Roman saint, St Cecilia is the patron of music and musicians. She was buried in the Catacombe di San Callisto and later moved to the Basilica di Santa Cecilia in Trastevere.

➡ **San Clemente** (d 97, b Rome) St Clement was ordained by St Peter and became the fourth pope in 88 AD. He was later banished to the Crimean mines by the emperor Trajan.

➡ **San Giovanni** (d c 101) Author of the gospel of St John and the Book of Revelation, St John was a travelling companion of Jesus and friend of St Peter. He was tortured by the emperor Domitian but apparently emerged unscathed from a cauldron of boiling oil. The Basilica di San Giovanni in Laterano is dedicated to him and St John the Baptist.

➡ **San Gregorio** (540–604, b Rome) St Gregory made his name as Pope Gregory the Great. He sent St Augustine to convert the Brits, built monasteries, and lent his name to a style of liturgical singing – the Gregorian chant. He is the patron saint of choirboys.

➡ **Sant'Ignazio di Loyola** (1491–1556, b Guipuzcoa, Spain) Spanish-born St Ignatius Loyola earned his Roman colours by founding the Jesuits in Rome in 1540. He spent his last years at the Chiesa del Gesù.

➡ **San Lorenzo** (c 225–258, b Huesca, Spain) A canny financial manager, St Lawrence safeguarded the assets of the 3rd-century Roman Church when not helping the sick, poor and crippled. His patronage of chefs and cooks results from his indescribably awful death – he was grilled to death on a griddle iron.

➡ **Santa Maria** (1st century BC – 1st century AD Nazareth) Venerated by Catholics, the Virgin Mary or Madonna, appears in paintings and sculptures across the city; Michelangelo famously depicts her in his Pietà in St Peter's Basilica.

➡ **San Marco** (1st century AD, b Libya) St Mark is said to have written the second gospel while in Rome. The Basilica di San Marco stands over the house where he used to stay when in town.

➡ **San Paolo** (c 3–65, b Turkey) Saul the Christian hater became St Paul the travelling evangelist after conversion on the road to Damascus. He was decapitated in Rome during Nero's persecution of the Christians. Along with St Peter, he's the capital's patron saint. Their joint feast day, a holiday in Rome, is 29 June.

➡ **San Pietro** (d 64, b Galilee) One of Rome's two patron saints, St Peter is said to have founded the Roman Catholic Church after Jesus gave him the keys to the Kingdom of Heaven. He was crucified upside down and buried on the spot where St Peter's Basilica now stands.

➡ **San Sebastiano** (d c 288, b France) St Sebastian distinguished himself as an officer in Diocletian's imperial army before converting to Christianity. Diocletian wasn't amused and had him tied to a tree and turned into an archery target. He survived, only to be beaten to death.

This focus on the human body led artists to develop a far greater appreciation of perspective. Early Renaissance painters had made great strides in formulating rules of perspective but they found that the rigid formulae they were experimenting with often made harmonious arrangements of figures difficult. This was precisely the challenge that

Raffaello Sanzio (Raphael; 1483–1520) tackled in *La Scuola di Atene* (The School of Athens; 1510–11) in the Stanze di Raffaello in the Vatican Museums and the *Trionfo di Galatea* (Triumph of Galatea) in Villa Farnesina.

Originally from Urbino, Raphael arrived in Rome in 1508 and went on to become the most influential painter of his generation. A paid-up advocate of the Renaissance exaltation of beauty, he painted many versions of the Madonna and Child, all of which epitomise the Western model of 'ideal beauty' that perseveres to this day.

Counter-Reformation & The Baroque

The baroque burst onto Rome's art scene in the early 17th century in a swirl of emotional energy. Combining a dramatic sense of dynamism with highly charged emotion, it was enthusiastically appropriated by the Catholic Church. At the time the Church was viciously persecuting Counter-Reformation heresy and the powerful popes of the day saw baroque art as an ideal propaganda tool. They eagerly championed the likes of Caravaggio, Gian Lorenzo Bernini, Domenichino, Pietro da Cortona and Alessandro Algardi.

Not surprisingly, much baroque art has a religious theme and you'll often find depictions of martyrdoms, ecstasies and miracles. The use of coloured marble, gold leaf and ornamental church settings are further trademarks.

Caravaggio

One of the key painters of the period was Caravaggio (1573–1610), the Milan-born *enfant terrible* of Rome's art world. A controversial and often violent character, he arrived in Rome around 1590 and immediately set about rewriting the artistic rule books. While his peers and Catholic patrons sought to glorify and overwhelm, he painted nature as he saw it. He had no time for 'ideal beauty' and caused uproar with his lifelike portrayal of hitherto sacrosanct subjects – his barefoot depiction of the Virgin Mary in the *Madonna dei Pellegrini* (Madonna of the Pilgrims) in the Chiesa di Sant'Agostino is typical of his audacious approach.

Gian Lorenzo Bernini

But while Caravaggio shocked his patrons, Gian Lorenzo Bernini (1598–1680) delighted them with his stunning sculptures. More than anyone else before or since, Bernini was able to capture a moment, freezing emotions and conveying a sense of dramatic action. His depiction of *Santa Teresa traffita dall'amore di Dio* (Ecstasy of St Teresa) in the Chiesa di Santa Maria della Vittoria does just that, blending realism, eroticism and theatrical spirituality in a work that is widely considered one of the greatest of the baroque period. Further evidence of his genius is on show at the Museo e Galleria Borghese, where you can marvel at his ability to make stone-cold marble seem soft as flesh in the *Ratto di Proserpina* (Rape of Persephone), and his magnificent depiction of Daphne transforming into a laurel tree in *Apollo e Dafne* (Apollo and Daphne).

Frescoes

Fresco painting continued to provide work for artists well into the 17th century. Important exponents include Domenichino (1581–1641), whose decorative works adorn the Chiesa di San Luigi dei Francesi and the Chiesa di Sant'Andrea della Valle; Pietro da Cortona (1596–1669), author of the *Trionfo della Divina Provvidenza* (Triumph of Divine Providence) in Palazzo Barberini; and Annibale Carracci (1560–1609), the

---

THE ARTS PAINTING & SCULPTURE

The most famous decorative artists of the 13th century were the Cosmati. This Roman family revolutionised the art of mosaic-making by slicing up ancient columns of coloured marble into circular slabs, which they then used to create intricate patterns.

Caravaggio took his trademark *chiaroscuro*, a technique involving the bold contrast of light and dark, to its extreme limits, giving rise to tenebrism, a style characterised by brightly lit figures set against solid dark backgrounds.

> ## NEOCLASSICISM
>
> Emerging in the late-18th and early-19th centuries, neoclassicism signalled a departure from the emotional abandon of the baroque and a return to the clean, sober lines of classical art. Its major exponent was the sculptor Antonio Canova (1757–1822), whose study of Paolina Bonaparte Borghese as *Venere Vincitrice* (Venus Victrix) in the Museo e Galleria Borghese is typical of the mildly erotic sculpture for which he became known.

genius behind the frescoes in Palazzo Farnese, said by some to equal those of the Sistine Chapel.

Emerging about 1520, mannerism bridged the gap between the Renaissance and baroque eras. Signature traits include the use of artificial colours and figures with elongated limbs posed in florid settings. It was much derided by later critics for distorting the balance of Renaissance art in favour of more emotional expression.

The 20th-century

In artistic terms, the early 20th century was marked by the development of two very different movements: futurism and metaphysical painting (*pittura metafisica*), an early form of surrealism.

Futurism

Often associated with fascism, Italian futurism was an ambitious movement, embracing not only the visual arts but also architecture, music, fashion and theatre. It started with the publication of Filippo Tommaso Marinetti's *Manifesto del futurismo* (Manifesto of Futurism) in 1909, which was backed up a year later by the futurist painting manifesto written by Umberto Boccioni (1882–1916), Giacomo Balla (1871–1958), Luigi Russolo (1885–1947) and Gino Severini (1883–1966). A rallying cry for modernism and a vitriolic rejection of artistic traditions, these manifestos highlighted dynamism, speed, machinery and technology as their central tenets. They were also nationalistic and highly militaristic.

One of the movement's founding fathers, Giacomo Balla encapsulated the futurist ideals in works such as *Espansione dinamica Velocità* (Dynamic Expansion and Speed), one of a series of paintings exploring the dynamic nature of motion, and *Forme Grido Viva l'Italia* (The Shout Viva l'Italia), an abstract work inspired by the futurists' desire for Italy to enter WWI. Both are on show at the Galleria Nazionale d'Arte Moderna.

Metaphysical Painting

In contrast to the brash vitality of futurism, metaphysical paintings were peopled by mysterious images conjured up from the subconscious world. Its most famous exponent was Giorgio de Chirico (1888–1978), whose visionary works were a major influence on the French surrealist movement. With their stillness and sense of foreboding they often show classical subjects presented as enigmatic mannequin-like figures. Good examples include *Ettore e Andromaca* (Hector and Andromache) in the Galleria Nazionale d'Arte Moderna, and *Orfeo Solitario* (Solitary Orpheus) in the Museo Carlo Bilotti.

Top Galleries & Museums

Vatican Museums

Museo e Galleria Borghese

Capitoline Museums

Museo Nazionale Romano: Palazzo Massimo alle Terme

Contemporary Scene

Rome's contemporary art scene is centred on the capital's two flagship galleries: the Museo Nazionale delle Arti del XXI Secolo, better known as MAXXI, and the Museo d'Arte Contemporanea di Roma, aka MACRO. Both have attracted widespread attention since they were opened in 2010 and 2011 respectively, but the jury remains out as to whether the exhibitions they host are equal to the sleek, architecturally innovative buildings that house them. More worryingly, recent austerity-driven cut-backs have begun to bite and a question mark currently hangs over MAXXI's future.

Other important galleries include the Gagosian, the Rome-branch of Larry Gagosian's contemporary arts empire, and MACRO Testaccio, an exhibition space in Rome's former slaughterhouse.

In terms of home-grown talent, Rome's artistic hub is the Pastificio Cerere in San Lorenzo. A pasta factory turned art studio, it's home to a number of working artists, including Maurizio Savini, best known for his sculptures made from pink chewing gum, and photographers Eligio Paoni and Gabriele Giugni. Other Rome-based artists to look out for include the video-artist Elisabetta Benassi, and Tiziano Lucci, who has exhibited in Britain, Germany, the US and Argentina.

Street art also thrives in Rome, particularly in the suburbs of San Lorenzo, Pigneto and Ostiense, where walls are covered in stencil art, poster work and graffiti. In recognition of this, Rome city council launched a ground-breaking initiative in 2012 giving local 'writers' – as Rome's graffiti artists call themselves – free use of 31 designated areas across town. These include spaces at the metro stations Monti Tiburtina, Santa Maria del Soccorso, Ponte Mammolo and Rebibbia (all line B).

Literature

A history of authoritarian rule has given rise to a rich literary tradition, encompassing everything from ancient satires to dialect poetry and anti-fascist prose. As a backdrop, Rome has inspired scribes as diverse as Goethe and Dan Brown.

Cicero, Virgil et al – the Classics

Famous for his blistering oratory, Marcus Tullius Cicero (106–43 BC) was the Roman Republic's pre-eminent author. A brilliant barrister, he became consul in 63 BC and subsequently published many philosophical works and speeches. Fancying himself as the senior statesman, Cicero took the young Octavian under his wing and attacked Mark Antony in a series of 14 speeches, the *Philippics*. These proved fatal, though, for when Octavian changed sides and joined Mark Antony, he demanded, and got, Cicero's head.

Poetry & Satire-

A contemporary of Cicero, Catullus (c 84–54 BC) cut a very different figure. A passionate and influential poet, he is best known for his epigrams and erotic verse.

On becoming emperor, Augustus (aka Octavian) encouraged the arts, and Virgil (70–19 BC), Ovid, Horace and Tibullus all enjoyed freedom to write. Of the works produced in this period, it's Virgil's rollicking *Aeneid* that stands out. A glorified mix of legend, history and moral instruction, it tells how Aeneas escapes from Troy and after years of mythical mishaps ends up landing in Italy where his descendants Romulus and Remus eventually found Rome.

Little is known of Decimus Iunius Iuvenalis, better known as Juvenal, but his 16 satires have survived as classics of the genre. Writing in the 1st century AD, he combined an acute mind with a cutting pen, famously scorning the masses as being interested in nothing but 'bread and circuses'.

Virgil gave us some of our most famous expressions – 'Fortune favours the bold', 'Love conquers all' and 'Time flies'. However, it was Juvenal who issued the classic warning: '*quis custodiet ipsos custodes?*' or 'who guards the guards?'.

Ancient Histories

The two major historians of the period were Livy (59 BC–AD 17) and Tacitus (c 56–116). Although both wrote in the early days of empire they displayed very different styles. Livy, whose history of the Roman Republic was probably used as a school textbook, cheerfully mixed myth with fact to produce an entertaining and popular tome. Tacitus, on the other hand, took a decidedly colder approach. His *Annals* and *Histories,* which cover the early years of the Roman Empire, are cutting and often witty, although imbued with an underlying pessimism.

Street Writing & Popular Poetry

Rome's tradition of street writing, which today survives in the form of colourful graffiti art, goes back to the dark days of the 17th century. With the Church systematically suppressing every whiff of criticism, Counter-Reformation Rome was not a great place for budding authors. As a way round censorship, disgruntled Romans began posting *pasquinades* (anonymous messages; named after the first person who wrote one) on the city's so-called speaking statues. These messages, often archly critical of the authorities, were sensibly posted in the dead of night and then gleefully circulated around town the following day. The most famous speaking statue stands in Piazza Pasquino near Piazza Navona.

Dialect Verse

Poking savage fun at the rich and powerful was one of the favourite themes of Gioacchino Belli (1791–1863), one of a trio of poets who made their names writing poetry in Roman dialect. Born poor, Belli started his career with conventional and undistinguished verse, but found the crude and colourful dialect of the Roman streets better suited to his outspoken attacks on the chattering classes.

Carlo Alberto Salustri (1871–1950), aka Trilussa, is the best known of the trio. He, too, wrote social and political satire, although not exclusively so, and many of his poems are melancholy reflections on life, love and solitude. One of his most famous works, the anti-fascist poem *All'Ombra* (In the Shadow), is etched onto a plaque in Piazza Trilussa, the Trastevere square named in his honour.

The poems of Cesare Pescarella (1858–1940) present a vivid portrait of turn-of-the-century Rome. Gritty and realistic, they pull no punches in describing everyday life as lived by Rome's forgotten poor.

Rome as Inspiration

With its magical cityscape and historic atmosphere, Rome has provided inspiration for legions of foreign authors.

Romantic Visions

In the 18th century the city was a hotbed of literary activity as historians and Grand Tourists poured in from northern Europe. The German author Johann Wolfgang von Goethe captures the elation of discovering ancient Rome and the colours of the modern city in his celebrated travelogue *Italian Journey* (1817).

Rome was also a magnet for the English Romantic poets. John Keats, Lord Byron, Percy Bysshe Shelley, Mary Shelley and other writers all spent time in the city. Byron, in a typically over-the-top outburst, described Rome as the city of his soul even though he visited only fleetingly. Keats came to Rome in 1821 in the hope that it would cure his ill

In 1559 Pope Paul IV published the *Index Librorum Prohibitorum* (Index of Prohibited Books), a list of books forbidden by the Catholic Church. Over the next 400 years, it was revised 20 times, the last edition appearing in 1948. It was officially abolished in 1966.

Rome's most influential contribution to literature was the Vulgate Bible. This dates to the 4th century when Pope Damasus (r 366–384) had his secretary Eusebius Hieronymous, aka St Jerome, translate the bible into accessible Latin. His version is the basis for the bible currently used by the Catholic Church.

health, but it didn't and he died of tuberculosis in his lodgings at the foot of the Spanish Steps.

Later, in the 19th century, American author Nathaniel Hawthorne penned his classic *The Marble Faun* (1860) after two years in Italy. Taking inspiration from a sculpture in the Capitoline Museums, he uses a murder story as an excuse to explore his thoughts on art and culture.

Rome as Backdrop

In the first decade of the 2000s it became fashionable for novelists to use Rome as a backdrop. Dan Brown's thriller *Angels and Demons* (2001) is set in Rome, as is Kathleen A Quinn's warm-hearted love story *Leaving Winter* (2003). Jeanne Kalogridis transports readers back to the 15th century in her sumptuous historical novel *The Borgia Bride* (2006), a sensual account of Vatican scheming and dangerous passions.

Robert Harris's accomplished fictional biography of Cicero, *Imperium* (2006), is one of a number of books set in 1st-century Rome. Steven Saylor's *The Triumph of Caesar* (2009) skilfully evokes the passion, fear and violence that hung in the air during Julius Caesar's last days. Similarly stirring is *Antony and Cleopatra* (2008), the last in Colleen McCollough's Masters of Rome series, which centres on the doomed love triangle between Octavian, Mark Antony and Cleopatra.

Into this historical genre you can add a further sub-genre – the ancient thriller. Good examples include Martha Marks' feminist-tinged mystery, *Rubies of the Viper* (2010), and *Vestal Virgin: Suspense in Ancient Rome* (2011), a dark tale of secret passions by Suzanne Tyrpak.

Literature & Fascism

A controversial figure, Gabriele D'Annunzio (1863–1938) was the most flamboyant Italian writer of the early 20th century. A WWI fighter pilot and ardent nationalist, he was born in Pescara and settled in Rome in 1881. Forever associated with fascism, he wrote prolifically, both poetry and novels. Of his books, perhaps the most revealing is *Il Fuoco* (The Flame of Life; 1900), a passionate romance in which he portrays himself as a Nietzschean superman born to command.

The Anti-Fascists

On the opposite side of the political spectrum, Roman-born Alberto Moravia (1907–90) was banned from writing by Mussolini and, together with his wife, Elsa Morante (1912–85), was forced into hiding for a year. The alienated individual and the emptiness of fascist and bourgeois society are common themes in his writing. In *La Romana* (The Woman of Rome; 1947) he explores the broken dreams of a country girl, Adriana, as she slips into prostitution and theft.

The novels of Elsa Morante are characterised by a subtle psychological appraisal of her characters and can be seen as a personal cry of pity for the sufferings of individuals and society. Her 1974 masterpiece, *La Storia* (History), is a tough tale of a half-Jewish woman's desperate struggle for dignity in the poverty of occupied Rome.

Taking a similarly anti-fascist line, Carlo Emilio Gadda (1893–1973) combines murder and black humour in his classic whodunnit, *Quer Pasticciaccio Brutto de Via Merulana* (That Awful Mess on Via Merulana; 1957). Although the mystery is never solved, the book's a brilliant portrayal of the pomposity and corruption that thrived in Mussolini's Rome.

Writing Today

Born in Rome in 1966, Niccolò Ammaniti is the best known of the city's current crop of writers. In 2007 he won the Premio Strega, Italy's top

Roman Reads

Roman Tales (Alberto Moravia)

That Awful Mess on Via Merulana (Carlo Emilio Gadda)

The Secrets of Rome, Love & Death in the Eternal City (Corrado Augias)

PIER PAOLO PASOLINI, MASTER OF CONTROVERSY

Poet, novelist and film-maker, Pier Paolo Pasolini (1922–75) was one of Italy's most important and controversial 20th-century intellectuals. His works, which are complex, unsentimental and provocative, provide a scathing portrait of Italy's postwar social transformation.

Although he spent much of his adult life in Rome, he had a peripatetic childhood. He was born in Bologna but moved around frequently and rarely spent more than a few years in any one place. He did, however, form a lasting emotional attachment to Friuli, the mountainous region in northeastern Italy where his mother was from and where he spent the latter half of WWII. Much of his early poetry, collected and published in 1954 as *La meglio gioventù,* was written in Friulano dialect.

Politically, he was a communist, but he never played a part in Italy's left-wing establishment. In 1949 he was expelled from the *Partito Comunista Italiano* (PCI; Italian Communist Party) after a gay sex scandal and for the rest of his career he remained a sharp critic of the party. His most famous outburst came in the poem *Il PCI ai giovani,* in which he dismisses left-wing students as bourgeois and sympathises with the police, whom he describes as *'figli di poveri'* (sons of the poor). In the context of 1968 Italy, a year marked by widespread student agitation, this was a highly incendiary position to take.

Pasolini was no stranger to controversy. His first novel *Ragazzi di Vita* (The Ragazzi), set in the squalor of Rome's forgotten suburbs, earned him success and a court case for obscenity. Similarly, his early films – *Accattone* (1961) and *Mamma Roma* (1962) – provoked righteous outrage with their relentlessly bleak depiction of life in the Roman underbelly.

True to the scandalous nature of his art, Pasolini was murdered in 1975. It was originally thought that his death was linked to events in the gay underworld but revelations in 2005 hinted that it might, in fact, have been a politically motivated killing.

literary prize for his novel, *Come Dio comanda* (As God Commands). He's probably best known for *Io Non Ho Paura* (I'm Not Scared; 2001), a soulful study of a young boy's realisation that his father is involved in a child kidnapping.

Another name to look out for is Alessandro Piperno, whose critically acclaimed novels have earned him comparisons with Marcel Proust and Philip Roth. His bestselling debut novel *Con le peggiore intenzioni* (The Worst Intentions; 2005) won the 2007 Premio Viareggio and in 2012 he went one better and won the Premio Strega for his Jewish family saga, *Inseparabili* (Inseparable).

Emanuele Trevi, a Rome-born critic and writer, has also been making a mark. His most high-profile novel is *Qualcosa di Scritto* (Something Written), a complex, quasi-autobiographical story of a writer's experience working in a Roman cultural foundation. In 2012, Trevi won the European Union Prize for Literature.

Coincidence? Nanni Moretti's 2011 comedy *Habemus Papam* centres on a pope who resigns after treatment for stress. Two years after the film was released Pope Benedict XVI became the first pope to resign in more than 600 years, claiming he no longer had the strength for the job.

Cinema & Television

Cinema

Since its inception in 2006, Rome's film festival has established itself on the European circuit, attracting Hollywood hotshots and hordes of paparazzi to the Auditorium Parco della Musica. However, controversy has rarely been far away, and in 2010 screenwriters and directors took to the red carpet to protest against government spending cuts. The Italian government is one of the major financiers of Italian cinema and over the past few years it has been systematically slashing investment leading to fears of future job losses.

Cannes & Cinecittà

Italian film-makers have long had a good relationship with Cannes and 2008 was a recent highpoint. Matteo Garrone, a talented Roman director, took the Grand Prix for *Gomorra* (Gomorrah), a hard-hitting exposé of the Neapolitan mafia, and Paolo Sorrentino scooped the Special Jury Prize for *Il Divo*, an ice-cold portrayal of Giulio Andreotti, Italy's most famous postwar politician.

The early noughties also witnessed a renewal of interest in Rome's film-making facilities. Private investment in Cinecittà lured a number of big-name directors to Rome's legendary studios, including Ron Howard for his 2009 thriller *Angels and Demons*, Mel Gibson for *The Passion of the Christ* (2004), and Martin Scorsese, who had 19th-century New York recreated for his 2002 epic *Gangs of New York*.

But competition from cheaper East European countries and a fall in domestic output – in 2011 only eight Italian films and six TV series were made at Cinecittà – have led to a serious decline in the studios' fortunes. To stop the rot the studio management is pinning its hopes on plans for a €500 million movie theme park and a glitzy on-site hotel complex. Predictably, though, these have been roundly criticised by studio employees who regard them as the opening gambit in a long-term project to do away with Cinecittà's movie-making facilities and focus on the 40-hectare site's real estate potential.

Cinecittà celebrated its 75th birthday in 2012. Inaugurated in 1937, the studios were originally intended to produce propaganda films for Mussolini. However, their golden age came in the 1950s and 1960s when Ben-Hur and Cleopatra were filmed there alongside Federico Fellini's La Dolce Vita and many other big-budget blockbusters.

THE ARTS CINEMA & TELEVISION

Roman Directors

Leading the new wave of Roman film-makers is Matteo Garrone (b 1968), whose award-winning *Gomorra* (Gomorrah; 2008) helped seal a reputation already on the up after his 2002 film *L'Imbalsamatore* (The Embalmer). In 2012, he won further honours, scooping the Grand Prix at Cannes for his sharply observed satire on the power of reality TV, *Reality*. The film, while a critical success, also made headlines for its casting – the lead actor was a former mafia hitman serving a life sentence for murder.

Other directors to have enjoyed recent critical acclaim included Emanuele Crialese (b 1965) who won the Jury Prize at Venice for *Terraferma*, a thought-provoking study of the effects of immigration on a small Sicilian island, and Saverio Costanzo (b 1975), who hit the bullseye with his 2010 film adaptation of Paolo Giordano's bestselling book *La solitudine dei numeri primi* (The Solitude of Prime Numbers). Gabriele Muccino (b 1967), director of the 2001 smash *L'Ultimo Bacio* (The Last Kiss) returned to his earlier success in 2010 with *Baciami ancora* (Kiss Me Again), a sequel to *L'Ultimo Baccio*.

Before Muccino, Rome was generally represented by Carlo Verdone (b 1950) and Nanni Moretti (b 1953). A comedian in the Roman tradition, Verdone has made a name for himself satirising his fellow citizens in a number of bittersweet comedies which, at best, are very funny, but which can be repetitive and predictable. His 1995 film *Viaggi di Nozze* (Honeymoons) is one of his best.

Moretti, on the other hand, falls into no mainstream tradition. A politically active writer, actor and director, his films are often whimsical and self-indulgent. Arguably his best work, *Caro Diario* (Dear Diary; 1994) earned him the best director prize at Cannes in 1994 – an award that he topped in 2001 when he won the Palme d'Or for *La Stanza del Figlio* (The Son's Room).

Throughout the 1960s and '70s Italy was one of the world's most prolific producers of horror films. Rome's master of terror was, and still is, Dario Argento (b 1940), director of the 1975 cult classic Profondo Rosso (Deep Red) and more than 20 other movies.

The Golden Age

For the real golden age of Roman film-making you have to turn the clocks back to the 1940s, when Roberto Rossellini (1906–77) produced

SERGIO LEONE, MR SPAGHETTI WESTERN

Best known for virtually single-handedly creating the spaghetti western, Sergio Leone (1929–89) is a hero to many. Martin Scorsese, Quentin Tarantino and Robert Rodriguez are among the directors who count him as a major influence, while Clint Eastwood owes him his cinematic breakthrough. Astonishingly, he only ever directed seven films.

The son of a silent-movie director, Leone cut his teeth as a screenwriter on a series of sword-and-sandal epics, before working as assistant director on *Quo Vadis?* (1951) and *Ben-Hur* (1959). He made his directorial debut three years later on *Il Colosso di Rodi* (The Colossus of Rhodes; 1961).

However, it was with his famous dollar trilogy – *Per un pugno di dollari* (A Fistful of Dollars; 1964), *Per qualche dollari in piu* (For a Few Dollars More; 1965) and *Il buono, il brutto, il cattivo* (The Good, the Bad and the Ugly; 1966) – that he really hit the big time. The first, filmed in Spain and based on the 1961 samurai flick *Yojimbo,* set the style for the genre. No longer were clean-cut, morally upright heroes pitted against cartoon-style villains, but characters were more complex, often morally ambiguous and driven by self-interest.

Stylistically, Leone introduced a series of innovations that were later to become trademarks. Chief among these was his use of musical themes to identify his characters. And in this he was brilliantly supported by his old schoolmate, Ennio Morricone. One of Hollywood's most prolific composers, Morricone (b 1928) has worked on more than 500 films, but his masterpiece remains his haunting score for *Il buono, il brutto, il cattivo* (The Good, the Bad and the Ugly). A unique orchestration of trumpets, whistles, gunshots, church bells, harmonicas and electric guitars, it was inducted into the Grammy Hall of Fame in 2009.

a trio of neo-realist masterpieces. The first and most famous was *Roma Città Aperta* (Rome Open City; 1945), filmed with brutal honesty in the Prenestina district east of the city centre. Vittorio de Sica (1901–74) kept the neo-realist ball rolling in 1948 with *Ladri di Biciclette* (Bicycle Thieves), again filmed in Rome's sprawling suburbs.

Federico Fellini (1920–94) took the creative baton from the neo-realists and carried it into the following decades. His disquieting style demands more of audiences, abandoning realistic shots for pointed images at once laden with humour, pathos and double meaning. Fellini's greatest international hit was *La Dolce Vita* (1960), starring Marcello Mastroianni and Anita Ekberg.

The films of Pier Paolo Pasolini (1922–75) are similarly demanding. A communist Catholic homosexual, he made films that not only reflect his ideological and sexual tendencies but also offer a unique portrayal of Rome's urban wasteland.

Woody Allen's celluloid homage to the Eternal City failed to impress local critics after it premiered in Rome in April 2012. Featuring four storylines and a glossy, picture-perfect portrayal of Rome, *To Rome With Love* was accused of being superficial and lacking in irony.

Television

The real interest in Italian TV is not so much what's on the screen as the political shenanigans that go on behind it. Unfortunately, none of this real-life drama translates to on-screen programming, which remains ratings-driven and advert-drenched. Soap operas, quizzes and reality shows are staples and homemade drama rarely goes beyond the tried and tested, with an incessant stream of films on popes, priests, saints and martyrs. Scantily-clad women, known as *veline,* appear in droves, particularly on the interminable variety shows that run on Saturday evenings and Sunday afternoons.

Music

Despite cut-backs in public funding, Rome's music scene is in rude health. International orchestras perform to sell-out audiences, jazz greats jam in steamy clubs and rappers rage in underground venues.

Castration & Choral Music

In a city of churches, it's little wonder that choral music has deep roots. In the 16th and 17th centuries, Rome's great Renaissance popes summoned the top musicians of the day to tutor the papal choir. Two of the most famous were Giovanni Pierluigi da Palestrina (c 1525–94), one of Italy's foremost Renaissance composers, and the Naples-born Domenico Scarlatti (1685–1757). Girolamo Frescobaldi (1583–1643), admired by the young JS Bach, was twice an organist at St Peter's Basilica.

The papal choirs, originally composed of priests, were closed to women and the high parts were taken by *castrati,* boys who had been surgically castrated before puberty to preserve their high voices. Although castration was punishable by excommunication, the Sistine Chapel and other papal choirs contained *castrati* as early as 1588 and as late as the early 20th century. The last known *castrato,* Alessandro Moreschi (1858–1922), known as *l'angelo di Roma* (the angel of Rome), was castrated in 1865, just five years before the practice was officially outlawed. He entered the Sistine Chapel choir in 1883 and 15 years later became conductor. He retired in 1913, 10 years after Pius X had banned *castrati* from the papal choirs. Boy sopranos were introduced in the 1950s.

In 1585 Sixtus V formally established the Accademia di Santa Cecilia as a support organisation for papal musicians. Originally it was involved in the publication of sacred music, although it later developed a teaching function, and in 1839 it completely reinvented itself as an academy with wider cultural and academic goals. Today it is one of the world's most highly respected conservatories, with its own orchestra and chorus.

Opera

Rome is often snubbed by serious opera buffs who prefer their Puccini in Milan, Venice or Naples. However, performances at the city's main opera house, the Teatro dell'Opera, are passionately followed. The Romans have long been keen opera-goers and in the 19th century a number of important operas were premiered in Rome, including Rossini's *Il Barbiere di Siviglia* (The Barber of Seville; 1816), Verdi's *Il Trovatore* (The Troubadour; 1853) and Giacomo Puccini's *Tosca* (1900).

Tosca not only premiered in Rome but is also set in the city. The first act takes place in the Chiesa di Sant'Andrea della Valle, the second in Palazzo Farnese, and the final act in Castel Sant'Angelo, the castle from which Tosca jumps to her death.

Adapted from a book by Giancarlo De Cataldo, the critically-acclaimed TV series *Romanzo Criminale* tells the story of a Rome-based criminal gang. The storyline and characters are based on the real-life Banda della Magliana which dominated Rome's criminal underworld in the late 1970s and early 1980s.

Jazz, Hip Hop & the Contemporary Scene

Jazz has long been a mainstay of Rome's music scene. Introduced by US troops during WWII, it grew in popularity during the postwar period and took off in the 1960s with the opening of the mythical Folkstudio club. Since then, it has gone from strength to strength and the city now boasts some fabulous jazz clubs, including Alexanderplatz, Big Mama and the Casa del Jazz. Big names to look out for include Enrico Pieranunzi, a Roman-born pianist and composer, and Doctor 3 whose idiosyncratic sound has earned them considerable acclaim.

Rome also has a vibrant rap and hip hop scene. Hip hop, which arrived in the city in the late 1980s and spread via the *centro sociale* (organised squat) network, was originally highly politicised and many early exponents associated themselves with Rome's alternative left-wing scene. But in recent years exposure and ever-increasing commercialisation has diluted this political element and the scene has largely gone mainstream. For a taste of genuine Roman rap tune into bands such as Colle der Fomento, Cor Veleno or the ragamuffin outfit Villa Ada Posse.

Rome's reputation in the world of dance rests more on its breakdancers than its corps de ballet

Dancehall is another popular music style and many of the capital's top clubs host regular dancehall nights.

Theatre & Dance

Surprisingly for a city in which art has always been appreciated, Rome has no great theatrical tradition. It has never had a Broadway or West End, and while highbrow imports are greeted enthusiastically, fringe theatre remains in the shadows. That said, theatres such as Teatro Vascello, Teatro Palladium and Teatro India stage wide-ranging programmes offering everything from avant-garde dance to cutting-edge street theatre. Adding to the mix, the annual Liberi Esperimenti Teatrali programme promotes workshops, laboratories and experimental performances.

Although not strictly speaking a Roman, Dacia Maraini (b 1936) has produced her best work while living in Rome. Considered one of Italy's most important feminist writers she has more than 30 plays to her name, many of which continue to be translated and performed around the world.

Dance is a major highlight of Rome's big autumn festival, Romaeuropa. But while popular, performances rarely showcase homegrown talent, which remains thin on the ground. In fact, Rome's reputation in the world of dance rests more on its breakdancers than its corps de ballet. The city's most celebrated crew is Urban Force which often represents the capital in national and international competitions and regularly performs live.

Major ballet performances are staged at the Teatro dell'Opera, home to Rome's principal ballet company, the Balletto del Teatro dell'Opera led by the Belgian choreographer and director, Micha van Hoecke.

Architecture

From ancient ruins and Renaissance basilicas to baroque churches and hulking fascist *palazzi*, Rome's architectural legacy is unparalleled. Michelangelo, Bramante, Borromini and Bernini are among the architects who have stamped their genius on its remarkable cityscape, which features some of the Western world's most celebrated buildings. But it's not all about history. In recent years a number of high-profile building projects have drawn the world's top architects to Rome, their futuristic designs provoking discussion, debate and soul-searching among the city's passionate critics.

The Ancients

Architecture was central to the success of the ancient Romans. In building their great capital, they were among the first people to use architecture to tackle problems of infrastructure, urban management and communication. For the first time, architects and engineers were asked to design houses, roads, aqueducts and shopping centres alongside temples, tombs and imperial palaces. To do this the Romans advanced methods devised by the Etruscans and Greeks, developing construction techniques and building materials that allowed them to build on a massive and hitherto unseen scale.

Etruscan Roots

By the 7th century BC the Etruscans were the dominant force on the Italian peninsula, with important centres at Tarquinia, Caere (Cerveteri) and Veii (Veio). These city-states were fortified with defensive walls and although little actually remains – the Etruscans generally built with wood and brick, which don't age well – archaeologists have found evidence of aqueducts, bridges and sewers, as well as sophisticated temples. In Rome, you can still see foundations of an Etruscan temple on the Campidoglio (Capitoline Hill).

But much of what we now know about the Etruscans derives from findings unearthed in their elaborate tombs. Like many ancient peoples, the Etruscans placed great emphasis on their dead and they built impressive cemeteries. These were constructed outside the city walls and harboured richly decorated stone vaults covered by mounds of earth. The best examples of Etruscan tombs are to be found in Cerveteri and Tarquinia, north of Rome (p244).

MAIN ARCHITECTURAL PERIODS

c 8th–3rd centuries BC
The Etruscans in central Italy and the Greeks in the southern Italian colony, Magna Graecia, lay the groundwork for later Roman developments. Particularly influential are Greek temple designs.

c 4th century BC–5th century AD
The ancient Romans make huge advances in engineering techniques, constructing monumental public buildings, bridges, aqueducts, houses and an underground sewerage system.

4th–12th century
Church building is the focus of architectural activity in the medieval period as Rome's early Christian leaders seek to stamp their authority on the city.

15th–16th century
Based on humanism and a reappraisal of classical precepts, the Renaissance hits an all-time high in the first two decades of the 16th century, a period known as the High Renaissance.

17th century
Developing out of the Counter-Reformation, the baroque flourishes in Rome, fuelled by Church money and the genius of Gian Lorenzo Bernini and Francesco Borromini.

ALL ROADS LEAD TO ROME

The Romans were the great road builders of the ancient world. Approximately 80,000km of surfaced highways spanned the Roman Empire, providing vital military and communication links. Many of modern Rome's roads retain the names of their ancient forebears and follow almost identical routes.

➡ **Via Appia** The 'queen of roads' ran down to Brindisi on the southern Adriatic coast.

➡ **Via Aurelia** Connected Rome with France by way of Pisa and Genoa.

➡ **Via Cassia** Led north to Viterbo, Siena and Tuscany.

➡ **Via Flaminia** Traversed the Apennines to Rimini on the east coast.

➡ **Via Salaria** The old salt road linked with the Adriatic port of Castrum Truentinum, south of modern-day Ancona.

Roman Developments

When Rome was founded in 753 BC (if legend is to be believed), the Etruscans were at the height of their power and Greeks colonists were establishing control over southern Italy. In subsequent centuries a three-way battle for domination ensued, with the Romans emerging victorious. Against this background, Roman architects initially borrowed heavily from Greek and Etruscan traditions.

Ancient Roman architecture was monumental in form and often propagandistic in nature. Huge amphitheatres, aqueducts and temples joined muscular and awe-inspiring basilicas, arches and thermal baths in trumpeting the skill and vision of the city's early rulers and the nameless architects who worked for them.

Rome's first aqueduct, the Aqua Appia is named after the censor Appius Claudius Caecus, the same man who built Via Appia Antica.

Temples

Early Republican-era temples were based on Etruscan designs, but over time the Romans turned to the Greeks for their inspiration. But whereas Greek temples had steps and colonnades on all sides, the classic Roman temple had a high podium with steps leading up to a deep porch. Good examples include the Tempio di Portunus near Piazza Bocca della Verità, and, though they're not so well preserved, the temples in the Area Sacra di Largo di Torre Argentina. These temples also illustrate another important feature of Roman architectural thinking. While Greek temples were designed to stand apart and be viewed from all sides, Roman temples were built into the city's urban fabric, set in busy central locations and designed to be approached from the front.

The Roman use of columns was also Greek in origin, even if the Romans favoured the more slender Ionic and Corinthian columns over the plain Doric pillars – to see how the columnar orders differ, study the exterior of the Colosseum, which incorporates all three styles.

To supply water to the Terme di Caracalla, a special aqueduct was built, the Aqua Antoniniana, linking the baths to the Aqua Marcia, which brought water in from hills near Subiaco.

Aqueducts & Sewers

One of the Romans' crowning architectural achievements was the development of a water-supply infrastructure, based on a network of aqueducts and underground sewers. In the early days, Rome got its water from the Tiber and natural underground springs, but as its population grew so demand outgrew supply. To meet this demand, the Romans constructed a complex system of aqueducts to bring water in from the hills of central Italy and distribute it around the city.

The first aqueduct to serve Rome was the 16.5km Aqua Appia, which became fully operational in 312 BC. Over the next 700 years or so, up to 800km of aqueducts were built in the city, a network capable of supplying up to one million cubic metres of water a day.

This was no mean feat for a system that depended entirely on gravity. All aqueducts, whether underground pipes, as most were, or vast overland viaducts, were built at a slight gradient to allow the water to flow. There were no pumps to force the water along so this gradient was key to maintaining a continuous and efficient flow.

At the other end of the water cycle, waste water was drained away via an underground sewerage system known as the Cloaca Maxima (Greatest Sewer) and emptied downstream into the river Tiber. The Cloaca was commissioned by Rome's seventh and last king, Tarquin the Proud (r 535–509 BC), as part of a project to drain the valley where the Roman Forum now stands. It was originally an open ditch, but from the beginning of the 2nd century BC it was gradually built over.

Residential Housing

While Rome's emperors and aristocrats lived in luxurious palaces on the Palatino (Palatine Hill), the city's poor huddled together in large residential blocks called *insulae*. These were huge, poorly built structures, sometimes up to six or seven storeys high, that accommodated hundreds of people in dark, unhealthy conditions. Little remains of these early *palazzi* but near the foot of the Aracoeli staircase – the steps that lead up to the Chiesa di Santa Maria in Aracoeli – you can still see a section of what was once a typical city-centre *insula*.

Concrete & Monumental Architecture

Most of the ruins that litter modern Rome are the remains of the ancient city's big, show-stopping monuments – the Colosseum, Pantheon, Terme di Caracalla, the Forums. These grandiose constructions, still standing some 2000 years after they were built, are not only reminders of the sophistication and intimidatory scale of ancient Rome – just as they were originally designed to be – they are also monuments to the vision and bravura of the city's ancient architects.

The Colosseum is not only an icon of Roman might, it is also a masterpiece of 1st-century engineering. Similarly, the Pantheon, with its

continued on p304

ARCHITECTURE THE ANCIENTS

18th century
A short-lived but theatrical style born out of the baroque, the florid rococo gifts Rome some of its most popular sights.

early 20th century
Muscular and modern, Italian rationalism plays to Mussolini's vision of a fearless, futuristic Rome, a 20th-century *caput mundi* (world capital).

1990s–
Rome provides the historic stage upon which some of the world's top contemporary architects experiment. Criticism and praise are meted out in almost equal measure.

OBELISKS

More readily associated with Egyptian temples than Roman piazzas, obelisks are a distinctive feature of Rome's cityscape. Many were brought over from Egypt after it was conquered by Augustus in 31 AD and used to decorate the *spina* (central spine) of the city's big circuses (chariot-racing arenas). Later the Romans began to make their own for their elaborate mausoleums.

The highest, and one of the oldest – it dates to the 15th century BC – towers 32.1m over Piazza San Giovanni in Laterano. The most curious sits atop Bernini's famous Elefantino statue outside the Chiesa di Santa Maria Sopra Minerva.

Rome's Signature Buildings

The result of 3000 years of urban evolution, Rome's cityscape is a magical mix of ruins, monuments, palaces, piazzas and churches. Here we trace the development of the city through its signature buildings, highlighting the history behind them and the architectural styles they represent.

Ancient Monuments & Medieval Churches

Driven by the wealth and ambition of their emperors, ancient Rome's architects and master builders created the greatest city the Western world had ever seen. In successive centuries, Christianity took root and the early popes led a bout of medieval church building.

Colosseum

Built in the 1st century AD as imperial Rome was approaching the pinnacle of its power, the Colosseum (p62) bears many of the hallmarks of ancient Roman architecture: arches (its first three tiers consist of 80 arches framed by Doric, Ionic and Corinthian columns), the use of various building materials (concrete, brick, travertine and tufa rock), and unprecedented scale. During the imperial age, the Romans built more than 200 amphitheatres across their empire as venues for gladiatorial games, animal shows, public executions and chariot races.

Pantheon

The use of the dome, one of the Romans' most important architectural innovations, finds perfect form in the Pantheon (p82). A squat rotunda, preceded by a columned portico and crowned by the largest unreinforced concrete dome ever built, the building was revolutionary in both concept and execution. The main technical challenge was how to keep the dome's weight down. To do this, the architects circled the cupola with five bands of decorative coffers (the rectangular recesses you see on the inside of the dome) and calibrated the concrete to ensure that it was lighter at the top than at the base. In the centre, the 8.7m-diameter oculus acts as a compression ring, absorbing and redistributing the huge structural forces centred on the dome's apex.

Basilica di Santa Maria Maggiore

This hulking cathedral (p162) exemplifies the early Christian basilicas that were being built in the 4th and 5th centuries. Although it has been much altered over the centuries, it is the only one of Rome's four papal basilicas to retain its original 5th-century layout. Signature features include the vast central nave, delineated by two rows of 20 columns, and the mosaics in the triumphal arch and nave. Mosaic decor was typical of early Christian design and many of the churches built in this period have stunning mosaics.

From Renaissance Basilicas to Contemporary Icons

Renaissance rigour and baroque flights of fancy found fertile soil as Italy's 16th- and 17th-century architects remodelled Rome. The 20th century saw further attempts to resurrect ancient glories as Mussolini restyled Rome as his fascist capital. A century later and Rome applauds the works of the world's top architects.

RECYCLING MARBLE

The building booms of the Renaissance and baroque periods transformed Rome in more ways than one. Just as spectacular new churches and *palazzi* went up, so the city's ancient buildings were stripped. The ancient Romans imported much of their marble from North Africa and Greece, but the papal paymasters preferred to plunder the city's abandoned marble-clad monuments. A particularly rich source was the Colosseum, which was systematically stripped for centuries and provided marble for St Peter's Basilica and other big projects. Its current form is largely the result of this relentless demolition.

Elsewhere, bronze was taken from the Pantheon for use on Castel Sant'Angelo and for the baldachin at St Peter's.

Tempietto di Bramante (p185)

Tempietto di Bramante

In architectural terms, Bramante's 1502 Tempietto (p185) is one of Rome's most influential buildings, a masterpiece of harmonious design that beautifully encapsulates High Renaissance ideals. A small circular temple capped by a dome and ringed by a columned peristyle, it's symmetrical and perfectly proportioned, its design clearly inspired by Rome's classical temples.

St Peter's Basilica

The greatest of all Renaissance churches, St Peter's (p138) was worked on by a small army of Renaissance and baroque architects, including Bramante, Bernini, Raphael and Michelangelo. In architectural terms, the two key features are Michelangelo's extraordinary dome – which at the time was the world's tallest structure – and Carlo Maderno's columned facade. Inside, the look is pure baroque with acres of polished marble and imposing sculptures set in niches.

Chiesa del Gesù

Counter-Reformation Rome saw an outbreak of artistic and architectural activity as the papacy sought to reassert its authority against the threat of Protestantism. One of the finest churches dating from this period is the late-16th-century Chiesa del Gesù (p93), whose Giacomo della Porta–designed facade proved highly influential. Originally the church had an austere look, in line with early Counter-Reformation thinking, but when the baroque took hold in the 17th century the decorators moved in and the interior now sports more ornate decor.

Auditorium Parco della Musica (p225), designed by Renzo Piano Building Workshop

Chiesa di San Carlo alle Quattro Fontane

It's seen better days, but this petite church (p122) is a prized example of baroque architecture. The first church built by the great 17th-century architect Francesco Borromini, it incorporates many of his trademark touches – a facade of convex and concave surfaces, the use of hidden windows to stream light onto decorative features and a complex elliptical plan to exploit the limited space.

Palazzo della Civiltà del Lavoro

Nicknamed the 'Square Colosseum', this iconic building (p213) is a signature work of 1930s Italian rationalism. With its plain, unadorned surfaces, it starkly captures the zeitgeist of the fascist age, while also exuding a sense of macho monumentality – a posture much appreciated by Italian dictator Benito Mussolini.

Auditorium Parco della Musica

Inaugurated in December 2002, Renzo Piano's startlingly original Auditorium (p225) is the most influential contemporary building in Rome, not so much in terms of its unique design – an eye-catching ensemble of iron-grey pods centred on an outdoor amphitheatre – as for the boost it has given Rome's cultural scene.

continued from p299

world-beating dome, is a wonderful example of an imperial-age temple while also being a building of quite staggering structural complexity.

One of the key breakthroughs the Romans made, and one that allowed them to build on an ever-increasing scale, was the invention of concrete in the 1st century BC. Made by mixing volcanic ash with lime and an aggregate, often tufa rock or brick rubble, concrete was quick to make, easy to use and cheap. Furthermore, it freed architects from their dependence on skilled masonry labour - up to that point construction techniques required stone blocks to be specially cut to fit into each other. Concrete allowed the Romans to develop vaulted roofing, which they used to span the Pantheon's ceiling and the huge vaults at the Terme di Caracalla among other places.

Concrete wasn't particularly attractive, though, and while it was used for heavy-duty structural work it was usually lined with travertine and coloured marble, imported from Greece and North Africa. Brick was also an important material, used both as a veneer and for construction.

Early Christian

The history of early Christianity is one of persecution and martyrdom. Introduced in the 1st century AD, it was legalised by the emperor Constantine in 313 AD and became Rome's state religion in 378. The most startling reminders of early Christian activity are the catacombs, a series of underground burial grounds built under Rome's ancient roads. Christian belief in the resurrection meant that the Christians could not cremate their dead, as was the custom in Roman times, and with burial forbidden inside the city walls they were forced to go outside the city.

Church Building

Ancient triumphal arches were designed as honorary monuments to commemorate military victory or an important individual. Only three of the 36 that stood in 5th-century Rome survive: the Arco di Tito and Arco di Settimio Severo in the Roman Forum, and the Arco di Costantino next to the Colosseum.

The Christians began to abandon the catacombs in the 4th century and increasingly opted to be buried in the churches the emperor Constantine was building in the city. Although Constantine was actually based in Byzantium, which he renamed Constantinople in his own honour, he nevertheless financed an ambitious building programme in Rome. The most notable of the many churches that he commissioned is the Basilica di San Giovanni in Laterano. Built between 315 and 324 and reformed into its present shape in the 5th century, it was the model on which many subsequent basilicas were based. Other showstoppers of the period include the Basilica di Santa Maria in Trastevere and the Basilica di Santa Maria Maggiore.

A second wave of church-building hit Rome in the period between the 8th and 12th centuries. As the early papacy battled for survival against the threatening Lombards, its leaders took to construction to leave some sort of historical imprint, resulting in the Basilica di Santa Sabina, the Chiesa di Santa Prassede and the 8th-century Chiesa di Santa Maria in Cosmedin, better known as home to the Bocca della Verità (Mouth of Truth).

The 13th and 14th centuries were dark days for Rome as internecine fighting raged between the city's noble families. While much of northern Europe and even parts of Italy were revelling in Gothic arches and towering vaults, little of lasting value was being built in Rome. The one great exception is the city's only Gothic church, the Chiesa di Santa Maria Sopra Minerva.

Basilica Style

In design terms, these early Christian churches were modelled on, and built over, Rome's great basilicas. In ancient times, a basilica was a large rectangular hall used for public functions, but as Christianity took hold they were increasingly appropriated by the city's church-builders. The main reason for this was that they lent themselves perfectly to the new style of religious ceremonies that the Christians were introducing, rites that required space for worshippers and a central focus for the altar. Rome's pagan temples, in contrast, had been designed as symbolic cult centres and were not set up to house the faithful – in fact, most pagan ceremonies were held outside, in front of the temple, not inside as Christian services required.

Over time, basilica design became increasingly standardised. A principal entrance would open onto an atrium, a courtyard surrounded by colonnaded porticoes, which, in turn, would lead to the narthex, or porch. The interior would be rectangular and divided by rows of columns into a central nave and smaller side aisles. At the far end, the main altar and bishop's throne (cathedra) would sit in a semicircular apse. In some churches a transept would bisect the central nave in front of the apse to form a Latin cross.

Early Basilicas

Basilica di San Giovanni in Laterano

Basilica di Santa Sabina

Basilica di Santa Maria Maggiore

Basilica di Santa Maria in Trastevere

ARCHITECTURE THE RENAISSANCE

The Renaissance

Florence, rather than Rome, is generally regarded as Italy's great Renaissance city. But while many of the movement's early architects hailed from Tuscany, the city they turned to for inspiration was Rome. The Eternal City might have been in pretty poor nick in the late 15th century, but as the centre of classical antiquity it was much revered by budding architects; a trip to study the Colosseum and the Pantheon was considered a fundamental part of an architect's training.

One of the key aspects they studied, and which informs much Renaissance architecture, is the idea of harmony. This is achieved, or sought, by the application of symmetry, order and proportion. To this end many Renaissance buildings incorporate structural features copied from the ancients – columns, pilasters, arches and, most dramatically, domes. The Pantheon's dome, in particular, proved immensely influential, serving as a blueprint for many later works.

Early Years

It's impossible to pinpoint the exact year the Renaissance arrived in Rome, but many claim it was the election of Pope Nicholas V in 1447 that sparked the artistic and architectural furore that swept the city in the next century or so. Nicholas believed that as head of the Christian world Rome had a duty to impress, a theory that was eagerly taken up by his successors, and it was at the behest of the great papal dynasties – the Barberini, Farnese and Pamphilj – that the leading artists of the day were summoned to Rome.

The Venetian Pope Paul II (r 1464–71) commissioned many works, including Palazzo Venezia, Rome's first great Renaissance *palazzo*. Built in 1455, when Paul was still a cardinal, it was enlarged in 1464 when he became pope. Sixtus IV (r 1471–84) had the Sistine Chapel built and enlarged the Chiesa di Santa Maria del Popolo.

Designed by Paolo Portoghesi, Rome's postmodernist mosque is one of Europe's largest. Its critically acclaimed design is centred on a beautiful, luminous interior capped by a cupola and 16 surrounding domes.

High Renaissance

It was under Pope Julius II (1503–13) that the Roman Renaissance reached its peak, thanks largely to a classically minded architect from Milan, Donato Bramante (1444–1514).

Considered the high priest of Renaissance architecture, Bramante arrived in Rome in 1499. Here, inspired by the ancient ruins, he developed a refined classical style that was to prove hugely influential. His 1502 Tempietto is a masterpiece of elegance. Similarly harmonious is his beautifully proportioned 1504 cloister at the Chiesa di Santa Maria della Pace near Piazza Navona.

In 1506 Julius commissioned him to start work on the job that would finally finish him off – the rebuilding of St Peter's Basilica. The fall of Constantinople's Aya Sofya (Church of the Hagia Sofia) to Islam in the mid-14th century had pricked Nicholas V into ordering an earlier revamp, but the work had never been completed and it wasn't until Julius took the bull by the horns that progress was made. However, Bramante never got to see how his original Greek-cross design was developed, as he died in 1514.

St Peter's Basilica occupied most of the other notable architects of the High Renaissance, including Giuliano da Sangallo (1445–1516), Baldassarre Peruzzi (1481–1536) and Antonio da Sangallo the Younger (1484–1546). Michelangelo (1475–1564) eventually took over in 1547, modifying the layout and creating the basilica's crowning dome. Modelled on Brunelleschi's design for the Duomo in Florence, this is considered the artist's finest architectural achievement and one of the most important works of the Roman Renaissance.

Mannerism

As Rome's architects strove to build a new Jerusalem, the city's leaders struggled to deal with the political tensions arising outside the city walls. These came to a head in 1527 when the city was invaded and savagely routed by troops of the Holy Roman Emperor, Charles V. This traumatic event forced many of the artists working in Rome to flee the city and ushered in a new style of artistic and architectural expression. Mannerism was a relatively short-lived form but in its emphasis on complexity and decoration, in contrast to the sharp, clean lines of traditional Renaissance styles, it hinted at the more ebullient designs that would later arrive with the onset of the 17th-century baroque.

One of mannerism's leading exponents was Baldassarre Peruzzi, whose Palazzo Massimo alle Colonne on Corso Vittorio Emanuele II, reveals a number of mannerist elements – a pronounced facade, decorative window mouldings and showy imitation stonework.

Architecture Reads

Rome (Amanda Claridge)

The Genius in the Design: Bernini, Borromini and the Rivalry that Transformed Rome (Jake Morrissey)

Rome and Environs: An Archaeological Guide (Filippo Coarelli)

BRAMANTE, THE ARCHITECT'S ARCHITECT

One of the most influential architects of his day, Donato Bramante (1444–1514) was the godfather of Renaissance architecture. His peers Michelangelo, Raphael and Leonardo da Vinci considered him the only architect of their era equal to the ancients.

Born near Urbino, he originally trained as a painter before taking up architecture in his mid-30s in Milan. However, it was in Rome that he enjoyed his greatest success. Working for Pope Julius II, he developed a monumental style that while classical in origin was pure Renaissance in its expression of harmony and perspective. The most perfect representation of this is his Tempietto, a small but much-copied temple. His original designs for St Peter's Basilica also revealed a classically inspired symmetry with a Pantheon-like dome envisaged atop a Greek-cross structure.

Rich and influential, Bramante was an adept political operator, a ruthless and unscrupulous manipulator who was not above badmouthing his competitors. It's said, for example, that he talked Pope Julius II into giving Michelangelo the Sistine Chapel contract in the hope that it would prove the undoing of the young Tuscan artist.

ROCOCO FRILLS

In the early days of the 18th century, as baroque fashions began to fade and neoclassicism waited to make its 19th-century entrance, the rococo burst into theatrical life. Drawing on the excesses of the baroque, it was a short-lived fad but one that left a memorable mark.

The Spanish Steps, built between 1723 and 1726 by Francesco de Sanctis, provided a focal point for the many Grand Tourists who were busy discovering Rome's classical past. A short walk to the southwest, Piazza Sant'Ignazio was designed by Filippo Raguzzini (1680–1771) to provide a suitably melodramatic setting for the Chiesa di Sant'Ignazio di Loyola, Rome's second Jesuit church.

Most spectacular of all, however, was the Trevi Fountain, one of the city's most exuberant and enduringly popular monuments. It was designed in 1732 by Nicola Salvi (1697–1751) and completed three decades later.

The Baroque

As the principal motor of the Roman Renaissance, the Catholic Church became increasingly powerful in the 16th century. But with power came corruption and calls for reform. These culminated in Martin Luther's *95 Theses* and the far-reaching Protestant Reformation. This hit the Church hard and prompted the Counter-Reformation (1560–1648), a vicious and sustained campaign to get people back into the Catholic fold. In the midst of this great offensive, baroque art and architecture emerged as a highly effective form of propaganda. Stylistically, baroque architecture aims for a dramatic sense of dynamism, an effect that it often achieves by combining spatial complexity with clever lighting and a flamboyant use of decorative painting and sculpture.

One of the first great Counter-Reformation churches was the Jesuit Chiesa del Gesù, designed by the leading architect of the day, Giacomo della Porta (1533–1602). In a move away from the style of earlier Renaissance churches, the facade has pronounced architectural elements that create a contrast between surfaces and a play of light and shade.

The end of the 16th century and the papacy of Sixtus V (1585–90) marked the beginning of major urban-planning schemes. Domenico Fontana (1543–1607) and other architects created a network of major thoroughfares to connect previously disparate parts of the sprawling medieval city, and decorative obelisks were erected at vantage points throughout town. Fontana also designed the main facade of Palazzo del Quirinale, the immense palace that served as the pope's summer residence for almost three centuries. His nephew, Carlo Maderno (1556–1629), also worked on the *palazzo* when not amending Bramante's designs for St Peter's Basilica.

Bernini vs Borromini

No two people did more to fashion the face of Rome than the two great figures of the Roman baroque – Gian Lorenzo Bernini (1598–1680) and Francesco Borromini (1599–1667). Two starkly different characters – Bernini was suave, self-confident and politically adept, while Borromini, from Lombardy, was a solitary and peculiar man – they led the transition from Counter-Reformation rigour to baroque exuberance.

Bernini is perhaps best known for his work in the Vatican. He designed St Peter's Square, styling the colonnade as 'the motherly arms of the Church', and was chief architect at St Peter's Basilica from 1629. While working on the basilica, he created the baldachin (altar canopy) over the main altar, using bronze stripped from the Pantheon.

Key Borromini Works

Chiesa di San Carlo alle Quattro Fontane

Chiesa di Sant'Agnese in Agone

Chiesa di Sant'Ivo alla Sapienza

Prospettiva, Palazzo Spada

Key Bernini Works

St Peter's Square

Chiesa di Sant'Andrea al Quirinale

Fontana dei Quattro Fiumi

Palazzo di Montecitorio

FIVE FLAMBOYANT FOUNTAINS

➡ **Trevi Fountain** Wild horses rise out of the rocks at this fantastical rococo extravaganza, Rome's largest and most celebrated fountain.

➡ **Fontana dei Quattro Fiumi** Topped by a tapering obelisk, Bernini's opulent baroque display sits in splendour on Piazza Navona.

➡ **Fontana delle Naiadi** The naked nymphs languishing around Piazza della Repubblica's scene-stealing fountain caused a scandal when revealed in 1901.

➡ **Fontana dell'Acqua Paola** Known to Romans as *il fontanone del Gianicolo*, this grandiose baroque fountain sits atop the Gianicolo Hill.

➡ **Barcaccia** The Spanish Steps lead down to this sunken-ship fountain, supposedly modelled on a boat dumped on the piazza by a flood in 1598.

Under the patronage of the Barberini pope Urban VIII, Bernini was given free rein to transform the city, and his churches, *palazzi*, piazzas and fountains remain landmarks to this day. However, his fortunes nose-dived when the pope died in 1644. Urban's successor, Innocent X, wanted as little contact as possible with the favourites of his hated predecessor, and instead turned to Borromini, Alessandro Algardi (1595–1654) and Girolamo and Carlo Rainaldi (1570–1655 and 1611–91, respectively). Bernini later came back into favour with his magnificent design for the 1651 Fontana dei Quattro Fiumi in the centre of Piazza Navona, opposite Borromini's Chiesa di Sant'Agnese in Agone.

Borromini, the son of an architect and well versed in stonemasonry and construction techniques, created buildings involving complex shapes and exotic geometry. A recurring feature of his designs is the skilful manipulation of light, often obtained by the clever placement of small oval-shaped windows. His most memorable works are the Chiesa di San Carlo alle Quattro Fontane, which has an oval-shaped interior, and the Chiesa di Sant'Ivo alla Sapienza, which combines a complex arrangement of convex and concave surfaces with an innovative spiral tower.

Throughout their careers, the two geniuses were often at each other's throats. Borromini was deeply envious of Bernini's early success and Bernini, in turn, was scathing of Borromini's complex geometrical style.

VIA DEI FORI IMPERIALI

Via dei Fori Imperiali, the road that divides the Roman Forums from the Imperial Forums, was one of Mussolini's most controversial projects. Inaugurated in 1932, it was conceived to link the Colosseum (ancient power) with Piazza Venezia (fascist power) but in the process tarmacked over much of the ancient forums.

Fascism, Futurism & the 20th Century

Rome entered the 20th century in good shape. During the last 30 years of the 19th century it had been treated to one of its periodic makeovers – this time after being made capital of the Kingdom of Italy in 1870. Piazzas were built – Piazza Vittorio Emanuele II, at the centre of a new upmarket residential district, and neoclassical Piazza della Repubblica, over Diocletian's bath complex – and roads were laid. Via Nazionale and Via Cavour were constructed to link the city centre with the new railway station, Stazione Termini, and Corso Vittorio Emanuele II to connect Piazza Venezia with the Vatican. To celebrate unification and pander to the ego of the ruling Savoy family, the Vittoriano monument was built between 1885 and 1911.

Rationalism & Rebuilding

Influenced by the German Bauhaus movement, architectural rationalism was all the rage in 1920s Europe. In its international form it advocated an emphasis on sharply defined linear forms, but in Italy it took on a slightly different look, thanks to the influence of the Gruppo Sette, its main Italian promoters, and Benito Mussolini, Italy's fascist dictator. Basically, the Gruppo Sette acknowledged the debt Italian ar-

Palazzo della Civiltà del Lavoro, EUR (p213)

chitecture owed to its classical past and incorporated elements of that tradition into their modernistic designs. Aesthetically and politically, this tied in perfectly with Mussolini's vision of fascism as the modern bearer of ancient Rome's imperialist ambitions.

A shrewd manipulator of imagery, Mussolini embarked on a series of grandiose building projects, including the 1928–31 Foro Italico sports centre, Via dei Foro Imperiali and the residential quarter of Garbatella. Garbatella, now a colourful neighbourhood in southern Rome, was originally planned as an English-style garden city to house the city's workers, but in the 1920s the project was hijacked by the fascist regime, which had its own designs. Central to these were innovative housing blocks, known as *alberghi suburbani* (suburban hotels), which were used to accommodate people displaced from the city centre. The most famous of these hotels, the *Albergo Rosso,* was designed by Innocenzo Sabbatini (1891–1983), the leading light of the Roman School of architecture. This local movement looked to ally modern functionalism with a respect for tradition and a utopian vision of urban development.

EUR

Mussolini's most famous architectural legacy is the EUR district in the extreme south of the city. Built for the Esposizione Universale di Roma in 1942, this strange quarter of wide boulevards and huge linear buildings owes its look to the vision of the *razionalisti* (rationalists). In practice, though, only one of their number, Adalberto Libera, actually worked on the project, as by this stage most of the Gruppo Sette had fallen out with the ruling junta. Libera's Palazzo dei Congressi is a masterpiece of rationalist architecture, but EUR's most iconic building

Modern Icons

Palazzo della Civiltà del Lavoro

Auditorium Parco della Musica

Museo dell'Ara Pacis

Museo Nazionale delle Arti del XXI Secolo (MAXXI)

is the 'Square Colosseum', the Palazzo della Civiltà del Lavoro, designed by Giovanni Guerrini, Ernesto Bruno La Padula and Mario Romano.

Postwar Developments

For much of the postwar period, architects in Rome were limited to planning cheap housing for the city's ever-growing population. Swathes of hideous apartment blocks were built along the city's main arteries, and grim suburbs sprang up on land claimed from local farmers.

The 1960 Olympics heralded a spate of sporting construction, and both Stadio Flaminio and Stadio Olimpico date to this period. Pier Luigi Nervi, Italy's master of concrete and a hugely influential innovator, added his contribution in the form of the Palazzetto dello Sport.

Modern Rome

Rome's recent past has witnessed a flurry of architectural activity. A clutch of archistars have worked on projects in the city, including Renzo Piano, Italy's foremost architect; renowned American Richard Meier; Anglo-Iraqi Zaha Hadid; Odile Decq, a major French architect; and Dutch legend Rem Koolhaas.

Controversy & Acclaim

The foundations of this building boom date to the early 1990s, when then-mayor Francesco Rutelli launched a major clean-up of the historic centre. As part of the process, he commissioned Richard Meier to build a new pavilion for the 1st-century-AD Ara Pacis. Predictably, Meier's glass-and-steel Museo dell'Ara Pacis caused controversy when it was unveiled in 2006. Vittorio Sgarbi, an outspoken art critic and politician, claimed that the American's design was the first step to globalising Rome's unique classical heritage. The Roman public appreciated the idea of modern architecture in the city centre, but few were entirely convinced by Meier's design and in 2010 Rome's mayor, Gianni Alemanno, met the architect to discuss modifications. The most important change they agreed on was to knock down the wall that separates the Ara Pacis from the Tiber-front road, as part of a planned renovation of the entire Piazza Augusto Imperatore area. As of yet, however, there's no sign of work starting on the project.

Meier won far more acclaim for a second project, his striking Chiesa Dio Padre Misericordioso in Tor Tre Teste, a dreary suburb east of the city centre. Another religious project that won widespread applause was Paolo Portoghesi's postmodern mosque, opened in 1995 in the upmarket Parioli district.

Back nearer the centre, Renzo Piano's Auditorium Parco della Musica has had a huge impact on Rome's music and cultural scene. Piano, the man behind London's Shard skyscraper and the *New York Times* building, is one of only a few Italian architects who can genuinely claim international celebrity status.

MAXXI

In 2010, archistar Zaha Hadid won the UK's prestigious RIBA (Royal Institute of British Architects) Stirling prize for her work on MAXXI. Her sinuous, curvaceous design beat out competition from projects in Berlin and Oxford.

Fuksas, Fendi & the Future

Born in Rome in 1944, Massimiliano Fuksas is known for his futuristic vision and while he has no signature building as such, his design for the Centro Congressi Italia, aka the Nuvola, comes as close as any to embodying his style. A rectangular 30m-high glass shell containing a 3500-sq-metre steel-and-Teflon cloud supported by steel ribs and suspended over a vast conference hall, its look is fearlessly modern. Yet it's not without its references to the past: in both scale and form it owes its inspiration to the 1930s rationalist architecture that surrounds it.

At the time of writing, construction of the Nuvola was moving towards completion as the curtain was going up on another Fuksas project. Crowning what is due to be a new flagship Benetton store on Via del Corso, the Lanterna is a low-lying irregularly shaped glass cupola that adds a decidedly contemporary touch to Rome's classical roof-scape.

In another fashion-funded initiative, the prize-winning French architect Jean Nouvel has been appointed to work on a contemporary arts centre for the Fondazione Alda Fendi. The centre, to be housed in an abandoned *casa popolare* – a fascist-era housing block – in the Forum Boarium area, will contain a museum, exhibition space, shops, restaurants and artists' studios. Work is due for completion in 2014.

Architecture Glossary

ambulatory	a place to walk in a cloister; also an aisle, often semicircular, running behind the high altar in a church
apse	a semicircular or polygonal recess with a domed roof over a church's altar
baldachino (baldachin)	a stone canopy built over an altar or tomb; often supported by columns and freestanding
baroque	style of European art, architecture and music of the 17th and 18th centuries
basilica	an oblong hall with an apse at the end of the nave; used in ancient Rome for public assemblies and later adopted as a blueprint for medieval churches
capital	the head of a pillar or column
cloister	enclosed court attached to a church or monastery; consists of a roofed ambulatory surrounding an open area
colonnade	a row of columns supporting a roof or other structure
crypt	an underground room beneath a church used for services and burials
cupola	a rounded dome forming part of a ceiling or roof
entablature	the part of a classical facade that sits on top of the columns; it consists of an architrave, on top of which is a decorative frieze and cornice
forum	in ancient Rome, a public space used for judicial business and commerce
frieze	a horizontal band, often with painted or sculptural decoration, that sits between the architrave and cornice
futurism	Italian early 20th-century artistic movement that embraced modern technology
loggia	a gallery or room with one side open, often facing a garden
nave	the central aisle in a church, often separated from parallel aisles by pillars
neoclassicism	dominant style of art and architecture in the late 18th and early 19th centuries; a return to ancient Roman styles
pilaster	a rectangular column attached to a wall from which it projects
portico	a porch with a roof supported by columns

rationalism	international architectural style of the 1920s; its Italian form, often associated with fascism, incorporates linear styles and classical references
relief	the projection of a design from a flat surface
Renaissance	European revival of art and architecture based on classical precedents between the 14th and 16th centuries
rococo	ornate 18th-century style of architecture
stucco	wall plaster used for decorative purposes
trompe l'œil	a visual illusion tricking the viewer into seeing a painted object as a three-dimensional image
transept	in a cross-shaped church, the two parts that bisect the nave at right angles, forming the short arms of the cross

The Roman Way of Life

As a visitor, it's often difficult to see beyond Rome's spectacular veneer to the large, modern city that lies beneath: a living, breathing capital that's home to more than two and a half million people. How do the Romans live in their city? Where do they work? Who do they live with? How do they let their hair down?

A Day in the Life

Rome's Mr Average, Signor Rossi, lives with his wife in a small, two-bedroom apartment in the suburbs and works in a government ministry in the city centre. His working day is typical of the many who crowd *i mezzi* (the means, ie public transport) in the morning rush hour.

His morning routine is the same as city dwellers the world over: a quick breakfast – usually nothing more than a sweet, black espresso – followed by a short bus ride to the nearest metro station. On the way he'll stop at an *edicola* (kiosk) to pick up his daily newspaper (*Il Messaggero*) and share a joke with the kiosk owner, a manic Roma supporter. A quick scan of the headlines reveals few surprises – the main political parties in turmoil as they try to form a workable coalition; Berlusconi in court again; a full-page match report on the previous evening's Roma–Lazio derby.

Rome's metro is not a particularly pleasant place to be in *l'ora di punta* (the rush hour), especially in summer when it gets unbearably hot, but the regulars are resigned to the discomfort and bear it cheerfully. On arriving at work Signor Rossi has time for another coffee and a *cornetto* at the bar underneath his office.

His work, like many in the swollen state bureaucracy, is not the most interesting in the world, nor the best paid, but it's secure and with a much sought-after *contratto a tempo indeterminato* (permanent contract) he doesn't have to worry about losing it. In contrast, many of his younger colleagues work in constant fear that their temporary contracts will not be renewed when they expire.

Lunch, which is typically taken around 1.30pm, is usually pizza *al taglio* (by the slice) from a nearby takeaway. It's eaten standing up and followed by a leisurely wander around the surrounding neighbourhood. Before heading back to the office for the afternoon session, another espresso is customary.

Clocking-off time in most ministries is typically from 5pm onwards and by about 7pm the evening rush hour is in full swing. Once home, our Signor Rossi changes out of his suit and at about 8.30pm sits down to a pasta supper and a discussion of plans for the weekend. There's an excellent art exhibition on at the Chiostro del Bramante and he's heard great things about a new trattoria in the Jewish Ghetto. Then, if it's a nice day on Sunday, he likes the idea of a day in the greenery of the Castelli Roman.

Rome is the fifth-most congested city in Europe according to a report by traffic navigator company TomTom. Topping the traffic blacklist are Istanbul, Warsaw, Marseille and Palermo.

RELIGION IN ROMAN LIFE

Rome is a city of churches. From the great headline basilicas in the historic centre to the hundreds of parish churches dotted around the suburbs, the city is packed with places to worship. And with the Vatican in the centre of town, the Church, with a capital C, is a constant presence in Roman life.

Yet the role of religion in modern Italian society is an ambiguous one. On the one hand, almost 90% of Italians consider themselves Catholic; on the other, only about a third attend church regularly. But while Romans don't go to church very often, they are, on the whole, a conformist bunch, and for many the Church remains a point of reference. The Church's line on ethical and social issues might not always meet with widespread support, but it's always given an airing in the largely sympathetic national press. Similarly, more than 60% of people who get married do so in church and first communions remain an important social occasion entailing gift-giving and lavish receptions.

Catholicism's hold on the Roman psyche is strong, but recent increases in the city's immigrant population have led to a noticeable Muslim presence – by the latest estimates about 110,000 out of a city population of 2.6 million. This has largely been a pain-free process, but friction has flared on occasion and in 2007 Rome's right-wing administration blocked plans to open a mosque in the multi-ethnic Piazza Vittorio Emanuele II area.

Work

Employment in the capital is largely based on Italy's bloated state bureaucracy. Every morning armies of suited civil servants pour into town and disappear into vast ministerial buildings to keep the machinery of government ticking over. Other important employers include the tourist sector, banking, finance and culture – Italy's historic film industry is largely based in Rome and there are hundreds of museums and galleries across town.

But times are tough and job opportunities are becoming increasingly rare, particularly for young people who struggle to get a foot in the door – unemployment among 15- to 24-year olds currently stands at 39.3% in central Italy. To land it lucky you really need to know someone. Official figures are hard to come by, but it's a universally accepted truth that personal connections are the best way of finding work. This system of *raccomandazioni* (recommendations) is widespread and covers all walks of life. In 2010, it was reported that the wife, daughter and son of the Rector of Rome's Sapienza University had all landed jobs in the university's medical faculty despite limited academic qualifications. The story, dubbed *parentopoli* (relative-gate), was echoed in a similar controversy that surrounded the employment of hundreds of wives, sons, in-laws and friends of powerful local politicians at the city's public transport company, ATAC. The newspapers screamed scandal, but, in truth, no one was all that surprised.

The average Italian earns US$23,917 per year. But according to Italy's retail association, Confcommercio, they then have to pay up to 55% tax on every euro they earn.

Like everywhere in Italy, Rome's workplace is largely a male preserve. After Malta, Italy has the worst female employment rate in the EU (46.5% in 2011), and Italian women continue to earn less than their male counterparts. They also have to face problems that their male colleagues don't. According to figures released by Istat, Italy's official statistics body, in 2008–09 up to 800,000 women were forced to leave work after giving birth. Italian law legislates against this – and in 2012 Mario Monti's technocrat government tightened the rules – but sexual discrimination remains a workplace reality for many women.

Rome's under 40s are another workplace minority with many young Romans forced to accept short-term contracts for jobs for which they are hugely overqualified, such as working in telephone call centres. These jobs typically offer no security, pension benefits or prospects.

Home Life & the Family

Romans, like most Italians, live in apartments. These are often small – 75 to 100 sq m is typical – and expensive. House prices in central Rome are among the highest in the country and many first-time buyers are forced to move out of town or to distant suburbs outside the GRA (the *grande raccordo anulare*), the busy ring road that marks the city's outer limit.

Almost all apartments are in self-managed *condominios* (blocks of individually owned flats), a fact which gives rise to no end of neighbourly squabbling. Regular *condominio* meetings are often fiery affairs as neighbours argue over everything from communal repairs and plumbing quotes to noisy dogs and broken lights.

Rates of home ownership are relatively high in Rome and properties are commonly kept in the family, handed down from generation to generation. People do rent, but the rental market is largely targeted at Rome's huge student population.

Staying at Home

Italy's single most successful institution, and the only one in which the Romans continue to trust, is the family. It's still the rule rather the exception for young Romans to stay at home until they marry, which they typically do at around 30. Figures report that up to 41.1% of 25- to 34-year olds still live at home with *mamma* and *papa*. To foreign observers this may seem strange, but there are mitigating factors: almost half (45%) of these stay-at-homes are out of work and property prices are high. There's also the fact that young Romans are generally reluctant to downgrade and move to a cheaper neighbourhood. In any case, Romans brought up in this tradition know that the *quid pro quo* comes later when they are expected to support their elderly parents. Seen from another perspective, though, it might simply mean that Roman families like living together.

But while faith in the family remains, the family is shrinking. Italian women are giving birth later than ever and having fewer children – in 2011, the average Italian mother had 1.39 children, fewer than most of her EU counterparts. Rome's army of *nonni* (grandparents) berate their children for this, as does the Vatican for whom procreation is a fundamental duty of marriage. For their part, Italy's politicians worry that such a perilously low birth rate threatens the future tax returns necessary for funding the country's pension payments.

Italy's adult stay-at-homes have given rise to various linguistic terms: *bamboccioni* (big babies), a word that came to prominence when it was used by Tommaso Padao-Schioppa during his term as Minister of Finance; the more commonly used *mammoni* (mummy's boys); and the female equivalent, *figlie di papa* (daddy's girls).

Paolo Virzi's 2008 film *Tutta la vita davanti* won critical praise for its bittersweet portrayal of a philosophy graduate who dreams of a job in research but ends up working the phones in a Roman call centre.

BELLA FIGURA

Making a good impression (*fare la bella figura*) is extremely important to Romans. For a style-conscious hipster that might mean wearing the latest designer fashions, having your hair cut just so or carrying a top-of-the-range smartphone. A cool car, perhaps a Smart or SUV, will help. For a middle-aged banker it will involve being impeccably groomed and dressed appropriately for every occasion. This slavish adherence to style isn't limited to clothes or accessories. It extends to all walks of life and hip Romans will frequent the same bars and restaurants, drink the same *aperitivi* and hang out on the same piazzas.

ROMAN QUEUES

Satirist Beppe Severgnini explains the Italian system of queuing, often a shock to first-time visitors, in *An Italian in Italy*: 'Here we favour more artistic configurations, such as waves, parabolas, herringbone patterns, hordes, groups, and clusters. Our choreography complicates waiting, but brightens our lives.'

Play

Despite the gloomy economic situation and all the trials and tribulations of living in Rome – dodgy public transport, iffy services and sky-high prices – few Romans would swap their city for anywhere else. They know theirs is one of the world's most beautiful cities and they enjoy it with gusto. You only have to look at the city's pizzerias, trattorias and restaurants – not those in the touristy centre, but those out in the dreary suburbs where most people live – to see that eating out is a much-loved local pastime. Groups of friends and relatives will typically get together in a favourite eatery to catch up over plateloads of pasta and pizza. It's a cliché of Roman life but food really is central to social pleasure.

Drinking, in contrast, is not a traditional Roman activity, at least not in the sense of piling into a pub for pints of beer. Romans have long enjoyed hanging out and looking cool – just look at all those photos of *dolce vita* cafe society – and today an evening out in a Roman bar is still as much about flirting and looking gorgeous as it is about consuming alcohol.

Clothes shopping is another popular Roman pastime alongside cinema-going and football. Interest in Rome's two Serie A teams, Roma and Lazio, remains high despite a dip in fortunes since the heady days of 2000 and 2001, and a trip to the Stadio Olimpico to watch the Sunday game is still considered an afternoon well-spent by many Romans. Depending on the result, of course.

Romans are inveterate car-lovers and on hot summer weekends they will often drive out to the coast or surrounding countryside. Beach bums make for nearby Ostia or more upmarket Fregene, while those in search of a little greenery make for the Castelli Romani, a pocket of green hills just south of town famous for its Frascati wine and foodie specialities such as *porchetta* (herbed, spit-roasted pork).

Survival Guide

Transport

ARRIVING IN ROME

Most people arrive in Rome by plane, landing at one of its two airports: Leonardo da Vinci, better known as Fiumicino, or Ciampino, hub for European low-cost carrier Ryanair. Flights from New York take around nine hours; from London 2¾ hours; from Sydney at least 22 hours.

Domestic flights connect Rome with airports across Italy.

As an alternative to short-haul flights, trains serve Rome's main station, Stazione Termini, from a number of European destinations, including Paris (about 15 hours), as well as cities across Italy.

Long-distance domestic and international buses arrive at the Autostazione Tiburtina.

You can also get to Rome by boat. Ferries serve Civitavecchia, some 80km north of the city, from a number of Mediterranean ports.

Flights, cars and tours may be booked online at lonely planet.com/bookings.

Leonardo da Vinci Airport

Rome's main international airport, **Leonardo da Vinci** (Fiumicino; ✆06 6 59 51; www. adr.it/fiumicino), is 30km west of the city. It's divided into four terminals: Terminals 1, 2 and 3 are for domestic and international flights; Terminal 5 is for

American and Israeli airlines flying to the US and Israel.

Terminals 1, 2 and 3 are within easy walking distance of each other in the main airport building; Terminal 5 is accessible by shuttle bus from Terminal 3.

The easiest way to get into town is by train, but there are also buses and private shuttle services.

Train

Leonardo Express (adult/child under 4 yr, €14/free) Runs to/from Stazione Termini. Departures from the airport every 30 minutes between 6.38am and 11.38pm; from Termini between 5.52am and 10.52pm. Journey time is 30 minutes.

FR1 (tickets €8) Connects to Trastevere, Ostiense and Tibur-

> ### CLIMATE CHANGE & TRAVEL
>
> Every form of transport that relies on carbon-based fuel generates CO_2, the main cause of human-induced climate change. Modern travel is dependent on aeroplanes which might use less fuel per kilometre per person than most cars but travel much greater distances. The altitude at which aircraft emit gases (including CO_2) and particles also contributes to their climate change impact. Many websites offer 'carbon calculators' that allow people to estimate the carbon emissions generated by their journey and, for those who wish to do so, to offset the impact of the greenhouse gases emitted with contributions to portfolios of climate-friendly initiatives throughout the world. Lonely Planet offsets the carbon footprint of all staff and author travel.

tina stations, but not Termini. Departures from the airport every 15 minutes (hourly on Sunday and public holidays) between 5.58am and 11.28pm; from Tiburtina every 15 minutes between 5.47am and 7.32pm, then half-hourly to 10.02pm Monday to Saturday, half-hourly between 6.02am and 10.02pm Sunday.

Bus

SIT (✆06 591 68 26; www. sitbusshuttle.it; one way €6 on bus/€5 online) Regular departures for Fiumicino from Stazione Termini from 5am to 8.30pm, and return trips from 8.30am to 12.30am, all calling at the Vatican en route. Journey time is one hour.

Cotral (www.cotralspa.it; one way €7 on bus/ €5 online)

Runs to/from Fiumicino from Stazione Tiburtina via Stazione Termini. Eight daily departures including night services from the airport at 1.15am, 2.15am, 3.30am and 5am, and from Tiburtina at 12.30am, 1.15am, 2.30am and 3.45am. There are also bus links to EUR Cornelia and Magliana. Journey time is one hour.

Terravision (www.terravision.eu; one way €6 on bus/€4 online) Regular services to Stazione Termini about every 30 minutes during the day; buses run to the airport from outside the Terracafè at Termini. Allow 45 minutes for the journey.

Private Shuttle

Airport Connection Services (☎06 338 32 21; www.airportconnection.it) Transfers to/from the city centre start at €27 per person.

Airport Shuttle (☎06 4201 3469; www.airportshuttle.it) Transfers to/from your hotel for €25 for one person, then €6 for each additional passenger up to a maximum of eight.

Taxi

The set fare to/from the city centre is €48, which is valid for up to four passengers including luggage. Note that taxis registered in Fiumicino charge €60, so make sure you catch a Comune di Roma taxi – these are white with a taxi sign on the roof and the words Roma Capitale on the door along with the taxi's licence number. Journey time is approximately 45 to 60 minutes depending on traffic.

Car

Follow signs for Roma out of the airport complex and onto the autostrada. Exit at EUR, following signs for the *centro*, to link up with Via Cristoforo Colombo, which will take you directly into the centre.

Ciampino Airport

Ciampino (☎06 6 59 51; www.adr.it/ciampino), 15km southeast of the city centre, is used by Ryanair. It's not a big airport but there's a steady flow of traffic and at peak times it can get extremely busy.

To get into town, the best option is to take one of the dedicated bus services. You can also take a bus to Ciampino station and then pick up a train to Termini.

Bus

Terravision (www.terravision.eu; one way €4) Twice-hourly departures to/from Via Marsala outside Stazione Termini. Services from the airport are between 8.15am and 12.15am; from Via Marsala between 4.30am and 9.20pm. Buy tickets at Terracafè in front of the Via Marsala bus stop. Journey time is 40 minutes.

SIT (www.sitbusshuttle.com; from/to airport €4/€6) Buses run from Ciampino between 7.45am and 11.30pm to Via Marsala 5 outside Stazione Termini; from Termini between 4.30am and 9.30pm. Get tickets on the bus. Journey time is 45 minutes.

Cotral (www.cotralspa.it; one way €3.90) Runs 17 daily services to/from Via Giolitti near Stazione Termini. Also buses to/from Anagnina metro station (€1.20) and Ciampino train station (€1.20), where you can get a train to Termini (€1.30).

Private Shuttle

Airport Connection Services (☎06 338 32 21; www.airportconnection.it) Transfers to/from the city centre from €22.

Airport Shuttle (☎06 4201 3469; www.airportshuttle.it) Transfers to/from your hotel for €25 for one person, then €5 for each additional passenger up to a maximum of eight.

Taxi

The set rate to/from the airport is €30. Journey time is approximately 30 minutes depending on traffic.

Car

Exit the station and follow Via Appia Nuova into the centre.

Termini Train Station

Almost all trains arrive at and depart from **Stazione Termini** (Piazza dei Cinquecento), Rome's main train station and principal transport hub. There are

BUSES FROM TERMINI

From Piazza dei Cinquecento outside Stazione Termini buses run to all corners of the city.

DESTINATION	BUS NO
St Peter's Square	40/64
Piazza Venezia	40/64
Piazza Navona	40/64
Campo de' Fiori	40/64
Pantheon	40/64
Colosseum	75
Terme di Caracalla	714
Villa Borghese	910
Trastevere	H

regular connections to other European countries, all major Italian cities and many smaller towns.

Train information is available from the Customer Service area on the main concourse to the left of the ticket desks. Alternatively, check www.trenitalia.com or phone ☎892021.

From Termini, you can connect with the metro or take a bus from Piazza dei Cinquecento out front. Taxis are outside the main exit.

Tiburtina Bus Station

Long-distance national and international buses use **Autostazione Tiburtina** (Piazzale Tiburtina).

From the bus station, cross under the overpass for the Tiburtina train station, where you can pick up metro

line B and connect with Termini for onward buses, trains and metro line A.

Civitavecchia Port

Rome's port is at Civitavecchia, about 80km north of Rome. Ferries sail here from destinations across the Mediterranean, as well as Sicily and Sardinia. Check out www.traghettiweb.it for route details, prices and bookings.

From Civitavecchia there are half-hourly trains to Stazione Termini (€5 to €14.50, forty minutes to one hour). Civitavecchia's station is about 700m from the entrance to the port.

GETTING AROUND ROME

Rome is a sprawling city, but the historic centre is rela-

tively compact and it's quite possible to explore much of it on foot. The city's public transport system includes buses, trams, metro and a suburban train system. Tickets, which come in various forms, are valid for all forms of transport.

Metro

➡ Rome has two main metro lines, A (orange) and B (blue), which cross at Termini, the only point at which you can change from one line to the other. A third line, 'B1', branches off line B and serves the northern suburbs, but you're unlikely to need it.

➡ Trains run between 5.30am and 11.30pm (to 1.30am on Friday and Saturday).

➡ All stations on line B have wheelchair access except Circo Massimo, Colosseo and

USEFUL BUS ROUTES

BUS NO	ROUTE	OPERATING HOURS	FREQUENCY
H	Termini, Via Nazionale, Piazza Venezia, Viale Trastevere	5.30am-midnight	up to 6 hourly
3	Ostiense, Testaccio, Circo Massimo, Colosseo, San Giovanni, Porta Maggiore, San Lorenzo, Villa Borghese	5.30am-10pm	up to 8 hourly
8 Tram	Largo di Torre Argentina, Trastevere, Gianicolo	5.10am-midnight	up to 17 hourly
23	Piazzale Clodio, Piazza del Risorgimento, Ponte Vittorio Emanuele II, Testaccio, Ostiense, Basilica di San Paolo	5am-midnight	up to 7 hourly
40	Termini, Via Nazionale, Piazza Venezia, Largo di Torre Argentina, Borgo Sant'Angelo	6am-midnight	up to 16 hourly
64	The same route as the 40 but slower with more stops	5am-midnight	up to 13 hourly
170	Termini, Via Nazionale, Piazza Venezia, Via del Teatro Marcello, Piazza Bocca della Verità, Testaccio, EUR	5.30am-midnight	up to 7 hourly
492	Stazione Tiburtina, San Lorenzo, Termini, Piazza Barberini, Largo di Torre Argentina, Corso Rinascimento, Piazza del Risorgimento, Cipro–Vatican Museums	5.15am-midnight	up to 6 hourly
590	Follows the route of metro line A	7.30am-10.30pm	1 hourly
660	Largo Colli Albani to Via Appia Antica	7am-8.30pm	2 hourly

Cavour. On line A, Cipro–Musei Vaticani station is one of the few central stations equipped with lifts.

➡ Take line A for the Trevi Fountain (Barberini), Spanish Steps (Spagna) and St Peter's (Ottaviano–San Pietro).

➡ Take line B for the Colosseum (Colosseo).

Bus & Tram

➡ Rome's buses and trams are run by **ATAC** (☏06 5 70 03; www.atac.roma.it).

➡ The main bus station is in front of Stazione Termini on Piazza dei Cinquecento, where there's an **information booth** (⊙7.30am-8pm). Other important bus stops are at Largo di Torre Argentina and Piazza Venezia.

➡ Buses generally run from about 5.30am until midnight, with limited services throughout the night.

➡ Rome's night bus service comprises more than 25 lines, many of which pass Termini and/or Piazza Venezia. Buses are marked with an 'n' before the number and bus stops have a blue owl symbol. Departures are usually every 15 to 30 minutes between about 1am and 5am, but can be much slower.

The most useful night routes:

➡ **n1** Follows the route of metro line A.

➡ **n2** Follows the route of metro line B.

➡ **n7** Piazzale Clodio, Via Zanardelli, Corso Rinascimento, Corso Vittorio Emanuele II, Largo di Torre Argentina, Piazza Venezia, Via Nazionale and Stazione Termini.

Car & Motorcycle

Driving around Rome is not recommended. Riding a scooter or motorbike is faster and makes parking easier, but Rome is no place for learners, so if you're not an experienced rider give it a miss. Hiring a car for a day trip out of town is worth considering.

Most of Rome's historic centre is closed to normal traffic from 6.30am to 6pm Monday to Friday, from 2pm to 6pm Saturday, and from 11pm to 3am Friday and Saturday. Evening restrictions also apply in Trastevere, San Lorenzo, Monti and Testaccio, typically from 9.30pm or 11pm to 3am on Friday and Saturday.

All streets accessing the 'Limited Traffic Zone' (ZTL) are monitored by electronic-access detection devices. If you're staying in this zone, contact your hotel. For further information, check www.agenziamobilita.roma.it.

Driving Licence & Road Rules

All EU driving licences are recognised in Italy. Holders of non-EU licences must get an International Driving Permit (IDP) to accompany their national licence. Apply to your national motoring association.

To ride a scooter up to 125cc, the minimum age is 18 and a licence (a car licence will do) is required. For anything over 125cc you need a motorcycle licence.

Other rules:

➡ Drive on the right, overtake on the left and give way to cars coming from the right.

➡ It's obligatory to wear seat belts, to drive with your headlights on outside built-up areas, and to carry a warning triangle and fluorescent waistcoat in case of breakdown.

➡ Wearing a helmet is compulsory on all two-wheeled vehicles.

➡ The blood alcohol limit is 0.05%.

Unless otherwise indicated, speed limits are as follows:

➡ 130km/h on autostradas

➡ 110km/h on all main, non-urban roads

➡ 90km/h on secondary, non-urban roads

➡ 50km/h in built-up areas

A good source of driving information is the **Automobile Club d'Italia** (ACI; www.aci.it), Italy's national motoring organisation.

Hire

Car hire is available at both Rome's airports and Stazione Termini.

Avis (www.avisautonoleggio.it)

Europcar (www.europcar.com)

Hertz (www.hertz.it)

Maggiore National (www.maggiore.it)

Reckon on €50 to €55 per day for a small car. Note also that most Italian hire cars have manual gear transmission.

To hire a scooter, prices range from about €20 for a 50cc scooter to €125 for a 1000cc motorbike. Reliable operators include the following:

Bici & Baci (☏06 482 84 43; www.bicibaci.com; Via del Viminale 5; ⊙8am-7pm)

Eco Move Rent (☏06 4470 4518; www.ecomoverent.com; Via Varese 48-50; ⊙8.30am-7.30pm)

Treno e Scooter (☏06 4890 5823; www.trenoescooter.com; Piazza dei Cinquecento; ⊙9am-2pm & 4-7pm)

On Road (☏06 481 56 69; www.scooterhire.it; Via Cavour 80; ⊙9am-7pm)

Parking

Blue lines denote pay-and-display parking – get tickets from meters (coins only) and *tabaccaio* (tobacconist shops). Expect to pay up to €1.20 per hour between 8am and 8pm (or to 11pm in some places). After 8pm (or 11pm) parking is generally free until 8am the next

TICKETS, PLEASE

Public-transport tickets are valid on all of Rome's bus, tram and metro lines, except for routes to Fiumicino airport. They come in various forms:

BIT (*biglietto integrato a tempo*, a single ticket valid for 100 minutes and one metro ride) €1.50

BIG (*biglietto integrato giornaliero*, a daily ticket) €6

BTI (*biglietto turistico integrato*, a three-day ticket) €16.50

CIS (*carta integrata settimanale*, a weekly ticket) €24

Abbonamento mensile (a monthly pass) €35

Children under 10 travel free. Buy tickets at *tabaccaio*, newsstands and from vending machines at main bus stops and metro stations. They must be purchased before you start your journey and validated in the machines on buses, at the entrance gates to the metro or at train stations. Ticketless riders risk an on-the-spot €50 fine.

The **Roma Pass** (www.romapass.it; 3 days €34) comes with a three-day travel pass valid within the city boundaries.

Travelling Out of Town

For destinations in the surrounding Lazio region, **Cotral** (☑800 174471; www.cotralspa.it) buses depart from numerous points throughout the city. The company is linked with Rome's public transport system, which means that you can buy tickets that cover city buses, trams, metro and train lines, as well as regional buses and trains. There are a range of tickets but your best bet is a daily BIRG (*biglietto integrato regionale giornaliero*) ticket, which allows unlimited travel on all city and regional transport. It's priced according to zones; tickets range from €3.30 to €14.

Get tickets from *tabaccaio* and authorised ATAC sellers.

---

morning. Traffic wardens are vigilant and fines are not uncommon.

If your car gets towed away, call ☑06 6769 2303.

There's a comprehensive list of car parks on www.060608.it – click on the transport tab then car parks.

Useful car parks include the following:

Piazzale dei Partigiani (per hr/day €0.77/5; ☺6am-11pm)

Stazione Termini (Piazza dei Cinquecento; per hr/day €2/18; ☺6am-1am)

Villa Borghese (Viale del Galoppatoio 33; per hr/day €2.20/20; ☺24hr)

Bicycle

The centre of Rome doesn't lend itself to cycling: there are steep hills, treacherous cobbled roads and the traffic is terrible. If you want to pedal around town, pick up *Andiamo in Bici a Roma* (€7), a useful map which details Rome's main cycle paths.

➡ You can take your bike on the metro all day Saturday and Sunday and on weekdays after 8pm. You can also take it on the Lido di Ostia train on Saturday and Sunday and on weekdays from the beginning of service to 10am and then from 8pm until the end of service. You have to buy a separate ticket for the bike.

➡ On regional trains marked with a bike icon on the timetable, you can carry a bike if you pay a €3.50 supplement.

Hire

Reckon on around €4 per hour, €15 per day.

Appia Antica Regional Park Information Point (☑06 513 53 16; www.parco-appiaantica.org; Via Appia Antica 58-60)

Eco Move Rent (☑06 4470 4518; www.ecomoverent.com; Via Varese 48-50; ☺8.30am-7.30pm)

Treno e Scooter (☑06 4890 5823; www.treno-escooter.com; Piazza dei Cinquecento; ☺9am-2pm & 4-7pm)

Villa Borghese (Largo Pablo Picasso)

Taxi

➡ Official licensed taxis are white with the symbol of Rome and an identifying number on the doors. Always go with the metered fare, never an arranged price (the set fares to and from the airports are exceptions).

➡ In town (within the ring road) flag fall is €3 between 6am and 10pm on weekdays, €4.50 on weekends and holidays, and €6.50 between 10pm and 6am. Then it's €1.10 per kilometre.

Official rates are posted in taxis and on www.viviromaintaxi.eu.

➡ You can hail a taxi, but it's often easier to wait at a rank or phone for one. There are taxi ranks at the airports, Stazione Termini, the Colosseum, Largo di Torre Argentina, Piazza San Silvestro, Piazza della Repubblica, Piazza Belli in Trastevere and in the Vatican at Piazza del Pio XII and Piazza del Risorgimento.

➡ You can book a taxi by phoning the Comune di Roma's automated taxi line on ☎06 06 09 or calling a taxi company direct.

➡ The website www.060608. it has a list of taxi companies – click on the transport tab, then getting around. then by taxi.

➡ Note that when you call for a cab, the meter is switched on straight away and you pay for the cost of the journey from wherever the driver receives the call.

Taxi companies:

La Capitale (☎06 49 94)
Pronto Taxi (☎06 66 45)
Radio Taxi (☎06 35 70)
Samarcanda (☎06 55 51)
Tevere (☎06 41 57)

Train

Apart from connections to Fiumicino airport, you'll probably only need the overground rail network if you head out of town.

➡ Train information is available from the Customer Service area on the main concourse at Stazione Termini. Alternatively, check www.trenitalia.com or phone ☎892021.

➡ Buy tickets at the station from automated ticket machines or from an authorised travel agency – look for an FS or *biglietti treni* sign in the window.

➡ Rome's second train station is Stazione Tiburtina, four stops from Termini on metro line B. Of the capital's eight other train stations, the most important are Stazione Roma-Ostiense and Stazione Trastevere.

TOURS

Walking Tours

A Friend in Rome (☎340 5019201; www.afriendinrome. it) Silvia Prosperi organises private tailor-made tours (on foot, by bike or scooter) to suit your interests. She covers the Vatican and main historic centre as well as areas outside the capital. Rates are €40 to €50 per hour, with a minimum of three hours for most tours. Silvia can also arrange kid-friendly tours, mosaic lessons, cooking classes and coastal cruises.

Dark Rome (☎06 8336 0561; www.darkrome.com) Runs a range of themed tours, costing from €20 to €150, including skip-the-line visits to the Colosseum and Vatican Museums and private visits to the Sistine Chapel. Other popular choices include a Crypts and Catacombs tour, which takes in Rome's buried treasures, and a day trip to Pompeii.

Enjoy Rome (Map p376; ☎06 445 18 43; www.enjoyrome.com; Via Marghera 8a) Offers three-hour walking (skip- the-line) tours of the Vatican (under/over 26yr €27/32) and Ancient & Old Rome (under/over 26yr €25/30) as well as various other tours – see the website for further details. Note that tour prices do not cover admission charges to the Vatican Museums and Colosseum.

Through Eternity Cultural Association (Map p370; ☎06 700 93 36; www. througheternity.com) A reliable operator offering a range of private and group (maximum 13 people) tours led by English-speaking experts. Walks include a group twilight tour of Rome's piazzas and fountains (€33, 2½ hours), the Vatican Museums (avoiding the queues) by day/ night (€54/66, 3½ hours), St Peter's Basilica (€62, five hours), and a Caravaggio tour (€48, three hours).

Roma Cristiana (Map p368; ☎06 6989 6380; www. operaromanapellegrinaggi. org) Runs various walking tours, including visits to the Vatican Museums (adult/reduced €26.50/19.50) and St Peter's Basilica (€25).

Arcult (Map p375; ☎339 6503172; www.arcult.it) Run by architects, Arcult offers excellent customisable group tours focusing on Rome's contemporary architecture. Prices depend on the itinerary.

Bus Tours

Trambus 110open (☎800 281281; www.trambusopen. com; family/adult/reduced €50/20/18; ⊙every 15min 8.30am-7pm) A hop-on, hop-off bus tour. It departs from Viale Einaudi near Termini, and stops at the Colosseum, Bocca della Verità, Piazza Venezia, St Peter's, Ara Pacis and Trevi Fountain. Tickets are valid for 48 hours and are available on board, from the info boxes on Piazza dei Cinquecento and at the Colosseum.

Trambus Archeobus (☎800 281281; www.trambusopen.com; family/adult €40/12; ⊙half-hourly 9am-12.30pm & 1.30-4.30pm) A stop-and-go bus that takes sightseers down Via Appia Antica, stopping at points of archaeological interest along the way. It departs from Viale Einaudi and tickets, valid for 48 hours, can be bought online, on board, at the Piazza dei Cinquecento or Colosseum info boxes and at authorised dealers.

Open Bus Cristiana
(www.operaromanapellegrinaggi.org; 24hr ticket €21; ⊘9am-5.30pm) The Vatican-sponsored Opera Romana Pellegrinaggi runs a hop-on, hop-off bus departing from Via della Conciliazione and Termini. Tickets are available on board, online or at the meeting point at Piazza Pio XII just off St Peter's Square.

Bike & Scooter Tours

Bici & Baci (☑06 482 84 43; www.bicibaci.com; Via del Viminale 5; tours €35; ⊘10am, 3pm & 7pm Mar-Oct, on request Nov-Feb) Bici & Baci runs daily bike tours of central Rome, taking in the historical centre, Campidoglio and the Colosseum, as well as tours on vintage Vespas and in classic Fiat 500 cars. For the Vespa and Fiat 500 tours you'll need to book 24 hours ahead.

Routes and prices vary according to your requests.

Boat Tours

Battelli di Roma (Map p360;☑06 9774 5498; www.battellidiroma.it; adult/reduced €16/12) From April to October it runs cruises along the Tiber. There's also a bus–boat combination tour (€35), and, on Thursdays, Fridays and Saturdays, a dinner cruise (€58, 2¼ hours) and wine-bar cruise (€39, 2¼ hours). Tickets are available online or at the embarkation points on Molo Sant'Angelo and Isola Tiberina.

Directory A–Z

Customs Regulations

Within the European Union you are entitled to tax-free prices on fragrances, cosmetics and skincare; photographic and electrical goods; fashion and accessories; and gifts, jewel-lery and souvenirs where they are available and if there are no longer any allowance restric-tions on these tax-free items.

If you're arriving from a non-EU country you can import, duty free, 200 cigarettes, 1L of spirits (or 2L fortified wine), 4L wine, 60ml perfume, 16L beer, and goods, including elec-tronic devices, up to a value of €300/430 (travelling by land/sea); anything over this value must be declared on arrival and the duty paid.

On leaving the EU, non-EU residents can reclaim value-added tax (VAT) on expensive purchases See p329 for more information.

DISCOUNT CARDS

DISCOUNT CARD	PRICE ADULT/ REDUCED	VALIDITY	ADMISSION TO
Appia Antica Card	€6/3	7 days	Terme di Caracalla, Mausoleo di Cecilia Metella and Villa dei Quintili.
Archaeologia Card	€23/12	7 days	Entrance to the Colosseum, Palatino, Terme di Caracalla, Museo Nazionale Romano (Palazzo Altemps, Palazzo Massimo alle Terme, Terme di Diocleziano, Crypta Balbi), Mausoleo di Cecilia Metella and Villa dei Quintili.
Roma Pass (www.romapass.it)	€34	3 days	Includes free admission to two museums or sites (you choose from a list of 38) as well as reduced entry to extra sites, unlimited public transport within Rome, access to the bike-sharing scheme, and reduced-price entry to other exhibitions and events. Roma & Più Pass includes some of the surrounding province.
OMNIA Vatican & Rome	€90/65	3 days	Includes fast-track entry to the Vatican Museums; to St Peter's Basilica/Vatican Gardens, plus a minibus tour; to the Basilica di San Giovanni, Colosseum, Roman Forum and Palatino with audio guides; and the Mamertine Prison. Free travel on the Roma Cristiana Open Bus; access to one of the other sites, and reductions for all others offered in the Roma Pass; unlimited public transport within Rome.

Note that EU citizens aged between 18 and 25 generally qualify for a discount at most galler-ies and museums, while those under 18 and over 65 often get in free. In both cases you'll need proof of your age, ideally a passport or ID card.

Electricity

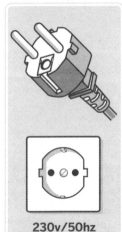

230v/50hz

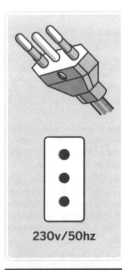

230v/50hz

Emergency

Ambulance (☑118)
Fire (☑115)
Police (☑113, 112)

Gay & Lesbian Travellers

Hardly San Fran on the Med, Rome nevertheless has a thriving, if low-key, gay scene. The big annual events: Gay Pride in June, Gay Village in the summer, are colourful crowd-pleasers and there are numerous gay and mixed nights in clubland, where gay is decidedly 'in' as well as out and proud. Close to the Colosseum, San Giovanni in Laterano is known as 'gay street', as it has several bars dotted along it, including **Coming Out** (Map p370; www.comingout.it; Via di San Giovanni in Laterano 8; ☉10.30am-2am; MColosseo) and **My Bar** (Map p370; Via di San Giovanni in Laterano 12; ☉9am-2am; MColosseo). There is also a popular gay beach, Settimo Cielo, outside Rome at Capocotta, accessible via bus 61 from Ostia Lido or bus 70 from EUR.

In terms of gay rights, Italy is a late bloomer. Homosexuality is legal (over the age of 16) and even widely accepted, but it is publicly frowned on by the government, whose views largely coincide with the Vatican's. And with the Catholic hierarchy decidedly against same-sex marriages and rights for common-law couples, both straight and gay, changes to the statute books are unlikely any time soon.

The main gay cultural and political organisation is the **Circolo Mario Mieli di Cultura Omosessuale** (☑800 110611; www.mariomieli.org; Via Efeso 2a), which organises debates, cultural events and social functions, including **Muccassassina** (www.muccassassina.com) club nights and the city's annual Gay Pride march. Its website has info and listings of forthcoming events.

The national organisation for lesbians is the **Coordinamento Lesbiche Italiano** (www.clrbp.it; Via San Francesco di Sales 1b), which holds regular conferences and literary evenings. There is also a women-only hostel, **La Foresteria Orsa Maggiore** (Map p372; ☑06 689 37 53; www.casainternazionaledelledonne.org; Via San Francesco di Sales 1a, 2nd fl; dm €26-42, s €55-75, d €110-150, without bathroom s €36-55, d €72-100, minimum 2-night stay; @☎; 🚌Piazza Trilussa).

Another useful listings guide is the international gay guide **Spartacus** (www.spartacusworld.com); available in app or book form. You can also go online at www.gayrome.com and www.gayfriendlyitaly.com.

The following might also be of help:

Arcigay Roma (☑06 6450 1102; www.arcigayroma.it; Via Nicola Zabaglia 14) The Roman branch of the national Arcigay organisation. Offers counselling, phone lines and general information.

Arcilesbica (☑06 6450 1102; www.arcilesbica.roma.it; Via Nicola Zabaglia 14) Organises social outings.

Zipper Travel Association (☑06 4436 2244; www.zippertravel.it; Via dei Gracchi 17) A specialist gay and lesbian travel agency.

Internet Access

There are plenty of internet cafes to choose from, particularly clustered around Termini station. Most hotels have wi-fi these days, though with signals of varying quality. There will usually be at least one fixed computer for guest use.

There are lots of wi-fi hotspots around the city, run by **Provincia di Roma** (www.provincia.roma.it), **Roma Wireless** (www.romawireless.com) and **Digit Roma** (www.digitroma.it), though to use any of these you will need to register online using an Italian mobile number. Once you've registered, you'll receive a call to check the line, and once you've answered (you don't need to speak), you'll be able to log in and use a password.

An easier option (no need for a local mobile number) is to head to a cafe or bar offering free wi-fi. Places offering wi-fi are indicated by the wi-fi icon 🛜 in this guide.

Legal Matters

The most likely reason for a brush with the law is to report a theft. If you do have something stolen and you want to claim it on insurance, you must make a statement to the police, as insurance companies won't pay up without official proof of a crime.

The Italian police is divided into three main bodies: the *polizia,* who wear navy-blue jackets; the *carabinieri,* in a black uniform with a red stripe; and the grey-clad *guardia di finanza* (fiscal police), responsible for fighting tax evasion and drug smuggling. If you run into trouble, you're most likely to end up dealing with the *polizia* or *carabinieri.*

If you are detained for any alleged offence, you should be given verbal and written notice within 24 hours of the charges laid against you. You have no right to a phone call upon arrest, but you can choose not to respond to questions without the presence of a lawyer.

Rome's **police station** (Questura; ☏06 4 68 61; http://questure.poliziadistato.it; Via San Vitale 15; ☑8.30am-11.30pm Mon-Fri, 3-5pm Tue & Thu), the police administrative headquarters, is just off Via Nazionale.

Drink & Drugs

Under Italian law there's no distinction between hard and soft drugs, so cannabis is effectively on the same legal footing as cocaine, heroin and ecstasy. If you're caught with what the police deem to be a dealable quantity, you risk a prison sentence of between six and 20 years. The offence of possession for personal use is punishable by administrative sanctions (such as suspension of your driving licence), which may have a duration of up to one year.

The legal limit for a driver's blood-alcohol reading is 0.05%.

Medical Services

Italy has a public health system that is legally bound to provide emergency care to everyone. EU nationals are entitled to reduced-cost, sometimes free, medical care with a European Health Insurance Card (EHIC), available from your home health authority – you can usually apply for it online. Non-EU citizens should take out medical insurance.

For emergency treatment, you can go to the *pronto soccorso* (casualty) section of an *ospedale* (public hospital). For less serious ailments call the **Guardia Medica** (☏06 7730 6650; Via Emilio Morosini 30).

A more convenient course, if you have insurance and can afford to pay up front, would be to call a private doctor to come to your hotel or apartment. Try **Roma Medica** (☏338 6224832; call out & treatment fee €150; ☑24hr) or the **International Medical Centre** (☏06 488 23 71; Via Firenze 47; call out & treatment fee €140; ☑24hr).

Pharmacists will serve prescriptions and can provide basic medical advice.

If you need an ambulance, call ☏118.

Emergency Rooms

Ospedale Bambino Gesù (☏06 6 85 91; www.ospedale-bambinogesu.it; Piazza di Sant'Onofrio 4) Rome's premier children's hospital, but be warned, the emergency section is very busy.

Ospedale di Odontoiatria G Eastman (☏06 84 48 31; Viale Regina Elena 287b) For emergency dental treatment.

Ospedale Fatebene-fratelli (☏06 6 83 71; www.fatebenefratelli-isolatiberina.it; Piazza Fatebenefratelli, Isola Tiberina)

Ospedale San Camillo Forlanini (☏06 5 87 01; www.scamilloforlanini.rm.it; Circonvallazione Gianicolense 87)

Ospedale San Giovanni (☏06 7 70 51; http://portale.hsangiovanni.roma.it; Via Amba Aradam 9)

Ospedale Santo Spirito (☏06 6 83 51; Lungotevere in Sassia 1) Near the Vatican.

Policlinico Umberto I (☏06 4 99 71; www.policlinicoumberto1.it; Viale del Policlinico 155) Near Stazione Termini.

Pharmacies

Marked by a green cross, *farmacie* (pharmacies) open from 8.30am to 1pm and 4pm to 7.30pm Monday to Friday and on Saturday mornings. Outside these hours they open on a rotational basis, and all are legally required to post a list of places open in the vicinity. Night pharmacies are listed in daily newspapers and in pharmacy windows.

If you think you'll need a prescription while in Rome, make sure you know the drug's generic name rather than the brand name. Regular medications available over the counter – such as antihistamines or paracetamol – tend to be expensive in Italy.

There's a 24-hour **pharmacy** (☏06 488 00 19; Piazza dei Cinquecento 51; ☑7.30am-10pm) on the western flank of

SMOKING

Smoking is banned in enclosed public spaces, which includes restaurants, bars, shops and public transport.

Piazza dei Cinquecento near Stazione Termini. In the station, you'll find a **pharmacy** (☏06 488 00 19; Piazza dei Cinquecento 51; ⏱7.30am-10pm) next to platform 1.

In the Vatican, the **Farmacia Vaticana** (☏06 6988 9806; Palazzo Belvedere; ⏱8.30am-6pm Mon-Fri Sep-Jun, 8.30am-3pm Mon-Fri Jul & Aug, plus 8.30am-1pm Sat year-round) sells certain drugs that are not available in Italian pharmacies and will fill foreign prescriptions (something local pharmacies can't do).

Money

For the latest exchange rates, check out www.xe.com.

ATMs

ATMs (known as *bancomat*) are widely available in Rome and most will accept cards tied to the Visa, MasterCard, Cirrus and Maestro systems. The daily limit for cash withdrawal is €250. It's a good idea to let your bank know when you are going abroad, in case it blocks your card when payments from unusual locations appear. If you are registered for online banking, you may be able to do this online.

Remember that every time you withdraw cash, your home bank charges you a foreign exchange fee (usually around 1% to 3%) as well as a transaction charge of around 1%. Check with your bank before you go to find out its specific charges.

Changing Money

You can change your money in banks, at post offices or at a *cambio* (exchange office). There are exchange booths at Stazione Termini and at Fiumicino and Ciampino airports. In the centre, there are numerous bureaux de change, including **American Express** (☏06 6 76 41; Piazza di Spagna 38; ⏱9am-5.30pm Mon-Fri, 9am-12.30pm

Sat). Post offices and banks tend to offer the best rates.

A few banks also provide automatic exchange machines that accept notes from most major currencies.

Always make sure you have your passport or some form of photo ID when exchanging money.

Credit Cards

Credit cards are widely accepted but it's still a good idea to carry a cash back-up. Virtually all midrange and top-end hotels accept credit cards, as do most restaurants and large shops. You can also use them to obtain cash advances at some banks. Some of the cheaper *pensioni* (guesthouses), trattorias and pizzerias accept nothing but cash.

Major cards such as Visa, MasterCard, Eurocard, Cirrus and Eurocheques are widely accepted. Amex is also recognised, although it's less common than Visa or MasterCard.

Note that using your credit card in ATMs can be costly. On every transaction there's a fee, which can reach US$10 with some credit-card issuers, as well as interest per withdrawal. Check with your issuer before leaving home.

If your card is lost, stolen or swallowed by an ATM, telephone to have an immediate stop put on its use.

The Amex office can issue customers with new cards, usually within 24 hours and sometimes immediately, if they have been lost or stolen.

As for your debit card, remember to let your bank know of your travel plans. Otherwise they might block the card when they see any unusual spending.

Amex (☏06 7290 0347)

Diners Club (☏800 393939)

MasterCard (☏800 870866)

Visa (☏800 819014)

Opening Hours

Banks	8.30am-1.30pm & 2.45-4.30pm Mon-Fri
Bars & cafes	7.30am-8pm, sometimes until 1am or 2am
Clubs	10pm-4am
Restaurants	noon-3pm & 7.30-11pm (later in summer)
Shops	9am-7.30pm or 10am-8pm Mon-Sat, some 11am-7pm Sun; smaller shops 9am-1pm & 3.30-7.30pm (or 4-8pm) Mon-Sat

Post

Italy's postal system, **Poste Italiane** (☏803160; www.poste.it), is not the world's best, but nor is it as bad as it's often made out to be. Parcels do occasionally go missing, however. The Vatican postal system, on the other hand, has long enjoyed a reputation for efficiency.

Stamps (*francobolli*) are available at post offices and authorised tobacconists (look for the official *tabaccheria* sign: a big 'T', usually white on black).

There are local post offices in every district. Opening hours vary but are typically 8.30am to 6pm Monday to Friday and 8.30am to 1pm on Saturday. All post offices close two hours earlier than normal on the last business day of each month.

Main post office (☏06 6973 7205; Piazza di San Silvestro 19; ⏱8.25am-7.10pm Mon-Fri, 8.25am-12.35pm Sat)

Vatican post office (☏06 6988 3406; St Peter's Square; ⏱8.30am-6.30pm Mon-Sat)

Letters can be posted in blue Vatican post boxes only if they carry Vatican stamps.

Rates

Letters up to 20g cost €0.85 to Zone 1 (Europe and the Mediterranean Basin), €2 to Zone 2 (other countries in Africa, Asia and the Americas) and €2.50 to Zone 3 (Australia and New Zealand). For more important items, use registered mail (raccomandata), which costs €4.80 to Zone 1, €5.60 to Zone 2 and €6 to Zone 3.

Public Holidays

Most Romans take their annual holiday in August. This means that many businesses and shops close for at least part of the month, particularly around Ferragosto (Feast of the Assumption) on 15 August.

Public holidays include the following:

Capodanno (New Year's Day) 1 January

Epifania (Epiphany) 6 January

Pasquetta (Easter Monday) March/April

Giorno della Liberazione (Liberation Day) 25 April

Festa del Lavoro (Labour Day) 1 May

Festa della Repubblica (Republic Day) 2 June

Festa dei Santi Pietro e Paolo (Feast of St Peter & St Paul) 29 June

Ferragosto (Feast of the Assumption) 15 August

Festa di Ognisanti (All Saints' Day) 1 November

Festa dell'Immacolata Concezione (Feast of the Immaculate Conception) 8 December

Natale (Christmas Day) 25 December

Festa di Santo Stefano (Boxing Day) 26 December

PRACTICALITIES

➡ Vatican Radio (www.radiovaticana.org; 93.3FM and 105FM in Rome) Broadcasts in Italian, English and other languages.

➡ RAI-1, RAI-2 and RAI-3 (www.rai.it) National broadcaster, running state TV and radio.

➡ Radio Città Futura (www.radiocittafutura.it) Great for contemporary and world music.

➡ Main commercial TV stations (mostly run by Silvio Berlusconi's Mediaset company): Canale 5 (www.mediaset.it/canale5), Italia 1 (www.mediaset.it/italia1), Rete 4 (www.mediaset.it/rete4) and La 7 (www.la7.it).

➡ Weights and measures use the metric system.

➡ Italy's currency is the euro. The seven euro notes come in denominations of €500, €200, €100, €50, €20, €10 and €5. The eight euro coins are in denominations of €2 and €1, and 50, 20, 10, five, two and one cents.

Safe Travel

Rome is not a dangerous city, but petty crime is a problem. Road safety is also an issue. The highway code is obeyed with discretion, so don't take it for granted that cars and scooters will stop at pedestrian crossings, or even at red lights.

Taxes & Refunds

A value-added tax of 20%, known as IVA (Imposta di Valore Aggiunto), is slapped on just about everything in Italy. If you are a non-EU resident and you spend more than €155 on a purchase, you can claim a refund when you leave the EU. The refund only applies to purchases from affiliated retail outlets that display a 'Tax Free' sign. When you make your purchase, ask for a tax-refund voucher, to be filled in with the date of your purchase and its value. When you leave the EU, get this voucher stamped at customs and take it to the nearest tax-refund counter where you'll get an immediate refund, either in cash or charged to your credit card.

Telephone

Domestic Calls

Rome's area code is ☑06. Area codes are an integral part of all Italian phone numbers and must be dialled even when calling locally. Mobile-phone numbers are nine or 10 digits long and begin with a three-digit prefix starting with a 3. Toll-free numbers are known as numeri verdi and usually start with 800. Some six-digit national-rate numbers are also in use.

For directory inquiries, dial ☑1240.

International Calls

To call abroad from Italy dial 00, then the relevant country and area codes, followed by the telephone number.

Try to avoid making international calls from a hotel, as you'll be stung by high rates. It's cheaper to call from a private call centre or from a public payphone with an international calling card. These are available at newsstands and tobacconists, and are often good value. Another alternative is to use a direct-dialling service such as AT&T's USA Direct

STOP, THIEF!

The greatest risk visitors face in Rome is from pickpockets and thieves. There's no reason for paranoia, but you need to be aware that the problem exists and protect your valuables with this in mind.

Pickpockets go where the tourists go, so watch out around the most touristed and crowded areas, such as the Colosseum, Piazza di Spagna, St Peter's Square and Stazione Termini. Note that thieves prey on disoriented travellers at the bus stops around Termini, fresh in from airports. Crowded public transport is another hot spot – the 64 Vatican bus is notorious. If travelling on the metro, try to use the end carriages, which are usually less busy.

A money belt with your essentials (passport, cash, credit cards) is a good idea. However, to avoid delving into it in public, carry a wallet with a day's cash. Don't flaunt watches, cameras and other expensive goods. If you're carrying a bag or camera, wear the strap across your body and away from the road – scooter thieves can swipe a bag and be gone in seconds. Be careful when you sit down at a streetside table – never drape your bag over an empty chair by the road or put it where you can't see it.

A common method is for one thief to distract you while their assistant makes away with your purse. Beware of gangs of kids or others demanding attention. If you notice that you've been targeted, either take evasive action or shout 'va via!' ('go away!') in a loud, angry voice. Remember also that some of the best pickpockets are well dressed.

Cars, particularly those with foreign number plates or rental-company stickers, also provide rich pickings for thieves. Never leave valuables in your car – try not to leave anything on display if you can help it. It's a good idea to pay extra to leave your car in supervised car parks.

Watch out also for short-changing – always check your change to see you haven't been 'accidentally' given a note too few.

In case of theft or loss, always report the incident to the police within 24 hours and ask for a statement.

(access number ☎800 172 444) or Telstra's Australia Direct (access number ☎800 172 610), which allows you to make a reverse-charge call at home-country rates. **Skype** (www.skype.com) is also available at most internet cafes.

To make a reverse-charge (collect) international call from a public telephone, dial ☎170. All phone operators speak English.

Mobile Phones

Italian mobile phones operate on the GSM 900/1800 network, which is compatible with the rest of Europe and Australia but not always with the North American GSM or CDMA systems – check with your service provider.

If you have a GSM dual-, tri- or quad-band phone that you can unlock (again, check with your service provider), it can cost as little as €10 to activate a prepaid (*prepagato*) SIM card in Italy. **TIM** (Telecom Italia Mobile; www.tim.it), **Wind** (www.wind.it) and **Vodafone** (www.vodafone.it) all offer SIM cards and have retail outlets across town. Note that by Italian law all SIM cards must be registered in Italy, so make sure you have a passport or ID card with you when you buy one.

Public Phones

You can still find public payphones around Rome. Most work and most take telephone cards (*schede telefoniche*), although you'll still find some that accept coins or credit cards. You can buy phonecards (€5, €10 or €20)

at post offices, tobacconists and newsstands.

Time

Italy is in a single time zone, one hour ahead of GMT. Daylight-saving time, when clocks move forward one hour, starts on the last Sunday in March. Clocks are put back an hour on the last Sunday in October.

Italy operates on a 24-hour clock, so 6pm is written as 18:00.

Toilets

Public toilets are not widespread and those that do exist are often closed; some make a small charge. The best thing to do is to nip into a cafe or bar, all of which are required by law to have a toilet.

Tourist Information

Telephone & Internet Resources

Comune Call Centre

(☑060606; ☉24hr) Very useful for practical questions such as: Where's the nearest hospital? Where can I park? When are the underground trains running? The centre is staffed 24 hours and staff speak English, Italian and Romanian. French, German, Spanish, Albanian and Polish speakers are available from 7am to 7pm Monday to Friday and 8am to 1pm on Saturday.

Tourist Information Line (☑060608; www.060608. it; ☉9am-9pm) A free multilingual tourist information line and website providing information on culture, shows, hotels, transport etc.

Turismo Roma (www. turismoroma.it) The official website of the Rome Tourist Board, with accommodation and restaurant lists, as well as details of upcoming events, museums and much more.

Tourist Offices

Centro Servizi Pellegrini e Turisti (☑06 6988 1662; St Peter's Square; ☉8.30am-6pm Mon-Sat) The Vatican's official tourist office.

Enjoy Rome (☑06 445 18 43; www.enjoyrome.com; Via Marghera 8a; ☉9am-5.30pm Mon-Fri, 8.30am-2pm Sat) An excellent private tourist office that runs tours and publishes the free and useful *Enjoy Rome* city guide.

Rome Tourist Board (APT;☑060608; www.turismoroma.it)

The Comune di Roma runs tourist information points throughout the city, including the following:

Castel Sant'Angelo Tourist Information (Piazza Pia; ☉9.30am-7pm)

Ciampino Airport (International Arrivals, baggage reclaim area; ☉9am-6.30pm)

Leonardo da Vinci– Fiumicino Airport (Terminal 3, International Arrivals; ☉8am-7.30pm)

Stazione Termini Tourist Information (☉8am-8.30pm) Next to platform 24.

Trevi Fountain Tourist Information (Via Marco Minghetti; ☉9.30am-7pm) This tourist point is nearer to Via del Corso than the fountain.

Via Nazionale Tourist Information (☉9.30am-7pm)

Travellers with Disabilities

Rome isn't an easy city for travellers with disabilities. Cobbled streets, blocked pavements and tiny lifts are difficult for the wheelchairbound, while the relentless traffic can be disorienting for partially sighted travellers or those with hearing difficulties.

Getting around on public transport is difficult. On metro line B all stations have wheelchair access except for Circo Massimo, Colosseo, Cavour and EUR Magliana, while on line A only Cipro–Musei Vaticani and Valle Aurelia have lifts. Note that bus 590 covers the same route as metro line A and is wheelchair accessible. Newer buses and trams have access for travellers with disabilities; it's indicated on bus stops which routes are wheelchair accessible.

If travelling by train, ring the national helpline ☑199 303060 to arrange assistance. At Stazione Termini, the **Sala Blu Assistenza Disabili** (salablu.roma@rfi.it;

☉6.45am-9.30pm) next to platform 1 can provide information on wheelchairaccessible trains and help with transport in the station. Contact the office 24 hours ahead if you know you're going to need assistance. There are similar offices at Tiburtina and Ostiense stations.

Airline companies should be able to arrange assistance at airports if you notify them of your needs in advance. Alternatively, contact **ADR Assistance** (www.adrassistance.it) for assistance at Leonardo da Vinci–Fiumicino Airport or Ciampino airports.

Some taxis are equipped to carry passengers in wheelchairs; ask for a taxi for a *sedia a rotelle* (wheelchair).

Organisations

The best point of reference is **CO.IN** (www.coinsociale.it; Via Enrico Giglioli 54a), an umbrella group for associations and cooperatives across the country, which can provide useful information and local contacts.

Other useful resources:

Handy Turismo (☑06 3507 5707; www.handyturismo.it) A comprehensive and easy-to-use website with information on travel, accommodation and access at the main tourist attractions.

Roma per Tutti (☑06 5717 7094; www.romapertutti.it) A council-backed venture to provide assistance and free guided museum visits.

Sage Traveling (☑1-888-645-7920; www.sagetraveling. com) This US-based agency, started by wheelchair user John Sage who has visited more than 70 countries, offers advice and tailor-made tours to assist travellers with disabilities, specialising in Europe.

Visas

EU citizens do not need a visa to enter Italy. Nationals

of some other countries, including Australia, Canada, Israel, Japan, New Zealand, Switzerland and the USA, do not need a visa for stays of up to 90 days.

Italy is one of the 15 signatories of the Schengen Convention, an agreement whereby participating countries abolished customs checks at common borders. The standard tourist visa for a Schengen country is valid for 90 days. You must apply for it in your country of residence and you cannot apply for more than two in any 12-month period. They are not renewable within Italy.

Technically, all foreign visitors to Italy are supposed to register with the local police within eight days of arrival. However, if you're staying in a hotel you don't need to bother as the hotel does this for you.

Up-to-date visa information is available on www. lonelyplanet.com – follow the links through to the Italy destination guide.

Permesso di Soggiorno

A *permesso di soggiorno* (permit to stay, also referred to as a residence permit) is required by all non-EU nationals who stay in Italy longer than three months. In theory, you should apply for one within eight days of arriving in Italy. EU citizens do not require a *permesso di soggiorno* but are required to register with the local registry office *(ufficio anagrafe)* if they stay for more than three months.

To get one, you'll need an application form; a valid passport, containing a stamp with your date of entry into Italy (ask for this, as it's not automatic); a photocopy of your passport with a visa, if required; four passport-style photographs; proof of your ability to support yourself financially (ideally a letter from an employer or school/ university); and a €14.62 official stamp.

Although correct at the time of writing, the documentary requirements change periodically, so always check before you join the inevitable queue. Details are available on www. poliziadistato.it – click on the English tab and then follow the links.

The quickest way to apply is to go with the relevant documents to the **Ufficio Immigrazione** (Via Teofilo Patini; ⊙8.30-11.30am Mon-Fri & 3-5pm Tue & Thu) in the city's eastern suburbs.

Study Visas

Non-EU citizens who want to study at a university or language school in Italy must have a study visa. These can be obtained at your nearest Italian embassy or consulate. You will normally require confirmation of your enrolment, proof of payment of fees and proof that you can support yourself financially. The visa only covers the period of the enrolment. This type of visa is renewable within Italy but, again, only with confirmation of ongoing enrolment and that you are still financially self-supporting.

Work Visas

To work in Italy all non-EU citizens require a work visa.

Apply to your nearest Italian embassy or consulate. You'll need a valid passport, proof of health insurance and a work permit. The work permit is obtained in Italy by your employer and then forwarded to you prior to your visa application.

Women Travellers

Rome is not a particularly dangerous city for women, but women should take the usual precautions as they would in any large city, and, as in most places, avoid wandering around alone late at night, especially in the area around Termini.

It's unusual for women to go out in the evening on their own, and if you do, be prepared for some unwanted attention or to feel quite conspicuous.

The most common source of discomfort is harassment. If you find yourself being pestered by local men and ignoring them isn't working, tell them that you are waiting for your husband *(marito)* or boyfriend *(fidanzato)*, and if necessary, walk away. Avoid becoming aggressive, as this may result in an unpleasant confrontation.

Gropers, particularly on crowded public transport, can also be a problem. If you do feel someone start to touch you inappropriately, make a fuss – a loud *'che schifo!'* (how disgusting!) should do the job. If a more serious incident occurs, report it to the police, who are then required to press charges.

Language

When in Rome, you'll find that locals appreciate you trying their language, no matter how muddled you may think you sound.

Italian is not difficult to pronounce as the sounds used in spoken Italian can all be found in English.

Note that, in our pronunciation guides, ai is pronounced as in 'aisle', ay as in 'say', ow as in 'how', dz as the 'ds' in 'lids', and that r is a strong and rolled sound. Keep in mind too that Italian consonants can have a stronger, emphatic pronunciation – if the consonant is written as a double letter, it should be pronounced a little stronger. This difference in the pronunciation of single and double consonants can mean a difference in meaning, eg *sonno son*·no (sleep) versus *sono so*·no (I am).

If you read our coloured pronunciation guides as if they were English, you'll be understood. The stressed syllables are indicated with italics.

BASICS

Italian has two words for 'you' – use the polite form *Lei* lay if you're talking to strangers, officials or people older than you. With people familiar to you or younger than you, you can use the informal form *tu* too.

In Italian, all nouns and adjectives are either masculine or feminine, and so are the articles *il/la* eel/la (the) and *un/una* oon/oo·na (a) that go with the nouns.

In this chapter the polite/informal and masculine/feminine options are included where necessary, separated with a slash and indicated with 'pol/inf' and 'm/f'.

WANT MORE?

For in-depth language information and handy phrases, check out Lonely Planet's *Italian phrasebook*. You'll find it at **shop.lonelyplanet.com**, or you can buy Lonely Planet's iPhone phrasebooks at the Apple App Store.

Hello.	Buongiorno.	bwon·jor·no
Goodbye.	Arrivederci.	a·ree·ve·der·chee
Yes.	Sì.	see
No.	No.	no
Excuse me.	Mi scusi. (pol)	mee skoo·zee
	Scusami. (inf)	skoo·za·mee
Sorry.	Mi dispiace.	mee dees·pya·che
Please.	Per favore.	per fa·vo·re
Thank you.	Grazie.	gra·tsye
You're welcome.	Prego.	pre·go

How are you?
Come sta/stai? (pol/inf) ko·me sta/stai

Fine. And you?
Bene. E Lei/tu? (pol/inf) be·ne e lay/too

What's your name?
Come si chiama? pol ko·me see kya·ma
Come ti chiami? inf ko·me tee kya·mee

My name is ...
Mi chiamo ... mee kya·mo ...

Do you speak English?
Parla/Parli par·la/par·lee
inglese? (pol/inf) een·gle·ze

I don't understand.
Non capisco. non ka·pee·sko

ACCOMMODATION

Do you have a ... room?	Avete una camera ...?	a·ve·te oo·na ka·me·ra ...
double	doppia con letto matrimoniale	do·pya kon le·to ma·tree·mo·nya·le
single	singola	seen·go·la
How much is it per ...?	Quanto costa per ...?	kwan·to kos·ta per ...
night	una notte	oo·na no·te
person	persona	per·so·na

Is breakfast included?
La colazione è
compresa?
la ko·la·tsyo·ne e
kom·pre·sa

air-con	aria condizionata	a·rya kon·dee·tsyo·na·ta
bathroom	bagno	ba·nyo
campsite	campeggio	kam·pe·jo
guesthouse	pensione	pen·syo·ne
hotel	albergo	al·ber·go
youth hostel	ostello della gioventù	os·te·lo de·la jo·ven·too
window	finestra	fee·nes·tra

DIRECTIONS

Where's ...?
Dov'è ...?
do·ve ...

What's the address?
Qual'è l'indirizzo?
kwa·le leen·dee·ree·tso

Could you please write it down?
Può scriverlo,
per favore?
pwo skree·ver·lo
per fa·vo·re

Can you show me (on the map)?
Può mostrarmi
(sulla pianta)?
pwo mos·trar·mee
(soo·la pyan·ta)

at the corner	all'angolo	a·lan·go·lo
at the traffic lights	al semaforo	al se·ma·fo·ro
behind	dietro	dye·tro
far	lontano	lon·ta·no
in front of	davanti a	da·van·tee a
near	vicino	vee·chee·no
next to	accanto a	a·kan·to a
opposite	di fronte a	dee fron·te a
straight ahead	sempre diritto	sem·pre dee·ree·to
to the left	a sinistra	a see·nee·stra
to the right	a destra	a de·stra

EATING & DRINKING

What would you recommend?
Cosa mi consiglia?
ko·za mee kon·see·lya

What's in that dish?
Quali ingredienti
ci sono in
questo piatto?
kwa·li een·gre·dyen·tee
chee so·no een
kwe·sto pya·to

What's the local speciality?
Qual'è la specialità
di questa regione?
kwa·le la spe·cha·lee·ta
dee kwe·sta re·jo·ne

That was delicious!
Era squisito!
e·ra skwee·zee·to

Cheers!
Salute!
sa·loo·te

KEY PATTERNS

To get by in Italian, mix and match these simple patterns with words of your choice:

When's (the next flight)?
A che ora è
(il prossimo volo)?
a ke o·ra e
(eel pro·see·mo vo·lo)

Where's (the station)?
Dov'è (la stazione)?
do·ve (la sta·tsyo·ne)

I'm looking for (a hotel).
Sto cercando
(un albergo).
sto cher·kan·do
(oon al·ber·go)

Do you have (a map)?
Ha (una pianta)?
a (oo·na pyan·ta)

Is there (a toilet)?
C'è (un gabinetto)?
che (oon ga·bee·ne·to)

I'd like (a coffee).
Vorrei (un caffè).
vo·ray (oon ka·fe)

I'd like to (hire a car).
Vorrei (noleggiare
una macchina).
vo·ray (no·le·ja·re
oo·na ma·kee·na)

Can I (enter)?
Posso (entrare)?
po·so (en·tra·re)

Could you please (help me)?
Può (aiutarmi),
per favore?
pwo (a·yoo·tar·mee),
per fa·vo·re

Do I have to (book a seat)?
Devo (prenotare
un posto)?
de·vo (pre·no·ta·re
oon po·sto)

Please bring the bill.
Mi porta il conto,
per favore?
mee por·ta eel kon·to
per fa·vo·re

I'd like to reserve a table for ...	Vorrei prenotare un tavolo per ...	vo·ray pre·no·ta·re oon ta·vo·lo per ...
(two) people	(due) persone	(doo·e) per·so·ne
(eight) o'clock	le (otto)	le (o·to)

I don't eat ...	Non mangio ...	non man·jo ...
eggs	uova	wo·va
fish	pesce	pe·she
nuts	noci	no·chee
(red) meat	carne (rossa)	kar·ne (ro·sa)

Key Words

bar	locale	lo·ka·le
bottle	bottiglia	bo·tee·lya
breakfast	prima colazione	pree·ma ko·la·tsyo·ne

cafe	bar	bar
cold	freddo	fre·do
dinner	cena	che·na
drink list	lista delle bevande	lee·sta de·le be·van·de
fork	forchetta	for·ke·ta
glass	bicchiere	bee·kye·re
grocery store	alimentari	a·lee·men·ta·ree
hot	caldo	kal·do
knife	coltello	kol·te·lo
lunch	pranzo	pran·dzo
market	mercato	mer·ka·to
menu	menù	me·noo
plate	piatto	pya·to
restaurant	ristorante	ree·sto·ran·te
spicy	piccante	pee·kan·te
spoon	cucchiaio	koo·kya·yo
vegetarian (food)	vegetariano	ve·je·ta·rya·no
with	con	kon
without	senza	sen·tsa

Meat & Fish

beef	manzo	man·dzo
chicken	pollo	po·lo
duck	anatra	a·na·tra
fish	pesce	pe·she
herring	aringa	a·reen·ga
lamb	agnello	a·nye·lo
lobster	aragosta	a·ra·gos·ta
meat	carne	kar·ne
mussels	cozze	ko·tse
oysters	ostriche	o·stree·ke
pork	maiale	ma·ya·le
prawn	gambero	gam·be·ro
salmon	salmone	sal·mo·ne

Signs

Entrata/Ingresso	Entrance
Uscita	Exit
Aperto	Open
Chiuso	Closed
Informazioni	Information
Proibito/Vietato	Prohibited
Gabinetti/Servizi	Toilets
Uomini	Men
Donne	Women

scallops	capasante	ka·pa·san·te
seafood	frutti di mare	froo·tee dee ma·re
shrimp	gambero	gam·be·ro
squid	calamari	ka·la·ma·ree
trout	trota	tro·ta
tuna	tonno	to·no
turkey	tacchino	ta·kee·no
veal	vitello	vee·te·lo

Fruit & Vegetables

apple	mela	me·la
beans	fagioli	fa·jo·lee
cabbage	cavolo	ka·vo·lo
capsicum	peperone	pe·pe·ro·ne
carrot	carota	ka·ro·ta
cauliflower	cavolfiore	ka·vol·fyo·re
cucumber	cetriolo	che·tree·o·lo
fruit	frutta	froo·ta
grapes	uva	oo·va
lemon	limone	lee·mo·ne
lentils	lenticchie	len·tee·kye
mushroom	funghi	foon·gee
nuts	noci	no·chee
onions	cipolle	chee·po·le
orange	arancia	a·ran·cha
peach	pesca	pe·ska
peas	piselli	pee·ze·lee
pineapple	ananas	a·na·nas
plum	prugna	proo·nya
potatoes	patate	pa·ta·te
spinach	spinaci	spee·na·chee
tomatoes	pomodori	po·mo·do·ree
vegetables	verdura	ver·doo·ra

Other

bread	pane	pa·ne
butter	burro	boo·ro
cheese	formaggio	for·ma·jo
eggs	uova	wo·va
honey	miele	mye·le
ice	ghiaccio	gya·cho
jam	marmellata	mar·me·la·ta
noodles	pasta	pas·ta
oil	olio	o·lyo
pepper	pepe	pe·pe

rice	riso	ree·zo
salt	sale	sa·le
soup	minestra	mee·nes·tra
soy sauce	salsa di soia	sal·sa dee so·ya
sugar	zucchero	tsoo·ke·ro
vinegar	aceto	a·che·to

Drinks

beer	birra	bee·ra
coffee	caffè	ka·fe
(orange) juice	succo (d'arancia)	soo·ko (da·ran·cha)
milk	latte	la·te
red wine	vino rosso	vee·no ro·so
soft drink	bibita	bee·bee·ta
tea	tè	te
(mineral) water	acqua (minerale)	a·kwa (mee·ne·ra·le)
white wine	vino bianco	vee·no byan·ko

EMERGENCIES

Help!
Aiuto! — a·yoo·to

Leave me alone!
Lasciami in pace! — la·sha·mee een pa·che

I'm lost.
Mi sono perso/a. (m/f) — mee so·no per·so/a

There's been an accident.
C'è stato un incidente. — che sta·to oon een·chee·den·te

Call the police!
Chiami la polizia! — kya·mee la po·lee·tsee·a

Call a doctor!
Chiami un medico! — kya·mee oon me·dee·ko

Where are the toilets?
Dove sono i gabinetti? — do·ve so·no ee ga·bee·ne·tee

I'm sick.
Mi sento male. — mee sen·to ma·le

It hurts here.
Mi fa male qui. — mee fa ma·le kwee

I'm allergic to ...
Sono allergico/a a ... (m/f) — so·no a·ler·jee·ko/a a ...

Question Words

How?	Come?	ko·me
What?	Che cosa?	ke ko·za
When?	Quando?	kwan·do
Where?	Dove?	do·ve
Who?	Chi?	kee
Why?	Perché?	per·ke

SHOPPING & SERVICES

I'd like to buy ...
Vorrei comprare ... — vo·ray kom·pra·re ...

I'm just looking.
Sto solo guardando. — sto so·lo gwar·dan·do

Can I look at it?
Posso dare un'occhiata? — po·so da·re oo·no·kya·ta

How much is this?
Quanto costa questo? — kwan·to kos·ta kwe·sto

It's too expensive.
È troppo caro/a. (m/f) — e tro·po ka·ro/a

Can you lower the price?
Può farmi lo sconto? — pwo far·mee lo skon·to

There's a mistake in the bill.
C'è un errore nel conto. — che oo·ne·ro·re nel kon·to

ATM	Bancomat	ban·ko·mat
post office	ufficio postale	oo·fee·cho pos·ta·le
tourist office	ufficio del turismo	oo·fee·cho del too·reez·mo

TIME & DATES

What time is it?	Che ora è?	ke o·ra e
It's one o'clock.	È l'una.	e loo·na
It's (two) o'clock.	Sono le (due).	so·no le (doo·e)
Half past (one).	(L'una) e mezza.	(loo·na) e me·dza

in the morning	di mattina	dee ma·tee·na
in the afternoon	di pomeriggio	dee po·me·ree·jo
in the evening	di sera	dee se·ra

yesterday	ieri	ye·ree
today	oggi	o·jee
tomorrow	domani	do·ma·nee

Monday	lunedì	loo·ne·dee
Tuesday	martedì	mar·te·dee
Wednesday	mercoledì	mer·ko·le·dee
Thursday	giovedì	jo·ve·dee
Friday	venerdì	ve·ner·dee
Saturday	sabato	sa·ba·to
Sunday	domenica	do·me·nee·ka

January	gennaio	je·na·yo
February	febbraio	fe·bra·yo
March	marzo	mar·tso
April	aprile	a·pree·le
May	maggio	ma·jo

June	*giugno*	*joo*·nyo
July	*luglio*	*loo*·lyo
August	*agosto*	a·*gos*·to
September	*settembre*	se·*tem*·bre
October	*ottobre*	o·*to*·bre
November	*novembre*	no·*vem*·bre
December	*dicembre*	dee·*chem*·bre

NUMBERS

1	*uno*	*oo*·no
2	*due*	*doo*·e
3	*tre*	tre
4	*quattro*	*kwa*·tro
5	*cinque*	*cheen*·kwe
6	*sei*	say
7	*sette*	*se*·te
8	*otto*	*o*·to
9	*nove*	*no*·ve
10	*dieci*	*dye*·chee
20	*venti*	*ven*·tee
30	*trenta*	*tren*·ta
40	*quaranta*	kwa·*ran*·ta
50	*cinquanta*	cheen·*kwan*·ta
60	*sessanta*	se·*san*·ta
70	*settanta*	se·*tan*·ta
80	*ottanta*	o·*tan*·ta
90	*novanta*	no·*van*·ta
100	*cento*	*chen*·to
1000	*mille*	*mee*·lel

TRANSPORT

At what time does the ... leave/arrive?
A che ora   a ke *o*·ra
parte/arriva ...?   *par*·te/a·*ree*·va ...

boat	*la nave*	la *na*·ve
bus	*l'autobus*	*low*·to·boos
ferry	*il traghetto*	eel tra·*ge*·to
metro	*la metro-*	la me·tro·
	politana	po·lee·*ta*·na
plane	*l'aereo*	la·e·*re*·o
train	*il treno*	eel *tre*·no

... ticket	*un biglietto ...*	oon bee·*lye*·to
one-way	*di sola*	dee *so*·la
	andata	an·*da*·ta
return	*di andata e*	dee an·*da*·ta e
	ritorno	ree·*tor*·no

bus stop	*fermata*	fer·*ma*·ta
	dell'autobus	del *ow*·to·boos
platform	*binario*	bee·*na*·ryo
ticket office	*biglietteria*	bee·lye·te·*ree*·a
timetable	*orario*	o·*ra*·ryo
train station	*stazione*	sta·*tsyo*·ne
	ferroviaria	fe·ro·*vyar*·ya

Does it stop at ...?
Si ferma a ...?   see *fer*·ma a ...

Please tell me when we get to ...
Mi dica per favore   mee *dee*·ka per fa·*vo*·re
quando arriviamo a ...   *kwan*·do a·ree·*vya*·mo a ...

I want to get off here.
Voglio scendere qui.   vo·lyo *shen*·de·re kwee

I'd like to hire a bicycle.
Vorrei noleggiare   vo·*ray* no·le·*ja*·re
una bicicletta.   *oo*·na bee·chee·*kle*·ta

I have a flat tyre.
Ho una gomma bucata.   o *oo*·na go·ma boo·*ka*·ta

I'd like to have my bicycle repaired.
Vorrei fare riparare la   vo·*ray* fa·re ree·pa·*ra*·re la
mia bicicletta.   *mee*·a bee·chee·*kle*·ta

GLOSSARY

abbazia – abbey

(pizza) al taglio – (pizza) by the slice

albergo – hotel

alimentari – grocery shop; delicatessen

anfiteatro – amphitheatre

aperitivo – pre-evening meal drink and snack

arco – arch

autostrada – motorway; highway

battistero – baptistry

biblioteca – library

biglietto – ticket

borgo – archaic name for a small town, village or town sector (often dating to Middle Ages)

camera – room

campo – field

cappella – chapel

Cappella Sistina – Sistine Chapel

carabinieri – police with military and civil duties

Carnevale – carnival period between Epiphany and Lent

casa – house

castello – castle

cattedrale – cathedral

catacomba – catacomb

centro sociale –social centre; often a venue for concerts, club nights, cultural events

centro storico – historic centre

chiesa – church

chiostro – cloister; covered walkway, usually enclosed by columns, around a quadrangle

città – town; city

colonna – column

comune – equivalent to a municipality or county; a town or city council; historically, a self–governing town or city

corso – boulevard

duomo – cathedral

enoteca – wine bar

espresso – short black coffee

EUR (Esposizione Universale di Roma) –outlying district in south Rome known for its rationalist architecture

ferrovia – railway

festa – feast day; holiday

fontana – fountain

foro – forum

fiume – river

gelateria – ice-cream shop

giardino – garden

grattachecca – ice drink flavoured with fruit and syrup

grotta – cave

isola – island

lago – lake

largo – small square

locanda – inn; small hotel

mar, mare – sea

mausoleo – mausoleum; stately and magnificent tomb

mercato – market

museo – museum

necropoli – ancient name for cemetery or burial site

nord – north

osteria – casual tavern or eatery presided over by a host

palazzo – mansion; palace; large building of any type, including an apartment block

palio – contest

Papa – Pope

parco – park

passeggiata – traditional evening stroll

pasticceria – cake/pastry shop

pensione – guesthouse

piazza – square

piazzale – large open square

pietà – literally 'pity' or 'compassion'; sculpture, drawing or painting of the dead Christ supported by the Madonna

pinacoteca – art gallery

PIT (Punto Informativo Turistico) – Tourist Information Point

ponte – bridge

porta – gate; door

porto – port

prenotare – to book or reserve

reale – royal

ristorante – restaurant

rocca – fortress

sala – room; hall

salumeria – delicatessen

santuario – sanctuary; 1. the part of a church above the altar; 2. an especially holy place in a temple (antiquity)

scalinata – staircase

scavi – excavations

spiaggia – beach

stadio – stadium

stazione – station

stazione marittima – ferry terminal

strada – street; road

sud – south

superstrada – expressway; highway with divided lanes

tartufo – truffle

tavola calda – literally 'hot table'; pre-prepared meat, pasta and vegetable selection, often self-service

teatro – theatre

tempietto – small temple

tempio – temple

terme – thermal baths

tesoro – treasury

Tevere – Tiber

torre – tower

trattoria – simple restaurant

Trenitalia – Italian State Railways; also known as Ferrovie dello Stato (FS)

via – street; road

Via Appia Antica – Appian Way

viale – avenue

vico – alley; alleyway

villa – town house; country house; also the park surrounding the house

Behind the Scenes

SEND US YOUR FEEDBACK

We love to hear from travellers – your comments keep us on our toes and help make our books better. Our well-travelled team reads every word on what you loved or loathed about this book. Although we cannot reply individually to postal submissions, we always guarantee that your feedback goes straight to the appropriate authors, in time for the next edition. Each person who sends us information is thanked in the next edition – the most useful submissions are rewarded with a selection of digital PDF chapters.

Visit **lonelyplanet.com/contact** to submit your updates and suggestions or to ask for help. Our award-winning website also features inspirational travel stories, news and discussions.

Note: We may edit, reproduce and incorporate your comments in Lonely Planet products such as guidebooks, websites and digital products, so let us know if you don't want your comments reproduced or your name acknowledged. For a copy of our privacy policy visit lonelyplanet.com/privacy.

OUR READERS

Many thanks to the travellers who used the last edition and wrote to us with helpful hints, useful advice and interesting anecdotes:

Ricardo Blasco, Graham Courtenay, Ben Smith, Kristin Vorbeck, Niko Waesche, Fred Woodcock, John Woodhouse

AUTHOR THANKS

Duncan Garwood

A big thanks to fellow scribe Abi Blasi for her suggestions and great work, and to Joe Bind-loss, Annelies Mertens and the SPP gurus for their in-house help and support. *Grazie* to Barbara Lessona for her pointers, and, as always, a big hug to Lidia, Ben and Nick for putting up with my long absences and deadline nerves.

Abigail Blasi

A huge thank you to Duncan, and to Joe Bind-loss, for giving me the chance to cover my favourite city once again. *Molto grazie* to Luca, Gabriel, Jack and Valentina, and to Anna, Marcello, Carlotta and Alessandro for all their help in Rome, to Georgina for help at home, and to Caroline and John for their care of Henry. For their help with research many thanks go to Barbara Lessona, Marco Messina (at the Parco Appia Antica), Cristiano Brughitta and Stéphanie Santini.

ACKNOWLEDGMENTS

Illustrations pp 68-9 by Javier Martinez Zarracina

Cover photograph: Angel on Ponte Sant'Angelo with St Peter's Basilica beyond at dusk, Rome, Brian Jannsen/Alamy©

THIS BOOK

This 8th edition of Lonely Planet's *Rome* guidebook was researched and written by Duncan Garwood and Abigail Blasi. The previous two editions were also written by Duncan Garwood and Abigail Blasi. This guidebook was commissioned in Lonely Planet's Melbourne office, and produced by the following:

Commissioning Editors Joe Bindloss, Helena Smith

Coordinating Editor Tracy Whitmey

Coordinating Cartographers Rachel Imeson, Chris Tsismetzis

Coordinating Layout Designer Carol Jackson

Managing Editors Brigitte Ellemor, Annelies Mertens

Managing Cartographers Anita Bahn, Anthony Phelan

Managing Layout Designer Chris Girdler

Assisting Editors Carolyn Boicos, Kellie Langdon, Christopher Pitts

Cover Research Naomi Parker

Internal Image Research Rebecca Skinner

Language Content Branislava Vladisavljevic

Thanks to Shahara Ahmed, Sasha Baskett, Yvonne Bischofberger, Bruce Evans, Ryan Evans, Larissa Frost, Jane Hart, Genesys India, Jouve India, Andi Jones, Wayne Murphy, Trent Paton, Wibowo Rusli, Carlos Solarte, Luna Soo, Kerrianne Southway, Gerard Walker, Dora Whitaker, Clifton Wilkinson, Amanda Williamson

See also separate subindexes for:

✕ **EATING P347**

🍷 **DRINKING & NIGHTLIFE P348**

☆ **ENTERTAINMENT P349**

🔒 **SHOPPING P349**

🛏 **SLEEPING P350**

Index

Sights 000
Map Pages **000**
Photo Pages **000**

NOTES

Rome Maps

Map Legend

Sights
- Beach
- Buddhist
- Castle
- Christian
- Hindu
- Islamic
- Jewish
- Monument
- Museum/Gallery
- Ruin
- Winery/Vineyard
- Zoo
- Other Sight

Eating
- Eating

Drinking & Nightlife
- Drinking & Nightlife
- Cafe

Entertainment
- Entertainment

Shopping
- Shopping

Sleeping
- Sleeping
- Camping

Sports & Activities
- Diving/Snorkelling
- Canoeing/Kayaking
- Skiing
- Surfing
- Swimming/Pool
- Walking
- Windsurfing
- Other Sports & Activities

Information
- Post Office
- Tourist Information

Transport
- Airport
- Border Crossing
- Bus
- Cable Car/Funicular
- Cycling
- Ferry
- Monorail
- Parking
- S-Bahn
- Taxi
- Train/Railway
- Tram
- Tube Station
- U-Bahn
- Underground Train Station
- Other Transport

Routes
- Tollway
- Freeway
- Primary
- Secondary
- Tertiary
- Lane
- Unsealed Road
- Plaza/Mall
- Steps
- Tunnel
- Pedestrian Overpass
- Walking Tour
- Walking Tour Detour
- Path

Boundaries
- International
- State/Province
- Disputed
- Regional/Suburb
- Marine Park
- Cliff
- Wall

Geographic
- Hut/Shelter
- Lighthouse
- Lookout
- Mountain/Volcano
- Oasis
- Park
- Pass
- Picnic Area
- Waterfall

Hydrography
- River/Creek
- Intermittent River
- Swamp/Mangrove
- Reef
- Canal
- Water
- Dry/Salt/ Intermittent Lake
- Glacier

Areas
- Beach/Desert
- Cemetery (Christian)
- Cemetery (Other)
- Park/Forest
- Sportsground
- Sight (Building)
- Top Sight (Building)

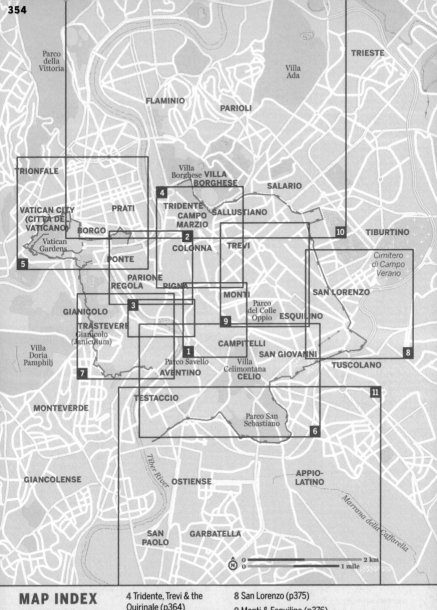

MAP INDEX

ANCIENT ROME

Key on p355

See map p361

See map p365

See map p377

MONTI

200 m
0.1 miles

Via del Plebiscito
Via Cesare Battisti
Piazza Venezia
Via degli Astalli
Via di San Marco
Piazza di San Marco
Via San Venazio
Piazza d'Ara Coeli
Via d'Aracoeli
Tor De' Specchi
Via Margana
Vic Margana
Via Tribuna di Tor De' Specchi

Via dei Fornari
Via della Sant'Eufemia
Via IV Novembre
Largo Magnanapoli
Via Nazionale
Largo Angelicum
Via Mazzarino
Via Panisperna
Via Cimarra
Via del Boschetto
Via dei Serpenti
Via degli Zingari
Piazza Madonna dei Monti
Via Leonina
Via Baccina
Via di Sant'Agata dei Goti
Via Alessandrina
Imperial Forums
Via dei Fori Imperiali
Via Tor de' Conti
Via della Madonna de' Monti
Via del Garofano
Via Baccina
Largo della Salara Vecchia
Via della Salara Vecchia
Via di San Pietro in Carcere
Campidoglio (Capitoline Hill)
Capitoline Museums
Via di San Pietro in Vincoli
Via del Teatro di Marcello
Via della Villa Caffarelli
Via del Monte Tarpeo
Clivus Capitolinus
Via del Foro Romano
Via Sacra
Roman Forum Entrance
Via della Curia
Via di Tulliano
Largo C Ricci
Via Cavour
Via Frangipane
Via dell'Agnello
Via del Colosseo
Via delle Carine
Via Vittorino da Feltre
Via degli Annibaldi
Via del Fagutale
Via Eudossiana
Piazza di San Pietro in Vincoli
Piazza San Francesco di Paola
Via di Paola Sette Sal
Via della Polveriera
Via di Monte Oppio

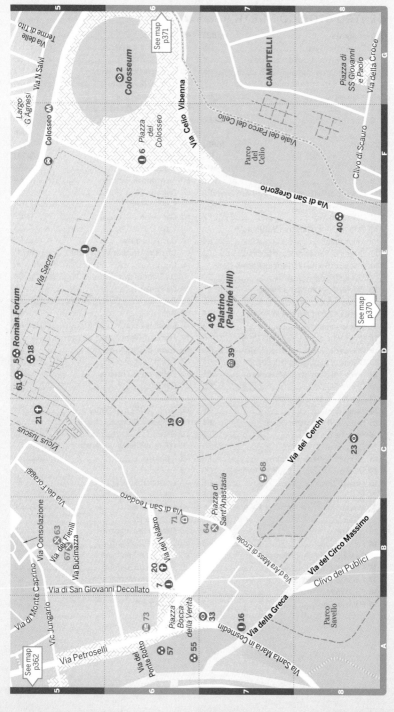

See map p371

Colosseum

Via delle Terme di Tito

Via N Salvi

Largo G Agnesi

Colosseo

2

6 Piazza del Colosseo

CAMPITELLI

Piazza di SS Giovanni e Paolo

Via della Croce

Clivo di Scauro

Via Celio Vibenna

Viale del Parco del Celio

Parco del Celio

Via di San Gregorio

40

Via Sacra

9

Roman Forum

5

18

61

21

Vicus Tuscus

Palatino (Palatine Hill)

4

39

19

See map p370

68

Via dei Cerchi

23

Piazza di Sant'Anastasia

Via di San Teodoro

71

64

Via dei Fienili

63

Via Bucimazza

67

Via Consolazione

Via dei Foraggi

Via di Monte Caprino

20

7

Via del Velabro

Via di San Giovanni Decollato

73

57

Piazza Bocca della Verità

55

33

16

Via Santa Maria in Cosmedin

Via della Greca

Via d'Ara Mass di Ercole

Via del Circo Massimo

Clivo dei Publici

Parco Savello

See map p362

Via Petroselli

Via del Ponte Rotto

Vic Jungario

CENTRO STORICO NORTH *Map on p360*

CENTRO STORICO NORTH

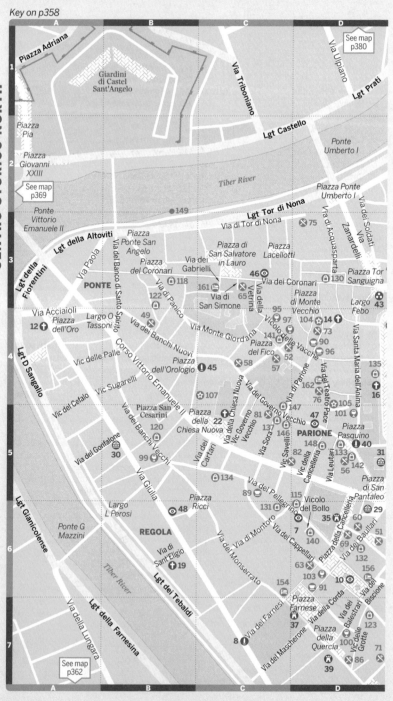

CENTRO STORICO NORTH

Piazza Adriana

Giardini
di Castel
Sant'Angelo

Via Triboniano

See map
p380

Via Ulpiano

Lgt Prati

Piazza
Pia

Lgt Castello

Piazza
Giovanni
XXIII

See map
p369

Tiber River

Ponte
Umberto I

Ponte
Vittorio
Emanuele II

Lgt Tor di Nona

Via di Tor di Nona

75

Piazza Ponte
Umberto I

Piazza Ponte
Umberto I

149

Lgt della Altoviti

Lgt della
Fiorentini

Via Paola

Piazza
Ponte San
Angelo

Piazza
del Coronari

Via del Banco di Santo Spirito

PONTE

118

122

Piazza di
San Salvatore
in Lauro

Via dei
Gabrielli

161

46

Via dei Coronari

130

Piazza
Lacelliotti

Via di
San Simone

Vetrina
65

Via della

Piazza
di Monte
Vecchio

Largo
Febo

43

Via Acciaioli

12

Piazza
dell'Oro

Largo O
Tassoni

49

Via dei Banchi Nuovi

Via di Panico

95

Vicolo delle Vacche

97

141

104

14

73

90

96

Via Santa Maria dell'Anima

Via Monte Giordana

Piazza
del Fico

52

57

58

Lgt D Sangallo

Corso Vittorio Emanuele II

Vic delle Palle

Vic del Cefalo

Vic Sugarelli

Piazza
dell'Orologio

45

Via di Parione

Via del Teatro Pace

162

76

105

101

135

16

107

Via dei Banchi Vecchi

Piazza San
Cesarini

120

Piazza
della
Chiesa Nuova

22

Via della Chiesa Nuova

Vic Governo
Vecchio

Via del Governo Vecchio

81

137

147

146

PARIONE

47

Piazza
Pasquino

40

31

Via del Gonfalone

30

99

Via di
Sant'Eligio

19

134

Piazza
Ricci

89

Via del Pellegrino

115

131

Vicolo
del Bollo

7

140

Via Sora

Vic Savelli

82

Via della Cancelleria

148

Via Leutari

56

133

142

Piazza
di San
Pantaleo

29

60

51

REGOLA

48

Largo
L Perosi

Ponte G
Mazzini

Via Giulia

Via dei Banchi Vecchi

Via del Monserrato

Via di Montoro

Via dei Cappellari

63

103

91

154

10

35

Piazza della Cancelleria

69

132

156

123

71

Lgt Gianicolense

Tiber River

Lgt dei Tebaldi

Via dei Farnesi

Piazza
Farnese

37

8

Via del Mascherone

Via della Corda

Piazza
della
Quercia

39

100

86

Via dei
Balestrari

Via dei
Biscione

Vic delle
Grotte

Lgt della Farnesina

Via della Lungara

See map
p362

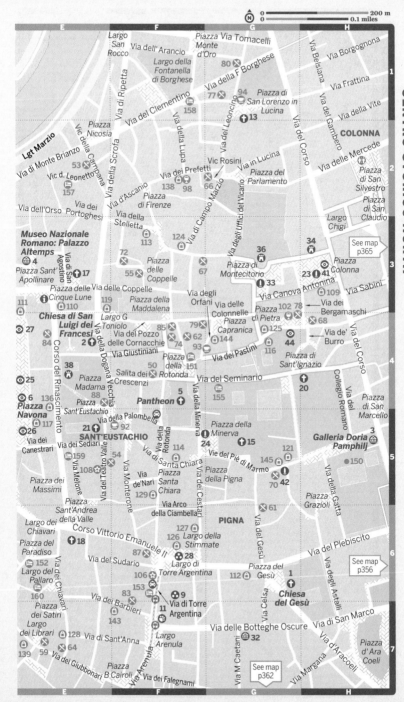

CENTRO STORICO SOUTH

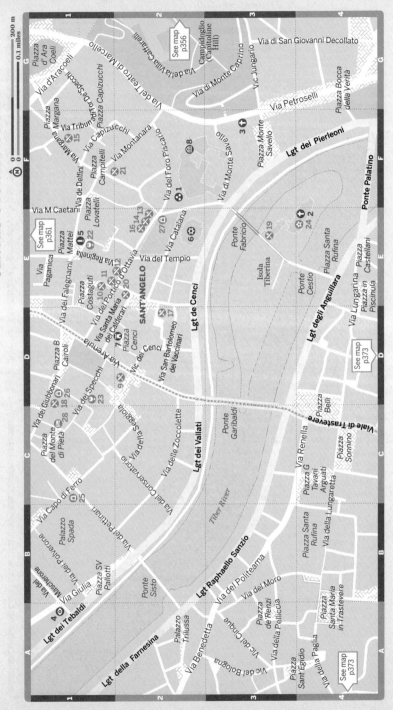

200 m
0.1 miles

See map p356

See map p361

See map p373

See map p373

Piazza d'Ara Coeli

Via d'Aracoeli

Via de' Specchi

Piazza Margana

Via Tribuna di Tor

Piazza Capizucchi

Via Marfana

Via Capizucchi

Via Montanara

Campidoglio (Capitoline Hill)

Via di San Giovanni Decollato

Via della Villa Caffarelli

Via di Monte Caprino

Vic. Jungario

Piazza Bocca della Verità

Via Petroselli

Piazza Monte Savello

Via del Foro Piscario

Via di Monte Savello

Lgt dei Pierleoni

Ponte Palatino

Piazza Campitelli

Via de Delfini

Via M Caetani

Via Lovatelli

Piazza Mattei

Via della Reginella

Via del Tempio

Via Catalana

Ponte Fabricio

Isola Tiberina

Ponte Cestio

Piazza Santa Rufina

Piazza Castellani

Via Paganica

Via dei Falegnami

Via del Portico d'Ottavia

SANT'ANGELO

Via Santa Maria del Calderari

Piazza Costaguti

Lgt de Cenci

Lgt degli Anguillara

Via Lungarina

Piazza in Piscinula

Via Arenula

Piazza B Cairoli

Via dei Giubbonari

Vic. de' Cenci

Via San Bartolomeo del Vaccinari

Piazza Cenci

Piazza Belli

Piazza del Monte di Pietà

Via dei Specchi

Via della Seggiola

Lgt dei Vallati

Viale di Trastevere

Via Renella

Piazza G Tavani Arguati

Piazza Sonnino

Via Capo di Ferro

Palazzo Spada

Via del Pettinari

Via del Conservatorio

Via delle Zoccolette

Ponte Garibaldi

Tiber River

Piazza Santa Rufina

Via della Lungaretta

Via del Mascherone

Via Giulia

Via dei Polverone

Piazza SV Pallotti

Ponte Sisto

Lgt Raphaello Sanzio

Via del Politeama

Via del Moro

Via della Lungaretta

Lgt dei Tebaldi

Palazzo Trilussa

Lgt della Farnesina

Via Benedetta

Vic del Cinque

Via della Pelliccia

Piazza de Renzi

Piazza Santa Maria in Trastevere

Piazza Sant'Egidio

Via della Paglia

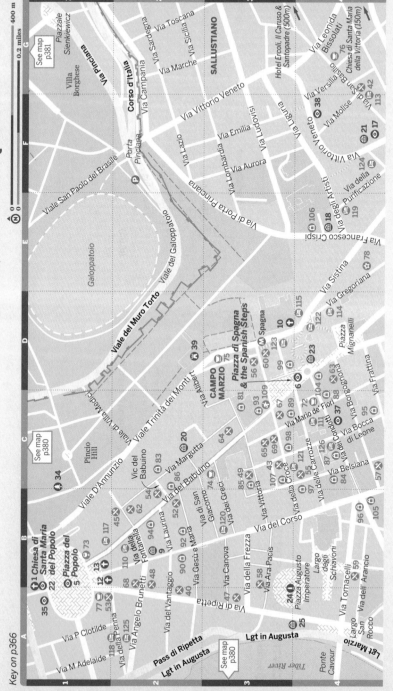

TRIDENTE, TREVI & THE QUIRINALE

Key on p366

See map p381

See map p380

See map p380

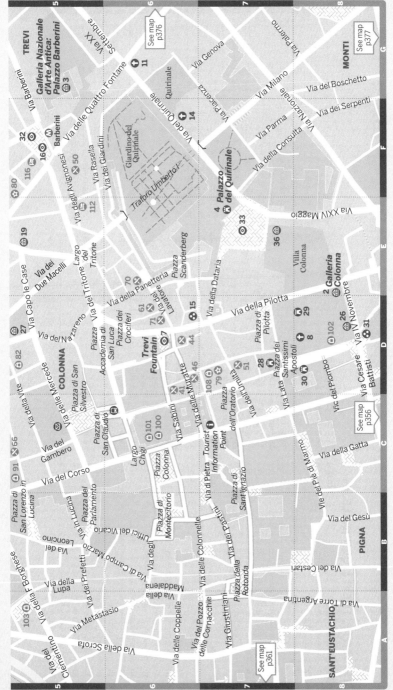

TRIDENTE, TREVI & THE QUIRINALE

TREVI

Galleria Nazionale
d'Arte Antica: Palazzo Barberini 3

MONTI

Via Barberini

Via XX Settembre

See map p376

11

Via del Boschetto

Via dei Serpenti

Via delle Quattro Fontane

Barberini

14

Quirinale

Via Piacenza

Via Milano

Via Nazionale

Via Parma

Via della Consulta

Giardino del
Quirinale

32

116

16

80

Via degli Avignonesi

Via Rasella

Via dei Giardini

50

112

Traforo Umberto I

4 Palazzo
del Quirinale

33

Via XXIV Maggio

19

Via dei
Due Macelli

Largo del
Tritone

Piazza
Scanderberg

36

Villa
Colonna

2 Galleria
Colonna

Via Capo le Case

Via del Tritone

70

Via della Panetteria

Piazza
dei
Crociferi

Via della Dataria

Via della Pilotta

Via IV Novembre

27

Via del Nazareno

Piazza di
Accademia di
San Luca

61

71

Via dei
Lavatore

15

Piazza della
Pilotta

26

82

Via del Mercede

COLONNA

Trevi
Fountain

7

Via delle Muratte

44

46

Piazza
dei Santissimi
Apostoli

29

8

31

102

30

Via Cesare
Battisti

91

66

Via della Vite

Piazza di San Silvestro

San Claudio

41

108

79

51

28

Via del Piombo

Via del Gambero

Piazza di
San Lorenzo in
Lucina

Via del Corso

Largo
Chigi

101

100

Piazza
Colonna

Via Sabini

Piazza
dell'Oratorio

Piazza di
Sant'Ignazio

Via della Gatta

See map
p356

103

Via della F Borghese

Via del Leoncino

Via in Lucina

Piazza di
Montecitorio

Via di Pietra

Tourist
Information
Point

Piazza
del Parlamento

Uffici del Vicario

Via degli

Via delle Colonnelle

Via del Piè di Marmo

Via del Gesù

PIGNA

Via del Clementino

Via della Lupa

Via dei Prefetti

Via di Campo Marzio

Via della Maddalena

Via del Pozzo
delle Cornacchie

Piazza della
Rotonda

Via del Cestari

Via di Torre Argentina

Via Metastasio

Via delle Coppelle

Via Giustiniani

Via della Scrofa

SANT'EUSTACHIO

See map
p361

TRIDENTE, TREVI & QUIRINALE *Map on p364*

VATICAN CITY, BORGO & PRATI

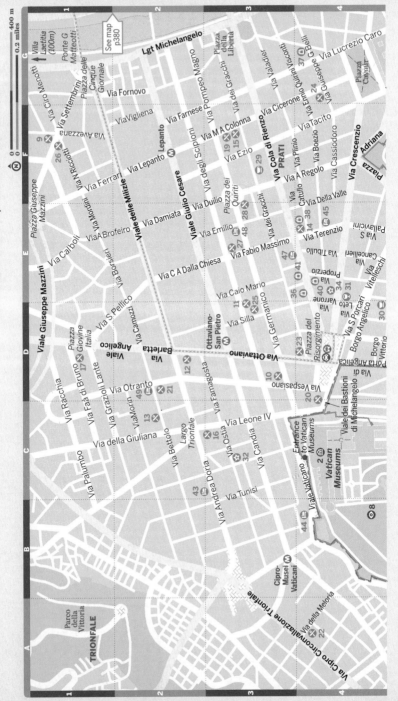

0.2 miles
400 m

See map p380

Lgt Michelangelo

Villa Laetitia (100m)
Ponte G Matteotti
Piazza delle Cinque Giornale

Piazza della Libertà

Via Ciro Menotti
Via N Ricciotti
Via Settembrini
Via Fornovo
Via Vigliena
Via Avezzana
Via Pompeo Magno
Via dei Gracchi
Via Farnese
Via M A Colonna
Via Ferrari
Via degli Scipioni
Via Ezio
Via Emio Quirini Visconti
Via Giuseppe G Belli
Via Lucrezio Caro

Piazza Cavour

Via Cicerone
Via Valadier
Via Emio Quirini Visconti
Via Cola di Rienzo
PRATI
Via Tacito

Piazza Giuseppe Mazzini

Viale Giuseppe Mazzini

Via Calboli
Via Mordini
Via A Brofeiro
Via Borsieri
Via delle Milizie
Viale delle Milizie
Via Damiata
Via Lepanto
Lepanto
Viale Giulio Cesare
Viale Giulio Cesare
Via Duilio

Piazza dei Quiriti

Via Plinio
Via A Regolo
Via Catullo
Via Crescenzio
Piazza Adriana

Via Boezio
Via Cassiodoro

Via Della Valle

Via C A Dalla Chiesa
Via Emilio
Via Fabio Massimo
Via dei Gracchi
Via Terenzio
Via S Pallavicini

Via Racchia
Via Faà di Bruno
Via Grazioli Lante
Via S Pellico
Via Camozzi
Via Caio Mario
Via Germanico
Via Silla
Via Tibullo
Via Properzio
Via Cancellieri
Via Vitelleschi

Piazza Giovine Italia

Viale Angelico
Via Barletta
Ottaviano-San Pietro
Via Ottaviano

Via Palumbo
Via Bettolo
Via Otranto
Via Famagosta
Via Vespasiano

Via Leto
Via Varrone
Via S Porcari
Borgo Angelico
Borgo Vittorio
Via di Porta Angelica

Piazza del Risorgimento

Via della Giuliana
Via Morin
Largo Trionfale
Via Ostia
Via Candia
Via Leone IV

Entrance to Vatican Museums

Via Andrea Doria
Via Tunisi

Vatican Museums

Viale Vaticano

Cipro-Musei Vaticani
Musei Vaticani

TRIONFALE

Parco della Vittoria

Via Cipro
Via Circonvallazione Trionfale
Viale Circonvallazione Trionfale
Via della Meloria

Viale dei Bastioni di Michelangelo

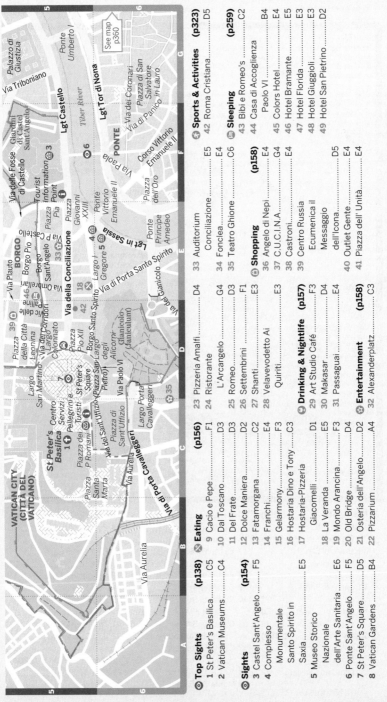

VATICAN CITY, BORGO & PRATI

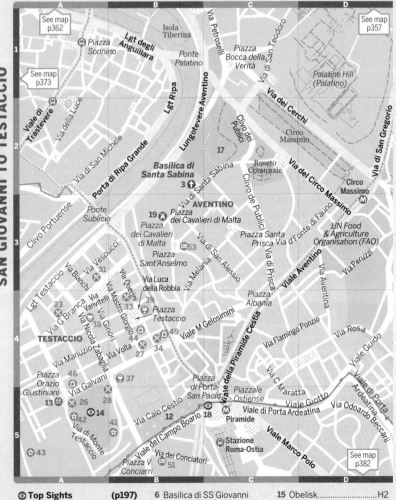

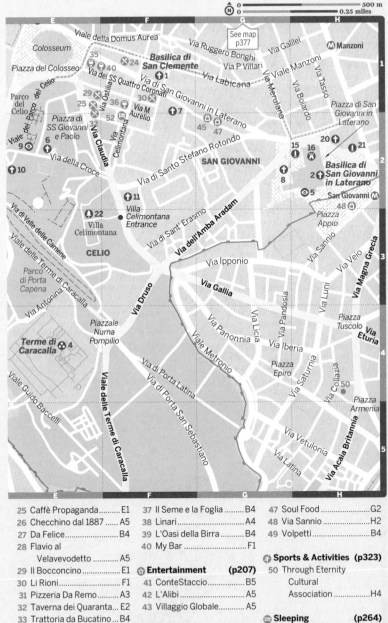

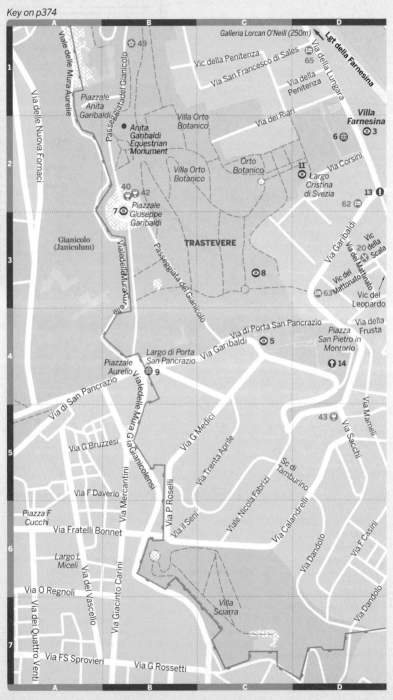

TRASTEVERE & GIANICOLO

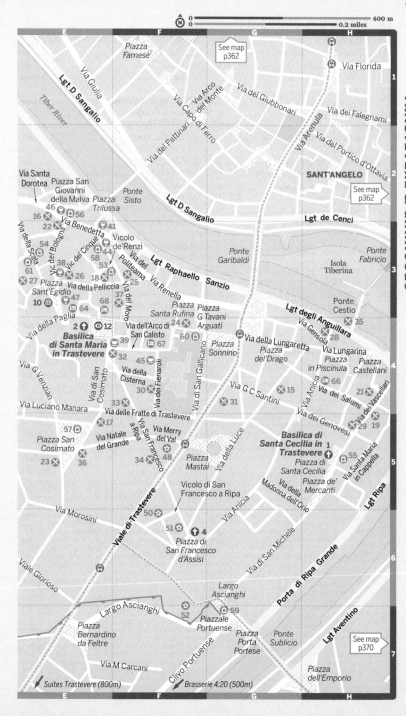

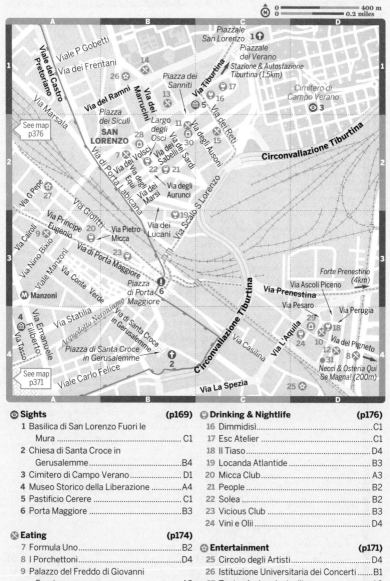

MONTI & ESQUILINO

Key on p378

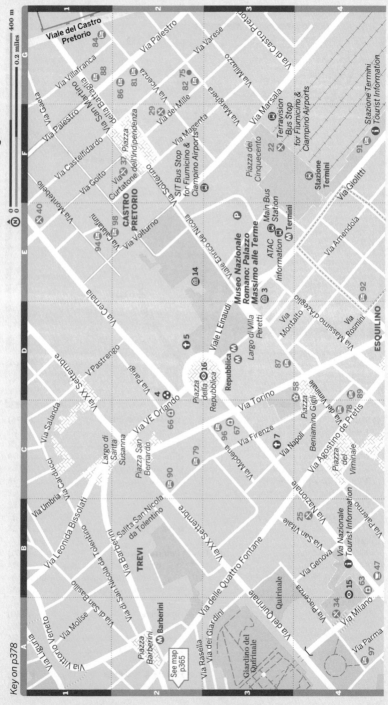

400 m
0.2 miles

See map p365

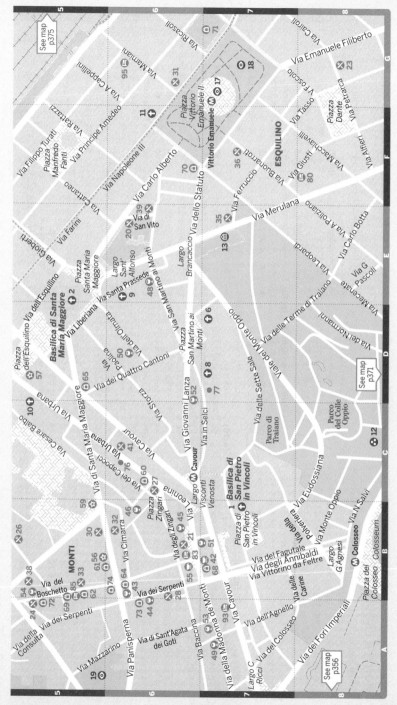

VILLA BORGHESE & NORTHERN ROME *Map on p380*

VILLA BORGHESE & NORTHERN ROME

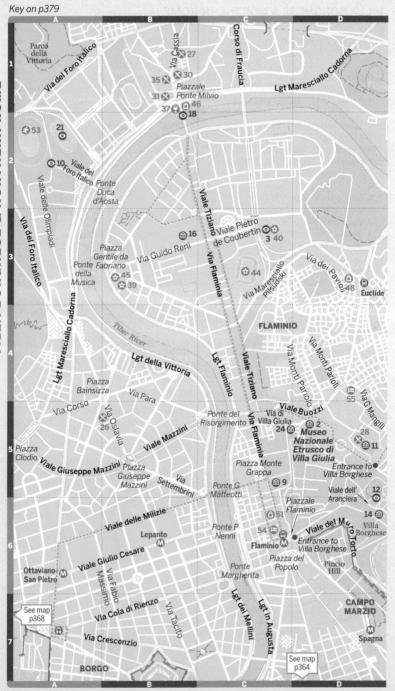

See map
p368

See map
p364

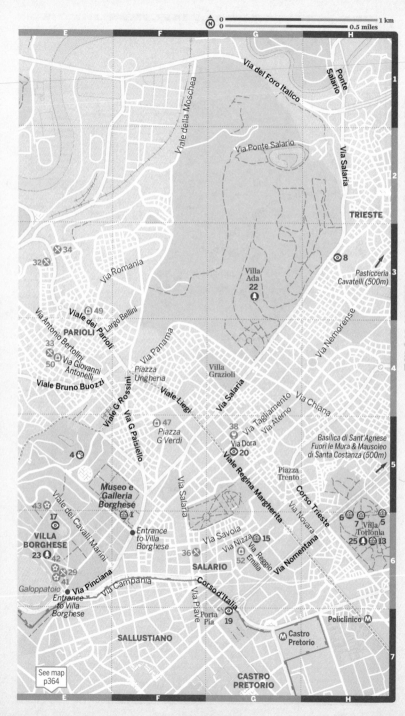

0 _____ 1 km
0 _____ 0.5 miles

Via del Foro Italico

Ponte Salario

Via Ponte Salario

Via Salaria

TRIESTE

8

Pasticceria
Cavatelli (500m)

34

32

Via Romania

Villa
Ada
22

Via Nemorense

49

Viale dei Parioli

Largo Bellini

PARIOLI

Via Antonio Bertolini

33

50

Via Giovanni
Antonelli

Viale Bruno Buozzi

Via Panama

Piazza
Ungheria

Villa
Grazioli

Viale G Rossini

Viale Liegi

Via Salaria

Via Tagliamento

Via Chiana

Via G Paisiello

Via Aterno

47

Piazza
G Verdi

38

Via Dora

20

Piazza
Trento

Basilica di Sant'Agnese
Fuori le Mura & Mausoleo
di Santa Costanza (500m)

4

Viale Regina Margherita

Corso Trieste

Via Novara

Museo e
Galleria
Borghese
1

Via dei Cavalli Marini

Via Salaria

6

7

5

Villa
Torlonia

43

17

Entrance
to Villa
Borghese

VILLA
BORGHESE

23

42

Via Savoia

Via Nizza

15

25

13

36

52

Via Reggio
Emilia

SALARIO

Via Nomentana

29

41

Galoppatoio

Via Pinciana

Entrance
to Villa
Borghese

Via Campania

Corso d'Italia

Policlinico M

Via Plave

Porta
Pia

19

Castro
Pretorio

SALLUSTIANO

CASTRO
PRETORIO

See map
p364

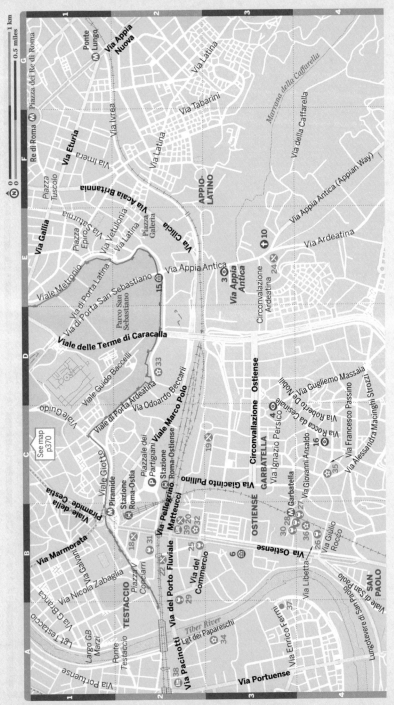

SOUTHERN ROME

382

0   0.5 miles
0   1 km

Via Portuense

Via Pacinotti

Lgt dei Papareschi

Tiber River

Via Enrico Fermi

🏛 38

🏛 34

Largo GB Marzi

Lgt Testaccio

Via G Branca

Via Nicola Zabaglia

Via Marmorata

TESTACCIO

Ponte Testaccio

Piazza V Conciarri

⊗ 22

🏛 29

Via del Porto Fluviale

Via del Commercio

⊗ 25

🏛 6

Via Portuense

Via Ostiense

Via Libetta

🏛 26

SAN PAOLO

Viale di San Paolo

Lungotevere di San Paolo

Via Giulio Rocco

Ⓜ 30 28 27
🏛 36

Viale della Piramide Cestia

Ⓜ Piramide

🏛 18

🏛 31

Stazione Roma-Ostia

🚉 Piramide

🚉 Stazione Roma-Ostia

Via Pallegrino Matteucci

🏛 39 20
🏛 32

OSTIENSE

Via Giacinto Pullino

GARBATELLA

Garbatella

Via Giovanni Ansaldo

🏛 35

Via Alessandra Macinghi Strozzi

Via Francesco Passino

Via Guglielmo Massaia

Circonvallazione Ostiense

Via Ignazio Persico

Via Rocca da Cesinale 🏛 4

Via Roberto De Nobili

🏛 16

Viale Giotto

Viale Guido

Viale Guido Baccelli

Piazzale dei Partigiani

Viale Marco Polo

Via Odoardo Beccari

Viale di Porta Ardeatina

⊗ 19

⊗ 33

See map p370

Parco San Sebastiano

Viale delle Terme di Caracalla

Via di Porta San Sebastiano

Via di Porta Latina

Viale Metronio

Via Appia Antica

🏛 15

🏛 3

Via Appia Antica

Circonvallazione Ardeatina

⊗ 24

🏛 10

Via Ardeatina

Via Appia Antica (Appian Way)

APPIO-LATINO

Via Clicia

Piazza Galeria

Via Latina

Via Acaia Britannia

Via Gallia

Via Vetulonia

Via Saturnia

Via Latina

Piazza Epiro

Piazza Tuscolo

Via Imera

Via Eturia

Via Eturia

Via Ivrea

Via Tabarini

Via Latina

Via Latina

Via Latina

Marrana della Caffarella

Via della Caffarella

Ⓜ Re di Roma

Piazza dei Re di Roma

🚇 Ponte Lungo

Via Appia Nuova

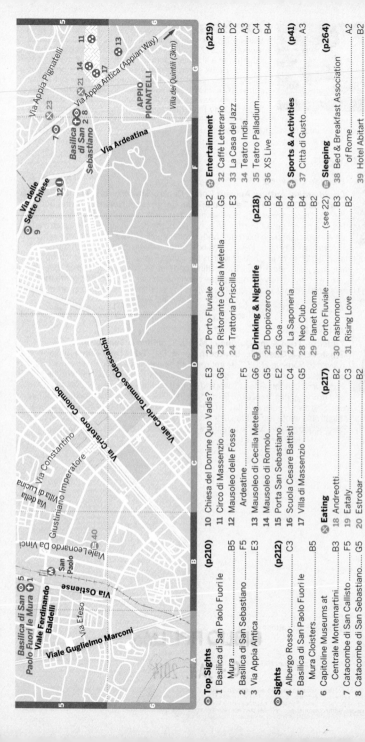

SOUTHERN ROME

◎ Top Sights (p210)
1 Basilica di San Paolo Fuori le Mura.........B5
2 Basilica di San Sebastiano...F5
3 Via Appia Antica...E3

◎ Sights (p212)
4 Albergo Rosso...C3
5 Basilica di San Paolo Fuori le Mura Cloisters...B5
6 Capitoline Museums at Centrale Montemartini...B3
7 Catacombe di San Callisto...F5
8 Catacombe di San Sebastiano...G5
9 Catacombe di Santa Domitilla...E5
10 Chiesa del Domine Quo Vadis?...E3
11 Circo di Massenzio...G5
12 Mausoleo delle Fosse Ardeatine...F5
13 Mausoleo di Cecilia Metella...G6
14 Mausoleo di Romolo...G5
15 Porta San Sebastiano...E2
16 Scuola Cesare Battisti...C4
17 Villa di Massenzio...G5

⊗ Eating (p217)
18 Andreotti...B3
19 Eataly...F5
20 Estrobar...G5
21 L'Archeologia...E5
22 Porto Fluviale...B2
23 Ristorante Cecilia Metella...G5
24 Trattoria Priscilla...E3

◐ Drinking & Nightlife (p218)
25 Doppiozeroo...B2
26 Goa...B4
27 La Saponeria...B4
28 Neo Club...B4
29 Planet Roma...B2
Porto Fluviale...(see 22)
30 Rashomon...B3
31 Rising Love...B2

◉ Entertainment (p219)
32 Caffè Letterario...B2
33 La Casa del Jazz...D2
34 Teatro India...A3
35 Teatro Palladium...C4
36 XS Live...B4

◉ Sports & Activities (p41)
37 Città di Gusto...A3

◉ Sleeping (p264)
38 Bed & Breakfast Association of Rome...A2
39 Hotel Abitart...B2
40 TwinCities Hostel...B5

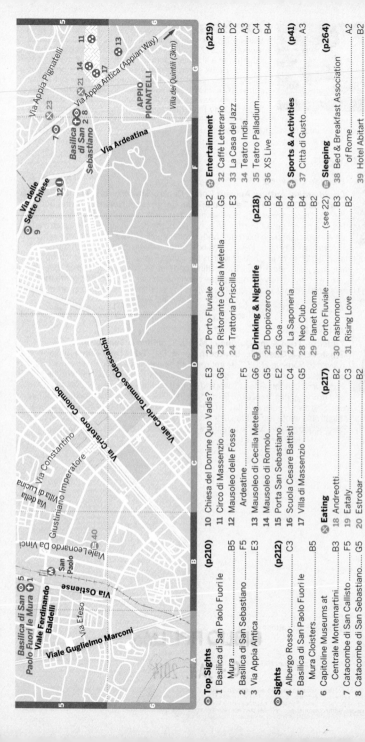

Our Story

A beat-up old car, a few dollars in the pocket and a sense of adventure. In 1972 that's all Tony and Maureen Wheeler needed for the trip of a lifetime – across Europe and Asia overland to Australia. It took several months, and at the end – broke but inspired – they sat at their kitchen table writing and stapling together their first travel guide, *Across Asia on the Cheap*. Within a week they'd sold 1500 copies. Lonely Planet was born.

Today, Lonely Planet has offices in Melbourne, London and Oakland, with more than 600 staff and writers. We share Tony's belief that 'a great guidebook should do three things: inform, educate and amuse'.

Our Writers

Duncan Garwood

Coordinating Author; Ancient Rome; Centro Storico; Vatican City, Borgo & Prati; San Giovanni to Testaccio; Villa Borghese & Northern Rome Born in the UK, Duncan now lives near Rome with his Italian wife and two bilingual kids. His first memories of the city he now calls home date to 1996 when he arrived on an overnight train from Bari and found himself virtually the only visitor in Piazza Navona and St Peter's Basilica. Since then he has worked on the past five editions of Lonely Planet's *Rome* guide as well as the *Rome Pocket* guide and a whole host of LP publications, including guidebooks to Sicily, Sardinia and Naples and the *Food Lover's Guide to the World*. He has also written on Italy for newspapers and magazines. Duncan also wrote the Plan Your Trip and Understand sections of this book as well as the Transport chapter and part of the Sleeping chapter.

Read more about Duncan at:
lonelyplanet.com/members/duncangarwood

Abigail Blasi

Tridente, Trevi & the Quirinale; Monti, Esquilino & San Lorenzo; Trastevere & Gianicolo; Southern Rome; Day Trips from Rome Abigail first moved to Rome in 2003. She got married alongside Lago Bracciano, her first son was born in Rome, and she nowadays divides her time between Rome, Puglia and London. She has worked on four editions of Lonely Planet's *Italy* and *Rome* guides, wrote the *Best of Rome* guide, and co-wrote the first edition of *Puglia & Basilicata*. She also regularly writes on Italy for various publications, including *Lonely Planet Traveller*. Abigail also wrote the Eating, Drinking & Nightlife, Entertainment and Shopping overviews in the Plan section, as well as the Directory A-Z and part of the Sleeping chapter.

Published by Lonely Planet Publications Pty Ltd
ABN 36 005 607 983
8th edition – Nov 2013
ISBN 978 1 74220 578 6
© Lonely Planet 2013   Photographs © as indicated 2013
10 9 8 7 6 5 4 3 2 1
Printed in China